W9-BSC-930

COOK'S ILLUSTRATED

2008

$35.00

Published by
America's Test Kitchen
17 Station Street
Brookline, MA 02445

ISBN-13: 978-1-933615-36-3
ISBN-10: 1-933615-36-2
ISSN: 1933-639X

To get home delivery of *Cook's Illustrated,* call 800-526-8442 inside the U.S., or 515-247-7571 if calling from outside the U.S., or subscribe online at www.cooksillustrated.com.

In addition to *Cook's Illustrated* Annual Hardbound Editions available from each year of publication (1993–2008), America's Test Kitchen offers the following cookbooks and DVD sets:

The America's Test Kitchen Family Cookbook
The America's Test Kitchen Family Baking Book

The Best Recipe Series
The Best Slow & Easy Recipes
The Best Chicken Recipes
The Best International Recipe
The Best Make-Ahead Recipe
The Best 30-Minute Recipe
The Best Light Recipe
The Cook's Illustrated Guide to Grilling and Barbecue
Best American Side Dishes
The Best Cover & Bake Recipes
The New Best Recipe
Steaks, Chops, Roasts, and Ribs
Baking Illustrated
Restaurant Favorites at Home
Perfect Vegetables
Italian Classics
The Best American Classics
The Best Soups & Stews

The Cook's Country Series
The Cook's Country Cookbook

Additional books from America's Test Kitchen
America's Best Lost Recipes
The Best of America's Test Kitchen 2008
The Best of America's Test Kitchen 2007
834 Kitchen Quick Tips
The Kitchen Detective
1993–2008 Cook's Illustrated Master Index

Cook's Country Hardbound Annual Editions
2008 Cook's Country Annual Edition
2007 Cook's Country Annual Edition
2006 Cook's Country Annual Edition
2005 Cook's Country Annual Edition

The America's Test Kitchen Series Companion Cookbooks
America's Test Kitchen: The TV Companion Cookbook (2009)
Behind the Scenes with America's Test Kitchen (2008)
Test Kitchen Favorites (2007)
Cooking at Home with America's Test Kitchen (2006)
America's Test Kitchen Live! (2005)
Inside America's Test Kitchen (2004)
Here in America's Test Kitchen (2003)
The America's Test Kitchen Cookbook (2002)

The America's Test Kitchen Series DVD Sets (from our hit public television series)
The *America's Test Kitchen* 2009 Season (4 DVD set)
The *America's Test Kitchen* 2008 Season (4 DVD set)
The *America's Test Kitchen* 2007 Season (4 DVD set)
The *America's Test Kitchen* 2006 Season (4 DVD set)
The *America's Test Kitchen* 2005 Season (4 DVD set)
The *America's Test Kitchen* 2004 Season (4 DVD set)
The *America's Test Kitchen* 2003 Season (4 DVD set)
The *America's Test Kitchen* 2002 Season (4 DVD set)
The *America's Test Kitchen* 2001 Season (2 DVD set)

To order any of our cookbooks and DVDs listed above, give us a call at 800-611-0759 inside the U.S., or at 515-246-6911 if calling from outside the U.S. You can order subscriptions, gift subscriptions, and any of our books by visiting our online store at www.cooksillustrated.com.

BC = Back Cover

COOK'S ILLUSTRATED INDEX 2008

A

B

C

D

E

N

O

P

R

S

T

V

W

Y

Z

NUMBER NINETY

JANUARY & FEBRUARY 2008

COOK'S ILLUSTRATED

No-Knead Bread 2.0
Dutch-Oven Method, Better Loaf

Cutting Boards
Wood, Plastic, Bamboo, or Composite?

Chicken in a Pot
French Method, Juiciest Bird

Dark Chocolate Taste Test
Pay Less, Get Better Chocolate!

Crunchy Baked Pork Chops

Sunday Roast Beef
Slow Cooking Transforms Cheap Cuts

Best French Onion Soup

Crispy Oatmeal Cookies

Mastering the Art of Stew

Sizzling Garlic Shrimp

Roasted Broccoli

www.cooksillustrated.com

$5.95 U.S./$6.95 CANADA

CONTENTS

January & February 2008

COOK'S ONLINE

Go to **www.cooksillustrated.com** to access all recipes from *Cook's Illustrated* since 1993 as well as updated tastings and testings. Watch videos of all the recipes in this issue being prepared and a special report on the cutting board testing.

EXOTIC MUSHROOMS Violet-stemmed blewit mushrooms, often called bluefoot, have a pronounced hominy or barley flavor and a firm, meaty texture. Fairy ring mushrooms have stems that are too tough to eat, but their dainty, bell-shaped caps yield a full-bodied, heady nuttiness. Mushrooms of the oyster variety include the hearty king oyster, silver-capped blue oyster, and abalone, which derives its name from its resemblance to the shellfish and rivals the blewit in meatiness. Oyster mushrooms are characterized by a clean, mild sweetness. Popular Japanese shimeiji mushrooms include the musky beech and the nutty pioppini. Namekos, also favored in Japanese cooking and similar in shape to the clustered shimeiji, are distinguished by their spongy, mucilaginous texture. Another textural oddity, the nearly translucent wood ear is rubbery and gelatinous when reconstituted from its more common dried form or when used fresh. Bear's head mushrooms have a flavor similar to asparagus and artichoke.

COVER: *Grapefruit* by Robert Papp; BACK COVER: *Exotic Mushrooms* by John Burgoyne

For list rental information, contact: Specialists Marketing Services, Inc., 1200 Harbor Blvd., 9th Floor, Weehawken, NJ 07087; 201-865-5800.
Editorial Office: 17 Station St., Brookline, MA 02445; 617-232-1000; fax 617-232-1572. Subscription inquiries, call 800-526-8442.
Postmaster: Send all new orders, subscription inquiries, and change-of-address notices to Cook's Illustrated, P.O. Box 7446, Red Oak, IA 51591-0446.

www.cooksillustrated.com
HOME OF AMERICA'S TEST KITCHEN

PRINTED IN THE USA

LOST RECIPES

The World's Food Fair. Boston. October 1896. Admission: 25 cents. Huge crowds throng the Mechanics Hall convention center. Women queue up for free samples from 200 different vendors: cereals, gelatins, extracts, candy, and custards. Table displays include "Edible Flowers" and "A Mermaid's Dinner." Luncheons are offered—a Dietetic Luncheon, a Hygienic Lunch—and teas as well, including Tennis Tea and Japanese Ceremonial Tea. Booths are constructed in the shape of buildings: a log cabin to sell pancake flour, a castle to sell all-purpose flour, and a Dutch cottage to promote Dutched cocoa. Other exhibits include a miniature margarine factory, a cereal machine that produces shredded wheat, an electrically operated dairy that churns out 3,000 pounds of butter each day, and a life-sized wax woman that promotes Pearline soap. Just like today, food and cooking were at the convergence of popular entertainment and capitalism.

Newspapers were raucous, loudmouthed, commercial, and utterly working class, and Boston's private clubs were much the same. Yes, in 1906 H.G. Wells accused the members of the Club of Odd Volumes of too much preoccupation with the past, but another private club of the period presented an evening entitled the Dime Museum, one of the features of which was the Bearded Lady, who was described by a reporter as an "exquisite picture of ravishing loveliness, whose heaving and sensitive bosom is concealed from view by her depending beard." Yet another bizarre dining establishment of the period featured a member who ate only with his toes and housed a live bear as a mascot.

The world was getting rapidly smaller. Three innovations—steamships, refrigeration, and railroads—meant that perishable goods could be transported across the country or across the Atlantic, both in and out of Boston. The S. S. Pierce supermarket offered more than 4,000 items for sale, including mushrooms grown in old quarries near Paris, the highest-quality Spanish olives, and isinglass, a precursor to modern gelatin (originally made from the bladders of Russian sturgeon, but a cheaper substitute was later made from cod). Quincy Market was a hotbed of local vendors, the original farmers' market, if you will, and Boston was also full of smaller establishments, many of which specialized in poultry (chicken, partridge, quail, woodcock, snipe, etc.), fruit, confectionary products (cream cakes, Washington pie, vanilla jumbles, charlotte russe, etc.), seafood (scallops, smelt, clams, whitefish, salt cod, shad roe, mackerel, etc.), or household dry goods.

Christopher Kimball

The *Boston Globe* contained two food columns: one entitled "The Housekeeper's Department" and the other penned by the Boston Cooking School. Recipes included Dewey's Fried Shortcakes (a recipe that was rediscovered in Pennsylvania almost 100 years later by Marion Cunningham, the author of the revised *Fannie Farmer Cookbook*), Stuffed Baked Tomatoes, Welsh Rarebit, Oatmeal Drink, Eggs Nest on Toast, Corn Bread, Salmon Croquettes, Chicken Paté, both Puff and Plain Paste, Brown Bread, Leap Year Cake, Pressed Cake, New Brides Cake, Pear and Rice Pudding, and Cinnamon Tea, to name a few. Staid? Repressed? Hardly. It was a mongrel mix of classic French (puff pastry and paté), Southern (corn bread), English (pudding), health food (oatmeal drink), pioneer (brown bread), and classic American (layer cakes). And what about taking a Victorian cooking class? Look no further than *Fannie Farmer* to learn about five types of acids (acetic, tartaric, malic, citric, and oxalic), four types of starch (cornstarch, arrowroot, tapioca, and sago), and three types of fermentation (alcoholic, acetic, and lactic). Readers of this publication will find those lists familiar. In addition, you would learn how to cook a live terrapin, including drawing out the head and removing the skin, and how to boil a calf's head for mock turtle soup.

You might ask about cooking technique. Sure, they were cooking on coal stoves, but they were thoroughly modern in their approach. Farmer suggested that when using only one set of measuring cups, start with dry, then liquid, and finally fat/shortening; to make coffee, steep 2 tablespoons grounds in 1 cup cold water overnight and then bring the mixture to a boil the next morning to serve; birds should be dredged in flour before roasting to create a better crust; and when baking bread, reduce the oven temperature for the last 15 minutes to cook the interior after the crust has been set. Not bad for 1896—or 2008, for that matter.

Many of you have, like me, a long reach back through history. I grew up on a small mountain farm, learned to simmer and bake over a wood stove, and extracted water from the well under the side porch using a loosely bolted green metal pump handle located in the pantry sink. I remember poor milk the color of an early morning sky—faint, powdery, and tinged with blue—hot baked potatoes opened with the swat of a fist, and baking powder biscuits stored in mistletoed Christmas tins separated by ragged, hoary rounds of waxed paper. A recently unearthed snapshot of my father standing arms stretched back, hat high, on an airfield in Egypt during the Second World War looks historical, but hoecakes, wine jelly, Irish moss, and chocolate cream do not. Good food lives on. If it pleases the palate, it's as timeless as an open-eyed kiss taken in the back of a school bus.

The history of food has sailed oceans to shipwreck on America's shores. Where this half-remembered flotsam has fetched up is sometimes hard to say, but the recipes are still there, buried perhaps, but not so far beneath our footsteps. We claim cooking as something new, yet another form of modern art, while the feasts of the ancients still echo through flickers of candlelight.

That is why so many of us stand at the stove to remember—to recall the wood smoke, the perfume of warm molasses, the fecund aroma of yeast. One lost recipe remembered is like love rediscovered, as fresh and unexpected as that first kiss.

FOR INQUIRIES, ORDERS, OR MORE INFORMATION:

www.cooksillustrated.com

At www.cooksillustrated.com, you can order books and subscriptions, sign up for our free e-newsletter, or renew your magazine subscription. Join the website and gain access to 15 years of *Cook's Illustrated* recipes, equipment tests, and ingredient tastings, as well as *Cook's Live* companion videos for every recipe in this issue.

COOKBOOKS

We sell more than 50 cookbooks by the editors of *Cook's Illustrated*. To order, visit our bookstore at www.cooksillustrated.com or call 800-611-0759 (or 515-246-6911 from outside the U.S.).

COOK'S ILLUSTRATED Magazine

Cook's Illustrated magazine (ISSN 1068-2821), number 90, is published bimonthly by Boston Common Press Limited Partnership, 17 Station St., Brookline, MA 02445. Copyright 2008 Boston Common Press Limited Partnership. Periodicals postage paid at Boston, Mass., and additional mailing offices USPS #012487. Publications Mail Agreement No. 40020778. Return undeliverable Canadian addresses to P.O. Box 875, Station A, Windsor, Ontario N9A 6P2. POSTMASTER: Send address changes to Cook's Illustrated, P.O. Box 7446, Red Oak, IA 51591-0446. For subscription and gift subscription orders, subscription inquiries, or change-of-address notices, call 800-526-8442 in the U.S. or 515-247-7571 from outside the U.S., or write us at Cook's Illustrated, P.O. Box 7446, Red Oak, IA 51591-0446.

NOTES FROM READERS

BY SANDRA WU AND DAVID PAZMIÑO

When to Oil a Grill Grate

Your recipes call for oiling the grill grate after it's heated, but my husband insists on oiling prior to heating. His premise is that the grilling surface is better able to hold the oil when it's still cool. Is one way better than the other?

SUZANNE EYERMAN
LONGMONT, COLO.

To prevent food from sticking, oiling your grill grate is essential. The reason we call for oiling the grate after it has been heated is because the grate always needs to be scraped down before it can be used. Debris is more readily removed from a hot grate than a cool one, and once these stuck-on bits are gone, the grate can be more effectively slicked down with an oil-dipped wad of paper towels.

Oiling the grill grate once it's hot also helps the oil to bond quickly to the metal and prevent proteins from sticking to the grill grate. When oil is added to a cold grill grate, the oil slowly vaporizes as the grill reaches the desired cooking temperature. The more the oil vaporizes, the less oil will be left on the grill grate, making sticking more likely. One more point: Never try to take a shortcut by spraying a hot cooking grate with nonstick cooking spray. You might save about 10 seconds, but risk having a flare-up on your hands.

Seasoning Cold Food

Is it true that cold food needs more salt to taste fully seasoned than the same food when eaten hot?

BILL SIEVER
NORTHAMPTON, MASS.

We often find that food that tastes great piping hot seems underseasoned when it is sampled again after refrigeration. To test this observation, we made some vichyssoise (cold potato-leek soup) and gazpacho. We divided the vichyssoise into two batches, then warmed one and kept the other ice-cold. For the gazpacho, we served one batch straight from the refrigerator and the second at room temperature. The results? Even though both versions of each soup contained the same amount of salt, tasters judged the hot and room-temperature soups saltier and better seasoned. This perception was particularly pronounced in the milder-tasting vichyssoise.

It turns out that chilling dulls all flavors, including saltiness, making them more difficult for the taste buds to perceive. But the next time you make a dish to serve cold, don't jump the gun by oversalting while the food is still hot. Instead, season as you would normally. Once the food is chilled, taste and add more salt as desired.

Keeping Waffles Warm

How can I keep waffles warm and crisp until I'm ready to serve them?

CRISWELL CHOI
SAN MATEO, CALIF.

We experimented with several methods of keeping waffles warm and crisp before finding one that worked well. First, we set the waffles on a baking sheet in a 200-degree oven, which was just hot enough to keep them warm without actually recooking them. But by the time the last batch was done, the ones that had been waiting in the oven the longest had lost their crispness. Next, we placed the waffles on a wire rack set in a baking sheet. Though this method improved matters dramatically by allowing hot air to circulate underneath and keep the waffles crisp, it also dried them out over time. To retain moisture, we covered the waffles with a clean kitchen towel, removing it only when the last waffle was in the oven. After a few more minutes in the oven, the waffles—held for about 30 minutes total—recrisped and tasted like they had just come from the waffle iron.

Sweet versus Hot Paprika

How can I substitute sweet paprika in recipes that call for hot paprika?

MELANIE FILES
MARTINSBURG, W.VA.

Both sweet and hot paprika come from the dried pods of *Capsicum annuum L.*, which includes a large swath of pepper varieties ranging from sweet red bell peppers to hot chile peppers. The type of pepper used will influence the flavor, spiciness, and intensity of the paprika. Sweet paprika is made from only the middle layer of the pepper's outer wall (the mesocarp), while hot paprika also contains some of the white veins (the placenta) and seeds, where most of the heat resides. Most paprika labeled "paprika" or "mild paprika" is of the sweet variety.

Heat aside, we wanted to find out if there were any other flavor differences between the two varieties and if one was better suited for a particular type of recipe than another. We took our winning brand (Penzeys Hungary Sweet Paprika) and its spicy counterpart (Penzeys Half-Sharp Paprika—the retailer's only type of hot paprika) and used each in three applications: chicken paprikash, barbecue sauce, and a dry rub for baked chicken breast. Most tasters found the sweet paprika, with its "bright," "well-balanced," and "smoky" flavors, to be a better choice in the chicken paprikash; the hot paprika was less flavorful, aside from its pronounced heat. The differences were even more apparent in the spice-rubbed chicken breasts, where the hot paprika took on an unpleasant bitter edge. In the barbecue sauce, however, tasters found both varieties perfectly acceptable, and some preferred the sauce made with the hot paprika. Here, its spiciness seemed less aggressive and was actually a virtue.

If yours is going to be a one-paprika household, we recommend stocking the more versatile sweet, as a pinch or two of cayenne pepper can be added to replicate the flavor of the hot stuff.

Hot paprika (left) lends spiciness but not much flavor; sweet paprika (right) provides earthy, smoky notes.

Raw-Milk Cheese

Is it possible to buy raw-milk cheese in the United States? My understanding is that the federal government requires all cheeses to be made from pasteurized milk. Is that true?

MILTON GARBER
JEFFERSON CITY, MO.

Raw-milk cheeses can be purchased domestically, but they may not be exactly like the raw-milk cheeses available in Europe. The U.S. Food and Drug Administration (FDA) requires that cheeses manufactured here and abroad from raw (unpasteurized) milk must be aged for at least 60 days at 35 degrees or higher at their point of origin before being imported or sold. Any cheese whose recipe precludes it from being aged longer than 60 days is affected by the regulation, including soft-ripened cheeses (such as Camembert and Brie), washed-rind cheeses (such as Epoisses), natural-rind goat's milk cheeses, and fresh (unaged) cheeses. The purpose of the FDA-enforced waiting period is to give the safe-to-ingest bacteria in the cheese (such as lactobacillus) sufficient time to multiply and become the dominant bacteria, which obstructs the potential growth of harmful bacteria such as E. coli, listeria, and salmonella.

As a result of the FDA rule, heavily pasteurized milk is often used to produce these cheeses in the United States, but not without a sacrifice in flavor. Cheese authority Steven Jenkins told us that a cheese will "immediately report" whether it was made from raw milk by the "depth, intensity, nuance, [and] rusticity" of its flavors. A heavily pasteurized cheese, he said, will be equally revealing, with flavors that are "muted, vitiated, absent, and blurry." Some cheese makers deal with the issue by pasteurizing milk slowly and gently at a low temperature. Jenkins said that this procedure, known as thermization, preserves flavor molecules and yields excellent cheese virtually indistinguishable from raw-milk cheeses. The only way to identify these lightly pasteurized cheeses is to ask your cheese monger.

Egg Substitutes

Is it okay to use egg substitutes instead of whole eggs for baking?

ELLEN McLAUGHLIN
VIA E-MAIL

➢In past tests using different brands of egg substitutes (yolk-free liquid-egg products composed mainly of egg whites, yellow coloring, flavorings, salt, and vegetable gums) to make scrambled eggs, we found Egg Beaters to be the best of the bunch. Despite an unnaturally bright yellow color and slightly spongy texture, Egg Beaters has decent flavor that tasters found acceptable. To see if this egg substitute would work in baking applications as well, we used it in place of real eggs in three recipes: yellow cake, peanut butter cookies, and custard pie filling.

The verdict? In all cases, tasters found Egg Beaters to be a reasonable substitute. The yellow cake made with engineered eggs didn't brown or rise quite as well as the one made with real eggs and had a slightly gummy top, but it was still acceptable, especially once the cake was frosted. The Egg Beaters and the real eggs turned out equally good results in the peanut butter cookies and the custard pie filling. (In fact, some tasters actually preferred the custard made with the egg substitute for its "less-eggy" flavor.)

While we still prefer real whole eggs to additive-laden egg substitutes, the vegetable gums in Egg Beaters do a good job of mimicking the texture of real yolks and will work just fine in most foods.

Good for more than just breakfast?

Turning Layer Cake into a Sheet Cake

Is there a rule of thumb to follow for converting layer cakes into sheet cakes? I find it much easier to frost a cake baked in a 13- by 9-inch baking dish than to frost a layer cake.

BETTY PARKER
FORT MYERS, FLA.

➢To answer your question, we followed our recipes for Rich and Tender Yellow Layer Cake (March/April 1999) and Old-Fashioned Chocolate Layer Cake (March/April 2006) without altering a thing in either batter. But instead of pouring each batter into two 9-inch round cake pans, we baked each cake in a 13- by 9-inch baking dish lined with parchment paper, following the baking times and oven temperatures in the recipes.

Each sheet cake required about five extra minutes of baking until a toothpick inserted in its center revealed a few moist crumbs: perfectly done. So the next time you want to prepare a recipe for two 9-inch layer cakes in a 13- by 9-inch baking dish, bake the cake as usual and add about five minutes of baking time to the original recipe (checking for doneness a few minutes early to prevent overbaking). Let the cake cool completely before frosting it in the pan or turning it out to be frosted.

WHAT IS IT?

I enjoy collecting antique kitchenware and recently bought this wire contraption. It looks like it may have been used to hold or lift things, but I'm not sure. Do you have any ideas?

KEUI-CHEN HSIEH, SAN DIEGO, CALIF.

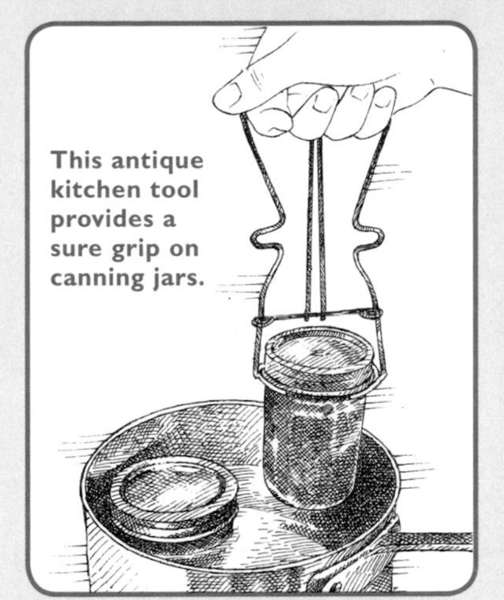
This antique kitchen tool provides a sure grip on canning jars.

We did some research and determined that this funny-looking gadget, made of wood and heavy-gauge wire, is an old-fashioned jar-lifter used to remove canning jars from their hot water baths, minimizing the risk of burns or broken jars. The gadget works like a pair of giant tongs. To use it, place your middle finger through the top loop and position the handles around the edge of the jar's ring top. Next, pull up on the wooden bars with your free fingers. The tension from the pulling action will cause the handles to close securely around the top of the lid, allowing jars of any size to be lifted up and out of the water. We found a few of these for sale online for about $6.

Grilling Safety

When grilling, is it OK to use the same pair of metal tongs to handle both raw and cooked chicken?

REBECCA FORMAN
STATEN ISLAND, N.Y.

➢You should never use the same tongs to handle both raw and fully cooked chicken (or any other meat) unless you wash them in hot, soapy water first. Using the same unwashed pair for both tasks would be an invitation for cross-contamination. Similarly, tongs used to pick up and flip raw or undercooked chicken should not be used to handle and serve grilled vegetables. We recommend buying a second pair of tongs.

Pastry Cloth

What exactly is pastry cloth? I've seen some recipes that call for it, but I wonder if using a floured work surface is good enough.

LAWRENCE ALDRED
PORTLAND, ORE.

➢Pastry cloth is a large, lightweight canvas cloth on which pastry dough can be rolled out. We found this item for sale on several cooking websites and tried it out for ourselves to see if it worked any better than a floured countertop.

We soon discovered that one key to using a pastry cloth successfully is making sure a little flour is rubbed into the fibers of the cloth. Otherwise, the dough tends to stick to the unfloured areas of the cloth, just as it will to the unfloured sections of a countertop. The pastry cloth made rolling out and transferring dough to a pie plate easier than doing the same on a countertop, but no easier than rolling out dough on a large piece of parchment paper or plastic wrap. Given that pastry cloths must be washed in between uses (fat residue gets stuck between the fibers and will become rancid if not removed, affecting the flavor of future dough), they are more trouble than they are worth.

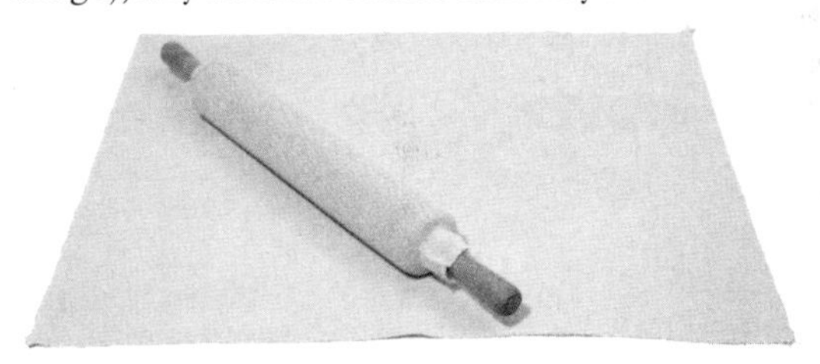
Pastry cloth is no better than parchment paper for rolling out dough.

Erratum

➢"Thinking Outside the Pantry" on page 17 of the November/December 2007 issue contained incomplete information. Here is the complete text. To replace 1 stick unsalted butter, use 1 stick salted butter - ½ teaspoon salt from recipe; to replace 1 cup buttermilk, use 1 cup milk + 1 tablespoon lemon juice allowed to thicken for 10 minutes; to replace 1 cup whole milk, use ⅝ cup skim milk + ⅜ cup half-and-half. We apologize for this error.

SEND US YOUR QUESTIONS We will provide a complimentary one-year subscription for each letter we print. Send your inquiry, name, address, and daytime telephone number to Notes from Readers, Cook's Illustrated, P.O. Box 470589, Brookline, MA 02447, or to notesfromreaders@americastestkitchen.com.

Quick Tips

COMPILED BY DAVID PAZMIÑO

No-Mess Measuring

It can be tricky to measure dry ingredients from small containers, such as cocoa powder or cornstarch boxes, without getting the work surface messy. To keep things tidy, Kate Griffin of Oakland, Calif., relies on a piece of parchment paper.

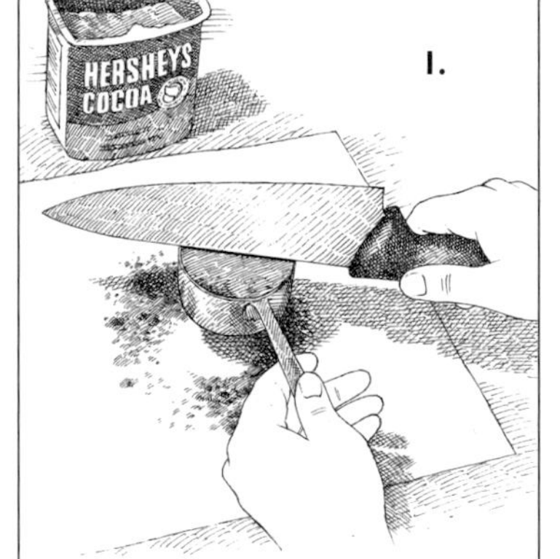

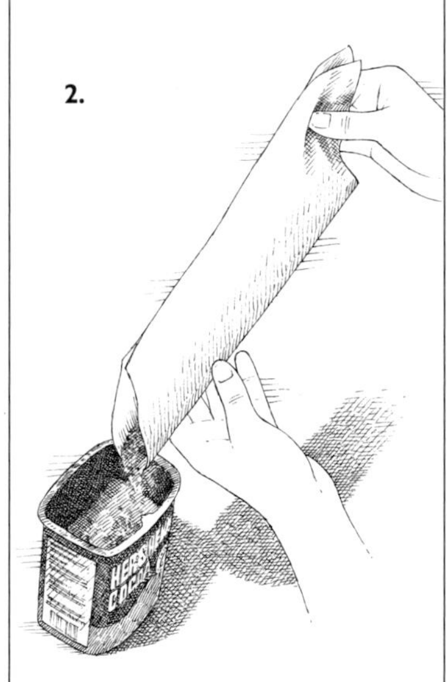

1. Place a dry measuring cup on a square of parchment or wax paper and measure the ingredient into the cup. Use a flat utensil to sweep excess onto the paper.
2. Holding the edges, pick up the paper and slide the excess ingredient back into the original container.

Cutting Marshmallows

Mini marshmallows are an important garnish for hot chocolate, but what if you only have large marshmallows on hand? Ari Wolfe of Princeton, N.J., found himself in such a predicament and reached for his kitchen shears, lightly spraying them with nonstick cooking spray to prevent the sticky marshmallows from adhering to the blades.

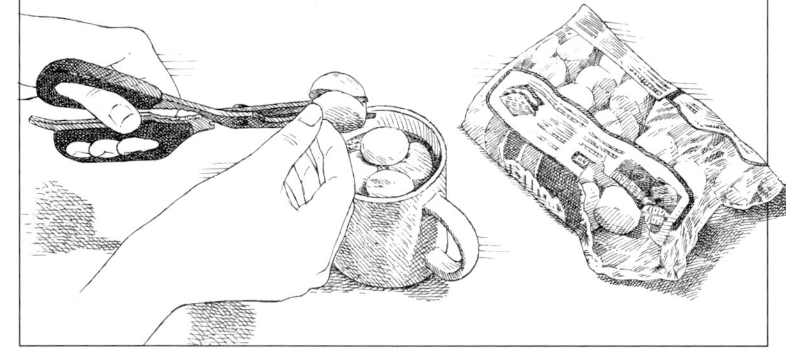

Portable Kitchen

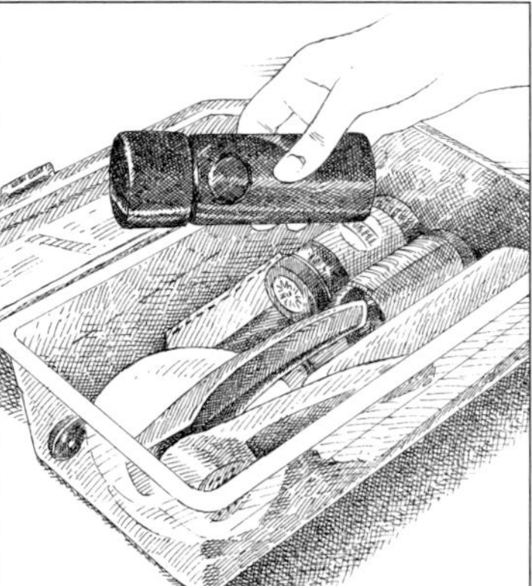

Robert Romano of San Diego, Calif., often misses must-have ingredients or favorite kitchen tools when cooking at friends' homes. His solution? He packs a few sharp knives and other indispensable items like a garlic press, a pepper grinder, his favorite type of salt, and a bottle of extra-virgin olive oil into a plastic container to take along. Multiple containers can easily be stacked on top of each other and lowered into a paper grocery bag.

Stacking Glass Measuring Cups

Stacking glass measuring cups can result in chipped and broken edges. Celeste Morien of Medina, N.Y., found that a small square of wax or parchment paper placed between the cups prevents them from chipping and makes them easier to separate when needed.

Removing Refrigerator Odors

Mary LeBrun of Raymond, Maine, came up with a technique that works better than baking soda to deodorize a refrigerator. She places a handful of charcoal briquettes in a disposable plastic container (with no lid) in the refrigerator or freezer. Once the offending smell has dissipated, she simply discards the container.

A Cleaner with Frills

Susannah Dickey of High Point, N.C., came up with an ingenious tool for removing bits of food from the nooks and crannies of hard-to-clean kitchen tools such as pastry tips, garlic presses, and rasp-style graters: the frilly end of a toothpick.

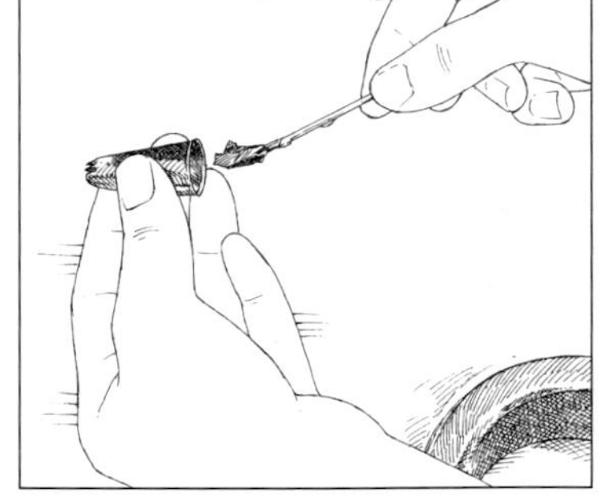

Unblemished Cauliflower

Even the freshest head of cauliflower can have minor blemishes. Sharon Cullinane of Farmington, N.Y., gently rubs a rasp-style grater over discolored areas until they disappear.

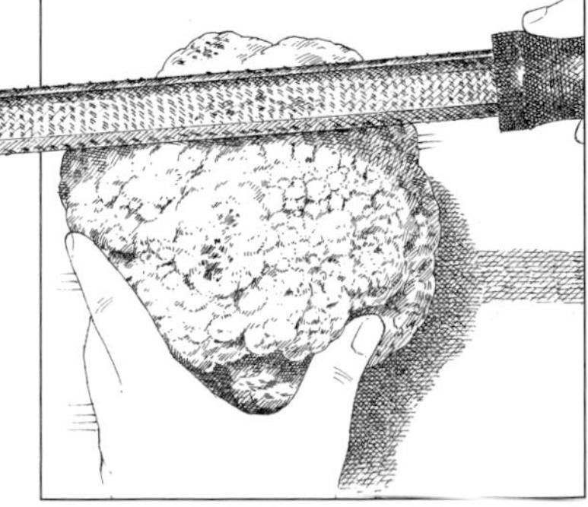

Send Us Your Tip We will provide a complimentary one-year subscription for each tip we print. Send your tip, name, and address to Quick Tips, Cook's Illustrated, P.O. Box 470589, Brookline, MA 02447, or to quicktips@americastestkitchen.com.

ILLUSTRATION: JOHN BURGOYNE

Citrus-Flavored Cocktails

Susan Abell of Hinesburg, Vt., came up with an idea for using up the zest taken from juiced lemons, limes, grapefruit, or oranges. Combine the grated zest from 1 to 2 pieces of fruit with 1 cup of vodka in a glass jar and refrigerate. When it's time to use the vodka in a citrusy cocktail, strain out the zest with a fine-mesh strainer.

Perfect Pie Pastry

Rolling pie dough into an even circle requires deft hands and experience. Joy Lillie of San Jose, Calif., uses parchment paper and a pencil to make the process less daunting.

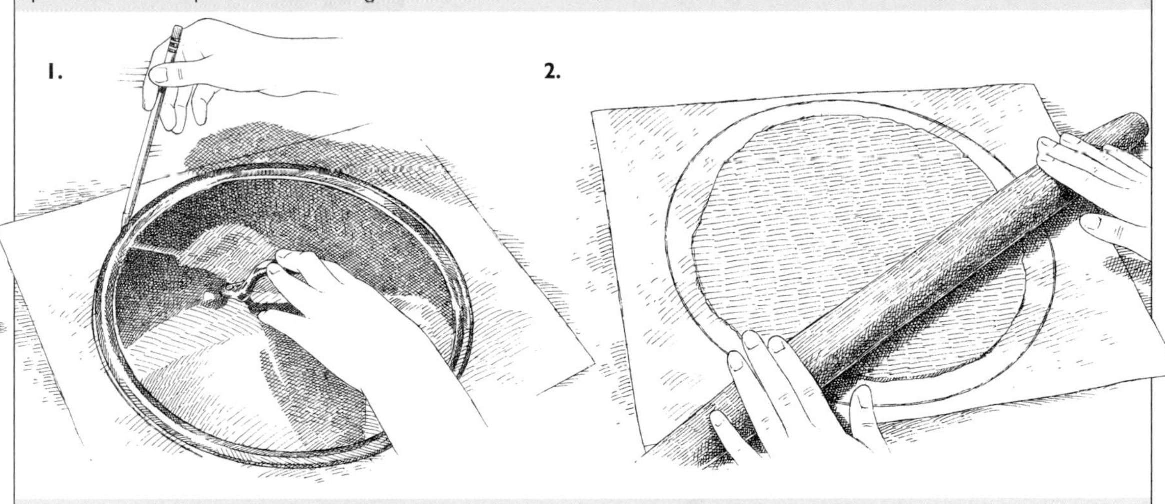

1. Place a 12-inch skillet lid on a sheet of parchment paper. Using a pencil, trace a circle around the lid.
2. Roll out a disk of lightly floured dough on the parchment, using the tracing as a guide and stopping when the dough reaches the line.

Makeshift Double Boiler

Many recipes call for melting chocolate in a homemade double boiler, which is created by suspending a heatproof bowl over a pot of simmering water. Finding herself with a bowl too small for her pot, Marika van Eerde of Santa Barbara, Calif., came up with a clever solution.

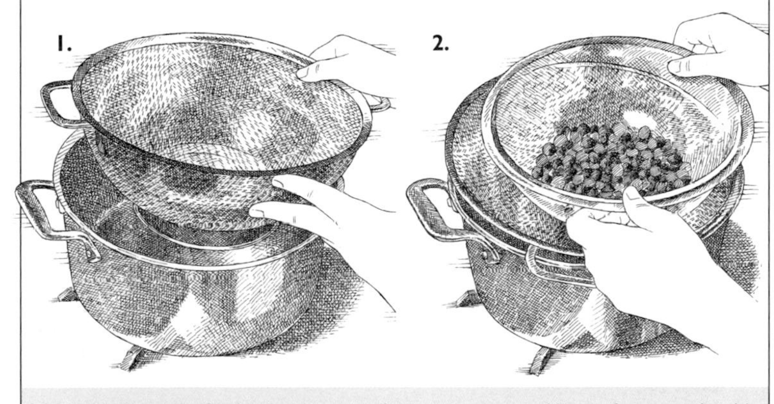

1. Place a heatproof colander in a pot of simmering water (the perforations should be above the level of the water).
2. Set a heatproof bowl with the chocolate inside the colander. Using an oven mitt to avoid a steam burn, stir the chocolate with a spatula until it melts.

Chemical-Free Cleaning

To avoid cleaning kitchen countertops with chemicals that might contaminate food, Carolyn Roberts of Vienna, Va., uses a spray bottle filled with equal parts white vinegar and water.

Scoring Chicken Skin

Cutting slashes in chicken skin with a knife to help render fat during cooking is a slippery job that often results in the meat being scored as well, leading to a loss of juices and drying out the meat. Tracey Bissell of West Hartford, Conn., found a better way: Pinch the chicken skin with one hand, then use kitchen shears in the other to snip the skin two or three times.

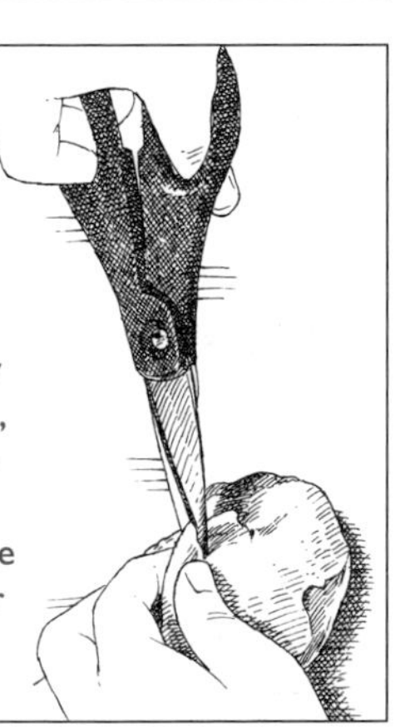

An Easier Squeeze

Pressing all the juice from a lemon or lime with a citrus juicer can be tricky. To ensure he gets every last drop, Fred Dunayer of Sarasota, Fla., employs the following technique:

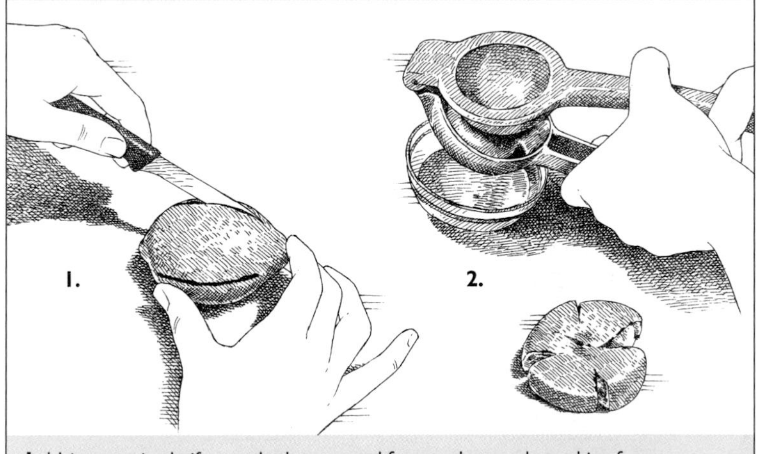

1. Using a paring knife, cut the lemon peel from pole to pole, making four ¼-inch-deep slits. Next, cut the lemon in half crosswise.
2. Place the lemon half in the juicer and squeeze to remove all of the juice.

Improving Cheap Roast Beef

Roasting inexpensive beef usually yields tough meat best suited for sandwiches. How do you transform a bargain cut into a tender, juicy roast that can stand on its own at dinner?

BY DAVID PAZMIÑO

For most families, Sunday roast beef isn't prime rib; it's a lesser cut that's sometimes good, sometimes not. The roasts my parents prepared throughout my childhood were typically tough and dried-out and better suited for sandwiches the next day. But when my grandfather was at the stove, he could take the same inexpensive cut and turn it into something special—tender, rosy, beefy-tasting meat that had everyone asking for seconds. I wanted to work the same kind of wizardry on my own Sunday roast.

First I needed to zero in on the most promising beef. After a week in the kitchen testing a slew of low-cost cuts (see "Low-Cost Lineup," right), I had a clear winner: the eye-round roast. Though less flavorful than fattier cuts from the shoulder (the chuck) and less tender than other meat from the back leg (the round), my eye roast had one key attribute the others lacked: a uniform shape from front to back. This was a roast that would not only cook evenly but look good on the plate as well.

Thinly slicing the eye round is the last step in transforming it from tough to tender.

The Showdown: High or Low Heat?

My next challenge was choosing between the two classic methods for roasting meat—high and fast or low and slow. I began with the more common high-heat approach, quickly searing the meat on the stovetop and then transferring it to a 450-degree oven for roasting. The technique works great with more upscale rib and loin cuts but showed its flaws with the leaner eye round, yielding meat that was overcooked and dried-out.

But before heading down the low-temperature path, which normally involves roasting meat in an oven set between 250 and 325 degrees, I wanted to try something more extreme. To extract maximum tenderness from meat, the popular 1960s nutritionist Adelle Davis advocated cooking it at the temperature desired when it was done. For a roast to reach an end temperature of 130 degrees for medium-rare, this process could involve 20 to 30 hours of cooking. Davis's advice wasn't new. Benjamin Thompson, the 18th-century physicist who invented the roasting oven, observed that leaving meat to cook overnight in an oven heated by a dying fire resulted in exceptional tenderness.

Tossing aside practical considerations like food safety and the gas bill, I decided I had to replicate these two experts' findings. I set the one oven in the test kitchen capable of maintaining such a low temperature to 130 degrees and popped in an eye round. Twenty-four hours later, I pulled out a roast with juicy, meltingly tender meat that tasters likened to beef tenderloin. What special beef magic was going on here?

The Lowdown

When I thought back to the test kitchen's discoveries in "The Problem with Thick-Cut Steaks" (May/June 2007), I had my answer: Beef contains enzymes that break down its connective tissues and act as natural tenderizers. These enzymes work faster as the temperature of the meat rises—but just until it reaches 122 degrees, at which point all action stops. Roasting the eye round in an oven set to 130 degrees allowed it to stay below 122 degrees far longer than when cooked in the typical low-temperature roasting range, transforming this lean, unassuming cut into something great.

But given that most ovens don't heat below 200 degrees—and that most home cooks don't want to run their ovens for a full day—how could I expect others to re-create my results? I would have

SHOPPING: Low-Cost Lineup

Not all bargain cuts have the potential to taste like a million bucks—or look like it when carved and served on a plate.

OUR FAVORITE
EYE-ROUND ROAST
($4.99 per pound)
We singled out this cut not only for its good flavor and relative tenderness but also for its uniform shape that guarantees even cooking and yields slices that look good on the plate.

TOO FATTY
CHUCK EYE
($3.99 per pound)
While undeniably tender and flavorful, its fat and gristle make this meat better for stew and pot roast than roast beef.

ODD SHAPE
TOP ROUND
($3.99 per pound)
A deli staple for sandwiches, this cut comes in irregular shapes that can cook unevenly.

TOUGH TO CARVE
BOTTOM ROUND RUMP
($4.29 per pound)
We ruled out this roast for being both tough and hard to carve against the grain.

COOK'S LIVE Original Test Kitchen Videos
www.cooksillustrated.com

HOW TO MAKE
- Slow-Roasted Beef

VIDEO TIPS
- Which cut of meat should I buy?
- How do I carve roast beef?
- Do I really need an instant-read thermometer?
- Can I check the temperature of my oven without an oven thermometer?

RECIPE SHORTHAND | THE TRANSFORMATION FROM TOUGH TO TENDER

Along with salting and searing, the key to our eye round's makeover into a tender, juicy roast is keeping its internal temperature below 122 degrees for as long as possible. Below 122 degrees, the meat's enzymes act as natural tenderizers, breaking down its tough connective tissues.

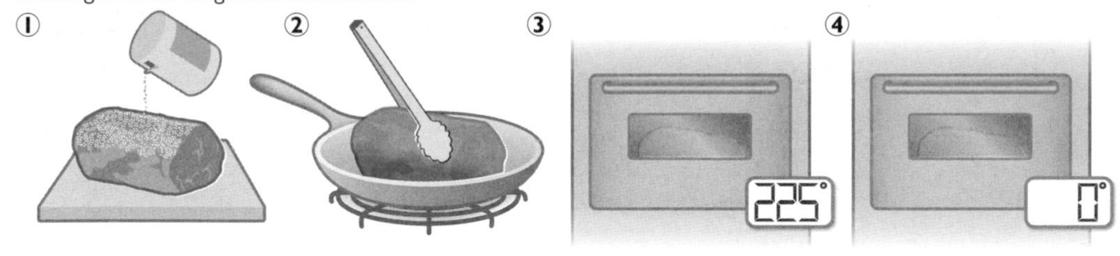

1. **SALT** Salt the roast and allow it to rest for 18 to 24 hours. Salt breaks down proteins to improve texture.
2. **SEAR** Sear the meat in a hot pan before roasting. While this won't affect tenderness, it will boost flavor.
3. **OVEN ON** Cook the meat in an oven set to 225 degrees and open the door as infrequently as possible.
4. **OVEN OFF** When the roast reaches 115 degrees, turn off oven and continue to cook the roast as the oven cools.

to go as low as I could and see what happened. To accommodate the widest possible range of ovens, I settled on 225 degrees as my lowest starting point. I also decided I would brown the meat first to give it nice color and a crusty exterior. (While tender, my 130-degree roast had an unappetizing gray exterior.) Searing would also help to ensure food safety, since bacteria on roasts are generally confined to the outside.

When I took the roast out of the oven, however, I was disappointed. It was tender, but nothing like the texture of the eye round cooked at 130 degrees. What could I do to keep the meat below 122 degrees longer? A new idea occurred to me: Why not shut off the oven just before the roast reached 122 degrees? As the oven cooled, the roast would continue to cook even more slowly.

Using a meat-probe thermometer to track the internal temperature of the roast, I shut off the oven when the meat reached 115 degrees. Sure enough, the meat stayed below 122 degrees 30 minutes longer, allowing its enzymes to continue the work of tenderizing, before creeping to 130 degrees for medium-rare. Tasters were certainly happy with this roast. It was remarkably tender and juicy for a roast that cost so little.

The Home Stretch

With the tenderness problem solved, it was time to tackle taste. So far I'd simply sprinkled salt and pepper on the roast just before searing it. Perhaps the flavor would improve if the meat were salted overnight or even brined. Brining—normally reserved for less fatty pork and poultry—certainly pumped more water into the beef and made it very juicy, but it also made it taste bland, watery, and less beefy. Next I tried salting the meat for first four, then 12, and finally 24 hours. As might be expected, the roast benefited most from the longest salting. Because the process of osmosis causes salt to travel from areas of higher to lower concentration, the full 24 hours gave it the most time to penetrate deep into the meat. There was another benefit: Salt, like the enzymes in meat, breaks down proteins to further improve texture.

At last I had tender, flavorful beef for a Sunday roast that even my grandfather would have been proud to serve to his family. The leftovers—if there were any—would have no need for mayonnaise or mustard to taste good.

SLOW-ROASTED BEEF

SERVES 6 TO 8

We don't recommend cooking this roast past medium. Open the oven door as little as possible and remove the roast from the oven while taking its temperature. If the roast has not reached the desired temperature in the time specified in step 3, heat the oven to 225 degrees for 5 minutes, shut it off, and continue to cook the roast to the desired temperature. For a smaller (2½- to 3½-pound) roast, reduce the amount of kosher salt to 3 teaspoons (1½ teaspoons table salt) and black pepper to 1½ teaspoons. For a 4½- to 6-pound roast, cut in half crosswise before cooking to create 2 smaller roasts. Slice the roast as thinly as possible and serve with Horseradish Cream Sauce, if desired (recipe follows).

- 1 **boneless eye-round roast (3½ to 4½ pounds) (see note above)**
- 4 **teaspoons kosher salt or 2 teaspoons table salt**
- 2 **teaspoons plus 1 tablespoon vegetable oil**
- 2 **teaspoons ground black pepper**

1. Sprinkle all sides of roast evenly with salt. Wrap with plastic wrap and refrigerate 18 to 24 hours.

2. Adjust oven rack to middle position and heat oven to 225 degrees. Pat roast dry with paper towels; rub with 2 teaspoons oil and sprinkle all sides evenly with pepper. Heat remaining tablespoon oil in 12-inch skillet over medium-high heat until starting to smoke. Sear roast until browned on all sides, 3 to 4 minutes per side. Transfer roast to wire rack set in rimmed baking sheet. Roast until meat-probe thermometer or instant-read thermometer inserted into center of roast registers 115 degrees for medium-rare, 1¼ to 1¾ hours, or 125 degrees for medium, 1¾ to 2¼ hours.

3. Turn oven off; leave roast in oven, without opening door, until meat-probe thermometer or instant-read thermometer inserted into center of roast registers 130 degrees for medium-rare or 140 degrees for medium, 30 to 50 minutes longer. Transfer roast to carving board and let rest 15 minutes. Slice meat crosswise as thinly as possible and serve.

HORSERADISH CREAM SAUCE

MAKES ABOUT 1 CUP

- ½ **cup heavy cream**
- ½ **cup prepared horseradish**
- 1 **teaspoon table salt**
- ⅛ **teaspoon ground black pepper**

Whisk cream in medium bowl until thickened but not yet holding soft peaks, 1 to 2 minutes. Gently fold in horseradish, salt, and pepper. Transfer to serving bowl and refrigerate at least 30 minutes or up to 1 hour before serving.

EQUIPMENT TESTING:

Meat-Probe Thermometers

Repeatedly opening the oven door to monitor the internal temperature of a roast can throw cooking times off kilter. One solution? Meat-probe thermometers. These remote devices transmit temperature from a long probe left in the meat and attached to a thin cord that snakes out of the oven to a digital console. But don't throw out your instant-read thermometer just yet. We tested 11 models—several by the same manufacturers—and not one was flawless. The ones that accurately measured temperature sported function buttons that were too slow or too hard to figure out. Others that were user-friendly were also unreliable.

The best of the bunch—an easy-to-use thermometer from ThermoWorks ($19)—was great when it worked but has probes that even its manufacturer admits are sometimes defective. Until a better meat probe comes on the market, we recommend this one—with reservations. Check the probe's accuracy by boiling water and taking a reading before trying it with a roast. If the probe doesn't read very close to 212 degrees, ask for a replacement. For complete testing results, go to www.cooksillustrated.com/february.

–Elizabeth Bomze

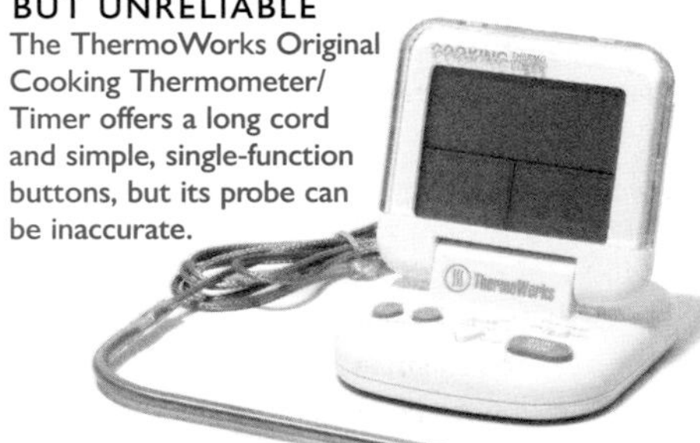

USER-FRIENDLY BUT UNRELIABLE
The ThermoWorks Original Cooking Thermometer/Timer offers a long cord and simple, single-function buttons, but its probe can be inaccurate.

Introducing French Chicken in a Pot

Taking cues from a French technique for cooking chicken in a covered pot, we forgo crispy skin for succulent meat and unforgettable flavor.

BY CHARLES KELSEY

I first encountered *poulet en cocotte* in a Parisian bistro last fall. Recommended to me by the waiter as a specialty of the house, the dish featured a whole chicken baked with a smattering of root vegetables in a covered pot. It was just the kind of homey comfort food I was craving on that cold, wet night. The bird arrived at my table in a cast-iron pot, and my anticipation grew as the waiter lifted the lid. At first glance, the chicken was nothing to rave about—it had pale, soft skin very unlike the crisp exterior of the roasted poultry I was used to—but its deep aroma was better than that of any roast chicken I could remember. My first bite confirmed that the dish was very special, indeed—the meat was incredibly tender and juicy, with a rich, soul-satisfying flavor.

As I continued to savor each bite, I began to think about the American obsession with crisp chicken skin. We are so bent on getting this one aspect right that we'll sacrifice what's really important—the meat. I'd certainly be willing to give up a crisp exterior if it meant I could have tender, succulent meat bursting with concentrated chicken flavor. I had to try making poulet en cocotte at home.

As it bakes in a Dutch oven, the chicken releases juices that stay in the pot, contributing to exceptionally moist meat and a rich-tasting jus.

Blowing Off Steam

The basic method for poulet en cocotte is simple: Place a seasoned chicken in a pot, scatter in a small handful of chopped vegetables, cover, and bake. Unlike braising, little to no liquid is added to the pot, resulting in a drier cooking environment. Many of the recipes I found called for auxiliary ingredients such as bacon, mushrooms, or tomatoes. But when I tried these extras, I found they served only to cover up what I was really after: great chicken flavor, pure and simple, like I'd had in Paris. I would stick with the chunks of potatoes, onions, and carrots I remembered from that meal.

As I continued to experiment with different recipes in the test kitchen, I realized the bistro had described their dish as a specialty of the house with good reason: Nothing I made could compare. Though most recipes did nothing to the chicken except season it before placing it in the pot to bake, I decided extra measures were necessary. I tried basting the bird, but going to the oven every 20 minutes was a hassle that had little impact on the taste. Next I tried lightly browning the top and bottom of the chicken on the stovetop before baking. Now I was getting somewhere—the flavor was beginning to deepen. But how could I get even more intense chicken flavor? I remembered earlier tests in which I'd added a splash of wine or broth to the pot at the start of cooking. These versions resulted in meat that was very juicy, but the steamier environment created a washed-out flavor. What if I actually *decreased* the humidity inside the pot? Would that give me the result I was looking for?

Eager for answers, I prepped a new chicken and a batch of vegetables, drying each thoroughly with paper towels before adding them to the pot. This had little effect. And then it dawned on me that the vegetables were releasing liquid and making the pot too steamy. To create something close to a one-pot meal, I had been using more vegetables and in larger chunks than I remembered from my bistro dish. But I'd gladly sacrifice the veggies if it meant a bird with better flavor.

My next go-round, I cooked a chicken by itself save for a little oil to prevent it from sticking. When I pulled the pot from the oven and removed the lid, a tiny puff of steam emerged—not the great whoosh that had been escaping from the tests with vegetables. This was a bird with great flavor that won over tasters and reminded me of my meal in Paris. And with no vegetables to soak them up, the flavorful juices remained in the pot. After defatting the liquid, I had a simple, richly flavored jus to accompany my chicken—a huge bonus. Still, the bird was not perfect. Tasters complained that the breast meat was a tad tough and fibrous, and I had to agree. I wondered what a lower oven temperature would do.

Timing Is Everything

Setting up a half dozen chickens in pots, I tested a range of oven temperatures below 400 degrees. To account for pots with poorly fitting lids, I sealed each with foil before adding the top, ensuring that as much of the chicken juices as possible would stay inside. Temperatures from 300 to 375 degrees produced better results, but even lower temperatures—between 250 and 300 degrees—yielded chickens with incredibly tender breast meat. And while these birds took much longer than average to cook (about an hour and a half—all walk-away time, mind you), tasters raved about the meat's rich, concentrated flavor, which was all thanks to the technique: slow-cooking the chicken in nothing more than its own juices.

The last cooking hurdle to clear was the matter of the dark meat not cooking quickly enough. By the time the breast meat was perfectly cooked to 160 degrees, the dark meat (which needs to be cooked to 175 degrees) still wasn't ready. Placing the oven rack on the lowest position, so it was closer to the heat source, combined with browning the dark meat for an extra minute or two, solved the problem.

With the cooking process under control, it was time to finesse the flavors. Two teaspoons of kosher salt was enough to season the chicken without making the jus too salty. And I discovered that I could get away with adding a small amount of potently flavored aromatic vegetables—chopped onion, celery, whole garlic cloves—to the pot. Lightly browning them along with the chicken helped wick away any excess moisture, and the caramelization added rich color and flavor to the jus. Stirring in a little fresh lemon juice to finish the jus brightened and balanced all of its flavors.

My French Chicken in a Pot will never place first in a beauty contest, of course, if a browned roast bird is the standard. But its tender, juicy, intensely flavored meat is sure to be a winner every time.

FRENCH CHICKEN IN A POT

SERVES 4

The cooking times in the recipe are for a 4½- to 5-pound bird. A 3½- to 4½-pound chicken will take about an hour to cook, and a 5- to 6-pound bird will take close to 2 hours. We developed this recipe to work with a 5- to 8-quart Dutch oven with a tight-fitting lid. If using a 5-quart pot, do not cook a chicken larger than 5 pounds. Use the best chicken available, such as a Bell & Evans. If using a kosher chicken, reduce the kosher salt to 1 teaspoon (or ½ teaspoon table salt). If you choose not to serve the skin with the chicken, simply remove it before carving. The amount of jus will vary depending on the size of the chicken; season it with about ¼ teaspoon lemon juice for every ¼ cup.

- 1 whole roasting chicken (4½ to 5 pounds), giblets removed and discarded, wings tucked under back (see note above)
- 2 teaspoons kosher salt or 1 teaspoon table salt
- ¼ teaspoon ground black pepper
- 1 tablespoon olive oil
- 1 small onion, chopped medium (about ½ cup)
- 1 small celery stalk, chopped medium (about ¼ cup)
- 6 medium garlic cloves, peeled and trimmed
- 1 bay leaf
- 1 medium sprig fresh rosemary (optional)
- ½–1 teaspoon juice from 1 lemon

1. Adjust oven rack to lowest position and heat oven to 250 degrees. Pat chicken dry with paper towels and season with salt and pepper. Heat oil in large Dutch oven over medium heat until just smoking. Add chicken breast-side down; scatter onion, celery, garlic, bay leaf, and rosemary (if using) around chicken. Cook until breast is lightly browned, about 5 minutes. Using a wooden spoon inserted into cavity of bird, flip chicken breast-side up and cook until chicken and vegetables are well browned, 6 to 8 minutes. Remove Dutch oven from heat; place large sheet of foil over pot and cover tightly with lid. Transfer pot to oven and cook until instant-read thermometer registers 160 degrees when inserted in thickest part of breast and 175 degrees in thickest part of thigh, 80 to 110 minutes.

2. Transfer chicken to carving board, tent with foil, and rest 20 minutes. Meanwhile, strain chicken juices from pot through fine-mesh strainer into fat separator, pressing on solids to extract liquid; discard solids (you should have about ¾ cup juices). Allow liquid to settle 5 minutes, then pour into saucepan and set over low heat. Carve chicken, adding any accumulated juices to saucepan. Stir lemon juice into jus to taste. Serve chicken, passing jus at table.

Dry Cooking versus Braising

French Chicken in a Pot shares some similarities with braised chicken—both are cooked in covered pots in low-temperature ovens to yield tender, flavorful meat. Unlike braising, however, where lots of liquid is added to the pot, our chicken is placed in a dry pot and left to cook in nothing more than the essence of its own juices.

DRY ENVIRONMENT
In a dry pot with no added liquid, juices that come out of the chicken go right back into it, undiluted by other flavors.

WET ENVIRONMENT
The wet environment of a braise creates an ongoing exchange between the flavors of the chicken as well as other ingredients, such as wine, broth, and vegetables.

EQUIPMENT TESTING:

Is a Clay Cooker Better?

Clay pot roasters have garnered fame for coaxing remarkable flavor from few ingredients and minimal work: You simply soak the cooker in water for 15 minutes, add the raw ingredients, and place the covered pot in a cold oven. You then crank the heat up to at least 400 degrees. Theoretically, the steam released from the water-soaked clay and the gradual temperature increase should yield tender, juicy meat.

Can a clay cooker outperform a Dutch oven? To find out, we compared two batches of our French Chicken in a Pot, one cooked in a Dutch oven and the other adapted for a clay roaster. We preferred the Dutch oven method. Though both chickens cooked up equally moist and fall-apart tender, clay cookers are not stovetop-safe, so we needed to brown the chicken in a skillet before transferring it to the clay pot. We'll stick with the Dutch oven.

–Elizabeth Bomze

ONLY IN A HOT OVEN
Clay cookers aren't stovetop-safe, so you'll need to brown chicken separately.

COOK'S LIVE Original Test Kitchen Videos

www.cooksillustrated.com

HOW TO MAKE
- French Chicken in a Pot

VIDEO TIPS
- Which Dutch oven should I buy?
- How can I separate fat without a fat separator?

KEYS TO SUCCESS | MOIST CHICKEN WITH CONCENTRATED FLAVOR

1. BROWN Sear chicken on both sides to enhance flavor.

2. SEAL Cover pot with foil before adding lid to trap chicken juices inside.

3. SLOW-COOK Cook chicken at 250 degrees for 80 to 110 minutes.

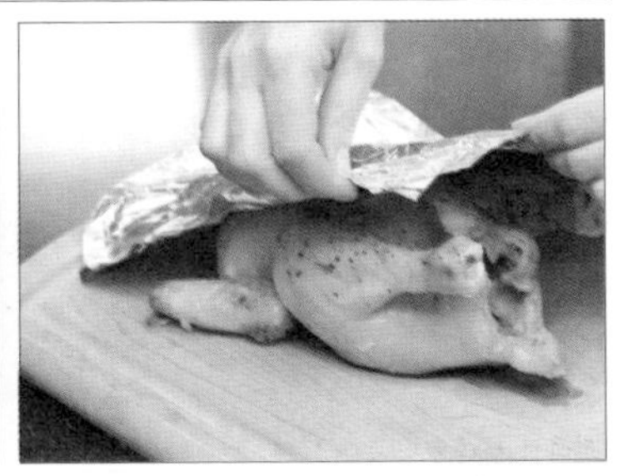

4. REST Transfer chicken to carving board to rest so juices can redistribute.

Ultracrunchy Baked Pork Chops

Pork chops with a thick coating that won't fall off require more than just a shake in a bag. We get rid of crumbly crusts and soggy bottoms to create chops with real crunch.

⋟ BY SANDRA WU ⋞

When done right, baked breaded pork chops are the ultimate comfort food: tender cutlets surrounded by a crunchy coating that crackles apart with each bite. But all too often, baked chops fall short of that ideal. Opt for the convenience of a shaky packaged product from the supermarket for your breading and you wind up with a bland-tasting chop with a thin, sandy crust. Make your own breading with fresh crumbs and the flaws are different—a soggy, patchy crust that won't stick to the meat. My goal was clear: to cook a juicy, flavorful chop with a crisp, substantial crust that would stay on the meat from fork to mouth.

A novel technique gives these chops their seriously crunchy coating.

Choice Chops

My first task was choosing the best cut of meat. Though bone-in chops retain moisture better, I decided on a boneless cut for this dish, so I wouldn't have to bread the bone and there would be no distraction from the crunchy crust. This gave me two options: sirloin or center-cut. I settled on center-cut boneless loin chops, which were not only easier to find in the supermarket but also cooked more evenly.

Next I needed to determine the chop size. The ½-inch-thick chops generally used for pan-frying were too easily overwhelmed by the kind of crust I wanted, and the 1½-inch-thick chops usually reserved for barbecuing or stuffing proved to be too thick, giving me too much meat and not enough crust. Pork chops that fell in between—¾ to 1 inch thick—were my tasters' top choice.

The test kitchen's standard breading method (dusting with flour, dipping in beaten egg, and rolling in toasted bread crumbs) was sufficient as I figured out the best cooking technique. Simply baking the breaded chops on a baking sheet, the most obvious method and one used in many recipes, made the bottoms soggy. I tried breading just the top and sides, and while this quick fix worked, tasters felt cheated. What if I let air circulation keep the bottom crumbs crisp? Placing the chops on a wire rack set inside the baking sheet definitely helped. Upping the oven temperature from 350 to 425 degrees helped even more. The coating crisped up more readily, and the excess moisture evaporated by the time the pork reached the requisite 150-degree serving temperature.

Crisp and Crunchy

I had figured out the right chops to use and the proper way to cook them. Now I could concentrate on the breading. Tasters deemed panko too fine-textured and bland. Crushed Melba toast was crunchier but didn't stick together. Ultimately, tasters preferred the fresh flavor and slight sweetness of crumbs made from white sandwich bread.

I tossed the fresh crumbs with a little salt, pepper, and oil; then I spread them on a baking sheet and toasted them until they were golden brown. The resulting crust was decently crisp but still not as good as I knew it could be. What if I took a cue from the supermarket coating and toasted the crumbs to a deeper brown? Though boxed crumbs produce a crust that is thin and sandy, the processed coating does have one thing going for it—a true crispness that I'd yet to achieve. For my next test, I left the crumbs in the oven until they looked dangerously overtoasted and was pleasantly surprised that this worked—the breading didn't burn when baked again on the chops, and my crumb coating was now seriously crisp. To add even more flavor, I stirred in some minced garlic and shallot with the crumbs before they went into the oven and tossed in some grated Parmesan cheese and minced herbs after they cooled. These chops tasted great. Everything would be perfect if I could just ensure one thing: that the crumbs stuck onto the pork evenly, rather than peeling off in patches.

Stick to It

With crumbs as thick and coarse as these, I knew I'd need something with more holding power than a typical egg wash to glue them to the pork. I recalled a cookbook recipe that used mustard instead of eggs to stick crumbs on chops. A straight swap made the taste too intense, but keeping the eggs and adding

RECIPE TESTING: Coatings without the Crunch

THIN
This popular boxed mix gives chops an insubstantial, bland crust.

PATCHY
The crust peels off chops dipped in a typical thin egg wash.

CRUMBLY
Fresh, untoasted crumbs have trouble sticking to the chop.

STEP-BY-STEP | SECRETS TO A CRISP COATING

1. DIP A thick batter of flour, mustard, and egg whites grips the bread crumbs like glue.

2. COAT Coating the chops with fresh, well-toasted bread crumbs results in a crust with flavor and crunch.

3. ELEVATE Baking the chops on a rack set in a baking sheet allows greater air circulation and prevents the bottoms from turning soggy.

The 30-Minute Brine

You might be tempted to skip the brining step when preparing Crunchy Baked Pork Chops. Don't. Center-cut chops are quite lean, and left untreated they will be very dry and chewy, even when cooked to medium (an internal temperature of 150 degrees). The salt in the brine changes the structure of the muscle proteins and allows them to hold on to more moisture when exposed to heat. My tasters had no trouble picking out the chops that I had brined versus chops that I had left untreated.

If you're accustomed to brining a turkey for the holidays, you might think you don't have time to brine pork chops for a weeknight recipe like this. But I found that making the brine super-concentrated (with ¼ cup of table salt dissolved in 1 quart of water) gets the job done in just 30 minutes—the time it will take you to prepare the fresh bread crumb coating. And my potent brine fits, along with four chops, in a medium container or gallon-sized zipper-lock bag. No brining bucket needed.

One exception: If you've purchased enhanced chops injected with a salt solution, don't brine them. The injected solution will make the chops moist, even spongy, and brining will make the meat way too salty. We prefer the flavor of natural chops and find that 30 minutes in a strong brine makes them plenty juicy. –S.W.

a few tablespoons of Dijon mustard thickened the mixture nicely and brought just enough new flavor to the mix. But while the crumbs stuck onto the baked chops better than they had with a simple egg wash, a few areas still flaked off.

A fellow test cook wondered aloud what would happen if I got rid of the egg wash altogether and dipped the floured chops into a thick batter before breading them. I laughed. After all, batter is for fried food. Who ever heard of using it for baking? I did it anyway, using a basic fritto misto batter of flour, cornstarch, water, oil, and eggs as my base. Fully expecting this experiment to tank, I was surprised when the pork chops came out with a crust that was crunchier than before and stayed on like a protective sheath. This batter, though, requires resting and seemed too fussy for a weeknight dish. But what if I made a quick egg wash that was more like a batter?

I whisked enough flour into the egg and mustard mixture to give it the thick consistency of mayonnaise. This adhering agent was now more of a spackle than a watery glue. After flouring the chops, I coated them evenly in the egg wash–batter hybrid, covered them in bread crumbs, and baked them again. Much better, but there was a soft, puffy layer directly beneath the crumbs. Replacing the whole eggs with egg whites, which have less fat but enough protein to lend sticking power, provided just the crisp, dry crust I was looking for. But even more impressive, the crumbs clung firmly onto the meat even during some heavy knife-and-fork action. This pork finally had some real chops.

CRUNCHY BAKED PORK CHOPS

SERVES 4

This recipe was developed using natural pork, but enhanced pork (injected with a salt solution) will work as well. If using enhanced pork, eliminate the brining in step 1. The bread crumb mixture can be prepared through step 2 up to 3 days in advance. The breaded chops can be frozen for up to 1 week. They don't need to be thawed before baking; simply increase the cooking time in step 5 to 35 to 40 minutes.

- Table salt
- 4 boneless center-cut pork chops, 6 to 8 ounces each, ¾ to 1 inch thick, trimmed of excess fat
- 4 slices hearty white sandwich bread, torn into 1-inch pieces
- 1 small shallot, minced (about 2 tablespoons)
- 3 medium garlic cloves, minced or pressed through garlic press (about 1 tablespoon)
- 2 tablespoons vegetable oil
- Ground black pepper
- 2 tablespoons grated Parmesan cheese
- ½ teaspoon minced fresh thyme leaves
- 2 tablespoons minced fresh parsley leaves
- ¼ cup plus 6 tablespoons unbleached all-purpose flour
- 3 large egg whites
- 3 tablespoons Dijon mustard
- Lemon wedges

1. Adjust oven rack to middle position and heat oven to 350 degrees. Dissolve ¼ cup salt in 1 quart water in medium container or gallon-sized zipper-lock bag. Submerge chops, cover with plastic wrap, and refrigerate 30 minutes. Rinse chops under cold water and dry thoroughly with paper towels.

2. Meanwhile, pulse bread in food processor until coarsely ground, about eight 1-second pulses (you should have about 3½ cups crumbs). Transfer crumbs to rimmed baking sheet and add shallot, garlic, oil, ¼ teaspoon salt, and ¼ teaspoon pepper. Toss until crumbs are evenly coated with oil. Bake until deep golden brown and dry, about 15 minutes, stirring twice during baking time. (Do not turn off oven.) Cool to room temperature. Toss crumbs with Parmesan, thyme, and parsley.

3. Place ¼ cup flour in pie plate. In second pie plate, whisk egg whites and mustard until combined; add remaining 6 tablespoons flour and whisk until almost smooth, with pea-sized lumps remaining.

4. Increase oven temperature to 425 degrees. Spray wire rack with nonstick cooking spray and place in rimmed baking sheet. Season chops with pepper. Dredge 1 pork chop in flour; shake off excess. Using tongs, coat with egg mixture; let excess drip off. Coat all sides of chop with bread crumb mixture, pressing gently so that thick layer of crumbs adheres to chop. Transfer breaded chop to wire rack. Repeat with remaining 3 chops.

5. Bake until instant-read thermometer inserted into center of chops registers 150 degrees, 17 to 25 minutes. Let rest on rack 5 minutes before serving with lemon wedges.

CRUNCHY BAKED PORK CHOPS WITH PROSCIUTTO AND ASIAGO CHEESE

Follow recipe for Crunchy Baked Pork Chops through step 3, omitting salt added to bread crumb mixture in step 2. Before breading, place ⅛-inch-thick slice Asiago cheese (about ½ ounce) on top of each chop. Wrap each chop with thin slice prosciutto, pressing on prosciutto so that cheese and meat adhere to one another. Proceed with recipe from step 4, being careful when handling chops so that cheese and meat do not come apart during breading.

COOK'S LIVE Original Test Kitchen Videos

www.cooksillustrated.com

HOW TO MAKE
- Crunchy Baked Pork Chops

VIDEO TIPS
- How do I mince a shallot?
- How do I mince parsley?

Best French Onion Soup

Most versions of this age-old recipe hide a mediocre broth under a crust of bread and a blanket of Gruyère. What is the secret to coaxing impressive flavor out of humble onions?

⋽ BY REBECCA HAYS ⋲

Legend has it that a hungry King Louis XV of France invented onion soup after returning home to an empty larder late one night from a hunting excursion. He took the few ingredients he could find—a sack of onions, leftover beef stock, and a bottle of Champagne—and created the now-famous recipe.

These days, the ideal French onion soup combines a satisfying broth redolent of sweet caramelized onions with a slice of toasted baguette and melted cheese. But the reality is that most of the onion soup you find isn't very good. Once you manage to dig through the layer of congealed cheese to unearth a spoonful of broth, it just doesn't taste like onions. I discovered the source of these watery, weak broths when I looked up some recipes. One was particularly appalling, calling for a mere 7 ounces of onions to make soup for six! Even more disturbing were those recipes that advised sautéing the onions for only five or six minutes—not nearly enough time for them to caramelize.

The French Connection

The good news is that I really didn't need these lackluster recipes. I knew of a terrific one introduced to the test kitchen by a friend visiting from France. Henri Pinon patiently cooked 3 pounds of onions in butter over very low heat until they were golden brown (this took about 90 minutes), then deglazed the pot with water. Nothing unusual there—deglazing is common in onion soup recipes. What followed, however, was something entirely new. Henri allowed the onions to recaramelize, and then he deglazed the pan again. And again. He repeated this process several more times over the course of another hour, finally finishing the soup by simmering the onions with water, white wine, and a sprig of thyme. He garnished the soup in the traditional way, with a slice of crusty toasted baguette and a very modest amount of shredded Gruyère, passing the crocks under the broiler to melt the cheese. How did it taste? Beyond compare—the broth was impossibly rich, with deep onion flavor that burst through the tanginess of the Gruyère and bread.

Having watched Henri make his soup, I couldn't wait to give the recipe a try. But before I started cooking, I pondered his technique. When onions caramelize, a complex series of chemical reactions takes place. Heat causes water molecules to separate from the onions' sugar molecules. As they cook, the dehydrated sugar molecules react with each other to form new molecules that produce new colors, flavors, and aromas. (This is the same series of reactions that occurs when granulated sugar is heated to make caramel.) Each time Henri deglazed the pan and allowed the onions to recaramelize, he was ratcheting up the flavor of the soup in a big way.

This soup is best finished under the broiler in oven-safe crocks. If using regular bowls, broil the cheese toasts separately.

Back in the test kitchen with Henri's recipe in hand, I started cooking, and a long while later, the soup was on. It was as delicious as when Henri had made it, yet after standing at the stove for more than two hours, I barely had the energy to enjoy it. Was there a way to borrow Henri's technique while cutting down on the active cooking time?

I cranked the heat from low to high to hurry the onions along, and my risk-taking was rewarded with burnt onions that ended up in the trash. I needed steady heat that wouldn't cause scorching—the stovetop was concentrating too much heat at the bottom of the pot. Why not use the oven? I spread oiled sliced onions on a baking sheet and roasted them at 450 degrees. Instead of caramelizing, however, they simply dried out. Lower temperatures caused the onions to steam. Next, I cooked as many sliced onions as I could squeeze into a Dutch oven (4 pounds), with far more promising results—the onions cooked slowly and evenly, building flavor all the while. After some trial and error, I finally settled on a method in which I cooked the onions covered in a 400-degree oven for an hour, then continued cooking with the lid ajar for another hour and a half.

With my new hands-off method, the onions emerged from the oven golden, soft, and sweet, and a nice fond had begun to collect on the bottom of the pot. Even better, I'd only had to tend to them twice in 2½ hours. Next, I continued the caramelization process on the stovetop. Because of their head start in the oven, deglazing only three or four times was sufficient (the process still took nearly an hour—but this was far better than the two-plus hours Henri spent

STEP-BY-STEP | GOLDEN ONIONS WITHOUT THE FUSS

Forget constant stirring on the stovetop. Cooking onions in the oven takes time but requires little attention.

1. RAW The raw onions nearly fill a large Dutch oven.

2. AFTER 1 HOUR IN OVEN The onions are starting to wilt and release moisture.

3. AFTER 2½ HOURS IN OVEN The onions are golden, wilted, and significantly reduced in volume.

PHOTOGRAPHY: CARL TREMBLAY

TECHNIQUE | TRIPLE DEGLAZE

Most recipes for French onion soup call for deglazing—loosening the flavorful dark brown crust, or fond, that forms on the bottom of the pot—only once, if at all. The secret to our recipe is to deglaze the pot at least three times.

on his dozens of deglazings). Once the onions were as dark as possible, I poured in a few splashes of dry sherry, which tasters preferred to sweet sherry, white wine, Champagne, red wine, and vermouth.

Finishing Touches

Settling on a type of onion from standard supermarket varieties was a snap. I quickly dismissed red onions—they bled out to produce a dingy-looking soup. White onions were too mild, and Vidalia onions made the broth candy-sweet. Yellow onions, on the other hand, offered just the sweet and savory notes I was after.

Henri had used only water for his soup, but after making batches with water, chicken broth, and beef broth alone and in combination, I decided the soup was best with all three. The broths added complexity, and my goal was to build as many layers of flavor as possible.

At last, I could focus on the soup's crowning glory: bread and cheese. So as to not obscure the lovely broth, I dialed back the hefty amounts that have come to define the topping in this country. Toasting the bread before floating a slice on the soup warded off sogginess. As for the cheese, Emmenthaler and Swiss were fine, but I wanted to stick to tradition. A modest sprinkling of nutty Gruyère (see "Gruyère Cheese," right) was a grand, gooey finish to a great soup.

BEST FRENCH ONION SOUP

SERVES 6

Sweet onions, such as Vidalia or Walla Walla, will make this recipe overly sweet. Be patient when caramelizing the onions in step 2; the entire process takes 45 to 60 minutes. Use broiler-safe crocks and keep the rim of the bowls 4 to 5 inches from the heating element to obtain a proper gratinée of melted, bubbly cheese. If using ordinary soup bowls, sprinkle the toasted bread slices with Gruyère and return them to the broiler until the cheese melts, then float them on top of the soup. We prefer Swanson Certified Organic Free Range Chicken Broth and Pacific Beef Broth. For the best flavor, make the soup a day or 2 in advance. Alternatively, the onions can be prepared through step 1, cooled in the pot, and refrigerated for up to 3 days before proceeding with the recipe.

Soup

- 3 tablespoons unsalted butter, cut into 3 pieces
- 6 large yellow onions (about 4 pounds), halved and cut pole to pole into ¼-inch-thick slices (see "Slicing Onions," page 30)
- Table salt
- 2 cups water, plus extra for deglazing
- ½ cup dry sherry
- 4 cups low-sodium chicken broth (see note above)
- 2 cups beef broth (see note above)
- 6 sprigs fresh thyme, tied with kitchen twine
- 1 bay leaf
- Ground black pepper

Cheese Croutons

- 1 small baguette, cut on bias into ½-inch slices
- 8 ounces Gruyère, shredded (about 2½ cups)

1. **FOR THE SOUP:** Adjust oven rack to lower-middle position and heat oven to 400 degrees. Generously spray inside of heavy-bottomed large (at least 7-quart) Dutch oven with nonstick cooking spray. Place butter in pot and add onions and 1 teaspoon salt. Cook, covered, 1 hour (onions will be moist and slightly reduced in volume). Remove pot from oven and stir onions, scraping bottom and sides of pot. Return pot to oven with lid slightly ajar and continue to cook until onions are very soft and golden brown, 1½ to 1¾ hours longer, stirring onions and scraping bottom and sides of pot after 1 hour.

2. Carefully remove pot from oven and place over medium-high heat. Using oven mitts to handle pot, cook onions, stirring frequently and scraping bottom and sides of pot, until liquid evaporates and onions brown, 15 to 20 minutes, reducing heat to medium if onions are browning too quickly. Continue to cook, stirring frequently, until pot bottom is coated with dark crust, 6 to 8 minutes, adjusting heat as necessary. (Scrape any fond that collects on spoon back into onions.) Stir in ¼ cup water, scraping pot bottom to loosen crust, and cook until water evaporates and pot bottom has formed another dark crust, 6 to 8 minutes. Repeat process of deglazing 2 or 3 more times, until onions are very dark brown. Stir in sherry and cook, stirring frequently, until sherry evaporates, about 5 minutes.

3. Stir in broths, 2 cups water, thyme, bay leaf, and ½ teaspoon salt, scraping up any final bits of browned crust on bottom and sides of pot. Increase heat to high and bring to simmer. Reduce heat to low, cover, and simmer 30 minutes. Remove and discard herbs, then season with salt and pepper.

4. **FOR THE CROUTONS:** While soup simmers, arrange baguette slices in single layer on baking sheet and bake in 400-degree oven until bread is dry, crisp, and golden at edges, about 10 minutes. Set aside.

5. **TO SERVE:** Adjust oven rack 6 inches from broiler element and heat broiler. Set individual broiler-safe crocks on baking sheet and fill each with about 1¾ cups soup. Top each bowl with 1 or 2 baguette slices (do not overlap slices) and sprinkle evenly with Gruyère. Broil until cheese is melted and bubbly around edges, 3 to 5 minutes. Let cool 5 minutes before serving.

TASTING: Gruyère Cheese

Though its fame derives mainly from its use in fondue and French onion soup, Gruyère is also a table cheese revered for its creamy texture and savory flavor. Both Switzerland and France make authentic versions that are crafted from raw cow's milk and aged for the better part of a year in government-designated regions (the French cheese is called Gruyère de Comté). Though labeled "Gruyère," domestic cheeses of this type bear little resemblance to the real thing. Made from pasteurized cow's milk, they are aged for fewer months and have a rubbery texture and bland flavor. In fact, in a blind taste test of nine brands, tasters overwhelmingly panned the two domestic versions, likening one (from Boar's Head) to "plastic." Imported Gruyères, on the other hand, received raves. The top picks in the lineup were three reserve cheeses, aged 10 or more months to develop stronger flavor: the Gruyère Reserve carried by Whole Foods Market, Emmi Le Gruyère Reserve, and a Gruyère Salé from a Boston-area cheese shop. For complete tasting results, go to www.cooksillustrated.com/february.

–Elizabeth Bomze

QUICKER FRENCH ONION SOUP

This variation uses a microwave for the initial cooking of the onions, which dramatically reduces the cooking time. The soup's flavor, however, will not be quite as deep as with the stovetop method. If you don't have a microwave-safe bowl large enough to accommodate all of the onions, cook in a smaller bowl in 2 batches.

Follow recipe for Best French Onion Soup, combining onions and 1 teaspoon salt in large microwave-safe bowl and covering with large microwave-safe plate (plate should completely cover bowl and not rest on onions). Microwave on high power for 20 to 25 minutes until onions are soft and wilted, stirring halfway through cooking. (Use oven mitts to remove bowl from microwave and remove plate away from you to avoid steam burn.) Drain onions (about ½ cup liquid should drain off) and proceed with step 2, melting butter in Dutch oven before adding wilted onions.

Spanish-Style Garlic Shrimp

Shrimp in garlicky olive oil is a tapas bar classic. But make this appetizer at home and suddenly the shrimp are rubbery and the garlic goes missing in a sea of olive oil.

⋟ BY J. KENJI ALT ⋞

If there is one thing that can catch attention in a Spanish tapas restaurant, it's the heady aroma wafting up from a dish of *gambas al ajillo*—little shrimp sizzling in a pool of olive oil and garlic. One bite will confirm that the garlic shares equal billing with the shrimp; when properly prepared, the shrimp is wonderfully sweet and tender and infused with deep garlic flavor. The key to achieving this flavor is the oil. A large quantity is heated along with sliced garlic, Spanish chiles, and bay leaves in a *cazuela* (an earthenware ramekin) until lightly sizzling. A handful of small shrimp are added, heated until just barely cooked through, and served directly out of the cooking vessel. The dish is always accompanied by crusty bread to soak up all the leftover garlic- and shrimp-flavored oil.

Shrimp and garlic share equal billing in this tapas bar favorite.

As perfect as the dish is, it needs some adjustments to work as an appetizer served at home. At a tapas restaurant, where your table is overflowing with other dishes, it's easy to be content with a few small shrimp. Back at home, where most cooks are going to prepare only a single appetizer, the dish needs to be more substantial, meaning either bigger shrimp or more small ones. Tasters in the test kitchen preferred bigger shrimp, and I settled on a pound of large shrimp as the ideal portion size for six people. But now that I was playing around with the size and quantity of shrimp, what would that mean for the rest of the dish?

Ensuring Tender Shrimp

Traditional recipes for gambas al ajillo call for completely submerging the shrimp in oil, where they can be heated very evenly and gently at a low temperature. Short of accidentally bringing the oil up to deep-fry temperatures, the shrimp are almost impossible to overcook. But to fully submerge the pound of large shrimp I wanted to use, I'd need nearly 2 cups of oil—far more than six people could ever finish. I wouldn't have to serve all that oil, of course, but why waste it? I wanted to find a way to reduce the amount (about half a cup was a reasonable quantity for six people) but still maintain the juiciness and garlic flavor that are the hallmarks of this dish.

With less oil, I figured using the smallest pan I could fit the shrimp into would be more effective, since a smaller pan size meant deeper oil. In an 8-inch saucepan, the oil came only ½ inch up the side, covering about half of the shrimp. The results? Overcooked shrimp on the bottom and raw shrimp on top. Even with almost constant stirring and tossing, I couldn't get the shrimp to cook as evenly as if they were completely submerged in oil.

I sat down and went back to thinking about cooking basics. In order to keep shrimp juicy and tender, it is important to not overcook them. My shrimp were partially overcooking because they were heating unevenly. They were heating unevenly because they were arranged in the pan in layers—some shrimp were closer to the heat source than others. I switched out the 8-inch pot for a 12-inch skillet. In the wider pan, the oil provided only a thin coating beneath the shrimp, but at least I could fit them in a single layer.

The new single-layer method meant that I would have to turn the shrimp halfway through cooking. With this many shrimp in the pan, I was afraid that turning them with tongs would take too long; by the time I had turned the last shrimp, the first ones would be overcooked. Keeping the heat at medium-low gave me plenty of time to turn each shrimp individually, so I managed to cook them as evenly and gently as if they had been completely submerged in oil.

I now had tender shrimp, but the other key characteristic of the dish was missing: great garlic flavor.

Building Garlic Flavor

With only a thin layer of oil in the pan, the shrimp were not absorbing enough garlic flavor. I increased the garlic from four thinly sliced cloves to eight, which provided the right proportion of shrimp to garlic, but the slices were still acting more like a garnish than a fully integrated part of the dish. More sliced garlic

SHOPPING: Choosing the Right Chile

AUTHENTIC CHOICE
The slightly sweet cascabel chile is the traditional choice for gambas al ajillo.

BEST SUBSTITUTE
New Mexico chile (aka California chile, chile Colorado, or dried Anaheim chile) is far more widely available and has the same bright freshness as the cascabel.

LAST RESORT
You won't have any trouble finding paprika, but its slightly stale flavor cannot compare with the complex taste of whole dried chiles.

PHOTOGRAPHY: CARL TREMBLAY

Garlic Flavor Three Ways

We imparted garlic flavor to the shrimp in three different ways for three different effects, resulting in a dish with multilayered garlic complexity.

RAW = PUNGENT
The minced garlic in the marinade gets cooked briefly with the shrimp, maintaining a hint of raw-garlic pungency.

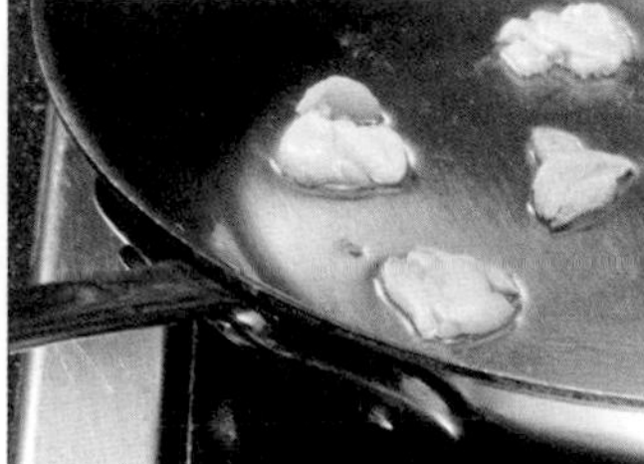

BROWNED = SWEET
Gently browning smashed whole garlic cloves infuses the olive oil with a sweet roasted-garlic flavor.

POACHED = MELLOW
Sliced garlic cooked gently in low-temperature olive oil loses its harsh flavor, becoming soft and mellow.

would just give me more garnish: I had to find a different way to get more garlic flavor into the shrimp.

I knew that allicin, the chemical responsible for garlic's flavor, is highly soluble in oil—which meant I could use the oil as a vehicle to deliver more flavor to the dish. Allicin is not formed until the garlic's cells are ruptured, so I smashed four garlic cloves before heating them in a fresh batch of olive oil. I allowed them to brown and impart a sweet roasted flavor to the oil, discarded the smashed cloves, and then added the shrimp. But to my frustration, despite the supercharged garlic base with its new type of garlic character, the shrimp were better but still not great.

I realized that the only way to get more garlic flavor into the shrimp was through a marinade. I minced two garlic cloves and combined them with 2 tablespoons of oil. Knowing that salt would draw flavorful juices out of the garlic through osmosis, I added a teaspoon to the marinade. After 30 minutes, I cooked the marinated shrimp and sliced garlic in the oil in which I had previously browned the smashed cloves. I waited with bated breath while my tasters bit into the shrimp. It was a resounding success.

Finally, I had juicy shrimp that were deeply flavored with garlic in a robust and complex sauce. By adding the garlic to the pan in three forms and at three different stages (minced raw garlic to provide pungency in the marinade, crushed and browned garlic to infuse sweetness into the oil, and slow-cooked sliced garlic to add mild garlic flavor), I was able to coax three distinct flavors from the versatile bulb. Not only did the olive oil evenly coat each shrimp with garlic flavor, it also provided protection for the garlic (see "Marinade Superheroes: Oil and Salt," below).

The traditional additions of bay leaf and red chile (see "Choosing the Right Chile," on page 14) were deemed essential to the recipe. Heating the aromatics in the pan along with the sliced garlic allowed them to flavor the oil, giving the finished dish a sweet, herbal aroma. While most recipes call for a splash of dry sherry or brandy, I found that sherry vinegar and chopped parsley were better suited to rounding out the flavors; they provided a jolt of brightness that cut through the richness of the olive oil.

As a finishing touch, I realized I could recapture some of the restaurant spirit by transferring the dish to a small cast-iron skillet that I'd heated on the stove. Placed on a trivet on the table, the shrimp and garlic continued to sizzle until my eager tasters downed the last one.

SPANISH-STYLE GARLIC SHRIMP

SERVES 6 AS AN APPETIZER

Serve shrimp with crusty bread for dipping in the richly flavored olive oil. The dish can be served directly from the skillet (make sure to use a trivet) or, for a sizzling effect, transferred to an 8-inch cast-iron skillet that's been heated for 2 minutes over medium-high heat. We prefer the slightly sweet flavor of dried chiles in this recipe, but ¼ teaspoon sweet paprika can be substituted. If sherry vinegar is unavailable, use 2 teaspoons dry sherry and 1 teaspoon white vinegar.

- 14 medium garlic cloves, peeled
- 1 pound large (31–40) shrimp, peeled, deveined, and tails removed
- 8 tablespoons olive oil
- ½ teaspoon table salt
- 1 bay leaf
- 1 (2-inch) piece mild dried chile, such as New Mexico, roughly broken, seeds included (see note above and page 14)
- 1½ teaspoons sherry vinegar (see note above)
- 1 tablespoon chopped fresh parsley leaves

1. Mince 2 garlic cloves with chef's knife or garlic press. Toss minced garlic with shrimp, 2 tablespoons olive oil, and salt in medium bowl. Let shrimp marinate at room temperature for 30 minutes.

2. Meanwhile, using flat side of chef's knife, smash 4 garlic cloves. Heat smashed garlic with remaining 6 tablespoons olive oil in 12-inch skillet over medium-low heat, stirring occasionally, until garlic is light golden brown, 4 to 7 minutes. Remove pan from heat and allow oil to cool to room temperature. Using slotted spoon, remove smashed garlic from skillet and discard.

3. Thinly slice remaining 8 cloves garlic. Return skillet to low heat and add sliced garlic, bay leaf, and chile. Cook, stirring occasionally, until garlic is tender but not browned, 4 to 7 minutes. (If garlic has not begun to sizzle after 3 minutes, increase heat to medium-low.) Increase heat to medium-low; add shrimp with marinade to pan in single layer. Cook shrimp, undisturbed, until oil starts to gently bubble, about 2 minutes. Using tongs, flip shrimp and continue to cook until almost cooked through, about 2 minutes longer. Increase heat to high and add sherry vinegar and parsley. Cook, stirring constantly, until shrimp are cooked through and oil is bubbling vigorously, 15 to 20 seconds. Serve immediately.

COOK'S LIVE Original Test Kitchen Videos
www.cooksillustrated.com

HOW TO MAKE
- Spanish-Style Garlic Shrimp

VIDEO TIP
- How do I peel and slice garlic?

SCIENCE: Marinade Superheroes: Oil and Salt

We found that omitting either the oil or the salt from our marinade significantly reduced garlic flavor in the cooked shrimp. Why? Oil protects and stabilizes allicin, the compound in garlic that is responsible for its characteristic flavor. Allicin is produced when garlic is cut or crushed, and it quickly degrades into less flavorful compounds when exposed to air. Once in oil, however, the allicin dissolves and is protected from air. With this protection in place, it can move into the shrimp. There's one more advantage to oil—it coats the shrimp and delivers flavor evenly, not just in areas directly in contact with the minced garlic. Salt contributes to the process by speeding things up. Salt draws water containing allicin out of the garlic at a faster rate than allicin would migrate on its own. –J.K.A.

OIL + SALT + GARLIC + SHRIMP = COMPLETE FLAVOR DISTRIBUTION
Oil protects garlic flavor, and salt speeds up the marinating time.

ILLUSTRATION: JAY LAYMAN

Mastering the Art of Stew

A little know-how goes a long way toward avoiding common mistakes when making stews. Here's how to get it right every time. BY KEITH DRESSER

Stew is kitchen alchemy that turns a marginal cut of meat and some basic vegetables into something rich, flavorful, and much more interesting. Even better, stew generally requires little preparation or effort; time and gentle simmering do all the work. That said, we've all had (or made) stews with tough meat, listless vegetables, and dull, watery broth. Over the years, we've learned which steps produce a superior stew.

Choosing the Right Meat

Choosing the proper cut of meat is the single most important part of making a great stew. We like to use cuts from the shoulder area, because they have the best combination of flavor and texture. Meat from this region is well marbled with fat, which means it won't dry out during long, slow cooking. In chicken, the high percentage of intramuscular fat in thigh meat makes this part the preferred choice. For the best results, we like to cut our own stew meat (see "Cut Your Own Meat," page 17).

PORK
We like pork butt (also called Boston shoulder or Boston butt) for its great flavor, but the less-expensive and slightly fattier picnic shoulder is also a fine choice.

PORK BUTT

BEEF
We love the beefy taste and exceptional tenderness of chuck-eye roast. Another good option: the chuck 7-bone roast.

CHUCK EYE

LAMB
Roasts from the lamb shoulder can be hard to find, so we rely on shoulder-cut chops such as the round-bone for our stews. This chop has bold taste mellowed by long cooking, and its bones are a bonus that add extra flavor to the pot. An alternative choice is the blade chop.

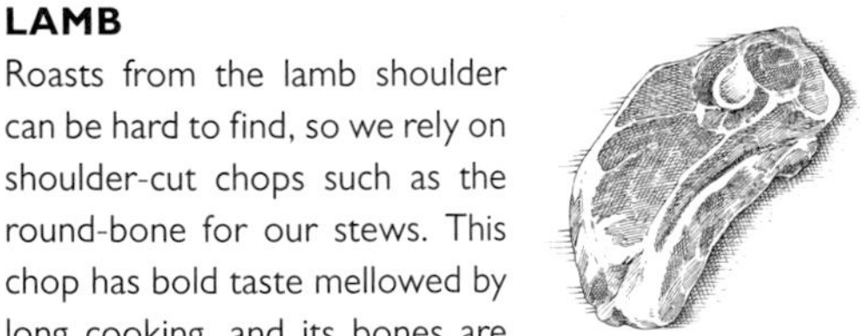

ROUND-BONE CHOP

CHICKEN
The extra fat and connective tissue in thigh meat make it better suited than breast meat for stew; it also separates more easily from the bone than does drumstick meat. We use skin-on thighs to protect the meat and keep it from overcooking and drying out during browning. Both the bones and fat lend stronger chicken flavor.

BONE-IN CHICKEN THIGH

KEY EQUIPMENT

DUTCH OVEN
A Dutch oven is essential for making stew. Look for one that is twice as wide as it is high, with a minimum capacity of 6 quarts (7 or 8 is even better). The bottom should be thick, so food browns evenly and the pot retains heat during cooking. The pot should also have a tight-fitting lid to prevent excess evaporation.

TEST KITCHEN WINNER:
➢**LE CREUSET** 7¼-Quart Round French Oven, $229.95

BEST BUY:
➢**TRAMONTINA** 6.5 Quart Cast Iron Dutch Oven, $39.86

HEATPROOF SPATULA
Wooden spoons are things of the past. Our favorite spatula is rigid enough to stir a thick stew yet flexible enough to get into the tight corners of a pot when deglazing. Throw in the fact that its surface won't stain, and what's not to like?

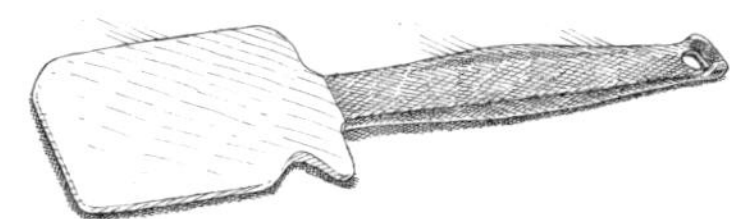

TEST KITCHEN WINNER:
➢**RUBBERMAID** 13.5-Inch High Heat Scraper, $11.40

TONGS
After flipping thousands of batches of cubed meat, we've come to value a good pair of tongs. Our favorite handily picks up the smallest pieces of meat without tearing or mashing.

TEST KITCHEN WINNER:
➢**OXO** Good Grips 12-Inch Locking Tongs, $10.39

LADLE
A ladle is definitely the best tool for dividing portions among individual bowls; it's also useful for skimming fat from the surface of the stew before serving.

TEST KITCHEN WINNER:
➢**RÖSLE** Ladle with Pouring Rim & Hook Handle, $26.95

KEY FLAVOR ENHANCERS

BROTH
While broth is not as central to the flavor of stew as it is to soup, choosing a high-quality brand is still important. And using a low-sodium broth is essential; as the liquid in a stew reduces, regular full-sodium broth can turn the stew too salty and ruin the flavor.

TEST KITCHEN WINNERS:
➢**SWANSON** Certified Organic Free Range Chicken Broth and **PACIFIC** Beef Broth

WINE
When a stew calls for wine, many cooks will grab the least-expensive bottle on hand. But even in small amounts, there is no hiding the taste of bad wine. In the test kitchen, we prefer the fuller, more complex flavor of wine made with more than one grape variety.

TEST KITCHEN WINNER:
➢**CÔTES DU RHÔNE** or other fruity wine with little or no oak

BEER
In general, we prefer darker ales to lighter lagers for the rich, full flavor they impart to stew (lager can leave stews tasting watery). As long as they're dark, nonalcoholic ales will work equally well.

TEST KITCHEN WINNERS:
➢**Amber and dark-colored ales**

TOMATO PASTE
A small amount of tomato paste added to a stew along with the aromatics brings depth and color, and its slight acidity enhances the flavor of other ingredients.

TEST KITCHEN WINNER:
➢**AMORE** Tomato Paste

ILLUSTRATION: JOHN BURGOYNE

10 STEPS TO BETTER STEW

1. CUT YOUR OWN MEAT

Packaged stew meat is often made up of irregularly shaped scraps that cook at varying rates. Cut your own stew meat to guarantee same-sized chunks that share the same flavor and cooking time. Use fatty, flavorful cuts from the shoulder, or chuck, that will stay moist with extended cooking.

2. SKIP THE FLOUR BEFORE BROWNING

Contrary to popular belief, dusting meat with flour before searing it doesn't help it brown better. In fact, we have found just the opposite. The flour itself darkens a little, but the meat remains pale and doesn't develop the intense flavor compounds that are the goal of browning. Instead of flouring, pat stew meat dry and season it with salt and pepper before browning.

3. BROWN MEAT PROPERLY

Crowding the pan with too much meat or using inadequate heat can cause meat to steam (rather than brown) and ultimately lose flavor. To avoid this problem, add the meat only after the oil begins to smoke and leave plenty of space (about ½ inch) between pieces (this means no more than 1 pound of meat per batch). Turn only when the first side is well seared.

4. IF FOND BURNS, REMOVE IT

Browning meat in more than two batches can lead to a pan covered by burnt (rather than browned) fond that can impart a bitter flavor to the stew. If the fond is blackening, add a little water to the empty pot and scrape the fond to loosen it. Discard burnt bits and water and wipe the pot clean. Add fresh oil and proceed with the next batch of meat.

5. SAUTÉ AROMATICS TO ENHANCE FLAVOR

Recipes that call for dumping spices and aromatics, such as garlic and onion, into the pot at the same time as the liquid fail to maximize their flavor. So hold the liquid and sauté these flavor-enhancing ingredients first.

6. FLOUR AROMATICS TO THICKEN STEW

Many recipes call for thickening a stew at the end of cooking by leaving the lid off, but this method risks overcooking. Thicken stew at the beginning of the cooking process by sprinkling flour over the sautéed aromatics. Cook the flour for a minute or two to remove any raw flour taste.

7. STAGGER ADDITION OF VEGETABLES

When vegetables are dumped indiscriminately into the pot at the outset of cooking, they not only lose flavor and turn mushy, but also water down the stew. Take into account the cooking time of individual vegetables (see "How Long Does It Take: Vegetables," above) and add them at the appropriate time.

HOW LONG DOES IT TAKE: VEGETABLES

Below are some common stew vegetables and general guidelines for how long to cook them. In many cases, you will be adding the vegetables once the stew has been cooking in the oven for a while.

VEGETABLE	PREPARATION	COOKING TIME
Potatoes	1- to 1½-inch cubes	1 hour
Carrots	sliced ¼ to ½ inch thick	1 hour
Parsnips	sliced ¼ to ½ inch thick	1 hour
Sweet Potatoes	quartered and sliced ¼ inch thick	1 hour
Turnips	½-inch dice	45 minutes
Peppers	½-inch dice	45 minutes
Canned Beans	rinsed	45 minutes
Frozen Vegetables	do not thaw	15 to 20 minutes
Hearty Greens	washed and chopped	20 to 30 minutes
Tender Greens	washed and chopped	1 to 2 minutes
Fresh Herbs	chopped	Stir in off heat

HOW LONG DOES IT TAKE: MEAT

Because meat varies in moisture and fat content, pinpointing cooking times is not an exact science. The chart below offers general guidelines.

MEAT	CUBE SIZE	APPROX. COOKING TIME
Beef, Pork, and Lamb	1 to 1½ inches	2 to 2½ hours
Beef, Pork, and Lamb	1½ to 2 inches	2½ to 3 hours
Chicken Thighs	whole	30 to 60 minutes

8. SIMMER STEW IN OVEN

To ensure a steady, gentle simmer that allows the internal temperature of the meat to rise slowly and eliminates the risk of scorching the pot bottom, cook the stew in a covered Dutch oven at 300 degrees. This will keep the temperature of the stewing liquid below the boiling point (212 degrees) and ensure meat that is tender, not tough.

9. COOK MEAT UNTIL FALL-APART TENDER

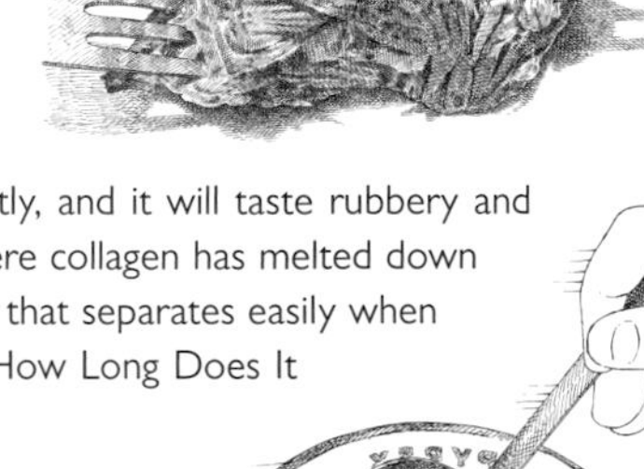

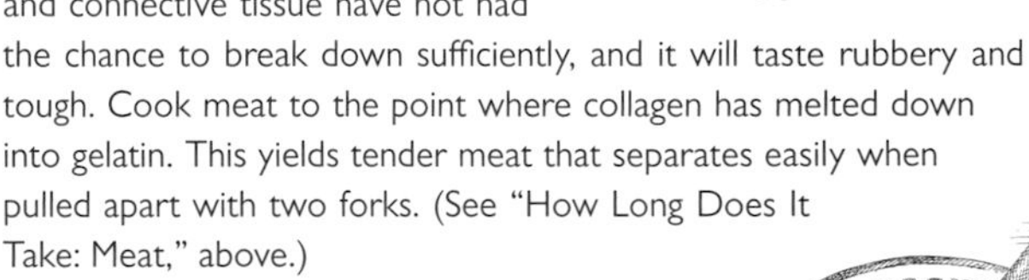

When meat is undercooked, its fat and connective tissue have not had the chance to break down sufficiently, and it will taste rubbery and tough. Cook meat to the point where collagen has melted down into gelatin. This yields tender meat that separates easily when pulled apart with two forks. (See "How Long Does It Take: Meat," above.)

10. DEFAT BEFORE SERVING

Pour stew liquid into a narrow container before defatting. This will create a thicker layer of fat that's easier to remove. Alternatively, refrigerate the stew overnight. When the fat solidifies, it can be lifted right off.

No-Knead Bread 2.0

A no-fuss recipe is revolutionizing home baking but trades flavor and reliability for ease. Could we improve the bread's bland taste and make it rise high every time?

BY J. KENJI ALT

In November 2006, *New York Times* writer Mark Bittman published a recipe developed by Jim Lahey of the Sullivan Street Bakery in Manhattan that promised to shake up the world of home baking. The recipe did the seemingly impossible. It allowed the average home cook to bake a loaf of bread that looked like it had been produced in a professional bakery. The recipe, which instantly won legions of followers, was exceedingly simple: Mix a few cups of flour, a tiny amount of yeast, and a little salt together in a bowl; stir in some water until the ingredients just come together; and leave the dough to rise. After 12 to 18 hours, the dough is turned a couple of times, shaped, risen, and baked in a Dutch oven. An hour later, out comes the most beautiful-looking loaf most people have ever baked at home—and all with no kneading.

Just a few seconds of kneading gives our loaf a perfect airy crumb.

At first, it seemed unlikely that there was anything to improve upon here. The no-knead recipe was remarkably easy and worlds better than other no-fuss breads. But threads on our bulletin board and other websites turned out some complaints amid all the praise. I decided to give the existing recipe to five inexperienced bakers in order to see what (if any) issues arose. I noticed a problem even before we sliced into the first loaf. While all were beautifully browned and crisp, the loaves varied wildly in size and shape, ranging from rounded mounds to flat, irregular blobs. Casting first impressions aside, I cut into each one and tasted a bite. Though the crusts were extraordinary—better than any I'd ever produced—the flavor of the crumb fell flat. It simply did not capture the complex yeasty, tangy flavor of a true artisanal loaf. I wondered if I could make this bread more consistent and better-tasting.

Analyzing Autolysis

I decided to tackle the problem of shape first. Thanks to the ingenious use of a Dutch oven, the bread always acquired a dark, crisp crust (see "Baking in a Dutch Oven," page 19), but the loaves took on a disconcertingly broad range of forms. After observing testers make the recipe a few times, I realized the problem: The wetness of the dough was making it too delicate to handle. Though it was well risen before baking, it was deflating on its way into the pot. In addition, because of its high moisture content, the dough was spreading out over the bottom of the pot before it could firm up properly. I analyzed the no-knead recipe and found that its dough is 85 percent hydrated—meaning that for every 10 ounces of flour, there are 8.5 ounces of water. Most rustic breads, on the other hand, max out at around 80 percent hydration, and standard sandwich breads hover between 60 percent and 75 percent hydration. So what would happen if I reduced the water?

To find out, I made a batch of dough in which I cut the hydration to 70 percent. Sure enough, this dough was much easier to handle and emerged from the oven well risen and perfectly shaped. But unfortunately, the texture was ruined. Instead of an open, airy crumb structure, it was dense and chewy, with rubbery pockets of unleavened flour. So more moisture led to an open but squat loaf, and less moisture led to a high but dense loaf. Was there a way to reconcile these two extremes?

Many bread recipes call for a rest period after adding water to the flour but before kneading. This rest is called "autolysis" (although most bakers use the French term *autolyse*). In most recipes, autolysis is just 20 to 30 minutes, but the no-knead bread calls for something completely out of the ordinary: a 12-hour rest. Was there something in the mechanics of such a lengthy autolysis that could help me solve the textural problem? The most common explanation for the autolysis process is simply that it allows time for the flour to hydrate and rest, making the dough easier to manipulate later on. But the word "autolysis" technically refers to the destruction of cells or proteins through enzymatic action. I decided to have a closer look at what really happens to the dough during the process.

The ultimate goal of making bread dough is to create gluten, a strong network of cross-linked proteins that traps air bubbles and stretches as the dough bakes, creating the bubbly, chewy crumb structure that is the signature of any good loaf. In order to form these cross links, the proteins in the flour need to be aligned next to each other. Imagine the proteins as bundled-up balls of yarn you are trying to tie together into one longer piece, which you'll then sew together into a wider sheet. In their balled-up state, it's not possible to tie them together; first you have to untangle and straighten them out. This straightening out and aligning is usually accomplished by kneading.

But untangling and stretching out short pieces of yarn is much easier than untangling entire balls. This is where autolysis comes in. As the dough autolyzes, enzymes naturally present in wheat act like scissors, cutting the balled-up proteins into smaller segments that are easier to straighten during kneading. This is why dough that has undergone

SCIENCE: How Beer Boosts Bread's Flavor

During a starter's fermentation, yeast produces alcohol, carbon dioxide, and sulfur compounds, all of which contribute to good bread's unique flavor. These three elements are present together in another location—a bottle of beer. But why choose lager over other types of beer? It's all about the fermentation. Most nonlager beers undergo a process called "top fermentation," whereby yeast floats on top of the wort (grain mashed in hot water), which is exposed to oxygen and kept warm. Oxygen and warmth persuade yeast to produce spicy, astringent flavor compounds called phenols and fruity, floral compounds called esters that are desirable in beer but not in bread. Lagers, on the other hand, undergo "bottom fermentation," where the yeast is kept submerged in the low-oxygen environment at the bottom of the wort at colder temperatures, which causes the yeast to produce fewer phenols and esters, so that the breadier yeast and sulfur flavors come forward. –J.K.A.

LET THERE BE LAGER Mild-flavored beer contains flavor compounds similar to those in a dough starter, which gives our bread a taste boost.

autolysis requires much less kneading than freshly made dough. And here's where the hydration level comes in: The more water there is, the more efficiently the cut-and-link process takes place.

So this was the explanation for how the no-knead bread recipe published in the *New York Times* worked. With 85 percent hydration and a 12-hour rest, the dough was so wet and had autolyzed for so long that the enzymes had broken the proteins down into extremely small pieces. These pieces were so small that, even without kneading, they could stretch out and cross-link during fermentation and the brief turning step. At 70 percent hydration, there simply was not enough water in my dough for the enzymes to act as efficiently as they had in the original recipe. As a result, many of the proteins in my finished bread were still in a semi-balled-up state, giving my bread the overly chewy texture.

What if the secret to making a better no-knead bread was actually adding in some kneading? I knew that even at a relatively dry 70 percent hydration, the proteins in my dough had already been broken down significantly by the long 12- to 18-hour autolysis. All they probably needed was a little kneading to untangle and create an airy, light crumb. I decided to make the leap.

I took the dough that I had resting from the day before and turned it out onto my board. Trusting that my understanding of autolysis was correct, I gave the dough the bare minimum of kneads—adding just 15 extra seconds to the no-knead recipe—and continued exactly as I had before. The dough emerged from the oven as beautifully browned and perfectly shaped as any I'd made so far. After letting it cool, I cut into it to reveal an ideal crumb structure: large pockets of air and stretched sheets of gluten. Not only that, I found that since such a small amount of kneading could develop gluten in a such a forceful manner, I could actually reduce the minimum time of the rest period from 12 hours to eight. That 15 seconds of kneading had reaped huge benefits.

No Substitute for Flavor

Now that I had bread with a great shape and texture, I turned my attention to the loaf's lackluster taste. To get a better sense of what specific flavors I was missing, I bought a loaf of bread from a bakery that makes dough the old-fashioned way—with a fermented starter. Because a starter contains a much more varied assortment of yeasts than the ones found in a packet, it yields more complex flavor. Tasting the bakery bread side by side with the no-knead bread confirmed this. But creating a starter is a multiday process. How could I get the flavors that a starter

Baking in a Dutch Oven

A major breakthrough in the no-knead bread recipe published in the *New York Times* was to bake the bread in a preheated Dutch oven, which creates the dramatic open-crumbed structure and the shatteringly crisp crust that was previously attainable only in a professional bakery. How does this work?

First, as the loaf heats it gives off steam to create a very humid environment inside the Dutch oven. Since moist air transfers heat much more efficiently than dry air, the loaf heats much more rapidly. This in turn causes the air bubbles inside to expand much faster, leading to a more open crumb structure. As a test, I baked two loaves of bread, one in a Dutch oven and the other on a preheated baking stone. After one minute in the oven, the surface temperature of the Dutch oven–baked loaf had risen past 200 degrees, while the other loaf had reached only 135 degrees.

Steam contributes to a great loaf a second way. As steam condenses onto the surface of the baking bread, it causes the starches to form a thin sheath that eventually dries out, giving the finished loaf a shiny crust that stays crisp.

Many recipes suggest adding water or ice cubes to the oven; the problem is home ovens cannot retain moisture in the way a professional steam-injected oven can. With its thick walls, small internal volume, and heavy lid, a Dutch oven is the ideal environment to create and trap steam.

STEP-BY-STEP | ALMOST NO-KNEAD BREAD

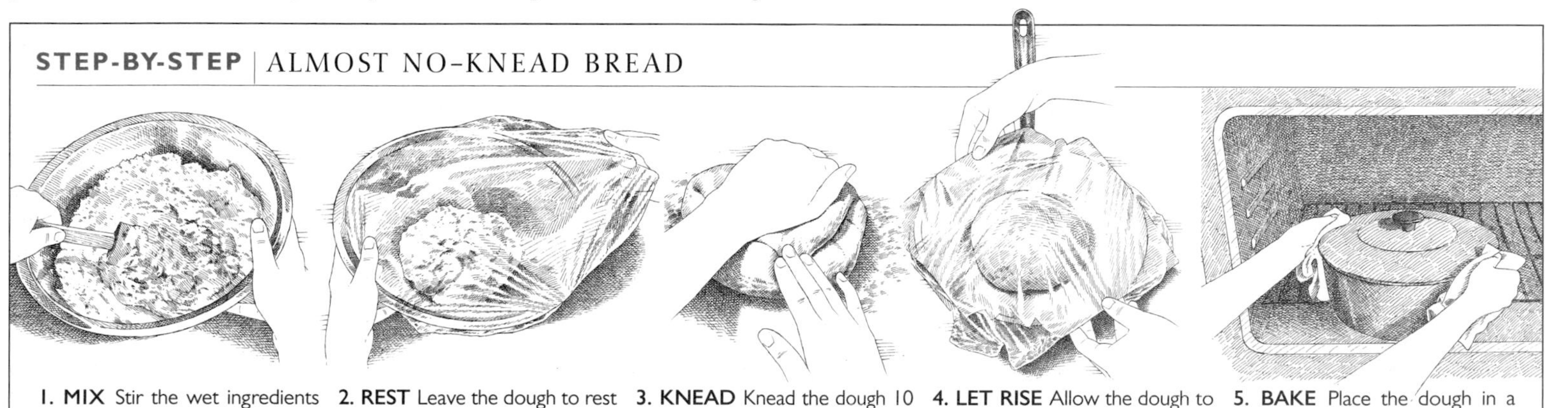

1. MIX Stir the wet ingredients into the dry ingredients with a spatula.

2. REST Leave the dough to rest for eight to 18 hours.

3. KNEAD Knead the dough 10 to 15 times and shape it into a ball.

4. LET RISE Allow the dough to rise for two hours in a parchment paper–lined skillet.

5. BAKE Place the dough in a preheated Dutch oven and bake it until it's deep brown.

ILLUSTRATION: JOHN BURGOYNE

TECHNIQUE | BREAD SLING

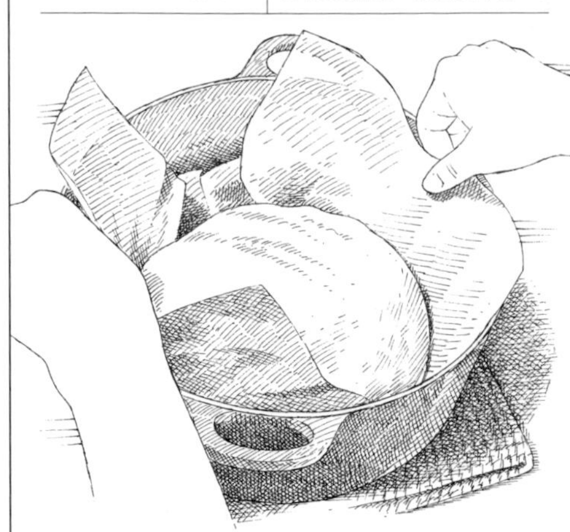

Transferring dough to a preheated Dutch oven to bake can be tricky. To avoid burnt fingers and help the dough hold its shape, we came up with a novel solution: Let the dough rise in a skillet (its shallow depth makes it better than a bowl) that's been lined with greased parchment paper, then use the paper's edges to pick up the dough and lower it into the Dutch oven. The bread remains on the parchment paper as it bakes.

produces without actually having to use one? Could I introduce a little tanginess another way?

Scanning the labels in our dry storage area, I saw that the majority of our bottled vinegars are 5 percent solutions of acetic acid—the same acid produced by bacteria during dough fermentation. Since other vinegars would introduce undesirable flavors to the bread, I experimented with different amounts of distilled white vinegar before settling on a single tablespoon.

My bread now had tang, but it lacked complexity. What I needed was a concentrated shot of yeasty flavor. As I racked my brain, I realized that beyond bread, there is another commonly available substance that relies on yeast for flavor: beer. Would its flavors compare to those produced in dough fermentation?

For the most part, no. I started my testing with dark ales, thinking their rich taste would lead to better flavor. The resulting bread had a strange spicy, fruity aftertaste and smelled like beer. Then I tried a light American-style lager. This time, the loaf came out with a distinct "bready" versus "beery" aroma that could fool anyone who had not seen the lager go into the dough. Why is it that the lighter beer produced the better taste? It turns out that the yeast in lagers is treated in a way that closely resembles the way yeast acts in dough, resulting in the production of similar flavor compounds (see "How Beer Boosts Bread's Flavor," page 19).

Through the simplest of tweaks—less hydration, the addition of vinegar and beer, and a few seconds of kneading—I had a loaf of bread that both looked and tasted incredible.

ALMOST NO-KNEAD BREAD

MAKES 1 LARGE ROUND LOAF

An enameled cast-iron Dutch oven with a tight-fitting lid yields best results, but the recipe also works in a regular cast-iron Dutch oven or heavy stockpot. Use a mild-flavored lager, such as Budweiser (mild non-alcoholic lager also works). The bread is best eaten the day it is baked but can be wrapped in aluminum foil and stored in a cool, dry place for up to 2 days.

- 3 cups (15 ounces) unbleached all-purpose flour, plus additional for dusting work surface
- ¼ teaspoon instant yeast
- 1½ teaspoons table salt
- ¾ cup plus 2 tablespoons water (7 ounces), at room temperature
- ¼ cup plus 2 tablespoons (3 ounces) mild-flavored lager
- 1 tablespoon white vinegar

1. Whisk flour, yeast, and salt in large bowl. Add water, beer, and vinegar. Using rubber spatula, fold mixture, scraping up dry flour from bottom of bowl until shaggy ball forms. Cover bowl with plastic wrap and let sit at room temperature for 8 to 18 hours.

2. Lay 12- by 18-inch sheet of parchment paper inside 10-inch skillet and spray with nonstick cooking spray. Transfer dough to lightly floured work surface and knead 10 to 15 times. Shape dough into ball by pulling edges into middle. Transfer dough, seam-side down, to parchment-lined skillet and spray surface of dough with nonstick cooking spray. Cover loosely with plastic wrap and let rise at room temperature until dough has doubled in size and does not readily spring back when poked with finger, about 2 hours.

3. About 30 minutes before baking, adjust oven rack to lowest position, place 6- to 8-quart heavy-bottomed Dutch oven (with lid) on rack, and heat oven to 500 degrees. Lightly flour top of dough and, using razor blade or sharp knife, make one 6-inch-long, ½-inch-deep slit along top of dough. Carefully remove pot from oven and remove lid. Pick up dough by lifting parchment overhang and lower into pot (let any excess parchment hang over pot edge). Cover pot and place in oven. Reduce oven temperature to 425 degrees and bake covered for 30 minutes. Remove lid and continue to bake until loaf is deep brown and instant-read thermometer inserted into center registers 210 degrees, 20 to 30 minutes longer. Carefully remove bread from pot; transfer to wire rack and cool to room temperature, about 2 hours.

ALMOST NO-KNEAD BREAD WITH OLIVES, ROSEMARY, AND PARMESAN

Follow recipe for Almost No-Knead Bread, adding 4 ounces finely grated Parmesan (about 2 cups) and 1 tablespoon minced fresh rosemary leaves to flour mixture in step 1. Add ½ cup pitted, chopped green olives with water in step 1.

EQUIPMENT UPDATE:

Inexpensive Dutch Ovens

Shelling out hundreds of dollars for a Dutch oven is less necessary than ever. We put two new low-cost models, one from Tramontina ($39.86) and another from Lodge ($49.86), to the test and liked what we found. Both are crafted from enameled cast iron, and both produced glossy, deeply flavored Belgian beef stew; fluffy white rice; and crispy French fries in the test kitchen. But the Tramontina oven's larger capacity (6.5 quarts to the Lodge's 6 quarts) and even lower price made it our preferred choice. We recommend the Tramontina as an inexpensive alternative to our favorite 7¼-quart Dutch oven by Le Creuset ($229.95). –Elizabeth Bomze

BEST BUY
Boasting both high quality and low cost, the Tramontina 6.5 Quart Cast Iron Dutch Oven is hard to beat.

ALMOST NO-KNEAD SEEDED RYE BREAD

Follow recipe for Almost No-Knead Bread, replacing 1⅜ cups (7 ounces) all-purpose flour with 1⅛ cups (7 ounces) rye flour. Add 2 tablespoons caraway seeds to flour mixture in step 1.

ALMOST NO-KNEAD WHOLE WHEAT BREAD

Follow recipe for Almost No-Knead Bread, replacing 1 cup (5 ounces) all-purpose flour with 1 cup (5 ounces) whole wheat flour. Stir 2 tablespoons honey into water before adding it to dry ingredients in step 1.

ALMOST NO-KNEAD CRANBERRY-PECAN BREAD

Follow recipe for Almost No-Knead Bread, adding ½ cup dried cranberries and ½ cup toasted pecan halves to flour mixture in step 1.

COOK'S LIVE Original Test Kitchen Videos
www.cooksillustrated.com

HOW TO MAKE
- Almost No-Knead Bread

VIDEO TIPS
- How does bread rise?
- Behind the Scenes: Developing the recipe

How to Roast Broccoli

Roasting can concentrate flavor to turn dull vegetables into something great. Could it transform broccoli?

⋑ BY MATTHEW CARD ⋐

While I'm a fan of the concentrated flavor and dappled browning that roasting lends vegetables, I'd never considered broccoli a suitable candidate. Its awkward shape, tough stems, and shrubby florets seemed ill suited for cooking via high, dry heat; moist cooking methods better accommodate its idiosyncrasies. However, there are plenty of people who do consider broccoli fit for roasting and wax poetic about the results.

Though skeptical, I roasted a bunch, following one of the recipes I had collected for the task. It tasted good—good enough to eat straight from the sizzling pan. That said, this recipe and the others I tried still had their flaws. First of all, none clearly addressed how best to prepare the broccoli for roasting. How big, for example, should you cut florets from the crown, and what should be done with the stalk to ensure that it cooked at the same rate? Second, except for the broccoli in direct contact with the baking sheet, browning was spotty. And last, the florets tended to char and taste bitter.

If contact with the baking sheet was the key to browning, I thought I'd try to cut the broccoli in a fashion that maximized this contact. I tackled the crown first, lopping it off the stalk, flipping it on its base, and cutting it crosswise into slabs. The cross sections fell apart into a jumble of odd sized pieces that cooked unevenly. Perhaps wedges would work. I sliced another crown in half, then cut each half into uniform wedges that lay flat on the baking sheet—much more promising. Turning my attention to the stalk, I sliced off the tough exterior, then cut the stalk into rectangular pieces slightly smaller than the more delicate wedges to help promote even cooking of both parts.

The most successful recipes from my initial survey dressed the broccoli simply, with salt, pepper, and a splash of extra-virgin olive oil. A 500-degree oven delivered the best browning, but it also increased the risk of charred florets. A couple of recipes blanched or steamed the broccoli before roasting, but I found these batches tasted bland, as if the flavor had been washed away. Eventually, I discovered that a preheated baking sheet cooked the broccoli in half the time and crisped the florets without any charring.

But despite the blazing heat and the fact that I had solved the problem of charred florets, the broccoli still wasn't as browned as I'd hoped. One of the more interesting recipes I found coated the broccoli in a lemon juice–based vinaigrette before roasting, which resulted in remarkably even browning. I wondered if it was the fruit sugars in the lemon juice that generated such browning. Skipping the juice, I tossed a scant ½ teaspoon of sugar over the broccoli along with the salt and pepper, and the results were the best yet: blistered, bubbled, and browned stems that were sweet and full, along with crispy-tipped florets that tasted even better, especially when dressed with a spritz of lemon juice. It turns out a spoonful of sugar really does help make the broccoli go down.

Flavor Boost for Broccoli

Tossing the broccoli with a little sugar before roasting helps it brown more evenly and taste even better.

ROASTED BROCCOLI

SERVES 4

Trim away the outer peel from the broccoli stalk, otherwise it will turn tough when cooked. For Roasted Broccoli with Garlic, stir 1 tablespoon minced garlic into the olive oil before drizzling it over the broccoli. Our free recipes for Roasted Broccoli for Two and Roasted Broccoli with Garlic and Anchovies are available at www.cooksillustrated.com/february.

- 1 large head broccoli (about 1¾ pounds)
- 3 tablespoons extra-virgin olive oil
- ½ teaspoon table salt
- ½ teaspoon sugar
- Ground black pepper
- Lemon wedges for serving

1. Adjust oven rack to lowest position, place large rimmed baking sheet on rack, and heat oven to 500 degrees. Cut broccoli at juncture of florets and stems; remove outer peel from stalk. Cut stalk into 2- to 3-inch lengths and each length into ½-inch-thick pieces. Cut crowns into 4 wedges if 3–4 inches in diameter or 6 wedges if 4–5 inches in diameter. Place broccoli in large bowl; drizzle with oil and toss well until evenly coated. Sprinkle with salt, sugar, and pepper to taste and toss to combine.

2. Working quickly, remove baking sheet from oven. Carefully transfer broccoli to baking sheet and spread into even layer, placing flat sides down. Return baking sheet to oven and roast until stalks are well browned and tender and florets are lightly browned, 9 to 11 minutes. Transfer to serving dish and serve immediately with lemon wedges.

ROASTED BROCCOLI WITH OLIVES, GARLIC, OREGANO, AND LEMON

SERVES 4

- 1 recipe Roasted Broccoli
- 2 tablespoons extra-virgin olive oil
- 5 medium garlic cloves, sliced thin
- ½ teaspoon red pepper flakes
- 2 tablespoons finely minced pitted black olives
- 1 teaspoon minced fresh oregano leaves
- 2 teaspoons juice from 1 lemon

Follow recipe for Roasted Broccoli, omitting black pepper. While broccoli roasts, heat oil, garlic, and pepper flakes in 8-inch skillet over medium-low heat. Cook, stirring frequently, until garlic is soft and beginning to turn light golden brown, 5 to 7 minutes. Remove skillet from heat; stir in olives, oregano, and lemon juice. Toss roasted broccoli with olive mixture and serve immediately.

ROASTED BROCCOLI WITH SHALLOT, FENNEL SEEDS, AND PARMESAN

SERVES 4

- 1 recipe Roasted Broccoli
- 1 tablespoon extra-virgin olive oil
- 2 large shallots, halved and sliced thin lengthwise (about ½ cup)
- 1 teaspoon fennel seeds, roughly chopped
- 1 ounce Parmesan, shaved (about ½ cup)

Follow recipe for Roasted Broccoli. While broccoli roasts, heat oil in 8-inch skillet over medium heat until just shimmering. Add shallots and cook, stirring frequently, until soft and beginning to turn light golden brown, 5 to 6 minutes. Add fennel seeds and continue to cook until shallots are golden brown, 1 to 2 minutes longer. Remove skillet from heat. Toss roasted broccoli with shallots, sprinkle with Parmesan, and serve immediately.

COOK'S LIVE Original Test Kitchen Videos
www.cooksillustrated.com
HOW TO MAKE
- Roasted Broccoli

Thin and Crispy Oatmeal Cookies

You may think an oatmeal cookie should be moist and chewy. Thin and crispy oatmeal cookies can be irresistible—if, that is, you can get the texture just right.

⋺ BY SANDRA WU ⋲

Most people's definition of the perfect oatmeal cookie is something big, hearty, and chewy, with raisins and nuts in every bite. That has never been my ideal. When I crave an oatmeal cookie, I look for something thin, crisp, and delicate that allows the simple flavor of buttery oats to really stand out. I want the refinement of a lace cookie combined with the ease of a drop cookie. The test kitchen has an excellent recipe for Big Chewy Oatmeal-Raisin Cookies (January/February 1997). Could I get the crisp, delicate cookie I wanted by simply adjusting the ingredients in this recipe?

Buttery oat flavor shines through in this thin, delicate cookie.

The Thick and Thin of It

Thick, chewy oatmeal cookies get their texture from generous amounts of sugar and butter (usually melted to lend even greater chewiness), a high ratio of oats to flour, and a modest amount of leavener. Most recipes beat in a couple of eggs and vanilla and finish with raisins and nuts, ingredients I knew wouldn't work in a thin, crisp cookie.

Because I wanted rich, buttery flavor, I rejected the idea of shortening from the get-go (even though it typically provides a crisper texture) and used the same amount of butter called for in chewy cookie recipes: two sticks. The sugar would take more finessing.

Most recipes use a combination of brown and granulated sugars. Brown sugar lends rich flavor and moisture, and granulated provides crispness and encourages exterior browning. Since the greater the amount of sugar in a cookie, the chewier it is, I began by scaling the sugar down from 2 cups to 1½, using equal amounts of light brown and granulated. But the cookies still had too much chew. When I switched to all granulated sugar, the cookies became hard and crunchy, with a one-dimensional, overly sweet flavor. Taking the granulated sugar down to 1 cup and adding ¼ cup of light brown sugar back in aided the flavor—it now had subtle caramel notes—without compromising the texture.

To contribute better structure and richer flavor to the cookies, an egg or two is beaten in next. One egg held the cookies together nicely, but two gave them a cakey texture. Along with the one egg, I added a teaspoon of vanilla to round out the flavor. Now that the wet ingredients were all set, I was ready to tackle the dry stuff.

Drawing on past experience baking cookies, I speculated that using less flour would likely yield a final product that was crisper rather than chewier, flatter rather than puffier. But without enough flour, the oatmeal cookies spread too much, becoming formless, gossamer-thin lace cookies. A fairly standard amount of 1½ cups of flour gave the cookies a thicker, oat cake–like texture. I slowly cut down the amount until I ended up with 1 cup of flour. Though these cookies emerged from the oven with enough structure and were crisper than their predecessors, they still weren't on the mark. Because they didn't spread enough, they lacked the thinness I was looking for, and the dry edges and slightly chewy centers were obviously wrong. Replacing some of the flour with ground-up oats—a technique I'd seen in some recipes—didn't work: The cookies became even chewier. Using quick or instant oats in lieu of old-fashioned oats made them dense and bland. What if I used less oats instead? It was worth a try.

The Full Spread

I tried reducing the amount of oats from 3 cups to 2½ cups to get rid of some of the unwanted bulk. As I watched them bake, I noticed that the balls of dough spread fairly quickly along the edges, which became dark and crisp, while the thicker, paler middles took much longer to catch up. Pressing the dough down into flat-topped cylinders helped the cookies bake more evenly, but they still weren't spreading enough. Could the leavener be the problem?

Baking powder—the leavener used in our Big Chewy Oatmeal-Raisin Cookies—is a mixture of baking soda and two kinds of acid salts, one that reacts at room temperature and one at high temperatures. These components react to create gas bubbles that help baked goods expand. I'd been using ½ teaspoon of baking powder, which clearly wasn't working too well. I tried taking it out completely, but that left me with leaden rocks that barely eased out of their initial raw dough form. To get the cookies to at least brown better, I replaced the ½ teaspoon of baking powder with baking soda: They spread even less.

The only thing left to try was using what seemed like too much leavener. The basic principles of leavener are as follows: Use too little and there won't be enough bubbles to help the dough rise; use too much and you end up with excess carbon dioxide, which causes the bubbles to get too big. These big bubbles eventually combine with one another, rise to the top

COOK'S LIVE Original Test Kitchen Videos

www.cooksillustrated.com

HOW TO MAKE

- Thin and Crispy Oatmeal Cookies

VIDEO TIPS

- Can I use quick or instant oats?
- Why does the test kitchen like parchment paper?
- Do I have to bake the cookies one sheet at a time?

More Leavener for Thinner Cookies

It may sound counterintuitive, but doubling the usual amount of leavener (we used both baking powder and baking soda) in oatmeal cookies is the key to crispiness. The amplified dose creates big bubbles that first help the dough rise, then combine and burst, resulting in a flat cookie.

MORE BAKING POWDER AND BAKING SODA LEADS TO CRISPIER COOKIES

of the dough, and burst, resulting in a flat product. But since what I wanted was a thin, flat cookie, perhaps I could make this "mistake" work to my advantage. After testing varying amounts and combinations of baking powder and baking soda, I found that ¾ teaspoon of baking powder coupled with ½ teaspoon of baking soda gave me exactly what I wanted. This time, the cookies puffed up in the oven, collapsed, and spread out, becoming a much thinner version of their former selves. Even better, they had no trace of the soapy aftertaste that is often a byproduct of too much leavener. I was finally getting somewhere.

Crisping It Up

Now the cookies were thin and had a nice buttery, oaty flavor. To address their slightly greasy aftertaste, I reduced the amount of butter by 2 tablespoons. Two issues remained: They were baking unevenly—the top tray was often darker than the bottom one, even after being rotated halfway through—and had a tendency to bend into nearly a **U** shape before breaking in half. They just weren't snappy enough.

To guard against the tough, dry cookies that can result from overbaking, most recipes for thick and chewy cookies say to remove them from the oven when they still look slightly raw. Suspecting this was a precaution I didn't need to heed, I tried baking my cookies all the way through until they were fully set and evenly browned from center to edge. Since the cookies were now thin, they didn't become tough. Instead, they were crisp throughout. Baking the cookies one sheet at a time ensured that they cooked evenly. And rather than transferring them warm from the baking sheet to a cooling rack, I accidentally discovered that the cookies got crisper when left to cool completely on the baking sheet. Less work, with even better results! I'd finally achieved my goal: a thin, delicate oatmeal cookie with buttery flavor and just the right amount of crunch. Who knows—a cookie this good might even convert the fans of chewiness over to my side.

RECIPE TESTING: The Right (and Wrong) Oats

TOO BLAND
Instant oats and quick-cooking oats create dense, mealy cookies lacking in good oat flavor.

JUST RIGHT
Old-fashioned oats produce perfectly crisp cookies that retain a nice, round shape.

THIN AND CRISPY OATMEAL COOKIES

MAKES 24 COOKIES

To ensure that the cookies bake evenly and are crisp throughout, bake them 1 tray at a time. Place them on the baking sheet in 3 rows, with 3 cookies in the outer rows and 2 cookies in the center row. If you reuse a baking sheet, allow the cookies on it to cool at least 15 minutes before transferring them to a wire rack, then reline the sheet with fresh parchment before baking more cookies. We developed this recipe using Quaker Old Fashioned Rolled Oats. Other brands of old-fashioned oats can be substituted but may cause the cookies to spread more. Do not use instant or quick-cooking oats.

- 1 cup (5 ounces) unbleached all-purpose flour
- ¾ teaspoon baking powder
- ½ teaspoon baking soda
- ½ teaspoon table salt
- 14 tablespoons (1¾ sticks) unsalted butter, softened but still cool, about 65 degrees
- 1 cup (7 ounces) granulated sugar
- ¼ cup (1¾ ounces) packed light brown sugar
- 1 large egg
- 1 teaspoon vanilla extract
- 2½ cups old-fashioned rolled oats (see note above)

1. Adjust oven rack to middle position and heat oven to 350 degrees. Line 3 large (18- by 12-inch) baking sheets with parchment paper. Whisk flour, baking powder, baking soda, and salt in medium bowl.

2. In standing mixer fitted with paddle attachment, beat butter and sugars at medium-low speed until just combined, about 20 seconds. Increase speed to medium and continue to beat until light and fluffy, about 1 minute longer. Scrape down bowl with rubber spatula. Add egg and vanilla and beat on medium-low until fully incorporated, about 30 seconds. Scrape down bowl again. With mixer running at low speed, add flour mixture and mix until just incorporated and smooth, 10 seconds. With mixer still running on low, gradually add oats and mix until well incorporated, 20 seconds. Give dough final stir with rubber spatula to ensure that no flour pockets remain and ingredients are evenly distributed.

3. Divide dough into 24 equal portions, each about 2 tablespoons (or use #30 cookie scoop), then roll between palms into balls. Place cookies on prepared baking sheets, spacing them about 2½ inches apart, 8 dough balls per sheet (see note above). Using fingertips, gently press each dough ball to ¾-inch thickness.

4. Bake 1 sheet at a time until cookies are deep golden brown, edges are crisp, and centers yield to slight pressure when pressed, 13 to 16 minutes, rotating baking sheet halfway through. Transfer baking sheet to wire rack; cool cookies completely on sheet.

THIN AND CRISPY COCONUT-OATMEAL COOKIES

Follow recipe for Thin and Crispy Oatmeal Cookies, decreasing oats to 2 cups and adding 1½ cups sweetened flaked coconut to batter with oats in step 2.

THIN AND CRISPY ORANGE-ALMOND OATMEAL COOKIES

Follow recipe for Thin and Crispy Oatmeal Cookies, creaming 2 teaspoons finely grated orange zest with butter and sugars in step 2. Decrease oats to 2 cups and add 1 cup coarsely chopped toasted almonds to batter with oats in step 2.

Cookies with a Twist: Sweet and Salty

A dusting of salt atop sweets such as chocolate and caramel is nothing new, but we recently came across Kayak Cookies, which gives a different item the salt treatment: their Salty Oats cookies. After sprinkling a few grains on our Thin and Crispy Oatmeal Cookies, we were hooked. Similar to its effect on caramel, salt's contrasting flavor adds a new dimension to the cookies and accentuates their rich, buttery taste.

SALTY THIN AND CRISPY OATMEAL COOKIES

MAKES 24 COOKIES

We prefer the texture and flavor of a coarse-grained sea salt, like Maldon or fleur de sel, but kosher salt can be used. If using kosher salt, reduce the amount sprinkled over the cookies to ¼ teaspoon.

- 1 recipe Thin and Crispy Oatmeal Cookies
- ½ teaspoon coarse sea salt

Follow recipe for Thin and Crispy Oatmeal Cookies, reducing the amount of table salt in dough to ¼ teaspoon. Lightly sprinkle sea salt evenly over flattened dough balls before baking.

Perfecting Spice Cake

Spice cakes can be bland and leaden. Could we create a tender, airy cake with convincing spice flavor that stands up to a rich cream cheese frosting?

⪢ BY KEITH DRESSER ⪡

The spice cake I remember most vividly is from my childhood. Though my grandmother baked it in a rectangular pan, this cake was light and airy and more akin to a layer cake than the heavy, dense snack cakes that all too often define the genre today. While it wasn't the fanciest dessert my grandmother served, it was company cake, something too special to serve every day. It was moist and substantial, with spices that were warm and bold without being overpowering, and its layer of rich cream cheese frosting was the perfect complement. I wanted to return to this classic, but the recipe for my grandmother's spice cake was never fixed in writing.

I decided to do a little research in our library, where I found as many variations on the spice cake theme as there are cooks to make them. I found Bundt cakes with raisins and nuts; squat, square versions that resembled gingerbread or carrot cake; cakes calling for everything from apples and stewed figs to chocolate chips and pumpkin puree. Some had spice overload, tasting gritty and dusty. Others were so lacking in spice flavor that it seemed as if a cinnamon stick had only been waved in their general direction. In fact, other than a mixture of warm spices, there were few common denominators linking any of these desserts. And, unfortunately, not one had the old-fashioned simplicity of the frosted spice cake from my childhood. I would have to begin from scratch.

Building Cake with the Right Heft

The texture of my grandmother's cake resembled the firm, moist, melt-in-your-mouth lightness of our Rich

Lightly spiced cream cheese frosting tops a moist, tender cake.

and Tender Yellow Cake (March/April 1999). But simply adding spices to this recipe didn't work. The cake crumbled under the heavy frosting, and the spice flavor was overwhelming. To add volume and heft, I replaced the cake flour used in that recipe with all-purpose flour. The switch made for a slightly tougher, drier cake. Adding more yolks to the batter increased the cake's tenderness; so did switching from milk to buttermilk, which also enriched the cake's flavor. Doubling the dairy from ½ cup to 1 cup was enough to fix the dryness issue.

But the most important adjustment I made involved the mixing technique. We make our yellow cake by reversing the usual order of things and mixing butter into the dry ingredients before adding the liquids, which yields a cake with a very fine-grained texture. I wanted a more open and substantial crumb, so I used the standard method of beating the softened butter with the sugar, incorporating the eggs, and adding flour and liquid alternately in small amounts.

Putting Spice into Spice Cake

I knew that simply adding more spice to something does not lead to increased spiciness. Most of what we experience when we consume a food containing spice is not actually the spice's taste but its aroma. These aromas are produced by volatile oils found within the spice cells. When spices are ground, these aromatic oils are released, which is why freshly ground whole spices are much "tastier" (i.e., more aromatic) than packaged ground spices (especially those that have been sitting on the shelf awhile). But in addition to being too much work, individually grinding the five spices I'd chosen for the recipe always imparted a faint but discernible grittiness to the cake, no matter how much time they spent in the spice grinder.

What about using techniques from the test kitchen to get the most out of the spices already in my cupboard? I knew from preparing curries and chili that heating spices (either through dry-toasting them or blooming them in hot oil) intensifies their aroma. This is because heat drives moisture out of the spice, carrying the aromatic oils along with it. While both techniques created a fuller-flavored cake, dry-toasting the spices was not as successful as blooming them in oil. Toasting allows more of the piquant aromas to escape into the air, but because the aromatic oils are soluble in cooking

AT A GLANCE | KEYS TO SPICE FLAVOR

1. BROWNED BUTTER
Browning the butter imparts a faint nuttiness that deepens the cake's spice flavor.

2. BLOOMED SPICES
Blooming the spices in the browned butter brings out their volatile oils, boosting their impact.

3. A HINT OF MOLASSES
Molasses adds a bittersweet note that underscores the warm flavor of the spices.

4. GRATED GINGER
Finely grated ginger adds a fresh, zesty quality to the cake that dried ginger can't provide.

TECHNIQUE | REMOVING TRAPPED AIR BUBBLES

In cakes with a thick batter, such as spice cake or carrot cake, trapped air bubbles can lead to a finished cake with unsightly holes. Here's how we got rid of them:

1. Run the tip of a metal spatula through the batter in a zigzag motion, pulling it to the edges of the pan.

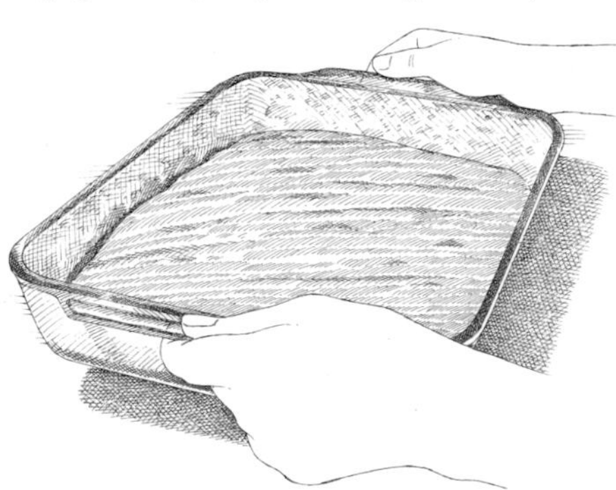

2. Gently tap the pan against the counter three or four times to release any air bubbles that have risen to the surface.

oil, blooming them was a more effective way of making sure they made it into the cake.

Up to this point, I had been using ground cinnamon, cloves, cardamom, allspice, and nutmeg. While the mixture contributed a respectable spiciness to the cake, I wanted more complexity. A coworker suggested steeping crushed fresh ginger in the buttermilk to extract maximum flavor. This brought slightly more depth of flavor to the cake but not enough to justify the extra work. A tablespoon of grated fresh ginger added directly to the batter, on the other hand, added noticeable zing. For yet another flavor dimension, I replaced the oil I had been using to bloom my spices with browned butter, which imparted a faint nuttiness and filled out the overall taste of the cake. As a finishing touch, I incorporated a couple tablespoons of molasses into the batter—just enough to balance the spices with a slight bittersweet nuance without turning the cake into gingerbread.

Topping It Off

All that remained was to create just the right frosting. Almost every frosting recipe for spice cake I'd come across in my initial research consisted of confectioners' sugar, cream cheese, and butter in varying amounts. To create a light, creamy frosting that would work well with the cake's tender crumb, I used a little less butter than called for in most of these recipes. When I frosted the cake, however, I was disappointed. The two elements lacked harmony and needed something to pull them into balance. Why shouldn't that be spice? I added ½ teaspoon of the spice mixture from the cake to the frosting, which lent a subtle yet perceptible flavor that made the two work beautifully together.

Maybe this cake will be one that my daughter will remember from her childhood. But unlike me, she'll have a recipe that will let her know exactly what to do to get it right.

SPICE CAKE WITH CREAM CHEESE FROSTING

SERVES 12 TO 14

To save time, let the eggs, buttermilk, and butter come up to temperature while the browned butter and spice mixture cools. To prevent unsightly air holes in the finished cake, be sure to follow the instructions for removing air bubbles in the batter (see illustrations at left). Leftover cake can be stored, covered with plastic wrap, in the refrigerator for up to 2 days. The cake should be brought to room temperature before serving.

Cake

- 2¼ cups (11¼ ounces) unbleached all-purpose flour, plus extra for dusting pans
- 1 tablespoon ground cinnamon
- ¾ teaspoon ground cardamom
- ½ teaspoon ground allspice
- ½ teaspoon ground cloves
- ¼ teaspoon ground nutmeg
- 16 tablespoons unsalted butter (2 sticks), softened
- ½ teaspoon baking powder
- ½ teaspoon baking soda
- ½ teaspoon table salt
- 2 large eggs plus 3 large yolks, at room temperature
- 1 teaspoon vanilla extract
- 1¾ cups (12¼ ounces) granulated sugar
- 2 tablespoons light or mild molasses
- 1 tablespoon grated fresh ginger
- 1 cup buttermilk, at room temperature

Frosting

- 5 tablespoons unsalted butter, cut into 5 pieces, softened
- 1¼ cups (4½ ounces) confectioners' sugar
- 8 ounces cream cheese, cut into 4 pieces, softened
- ½ teaspoon vanilla extract
- ¾ cup coarsely chopped walnuts, toasted (optional)

1. **FOR THE CAKE:** Adjust oven rack to middle position and heat oven to 350 degrees. Grease and flour 13- by 9-inch baking pan. Combine spices in small bowl; reserve ½ teaspoon for frosting.

2. Heat 4 tablespoons butter in 8-inch skillet over medium heat until melted, 1 to 2 minutes. Continue to cook, swirling pan constantly, until butter is light brown and has faint nutty aroma, 2 to 4 minutes. Add spices and continue to cook, stirring constantly, 15 seconds. Remove from heat and cool to room temperature, about 30 minutes.

3. Whisk flour, baking powder, baking soda, and salt in medium bowl. In small bowl, gently whisk eggs, yolks, and vanilla to combine. In standing mixer fitted with paddle attachment, cream remaining 12 tablespoons butter with sugar and molasses at medium-high speed until pale and fluffy, about 3 minutes, scraping down sides and bottom of bowl twice with rubber spatula. Reduce to medium speed and add cooled butter and spice mixture, ginger, and half of egg mixture; mix until incorporated, about 15 seconds. Repeat with remaining egg mixture; scrape down bowl again. Reduce to low speed; add about one-third flour mixture, followed by half of buttermilk, mixing until just incorporated after each addition, about 5 seconds. Repeat using half of remaining flour mixture and all of remaining buttermilk. Scrape bowl and add remaining flour mixture; mix at medium speed until batter is thoroughly combined, about 15 seconds. Remove bowl from mixer and fold batter once or twice with rubber spatula to incorporate any remaining flour.

4. Transfer batter to prepared pan; following illustrations at left, zigzag tip of metal spatula through batter, pulling it to pan edges. Lightly tap pan against counter 3 or 4 times to dislodge any large air bubbles; smooth surface with spatula.

5. Bake until toothpick inserted in center of cake comes out clean, 32 to 37 minutes. Cool cake to room temperature in pan on wire rack, about 2 hours.

6. **FOR THE FROSTING:** In bowl of standing mixer fitted with paddle attachment, beat butter, sugar, and reserved ½ teaspoon spice mixture at medium-high speed until light and fluffy, 1 to 2 minutes. Add cream cheese one piece at a time, beating thoroughly after each addition. Add vanilla and beat until no lumps remain, about 30 seconds.

7. Run paring knife around edge of cake to loosen from pan. Using spatula, spread frosting evenly over surface of cake. Sprinkle cake with walnuts, if using. Cut into squares and serve.

SPICE CAKE WITH ORANGE CREAM CHEESE FROSTING

Follow recipe for Spice Cake with Cream Cheese Frosting, adding 1½ teaspoons finely grated orange zest to frosting with the vanilla in step 6. Substitute toasted slivered almonds or roughly chopped hazelnuts for walnuts in step 7.

The Truth About Dark Chocolate

Does spending more for "gourmet" chocolate buy richer, more complex flavor and yield better baking results?

BY LISA McMANUS

Just a few years ago, selecting dark chocolate for your dessert recipe seemed pretty simple: You went to the supermarket and bought a bar of baking chocolate. These days, there are dozens of choices, and you can spend hours poring over the cacao percentages and exotic provenances on the labels. You can pay a lot more, too. But does any of it really matter? Does spending more get you better chocolate flavor? And can your choice of chocolate change your baking results?

Chocolate Basics

First, we looked into the definition of "dark chocolate" and discovered it's a pretty loose term. The U.S. Food and Drug Administration doesn't distinguish between bittersweet and semisweet chocolate—it simply requires that products by either name contain at least 35 percent cacao (the cocoa solids and cocoa butter from the cacao bean). Companies use the names cacao and cocoa interchangeably, but in general, when there is more cacao in the chocolate, there is less sugar, and bittersweet chocolate tends to be less sweet and have more cacao than semisweet. Even darker chocolates, with higher cacao percentages, will be correspondingly less sweet (100 percent cacao chocolate is completely unsweetened).

Understanding Cacao Percentages

In a recipe specifying a bittersweet or semisweet chocolate, can you substitute a chocolate with a higher cacao percentage than the 60 percent generally used for cooking, making no other adjustments? Not if you expect identical results. We tasted brownies and pots de crème made with our two top-ranked dark chocolates, by Callebaut and Ghirardelli, which have 60 percent cacao, alongside ones made with the same brands' 70 percent cacao offerings.

While all four versions were acceptable, tasters strongly preferred the 60 percent cacao chocolates in these recipes, complaining of the 70 percent versions' dryness and lack of sweetness (and in the case of the pots de crème, a thicker, stiffer consistency), although some tasters noted their "deeper" chocolate flavor. When chocolate manufacturers increase cacao content, they correspondingly decrease the amount of sugar and usually add less cocoa butter. With less sugar and fat, it's no wonder the results were distinctly different. –L.M.

Any number of variables—the type of bean, where it's grown, and when it's harvested; the length and conditions of fermentation; the roasting and grinding methods; and the quality and quantity of any additives (such as vanilla)—can contribute to differences in flavor and texture. Chocolate makers claim that every detail is critical—and are loath to share too many specifics.

We'd heard a lot about the type of cacao bean being extremely important. There are only three types. The most prized (and expensive) bean, the criollo, grown mainly in the Caribbean and Central America, makes up less than 2 percent of the world's cacao. Most chocolate is made from forastero beans, generally from Africa. These beans are harvested from hardier trees, which makes them cheaper. The third, trinitario, is a hybrid of the other two beans and comprises about 5 percent of the total harvest.

The Cook's Chocolate—60 Percent Cacao

To choose chocolate for our testing lineup, we ignored "bittersweet" or "semisweet" nomenclature and concerned ourselves with chocolate containing roughly 60 percent cacao—the type that most recipes calling for dark chocolate have been developed to use. (Even darker chocolates, with 70 percent or more cacao, usually require recipe adjustments to get good results; see "Understanding Cacao Percentages," left). Not confining ourselves to baking chocolate, we included chocolate from the candy aisle in selecting 12 widely available brands. Prices varied wildly: We spent from 44 cents per ounce to nearly four times as much.

Seeking a chocolate that would perform well in various applications, we held three blind tastings: first eating the bars plain, then melting them into chocolate pots de crème, and finally baking them into brownies. In each tasting, we rated the chocolate on sweetness, intensity of flavor, texture, and overall appeal. And since many chocolate makers are secretive about their proprietary methods and formulas, we sent samples of each to an independent laboratory to confirm levels of cocoa solids, cocoa butter, and sugar.

Chocolate Myths and Chocolate Truths

So which chocolates won favor with our tasters? The results were surprising. The chocolate with the fanciest pedigree in our lineup, El Rey, made exclusively from Venezuelan criollo beans, wound up in the lower half of the rankings. The other single-origin sample, produced by Lindt from criollo and trinitario beans grown in Madagascar, came in last. Our two top-rated chocolates, Callebaut and Ghirardelli, came from blends relying primarily on the inexpensive forastero bean. Both were purchased at the supermarket, and they cost just 53 cents and 75 cents per ounce, respectively.

Our second discovery also defied expectations. We assumed that if one brand of chocolate is 60 percent cacao, it would be pretty similar in sweetness, chocolate intensity, and creaminess to another brand's 60 percent cacao chocolate. Not so. When chocolate makers grind shelled cacao beans, known as nibs, to create the thick paste called chocolate liquor, this paste contains both cocoa solids and cocoa butter. Most manufacturers then add even more cocoa butter, in varying amounts, to help create the texture of the final chocolate. A few, like our winner, also add extra cocoa solids to intensify the chocolate flavor. Ultimately, however, the cacao percentage on the label of a chocolate bar is a total that includes both cocoa solids and cocoa butter—meaning that different chocolates can have different proportions of each and still share the 60 percent cacao designation. As our lab tests showed, the cocoa solids in our lineup ranged from about 17 percent of a bar's total weight to more than 30 percent, while fat ranged from a third of the weight to nearly half of it. Sugar levels varied by nearly 20 percent as well.

So would the chocolate with the most cocoa butter make the biggest splash, bringing richer, extra-creamy, flavor to your desserts? No. In fact, our lab results revealed that the chocolate with the lowest fat won the day, while the one with the most fat came in dead last. And would having the most cocoa solids make a chocolate superior? Again, no. Our tasters preferred chocolates with only a moderate amount. Sweetness wasn't the explanation, either: Chocolates in the middle range of sugar levels were preferred over those with the most sugar, though overall the top half of the rankings had more sugar than the bottom half.

In the end, we preferred dark chocolate that achieved the best balance of all three major components—cocoa butter, cocoa solids, and sugar. Callebaut Intense Dark Chocolate L-60-40NV was favored for its rich chocolate flavor, moderate sugar and cocoa solids, and comparatively low fat. Tasters appreciated its "intensely chocolaty," "rich," "espresso" flavor and "caramel aftertaste." It excelled in every application. San Francisco–based Ghirardelli's Bittersweet Chocolate Baking Bar came in a close second, with praise for its "smoky," "fruity" notes. It also demonstrated that balanced chocolate flavor derived from moderate levels of sugar, cocoa solids, and cocoa butter.

TASTING DARK CHOCOLATE

Twenty-four members of the *Cook's Illustrated* staff tasted 12 dark chocolates, all containing around 60 percent cacao. We sampled them plain, in chocolate pots de crème, and baked into brownies. Results were averaged, and the chocolates appear in order of preference. We purchased the chocolates at Boston stores or online (see page 32).

RECOMMENDED

CALLEBAUT Intense Dark Chocolate, L-60-40NV
➤ 60 percent cacao ➤ **Price:** 53 cents per ounce
Country of Origin: Belgium

Comments: "Complex flavor, creamy and thick," "dark and earthy," with a "rich cocoa flavor" and "a nice balance of sweetness and bitterness." Tasters picked up "caramel, smoke, and espresso" in the plain tasting. It baked into "what a brownie should be."

GHIRARDELLI Bittersweet Chocolate Baking Bar
➤ 60 percent cacao ➤ **Price:** 75 cents per ounce
Country of Origin: USA

Comments: Tasters discerned "coffee, smoke, and dried fruit" in this "creamy, rich, glossy" chocolate, with a "slight sour aftertaste." In brownies, it had "quintessential brownie flavor" that was "assertive," "like dark chocolate but not cocoa-y or bitter like some others; a really good blend of tastes."

DAGOBA Organic Semisweet Dark Chocolate
➤ 59 percent cacao ➤ **Price:** $1.30 per ounce
Country of Origin: USA

Comments: "Fairly sweet" (a few said "cloyingly" so), with "great chocolate flavor," it had "hints of fruit" and "apricot and almond." In pots de crème, it was "very buttery and chocolaty, with a silky texture" and a flavor that was "smooth yet strong." In brownies: "a good one all-around," "malty, sweet, rich, slightly floral."

MICHEL CLUIZEL Noir de Cacao Dark Chocolate
➤ 60 percent cacao ➤ **Price:** $1.43 per ounce
Country of Origin: France

Comments: "Creamy, not bitter. Nice for an eating chocolate," "complex and earthy," but tasters were reminded of "olive oil" or "mayonnaise." In brownies, it was "very smooth and well balanced," if a bit "bland"; in pots de crème, it was "supercreamy," "like milk chocolate."

VALRHONA Le Noir Semisweet Chocolate
➤ 56 percent cacao ➤ **Price:** $1.37 per ounce
Country of Origin: France

Comments: "A nondark-chocolate-lover's dark chocolate," this was "well balanced" and "creamy," with "a sharp chocolate flavor" and "not much aftertaste." In pots de crème, it was "supersmooth and cushiony" and "almost too creamy"; "fudgy" brownies were "very sweet."

RECOMMENDED WITH RESERVATIONS

E. GUITTARD Tsaratana Pure Semisweet Dark Chocolate
➤ 61 percent cacao ➤ **Price:** $1.45 per ounce
Country of Origin: USA

Comments: "Fruity, spicy," "sweet and smoky," this "very creamy" chocolate had slightly "odd" flavors, including banana, tobacco, beef, and leather, along with caramel and honey. While it had some fans, others observed that it made drier, cakier brownies and slightly "chalky" pots de crème.

HERSHEY'S All-Natural Extra Dark Pure Dark Chocolate
➤ 60 percent cacao ➤ **Price:** 63 cents per ounce
Country of Origin: USA

Comments: A "chalky" texture was decried by many tasters, both when eaten plain and in brownies, though the brownies were praised for "rich, roasted chocolate flavor." In pots de crème, it was "dark and glossy," but "very gloppy" and "too gummy and dense—flavor is good, though."

EL REY MIJAO Dark Chocolate, Venezuelan Single Bean, Carenero Superior
➤ 61 percent cacao ➤ **Price:** 50 cents per ounce
Country of Origin: Venezuela

Comments: "Not very complex" and "mild," with a slightly "sour" aftertaste, it was "sweet and buttery" in pots de crème and "kinda flat" and "dull" in brownies, where it was also deemed "toothachingly sweet." "Solid, if unspectacular."

SCHARFFEN BERGER Fine Artisan Semisweet Dark Chocolate
➤ 62 percent cacao ➤ **Price:** $1.03 per ounce
Country of Origin: USA

Comments: "Lots of fruit" here: Tasters noted cherry (some said "cough syrup"), grape, raspberry, raisins, and prunes. "Complex, but I didn't care for it," said one. "Gluey" in pots de crème, it had a "roasty" quality in brownies, but "lacked choco-oomph."

NESTLÉ CHOCOLATIER Premium Baking Chocolate Bittersweet Chocolate Bar
➤ 62 percent cacao ➤ **Price:** 56 cents per ounce
Country of Origin: USA

Comments: "Dry and chalky," "grainy," and "gritty," agreed tasters when it was sampled plain and in pots de crème. In brownies, it was "rich" and "fudgy," but again "a bit grainy," with an "almost sour milk taste." Others noted off-flavors that were "metallic," "tannic," "bitter," or "chemical."

BAKER'S Semi-Sweet Baking Chocolate Squares (USA)
➤ 54 percent cacao ➤ **Price:** 44 cents per ounce
Country of Origin: USA

Comments: "Very sweet, you can almost taste the sugar granules," with a "bitter coffee flavor." "Very cocoa-y, but otherwise pretty boring." "Tastes like cheap chocolate." It rated poorly when tasted plain and in pots de crème due to its granular texture, but shone in brownies as "very moist, chewy," and "fudgy."

LINDT Excellence Madagascar Extra Fine Mild Dark Chocolate
➤ 65 percent cacao ➤ **Price:** $1.08 per ounce
Country of Origin: Switzerland

Comments: Lab tests showed it had the highest fat content of the lineup by far, and also the lowest cocoa solids. Tasters noted a "very creamy" but "waxy" texture and a "one-dimensional" flavor with "very vanilla" notes. In pots de crème, it was "creamy, but strange and acidic." In brownies, it was "funky."

A Cut Above

Cutting boards made from bamboo and wood composite are flooding the market. Is there any reason to choose these new-fangled materials over traditional wood and plastic?

BY LISA McMANUS

Buying a cutting board starts with deciding on its material. Until recently, there were just two good options: wood and plastic. Wood boards appeal to cooks who love how they feel and don't mind that they need to be hand-washed. Fans of plastic rate a dishwasher-safe, maintenance-free board over everything else—even if it means a surface that will never feel as cushiony as wood. Recently, eco-friendly bamboo boards claiming to match and even surpass the benefits of wood have appeared in kitchenware stores everywhere. Alongside them are lightweight composite boards, fashioned from laminated wood fiber, which look like wood but clean up like plastic. Do these newcomers offer anything better than the old standbys?

To find out, we gathered a lineup made from all four materials (plus a glass board; we haven't liked glass in the past, but we know many people do). We whacked at them with a cleaver, subjected them to hundreds of cuts with a new, factory-sharpened knife, and repeatedly knocked them off the counter. When we were done, we chopped chipotle chiles in brick-red adobo sauce to see how easily they would clean up. Our ultimate goal was to find the ideal surface: soft enough to keep your knife and hands in good shape but sturdy enough to take on any cutting job without undue damage.

The Tried and True

At the outset, we were impressed by what many consider the king of cutting boards: a 10-pound maple butcher block from John Boos. Heavy and solid (with a $75 price tag to match), this board's end-grain wood took cleaver strikes and repetitive cuts without showing any damage to its surface or the knife. But the board's virtues were also its undoing: its heft made it uncomfortable to set up, wash, and put away. And despite being oiled, it split along a glue line after routine use. We preferred a lighter yet still substantial maple board from J.K. Adams, which had a convenient size—roomy but not unwieldy or heavy—that felt great under the knife and took all the abuse we could dish out.

In the plastic category, two didn't measure up—a folding board that proved more gimmicky than useful and a plain plastic board that was too slick, making the knife, food, and board itself skid around as we worked. This board's soft surface also became deeply stained and cut up. But the Architec Gripper board we've loved in the past remains highly recommended for its durable surface and hundreds of rubber feet, thermally bonded to the plastic, which make the board a pleasure to cut on by keeping it rock-solid on the counter. Any stains on this board were blasted clean in the dishwasher, but we weren't influenced by its sanitized appearance. Our lab tests have shown that, contrary to popular belief, bacteria doesn't wash off plastic boards any more easily than it does off wood ones (see "Bacteria on Board," left).

Composed of Composite

We were most skeptical about wood-composite boards. Despite their purported resemblance to real wood, the two first boards we tested looked like the thin, hard particleboard they were. The Epicurean model (a product we see everywhere) immediately lived down to our low expectations, making a nasty clack under the knife and giving off sawdust under repeated cuts.

However, the Snow River composite board took us by surprise, winning some of our highest accolades. An innovative twist to its design—softer layers of maple veneer surrounding a hard inner core—made it almost as comfortable to cut on as wood. This board held up extremely well under abuse. When we checked with the manufacturer, we found out why: The board's maple veneer is not simply glued onto the core, but bonded with it from the beginning through the application of resin, high heat, and thousands of pounds of compression. The fact that the board can go in the dishwasher, like all boards of this type, made us appreciate it all the more.

The Bamboo Advantage

Bamboo boards are lightweight and attractive, but we wondered about their endurance. This material is often misunderstood to be a type of hardwood; it's actually a kind of grass. Bamboo does have definite advantages over wood: It grows in poor soil and in almost any climate, and it renews itself in years rather than decades.

Like our favorite composite board, the butcher-block-style Totally Bamboo Congo Board turned out to be a pleasant surprise. In test after test, it matched the outstanding comfort and ease of cutting on a classic maple butcher block—and it was so impervious to abuse that it looked new after hundreds of cuts. Like wood, this board can't go into the dishwasher and would benefit from occasional oiling, but we were more than willing to trade those inconveniences for its superior feel. An unexpected bonus: Lab tests confirmed bamboo has natural antimicrobial properties that help kill bacteria even before you wash it.

But not all bamboo boards are created equal. The other bamboo boards' surfaces were not as durable or forgiving as the Congo's, due in part to their construction and possibly also to the age of the bamboo at harvest—the younger it is, the softer the cane and the cheaper the board.

The Final Cut

So are the new materials any better than wood and plastic? If you choose overall design and construction carefully, the answer is yes—but only by a hair. In the final analysis, our top-rated boards cut across material distinctions, displaying similar features of comfort, durability, and solid construction. If you're willing to wash by hand and do occasional maintenance to keep your board in peak form, the top-performing Totally Bamboo Congo board and J.K. Adams's Takes Two maple board are good choices. If the dishwasher is the only way you'll go, you have two fine options: the composite Snow River Utility board and the plastic Architec Gripper Nonslip board.

COOK'S LIVE Original Test Kitchen Videos

www.cooksillustrated.com

- Behind the Scenes: Cutting Board Testing

VIDEO TIP

- What's the best way to clean a cutting board?

SCIENCE: Bacteria on Board

In 2004, we asked an independent laboratory to compare wood and plastic cutting boards to see which harbors more harmful bacteria. The answer? There's no difference—both are equally safe as long as you scrub them in hot, soapy water. We repeated the tests on bamboo and composite boards, which are new to the market since we conducted the earlier tests. Just as with wood and plastic, if you wash these boards with soap and water, the bacteria will die. Interestingly, even before being washed, the bamboo board's natural antimicrobial properties helped kill off much of the bacteria. You shouldn't skip washing bamboo—but it's nice to have a built-in head start. –L.M.

KEY

GOOD: ★★★
FAIR: ★★
POOR: ★
DISHWASHER-SAFE: DW

We tested 13 cutting boards by evaluating their design, durability, wear on a chef's knife, and suitability for a variety of kitchen tasks. Boards appear in order of preference. Sources for the winning boards are on page 32.

Maintaining Your Cutting Board

Over the years, we have conducted many lab and kitchen tests to determine the best methods for cleaning and deodorizing cutting boards. Here are our recommendations.

ROUTINE CLEANING

After each use, scrub your board thoroughly in hot, soapy water (or put it through the dishwasher if it's dishwasher-safe). This kills nearly all harmful bacteria on any type of cutting board. Rinse well and dry thoroughly.

TO REMOVE FOOD ODORS (SUCH AS GARLIC)

Scrub with a paste of 1 tablespoon of baking soda and 1 teaspoon of water, followed by routine washing with hot, soapy water.

TO REMOVE STAINS FROM PLASTIC BOARDS

An overnight bleach bath leaves stained plastic boards pristine and sanitized. Put 1 tablespoon of bleach per quart of water in the sink and immerse the board, fouled-side up. When the board rises to the surface, drape a clean white kitchen towel or two over its surface and splash the towel with about ¼ cup of additional bleach.

TO MAINTAIN A WOOD OR BAMBOO BOARD

Apply food-grade mineral oil every few weeks when the board is new and a few times a year thereafter. The oil soaks into the fibers, creating a barrier to excess moisture. (Don't use olive or vegetable oil, which can become rancid.) Avoid leaving wood or bamboo boards resting in water, or they will eventually split.

TESTING CUTTING BOARDS

HIGHLY RECOMMENDED	PERFORMANCE	TESTERS' COMMENTS
Totally Bamboo Congo PRICE: $39.99 MATERIAL: Butcher-block-style bamboo WEIGHT: 5 pounds	CUTTING: ★★★ DURABILITY: ★★★ CLEANUP: ★★★ USER-FRIENDLINESS: ★★★	Solid and cushy surface of a wooden butcher block, but lightweight, with nicely rounded edges that are easy to grasp. Perfect score in every test.
Snow River Utility (DW) PRICE: $16.99 MATERIAL: Wood-laminate composite with maple surface WEIGHT: 1.7 pounds	CUTTING: ★★★ DURABILITY: ★★★ CLEANUP: ★★★ USER-FRIENDLINESS: ★★★	Looks and feels like wood but can go in the dishwasher. Cleaver cut deeply, but cuts closed up after washing. Softer veneer mitigated the core's hardness and made it very enjoyable to use.
J.K. Adams Takes Two PRICE: $22 MATERIAL: Hard rock sugar maple WEIGHT: 3.7 pounds	CUTTING: ★★★ DURABILITY: ★★★ CLEANUP: ★★ USER-FRIENDLINESS: ★★★	Classic plank board is solid but light enough to be convenient for frequent use. Knife felt cushioned during use; board showed few marks of cuts; blade stayed sharp after 750 cuts. Chipotle stain hung on.
Architec Gripper Nonslip (DW) PRICE: $14.99 MATERIAL: Polypropylene (plastic) WEIGHT: 0.9 pounds	CUTTING: ★★ DURABILITY: ★★★ CLEANUP: ★★★ USER-FRIENDLINESS: ★★★	Nonslip "gripper" underside keeps board extremely stable but makes it one-sided. Pleasant cutting surface, but it slightly dulled a new knife.

RECOMMENDED	PERFORMANCE	TESTERS' COMMENTS
Totally Bamboo Kauai PRICE: $28 MATERIAL: Vertical-grain bamboo WEIGHT: 2.7 pounds	CUTTING: ★★★ DURABILITY: ★★ CLEANUP: ★★★ USER-FRIENDLINESS: ★★★	This pretty board was easy to handle, felt solid and well cushioned under the knife, and was tough enough to handle the cleaver. Surface became deeply incised in one area after 750 cuts, but it didn't stain.
John Boos Chopping Block PRICE: $74.95 MATERIAL: Northern hard rock maple WEIGHT: 10.4 pounds	CUTTING: ★★★ DURABILITY: ★★ CLEANUP: ★ USER-FRIENDLINESS: ★★★	This deluxe cutting board is mighty heavy to hoist around the kitchen. Feels great under the knife, keeping blade sharp after 750 cuts; definitely needs oiling and careful drying to keep its good looks and avoid splitting, as our first sample did.
TruBamboo Palm Beach PRICE: $39.99 MATERIAL: Flat-grain bamboo WEIGHT: 5.2 pounds	CUTTING: ★★★ DURABILITY: ★★ CLEANUP: ★★ USER-FRIENDLINESS: ★★	Board did the job but was unremarkable. Surface showed faint cuts and became increasingly fuzzy, with tiny raised fibers, as we used and cleaned it.

RECOMMENDED WITH RESERVATIONS	PERFORMANCE	TESTERS' COMMENTS
The Cutting Board Company (DW) PRICE: $11.35 MATERIAL: Polypropylene (plastic) WEIGHT: 3.7 pounds	CUTTING: ★★ DURABILITY: ★★ CLEANUP: ★★ USER-FRIENDLINESS: ★★	Surface was too slick when new—onion skidded as we cut. Cleaver made deep cuts, raised ridges on surface. This board slipped around if we didn't use a mat underneath, and it stained deeply.
Epicurean Cutting Surfaces, Kitchen Series (DW) PRICE: $24.95 MATERIAL: Wood-laminate composite WEIGHT: 1.9 pounds	CUTTING: ★★ DURABILITY: ★★ CLEANUP: ★★ USER-FRIENDLINESS: ★★	Hard board clacked loudly under the knife; surface gave off sawdust after repeated cuts. Board smells like a wet dog when washed (it's the glue).
Architec Gripper Bamboo PRICE: $14.99 MATERIAL: Vertical-grain bamboo WEIGHT: 2.4 pounds	CUTTING: ★★ DURABILITY: ★★ CLEANUP: ★ USER-FRIENDLINESS: ★★	Four rubber feet trapped wetness and gave board a hollow feel. More difficult to cut across planks than along them. Showed every cut, and stains hung on.

NOT RECOMMENDED	PERFORMANCE	TESTERS' COMMENTS
OXO Good Grips Folding Utility (DW) PRICE: $24.99 MATERIAL: Polypropylene (plastic) WEIGHT: 3.8 pounds	CUTTING: ★★ DURABILITY: ★ CLEANUP: ★★★ USER-FRIENDLINESS: ★	Rubbery surface of board felt pleasant, but center-fold ridge got in the way of cutting. Board ripped in two at fold when swept off counter.
Architec Gripperwood  PRICE: $24.99 MATERIAL: Beechwood with rubber feet WEIGHT: 5.2 pounds	CUTTING: ★★ DURABILITY: ★ CLEANUP: ★★ USER-FRIENDLINESS: ★	Wood felt lightweight but cheap; made hollow sound when knife struck. Soft surface was heavily damaged, giving off ⅛ teaspoon of sawdust as we cut. Board split in two when swept off the counter.
Pyrex Glass (DW)  PRICE: $17.99 MATERIAL: Tempered glass WEIGHT: 3.2 pounds	CUTTING: DURABILITY: ★★★ CLEANUP: ★★★ USER-FRIENDLINESS:	Clacked with every cut; dulled new knife after 10 cuts. Didn't break (even when knocked off counter and whacked with a cleaver), but horrible as a cutting board.

KITCHEN NOTES

⋛ BY J. KENJI ALT ⋚

Clean Break for Eggs

When recipes for baked goods, such as our Spice Cake (page 25), call for yolks at room temperature, most cooks wait to separate them until the eggs have already warmed up. We find the process is easier if you do it when the eggs are still cold. Just out of the refrigerator, the membranes surrounding the white and the yolk are much firmer and separate more cleanly and easily.

Hot or Cold Water for Washing?

We've always believed the conventional wisdom that cold water works better than hot when washing flour off bowls and boards. The theory is that hot water hydrates the starch, causing it to become sticky, while cold water simply dilutes the flour. Washing hundreds of dirty bowls for our Almost No-Knead Bread (page 20) recipe gave us the perfect opportunity to test this. Our finding: When it comes to removing flour, water temperature makes no difference at all. Both hot and cold water work equally well.

Broccoli Resurrection

We recently tried reviving limp broccoli by soaking florets and whole heads overnight in three different liquids: plain water, sugar water, and salt water. The sugar, we thought, might provide food that would revive the vegetable, while the salt might work like a brine, adding moisture and seasoning. The next day, we examined the broccoli raw and then pan-roasted it. In both the cooked and raw states, the broccoli left standing in plain water was the clear winner. The broccoli placed in sugar water was nearly as limp as before, and the broccoli from salty water was even more dehydrated.

PLUMP IT UP
To revive limp broccoli, trim the stalk, stand it in an inch of water, and refrigerate it overnight.

Breathable Bags

Spinach used to come in perforated plastic bags that allowed the greens to breathe and stay fresh longer. These days, the bags of greens we buy no longer have the holes. Why the change? Plastic bag technology has come a long way over the years. Though they appear solid, the bags in which spinach and other greens are now sold are made of a polymer that allows the ripening gases that all produce emits to pass through freely. Because of this, leftover packaged spinach or greens will do much better stored in their original bags than in ordinary plastic ones. To ensure freshness for as long as possible, fold the bag over and tape it shut.

STILL FRESH
Bagged spinach stored in its original breathable plastic bag is still fresh one week later.

STARTING TO SPOIL
This spinach was stored in a sealed airtight bag, rather than its original packaging, causing it to spoil prematurely.

Oven Calibration

A properly calibrated oven is essential for ensuring consistent cooking results. Because many people don't have an oven thermometer, we developed an easy method to test for accuracy using an instant-read thermometer. Here's how to do it.

Set an oven rack to the middle position and heat your oven to 350 degrees for at least 30 minutes. Fill an ovenproof glass 2-cup measure with 1 cup of water. Using an instant-read thermometer, check that the water is exactly 70 degrees, adjusting the temperature with hot or cold water as necessary. Place the cup in the center of the rack and close the oven door. After 15 minutes, remove the cup and insert the instant-read thermometer, making sure to swirl the thermometer around in the water to even out any hot spots. If your oven is properly calibrated, the water should be at 150 degrees (plus or minus 2 degrees). If the water is not at 150 degrees, then your oven is running too hot or too cold and needs to be adjusted accordingly. We tested this method in multiple ovens, both gas and electric, and all worked well. (Note: To avoid shattering the glass cup, allow the water to cool before pouring it out.)

SPICE ADVICE: **Toast, then Grind**

It's best to toast whole spices before grinding them. Here's why:

STAYING PUT
Toasting a spice whole brings its aromatic oils to the surface, contributing to a stronger, more complex aroma when ground.

CARRIED AWAY
Grinding a spice releases moisture and aromatic oils into the air, subsequently leaving the spice with less to give when toasted.

Garlic Guide

Sometimes when we're shopping for a recipe that calls for a large amount of minced garlic, we wonder how many heads we'll need to buy to complete the recipe. We bought heads of garlic from several different stores. While the size and number of cloves in a single head ranged from 15 large to 25 small, the total amount of minced garlic from each head was very similar across the board. A medium head of garlic (about 2½ inches across) will yield a little over 2 tablespoons of minced garlic.

Holey Foil

We don't recommend covering acidic foods stored in open metal containers (like baking pans) directly with foil. Recently, rushing to refrigerate a batch of our Skillet Apple Brown Betty (January/February 2004) at the end of the day, we forgot and covered the pan with foil. When we

---

TECHNIQUE | **SLICING ONIONS**

Slicing against the grain results in cooked onions with a lifeless, stringy texture. Onions that are cut pole to pole maintain their shape during our Best French Onion Soup's (page 13) long cooking process.

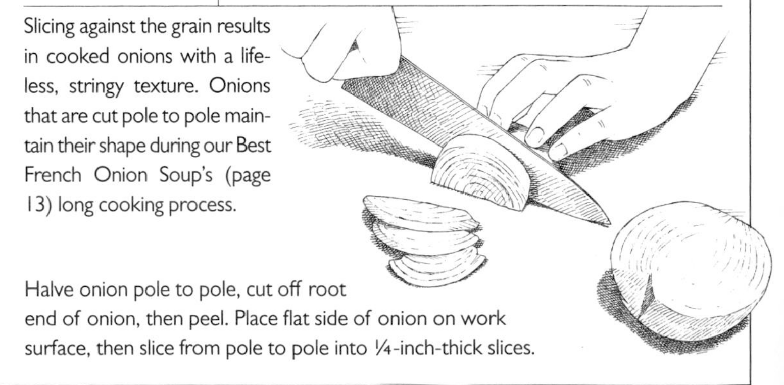

Halve onion pole to pole, cut off root end of onion, then peel. Place flat side of onion on work surface, then slice from pole to pole into ¼-inch-thick slices.

removed the foil the next morning, it was riddled with holes, and the top of the dessert was discolored. What was going on here?

Aluminum is what's called an "active metal"—a material that readily sheds electrons. Because of this, when aluminum is in contact with an acidic medium and a nonaluminum metal like the skillet in which our brown betty was stored, it will steadily lose electrons and change into a form that's dissolvable by the acid in the food. We found that even in nonmetal containers, after several days of storage, the foil wound up discoloring where it was in contact with the acidic food, as the aluminum had shed electrons to the electron-hungry acids.

To prevent this, we recommend that you store acidic leftovers in nonmetal containers and make sure the foil doesn't come in direct contact with the food.

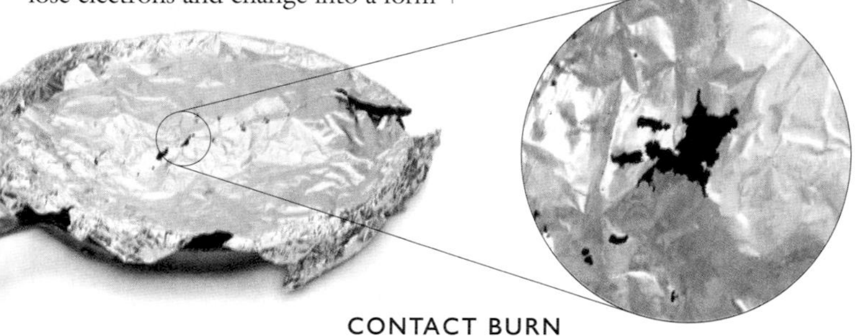

CONTACT BURN
An electrolytic reaction causes holes to appear in foil placed directly on acidic food stored in a metal container.

TASTING: Dried Chiles

Though chiles are available in a wider variety than ever, most stores still don't carry an exhaustive selection. So what to do when you can't find the specific dried chile a recipe calls for? After holding a blind tasting of several of the most commonly available chiles, we found that each fell into one of four broad flavor categories. Widely available chiles for each flavor category are listed below. The substitute chiles have subtle flavor variations but can successfully replace any other in the grouping.

CHILE TYPE	DESCRIPTION	SUBSTITUTES
SWEET New Mexico (California, Anaheim, or chile Colorado)	These chiles share fresh, sweet flavors reminiscent of roasted red peppers and tomatoes.	Cascabel (chile bola) Choricero Costeño
EARTHY Ancho (dried poblano)	Deep, rich flavors that bring to mind chocolate, coffee, raisins, and licorice characterize these chiles.	Mulato Pasilla (chile negro)
SMOKY Chipotle	These chiles have charred wood, tobacco, and barbecue flavors balanced by subtle sweetness.	Guajillo Ñora
HOT Arbol	The overwhelming heat of these chile varieties masks their other flavors.	Cayenne Guindilla Pequeño Thai (bird's beak)

RECIPE UPDATE

Garlicky Scallops with Bread Crumbs

For a different spin on our one-skillet recipe for Garlicky Shrimp with Bread Crumbs (March/April 2007), we substituted sea scallops. We quickly discovered the swap produced a sauce that was too watery, because scallops shed more liquid than shrimp. Addressing the issue would mean reducing the clam juice called for in the original recipe. But by how much? The moisture content varies from scallop to scallop. Our solution: We placed the seared scallops in a strainer set over a bowl to collect the juice, then poured it into a measuring cup and added enough clam juice (if needed) to equal ⅔ cup. Since scallops are naturally sweeter than shrimp, we omitted the sugar in the recipe. Go to www.cooksillustrated.com/february for our free recipe for Garlicky Scallops with Bread Crumbs.

Simple Turkey Chili with Kidney Beans

Readers wanted to know the best way to use ground turkey in place of the ground beef in our Simple Beef Chili with Kidney Beans (March/April 2003). Since the key to the recipe is its long simmering process, we avoided extra-lean ground turkey, which we knew would turn mealy and flavorless with prolonged cooking. We used 93 percent lean instead. Nevertheless, after two hours of simmering, the turkey had disintegrated and the chili resembled Bolognese sauce. We solved this problem by dividing the meat in half and adding one installment at the beginning of cooking and the second an hour later, pinching off teaspoon-sized lumps of turkey for a chunkier texture. Our final adjustment was to reduce the total cooking time by 20 minutes. Go to www.cooksillustrated.com/february for our free recipe for Simple Turkey Chili with Kidney Beans.

TOO FINE

JUST RIGHT

Ground turkey broke down too much when simmered for hours in our chili recipe (left). But when we added the delicate meat at different stages during cooking (and in larger pieces), we achieved the perfect texture (right).

New York–Style Crumb Cake Muffins

Transforming our New York–Style Crumb Cake (May/June 2007) into muffins seemed like a doable task, and it was. The batter from the existing recipe was just enough to apportion ¼ cup to each of the 12 cups in a standard-sized muffin tin. After experimenting with various baking times, we arrived at 20 minutes as the right amount to turn out tender, light interiors. But although the insides of the muffins were baking up perfectly, the exteriors were dry, tough, and overly brown. When lowering the oven temperature didn't solve the problem, we tried lining the muffin tin with parchment baking cups. This did the trick. The liners prohibited browning and kept the outside of the muffins insulated, tender, and moist. Go to www.cooksillustrated.com/february for our free recipe for New York–Style Crumb Cake Muffins.

–Charles Kelsey

IF YOU HAVE A QUESTION about a recipe, let us know. Send your inquiry, name, address, and daytime telephone number to Recipe Update, Cook's Illustrated, P.O. Box 470589, Brookline, MA 02447, or write to recipeupdate@americastestkitchen.com.

EQUIPMENT CORNER

BY ELIZABETH BOMZE

NEW PRODUCT:

Spin'n Stor Produce Bags

In smaller kitchens, it can be hard to find space for bulky salad spinners. Argeecorp Spin'n Stor Produce Spinning Bags ($3.49 for four reusable bags) condense the drying and storing of greens into one bag. You put washed produce into the 11- by 6-inch bag and spin it around in the air; the water pools into a reservoir and feeds into a drainable channel along the bag's side. Once drained, the bag of greens can be sealed and stored in the refrigerator. To test the bag's effectiveness against our preferred OXO Salad Spinner, we divided a head of romaine, washed the leaves, and put half in the bag and the other half in the spinner. Both methods dried the leaves equally well.

BAG THE SPINNER?
Spin'n Stor produce bags dried salad greens just as well as our preferred salad spinner—and stored them to boot. They're a great alternative if you're short on space.

EQUIPMENT TESTING:

Universal Knife Blocks

Do "universal" knife blocks hold knives of every shape, size, and make? We tested three models. The Viva Terra Bamboo Box Knife Holder ($89) is a simple wooden box of tightly packed bamboo skewers meant to cradle the knives. It holds knives at an awkward 90-degree angle, and when you pull them out, unattached skewers pop up, too. It's also flimsily constructed: Three of the four we ordered arrived broken. A bit better, the Bisbell Magnabloc ($143.50) is a magnetized wooden block that grips up to 10 knives (but not ceramic ones) along its surface. Unfortunately, its grasp is almost too strong: Knives release only with a vigorous tug that makes the tall, narrow structure wobble. The best (and cheapest) of the lot, the oak-framed Igo Home Kapoosh Universal Knife Block ($29.99), comfortably shelters up to 10 tools in its dishwasher-safe nest of spaghetti-like plastic rods, and the sturdy box's opening is at an accessible angle. Though we wish it were deeper—handles of blades over 8 inches stuck out—it makes a practical home for most knives.

UNIVERSAL PROTECTION
The Igo Home Kapoosh Universal Knife Block contains thousands of fine plastic rods that easily accommodate up to 10 knives and tools.

EQUIPMENT UPDATE:

Toaster Oven/Toaster Combo

Our favorite toaster oven, the Krups 6-Slice Digital Convection Toaster Oven FBC4-12 ($199.99), is handy for small-scale cooking and makes decent toast, but it takes a toll on both your counter space and your wallet. That's why we were hopeful when we found the Hamilton Beach Toastation Toaster & Oven 22708H ($49.99), which combines a regular toaster and toaster oven. A wide toaster slot runs across its top, and a mini-oven opens from the front. Unfortunately, the two can't operate simultaneously, and the appliance is too small to accommodate an average-sized spud or slice of pizza.

EQUIPMENT TESTING:

Dry Storage Containers

When it comes to storing flour and sugar, we like an airtight container that can easily accommodate an entire five-pound bag, with an opening wide enough to dip in a measuring cup and level off the excess right back into the container. After testing six models, we found that all fit the bill. Each container locked tightly enough to keep a slice of white sandwich bread soft and mold-free for over two weeks. That said, a few extra features caught our attention: clear plastic for easy visibility, measurement markers along the sides, and sturdy handles. Our favorite, the Rubbermaid 4 Qt. Carb-X Commercial Food Storage ($8.99), includes these; plus it also comes in an 8-quart size.

Sources

The following are sources for items recommended in this issue. Prices were current at press time and do not include shipping. Contact companies to confirm information or visit www.cooksillustrated.com for updates.

Page 7: MEAT-PROBE THERMOMETER

- ThermoWorks Original Cooking Thermometer/Timer: $19, item #TW362A, ThermoWorks (800-393-6434, www.thermoworks.com).

Page 20: DUTCH OVEN

- Tramontina 6.5 Quart Cast Iron Dutch Oven: $39.86, item #80131/504, Wal-Mart (800-966-6546, www.walmart.com).

Page 27: DARK CHOCOLATE

- Callebaut Intense Dark Chocolate L-60-40NV: $17.95 for 2.2 pounds of callets (chocolate bits), World Wide Chocolate (800-664-9410, www.worldwidechocolate.com). Also available at Whole Foods Market in smaller portions.
- Ghirardelli Bittersweet Chocolate Baking Bar: $2.99 for 4 ounces, World Wide Chocolate.

Page 29: CUTTING BOARDS

- Totally Bamboo Congo Parquet End Grain Cutting Board: $39.99, item # B000A389GE, www.amazon.com.
- Snow River Utility Board: $16.99, item # B0006FRAGQ www. amazon.com.

Page 32: PRODUCE BAGS

- Spin'n Stor Produce Spinning Bags: $3.49 for four bags, item #17764, Camping World (888-626-7576, www.campingworld.com).

Page 32: UNIVERSAL KNIFE BLOCK

- Igo Home Kapoosh Universal Knife Block: $29.99, Bed Bath & Beyond (800-462-3966, www.bedbathandbeyond.com).

Page 32: DRY STORAGE CONTAINERS

- Rubbermaid 4-Qt. Carb-X Commercial Food Storage: $8.99, item #576440, The Container Store (888-266-8246, www.containerstore.com).

UNITED STATES POSTAL SERVICE

Statement of Ownership, Management, and Circulation (All Periodicals Publications Except Requester Publications)

1. Publication Title	2. Publication Number	3. Filing Date
Cook's Illustrated	1068-2821	9-28-07
4. Issue Frequency	**5. Number of Issues Published Annually**	**6. Annual Subscription Price**
Bi-Monthly	6 Issues	$35.70

7. Complete Mailing Address of Known Office of Publication (Not printer) (Street, city, county, state, and ZIP+4®)
17 Station Street, Brookline, MA 02445
Contact Person
Telephone (Include area code) 617-232-1000

8. Complete Mailing Address of Headquarters or General Business Office of Publisher (Not printer)
Same as Publisher

9. Full Names and Complete Mailing Addresses of Publisher, Editor, and Managing Editor (Do not leave blank)
Publisher (Name and complete mailing address)
Christopher P. Kimball, Boston Common Press,
17 Station Street, Brookline, MA 02445
Editor (Name and complete mailing address)
Same as Publisher
Managing Editor (Name and complete mailing address)
Jack Bishop, Boston Common Press,
17 Station Street, Brookline, MA 02445

10. Owner (Do not leave blank. If the publication is owned by a corporation, give the name and address of the corporation immediately followed by the names and addresses of all stockholders owning or holding 1 percent or more of the total amount of stock. If not owned by a corporation, give the names and addresses of the individual owners. If owned by a partnership or other unincorporated firm, give its name and address as well as those of each individual owner. If the publication is published by a nonprofit organization, give its name and address.)

Full Name	Complete Mailing Address
Boston Common Press Limited Partnership	17 Station Street, Brookline, MA 02445
(Christopher P. Kimball)	

11. Known Bondholders, Mortgagees, and Other Security Holders Owning or Holding 1 Percent or More of Total Amount of Bonds, Mortgages, or Other Securities. If none, check box ☐ None

Full Name	Complete Mailing Address
N/A	

12. Tax Status (For completion by nonprofit organizations authorized to mail at nonprofit rates) (Check one)
The purpose, function, and nonprofit status of this organization and the exempt status for federal income tax purposes:
☐ Has Not Changed During Preceding 12 Months
☐ Has Changed During Preceding 12 Months (Publisher must submit explanation of change with this statement)

PS Form 3526, September 2006 (Page 1 of 3 (Instructions Page 3)) PSN 7530-01-000-9931 PRIVACY NOTICE: See our privacy policy on www.usps.com

13. Publication Title	14. Issue Date for Circulation Data Below	
Cook's Illustrated	September/October 2007	
15. Extent and Nature of Circulation	**Average No. Copies Each Issue During Preceding 12 Months**	**No. Copies of Single Issue Published Nearest to Filing Date**
a. Total Number of Copies (Net press run)	1,135,802	1,140,323
b. Paid Circulation (By Mail and Outside the Mail) (1) Mailed Outside-County Paid Subscriptions Stated on PS Form 3541 (Include paid distribution above nominal rate, advertiser's proof copies, and exchange copies)	891,971	894,020
(2) Mailed In-County Paid Subscriptions Stated on PS Form 3541 (Include paid distribution above nominal rate, advertiser's proof copies, and exchange copies)	0	0
(3) Paid Distribution Outside the Mails Including Sales Through Dealers and Carriers, Street Vendors, Counter Sales, and Other Paid Distribution Outside USPS®	96,625	97,669
(4) Paid Distribution by Other Classes of Mail Through the USPS (e.g. First-Class Mail®)	0	0
c. Total Paid Distribution (Sum of 15b (1), (2), (3), and (4))	988,596	991,689
d. Free or Nominal Rate Distribution (By Mail and Outside the Mail) (1) Free or Nominal Rate Outside-County Copies included on PS Form 3541	4,506	4,341
(2) Free or Nominal Rate In-County Copies Included on PS Form 3541	0	0
(3) Free or Nominal Rate Copies Mailed at Other Classes Through the USPS (e.g. First-Class Mail)	0	0
(4) Free or Nominal Rate Distribution Outside the Mail (Carriers or other means)	94	65
e. Total Free or Nominal Rate Distribution (Sum of 15d (1), (2), (3) and (4)	4,600	4,406
f. Total Distribution (Sum of 15c and 15e)	993,196	996,095
g. Copies not Distributed (See Instructions to Publishers #4 (page #3))	142,606	144,228
h. Total (Sum of 15f and g)	1,135,802	1,140,323
i. Percent Paid (15c divided by 15f times 100)	99.54%	99.56%

16. Publication of Statement of Ownership
☒ If the publication is a general publication, publication of this statement is required. Will be printed in the Jan/Feb 2008 issue of this publication. ☐ Publication not required.

17. Signature and Title of Editor, Publisher, Business Manager, or Owner — Date 8/16/07.

I certify that all information furnished on this form is true and complete. I understand that anyone who furnishes false or misleading information on this form or who omits material or information requested on the form may be subject to criminal sanctions (including fines and imprisonment) and/or civil sanctions (including civil penalties).

PS Form 3526, September 2006 (Page 2 of 3)

INDEX

January & February 2008

RECIPES

COOK'S LIVE Original Test Kitchen Videos www.cooksillustrated.com

MAIN DISHES
- **How to Make Crunchy Baked Pork Chops**
- How do I mince a shallot?
- How do I mince parsley?

- **How to Make French Chicken in a Pot**
- Which Dutch oven should I buy?
- How can I separate fat without a fat separator?

- **How to Make Slow-Roasted Beef**
- Which cut of meat should I buy?
- How do I carve roast beef?
- Do I really need an instant-read thermometer?
- Can I check the temperature of my oven without an oven thermometer?

SIDE DISH
- **How to Make Roasted Broccoli**

BREAD
- **How to Make Almost No-Knead Bread**
- Behind the Scenes: Developing the recipe
- How does bread rise?

SOUP AND APPETIZER
- **How to Make Best French Onion Soup**
- How do I peel and slice an onion?
- What size onions should I buy?

- **How to Make Spanish-Style Garlic Shrimp**
- How do I peel and slice garlic?

DESSERTS
- **How to Make Thin and Crispy Oatmeal Cookies**
- Can I use quick or instant oats?
- Why does the test kitchen like parchment paper?
- Do I have to bake the cookies one sheet at a time?

- **How to Make Spice Cake with Cream Cheese Frosting**
- How do I know when the butter is brown enough?

TESTING
- **Buying Guide to Cutting Boards**
- Behind the Scenes: Cutting Board Testing
- What's the best way to clean a cutting board?

Slow-Roasted Beef, 7

French Chicken in a Pot, 9

Best French Onion Soup, 13

Crunchy Baked Pork Chops, 11

Almost No-Knead Bread, 20

Spanish-Style Garlic Shrimp, 15

Roasted Broccoli, 21

Spice Cake with Cream Cheese Frosting, 25

Thin and Crispy Oatmeal Cookies, 23

PHOTOGRAPHY: CARL TREMBLAY, STYLING: MARIE PIRAINO

EXOTIC MUSHROOMS

NUMBER NINETY-ONE

MARCH & APRIL 2008

COOK'S ILLUSTRATED

Crisp Roast Chicken
New Baking Powder Method

Premium OJ Taste Test
Tropicana Squeezes Competition

Oven-Roasted Salmon
Quick High-Low Method

One-Minute Chocolate Frosting

Better Mashed Potatoes
Faster, Lighter, and Fluffier

Rating Serrated Knives

Italian-Style Meat Sauce

Roasted Vegetable Salads

Chicken Saltimbocca

Hearty Tuscan Bean Stew

Perfect Meringue Cookies

Fluffy Yellow Cake

www.cooksillustrated.com

$5.95 U.S./$6.95 CANADA

CONTENTS

March & April 2008

COOK'S ONLINE

Go to **www.cooksillustrated.com** to access all recipes from *Cook's Illustrated* since 1993. Watch videos of all the recipes in this issue being prepared and a report on serrated knives.

INDIAN HERBS AND SPICES The intricate architecture of Indian cuisine depends on the precise melding of exotic spices and fragrant herbs. Sweet and savory dishes benefit from the bittersweet muskiness of golden saffron threads. Turmeric is used not only as a spice but also as a preservative and food colorant in pickling blends, curry powders, and tandoori pastes. Fresh curry leaves are sizzled in oil to extract the pungent, sweet flavors that add depth to dals, curries, soups, and breads. Less-assertive fenugreek leaves lend a bitter, celerylike flavor to dishes. The peppery warmth of nutmeg makes it versatile in a variety of applications. Culinary twins are harvested from the cassia tree: cassia bark (which boasts an astringency that distinguishes it from its cinnamon relation) and the glossy, green, cinnamon-scented Indian bay leaf. Licorice notes are detected in star anise, the seedpod of the Asian magnolia tree. Mint contributes a refreshing element to chutneys, sauces, and teas. Green and black cardamom pods are valued for their spicy sweetness.

COVER (*Radishes*): Robert Papp, BACK COVER (*Indian Herbs and Spices*): John Burgoyne

For list rental information, contact: Specialists Marketing Services, Inc., 1200 Harbor Blvd., 9th Floor, Weehawken, NJ 07087; 201-865-5800.
Editorial Office: 17 Station St., Brookline, MA 02445; 617-232-1000; fax 617-232-1572. Subscription inquiries, call 800-526-8442.
Postmaster: Send all new orders, subscription inquiries, and change-of-address notices to Cook's Illustrated, P.O. Box 7446, Red Oak, IA 51591-0446.

COOK'S ILLUSTRATED
www.cooksillustrated.com
HOME OF AMERICA'S TEST KITCHEN

PRINTED IN THE USA

OLD BONES

Jack just celebrated his 90th birthday. He lives across the valley in a white clapboard farmhouse owned by his girlfriend, Jean, who is younger, a late-October/December relationship, if you will. He has good bones; his fat and muscle hang on a stout frame, barrel-chested, the cooper having selected aged oak for the staves. Jack is a solid construct of fine mortise and tenon, the joinery expertly chiseled and built to last. He walks as if on timbers: a bit stiff, perhaps, but hip is connected to ground like a tall, straight ash, firmly rooted. If you were to meet him, you would come to notice that his peripheral vision is a better bet than looking straight ahead, but he gets around well enough. I think he can tell a pretty girl when he sees one, since he always goes to bear hug them first the moment he half-steps into a room. Yet Jack is clearly in love, telling Jean that he is looking forward to spending eternity with her, both of their headstones already carved and placed on a side hill in a cemetery up in Wallingford. Jean picked the spot for the view to the west. It will be hard not to remember Jack each day at sunset.

He is the exact opposite of my great-uncle Jack, who, after being bedridden for half a year, decided that he did not wish to regain the use of his legs. He spent the rest of his life in a cane-seated wheelchair, legs covered in a tartan blanket, playing solitaire at a card table in the corner of the great room of his house outside of Baltimore, attended to by his daughter, Snoozie, and his wife, Dorothy. The latter spent much of her time constructing sculptures of chicken bones and colored glass, wrapped in delicate white paper, like small origami jewels. I discovered an entire chest of her works when I was 8 years old, opening a door onto this private world of adults, where old bones were boiled and hidden instead of used for walking.

Our family recently purchased a house (now the home of *Cook's Country* magazine) that was once owned by the Sheldons, who pretty much ran the north end of town, whereas the Shermans were located a few miles south (where Sherman's store still operates today). It is a classic colonial structure, upstanding and squared-off, the horse barn in good repair, the dairy barn settling into the weeds, plus a milk house and a smokehouse. It had fallen into bad disrepair, almost entirely hidden in a stand of pine, poplar, and maple, the joists punky and rotten, the putty-colored paint scaled and rippled, the floor so warped that a second floor was nailed on top to provide a sense of level well-being just inches above the damp.

Christopher Kimball

But the house has good bones. I know this because the building was stripped down to its load-bearing beams, evenly spaced ax cuts still visible along their length two centuries later. With nothing more than a roof and strapping along the exterior walls, the house stood jacked up on heavy timber pylons while the foundation was removed and poured anew, a skeleton standing in the north end of town, bare but still strong, stiff, and alive, having settled into its shape long before the Civil War.

Last summer, my 17-year-old daughter, Caroline, and I headed out to post our property in order to reduce the constant flow of out-of-state hunters and four-wheelers. We carried knapsacks filled with orange and black No Hunting signs, roofing nails, hammers, water, sandwiches, and apples. We headed up onto the ridges that flow, serpentine, through the hills and hollows and walked on the very spines of the hills, through bright spots of birches and small patches of wavy lime-colored grass, and we scrabbled over rocky outcroppings where the schist and limestone showed through. We turned this way and that, descended through a wild stand of fresh-scented balsam pine, crossed deer trails so clear they needed no highway sign, and then scrambled back down an embankment and onto a logging road. Soon, we headed back up into the mountains, back behind the LeShane property and then up toward Orval and Delores Thompson's. It was steep and recently logged, which made walking treacherous, but we found a good spot for lunch about 50 yards below the ridge, with a clear view down the valley.

Parents often say that teenagers are awkward, the distance in age and experience too great for normal conversation. Maybe it is the toll of mileage, the old joints and sinews that still take us through the woods but with a bit less certainty and speed as the younger frame makes better time and the gap between us widens. But sitting back propped up against a red maple on that late-August day, the two of us were both young enough compared to the old oaks, elm, and hickory, some of them so ancient that the wood had swallowed lengths of barbed wire and sheep fence that was once nailed to the outer bark. When you sit on the very back of the beast, the mountains that run up through Camel's Hump and Mount Mansfield and then up toward Canada and the frozen north, you become fellow travelers, hitching a ride on weather and geology and history. Far from the city, the differences diminish to a finite point; who can hit a distant tree stump with an apple core or find the next marked tree along the property line. Ponce de León was wrong. The fountain of youth is not in Florida; it is up in the Verts Monts, where one can walk on the very rim of time and become timeless oneself, keeping pace with the cheerful stride of youth.

At the table, over Thanksgiving or a summer spread of pies and cobblers, Jack and Caroline often sit side by side, old and new, it makes no difference. And when the bones go back into the ground, they are not buried for memory's sake but held in living memory, as what is bred in the bone still enjoys a sheltered view, one that marks the ancient descent of the sun, far past the valleys and mountains on to the birthplace of our hope, somewhere beyond time, to the west.

FOR INQUIRIES, ORDERS, OR MORE INFORMATION:

www.cooksillustrated.com

At www.cooksillustrated.com, you can order books and subscriptions, sign up for our free e-newsletter, or renew your magazine subscription. Join the website and gain access to 15 years of *Cook's Illustrated* recipes, equipment tests, and ingredient tastings, as well as *Cook's Live* companion videos for every recipe in this issue.

COOKBOOKS

We sell more than 50 cookbooks by the editors of *Cook's Illustrated*. To order, visit our bookstore at www.cooksillustrated.com or call 800-611-0759 (or 515-246-6911 from outside the U.S.).

COOK'S ILLUSTRATED Magazine

Cook's Illustrated magazine (ISSN 1068-2821), number 91, is published bimonthly by Boston Common Press Limited Partnership, 17 Station St., Brookline, MA 02445. Copyright 2008 Boston Common Press Limited Partnership. Periodicals postage paid at Boston, Mass., and additional mailing offices USPS #012487. Publications Mail Agreement No. 40020778. Return undeliverable Canadian addresses to P.O. Box 875, Station A, Windsor, Ontario N9A 6P2. POSTMASTER: Send address changes to Cook's Illustrated, P.O. Box 7446, Red Oak, IA 51591-0446. For subscription and gift subscription orders, subscription inquiries, or change-of-address notices, call 800-526-8442 in the U.S. or 515-247-7571 from outside the U.S., or write us at Cook's Illustrated, P.O. Box 7446, Red Oak, IA 51591-0446.

NOTES FROM READERS

COMPILED BY DAVID PAZMIÑO

Hand-Kneading Bread

I don't have a stand mixer and was wondering how to convert stand-mixer kneading times to hand kneading.

JESSICA VOLOUDAKIS
BRAINTREE, MASS.

➣To answer your question, we made a few batches of white bread and whole wheat bread, mixing some of the dough with a stand mixer and some by hand. To take different hand sizes and strengths into account, we asked several test cooks to knead the dough. They hand-kneaded for the same amount of time suggested in the stand-mixer recipe, about 10 minutes. The hand-kneaded and machine-kneaded doughs were then allowed to rise in the same spot in the test kitchen. Once baked and cooled, the loaves were nearly identical. Some tasters preferred the machine-kneaded bread, which was somewhat lighter and less dense, but others preferred the chewier texture of the hand-kneaded bread. Overall, the differences were slight, so no conversions are necessary: Simply hand-knead bread dough for the same amount of time as you would knead it in a machine.

Buttermilk Substitute

In your New York–Style Crumb Cake recipe (May/June 2007), you say that it is possible to replace the buttermilk with plain low-fat yogurt. Is it possible to use the same substitution in other recipes?

ELISABETH KULAWICK
OTTAWA, ONTARIO

➣To find out if there is a simple conversion for replacing buttermilk with yogurt, we went into the test kitchen and cooked up our recipes for Tall and Fluffy Buttermilk Biscuits (July/August 2004), Best Buttermilk Waffles (November/December 1993), and Buttermilk Mashed Potatoes (November/December 2005).

At first we tried simply substituting equal amounts of plain whole-milk yogurt for buttermilk. The resulting biscuits and waffles were a bit dense and dry, and the mashed potatoes were somewhat stiff. To improve the texture, we next thinned the yogurt with milk, using 3 parts yogurt to 1 part milk. While the yogurt-based biscuits and waffles were slightly less tangy than the buttermilk versions, tasters found that thinned yogurt (whole-milk or low-fat) was a perfectly acceptable substitution. (Avoid nonfat yogurt; it produced biscuits and waffles that were too dry.)

The mashed potatoes were a different story. While their consistency remained the same with yogurt, the lack of the buttermilk's tang was noticeable in this savory dish. Our advice? For baked goods, a mixture of 3 parts plain whole-milk or low-fat yogurt to 1 part milk can be swapped for buttermilk (that translates to ¾ cup yogurt plus ¼ cup milk to replace 1 cup buttermilk). For savory recipes, stick with the real thing.

BUTTERMILK SUBSTITUTE
For baking, substitute plain yogurt thinned with milk for buttermilk.

Toasted-Nut Controversy

Is it better to toast nuts on the stovetop or in the oven?

HARRY HOLMBERG
POST FALLS, IDAHO

➣A quick straw vote in the test kitchen revealed a divided camp on this issue. To settle the matter once and for all, we toasted a range of different-sized nuts (slivered almonds, sliced almonds, walnut halves, pecan halves, and whole pine nuts) in a 10-inch skillet over medium heat and on a baking sheet in a 350-degree oven. After comparing the cooled nuts, we found no flavor differences. As for technique, toasting nuts on the stovetop requires more attention from the cook: Frequent stirring is a necessity. Another strike against the stovetop is that large amounts of nuts can crowd a skillet, preventing thorough toasting. The bottom line: For more than 1 cup of nuts (or if you happen to have the oven on already), use your oven. For smaller quantities, pull out a skillet; just remember to stir the nuts often to prevent them from burning.

High-Heat Cooking Spray

I recently noticed a new PAM cooking spray product, PAM Professional High Heat, in my supermarket. What do you think of it?

JILL KINTON
WINCHESTER, MASS.

➣After purchasing a few cans of PAM Professional High Heat, we headed into the test kitchen to see how it compared with the original PAM. We sprayed one skillet with the original and another with PAM Professional, then placed both over a medium-high flame. After 2½ minutes, the original PAM was nearly black and smoking, and the PAM Professional was crystal clear, just as it had been when it went into the skillet.

A look at the label revealed that the original PAM contains four ingredients: canola oil, grain alcohol, soy lecithin, and propellant. Canola oil is high in polyunsaturated fats, which oxidize, or break down, when heated. These oxidized fats burn rather easily. To reduce the risk of scorching, PAM Professional swaps canola oil for partially hydrogenated soybean and canola oils. These fats are more saturated, making them less prone to oxidation and burning. PAM Professional also contains calcium carbonate, an ingredient that helps fats resist the oxidation process.

For our next test, we cooked beef stir-fries using a few sprays of each type of PAM instead of the 2 teaspoons of oil called for in the recipe. The stir-fry cooked with the original PAM was burnt and blackened, with beef drippings that were hard to remove from the pan. The pan sprayed with PAM Professional exhibited only minor charring and cleaned up much more easily. While there might be minor health drawbacks to eating the hydrogenated oils in PAM Professional, very little spray is used for most cooking tasks. If you use cooking spray for high-heat stovetop cooking, you should consider PAM Professional. If you use cooking spray only for baking, there is no reason to add a second can to your arsenal.

ORIGINAL PAM
The oils in original PAM break down and burn at high temperatures.

PAM PROFESSIONAL HIGH HEAT
PAM Professional doesn't burn when heated.

Rancid Oil

I bought a giant bottle of canola oil two years ago. How can I tell if it has gone bad?

PATRICK MULLANE
NEWTON, MASS.

➛Because we go through oil so quickly in the test kitchen, we had to scrounge through some of our home cupboards to get our hands on properly aged specimens. In the end, we found several bottles of canola and soybean oil ranging in age from about a year to "Not sure; it was in the cabinet when I moved in." Rather than subjecting tasters to slurping potentially rancid oil, we asked them to sniff it directly from the bottle and after it was gently heated in a pan. At room temperature, some of the older oils were clearly rancid, with odors variously described as akin to "crayons," "musty paint," and "paint thinner." By contrast, new bottles of oil were completely odorless. The tricky oils were the aged ones that fell in between. When heated, the odor of the obviously bad oils became even more pronounced, and, more important, the iffy ones were exposed as rancid. We also noticed the over-the-hill oils tended to be more viscous than the fresh oils, as well as sticky under the cap, making some caps difficult to remove.

So if you have doubts about the freshness of your oil that a quick sniff can't erase, warm a couple of tablespoons in a pan and then take a whiff. If it smells anything other than neutral, buy a new bottle.

WHAT IS IT?

I recently moved into a house and found a large box of old kitchen gadgets in the basement. Although I knew what most things were, this little contraption bewildered me. Is it a type of funnel?

DRUH KOLYR, WRENTHAM, MASS.

Your basement find stumped many of us here in the test kitchen. After some digging, we determined that this antique metal device is not a funnel, but an automatic baster. Made by the Paul V. Shell Company in 1949, the Percomatic Baster promises to continuously baste a chicken so the cook doesn't have to. To use the baster, the 5½-inch metal support bar is positioned under a chicken (or turkey, roast, or ham) with the circular base resting beside the bird. Similar to the action of a coffee percolator, the hot drippings from the chicken collect in the bottom of the roasting pan and are pulled up through the base into a curved 6-inch tube, from which drippings spray onto the bird. When we gave it a try in the test kitchen, however, the basting action was unreliable. Sometimes the basting liquid dribbled out of the tube and back onto itself; other times it overshot the chicken, missing it altogether. We found this tool for sale at online auctions.

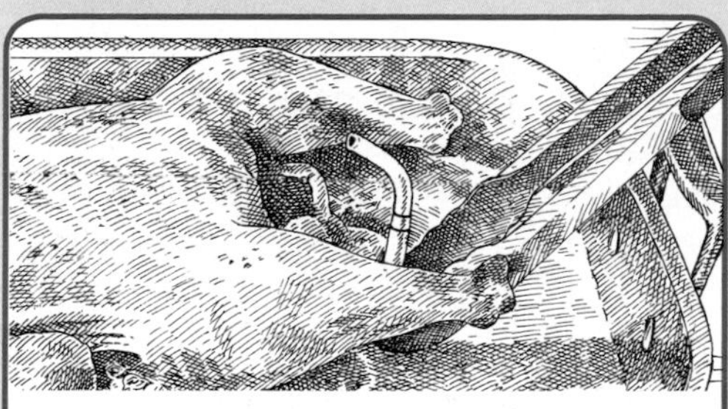

This gadget is designed to automatically baste a chicken, without the cook ever having to open the oven door.

Resurrecting Pancake Batter

I often mix pancake batter first thing in the morning for my early-rising daughter, saving some of the batter for later in the morning, when my son rolls out of bed. But by that time, the pancakes always turn out thin and flat. Is there a way to revive the batter?

ELIZABETH BASS
TAMPA, FLA.

➛To answer your question, we mixed up a few batches of basic pancake batter and held them for different lengths of time before cooking: one hour, two hours, and three hours. Holding the batter for one hour had no detrimental effect on the pancakes. After two and three hours, however, the batter spread out too easily, producing thin, floppy cakes that were much less appealing than the ones made from fresh batter. Here's why: In fresh pancake batter, baking powder reacts quickly, releasing most of its gas in a short period of time. The longer the batter sits, the fewer bubbles there are left when it's time to cook, increasing the likelihood of flat flapjacks.

FLAT
Pancake made with old batter

FLUFFY
Pancake made with batter rejuvenated by an egg white

At first we thought we could add a bit more baking powder to the batter to provide some extra lift, but this merely lent an unpleasant chemical taste to the pancakes. Next, we tried adding a stiffly beaten egg white to the batter. The resulting pancakes were not quite as fluffy as those from fresh batter, but the egg white added a good amount of height. So the next time you find yourself with pancake batter past its prime, simply add a stiffly beaten egg white.

Is Draining Canned Beans Necessary?

Why do most recipes call for canned beans to be drained and rinsed? Is rinsing necessary?

MAURICE DIONNE
ST. LOUIS, MO.

➛Canned beans are made by pressure-cooking dried beans directly in the can with water, salt, and preservatives. As the beans cook, starches and proteins leach into the liquid, thickening it. To find out if rinsing the beans is really necessary, we used canned beans in two recipes: chickpeas for hummus and red kidney beans for Simple Beef Chili (March/April 2003). Tasters found no difference in the chili; there are so many bold flavors and contrasting textures in this dish that rinsing the beans didn't matter.

We detected notable differences in the hummus. Most tasters thought the version with rinsed beans was brighter in flavor and less pasty than the version with unrinsed beans. So while rinsing the beans may not be necessary for a robust dish like chili, a thick, salty bean liquid does have the potential to throw a simpler recipe off-kilter. As rinsing beans only takes a few seconds, we recommend doing so.

Natural Glutamates versus MSG

I enjoyed your recipe for Beef and Vegetable Soup (September/October 2007). The story mentioned that foods containing glutamates were used to enhance the soup's flavor. How do these compounds differ from monosodium glutamate?

ROD SHAND
WEST VANCOUVER, BRITISH COLUMBIA

➛Glutamates are natural compounds found in foods from onions and soy sauce to tomatoes and wine. Being a natural amino acid, the same molecule that builds proteins, glutamate leaves a savory, meaty taste on the tongue. Monosodium glutamate (MSG) is produced by growing bacteria on sugar or molasses and corn. It is commonly added to Chinese food, canned vegetables, soups, and meat to enhance flavor. MSG is also commercially available in powdered form under the brand name Accent.

Although the Food and Drug Administration has classified MSG as a food ingredient that is "generally recognized as safe," its use remains controversial. Reports abound of adverse reactions to MSG, including headaches, numbness, and shortness of breath. Scientific studies, however, have yet to find evidence of a definitive link between MSG and such symptoms.

We have found without a doubt that MSG bumps up the flavor of food. When we added MSG in the form of Accent to our Beef and Vegetable Soup, tasters raved about the "rich," "ultrabeefy" results. But given the controversy over MSG, we'll stick to figuring out other ways to increase savory flavor.

SEND US YOUR QUESTIONS We will provide a complimentary one-year subscription for each letter we print. Send your inquiry, name, address, and daytime telephone number to Notes from Readers, Cook's Illustrated, P.O. Box 470589, Brookline, MA 02447, or to notesfromreaders@americastestkitchen.com.

Quick Tips

⋟ COMPILED BY DAVID PAZMIÑO WITH YVONNE RUPERTI ⋞

Thin Spatula Stand-In

If you have only a thick plastic spatula, it can be difficult to remove warm cookies from a baking sheet without breaking them. Finding herself in such a situation, Olga Marino of Baltimore, Md., reached for a metal cheese slicer. With its thin, sharp blade, it's the perfect tool for sliding under warm cookies and transferring them to a cooling rack without breaking or tearing.

Preventing Dough from Sticking

Gina Colby of Austin, Texas, found that lightly spraying her dough hook with nonstick cooking spray before mixing bread dough prevented dough from edging up the hook and made cleanup a breeze.

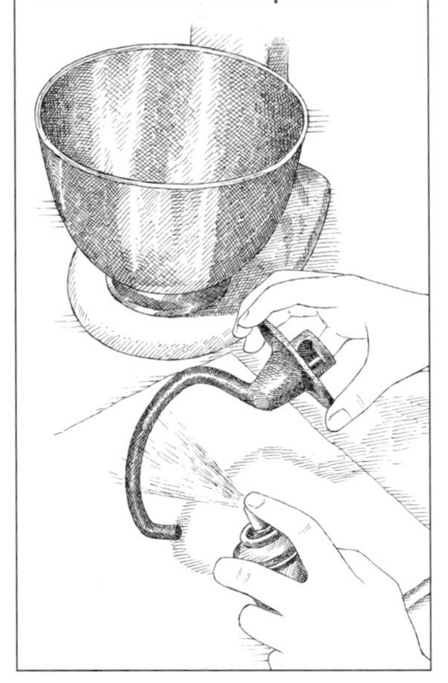

Remembering If Water Is Salted

Charley Eastman of Needham, Mass., could never remember if he had salted the water he was bringing to a boil for pasta or vegetables. After burning his tongue one too many times to determine if the water was salted, he thought of a way to remember: Every time he adds the salt, he now also puts one whole black peppercorn in the water as a reminder.

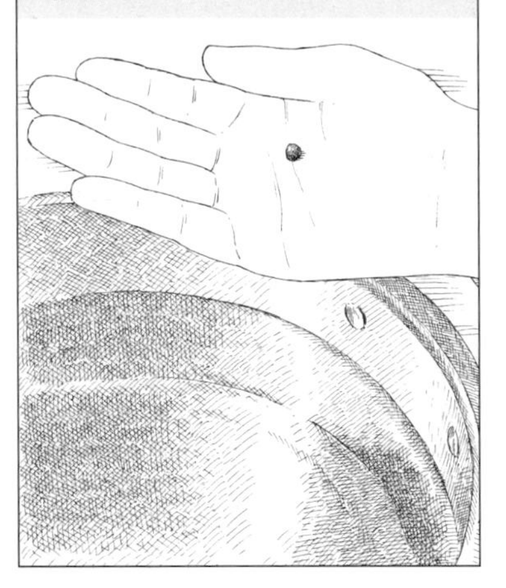

Slippery Chicken Solution

Halving a chicken breast horizontally to form thin cutlets is a slippery proposition. Looking for a safer way to accomplish this task, Manny Landron of Raleigh, N.C., came up with the following approach: Using tongs, hold a chicken breast that has been frozen for 15 minutes perpendicular to the work surface. Cut through the chicken to make two even cutlets.

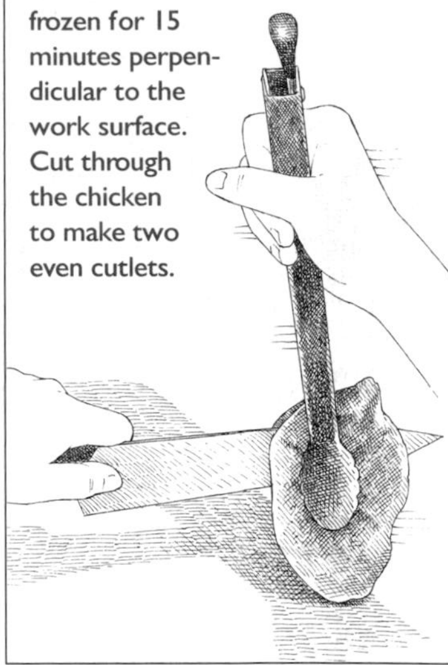

Roasted Garlic

When using all of her stovetop burners in preparation for a dinner party, Linda Moore of Richmond, Va., preferred not to turn the oven on just to roast garlic. Instead, she used her toaster oven.

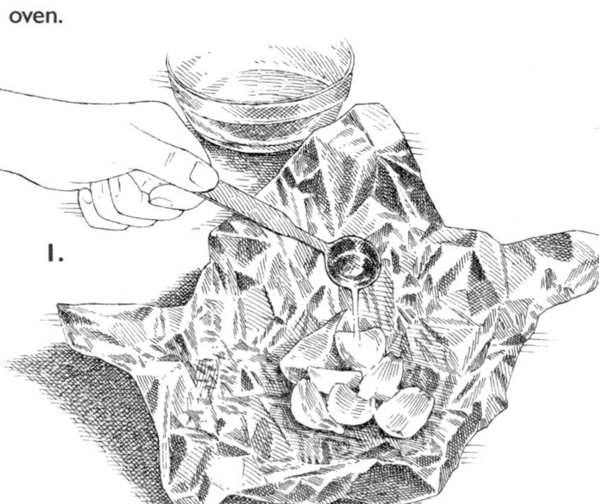

1. Loosely wrap up to eight unpeeled garlic cloves in a small pouch of aluminum foil with 1 teaspoon of olive or canola oil.
2. Bake the packet in the toaster oven at 375 degrees for about 20 minutes, or until the cloves soften. The cloves should be briefly cooled and then peeled.

Quick Cookies

Renata Mangrum of Wake Forest, N.C., often bakes a few frozen balls of cookie dough in her toaster oven for a quick snack. Instead of cutting up parchment paper to line a small toaster-oven baking sheet, she uses paper muffin-tin liners.

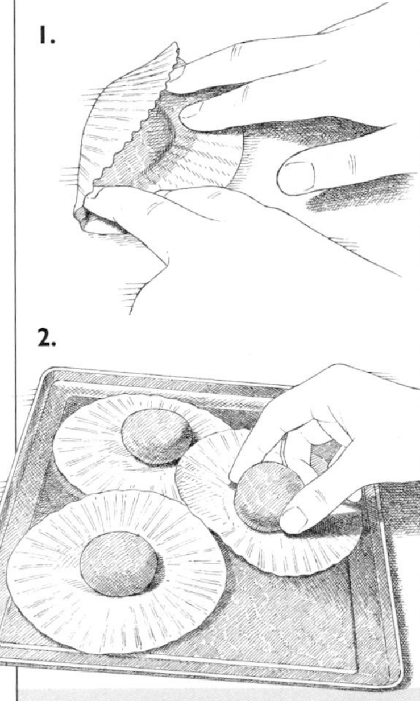

1. Flatten three or four paper muffin-tin liners on a toaster-oven baking sheet.
2. Place a ball of dough on each liner and bake the cookies as usual.

Send Us Your Tip We will provide a complimentary one-year subscription for each tip we print. Send your tip, name, and address to Quick Tips, Cook's Illustrated, P.O. Box 470589, Brookline, MA 02447, or to quicktips@americastestkitchen.com.

Moistening Dry Cake

Finding herself with a dry, overbaked cake, Gina Jamieson of Dublin, Calif., discovered that brushing the cake with a flavored simple syrup restored moistness. The technique works with yellow, white, and chocolate cakes.

1. Bring ½ cup each of water and sugar to a simmer in a small saucepan. Cook, stirring occasionally, until the sugar dissolves. Remove from heat and add 2 tablespoons of liqueur, such as Framboise, Frangelico, Chambord, or Kahlúa.
2. Brush each cake layer with a few tablespoons of the flavored syrup before frosting the cake.

Steady Stuffed Tomatoes

Stuffed tomatoes have the tendency to slip and slide all over the pan when they're being transferred in and out of the oven. Harry Lipman of Brooklyn, N.Y., came up with a resourceful solution that uses all parts of the tomato.

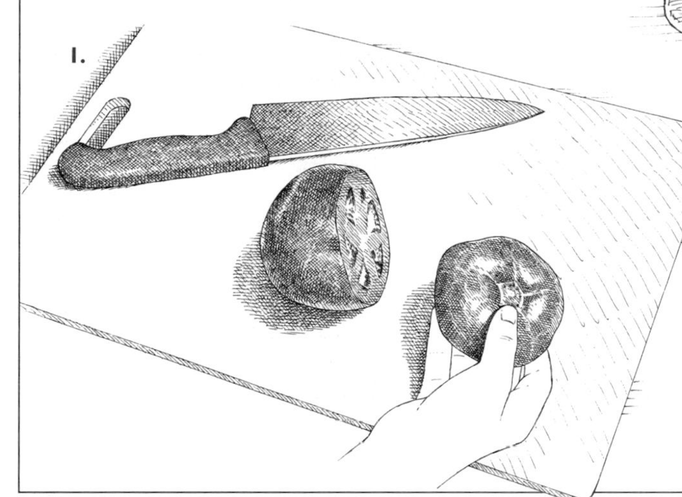

1. Slice the blossom end off of each tomato and arrange, cut-side down, in a baking dish.
2. Place the stuffed tomatoes on the blossom-end slices to keep them in place during baking.

Sugar-Coated Cookies

Rather than rolling balls of gingersnap or sugar-cookie dough individually in sugar, Mary Moltman of Vancouver, British Columbia, fills a small plastic container with sugar, then places the dough balls in the container and secures the lid. After a gentle shake, she removes the lid to reveal dough balls that are completely coated in sugar.

Safer Way to Cut Bagels

Slicing a bagel evenly and safely is a challenge. Donna Williams of Burton, Ohio, has the solution.

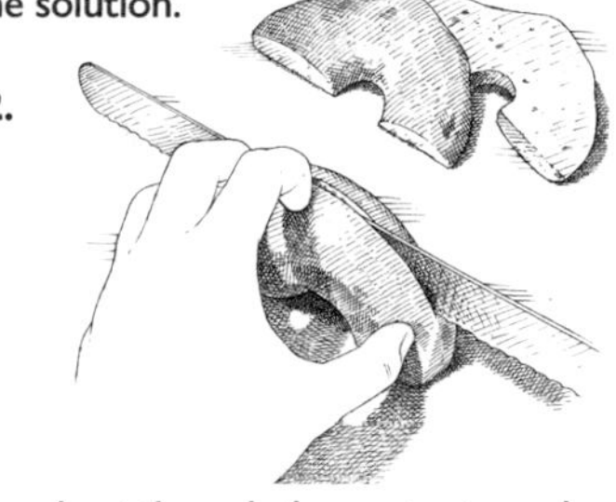

1. Lay the bagel flat on the work surface and cut through the center to make two pieces.
2. Place each piece, cut-side down, on the work surface to safely slice in half.

No-Slip Strainer

When straining vegetables or broths, Kristi Shawl of Spreckels, Calif., always found it difficult to keep the lip of her fine-mesh strainer from falling into the bowl or pot she was straining into. Her solution? She wraps a thick rubber band around the balancing loop of the strainer to create a no-slip grip that stays in place.

Easy Butter Cubes

Carolyn Winslow of Bellingham, Wash., uses an egg slicer to quickly and precisely cut butter into small pieces for pie dough and biscuits.

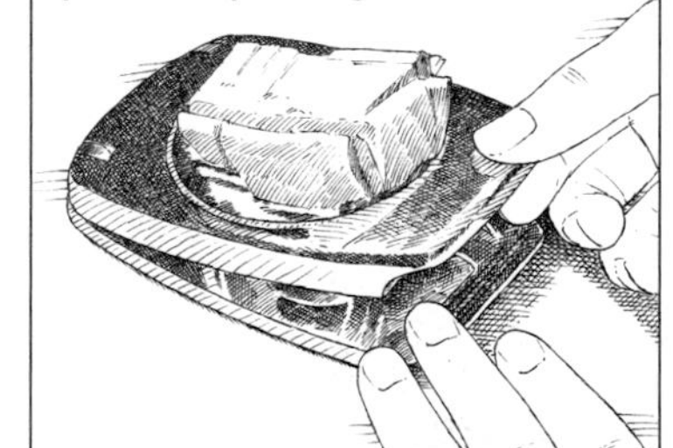

1. Place up to 4 tablespoons of butter into an egg slicer and push down on the slicing blades to create planks.
2. Rotate the butter a quarter turn, then push down on the slicing blades to create small pieces.

Testing Frying Oil Temperature

Amy Malek of Houston, Texas, has a trick that takes the guesswork out of determining when frying oil is hot. She simply places a kernel of popcorn in the oil as it heats up. The kernel will pop when the oil is between 350 and 365 degrees, just the right temperature for deep-frying.

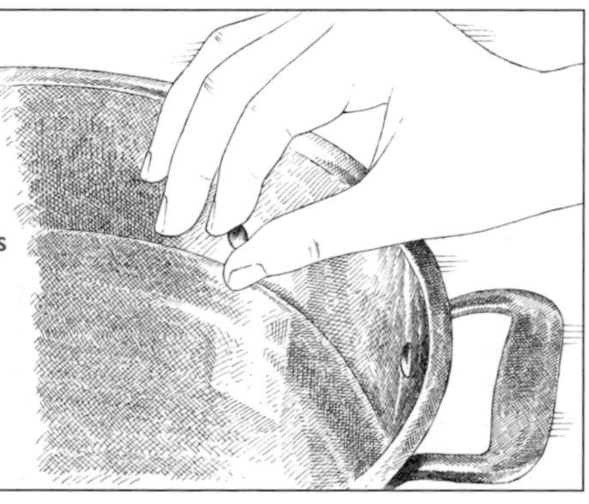

Crisp-Skinned Roast Chicken

Years ago, we developed an ideal roasting method for tender, juicy meat. Now could we figure out how to get supercrisp skin?

⋺ BY J. KENJI ALT ⋹

Back in 1996, our Easy Roast Chicken recipe solved the biggest problem with roasting chicken: getting both the breast and leg meat to stay juicy and finish cooking at the same time. The remaining problem? We've always put juiciness and evenly cooked meat first and have simply made do with so-so skin. That's not to say the skin on our Easy Roast Chicken isn't good—it has a burnished golden brown finish and a nice roasted flavor. But chicken skin has much more potential. The best skin should crackle against your teeth with every bite before melting into rich chicken flavor. Could we develop a method that would deliver both juicy meat and crisp, flavorful skin?

A study in contrasts: ultracrisp skin and extremely moist meat.

Hanging Out to Dry

In order to isolate all the variables that contribute to skin crisping, I decided to work with skin alone. To this end, I removed the skin from a few dozen chickens. Because I knew that meat (or skin) can't brown until all its surface moisture has evaporated, I decided to see what would happen if I dried out the skin before cooking—a standard method in recipes for Peking duck. I stretched a piece of skin on a wire rack and left it overnight in the refrigerator to dry out. The next day, I roasted it side by side with a moist piece of skin I had just removed from the chicken. The difference was striking: After 20 minutes, the dried skin had turned golden brown and crisp, while the fresh skin remained pale and limp. Could I dry out the skin even more with salt? I rubbed a new piece with salt and again left it to dry overnight. The next day, the skin looked shriveled as it came out of the refrigerator but cooked up even crisper than before.

Encouraged by this success, I pushed on with my experiments. I recalled a technique I'd witnessed for cooking *chicharrónes*—crisp pieces of deep-fried pork belly—during a recent trip to South America. To get these pieces to crisp to the point of brittleness, they are coated with baking soda and allowed to rest before cooking. I got to thinking about why such a thing would work. The Maillard reaction that occurs during browning (in which proteins denature and recombine with sugar molecules to create hundreds of new flavor compounds) is speeded up in an alkaline environment. When I tried mixing baking soda into my salt rub, it left a bitter aftertaste. Baking powder (which is also alkaline, though less so than baking soda), however, produced a markedly crisper skin without otherwise announcing its presence. A bit of research revealed two more effects this leavening agent produces on chicken skin: Baking powder helps chicken skin dehydrate more readily, enhancing the effects of overnight air-drying. In addition, it reacts with the proteins in chicken skin to produce a crunchier texture (see "New Powers for Baking Powder," page 7).

I was ready to try this technique on the whole bird. I combined baking powder with salt and rubbed the mixture evenly over a chicken, then let it rest overnight in the refrigerator. The next day I put the chicken in the oven and cooked it according to our Easy Roast Chicken recipe. It was a qualified success: The skin came out much crisper than usual for this recipe, but it was nowhere near as crisp as it had been when I roasted it on its own.

Skin Conditioning

Two pieces of skin removed from two chickens received different treatment before being roasted. One piece was left au naturel; the other was conditioned with a rub of baking powder and salt and allowed to dry out overnight.

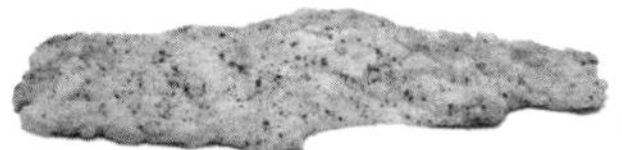

AU NATUREL: SOFT AND SOGGY

RUBBED AND AIR-DRIED: ULTRACRISP

Escape Route for Juice

As I cooked another chicken, I peered through the oven's glass door for ideas. Thirty minutes into the roast, I got an important clue: Juices and rendered fat were accumulating beneath the chicken's skin with nowhere to go, turning my once-dry skin wet and flabby. Clearly, for maximum crispness, the skin would need more than just an overnight rub to dry out; it would need a way for liquid to escape during cooking. For my next test, I used a metal skewer to poke about 20 holes in the fat deposits of each breast half and thigh, then proceeded to roast the chicken. The total amount of fat under the skin was now greatly reduced, but stubborn pockets remained, which led to flabby spots on the finished bird.

Would kicking up the oven temperature correct this? I upped it from 350 degrees to 450 for the majority of the cooking time, then increased it all the way to 500 for the last few minutes. I was worried that the high heat would dry out the breast, but I found that by starting the chicken breast-side down and flipping it midway through cooking, the breast meat was amply protected and cooked gently enough to come out tender and juicy. One unfortunate consequence: The high heat caused the drippings in the pan to burn, creating clouds of smoke. This was easily fixed by placing a sheet of aluminum foil with holes punched in it under the chicken to shield the rendered fat from direct oven heat.

And the skin? Better than before, but still not perfect. I was nearly tempted to remove the skin from the chicken and cook the two separately. Then

COOK'S LIVE Original Test Kitchen Videos
www.cooksillustrated.com

HOW TO MAKE
- Crisp Roast Chicken

VIDEO TIPS
- How do I carve a chicken?
- What's the difference between kosher and table salt?

STEP-BY-STEP | CRISP-SKIN MAKEOVER

A little advance prep and a high-heat roast give our chicken skin so crisp it crackles.

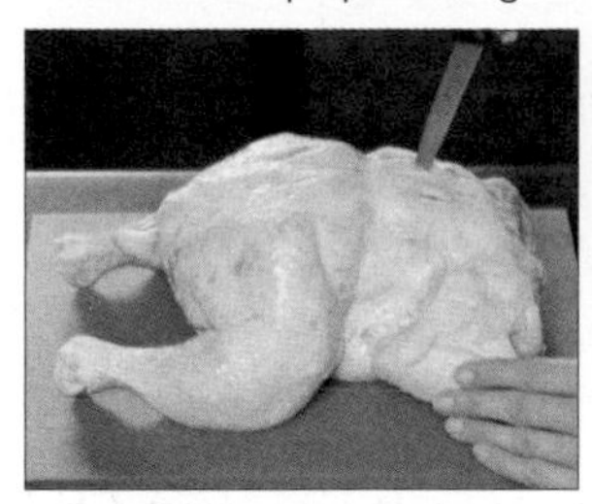

1. CUT CHANNELS FOR FAT
Cutting incisions in the skin along the chicken's back creates openings for fat to escape.

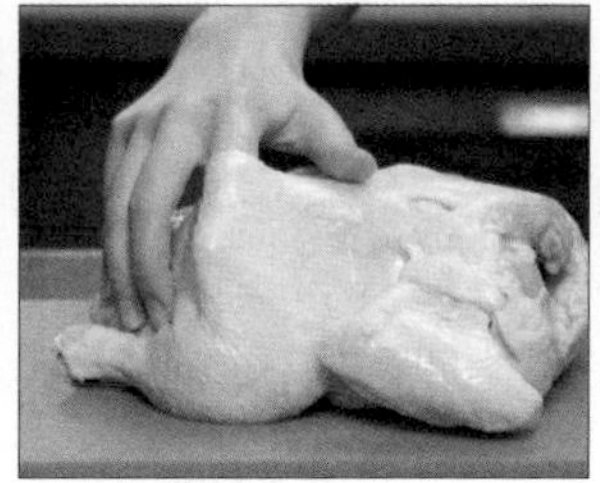

2. LOOSEN SKIN
Loosening the skin from the thighs and breast allows rendering fat to trickle out the openings.

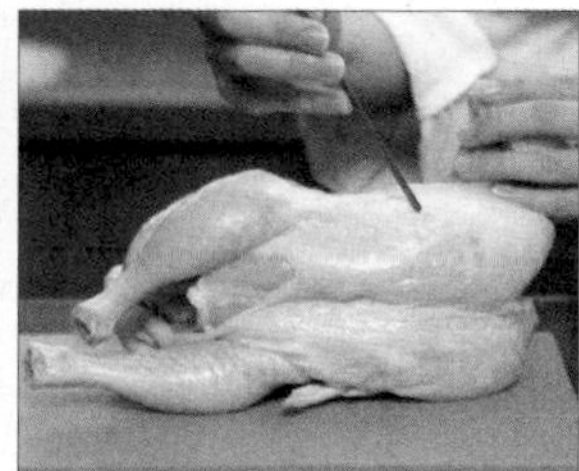

3. POKE HOLES
Poking holes in the skin of the breast and thighs creates additional channels for fat and juices to escape.

4. RUB AND CHILL-OUT
Rubbing baking powder and salt into the skin and air-drying the chicken in the refrigerator helps the skin crisp and brown.

5. ROAST AT HIGH HEAT
Roasting at 450 degrees (with a final blast at 500 degrees) speeds browning.

I realized the answer: To allow fat to flow freely from my roasting chicken, I would have to separate the skin from the meat over much of the bird. For my next test, I carefully ran my hand between the meat and the skin all over the bird (making sure not to tear it). Hoping that gravity would do some of the work for me, I also cut a few holes in the skin near the back of the bird to provide extra-large channels for the rendering fat to drip down and escape. When I pulled the chicken out, the proof was in the pan: a large amount of rendered fat, far more than before. There was so much fat that I couldn't help wondering if the meat would be less flavorful. But the skin was now better than anything I could have hoped for: deep, even brown and cracklingly crisp to the touch. The speed at which my tasters ate every bite proved that this chicken's beauty wasn't only skin-deep—underneath the crisp exterior, the meat was tender, juicy, and flavorful to the bone.

CRISP ROAST CHICKEN

SERVES 2 TO 3

For best flavor, use a high-quality chicken, such as one from Bell & Evans. Do not brine the bird; it will prohibit the skin from becoming crisp. The sheet of foil between the roasting pan and V-rack will keep the drippings from burning and smoking.

- 1 whole chicken (3½–4½ pounds), giblets removed and discarded (see note)
- 1 tablespoon kosher salt or 1½ teaspoons table salt
- 1 teaspoon baking powder
- ½ teaspoon ground black pepper

1. Place chicken breast-side down on work surface. Following photos above, use tip of sharp knife to make four 1-inch incisions along back of chicken. Using fingers or handle of wooden spoon, carefully separate skin from thighs and breast. Using metal skewer, poke 15 to 20 holes in fat deposits on top of breast halves and thighs. Tuck wing tips underneath chicken.

2. Combine salt, baking powder, and pepper in small bowl. Pat chicken dry with paper towels and sprinkle all over with salt mixture. Rub in mixture with hands, coating entire surface evenly. Set chicken, breast-side up, in V-rack set on rimmed baking sheet and refrigerate, uncovered, for 12 to 24 hours.

3. Adjust oven rack to lowest position and heat oven to 450 degrees. Using paring knife, poke 20 holes about 1½ inches apart in 16- by 12-inch piece of foil. Place foil loosely in large roasting pan. Flip chicken so breast side faces down, and set V-rack in roasting pan on top of foil. Roast chicken 25 minutes.

4. Remove roasting pan from oven. Using 2 large wads of paper towels, rotate chicken breast-side up. Continue to roast until instant-read thermometer inserted in thickest part of breast registers 135 degrees, 15 to 25 minutes.

5. Increase oven temperature to 500 degrees. Continue to roast until skin is golden brown, crisp, and instant-read thermometer inserted in thickest part of breast registers 160 degrees and 175 degrees in thickest part of thigh, 10 to 20 minutes.

6. Transfer chicken to cutting board and let rest, uncovered, for 20 minutes. Carve and serve immediately.

SCIENCE: New Powers for Baking Powder

Our recipe relies on an overnight rub made with baking powder and salt to guarantee supercrisp skin. The process works in two ways. First, baking powder has alkaline properties that speed up dehydration in the skin, leading to better, faster browning as the chicken roasts. Second, baking powder reacts with the proteins in the chicken skin over the course of its overnight rest, prodding them to break down more readily to produce crisper skin. –J.K.A.

SKIN TONIC

TASTING: Is a $35 Chicken Worth the Splurge?

Rare breeds of chicken allowed to mature for longer periods than the supermarket variety are touted for their rich taste. But are they really worth the sticker-shock prices and overnight shipping costs? We compared three specialty birds with our favorite supermarket chicken, from Bell & Evans ($2.29 per pound). The winning birds bested the Bell & Evans chicken and are highly recommended—for those with unlimited chicken budgets. –Elizabeth Bomze

HIGHLY RECOMMENDED

D'Artagnan Heritage Blue Foot
Price: $20.99 for one 3¼- to 4-pound chicken, plus overnight shipping
Comments: This California-raised bird engineered to share the physical traits and flavor profile of the French gold standard in poultry, Poulet de Bresse, completely won over tasters with its "exceptional" flavor and "sweet, tender meatiness."

RECOMMENDED

Joyce Foods Poulet Rouge Fermier du Piedmont
Price: $15–$17 per bird, depending on size, plus overnight shipping
Comments: Tasters liked the "high-tone chickeny" flavor of these birds raised on small North Carolina farms inspired by the famous French slow-growth program, Label Rouge.

RECOMMENDED WITH RESERVATIONS

Good Shepherd Turkey Ranch Dark Cornish Indian Game Chicken
Price: $69 for two 3- to 3½-pound chickens, shipping included
Comments: A different breed than the Cornish Rock chickens that account for most supermarket poultry, this bird garnered mixed reviews. Praised for its "excellent, slightly gamy flavor," it was also criticized for "rubbery skin" and "dry" white meat.

Simple Italian-Style Meat Sauce

In this country, meat sauce usually means a hastily made dish with rubbery ground beef and no flavor. We wanted something simple—but a lot better.

⋟ BY CHARLES KELSEY ⋞

In Italy, cooking a meaty pasta sauce is an all-day affair. Whether using ground meat for a *ragù alla Bolognese* or chunks of meat for a rustic sauce, one thing is for sure: These sauces slowly simmer for three or four hours—or even longer. This long simmer develops concentrated flavor and, more important, breaks down the meat, giving it a soft, lush texture.

In America, "Italian meat sauce" has typically come to mean a shortcut version in which ground beef, onions, garlic, and canned tomatoes are thrown together in a pot and cooked for half an hour. While such sauces may be quick, their lackluster flavor and rubbery meat bear no resemblance to their Italian cousins. But the trouble is, when I crave pasta with meat sauce, I don't always have hours to spend on a Bolognese. Could I develop a meat sauce to make on a weeknight that tasted like it had been simmering for, if not all day, at least a good portion of it?

With its supple bits of meat and rich flavor, you'd never guess our meat sauce simmers for less than an hour.

Meat of the Matter

My search started with analyzing Bolognese recipes, and I discovered right away that the best ones don't brown the meat. Instead, they call for cooking the ground meat until it loses its raw color, then adding the liquid ingredients one by one, slowly reducing each and building flavor before adding the next. One of the first liquids in the pot is usually some form of dairy, a Bolognese sauce's signature ingredient that imparts a sweet creaminess to the dish. Most American meat sauces, on the other hand, brown the beef first—a step that adds flavor but toughens the meat. They also skip the dairy in favor of tomato sauce, which doesn't provide the milk fat or the same layers of complex flavor.

Would eliminating the browning step and adding milk work better? I headed to the test kitchen to find out. After sautéing onion and garlic, I stirred in a pound of ground beef, breaking it up with a wooden spoon. As soon as it started to lose its raw color, I immediately added ½ cup of milk along with the tomatoes, and then simmered the sauce for 30 minutes or so. The results were disappointing: Some of the meat was tender and moist, but most of it was tough and mealy. And despite the milk, the sauce lacked flavor overall. If anything, without sufficient time to reduce, the milk actually overpowered the meat flavor in the sauce. It occurred to me that in order for the milk to develop the new flavor compounds that are its key contribution to a Bolognese sauce, a lengthy simmer was necessary. Would cooking the sauce a little longer—45 minutes instead of 30—help? Not enough to notice. Furthermore, the extra 15 minutes of simmering had little impact on the meat, which was still more rubbery than not.

It was time to look beyond Bolognese for ways to improve my simple weeknight sauce. Meat tenderizer seemed like an obvious place to start. A few teaspoons did soften the beef, but it also made it spongy. Would soy sauce work? Soy sauce is a base ingredient in many of our steak marinades, where it acts much like a brine, tenderizing meat by helping it retain moisture. But I quickly discovered that while soy minimizes moisture loss in large pieces of meat, such as steak, it has virtually no impact on tiny bits of ground beef. After a little research I found out why: Bigger pieces of meat contain more water, which takes a longer time to evaporate during cooking. The water in small pieces of ground meat, on the other hand, evaporates almost immediately, and not even soy sauce can help prevent this.

A colleague suggested a trick that hadn't occurred to me: mixing in a panade. This paste of bread and milk is often blended into meatballs and meatloaf to help them hold their shape and retain moisture during cooking. It was worth a try. Using a fork, I mashed up a piece of bread with some milk until I had a smooth paste and mixed it into the ground beef until well combined. I then proceeded as usual with the rest of the recipe: stirring the beef mixture into the sautéed onions and garlic, adding the tomatoes, and simmering. I noticed a difference in the sauce even before I ladled it over pasta for tasters. The meat looked moister and, sure enough, tasters confirmed that it was. It turns out that starches from the bread absorb liquid from the milk to form a gel that coats and lubricates the meat, much in the same way as fat (see "Panade to the Rescue," page 9). But all was not perfect: Tasters were pleased with the meat's tenderness but complained that the sauce was too chunky and resembled chili. No problem. I pulsed the meat and panade together in a food processor to create finer pieces of supple, juicy meat.

Keys to Great Flavor

MUSHROOMS | TOMATO PASTE | PARMESAN CHEESE

Minced mushrooms browned in oil boost the sauce's meaty taste. A spoonful of tomato paste and a sprinkle of Parmesan cheese add complexity.

Beefing Up Flavor

With the meat issue solved, it was time to turn my attention to flavor. Without browning or a lengthy simmer to concentrate and build new layers of flavor, complexity and depth were noticeably lacking from my sauce. Could the type of ground beef I used enhance flavor? I bought four different kinds—ground round, chuck, and sirloin, as well as meat labeled "ground beef" (a mix of various beef cuts and trimmings)—and made four sauces. The ground round was bland and spongy, but tasters liked the other three equally well. Eighty-five percent lean beef proved to have just the right degree of leanness, adding richness without making the sauce greasy. Still, tasters were pressing, "Where's the beef [flavor]?"

Next, I tested a range of ingredients that are often used to boost meaty flavor. Beef broth ended up imparting a tinny taste to the sauce. Worcestershire and steak sauce overwhelmed it with their potent flavorings, and red wine lent a sour taste. Finally, I tried mushrooms—and at last I had a winner. The mushrooms brought a real beefiness to the sauce. After experimenting with different types, I discovered that plain white mushrooms worked just fine. The key was browning them. I minced a modest amount (about 4 ounces) and added them to the pan with the onions. Browning concentrated their flavor but left them tender and supple, allowing them to add complexity without otherwise letting their presence be known.

When it came to other components of the sauce, tasters liked a mix of diced and crushed tomatoes. The diced tomatoes brought a chunky texture, and the crushed provided a smooth foundation. I reserved a small amount of juice from the drained diced tomatoes to deglaze the pan after browning the mushrooms. This little trick gave the sauce's tomato flavor a boost, as did a tablespoon of tomato paste. Earlier, I had ruled against milk in the sauce (except for the couple of tablespoons in the panade), but I reinstated dairy in the form of a handful of grated Parmesan, which brought a welcome tanginess. With a dash of red pepper flakes and some fresh oregano, I was done.

I now had a sauce with meltingly tender meat that was as complex and full-bodied as any sauce simmered for under an hour could be. True, no one would mistake it for a Bolognese—but no one would ever believe I hadn't rushed home early to put it on the stove, either.

SHOPPING: Ground Beef

Ground beef can be made from a variety of cuts, and fat levels vary from 70 to 95 percent lean. Our meat sauce recipe calls for any 85 percent lean ground beef other than ground round. But when a recipe doesn't specify, how do you know what to buy? Here's a guide:

GROUND CHUCK: Cut from the shoulder, ground chuck is distinguished by its rich, beefy flavor and tender texture.

GROUND SIRLOIN: This cut from the cow's midsection near the hip offers good beefy flavor, but it can be on the dry side. Generally fairly lean.

GROUND BEEF: A mystery meat of sorts, ground beef can be any cut or combination of cuts, which means flavor and texture are rarely consistent.

GROUND ROUND: Lean, tough, and often gristly, ground round comes from the rear upper leg and rump of the cow. –Elizabeth Bomze

SIMPLE ITALIAN-STYLE MEAT SAUCE

MAKES ABOUT 6 CUPS

Except for ground round (which tasters found spongy and bland), this recipe will work with most types of ground beef, as long as it is 85 percent lean. (Eighty percent lean beef will turn the sauce greasy; 90 percent will make it fibrous.) Use high-quality crushed tomatoes; our favorite brands are Tuttorosso, Muir Glen Organic, and Hunt's Organic. If using dried oregano, add the entire amount with the canned tomato liquid in step 2. The sauce makes enough for nearly 2 pounds of pasta. Leftover sauce can be refrigerated in an airtight container for 3 days or frozen for 1 month.

- 4 ounces white mushrooms, cleaned, stems trimmed, and broken into rough pieces
- 1 large slice high-quality white sandwich bread, torn into quarters
- 2 tablespoons whole milk
- Table salt and ground black pepper
- 1 pound 85 percent lean ground beef (see note and box at left)
- 1 tablespoon olive oil
- 1 large onion, chopped fine (about 1½ cups)
- 6 medium garlic cloves, minced or pressed through garlic press (about 2 tablespoons)
- ¼ teaspoon red pepper flakes
- 1 tablespoon tomato paste
- 1 (14.5-ounce) can diced tomatoes, drained, ¼ cup liquid reserved
- 1 tablespoon minced fresh oregano leaves or 1 teaspoon dried (see note)
- 1 (28-ounce) can crushed tomatoes
- ½ ounce grated Parmesan cheese (about ¼ cup)

1. Process mushrooms in food processor until finely chopped, about eight 1-second pulses, scraping down side of bowl as needed; transfer to medium bowl. Add bread, milk, ½ teaspoon salt, and ½ teaspoon pepper to now-empty food processor and process until paste forms, about eight 1-second pulses. Add beef and pulse until mixture is well combined, about six 1-second pulses.

2. Heat oil in large saucepan over medium-high heat until just smoking. Add onion and mushrooms; cook, stirring frequently, until vegetables are browned and dark bits form on pan bottom, 6 to 12 minutes. Stir in garlic, pepper flakes, and tomato paste; cook until fragrant and tomato paste starts to brown, about 1 minute. Add ¼ cup reserved tomato liquid and 2 teaspoons fresh oregano (if using dried, add full amount), scraping bottom of pan with wooden spoon to loosen browned bits. Add meat mixture and cook, breaking meat into small pieces with wooden spoon, until beef loses its raw color, 2 to 4 minutes, making sure that meat does not brown.

3. Stir in crushed and drained diced tomatoes and bring to simmer; reduce heat to low and gently simmer until sauce has thickened and flavors have blended, about 30 minutes. Stir in cheese and remaining teaspoon fresh oregano; season with salt and pepper to taste.

SCIENCE: Panade to the Rescue

A paste of milk and bread, called a panade, is responsible for keeping the ground beef in our meat sauce moist and tender. Because panades are typically used to help foods like meatballs and meatloaf hold their shape (and moisture), adding a panade to a meat sauce where the beef is crumbled seemed like an odd idea. Wouldn't the mashed-up milk and bread just dissolve into the sauce? We were left scratching our heads when the panade worked.

Our science editor explained what was happening: Starches from the bread absorb liquid from the milk to form a gel that coats and lubricates the protein molecules in the meat, much in the same way as fat, keeping them moist and preventing them from linking together to form a tough matrix. Mixing the beef and panade in a food processor helps to ensure that the starch is well dispersed so that all the meat reaps its benefits. –C.K.

COOK'S LIVE Original Test Kitchen Videos
www.cooksillustrated.com

HOW TO MAKE
- Simple Italian-Style Meat Sauce

VIDEO TIPS
- Can I wash mushrooms?
- Buying Guide: Tomato Paste

Perfecting Oven-Roasted Salmon

Most recipes for salmon create either a nicely browned exterior or a silky, moist interior. Why shouldn't we have our salmon both ways?

≥ BY KEITH DRESSER ≤

In the two decades since improved fish-farming techniques began to make good-quality fresh salmon available year-round, this fish has become one of America's favorites; salmon is second to canned tuna in per capita consumption. The reasons for its popularity are simple: Salmon is rich without being aggressively fishy, and, unlike a lot of white fish, it needs no dressing up to taste good.

Steaming and poaching are two of the best methods for achieving the silky, almost buttery, texture that is salmon's signature trait; pan-searing is the best way to exploit its high fat content to produce a flavorful, caramelized crust. But what if you want both qualities—moist, succulent flesh inside, and, if not a crust, at least a contrasting texture on the outside? Recipes for roasting salmon promise just that.

I knew that roasting at a high temperature (from 400 to 475 degrees) can create browning on the exterior of the fish, but by the time that point is reached, you've got a well-done piece of salmon. Slow-roasting at a very gentle oven temperature, between 250 and 300 degrees, seemed like a better place to start. To ensure uniform pieces that would cook evenly, I bought a whole center-cut fillet and divided it into four pieces that I cooked at 275 degrees for about 20 minutes. This method resulted in moist, near-translucent flesh through and through, but the fish was a little mushy, and there was no contrast in texture whatsoever. Cranking the temperature higher would definitely create a more golden exterior, but it would also sacrifice some of the medium-rare flesh inside.

A bright tomato relish complements the salmon's richness.

Perhaps a hybrid cooking technique combining high and low heat, as we often use for roasting chicken with crisp skin and tender, juicy meat, would work. After a bit of experimentation, I settled on a starting temperature of 500 degrees, which I reduced to 275 degrees immediately upon placing the fish in the oven. The initial blast of high heat firmed the exterior of the salmon and helped render some of the excess fat that had made the slower-roasted fish mushy. To prevent the oven temperature from dropping too rapidly, I also preheated the baking sheet. This necessitated cooking the fish with its skin on, so the fillets could be placed skin-side down in the pan to protect the flesh. The fish tasted a little too fatty on my first try with this new approach, but making several slits through the skin before placing it in the pan allowed most of the fat residing directly beneath the skin to render off onto the baking sheet.

The fish then gently cooked while the oven temperature slowly dropped. Though the temperature was never really in a range that I would consider true slow-roasting, this technique did rely on the declining ambient temperature, as opposed to constant heat, to slowly cook the fish. It worked beautifully: I now had salmon with a little firmness on the outside and a lot of moist, succulent meat on the inside.

I was inspired to dress up this perfectly cooked salmon to make it more of a company meal. I dismissed spice rubs and glazes, which require sustained high heat to fully flavor the fish. I tried several marinades, but their impact was more subtle than I wanted. Quick salsas and easy, no-cook relishes were the answer. After trying dozens of combinations, I found those with an acidic element worked best to balance the richness of the fish. Tasters liked a tomato-basil relish, a spicy cucumber version, a tangy tangerine and ginger combo, and a tart grapefruit-basil pairing. In addition to bright flavor, each relish provided a further contrast in texture to complement the salmon's silkiness.

STEP-BY-STEP | PREPARING SALMON FOR ROASTING

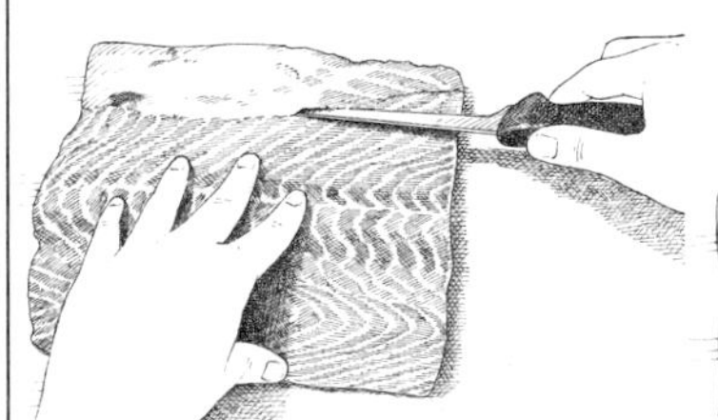

1. Hold a sharp knife at a slight downward angle to the flesh and cut off the whitish, fatty portion of the belly.

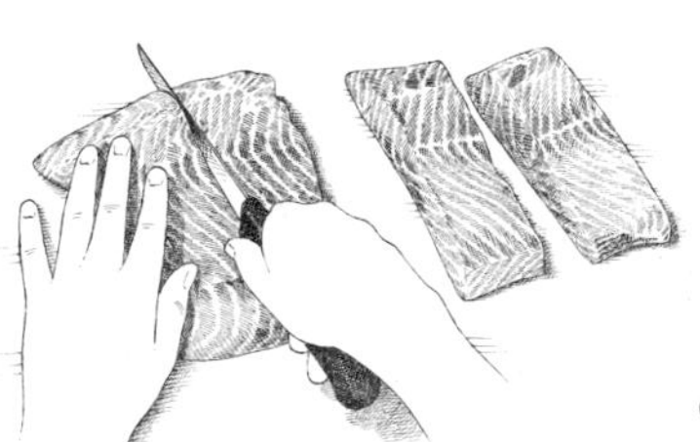

2. Cut the salmon fillet into four pieces of equal size to help ensure that they cook at the same rate.

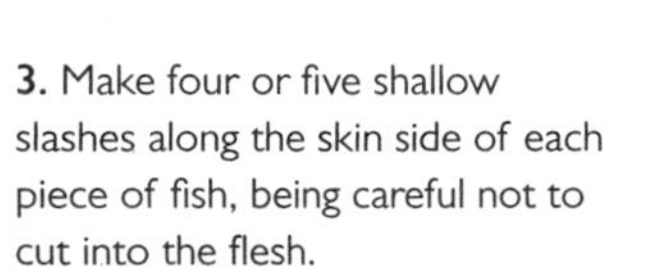

3. Make four or five shallow slashes along the skin side of each piece of fish, being careful not to cut into the flesh.

COOK'S LIVE Original Test Kitchen Videos
www.cooksillustrated.com

HOW TO MAKE
- Oven-Roasted Salmon

VIDEO TIP
- Buying Guide: Salmon

OVEN-ROASTED SALMON

SERVES 4

To ensure uniform pieces of fish that cook at the same rate, buy a whole center-cut fillet and cut it into 4 pieces. If your knife is not sharp enough to easily cut through the skin, try a serrated knife. It is important to keep the skin on during cooking; remove it afterward if you choose not to serve it. Our recipe for Orange-Mint Relish is available free at www.cooksillustrated.com/april.

- 1 skin-on salmon fillet (1 ¾–2 pounds), about 1 ½ inches at thickest part (see note)
- 2 teaspoons olive oil
- Table salt and ground black pepper
- 1 recipe relish (recipes follow)

1. Adjust oven rack to lowest position, place rimmed baking sheet on rack, and heat oven to 500 degrees. Following illustrations on page 10, use sharp knife to remove any whitish fat from belly of fillet and cut into 4 equal pieces. Make 4 or 5 shallow slashes about an inch apart along skin side of each piece, being careful not to cut into flesh.

2. Pat salmon dry with paper towels. Rub fillets evenly with oil and season liberally with salt and pepper. Reduce oven temperature to 275 degrees and remove baking sheet. Carefully place salmon skin-side down on baking sheet. Roast until centers of thickest part of fillets are still translucent when cut into with paring knife or instant-read thermometer inserted in thickest part of fillets registers 125 degrees, 9 to 13 minutes. Transfer fillets to individual plates or platter. Top with relish and serve.

FRESH TOMATO RELISH

MAKES ABOUT 1 ½ CUPS

- ¾ pound ripe tomatoes, cored, seeded, and cut into ¼-inch dice (about 1 ½ cups)
- ½ small shallot, minced (about 1 tablespoon)
- 1 small garlic clove, minced or pressed through garlic press (about ½ teaspoon)
- 1 tablespoon extra-virgin olive oil
- 1 teaspoon red wine vinegar
- 2 tablespoons chopped fresh basil leaves
- Table salt and ground black pepper

Combine all ingredients in medium bowl. Season to taste with salt and pepper.

SPICY CUCUMBER RELISH

MAKES ABOUT 2 CUPS

- 1 medium cucumber, peeled, seeded, and cut into ¼-inch dice (about 2 cups)
- ½ small shallot, minced (about 1 tablespoon)
- 1 serrano chile, seeds and ribs removed, minced (about 1 tablespoon)
- 2 tablespoons chopped fresh mint leaves
- 1–2 tablespoons juice from 1 lime
- Table salt

Combine cucumber, shallot, chile, mint, 1 tablespoon lime juice, and ¼ teaspoon salt in medium bowl. Let stand at room temperature to blend flavors, 15 minutes. Adjust seasoning with additional lime juice and salt.

TANGERINE AND GINGER RELISH

MAKES ABOUT 1 ¼ CUPS

- 4 tangerines, rind and pith removed and segments cut into ½-inch pieces (about 1 cup)
- 1 scallion, sliced thin (about ¼ cup)
- 1 ½ teaspoons grated fresh ginger
- 2 teaspoons juice from 1 lemon
- 2 teaspoons extra-virgin olive oil
- Table salt and ground black pepper

1. Place tangerines in fine-mesh strainer set over medium bowl and drain for 15 minutes.

2. Pour off all but 1 tablespoon tangerine juice from bowl; whisk in scallion, ginger, lemon juice, and oil. Stir in tangerines and season to taste with salt and pepper.

GRAPEFRUIT AND BASIL RELISH

MAKES ABOUT 1 CUP

- 2 red grapefruit, rind and pith removed and segments cut into ½-inch pieces (about 1 cup)
- ½ small shallot, minced (about 1 tablespoon)
- 2 tablespoons chopped fresh basil leaves
- 2 teaspoons juice from 1 lemon
- 2 teaspoons extra-virgin olive oil
- Table salt and ground black pepper

1. Place grapefruit in fine-mesh strainer set over medium bowl and drain for 15 minutes.

2. Pour off all but 1 tablespoon grapefruit juice from bowl; whisk in shallot, basil, lemon juice, and oil. Stir in grapefruit and season to taste with salt and pepper.

TASTING: Salmon Primer

In season, we've always preferred the more pronounced flavor of wild-caught salmon to farmed Atlantic salmon, which has traditionally been the main farm-raised variety for sale in this country. But with more species of wild and farmed salmon available these days, we decided to see what distinguishes one from the next. We tasted three kinds of wild Pacific salmon alongside two farmed kinds; they ranged in price from $9 to $20 per pound. While we loved the generally stronger flavor of the wild-caught fish, our tasting confirmed: If you're going to spend the extra money on wild salmon, make sure it looks and smells fresh, and realize that high quality is available only from late spring through the end of summer.

—Meredith Smith

FARMED SPECIES

ATLANTIC
$9/lb.
Season: year-round
The sedentary, farm-bound lifestyle of this fish gave it a "buttery" texture enjoyed by some tasters, but its farm diet may account for the "bland," "vegetal" flavors noted by others. Tasters were divided on texture: Some praised its "supple" consistency, but others called it "squishy" or "mushy."

KING
$12/lb.
Season: year-round
TEST KITCHEN FAVORITE
Tasters loved this variety's "custardy" texture and "rich" yet "mild" flavor that "tasted of the sea." But this farmed species is not as widely available as its Atlantic counterpart and may require a trip to a specialty store.

WILD SPECIES

COHO
$12/lb.
Season: July through September
This species of wild salmon has never enjoyed the popularity of king or sockeye, perhaps due to its far leaner constitution. Many of our tasters found it to be "mealy," comparing its texture to that of canned fish. Coho was praised, however, for a flavor that was "just right"—neither too fishy nor too mild.

KING $20/lb.
Season: May through September
This prized variety winds up on the menus of many top restaurants, which pushes the retail price to about $20 per pound. Wild king has to travel father than coho salmon to reach its spawning grounds, and thus boasts far fattier flesh. Tasters found the fish to have a strong flavor and a "meaty" texture. However, the firmness of this fish's flesh was considered by some to be overly "rubbery."

SOCKEYE
$13/lb.
Season: May through September
TEST KITCHEN FAVORITE
In great demand in Japan, the sockeye (its name is a corruption of an American Indian word and has nothing to do with the fish's eyes) was distinguished by its "clean, briny" notes and deep reddish color—the darkest of all the species. Some found the "big flavor" off-putting, but others praised the same assertiveness. Tasters also liked the "smooth," "firm" texture that gave the sockeye a "good bite."

Rethinking Mashed Potatoes

Spuds boiled in their jackets make great mashed potatoes. But who wants burnt fingers from peeling hot potatoes before dinner?

BY DAVID PAZMIÑO

Our favorite mashed potato recipe calls for boiling whole potatoes in their jackets, then peeling and mashing them right before serving. Keeping the skins on during cooking yields the best potato flavor, but the method itself isn't all that convenient. After boiling the potatoes for 30 minutes, there you are, right before dinner, burning your fingers on hot skins. We decided it was time to revisit this recipe to come up with something that allowed a little more of the prep work to be done in advance.

Starch Management

Ask people their favorite way to make mashed potatoes and most will say the same thing: They peel the skins, chop the spuds, then throw them into a pot of cold water to boil. We like cooking the potatoes in their jackets because it keeps the earthy potato flavor from leeching out into the water, and also because we find it yields the creamiest texture. The skins prevent the starch granules in the potato cells from absorbing too much water and bursting like overfilled water balloons when mashed, spilling their sticky, gluey contents into the mix. But to meet my goal of cutting back on last-minute prep, clearly the skins would have to go before cooking. Waterlogged starch granules, then, were a given. Was there a way to prevent at least some of them from bursting?

A unique cooking method gives these mashed potatoes their light, fluffy texture.

One way is to use a ricer, rather than a potato masher, to finish the dish. Potatoes pass through the sievelike hopper of this tool only once, avoiding the repeated abuse of mashing. (Pounding already-mashed portions over and over greatly increases the chance of bursting starch granules.) Ricing aside, what else could I do?

I tried a lot of unlikely techniques, most of which yielded poor results. One bright light during this early testing was a recipe in Jeffrey Steingarten's book *The Man Who Ate Everything* that employed a technique invented by the instant-mashed-potato industry. Steingarten partially cooks the spuds in simmering water, drains and rinses them under cool water, and sets them aside for half an hour. Once fully cooled, the potatoes are cooked again and mashed. Cooling the potatoes partway through cooking causes the sticky gel in the starch granules to crystallize and become resistant to dissolving in water or milk (even if the cell walls surrounding them subsequently rupture), leading to fluffier potatoes. The only problem: This meant cooking potatoes for over an hour in numerous changes of hot and cold water. This was not the "advance prep" I had in mind.

Another method, recommended on the website of the Idaho Potato Board, was simpler and equally intriguing. To avoid gluey mashed potatoes, the site suggests a two-step cooking process that has you start the potatoes in actively boiling water (rather than the traditional cold water) and then immediately reduce the temperature to keep the water at a bare simmer. After 20 minutes, you crank up the heat and boil the spuds until soft. The idea is to keep the pectin that glues individual potato cells together (and helps keep water out) from degrading too quickly. At temperatures below the boiling point, the pectin won't dissolve and can continue to act as a barrier to water.

Tasted side by side with conventional one-step potatoes started in cold water, the two-step spuds were definitely lighter. But they still tasted more thin and watery than the potatoes cooked with their jackets on. To get both fluffy consistency and great flavor, I was going to have to keep excess water from getting into the starch granules in the first place. Why not just forget simmering and boiling and go with a method that would expose the potatoes to little or no water?

Full Steam Ahead

Baking the potatoes was out—it would take too long (plus, if I cooked potatoes with their skins on, I was back where I started). Microwaving produced a starchy, pasty mash. Steaming was my best bet.

RECIPE SHORTHAND | FLUFFY MASHED POTATOES

1. RINSE Washing off excess starch from cut potatoes is the first step in preventing dense mashed potatoes.
2. STEAM Cooking the potatoes over simmering water maintains flavor and cuts down on burst starches.
3. RINSE Rinsing the potatoes halfway through cooking washes away any sticky starches that do burst.
4. RICE Pushing the potatoes through a ricer is another way to prevent the swollen starch granules from bursting.

SCIENCE: How Steaming and Rinsing Help Prevent Gluey Potatoes

We found that rinsing steamed potatoes halfway through cooking produced mashed potatoes with a particularly light and fluffy texture and rich potato flavor. What was going on?

Potatoes contain two starches, including one called amylose that can be the enemy of a fluffy consistency. If these starch granules absorb too much water during cooking, they will eventually burst, spilling a sticky gel that turns potatoes gluey. Because steaming exposes the potatoes to less water, it reduces the chance of these granules swelling to the point of bursting. Some granules will inevitably burst anyway, from overfilling with water due to heat breaking down the pectin that surrounds the potato cells. Rinsing midway through cooking helps remove some of this free, or escaped, amylose, leading to potatoes with a lighter, silkier texture. –D.P.

WHAT MAKES POTATOES GLUEY?

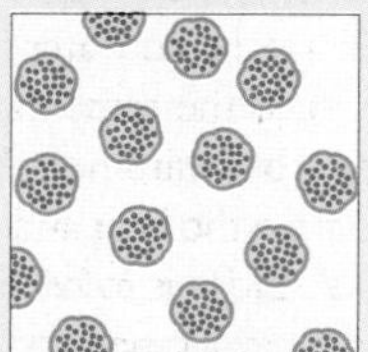

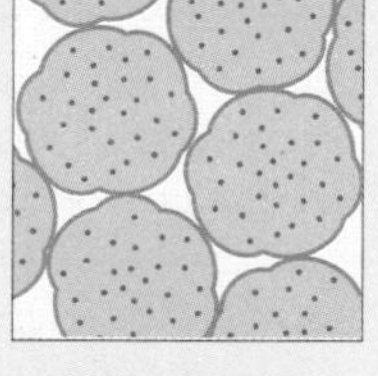
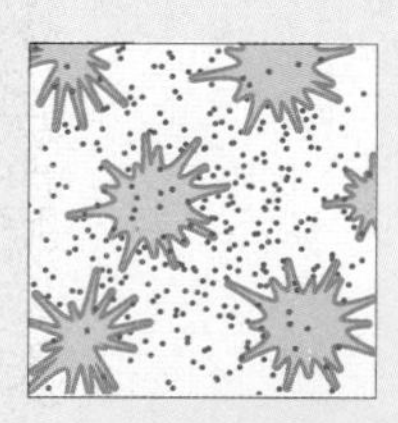
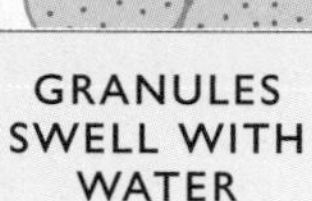

UNCOOKED STARCH GRANULES

GRANULES SWELL WITH WATER

SWOLLEN GRANULES BURST

I fashioned a steamer by placing a colander in a Dutch oven, then brought a few inches of water to a boil. I peeled, cut, and rinsed the spuds (to remove any surface starch) and dropped them into the colander. About 20 minutes later, the potatoes were soft and ready for mashing. They were also covered in a sticky substance that I knew to be free amylose, the very thing that turns potatoes gluey (see "How Steaming and Rinsing Help Prevent Gluey Potatoes," above). I tried rinsing the potatoes before ricing to get rid of the amylose, but some of the potato flavor washed away as well, resulting in a mash that was as bland as the two-step potatoes. And the potatoes were now cold. Would rinsing the potatoes earlier in the process, before they got fully cooked, bring me better results?

I put a new batch of spuds into the steamer. Peeking after 10 minutes, I saw they were already covered in gluey amylose. I took the colander out of the pot, rinsed the hot potatoes under cold water for a couple of minutes, then returned them to the pot of still-boiling water to finish cooking. When riced, these potatoes were wonderfully light and fluffy and had the best flavor yet.

Back to Basics

Ideally, this recipe should work with a wide range of potatoes: Russets, Yukon Golds, red potatoes, and white potatoes. But due to their low starch content, the red potatoes were a bust, tasting bland and uninspiring no matter how much butter was added to the mix. While the other potatoes worked fine, tasters liked the deeper flavor of the Yukon Golds best.

With my cooking method solved and the type of potato chosen, I was ready to tackle the butter and mashing liquid. Up to this point, I had been using a stick of butter and a cup of cream. I had been getting complaints all along that the potatoes tasted a little rich—surprising, since these are the very proportions we have loved for so long in our favorite recipe. Could it be that my cooking method was creating so much rich potato flavor on its own that less butter or cream was now necessary? As it turned out—yes. Just 4 tablespoons of butter yielded the right amount of richness. As for liquid, my potatoes needed less than the full cup of cream. Two-thirds of a cup of cream created the right consistency but still left the potatoes too heavy. In head-to-head tests, my tasters actually preferred whole milk to cream or half-and-half.

I now had a fluffy, smooth mash with robust, earthy potato flavor. And I was able to get it on the table without burning my fingers once on hot skins.

FLUFFY MASHED POTATOES

SERVES 4

This recipe works best with either a metal colander that sits easily in a Dutch oven or a large pasta pot with a steamer insert. To prevent excess evaporation, it is important for the lid to fit as snugly as possible over the colander or steamer. A steamer basket will work, but you will have to transfer the hot potatoes out of the basket to rinse them off halfway through cooking. For the lightest, fluffiest texture, use a ricer. A food mill is the next best alternative. Russets and white potatoes will work in this recipe, but avoid red-skinned potatoes.

- 2 pounds Yukon Gold potatoes (4 to 6 medium), peeled, cut into 1-inch chunks, rinsed well, and drained
- 4 tablespoons unsalted butter, melted
- Table salt
- ⅔ cup whole milk, warm
- Ground black pepper

1. Place metal colander or steamer insert in large pot or Dutch oven. Add enough water for it to barely reach bottom of colander. Turn heat to high and bring water to boil. Add potatoes, cover, and reduce heat to medium-high. Cook potatoes 10 minutes. Transfer colander to sink and rinse potatoes under cold water until no longer hot, 1 to 2 minutes. Return colander and potatoes to pot, cover, and continue to cook until potatoes are soft and tip of paring knife inserted into potato meets no resistance, 10 to 15 minutes longer. Pour off water from Dutch oven.

2. Set ricer or food mill over now-empty pot. Working in batches, transfer potatoes to hopper of ricer or food mill and process, removing any potatoes stuck to bottom. Using rubber spatula, stir in melted butter and ½ teaspoon salt until incorporated. Stir in warm milk until incorporated. Season to taste with salt and pepper; serve immediately.

EQUIPMENT TESTING: Potato Ricers

For silky-smooth mashed potatoes, the best tool is a potato ricer—a device that resembles an oversized garlic press. Cooked spuds are loaded into a hopper and squeezed (or "riced") through a sievelike disk: brilliant, but not complicated. How much difference could there really be from model to model? We pressed our way through seven ricers to find out.

Most models riced potatoes acceptably. Beyond that, testers appreciated large hoppers—both of our recommended models hold at least 1 ¼ cups of sliced potatoes—as well as interchangeable fine and coarse disks; sturdy, ergonomic handles that don't require brute force to squeeze; and a pot extension grip to hold the ricer steady. For complete testing results, go to www.cooksillustrated.com/april.

–Elizabeth Bomze

TOP CHOICE

➢ **R.S.V.P. International Classic Kitchen Basics Potato Ricer ($11.99)** The only plastic model in the mix impressed us with a clamp to hold the ricer disk in place and a masher plate that opened nearly 180 degrees to more easily fill the hopper.

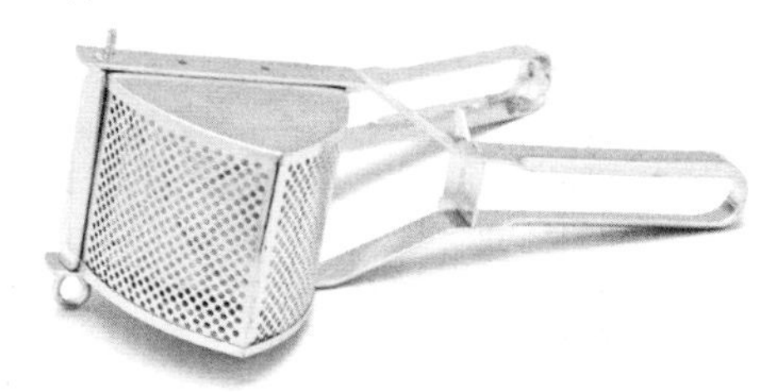

RUNNER UP

➢ **Bethany Housewares Potato Ricer ($16.99)** The hopper of this traditionally designed ricer sported two walls of holes for efficient ricing, but offered no pot grip and was a bit stiff to open.

COOK'S LIVE Original Test Kitchen Videos

www.cooksillustrated.com

HOW TO MAKE

- Fluffy Mashed Potatoes

Hearty Tuscan Bean Stew

In Tuscany, creamy, flavorful beans transform rustic soups and stews into something special. We were determined to avoid tough, exploded beans.

BY CHARLES KELSEY

The people of Tuscany are known as *mangiafagioli*, or "bean eaters," for the prominent role beans play in their cuisine. Cannellini (white kidney beans) are the region's most famous legume, and Tuscan cooks go to great extremes to ensure that these beans are worthy of star status. Simmering the cannellini in rainwater to produce a creamy, almost buttery texture is not uncommon. And putting the beans in an empty wine bottle to slow-cook overnight in a fire's dying embers is not unheard of.

When I set out to make a heartier stew version of the region's classic white bean soup, I wanted my cannellini to be as memorable as any you would find in Tuscany. Collecting rainwater and cooking in my fireplace would be one way to go about it—but I hoped to use a more practical approach.

Chunks of vegetables distinguish our stew from ordinary Tuscan bean soup.

Sorting the Beans

The first task was to sort through all the contradictory advice given for dried-bean cookery. I began with the most hotly contested issue: how long to soak beans before cooking. Some recipes swear that a lengthy soak leads to beans with a more tender, uniform texture. Others insist that a quick soak—an hour-long rest off the stove covered in just-boiled water—is best. In the past, our recipes have maintained that no soak at all can be the way to go.

To judge for myself, I cooked up batches of beans using all three approaches. To my surprise, I found relatively minor differences. The biggest difference was in cooking time: The no-soak beans took 45 minutes longer to soften fully than the other two methods. But I was seeking perfection. And since the beans soaked overnight were, in fact, the most tender and evenly cooked of the bunch and had the least number of exploded beans, that's the method I settled on.

But while the beans' interiors were creamy, their skins remained tough, and overall they were not yet what I imagined a Tuscan cook would be proud to serve. Like length of soaking, when to add salt is another much-debated topic in bean cookery. Was there something to investigate here that could help me cook up perfect beans?

The conventional wisdom is that salt added to beans at the beginning of cooking will prevent them from ever fully softening. Paradoxically, other advice maintains that salting beans too early can create a mushy texture. When I added salt to a batch of beans at the outset of cooking, I found it made some of the beans mealy. I checked with our science editor and learned that the salt effect may be a matter of semantics. As beans cook, their starch granules swell with water, softening to a creamy texture and eventually bursting. The presence of salt in the cooking water causes the starch granules to swell less, so that fewer reach the point of bursting. The result: beans that have a lot of starch granules still intact. To me, the texture of such beans is mealy; others may call the same effect gritty.

Though the texture of the beans was now inferior, their skins were exactly what I wanted: soft and pliable. Was there a different way to use salt to get the same effect? My thoughts turned to brining, which we use in the test kitchen to help meat trap water and remain moist during cooking. Over the years, we've brined everything from poultry and pork to beef and even shrimp. Why not beans? Back in the test kitchen, I made a brine by dissolving a few tablespoons of salt in water and left the beans to soak overnight in the solution. The next day, I rinsed the beans thoroughly before proceeding with the recipe. My experiment was a success: The cannellini now boasted tender, almost imperceptible skins with interiors that were buttery soft. Why the change? When beans are soaked in salted water, rather than being cooked in it, not as much salt enters the beans. Its impact is confined mainly to the skins, where sodium ions interact with the cells to create a softer texture (see "Brining Beans," page 15).

Although tasters were impressed with this technique, I knew that no Tuscan would stand for the number of exploded beans in the pot. Usually, the culprit is an over-vigorous bubbling of cooking liquid, which disturbs the beans and causes them to blow out and disintegrate. I would need to simmer the beans very gently—with no perceptible bubbling and no stirring. Thinking back to the Tuscan technique of cooking beans overnight in a dying fire, I wondered if I might simply try cooking my beans in a 250-degree oven. In my next test, I brought the beans and water to a simmer on the stovetop, then covered the pot and placed it in the oven. This method required a little more time, but it worked beautifully, producing perfectly cooked beans that stayed intact.

Simmer Down

The bubbling action of stew simmered on the stovetop caused our beans to fall apart. Cooking the beans at a near-simmer in a covered pot in a 250-degree oven kept them intact.

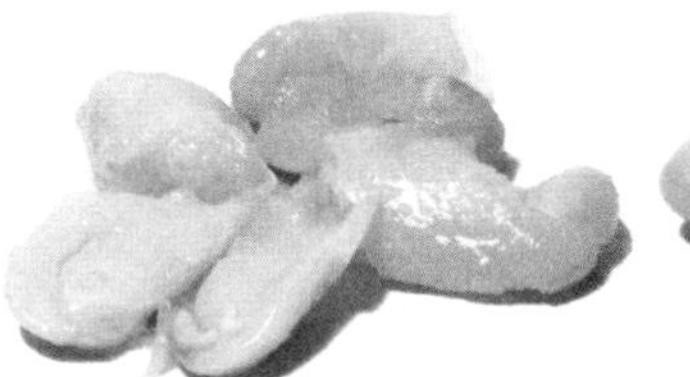

SIMMERED ON STOVETOP

NEAR-SIMMERED IN OVEN

Keys to Tender, Flavorful Beans

1. SALTWATER SOAK
Soaking the beans in salt water overnight helps them cook up creamy, with tender skins.

2. LOW-TEMPERATURE OVEN
Cooking the beans at a near-simmer in a 250-degree oven leads to fewer exploded beans in the finished stew.

3. WAIT TO ADD TOMATOES
The acid in tomatoes can interfere with the beans' tender texture. Add them toward the end of cooking, after the beans have already softened.

Nothing to Stew About

With tender, creamy beans in my pot, it was time to work on the stew's other flavors. Salt-cured Italian bacon, or pancetta, is traditional in Tuscan white bean stew, lending depth and flavor. I still needed a few more ingredients to transform the dish into a one-pot meal. My tasters and I settled on chewy, earthy-tasting kale, another Tuscan favorite, along with canned diced tomatoes, carrots, celery, onion, and lots of garlic. For extra richness, I also replaced some of the water in the stew with chicken broth (low-sodium, of course, to mitigate any impact on the beans).

I sautéed all the vegetables (except the kale and tomatoes) with the pancetta, added the beans and water, and placed the stew in the oven. The acid in tomatoes can toughen beans, so I waited until the beans were sufficiently softened, about 45 minutes, before adding the tomatoes to the pot, along with the kale. The final touch: a sprig of rosemary, steeped in the stew just before serving, which infused the broth with a delicate herbal aroma.

Borrowing from a classic Tuscan dish called ribollita—leftover bean soup thickened with bread—I made my stew even more substantial by serving it atop slabs of toasted country bread. Drizzled with fruity extra-virgin olive oil, the stew was pure comfort food. And I hadn't even needed to collect rainwater or bank a fire to make it.

SCIENCE: Brining Beans

Why does soaking dried beans in salted water make them cook up with softer skins? It has to do with how the sodium ions in salt interact with the cells of the bean skins. As the beans soak, the sodium ions replace some of the calcium and magnesium ions in the skins. Because sodium ions are weaker than mineral ions, they allow more water to penetrate into the skins, leading to a softer texture. During soaking, the sodium ions will only filter partway into the beans, so their greatest effect is on the cells in the outermost part of the beans. –C.K.

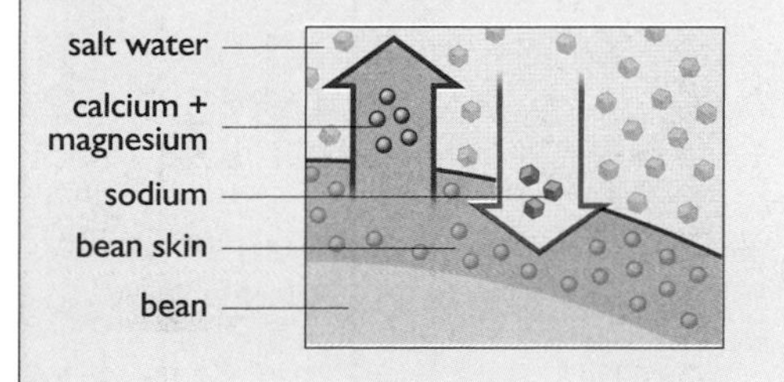

HEARTY TUSCAN BEAN STEW

SERVES 8

We prefer the creamier texture of beans soaked overnight for this recipe. If you're short on time, quick-soak them: Place the rinsed beans in a large heat-resistant bowl. Bring 2 quarts of water and 3 tablespoons of salt to a boil. Pour the water over the beans and let them sit for 1 hour. Drain and rinse the beans well before proceeding with step 2. If pancetta is unavailable, substitute 4 ounces of bacon (about 4 slices). For a more substantial dish, serve the stew over toasted bread. Our recipes for Quick Hearty Tuscan Bean Stew (with canned beans) and Vegetarian Hearty Tuscan Bean Stew are available free at www.cooksillustrated.com/april.

- Table salt
- 1 pound dried cannellini beans (about 2 cups), rinsed and picked over
- 1 tablespoon extra-virgin olive oil, plus extra for drizzling
- 6 ounces pancetta, cut into ¼-inch pieces (see note)
- 1 large onion, chopped medium (about 1½ cups)
- 2 medium celery ribs, cut into ½-inch pieces (about ¾ cup)
- 2 medium carrots, peeled and cut into ½-inch pieces (about 1 cup)
- 8 medium garlic cloves, peeled and crushed
- 4 cups low-sodium chicken broth
- 3 cups water
- 2 bay leaves
- 1 bunch kale or collard greens (about 1 pound), stems trimmed and leaves chopped into 1-inch pieces (about 8 cups loosely packed)
- 1 (14.5-ounce) can diced tomatoes, drained and rinsed
- 1 sprig fresh rosemary
- Ground black pepper
- 8 slices country white bread, each 1¼ inches thick, broiled until golden brown on both sides and rubbed with garlic clove (optional)

1. Dissolve 3 tablespoons salt in 4 quarts cold water in large bowl or container. Add beans and soak at room temperature for at least 8 hours and up to 24 hours. Drain and rinse well.

2. Adjust oven rack to lower-middle position and heat oven to 250 degrees. Heat oil and pancetta in large Dutch oven over medium heat. Cook, stirring occasionally, until pancetta is lightly browned and fat has rendered, 6 to 10 minutes. Add onion, celery, and carrots. Cook, stirring occasionally, until vegetables are softened and lightly browned, 10 to 16 minutes. Stir in garlic and cook until fragrant, about 1 minute. Stir in broth, water, bay leaves, and soaked beans. Increase heat to high and bring to simmer. Cover pot, transfer to oven, and cook until beans are almost tender (very center of beans will still be firm), 45 minutes to 1 hour.

3. Remove pot from oven and stir in greens and tomatoes. Return pot to oven and continue to cook until beans and greens are fully tender, 30 to 40 minutes longer.

4. Remove pot from oven and submerge rosemary sprig in stew. Cover and let stand 15 minutes. Discard bay leaves and rosemary sprig and season stew with salt and pepper to taste. If desired, use back of spoon to press some beans against side of pot to thicken stew. Serve over toasted bread, if desired, and drizzle with olive oil.

HEARTY TUSCAN BEAN STEW WITH SAUSAGE AND CABBAGE

This variation has much more meat and is made with crinkly Savoy cabbage.

Follow recipe for Hearty Tuscan Bean Stew, substituting 1½ pounds sweet Italian sausage, casings removed, for pancetta; ½ medium head Savoy cabbage, cut into 1-inch pieces, for kale; and 1 sprig fresh oregano for rosemary. Cook sausage in oil in step 2, breaking meat into small pieces with wooden spoon until it loses its raw color, about 8 minutes. Transfer sausage to paper towel–lined plate and place in refrigerator. Proceed with recipe as directed, stirring sausage and cabbage into stew along with tomatoes in step 3.

COOK'S LIVE Original Test Kitchen Videos
www.cooksillustrated.com

HOW TO MAKE
- Hearty Tuscan Bean Stew

VIDEO TIP
- How do I chop greens?

Roasting Meat 101

A properly cooked roast is simple and satisfying. It is also a rarity. Here's how to make a great roast every time.

BY KEITH DRESSER

Few cooking methods can beat roasting for ease—the process is largely unattended. And when done right, roasting builds rich, concentrated flavor and yields a tender, juicy texture in meat. But the unfortunate reality is that most roasts are dry, bland, and overcooked. And what works for one cut of meat doesn't necessarily work for another. Years of roasting countless cuts of meat in the test kitchen have taught us the best techniques for producing superior results.

CHOOSING THE RIGHT CUT AND THE RIGHT METHOD

Choosing a roast can be a confusing endeavor, and once you've made a selection it's important to use the right roasting method. We've developed two categories of roasting that work best for different kinds and cuts of meat: fast and high and slow and low. Here is a list of our favorite cuts of beef, pork, and lamb, along with the best way to roast them.

ROASTING METHOD

Fast and High

Though lower oven temperatures generally guarantee more evenly cooked meat, small, narrow roasts like beef tenderloin and rack of lamb depend on a relatively quick cooking time to ensure juicy, tender meat. Roast these cuts at an oven temperature of 450 degrees.

Favorite Cuts:

BEEF

Tenderloin

The most tender cut of beef money can buy, but the flavor is mild.

Top Sirloin Roast

As flavorful and juicy (though not as tender) as a rib roast at a fraction of the cost.

LAMB

Rack of Lamb

The extreme tenderness of this mild-tasting cut commands a high price tag. It usually contains eight or nine ribs, depending on how the meat has been butchered.

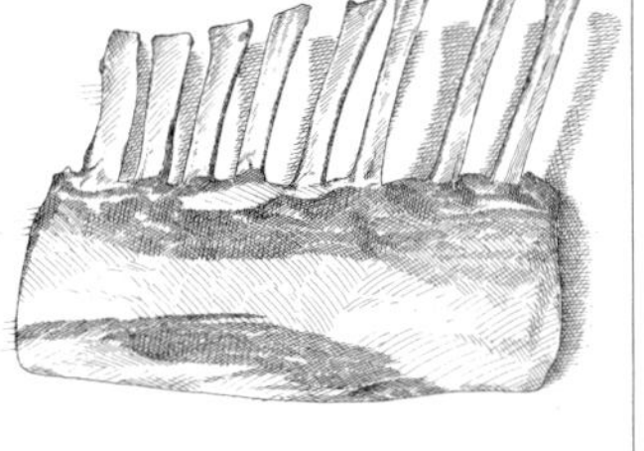

ROASTING METHOD

Slow and Low

Heat takes a long time to penetrate into the center of large cuts of meat such as prime rib, leg of lamb, and rack of pork, making them susceptible to a thick outer swath of gray, overcooked meat. To prevent this problem, roast large cuts slowly at 250 degrees for beef and 325 degrees for pork.

Favorite Cuts:

BEEF

Rib Roast, First Cut

The standard for roast beef. This cut is extremely tender and flavorful, albeit on the expensive side.

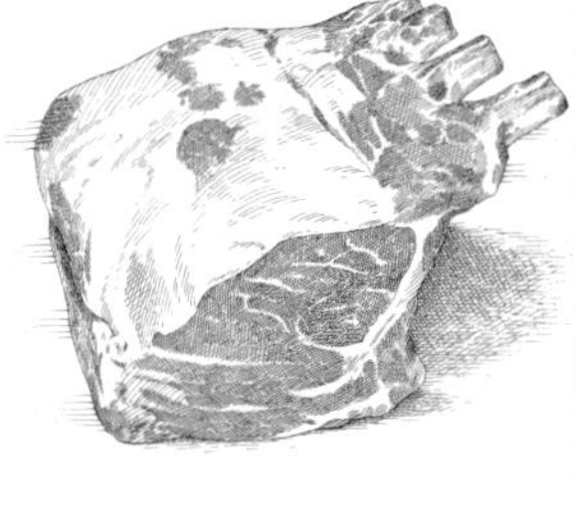

PORK

Boneless Blade Roast

The most flavorful cut from the loin, with a fair amount of fat that allows it to remain juicy when roasted.

Center Rib Roast

Though not as juicy as a blade roast, this lean roast is flavorful and widely available.

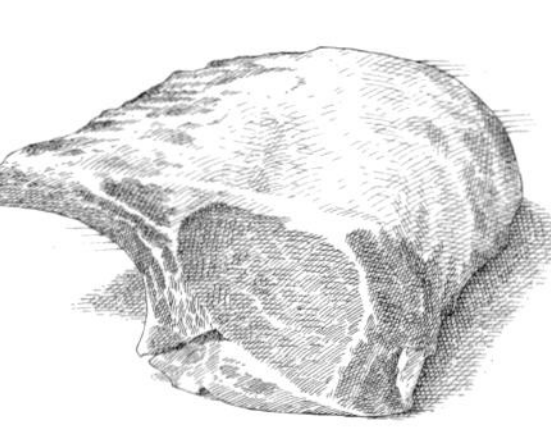

LAMB

Leg of Lamb

This cut is not as tender as the rack, but it boasts fuller flavor. It may be sold with the bones in but is more commonly found butterflied and boneless, making preparation easier.

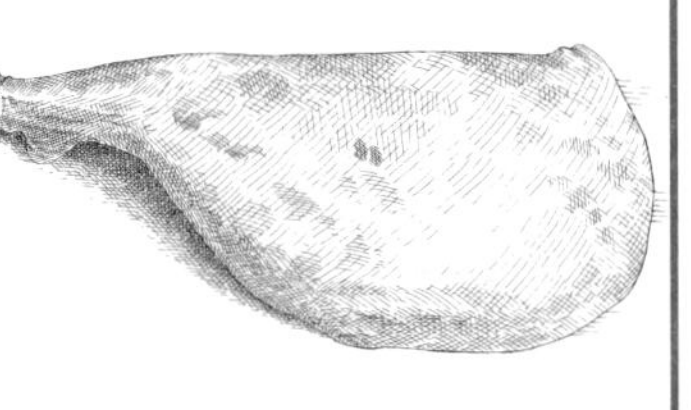

Roasting: Essential Equipment

Although roasting requires very few pieces of equipment, we've learned that these items are essential.

INSTANT-READ THERMOMETER

An instant-read thermometer is by far the best way to gauge when a roast is done. We prefer digital to dial-face models for their speed, accuracy, and ease of reading.

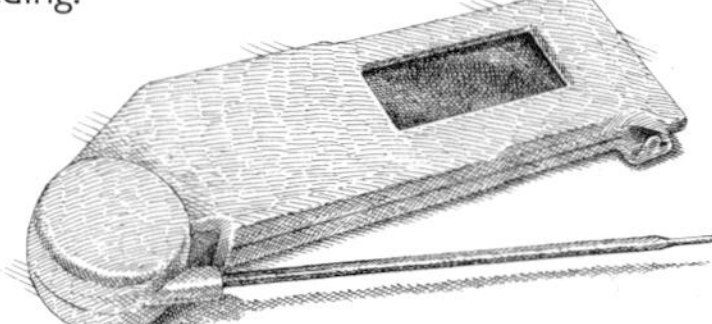

TEST KITCHEN WINNER:

➢ **THERMOWORKS** Super-Fast Thermapen $85

BEST BUY:

➢ **CDN** ProAccurate DTQ450 $17.95

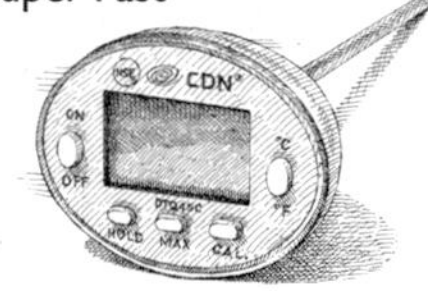

ROASTING PAN

Size and construction are the most important factors to consider when selecting a roasting pan. Because we often sear meat before we roast it, we like a flameproof pan that can be used on the stovetop. We avoid pans with nonstick finishes, because they can't handle high oven temperatures. The perfect pan should accommodate a big holiday turkey with ease, so 15 by 11 inches is our preferred size.

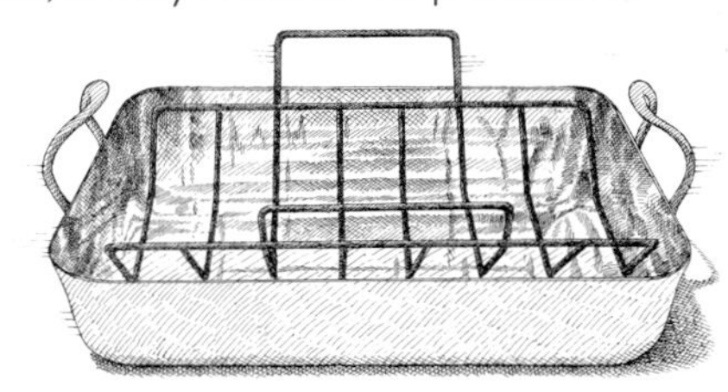

TEST KITCHEN WINNER:

➢ **CALPHALON** Contemporary Roasting Pan $99.99 (comes with roasting rack)

ROASTING RACK

A rack elevates the roast above drippings and grease, preventing the meat's exterior from becoming fatty and soggy. It also allows for rotation of the meat and air circulation around the roast, ensuring even cooking. We prefer a sturdy-handled V-shaped rack that holds a roast snugly in place and can be easily removed from the pan.

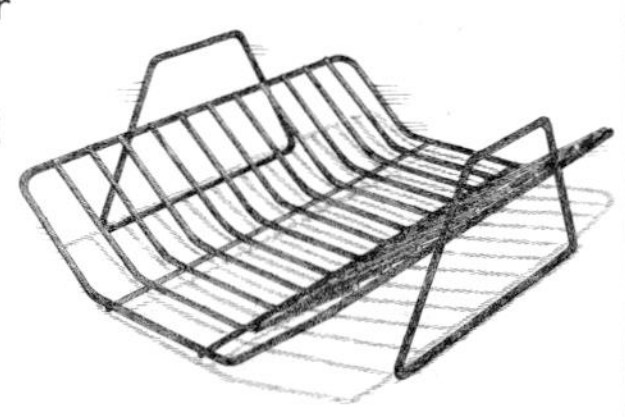

TEST KITCHEN WINNER:

➢ **ALL-CLAD** Non-Stick Roasting Rack $24.95

5 STEPS TO A GREAT ROAST

Beef, pork, and lamb roasts come in a variety of shapes and sizes that can make it challenging to produce well-browned, flavorful, evenly cooked meat. Follow these tips to ensure success.

1. Season and let stand

Sprinkle the exterior of the roast with salt (preferably kosher) and let it stand at room temperature for at least an hour. As the roast sits, the salt draws out its juices, which then combine with the salt before being reabsorbed into the meat. The result: a roast that is flavorful both inside and out.

2. Tie before cooking

Tying a roast forces it into a more even shape, ensuring that the thin, narrow ends won't overcook before the thick middle part is done. Tying also makes for a nicer presentation and easier slicing.

3. Sear before roasting

Browning meat produces new flavor compounds that are essential to the success of a roast. But blasting the oven temperature to accomplish this can dry out the meat's exterior and doesn't uniformly brown the entire roast. To guarantee a well-caramelized crust, sear the roast in 1–2 tablespoons of oil for two to three minutes per side, either in the roasting pan or a skillet, before putting it into the oven.

4. Choose appropriate roasting method

Most recipes call for cooking roasts in a moderately hot (350- to 400-degree) oven, but this method can lead to an overcooked exterior and unevenly cooked interior. Depending on the meat's size and shape, we prefer to roast at temperatures as high as 450 degrees or as low as 250 degrees. (See "Choosing the Right Cut and the Right Method," left.)

5. Let meat rest

All roasts should rest under a foil tent for 10 to 20 minutes before being carved. As the protein molecules in the meat cool, they will reabsorb any accumulated juices and redistribute them throughout the roast.

When Is It Done?

A thermometer takes the guesswork out of knowing when a roast is done. To ensure that the probe stays in the roast, insert the thermometer at an angle. To get an accurate reading, push the probe deep into the roast and then slowly draw it out until you locate the center of the meat (indicated by the lowest temperature). Avoid bones and pan surfaces. And take more than one reading.

The ideal serving temperatures for optimal flavor and juiciness are listed below. If food safety is your primary concern, cook all meat until well-done. Note: The meat should come off the heat 5 to 10 degrees below the desired final temperature, as the internal temperature will continue to rise as the meat rests.

TEMPERATURE

TYPE OF MEAT	RARE	MEDIUM-RARE	MEDIUM	WELL-DONE
Beef	125	130	140	160
Lamb	125	130	140	160
Pork	*	*	150	160

* Not recommended

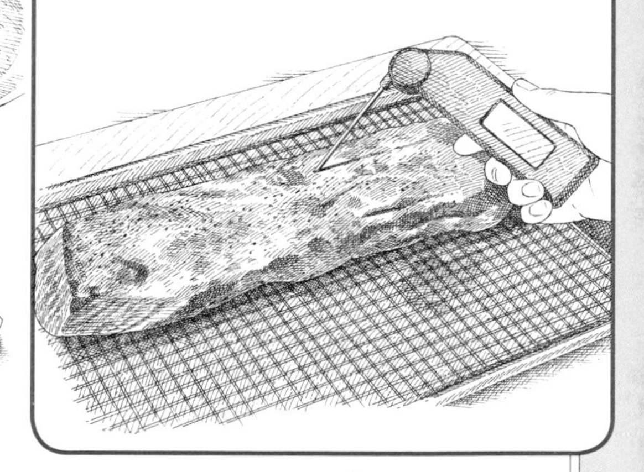

Outdoor Roasting on the Grill

The oven isn't your only option for roasting meat. For tender cuts that don't require slow cooking over low heat, such as beef tenderloin, the grill works just as well. Grill-roasting relies on indirect heat between 300 and 400 degrees (in contrast to true grilling, which occurs at temperatures in excess of 500 degrees). Coals are banked on one side of the grill, and meat roasts on the "cool" side, with the lid kept down to trap heat and create an environment much like the oven. With a gas grill, the primary burner is kept on and the others are turned off.

SECRETS TO SUCCESS

1. Season, let meat stand 1 hour, and tie before grill-roasting
(see steps 1 and 2 in "5 Steps to a Great Roast," above). For lean cuts of pork, skip the salt and brine the meat before placing it on the grill.

2. Use wood chunks or chips to enhance smoky flavor
While charcoal will impart some flavor to the meat, wood chunks or chips are necessary to achieve true smokiness (especially with a gas grill). Place soaked, drained chunks directly on charcoal; wrap wood chips in a foil packet poked with holes (or place in a foil tray for a gas grill). To keep the fire burning as long as possible, we also prefer to use briquettes rather than hardwood charcoal.

3. Bank coals on one side of grill
Many recipes recommend banking coals on both sides of the grill. We find the edges of large roasts can burn with this method. We prefer to transfer all coals to one side of the grill, leaving half of the grill free of coals so meat can cook without danger of burning. To ensure even cooking, it is a good idea to rotate the meat halfway through cooking.

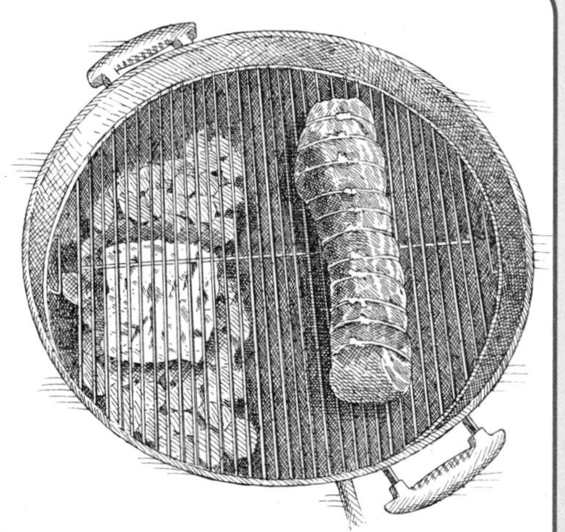

4. Use vents to regulate heat
To help regulate heat, adjust vents on both the lid and grill bottom. We prefer to close vents partially to keep the coals from burning up too fast and to help the grill retain heat.

Chicken Saltimbocca Done Right

Adaptations of this Italian classic smother it in breading, stuffing, and cheese. We wanted a dish that would give the chicken, prosciutto, and sage their proper due.

BY DAVID PAZMIÑO

I can never find enough quick and easy chicken dishes for my weeknight repertoire. So when I came across a new chicken spin on an old Italian classic—veal saltimbocca—I was immediately intrigued. The traditional version has long been a standard menu item in the trattorias of Italy as well as Italian restaurants in this country. Made by sautéing veal cutlets with prosciutto and sage, this simple yet elegant dish promises, literally, to "jump in your mouth" with its distinctive blend of flavors.

But as happens all too often when cooks start to meddle with a perfectly good thing, most chicken adaptations I found took the dish too far from its roots, wrapping the cutlet around stuffing or adding unnecessary breading or cheese. Others fiddled with the proportions, allowing a thick slab of prosciutto to share equal billing with the chicken and knock the balance of flavors out of whack. Perfecting chicken saltimbocca, then, would be a matter of avoiding the temptation to overcomplicate the dish with extraneous ingredients and figuring out how to give each of the three key elements—chicken, prosciutto, and sage—its due.

Fried sage leaves make an elegant (but optional) garnish.

Flour Power

Though we generally prefer to make our own cutlets to ensure that pieces are of uniform size and shape, I decided to forgo butchering and buy commercially prepared cutlets to keep the process as streamlined as possible. I opted for mass-produced supermarket cutlets and trimmed their edges to remove any thin, tattered pieces.

Most of the simpler chicken saltimbocca recipes I came across followed the traditional practice of threading a toothpick through the prosciutto and a whole sage leaf to attach them to the cutlet, then dredging the entire package in flour before sautéing it on both sides. I found this method to be problematic. Flour got trapped in the small gaps where the ham bunched up around the toothpick, leaving sticky, uncooked spots. I wondered if I could skip the flouring and sauté the chicken and prosciutto without any coating. This worked fine for the ham, which crisped nicely without help from the flour. The chicken, on the other hand, browned unevenly and tended to stick to the pan. Surprisingly, flouring only the cutlet—before attaching the ham—proved to be the solution. And by sautéing the cutlet prosciutto-side down first, I was able to keep the flour under the prosciutto from turning gummy.

Balancing Act: Green Sage and Ham

With my flouring method under control, it was time to turn my attention to proportions. While we liked high-end prosciutto for the rich flavor it added to the overall dish (see "Can Any Prosciutto Be Worth $60 per Pound?" on page 19), if the slice was too thick, the taste overwhelmed everything else and the ham had trouble staying put. If the slice was ultrathin, however, it fell apart too easily. The ideal slice was just thick enough to hold its shape—about the thickness of two or three sheets of paper. Though some recipes folded the slice to make it fit on the cutlet, this resulted in ham that was only partially crisped and overpowered the chicken with its flavor. I found trimming the ham to fit the cutlet in a single layer worked best on all counts.

While the prosciutto needed to be tamed, the sage flavor needed a boost. In the traditional dish, each cutlet features a single sage leaf (fried in oil before being attached), so that the herbal flavor imparted is very subtle. Perhaps the sage of yore boasted far bigger leaves than are grown today, but this was one aspect of the original that I found lacking. Tethering additional leaves to the cutlet with the toothpick, however, was cumbersome and still resulted in adding flavor only to bites that actually contained sage.

I wanted a more even distribution of herbal flavor. Would infusing the cooking oil with sage be a way to diffuse—and heighten—its flavor? I tossed a handful of leaves into the cooking oil before sautéing the cutlets, removing the herbs before they burned. Tasters, however, detected only a

RECIPE TESTING: Saltimbocca Gone Wrong

As we discovered, many saltimbocca recipes add extraneous elements when switching from veal to chicken, ruining the simplicity of the dish.

CHOCK TOO FULL
Stuffing the cutlet with extra ingredients, such as spinach, dilutes the impact of the other flavors.

BREADED AND BLAND
Breading requires additional prep time and means that the flavorful pan sauce is out.

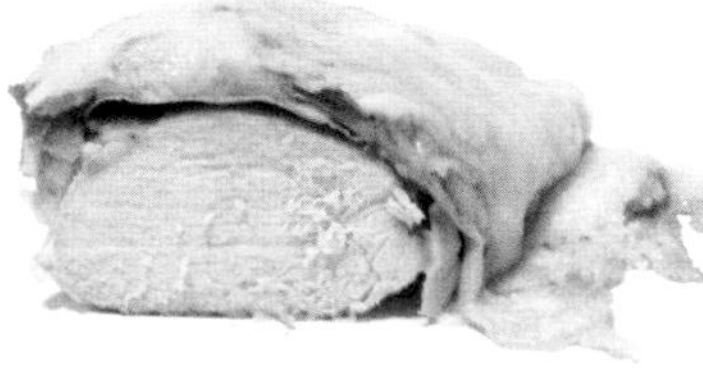

CHEESY AND GREASY
Cheese adds unnecessary richness that masks the more subtle flavors of sage and wine.

COOK'S LIVE Original Test Kitchen Videos
www.cooksillustrated.com

HOW TO MAKE
- Chicken Saltimbocca

VIDEO TIP
- How do I cut chicken breasts into cutlets?

very slight flavor boost in the finished dish. The way to more intense and evenly distributed sage flavor turned out to be as simple as chopping the leaves and sprinkling them over the floured cutlet before adding the ham. The only thing missing was the pretty look of the whole sage leaf. While not necessary, frying extra sage leaves to place on the cooked cutlets is an elegant finishing touch.

Skip the Pick

The only aspect of the dish I had not yet examined was the toothpick. After skewering prosciutto to 150 cutlets in the course of my testing, I decided enough was enough. What would happen if I just omitted the toothpick? After flouring the cutlet, sprinkling it with sage, and placing the prosciutto on top, I carefully lifted the bundle and placed it as I had been doing, prosciutto-side down, in the hot oil. Once the edges of the chicken on the bottom had browned, I flipped the cutlet, revealing ham that seemed almost hermetically sealed to the chicken.

A quick pan sauce made from vermouth, lemon juice, butter, and parsley was all I needed to accentuate the perfect balance of flavors. I now had a quick Italian food fix with all the jumping in my mouth, not the kitchen.

STEP-BY-STEP | SALTIMBOCCA MADE SIMPLE

1. FLOUR CHICKEN ONLY No need to flour the prosciutto before sautéing, just the chicken.

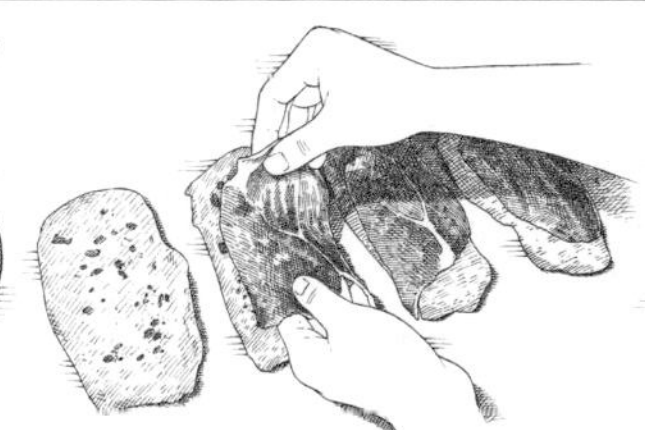

2. SPREAD SAGE FLAVOR Sprinkling the cutlets with sage and topping with prosciutto distributes flavor evenly.

3. FORGET THE TOOTHPICK Searing the cutlets prosciutto-side down first helps the ham stick.

4. MAKE SAUCE Stir the vermouth into the pan, reduce, and finish with butter. Spoon over cutlets.

CHICKEN SALTIMBOCCA

SERVES 4

Buy cutlets that are approximately 5 to 6 inches long. If the tip is too thin, trim back 1 to 2 inches to make the cutlet of uniform thickness. If cutlets are unavailable, you can make your own with four (8-ounce) boneless, skinless chicken breasts (see "Cutting Your Own Cutlets," page 31). Although whole sage leaves make a beautiful presentation, they are optional and can be left out of step 3. Make sure to buy prosciutto that is thinly sliced, not shaved; also avoid slices that are too thick, as they won't stick to the chicken.

- ½ cup unbleached all-purpose flour
- Ground black pepper
- 8 thin boneless, skinless chicken breast cutlets (about 2 pounds), trimmed of ragged edges as necessary (see note)
- 1 tablespoon minced fresh sage leaves, plus 8 large leaves (optional)
- 8 thin slices prosciutto, cut into 5- to 6-inch-long pieces to match chicken (about 3 ounces)
- 4 tablespoons olive oil
- 1¼ cups dry vermouth or white wine
- 2 teaspoons juice from 1 lemon
- 4 tablespoons unsalted butter, cut into 4 pieces and chilled
- 1 tablespoon minced fresh parsley leaves
- Table salt

1. Adjust oven rack to middle position and heat oven to 200 degrees. Combine flour and 1 teaspoon pepper in shallow dish.

2. Pat cutlets dry with paper towels. Dredge chicken in flour, shaking off any excess. Lay cutlets flat and sprinkle evenly with minced sage. Place 1 prosciutto slice on top of each cutlet, pressing lightly to adhere; set aside.

3. Heat 2 tablespoons oil in 12-inch skillet over medium-high heat until beginning to shimmer. Add sage leaves (if using) and cook until leaves begin to change color and are fragrant, about 15 to 20 seconds. Using slotted spoon, remove sage to paper towel–lined plate; reserve. Add half of cutlets to pan, prosciutto-side down, and cook until light golden brown, 2 to 3 minutes. Flip and cook on other side until light golden brown, about 2 minutes more. Transfer to wire rack set on rimmed baking sheet and keep warm in oven. Repeat with remaining 2 tablespoons oil and cutlets, then transfer to oven to keep warm while preparing sauce.

4. Pour off excess fat from skillet. Stir in vermouth, scraping up any browned bits, and simmer until reduced to about ⅓ cup, 5 to 7 minutes. Stir in lemon juice. Turn heat to low and whisk in butter, 1 tablespoon at a time. Off heat, stir in parsley and season with salt and pepper. Remove chicken from oven and place on platter. Spoon sauce over cutlets before serving.

TASTING: Can Any Prosciutto Be Worth $60 per Pound?

Americans have long looked to Italy for the best prosciutto. After all, Italy invented the method used to produce this salt-cured and air-dried ham. So when we heard about a new prosciutto on the market crafted not in Italy but in Iowa—and commanding three times the price of the imports—we were more than curious.

Tasted side-by-side with prosciutto di Parma and prosciutto San Daniele, both of which are crafted under the strict specifications of two Protected Designations of Origin (PDO), the newcomer from Iowa, La Quercia Prosciutto Americana, was the hands-down winner. But at $69 for 18 ounces, we'll stick with classic prosciutto di Parma for all but the most special of occasions. The other domestic brands we tasted simply aren't worth buying.

–Elizabeth Bomze

TOO GOOD FOR COOKING

➢ **La Quercia Prosciutto Americana (USA)**
Price: $69 for six 3-oz. packages, including shipping
Comments: Tasters marveled at the "deep," "earthy" flavor, "creamy" texture, and "melt-in-your-mouth," "porky yumminess" of this premium-priced prosciutto produced on a relatively small scale in Iowa.

BEST BUY

➢ **Prosciutto di Parma (Italy)**
Price: $18.99/lb.
Comments: This "lovely," "meaty and rich" Italian staple garnered much praise. Its "nutty undertones" come from the whey of the Parmiggiano-Reggiano cheese that producers add to their pigs' diet.

MILD-MANNERED IMPORT

➢ **Prosciutto San Daniele (Italy)**
Price: $14.98/lb.
Comments: "Sweeter" and more "mellow" than the Parma pig, this ham with "good, clean flavor" was the favorite among tasters who preferred a slightly milder sample.

EXPENSIVE DISAPPOINTMENT

➢ **Citterio Fresco Prosciutto (USA)**
Price: $5.99 for a 4-oz. package
Comments: Many thought this mass-produced, prepacked American product looked like "plastic prosciutto," while others noted a "silky" texture.

JUST AWFUL

➢ **Generic Domestic Prosciutto (USA)**
Price: $9.99/lb.
Comments: "Baloney," wrote one taster in reference to this ham's claim to be prosciutto. Some noted a resemblance to "bad pastrami." Others found it just plain "horrible."

Roasted Vegetable Salads

Roasting can give new life to tired produce. It can also make for limp, soggy salad.

⋟ BY REBECCA HAYS ⋞

Fresh-from-the-farm produce needs little adulteration—a quick steam or sauté and a drizzle of extra-virgin olive oil will suffice. But the reality is that most of us have to make do with ordinary supermarket vegetables, especially at this time of year.

The good news is that roasting can transform tired produce through the development of hundreds of new flavor compounds. But while roasting is straightforward for individual vegetables, roasting a few veggies together, as I wanted to do for a light side salad, can be tricky. To begin, I sketched out some combinations, taking color, flavor, and texture into account. I took advantage of the test kitchen's experience to determine the best approach to roasting. First I tossed my selections with a little olive oil and seasoned them with salt and pepper, plus a pinch of sugar to aid in caramelization. To guarantee maximum browning—a crucial requirement—I placed them on a baking sheet I had heated in a 500-degree oven. By the time I put the sheet back into the oven, the vegetables were sizzling.

Twenty-five minutes later, the results were in. I quickly eliminated porous vegetables like eggplant and zucchini from the lineup, because they were simply too limp and soggy to even consider tossing with dressing for a salad. Winning combos were beets and carrots, cremini mushrooms and fennel, and potatoes and green beans. These particular pairings maintained their structure after roasting and, thanks to the care I had taken to cut them into same-sized pieces, they cooked to a similarly firm yet tender consistency.

Now to figure out the dressing. Using just a tablespoon of oil kept the salads from being greasy, and a similarly light hand with the vinegar (or lemon juice) let the sweetness of the vegetables dominate. Tossing the vegetables with the vinaigrette while they were still hot allowed them to better absorb its flavors.

To make roasted vegetables a proper salad, I went back to the produce aisle for inspiration and decided that something crisp and raw was the missing link. Added to the cooled roasted vegetables, slightly bitter radicchio, spicy radishes, and peppery watercress each contributed the freshness and vibrancy that every self-respecting salad needs.

ROASTED GREEN BEAN AND POTATO SALAD WITH RADICCHIO

SERVES 4

For this recipe and those that follow, if using a dark-colored nonstick baking sheet, line the pan with aluminum foil to prevent scorching.

- 1 pound green beans, trimmed and cut into 1½-inch pieces
- 1 pound Red Bliss potatoes, scrubbed and cut into ½-inch pieces
- 3 tablespoons extra-virgin olive oil
- Table salt and ground black pepper
- ¼ teaspoon sugar
- 2 tablespoons red wine vinegar
- 1 small garlic clove, minced or pressed through garlic press (about ½ teaspoon)
- 1 small head radicchio (about 6 ounces), washed and cut into 2-inch by ¼-inch slices (about 4 cups)

1. Adjust oven rack to lowest position, place large rimmed baking sheet on rack, and heat oven to 500 degrees. Toss beans and potatoes with 2 tablespoons oil, ½ teaspoon salt, ¼ teaspoon pepper, and sugar in large bowl. Remove baking sheet from oven and, working quickly, carefully transfer beans and potatoes to sheet and spread in even layer. (Do not wash bowl.) Roast until vegetables are tender and well-browned on one side, 20 to 25 minutes (do not stir during roasting).

2. Meanwhile, whisk remaining tablespoon oil, vinegar, garlic, ¼ teaspoon salt, and ⅛ teaspoon pepper in now-empty bowl.

3. Toss hot vegetables with vinaigrette and cool to room temperature, about 30 minutes. Stir in radicchio, transfer to serving platter, and serve.

ROASTED BEET AND CARROT SALAD WITH WATERCRESS

SERVES 4

- 1 pound beets, peeled and cut into ½-inch-thick wedges, wedges cut in half crosswise if beets are large
- 1 pound carrots, peeled and cut on bias into ¼-inch-thick slices
- 3 tablespoons extra-virgin olive oil
- Table salt and ground black pepper
- ¼ teaspoon sugar
- 2 tablespoons white wine vinegar
- 1 teaspoon honey
- 1 medium shallot, minced (about 3 tablespoons)
- 6 ounces watercress, washed and trimmed (about 4 cups)

1. Adjust oven rack to lowest position, place large rimmed baking sheet on rack, and heat oven to 500 degrees. Toss beets and carrots with 2 tablespoons oil, ½ teaspoon salt, ¼ teaspoon pepper, and sugar in large bowl. Remove baking sheet from oven and, working quickly, carefully transfer beets and carrots to sheet and spread in even layer. (Do not wash bowl.) Roast until vegetables are tender and well-browned on one side, 20 to 25 minutes (do not stir during roasting).

2. Meanwhile, whisk remaining tablespoon oil, vinegar, honey, shallots, ¼ teaspoon salt, and ⅛ teaspoon pepper in now-empty bowl.

3. Toss hot vegetables with vinaigrette and cool to room temperature, about 30 minutes. Stir in watercress, transfer to serving platter, and serve.

ROASTED FENNEL AND MUSHROOM SALAD WITH RADISHES

SERVES 4

If fennel fronds (the delicate greenery attached to the fennel stems) are unavailable, substitute 1 to 2 tablespoons chopped fresh tarragon leaves.

- 2 medium bulbs fennel (about 1½ pounds), bulbs quartered, cored, and cut crosswise into ½-inch-thick slices; ⅓ cup fronds reserved and chopped (see note)
- 20 ounces cremini mushrooms, trimmed, cleaned, and cut into quarters if large or halved if medium
- 3 tablespoons extra-virgin olive oil
- Table salt and ground black pepper
- ¼ teaspoon sugar
- 2 tablespoons juice from 1 lemon
- 1 teaspoon Dijon mustard
- 4–6 radishes, cut in half and sliced thin (about ¾ cup)

1. Adjust oven rack to lowest position, place large rimmed baking sheet on rack, and heat oven to 500 degrees. Toss fennel and mushrooms with 2 tablespoons oil, ½ teaspoon salt, ¼ teaspoon pepper, and sugar in large bowl. Remove baking sheet from oven and, working quickly, carefully transfer fennel and mushrooms to sheet and spread in even layer. (Do not wash bowl.) Roast until vegetables are tender and well-browned on one side, 20 to 25 minutes (do not stir during roasting).

2. Meanwhile, whisk remaining tablespoon oil, lemon juice, mustard, ¼ teaspoon salt, and ⅛ teaspoon pepper in now-empty bowl.

3. Toss hot vegetables with vinaigrette and cool to room temperature, about 30 minutes. Stir in radishes and reserved fennel fronds, transfer to serving platter, and serve.

Fluffy Yellow Layer Cake

Box mixes are famous for engineering cake with ultralight texture. We set out to make an even fluffier cake—without the chemicals and additives.

BY YVONNE RUPERTI

When the first Betty Crocker boxed cake mix hit store shelves shortly after World War II, it introduced Americans to a convenience food many have never lost their taste for. It also introduced the country to a whole new kind of cake—one so light, soft, and moist that it practically melted on the tongue. As a kid, I could never get enough of this chemically engineered confection, so different was it from the dense and crumbly cakes my mother baked from scratch. Eventually, of course, I came to my senses and could no longer tolerate the box cake's cloying artificial flavors. But one thing I've never gotten over is its supreme fluffiness. I wondered: Without the help of mono- and diglycerides, cellulose gum, and other additives, was it possible to create a yellow layer cake with the same ethereal texture but also the great flavor of natural ingredients?

Our cake's fresh, buttery goodness could never have come from a box.

To answer that question, I began by researching recipes for basic yellow butter cake, the prototype after which the box-mix yellow version is modeled. Very quickly, I made a surprising discovery: Yellow cake with the kind of soft and fluffy texture I was looking for doesn't actually exist. Of the half-dozen yellow or gold layer cakes I tested, not one had the supermoist lightness I wanted. The best of the bunch, our Rich and Tender Yellow Cake (March/April 1999), while definitely worthy of its name, was still more dense—and rich—than the box-mix version.

Mixing Up the Method

It was time to step back and really think about the mechanics of cake making. I knew that along with the ingredients, mixing methods play a major role in cake volume and texture. To achieve their relative lightness and tenderness, the yellow butter cakes I tested relied on one of two methods: conventional creaming and reverse creaming (also known as the two-stage method). With conventional creaming, butter and sugar are whipped together before any other ingredients are added, creating lots of air bubbles that produce lightness and volume in the cake. Reverse creaming, used in our Rich and Tender Yellow Cake, has a different impact on texture: Soft butter is blended with the flour (and other dry ingredients) to coat the flour proteins with fat and prevent them from forming tough gluten, leading to a more tender cake.

What if I widened my net beyond yellow cake and tested a chiffon cake, which uses a large quantity of whipped egg whites, instead of a creaming method, to get its mile-high volume and feathery texture? First, the batter is made as if for pancakes, with the dry ingredients (flour, sugar, leavener) dumped into a bowl with the liquid ingredients (yolks, water, oil). The egg whites are then aerated through vigorous whipping and folded into the batter, creating height and super fluffiness. The test kitchen's chiffon cake is especially weightless, springy, and moist. Unfortunately, with its five whipped egg whites (in addition to two whole eggs), the cake had too much of a good thing—it was too ethereal and light. It would never be a proper substitute for a layer cake that could stand up to a serious slathering of frosting.

Besides employing a different mixing method, butter cakes differ from chiffon cakes by using butter as their fat, fewer eggs (usually three or four, left whole), a greater proportion of flour, and a liquid, usually some type of dairy. On a whim, I decided to see what would happen if I took these butter-cake ingredients and combined them using a chiffon-cake technique: I would separate my eggs; mix the rest of my ingredients together, except the whites; and then whip the whites and fold them in at the end. The only other change: Since I needed a liquid fat, I would use melted butter instead of solid. This mixing of chiffon-cake method and butter-cake ingredients worked beautifully. After adding extra egg yolks to enrich the crumb, I had a light, porous cake that still had enough heft to hold a frosting.

Maximizing Moisture

While my cake now had the fluffiness I was after, it still didn't have the moistness I wanted. I knew that oil, even more than butter, can be a key factor in the moisture level of a cake. (Butter contains about 20 percent water, which can evaporate in the oven and leave a cake dry.) Could I use a combination of both types of fat? After testing different proportions of each, I found that 10 tablespoons of butter plus 3 tablespoons of oil kept my butter flavor intact and improved the moistness of the cake. But could I get it even more soft and tender?

Adding more sugar was my first thought. Sugar is well known for increasing tenderness in cakes by attracting and bonding with water, thus preventing the water from hydrating the proteins in the flour. With less liquid available to them, fewer proteins can link together, resulting in weaker gluten. I found that an additional ½ cup of sugar did the trick. My cake was very moist and now had nice

Turning Up the Volume

HIGH
The chief hallmark of a box-mix cake is a feather-light (and chemical-laden) crumb.

HIGHER
Our Fluffy Yellow Layer Cake has an even more ethereal texture—plus it tastes good, too.

PHOTOGRAPHY: CARL TREMBLAY

caramelization on its sides and bottom. Tasters also liked its sweeter flavor.

Up to now I had been using milk in my working recipe, but yellow-cake recipes often call for buttermilk, sour cream, or yogurt. In the end, buttermilk was tasters' clear favorite, producing a crumb that was slightly porous and so fine it was almost downy. The buttermilk's tang also brought a new flavor dimension to my cake—an added bonus. With acidic buttermilk in my recipe, I needed to replace some of the baking powder with a little baking soda to ensure an even rise.

A slight tweaking of the salt and vanilla was all that was needed to finish the recipe. I now had a cake that was so moist and fluffy that I could almost patent it. Of course, there would be no way to patent its fresh, all-natural taste.

FLUFFY YELLOW LAYER CAKE

MAKES TWO 9-INCH CAKE LAYERS

Nonstick cooking spray can be used for greasing the pans (proceed with flouring as directed). Bring all ingredients to room temperature before beginning. Frost the cake with our Foolproof Chocolate Frosting (page 23) or your favorite topping.

- 2½ cups (10 ounces) cake flour, plus extra for dusting pans
- 1¼ teaspoons baking powder
- ¼ teaspoon baking soda
- ¾ teaspoon table salt
- 1¾ cups (12¼ ounces) sugar
- 10 tablespoons (1¼ sticks) unsalted butter, melted and cooled slightly
- 1 cup buttermilk, room temperature
- 3 tablespoons vegetable oil
- 2 teaspoons vanilla extract
- 6 large egg yolks plus 3 large egg whites, room temperature

1. Adjust oven rack to middle position and heat oven to 350 degrees. Grease two 9-inch-wide by 2-inch-high round cake pans and line bottoms with parchment paper. Grease paper rounds, dust pans with flour, and knock out excess. Whisk flour, baking powder, baking soda, salt, and 1½ cups sugar together in large bowl. In 4-cup liquid measuring cup or medium bowl, whisk together melted butter, buttermilk, oil, vanilla, and yolks.

2. In clean bowl of stand mixer fitted with whisk attachment, beat egg whites at medium-high speed until foamy, about 30 seconds. With machine running, gradually add remaining ¼ cup sugar; continue to beat until stiff peaks just form, 30 to 60 seconds (whites should hold peak but mixture should appear moist). Transfer to bowl and set aside.

3. Add flour mixture to now-empty mixing bowl fitted with whisk attachment. With mixer running at low speed, gradually pour in butter mixture and mix until almost incorporated (a few streaks of dry flour will remain), about 15 seconds. Stop mixer and scrape whisk and sides of bowl. Return mixer to medium-low speed and beat until smooth and fully incorporated, 10 to 15 seconds.

4. Using rubber spatula, stir ⅓ of whites into batter to lighten, then add remaining whites and gently fold into batter until no white streaks remain. Divide batter evenly between prepared cake pans. Lightly tap pans against counter 2 or 3 times to dislodge any large air bubbles.

5. Bake until cake layers begin to pull away from sides of pans and toothpick inserted into center comes out clean, 20 to 22 minutes. Cool cakes in pans on wire rack for 10 minutes. Loosen cakes from sides of pans with small knife, then invert onto greased wire rack and peel off parchment. Invert cakes again and cool completely on rack, about 1½ hours.

COOK'S LIVE Original Test Kitchen Videos

www.cooksillustrated.com

HOW TO MAKE
- Fluffy Yellow Layer Cake

VIDEO TIPS
- Should I use a stand or hand-held mixer?
- Buying Guide: Stand Mixers

The Miracle of Yellow Cake Mix

CHEMICAL WONDER

Cake mixes contain all the same ingredients as a from-scratch cake, plus a whole lot of additives that help ensure that each cake is a replica of the one that came before it, with the same look, taste, and texture. Chief among them are a slew of chemically engineered emulsifiers and leavening agents that work in tandem to guarantee a mix that is virtually foolproof—no matter if the cook overbeats, adds too much or too little water, or pours the batter into the wrong-sized pan.

Emulsifiers like mono- and diglycerides help incorporate more air into the batter than do the eggs that are the sole emulsifiers in homemade cakes, as well as holding all the ingredients together. The emulsifiers also work to improve the effectiveness of the leaveners (baking soda or powder along with monocalcium and dicalcium phosphates) by helping the batter hold more of the gas these agents produce, which in turn ensures greater volume and lightness in the cake. Beyond these additives, cake mix contains hydrogenated fats and artificial food coloring—the latter imparting a deep golden hue that hasn't been common in all-natural yellow cake since mass-produced eggs with uniformly pale yolks began dominating supermarket shelves decades ago.

We'll stick with the fresh, honest flavors of an all-natural cake. –Y.R.

EQUIPMENT TESTING:

Stand Mixers

The KitchenAid Professional 600 ($399.95), earned its spot on the test kitchen counter in 2005 for mastering tasks that ranged from churning cookie dough and kneading bread and pizza dough to whipping air into heavy cream and egg whites. We wondered how three newer models would compare. The West Bend 12-Speed Stand Mixer ($99.99) was disqualified during round one (kneading bread dough) when its dough hook caused the machine to shudder so fiercely it almost fell off the counter. Brawnier rivals—the Cuisinart 5.5 Quart Stand Mixer ($349) and the Wolfgang Puck Bistro Stand Mixer ($249.90)—whisked their way through all manner of tasks (though the Wolfgang Puck machine tended to tremble while kneading). Both models sport an ingenious disk that caps their nonstick dough hook and prevented pizza dough from riding up and sticking, as it did in the KitchenAid. Add that to Cuisinart's handful of modern perks and it's clear why this mixer has overthrown KitchenAid for a place on our countertop. For complete testing results, go to www.cooksillustrated.com/april.

–Elizabeth Bomze

TEST KITCHEN FAVORITE
★ NEW WINNER ★

Cuisinart 5.5 Quart Stand Mixer
Price: $349
Comments: Besides acing its way through tasks like kneading bread and pizza dough and churning cookie dough full of nuts and dried fruit, this machine offers a host of modern updates including a digital timer with automatic shutoff and a splashguard attachment with a built-in feed tube.

RECOMMENDED

KitchenAid Professional 600 Stand Mixer
Price: $399.95
Comments: Still a true kitchen workhorse, this cookware standard is strong enough for the thickest cookie dough and the tackiest bread dough.

RECOMMENDED WITH RESERVATIONS

Wolfgang Puck Bistro Stand Mixer

Price: $249.90
Comments: It whipped stiff peaks into cream in no time and breezed through chunky cookie dough but rattled on heavier, yeasted bread dough. The suction counter-grips were too strong at first, then weakened too much after one day of use.

Foolproof Chocolate Frosting

We wanted a frosting that wouldn't curdle or deflate—or take an hour to set.

BY YVONNE RUPERTI

In the world of chocolate frosting, rich, dense ganaches and billowy buttercreams are the archetypes you turn to when you want to impress. But they're also the frostings you steer clear of when you're looking for something fast and foolproof. Ganache involves whisking hot cream into chopped chocolate and waiting at least an hour for the warm mixture to set. Traditional buttercream requires you to stand over a pot of boiling sugar syrup with a candy thermometer, keeping your fingers crossed that things will go well when you mix it with egg yolks and butter.

At the other end of the spectrum are quick chocolate buttercreams. Simple and no-nonsense, these call for beating butter with cooled, melted chocolate and confectioners' sugar—and they're ready to spread. But such frostings also have their flaws: Confectioners' sugar gives them an underlying graininess and blunts their chocolate flavor. Worse, they often deflate or harden a few hours after they're made.

I had several goals for a chocolate frosting. I wanted it to be easy and foolproof and require no special equipment. I wanted it to have a light, satiny consistency that would spread like a dream. I wanted to be able to use it immediately—or to know that it wouldn't harden or deflate if I left it sitting on the counter for an hour or two. And above all, I wanted it to have deep chocolate flavor.

A Better Quick Fix

I began my testing on the quick buttercream end of things, with a base of butter, confectioners' sugar, and 8 ounces of melted chocolate—the fairly modest standard amount in most recipes I'd come across. My first task was to bump up the chocolate flavor. Could this be as simple as adding a few ounces more? No. As I mixed in more melted chocolate, my frosting became gooey, waxy, and too thin to spread.

Up to this point, I had been avoiding cocoa powder. Graininess was already an issue due to the confectioners' sugar, and I feared adding more powdery solids would make the problem even worse. But with no other options for intensifying chocolate flavor, I decided to give it a try. I began cautiously, with a few tablespoons, then added a few tablespoons more until I'd incorporated ¾ cup. To my surprise, the cocoa powder remained undetectable, except for its rich flavor. When I checked with our science editor, I found out why: The cocoa butter crystals in cocoa powder blend with the fat in butter (I was using two and a half sticks) to coat and lubricate particles of cocoa powder, helping mask any grittiness.

Our frosting takes just one minute to make.

The ¾ cup of cocoa powder combined with 8 ounces of melted chocolate gave me the big chocolate boost I was looking for. It was time to tackle the graininess that the confectioners' sugar was causing. A little research revealed the reason: Confectioners' sugar is soluble only in water, not fat, and my recipe had very little water (in the butter). Was there a liquid ingredient that could sweeten the frosting? I thought back to traditional buttercreams and how they use boiled sugar syrup to achieve their luxuriously silky texture. I already had a type of dissolved sugar syrup sitting right in the pantry—corn syrup. Simply swapping one sweetener out for the other was not an option; too much corn syrup would have made my frosting runny. After testing a few amounts, my tasters and I agreed that replacing 1 cup of the confectioners' sugar with ¾ cup of corn syrup was the right proportion. And because of the water content in the syrup, the confectioners' sugar could at least partially dissolve. My frosting was now smooth, glossy, and practically grainless.

Getting a Bead on the Beating

All that was left to figure out was how to keep the frosting from separating and turning greasy as the ingredients were whipped together and from deflating after all was done—problems common to both quick and traditional buttercreams as well as the whipped form of ganache. My working recipe followed the typical buttercream protocol of beating the ingredients together in a standing mixer. With a mixer, care must be taken to not overbeat, or friction will make the butter break down and melt. Overbeating can also pump in too much air, causing the frosting to become frothy and unstable. I needed a technique that could blend my ingredients quickly without melting the butter and without incorporating too much air.

I thought back to some of the frosting recipes I'd come across that used a food processor instead of a mixer—a faster method that creates less aeration. Would this method help my frosting? The proof was in the waiting: Three hours after processing, the frosting still looked perfectly smooth and fluffy.

Easy, foolproof, with a rich chocolate flavor and a light, satiny texture, this frosting was truly the icing on the cake—whether I used it right out of the processor bowl or chose to wait.

FOOLPROOF CHOCOLATE FROSTING

MAKES ABOUT 3 CUPS, ENOUGH TO FROST ONE 9-INCH 2-LAYER CAKE

This frosting may be made with milk, semisweet, or bittersweet chocolate. For our Fluffy Yellow Layer Cake (page 22), we prefer a frosting made with milk chocolate. Cool the chocolate to between 85 and 100 degrees before adding it to the butter mixture. The frosting can be made 3 hours in advance. For longer storage, refrigerate the frosting, covered, and let it stand at room temperature for 1 hour before using.

- 20 tablespoons (2½ sticks) unsalted butter, softened (60 to 65 degrees)
- 1 cup (4 ounces) confectioners' sugar
- ¾ cup Dutch-processed cocoa
- Pinch table salt
- ¾ cup light corn syrup
- 1 teaspoon vanilla extract
- 8 ounces chocolate, melted and cooled slightly (see note)

In food processor, process butter, sugar, cocoa, and salt until smooth, about 30 seconds, scraping sides of bowl as needed. Add corn syrup and vanilla and process until just combined, 5 to 10 seconds. Scrape sides of bowl, then add chocolate and pulse until smooth and creamy, 10 to 15 seconds. Frosting can be used immediately or held (see note).

How to Make Meringue Cookies

These classic cookies can have a Styrofoam-like texture and a saccharine-sweet flavor. How could we avoid these pitfalls?

BY J. KENJI ALT

A classic meringue cookie consists of just two ingredients—egg whites and sugar—whipped together, then baked. If all goes right, the cookie that emerges from the oven is glossy and white, with a shatteringly crisp texture that dissolves instantly in your mouth. But when things go wrong, you wind up with meringues as dense as Styrofoam or weepy, gritty, and cloyingly sweet. How can a cookie with so few ingredients produce such unreliable results?

Use a pastry bag (or a zipper-lock bag with a corner cut off) to pipe uniformly shaped cookies that cook evenly.

Whipping Up a Froth

Almost every meringue recipe I found fell into one of two categories: French meringue, in which egg whites are whipped with sugar, and fussier Italian meringue that calls for pouring hot sugar syrup into the whites as they are being beaten. The Italian meringue produced cookies that were dense and candylike, so I decided to go with the French version. Though the French method was the simpler of the two, these meringues proved just as finicky. Add sugar too soon and the meringue doesn't fully expand, resulting in flat, dense cookies. Add sugar too late and you get a meringue that is voluminous when raw but weepy and gritty when cooked. Why such different results? It turns out that with egg whites, it's all about timing.

As an egg white is beaten, its proteins unfold and cross-link to create a network of bonds that reinforce the air bubbles produced in a sea of water (egg whites are composed mainly of water). Early in the process, the proteins have not completely unfurled and linked together, so the bubbles can't hold a firm shape. Sugar added at this stage will grab water molecules from the egg whites, lending stability to the bubbles. Sugar, however, interferes with the ability of proteins to cross-link; if it's added too early, fewer proteins will bond and trap air, resulting in a meringue that is less voluminous.

If, on the other hand, you continue to beat the whites without adding sugar, more air bubbles will form, more proteins will bond to reinforce them, and the meringue will puff up and take on the firm texture of shaving cream. Sugar added after this stage has been reached will have less water to dissolve in, giving the finished meringues a gritty texture and a tendency to weep out drops of sugar syrup during baking.

So the key is to add sugar only when the whites have been whipped enough to gain some volume but still have enough free water left in them for the sugar to dissolve completely. After some experimentation, I discovered that the best time to add sugar is just before the soft peak stage, when the meringue is very frothy and bubbly but not quite firm enough to hold a peak (see "Stabilizing Meringue with Sugar," below). Adding the sugar in a slow stream down the side of the bowl of a running stand mixer helped distribute the sugar more evenly, which created a smoother meringue.

Many recipes call for adding an acid such as cream of tartar before whipping the whites. In theory, acid helps the egg proteins unwind faster and bond more efficiently. But I got the best results when I left the acid out. Without acid, the whites formed peaks more slowly, giving me a wider time frame in which to add the sugar, leading to a more stable meringue.

Time to Shape

Now that I had a smooth and stable meringue, I was ready to shape it into cookies and bake. I figured the simplest approach would be to scoop a small amount of meringue with a spoon and use a second spoon to drop the dollop onto a baking sheet. After much effort, however, I ended up with two baking sheets of misshapen blobs that didn't bake properly. Some came out browned and crumbly; others were wet in the center. To guarantee uniform shape and proper cooking, I would have to pipe them. A pastry bag produced perfectly shaped meringues, and a zipper-lock bag with a corner cut off worked nearly as well.

Traditionally, meringues are baked at a very low temperature and then left in the turned-off oven, sometimes for as long as overnight. The idea is to completely dry out the cookies while allowing them

TECHNIQUE | STABILIZING MERINGUE WITH SUGAR

The key to glossy, even-textured meringue is adding sugar at just the right time.

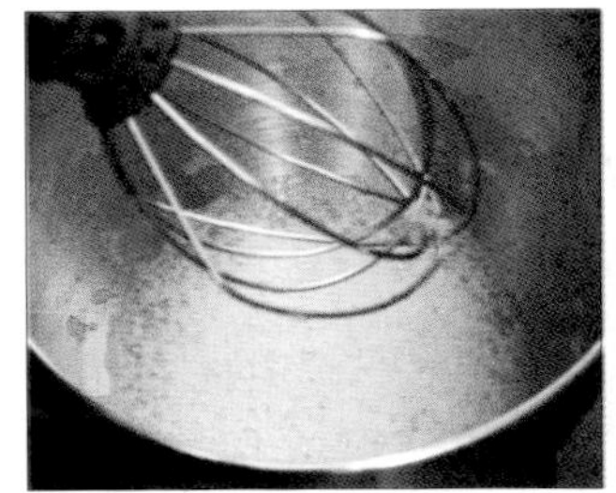

TOO SOON
After 15 seconds, the egg whites begin to get foamy, but it's too early to add the sugar.

JUST RIGHT
Adding sugar just as the foam starts to gain volume yields a stable, voluminous meringue.

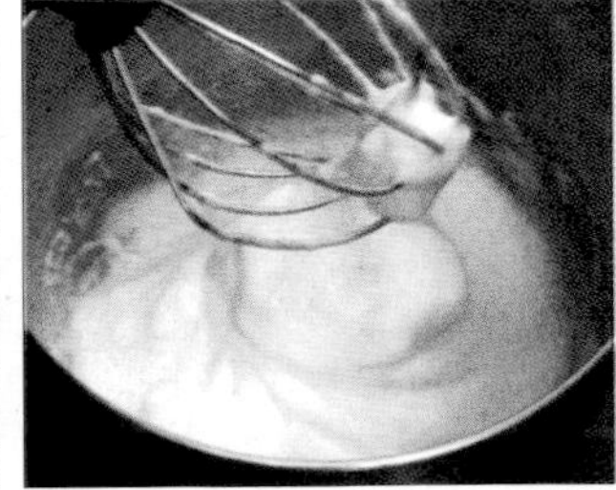

TOO LATE
Adding sugar once the egg whites form stiff peaks will result in a gritty meringue.

SCIENCE: Twin Stabilizers—Sugar and Cornstarch

We wanted meringue cookies that were less sweet than the traditional kind, but when we cut back on sugar, our cookies collapsed in the oven. What was going on? In their raw state, the tiny bubbles that form a meringue get their structure from two things: the cross-linking of egg-white proteins and the surface tension of water. As a meringue bakes, its moisture slowly evaporates, weakening its structure. At the same time, the egg-white protein ovalbumin is becoming stronger, providing additional structure for the foam. Because sugar has a tendency to hold on to water molecules, if there is not enough in the meringue, the water evaporates too quickly, causing the cookies to collapse before the ovalbumin has time to strengthen. We found that cornstarch, which shares the water-clinging property of sugar, could perform the same role in our recipe, allowing us to cut back on sweetness without compromising structure. –J.K.A.

SUGAR WITHDRAWAL Removing too much sugar causes meringues to collapse in the oven.

FORTIFIED FOAM Replacing a little sugar with cornstarch helps meringues keep their shape while baking.

to remain snow-white. I tried baking at temperatures as low as 175 degrees, but our ovens had trouble maintaining this temperature, leading to inconsistent results. An hour in a 225-degree oven followed by another hour in the turned-off oven produced perfectly cooked meringues every time.

Perfecting Sweetness and White

It was time to shift my attention to flavor. There was one complaint common to every cookie I'd made so far: They were too sweet. My working recipe used 1 cup of sugar for four egg whites (the lowest amount I could find in any recipe). Could I cut back the sugar to ¾ cup with no adverse effects? I made up a new batch of meringues with less sugar, and everything was fine until I put them into the oven. Then disaster struck. The meringues, which up to now had been holding their shape perfectly, started collapsing and shrinking. Why would reducing the amount of sugar suddenly ruin my cookies?

It turns out that beyond its stabilizing role in the mixing bowl, sugar also plays a stabilizing role in the oven. Without sufficient sugar, the meringues lose moisture too rapidly as they bake, causing them to collapse. In order to solve this problem, I needed to find something with the hygroscopic (water-clinging) property of sugar, but without the sweetness. My first thought was to swap some of the sugar with corn syrup, which is made from glucose and is about 75 percent as sweet as the sucrose in table sugar. This trick works—as long as you don't mind brown meringues. I had forgotten that corn syrup browns much more easily than regular sugar, and my meringues emerged from the oven a light amber color instead of the pure white I wanted. I decided to try another corn product that is also hygroscopic and would add no sweetness to the meringues: cornstarch. Moderation was key; too much cornstarch and tasters complained the cookies left a starchy aftertaste. With 2 teaspoons of cornstarch and ¾ cup of sugar, complaints disappeared.

All that remained to complete my cookies were a little vanilla and a pinch of salt (both found in many recipes that my tasters liked). As a final measure, I developed a few flavor variations with chocolate, citrus, and nuts. Plain or flavored, I finally had snow-white meringues that were light and crisp, with just the right amount of sweetness.

MERINGUE COOKIES

MAKES 48 SMALL COOKIES

Meringues may be a little soft immediately after being removed from the oven but will stiffen as they cool. To minimize stickiness on humid or rainy days, allow the meringues to cool in a turned-off oven for an additional hour (for a total of 2) without opening the door, then transfer them immediately to airtight containers and seal. Cooled cookies can be kept in an airtight container for up to 2 weeks. Our recipe for Espresso Meringue Cookies is available free at www.cooksillustrated.com/april.

- ¾ cup (5¼ ounces) sugar
- 2 teaspoons cornstarch
- 4 large egg whites
- ¾ teaspoon vanilla extract
- ⅛ teaspoon table salt

1. Adjust oven racks to upper-middle and lower-middle positions and heat oven to 225 degrees. Line 2 baking sheets with parchment paper. Combine sugar and cornstarch in small bowl.

2. In stand mixer fitted with whisk attachment, beat egg whites, vanilla, and salt at high speed until very soft peaks start to form (peaks should slowly lose their shape when whisk is removed), 30 to 45 seconds. With mixer running at medium speed, slowly add sugar mixture in steady stream down side of mixer bowl (process should take about 30 seconds). Stop mixer and scrape down sides and bottom of bowl with rubber spatula. Return mixer to high speed and beat until glossy, stiff peaks have formed, 30 to 45 seconds.

3. Working quickly, place meringue in pastry bag fitted with ½-inch plain tip or large zipper-lock bag with ½ inch of corner cut off (see page 30). Pipe meringues into 1¼-inch-wide mounds about 1 inch high on baking sheets, 6 rows of 4 meringues on each sheet. Bake 1 hour, rotating pans front to back and top to bottom halfway through baking. Turn off oven and allow meringues to cool in oven at least 1 hour. Remove from oven and let cool to room temperature before serving, about 10 minutes.

EQUIPMENT TESTING: Pastry Bags

Pastry chefs can make decorative work like piping perfect meringues or buttercream rosettes look easy. But as we piped out meringues with five different sacks, we found that the bag itself can make a difference. We preferred larger models of about 18 inches, which give you enough length to grip and twist the top. While canvas is traditional, we liked materials such as plastic and coated canvas that are easier to clean. Finding the apertures of our bags sometimes too large or too small to work with tips bought separately, we learned that pastry bags have larger openings for handling jobs such as meringues or mashed potatoes, while decorating bags' smaller openings fit the tiny piping tips for fine scrollwork and writing. If your pastry-tip set didn't come with a coupler to help adapt tips to your bag, you can buy one at any kitchen store.

Once fitted with the right size tip, each bag piped both heavy frosting and ethereal meringue equally well. Cut-to-fit disposable plastic bags from Thermohauser ($17.98 for 100) made for mess-free cleanup, but we ultimately preferred the more durable, reusable Ateco 18-Inch Plastic Coated Pastry Bag ($4.45). For complete testing results, go to www.cooksillustrated.com/april.

–Elizabeth Bomze

CHOCOLATE MERINGUE COOKIES

Follow recipe for Meringue Cookies, gently folding 2 ounces finely chopped bittersweet chocolate into meringue mixture at end of step 2.

TOASTED ALMOND MERINGUE COOKIES

Follow recipe for Meringue Cookies, substituting ½ teaspoon almond extract for vanilla extract. In step 3, sprinkle meringues with ⅓ cup coarsely chopped toasted almonds and 1 teaspoon coarse sea salt, such as Maldon (optional), before baking.

ORANGE MERINGUE COOKIES

Follow recipe for Meringue Cookies, stirring 1 teaspoon finely grated orange zest into sugar mixture in step 1.

COOK'S LIVE Original Test Kitchen Videos

www.cooksillustrated.com

HOW TO MAKE
- Meringue Cookies

VIDEO TIPS
- How do I use a pastry bag?
- How do I whip egg whites?

Is Super-Premium Orange Juice Worth the Super-Premium Price?

High-end orange juices claim to taste better and fresher than ordinary not-from-concentrates. At twice the price, are they a sweet deal?

BY LISA McMANUS

We've always grabbed our weekly carton of orange juice in the dairy section of the supermarket, right next to the milk and cream. But a growing number of fresh squeezed–style orange juices have been popping up in the produce department, where their makers clearly are hoping to encourage customers to associate them with fresh fruit. The industry term for these brands is "super-premium juice," and they're often packaged in fancier bottles that cultivate this image. But so-called super-premium juice costs nearly twice as much as "not from concentrate" brands from the dairy section, such as Tropicana or Minute Maid. Is it worth it?

To find out, we compared five of these upscale juices with ordinary Tropicana Pure Premium, the not-from-concentrate winner of our previous tasting, which focused on middle-market juices including frozen concentrates. Prices ranged from $3.99 for a 64-ounce container of Tropicana to $9.99 for the same quantity of a gourmet brand.

From Tree to Jug (Psst—Plus Processing)

Super-premium juices take pains to suggest on their labels that they're nothing more than squeezed fruit that's been poured into a jug and shipped to your store. The reality is that they undergo many of the same processes as any bottled orange juice, including those at the lowest end of the scale. And, like these other products, they may be doctored to improve flavor without this fact being broadcast to consumers.

Here's how it works: The freshly picked fruit is trucked to a processing plant to be washed and sorted, after which it is put in a machine that extracts the juice and strips off the pith and peel (for cattle feed and other byproducts), all in a matter of seconds. If the juice is destined to become lower-end concentrated juice, it goes to an evaporator before being pasteurized. If it is slated for middle-market "not-from-concentrate" juice, it is pasteurized immediately at a high temperature to kill harmful bacteria, deactivate enzymes, and extend shelf life.

It is at the pasteurization point that super-premium juices take a turn. Many of these brands got their start two decades ago selling fresh, unpasteurized juice. Following health scares in the late 1990s, most adopted "flash" pasteurization after the FDA began requiring unpasteurized juice to carry warning labels and demanded juice makers follow strict bacterial control measures. Flash pasteurization involves heating the juice for a shorter time and at a lower temperature than full pasteurization, preserving more of the fresh taste. While the process doubles the juice's shelf life, it doesn't remain viable nearly as long as the fully pasteurized product.

Flavor Fix

Fresh orange juice is a fragile and finicky product. The downside of any pasteurization is that heat destroys flavor and aroma compounds that make the juice taste fresh and, at worst, can lead to a flat, cooked taste. To restore some of those lost qualities, or to make up for a batch of oranges that falls short of the brand's desired flavor profile, not-from-concentrate manufacturers mix in juice from other batches. (These held-over batches may have been stored frozen or just above the freezing point for months or even years.) They also mix in special "flavor packets" made from orange essence and other orange parts to correct deficiencies in taste, color, or aroma. There's no way to tell from the label when flavor packets have been added or held-over juice was blended in, since juice makers are not required to specify this. Super-premium juice makers may also blend in held-over juice and add flavor packets, but most play that down.

"Ideally, you shouldn't have to add anything, but you can use [flavor packets] to enhance certain features," said Russel Rouseff, professor of food chemistry at the University of Florida and co-director of its Citrus and Beverage Technology Center.

Squeezing Out the Competition

So does what manufacturers describe as "light," "gentle," "delicate" pasteurization actually make their juice taste more like fresh and therefore worth the extra cost? Much to our surprise, the answer is no, with one notable exception—our winner, Natalie's Orchid Island Gourmet Pasteurized Orange Juice. The other gourmet juices rated abysmally. The even bigger surprise? Everyday dairy-section Tropicana came in second, beating out juices twice its price, as well as its own fancier sister brand, Tropicana Pure Valencia.

Tasters praised the Natalie's brand for a fresh taste that was just a notch below the true fresh-squeezed juice we included in the lineup. They were also impressed by its superior blend of both sweet and tart flavors. Tropicana got high marks not for tasting particularly fresh, but for its overall good flavor. The rest of the super-premium juices, on the other hand, were panned for being acidic and sour and tasting closer to concentrate than to anything approaching fresh-squeezed. One of the most expensive juices in the lineup, Odwalla, was also criticized for containing strange flavors reminiscent of cardamom and even pine, landing it at the bottom of the list.

What accounts for the striking difference in flavor among the super-premium juices? Part of the answer may lie in the specifics of how each company conducts its flash pasteurization. Most juice makers told us that details of their process are proprietary and would only admit it's not identical from one company to the next. Only Natalie's Orchid Island was willing to share its formula: "We do six seconds at 170 degrees, then drop it down to 33 (degrees) immediately," noted Michael D'Amato, director of sales for Natalie's Orchid Island Juice, based in Fort Pierce, Fla. Other companies, D'Amato maintains, bring the juice up to as high as 200 degrees and "cook the heck out of it."

A more transparent part of the answer may have to do with the oranges themselves. In our tasting, all the top juices (Natalie's, Tropicana Pure Premium, and Tropicana Pure Valencia) relied mainly on oranges grown in Florida; juices squeezed from California-grown oranges (Bolthouse Farms, Naked, and Odwalla) took the bottom three spots. The fact that the Florida juices didn't have as far to travel to us here in our offices in the Northeast may have contributed to a better and literally fresher taste. (There is no way for a consumer to know when, exactly, a juice left the warehouse; all we could do is confirm that the juices

Ordinary OJ Beats Super-Premium Brands

Tasters gave high marks to plain Tropicana Pure Premium orange juice, preferring it to most of the less-pasteurized and more expensive super-premium brands.

TASTING ORANGE JUICE

We tasted six nationally available brands of orange juice alongside freshly squeezed juice made from oranges in our test kitchen. To ensure consistency, we pretasted and blended together all bottles of each brand of juice. We sent samples of the blended juice to an independent laboratory, testing brix (sugar content) and percentage of acidity. To find out how visual perception influences taste, we also sampled the juices a second time in covered cups—and reached identical conclusions about their rankings. The juices are listed below in order of preference.

HIGHLY RECOMMENDED

NATALIE'S ORCHID ISLAND JUICE COMPANY
Gourmet Pasteurized Orange Juice

➢ **Acidity:** 0.86 percent ➢ **Brix:** 14 percent
➢ **Origin:** Florida
➢ **Types of Oranges:** Includes Valencia, Hamlin, and Pineapple
➢ **Price:** $4.99 for 64-ounce jug (8 cents per ounce)
Comments: The only juice to give fresh-squeezed a run for its money, Natalie's was deemed "very sweet and fruity" with "nice bits of pulp" and a "strong floral smell." Tasters praised its "well-balanced and fresh-tasting" flavors with notes of "tropical fruit."

RECOMMENDED

TROPICANA **Pure Premium 100% Pure and Natural Orange Juice with Some Pulp**

➢ **Acidity:** 0.81 percent ➢ **Brix:** 13.6 percent
➢ **Origin:** Florida
➢ **Types of Oranges:** Includes Valencia, Hamlin, and Pineapple
➢ **Price:** $3.99 for 64-ounce carton (6 cents per ounce)
Comments: While its scores were a notch down from Natalie's, this dairy-case staple and winner of our previous orange juice tasting came in above the rest of the fresh squeezed–style pack. Tasters admired its "bright, clean" taste with a "nice amount of pulp and good balance of sweet to acidic flavor." "Good overall flavor."

TROPICANA **Pure Valencia Orange Juice**

➢ **Acidity:** 0.82 percent ➢ **Brix:** 13.2 percent
➢ **Origin:** Florida
➢ **Types of Oranges:** Valencia, with a blend of other varietals (at the time of our tasting). Company announced new 100% Valencia juice at press time.
➢ **Price:** $3.50 for 33.8-ounce bottle (10 cents per ounce)
Comments: "Tastes more like tangerine than orange," "perfumy and flowery," with a "low acidity." Some liked its "nice, sweet flavor," others called it "sugary" and "supersweet" like "orange candy or Tang."

RECOMMENDED WITH RESERVATIONS

BOLTHOUSE FARMS **100% Valencia Orange Juice**

➢ **Acidity:** 1.01 percent ➢ **Brix:** 14.2 percent
➢ **Origin:** California
➢ **Type of Oranges:** Valencia
➢ **Price:** $3.99 for 33.8-ounce bottle (12 cents per ounce)
Comments: This high-acid, high-sugar juice "tastes like the oranges were slightly unripe" and has an "unpleasant, acidic taste—makes my mouth pucker." Tasters were split on the texture: "If you don't want pulp, this is good: has body and density," though some deemed it "a bit thick," asking, "Is this from concentrate?" A few really disliked it: "I wouldn't waste vodka on this." "Overall, not fresh."

NOT RECOMMENDED

NAKED **All Natural Just Juice 100% Orange Juice**

➢ **Acidity:** 0.87 percent ➢ **Brix:** 12.8 percent
➢ **Origin:** California (supplemented with Florida oranges if crops are diminished by natural disasters such as frost or wildfire)
➢ **Type of Oranges:** Valencia
➢ **Price:** $9.99 for 64-ounce jug (16 cents per ounce)
Comments: This juice was "not fresh-tasting." Some said it was "floral, without much orange flavor." Others called it "thin" and "smooth, with no pulp." A few tasters found it "bleh." "Very plain. Nothing stood out." "It puckers up your mouth." Some disliked its "cooked-cardboard taste."

ODWALLA **Orange Juice**

➢ **Acidity:** 0.89 percent ➢ **Brix:** 12.4 percent
➢ **Origin:** California (supplemented with oranges from around the world)
➢ **Types of Oranges:** Mostly Navel and Valencia, but all Valencia in summer and fall (label changes accordingly)
➢ **Price:** $7.59 for 64-ounce jug (12 cents per ounce)
Comments: "Tastes like orange rind," "thin," "piney and pithy," and "not overpowering in sweetness." One taster said it "tastes strangely of cardamom." Most disliked its "acidic" character, but a few found it "refreshing."

were tested well before their expiration dates.) But experts do agree that an identical variety of orange will develop distinctly different characteristics depending on where it is grown. Florida's warm, humid days and nights produce a larger, sweeter orange, with a thinner peel and more juice. California's dry desert climate and cool nights lead to smaller oranges with thicker peels and a more tart juice. In general, our tasters preferred the sweeter juices made with Florida oranges. The juices from California tasted slightly more sour and acidic. Lab results confirmed it, too. The bottom-rated California juices were higher in acidity.

The Power of Processing

The origin of oranges and the length and level of heat used in flash pasteurization may help explain why Natalie's rated so much higher than the other super-premium juices. But it doesn't explain why a super-processed brand of not-from-concentrate juice like Tropicana so soundly trounced the less-processed competition. Could it be that lots of processing, at least in the case of Tropicana Pure Premium, actually helps?

By all indications—yes. Tropicana's pasteurizing machines heat the juice to 205 degrees for five seconds, then cool it down almost instantly to 36 degrees, thereby destroying far more of the fresh-squeezed flavor than Natalie's does pasteurizing at a comparatively gentle 160 degrees. But Tropicana is also an industry giant that buys 40 percent of all oranges grown in Florida and processes more than one million gallons of juice a day. Over the years, the company has poured millions of dollars into figuring out how to successfully put flavor back in. Its goal, according to Rachel Jordan, principal scientist for Tropicana, is to have every container of juice taste exactly the same. It analyzes more than 300 attributes of the juice and adjusts each batch with techniques including adding flavor packets and held-over juice to re-create the same taste every time. Its blend of Hamlin, Pineapple, and Valencia oranges also seems like a winning combo; it's the same mix used by Natalie's. Other brands bragged that they used all or predominately Valencia oranges, considered the very best oranges for juice, but that didn't impress our tasters.

In the end, none of the juices in the lineup (not even our winner) could beat the juice we had squeezed ourselves. However, we calculated that buying oranges and squeezing them ourselves made the juice cost about $1.84 for an 8-ounce glass, or 23 cents per ounce—about three times the price of our winning super-premium juice.

Can One Serrated Knife Do It All?

Do you really need a bread knife, a tomato knife, a sandwich knife, and a cake splitter? We wanted one all-purpose serrated knife.

BY LISA McMANUS

Serrated knives are an indispensable part of any cook's kitchen arsenal, slicing through squishy tomatoes and foods with a hard exterior and soft interior (like bread) that the straight edge of a chef's knife has trouble tackling. But choosing a serrated knife isn't as simple as it sounds. Do you want serrations that are pointed, scalloped, or saw-toothed? Big and spread-out or tiny and crowded? Or maybe a mix of styles and shapes on one knife? Do you want a blade that's forged or stamped? One that sticks straight out from the handle, one that curves—a little or a lot—or even one where the handle is tilted downward from the blade? What about offset serrated knives, where the blade drops down from the handle into an L shape?

And must you buy different serrated knives for different tasks? Can a knife that's good for cutting bread and sandwiches also cut tomatoes, split cake layers, and separate dough for sticky buns? We have always wanted a good serrated knife that can do it all. We bought 12 knives of all shapes and sizes and began cutting into food to see if our frugal dream of the perfect all-purpose tool could be fulfilled.

Different Strokes

In contrast to a chef's knife, which works best when its straight edge is pushed through food, a serrated knife relies on a slicing motion in which the blade is dragged across the food's surface as it moves down through it. To excel in our testing, the serrations had to exert just the right amount of grip on the food's surface. In the past, we've found that scalloped edges (also known as reverse serrations) provide too little grip, skidding before biting in; the one model of this type we included in our lineup lived down to this expectation. Pointed serrations, on the other hand, needed to be just the right size—too long and they had too much grip, snagging and tearing at the soft interiors of the bread, cake, and sandwich; too small and they were ineffectual (see "Serration Styles," right) on the tougher tasks.

But it's not just point size that matters in a serrated knife; blade size is equally important. Blades shorter than 10 inches just couldn't cut across larger foods like 9-inch cake rounds or big loaves of bread without getting lost inside. We were excited about a 14-inch knife, but while its serrations did every task exceptionally well, it was just too much knife—we kept bumping into objects at the back of the counter as we worked on the cutting board.

Cutlery companies keep tinkering with serrated knife design. We tested offset serrated knives, where the blade is lower than the handle by a few inches, making an L-shaped profile. The idea is to give the cook additional leverage, but these knives didn't offer enough control when cutting through foods; the blades felt too removed from the testers' hands. Another new-style knife sported a downward-sloping handle designed to be more ergonomic and comfortable for the cook. But combined with an offset blade, the sloping handle just gave this knife too many odd angles. In the end, none of the innovations we sampled were improvements over classic serrated knives.

Like chef's knives, serrated knives are manufactured in one of two ways: stamping (cutting the blade out of a sheet of metal) or forging (the age-old technique of heating and hammering a rough shape of metal into a knife). Forged knives tend to have heavier blades, but our longtime favorite 8-inch chef's knife, by Victorinox, is stamped, so we didn't think it would matter whether a serrated knife was forged or stamped. And, for the most part, it didn't—our top two knives were one of each. However, we did appreciate the way the heavier blade and more steeply tapered serrations of our top-rated knife, which is forged, sliced into food with greater power and ease.

Regardless of how they were manufactured, we found that bad serrated knives often failed on opposite extremes: They felt like either blunt instruments or wet noodles. A few knives were so rigid that they were hard to manipulate, making them poorly suited for precise work. With one particularly unbendable blade, if you tried to correct your angle of attack through a soft cake layer, there was no bringing it back, resulting in a lopsided slice. Both of our top-ranked knives hit a nice middle ground, being slightly bendable for better maneuverability yet firm enough to allow for proper control.

Cut to the Chase

We found that for a knife to be a great all-purpose tool that excelled at cutting bread and soft, ripe tomatoes as well as cake layers and gooey sticky-bun dough, it needed three main traits: a slightly flexible blade between 10 and 12 inches long, with serrations that are both uniformly spaced and moderate in length. We highly recommend two knives that boast all three qualities. Wüsthof's Classic Bread Knife, 10-Inch ($79.95), edged out the competition as the best all-purpose serrated knife, and the Victorinox Forschner 10¼-Inch Curved Blade Bread Knife with Black Fibrox Handle ($24.95) performed almost as well for about a third of the price.

Crumby Knives

Serrated knives are like roommates. Some make a huge mess, leaving piles of crumbs everywhere. Others are neat and clean-cut. What accounts for the difference? To find out, I toasted three dozen slices of bread and quartered three pieces with each of the 12 serrated knives in our lineup. I tapped each piece of toast exactly three times after it was cut, then carefully weighed the crumbs on our most precise scale, averaging the results to get the most accurate tally for each knife.

The results were all over the place: Many knives that did well in other applications failed in this one and vice versa. Even more befuddling, a knife's crumb production seemed unrelated to serration style, weight, or whether the blade was forged or stamped. We can't say why, but our two top-rated serrated knives, by Wüsthof and Victorinox, both performed splendidly in the crumb test. I'll let them move into my kitchen anytime. As for the third-ranked Viking knife, its other lovable qualities just might make up for its crumby cuts. –L.M.

SERRATION STYLES

Good Points
Uniformly spaced, moderately sized serrations, such as those on the Wüsthof Classic, excelled at cutting through all foods.

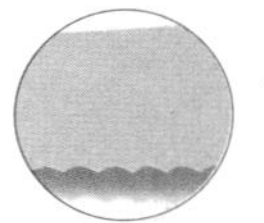

Too Toothy
The LamsonSharp Wave Edge's overly large pointed serrations snagged and tore at foods.

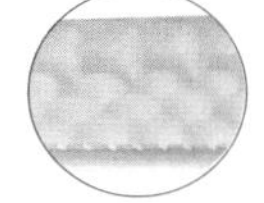

Too Tiny
Saw-toothed microserrations on the Warther knife struggled to make the cut.

Too Rounded
Scalloped serrations on the Mac knife slid over food too many times before cutting in.

KEY
GOOD: ★★★
FAIR: ★★
POOR: ★

TESTING SERRATED KNIVES

Testing Serrated Knives

We tested 12 serrated knives, using them to split cake layers, slice bread and ripe tomatoes, and cut sticky-bun dough and club sandwiches. Testers included a left-handed cook (serrations tend to pull in the wrong direction for lefties) and cooks with large hands (who prefer blades that are taller and curved, as both qualities help keep their knuckles off the cutting board). The results were averaged, and the knives appear in order of preference. Prices were paid at Boston-area retail stores or online. Sources for the winners appear on page 32.

BREAD & TOMATOES: We sliced large ripe tomatoes and loaves of artisanal bread with a strong, chewy crust and a soft, open-crumbed interior, averaging the results. Knives that cut the tomatoes into paper-thin slices without squishing them and the bread into clean-edged slices of even thickness received top marks.

CLUB SANDWICH: We quartered club sandwiches, preferring knives that cut neatly without squashing, keeping all the sandwich layers tall and intact.

CAKE: We split 9-inch cake rounds horizontally, rating highly knives that made it easy to produce evenly sized halves with clean edges and few crumbs.

STICKY DOUGH: We cut rolled, filled sticky-bun dough into pieces for baking. We preferred knives that cut through the gooey dough easily without sticking or flattening the roll.

COOK'S LIVE
Original Test Kitchen Videos
www.cooksillustrated.com
BEHIND THE SCENES
• Testing Serrated Knives

HIGHLY RECOMMENDED	PERFORMANCE	TESTERS' COMMENTS
Wüsthof Classic Bread Knife, 10 Inches PRICE: $79.95 STYLE: Forged construction, pointed serrations	BREAD & TOMATOES: ★★★ CLUB SANDWICH: ★★★ CAKE: ★★★ STICKY DOUGH: ★★★	Well-balanced knife with deeply tapered pointed serrations handled every task with exceptional ease and control, even for our left handed tester. Not as good for large hands.
Victorinox Forschner 10¼-Inch Curved Blade Bread Knife, Black Fibrox Handle (BEST BUY) PRICE: $24.95 STYLE: Stamped construction, pointed serrations	BREAD & TOMATOES: ★★★ CLUB SANDWICH: ★★★ CAKE: ★★★ STICKY DOUGH: ★★★	Comfortable, sharp blade and pointed serrations performed almost as well as our top knife, struggling a tad more with crusty bread. Taller blade was easier on large-handed testers. Good for lefties.

RECOMMENDED	PERFORMANCE	TESTERS' COMMENTS
Viking 10-Inch Serrated Slicer PRICE: $108 STYLE: Forged construction, pointed serrations	BREAD & TOMATOES: ★★★ CLUB SANDWICH: ★★★ CAKE: ★★★ STICKY DOUGH: ★★★	Lethally sharp forged blade with deeply tapered pointed serrations was easy to control during delicate tasks. Feels (and is) expensive and isn't good for lefties or cooks with large hands.

RECOMMENDED WITH RESERVATIONS	PERFORMANCE	TESTERS' COMMENTS
Victorinox Forschner 14-Inch Bread/ Serrated Slicing Knife, Black Fibrox Handle PRICE: $30.95 STYLE: Stamped construction, pointed serrations	BREAD & TOMATOES: ★★ CLUB SANDWICH: ★★★ CAKE: ★★★ STICKY DOUGH: ★★★	Extra-long blade excelled at tackling a large, crusty loaf and splitting a cake round. But its length kept us poking at the back of the kitchen counter when cutting smaller foods such as tomatoes.
MAC Bread/Roast Knife, Superior Series, 10½ Inches PRICE: $28 STYLE: Stamped construction, scalloped ("reverse") serrations	BREAD & TOMATOES: ★★ CLUB SANDWICH: ★★★ CAKE: ★★★ STICKY DOUGH: ★★★	Comfortable, fairly lightweight, sharp knife, but scallop-shaped serrations slid over bread crust and tomato skin for several strokes before biting in. But for its rounded edges, it would be a winner.
F. Dick Utility Serrated Edge Knife, 1905 Series, 10 Inches PRICE: $74.95 STYLE: Forged construction, pointed serrations	BREAD & TOMATOES: ★★ CLUB SANDWICH: ★★ CAKE: ★★ STICKY DOUGH: ★★★	Thick, forged knife weighed nearly twice as much as the top-ranked knives. It glided through bread but was described as feeling "like an ax" cutting a tomato or splitting a cake.
Global 10-Inch Bread Knife, Serrated PRICE: $122.95 STYLE: Forged construction, pointed serrations	BREAD & TOMATOES: ★★ CLUB SANDWICH: ★★★ CAKE: ★ STICKY DOUGH: ★★★	Priciest knife in the lineup looks and feels like a chef's knife with serrations. The alleged 10-inch blade is only 9½ inches. Acceptable, but not stellar, performance.

NOT RECOMMENDED	PERFORMANCE	TESTERS' COMMENTS
Warther Serrated Knife, 9-Inch PRICE: $48.50 STYLE: Stamped construction, microserrations	BREAD & TOMATOES: ★★ CLUB SANDWICH: ★★★ CAKE: ★ STICKY DOUGH: ★★★	Saw-toothed serrations and too-short blade (just 8¾ inches) were not up to tackling big bread loaves or cake rounds. Praised for paper-thin slices of tomato.
Messermeister 10-Inch Park Plaza Bread/Serrated Slicing Knife PRICE: $39.95 STYLE: Stamped construction, mixed-shape serrations	BREAD & TOMATOES: ★★ CLUB SANDWICH: ★★★ CAKE: ★★ STICKY DOUGH: ★	An odd mix of wavy, pointed, and rounded serrations lacked bite and held this knife back, particularly when trying to slice through thick, leathery bread crust.
LamsonSharp Forged Offset Bread Knife with Ebony Handle, 9 Inches PRICE: $67.95 STYLE: Forged construction, tiny pointed serrations	BREAD & TOMATOES: ★★ CLUB SANDWICH: ★★★ CAKE: ★★ STICKY DOUGH: ★	While this knife felt solidly built, its blade was too short and its pointed serrations too tiny, making it struggle through both hard bread and sticky dough.
Ergo Chef 9-Inch Pro-Series Offset Serrated Bread/Multi-Purpose Knife PRICE: $79.99 STYLE: Forged construction, pointed serrations	BREAD & TOMATOES: ★ CLUB SANDWICH: ★★★ CAKE: ★★ STICKY DOUGH: ★★	This knife's downward-tilting handle unnerved testers. Ranked last for slicing bread: Too-short blade and offset heel got trapped inside the loaf. Uncomfortable held sideways to halve a cake layer.
LamsonSharp 10-Inch Wave Edge Curved Bread Knife PRICE: $30 STYLE: Stamped construction, pointed serrations	BREAD & TOMATOES: ★★ CLUB SANDWICH: ★ CAKE: ★★ STICKY DOUGH: ★	Like a caricature of our favorite models, this knife was called "overly curved and overly pointed." It snagged and tore the soft sticky-bun dough, chewed up toast, and made a disheveled club sandwich.

KITCHEN NOTES

BY J. KENJI ALT

Beating Beet Stains

Prepping the beets for our Roasted Beet and Carrot Salad with Watercress (page 20) left the cutting board with dark stains that discolored other foods we put on it. Instead of stopping to wash the board between uses, we had a better idea: giving its surface a light coat of nonstick cooking spray before chopping. This thin coating added no discernible slickness under our knife and allowed us to quickly wipe the board clean with a paper towel before proceeding with our next task.

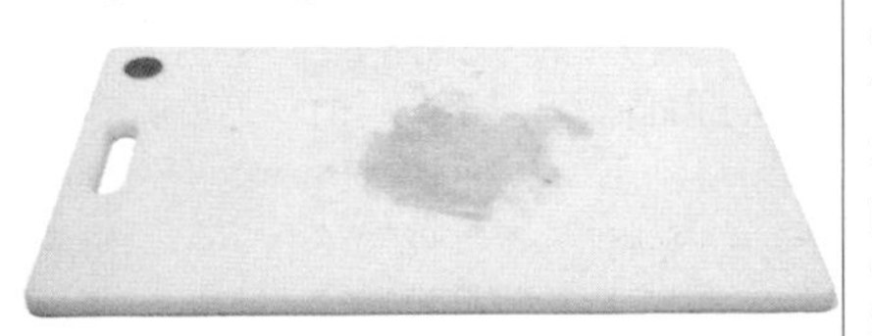

SLICK SOLUTION
A light coat of nonstick cooking spray allows beet stains like this one to be easily wiped away.

Cold Water Storage for Yolks

Making Meringue Cookies (page 25) left us with lots of extra egg yolks, and we wanted to find the best way to store them. Placed in nothing more than a sealed container, the yolks developed a dried-out skin. As long as the yolks were unbroken, we found we could refrigerate them for a week by covering them in cold water. Simply drain off the water and use the yolks as directed in any recipe.

Hard Water = Hard Beans

Developing our recipe for Hearty Tuscan Bean Stew (page 15) made us wonder how the mineral content of water affects bean texture. To find out, we compared a batch of dried white beans soaked and cooked in mineral-free distilled water with a batch prepared with tap water containing dissolved minerals. The beans cooked in this hard tap water came out with tougher skins. Why? Two of the minerals in tap water, magnesium and calcium, are enemies of beans. If given the chance, each will grip tightly to the cell walls of the bean skins, lending reinforcement that creates harder, tougher skins. But you don't need distilled water to prevent this; salt will do.

Salt added to bean-soaking water will stop magnesium and calcium from binding to the cell walls, and it will also displace some of the minerals that occur naturally in the skins. And because salt's grip on the cell walls of the bean skins is less firm than that of magnesium or calcium, it will turn beans softer and more pliable. We found that 3 tablespoons of salt per gallon of soaking water was enough to guarantee soft skins.

Whipping Warmed-Up Whites

Baking books often recommend allowing egg whites to come to room temperature so they form peaks more quickly, but we wondered if the whipping time saved was significant. Armed with a stopwatch, we whipped our way through several dozen egg whites. We found that room-temperature eggs took, on average, 1 minute and 7 seconds to whip up to stiff peaks, while cold eggs took 1 minute and 9.5 seconds—a grand savings of 2.5 seconds.

Our conclusion? An extra 2.5 seconds of whipping makes more sense than waiting for cold whites to come up to room temperature. (But regardless of the temperature of your whites when you begin whipping, do try to separate the eggs when they are still cold—it's a lot easier.)

Air-Chilled versus Water-Chilled Chicken

When working on chicken recipes, we almost always use a high-quality bird from one of our favorite brands, Bell & Evans. One morning when these chickens weren't available, we tested our recipe for Crisp Roast Chicken (page 7) using a regular supermarket brand instead. The chicken behaved completely differently—the skin did not brown as much, and the meat tasted bland and washed-out. When we read the fine print on the label—"Contains up to 4% retained water"—we understood why.

Unlike Bell & Evans chickens, which are air-chilled soon after slaughtering in order to cool to a safe temperature, most supermarket birds are submerged in a 34-degree water bath. According to the USDA's Agricultural Research Service, chickens can absorb up to 12 percent of their body weight in moisture during this process; the amount drops down to about 4 percent by the time they are sold. Air-chilled chickens, on the other hand, are not exposed to water and thus do not absorb additional moisture, which helps to account for the more concentrated flavor of their meat and better browning of their skin.

Putting the Yellow into Yolks

As we developed the recipe for our Fluffy Yellow Layer Cake (page 22), we were surprised by the lack of any real yellow color to the cake. A closer look at the standard supermarket eggs we were using provided a clue: The yolks were all relatively pale. When we compared them with yolks from free-range eggs bought fresh at the farmers' market, the contrast was striking: The yolks were much darker. What accounts for the difference in color? It all boils down to the hens' diet. Bright golden-yellow yolks show that the hens are well supplied with carotenoids. These substances are found in a wide range of plants that a true free-range hen could find merely by pecking around the farmyard.

Cakes made with light and dark yolks actually tasted the same; the difference was merely aesthetic.

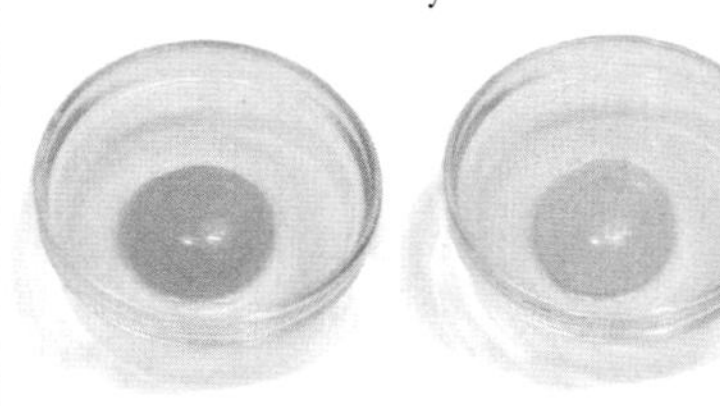

FARM-FRESH   MASS-PRODUCED
Free-range eggs from the farmers' market typically have darker yolks than the mass-produced supermarket variety.

Red Meat, Brown Meat

Ever find that the ground meat you just brought home from the supermarket is red on the outside but dark purple or brown on the inside? We noticed this phenomenon with ground

TECHNIQUE | MAKE YOUR OWN PASTRY BAG

If you don't have a pastry bag, there's no need to rush out and buy one if the recipe merely calls for simple piping (as for our Meringue Cookies, page 25). A zipper-lock bag will do just as well for this and other jobs that don't require lots of precision.

1. LOAD Steady an open zipper-lock bag inside a measuring cup and fold the top edge over your fingertips. Load the bag using a large rubber spatula or spoon.

2. SEAL AND CUT Squeeze out excess air and seal the bag. Use scissors to cut off the bottom corner of the bag.

3. SQUEEZE AND PIPE Hold the bag from the back (behind the filling) and squeeze gently, guiding the tip with your free hand.

SCIENCE: For Quicker Thaw, Put Meat on Metal

In the test kitchen, we've noticed that meat seems to thaw more quickly when left on a metal surface rather than a wood or plastic one. To confirm our observation, we froze inch-thick steaks, pork chops, and ground beef overnight and defrosted them the next day on a variety of surfaces: wood and plastic cutting boards; heavy stainless steel, cast-iron, and nonstick skillets; and lightweight aluminum baking trays. After one hour, the meat on the cutting boards was still frozen solid, the meat on the aluminum trays had made slightly more progress, and the meat on the heavy pans was almost completely thawed. What process was at work?

Unlike plastic and wood, which contain atoms bound together in a relatively rigid matrix, metal contains lots of moving atoms that allow it to transfer ambient heat much more quickly. We found heavy steel and cast-iron skillets worked best—which makes sense, given that the heavier and thicker the metal, the more efficient the transference of heat. To thaw frozen wrapped steaks, chops, or ground meat (flattened to 1 inch thick before freezing), place them in a skillet in a single layer (keep the wrapping on). Flip the meat every half hour until it's thawed. Irregularly shaped meats such as poultry or whole roasts that can't make good contact with the skillet will not benefit from this method.

beef bought for our Simple Italian-Style Meat Sauce (page 9). Is this an indication of meat past its prime? Fortunately, no. The color in meat comes from a muscle protein called myoglobin. When the meat is freshly cut, this protein is deep purple. As the meat sits in its packaging (or in the butcher's display case), the myoglobin will convert to bright red oxymyoglobin on the meat's exterior, where it is exposed to more oxygen. Inside the meat, where less oxygen can penetrate, it will slowly convert to brown metmyoglobin. Color changes of this nature are purely cosmetic—they have no bearing on the meat's flavor or wholesomeness.

TECHNIQUE | CUTTING YOUR OWN CUTLETS

Buying commercially prepared chicken cutlets is the most convenient option for preparing our Chicken Saltimbocca (page 19). But if your supermarket doesn't carry them, you can also make your own cutlets from boneless skinless breasts.

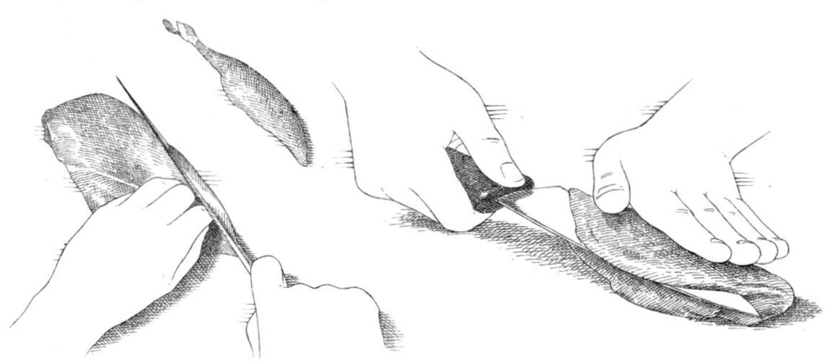

1. TRIM Remove the tenderloin (if present) from the underside of the chicken breasts. Trim any excess fat, gristle, or bones where the wing or ribs were attached. Freeze breasts for 15 minutes until firm but not fully frozen.

2. SLICE Place the chicken breast smooth-side up on the work surface. Place one hand on top of the breast and, with a sharp chef's knife held parallel to the work surface, carefully slice through the middle of the breast horizontally to yield two ¼- to ½-inch-thick pieces.

RECIPE UPDATE

Shrimp Tikka Masala

We wondered if shrimp could be substituted for the chicken breasts in our **Chicken Tikka Masala** recipe (September/October 2007). The recipe calls for salting boneless, skinless chicken breasts for 30 to 60 minutes (to flavor and tenderize the meat) as the sauce cooks on the stovetop. The chicken is then dipped in yogurt, broiled, cut up, and combined with the sauce (a mix of onion, garlic, ginger, chile, crushed tomatoes, spices, and cream). When we tried a simple swap of one ingredient for another (with our only adjustment being to broil the shrimp for less time), tasters complained that the shrimp were rubbery. After a few tests, we discovered the salting process was to blame. If exposed to salt for too long, raw shrimp will actually begin to cook and will turn tough when heated, so we found it was best to simply leave the salt out. Go to www.cooksillustrated.com/april for our free recipe for Shrimp Tikka Masala.

Olive-Rosemary Rolls

Fans of our **Olive-Rosemary Bread** (March/April 2007) wanted to know how to turn these hearty, rustic loaves into rolls. After determining that our recipe was best divided into 16 portions, we then focused on a fuss-free way to bake the small pieces of dough. Baking directly on a preheated baking stone worked with loaves but proved unwieldy with 16 rolls. Instead of a baking stone, we divided the rolls evenly among two rimmed baking sheets. But no stone meant less heat retention in the oven and less crust on the rolls. Starting the rolls in a 500-degree oven (50 degrees hotter than in the original recipe) for five minutes and then lowering the temperature to 400 degrees to finish baking gave them the thick, burnished crust we were after. Go to www.cooksillustrated.com/april for our free recipe for Olive-Rosemary Rolls.

Make-Ahead Garlic-Potato Soup

We didn't design our **Garlic-Potato Soup** (March/April 2007) to be made ahead, but enough readers have told us that they freeze the soup anyway—with poor results—for us to decide it was time to figure out the right way to go about it. This velvety smooth soup is a delicate emulsion of leeks, garlic, and potato blended with heavy cream. Under the duress of freezing and reheating, the fat separates from the starch, turning the soup grainy (think broken mayonnaise or hollandaise). Making, then freezing, the soup base without the cream (which we added to the soup upon reheating) fixed the graininess issue. The remaining problem? The potato chunks were watery and mushy from being twice-cooked. We got around this by only partially cooking the potatoes before freezing the soup. The potatoes finished cooking as the soup reheated, and everything tasted as good as if it had never been frozen. Go to www.cooksillustrated.com/april for our free recipe for Make-Ahead Garlic-Potato Soup.

–Charles Kelsey

FULLY COOKED: MUSHY

PARTIALLY COOKED: JUST RIGHT

Partially cooking the potatoes before freezing leads to better texture when the soup is reheated.

If you have a question about a recipe, let us know. Send your inquiry, name, address, and daytime telephone number to Recipe Update, Cook's Illustrated, P.O. Box 470589, Brookline, MA 02447, or write to recipeupdate@americastestkitchen.com.

EQUIPMENT CORNER

BY ELIZABETH BOMZE WITH MEREDITH SMITH

EQUIPMENT TESTING: Electric Kettles

Electric kettles promise to shave minutes off the wait for boiling water and save space on your stovetop, too. We tested eight brands, ranging in price from $9.99 to $89.99, for speed, safety, and ease of use. All but one (the Proctor Silex K2070; $9.99) beat the time it took to boil water on the powerful gas stovetops we use in the test kitchen. Unfortunately, the Proctor Silex and the other under-$25 model we tested (Melitta MEK17W; $24.95) also lacked the automatic shutoff/boil-dry safeguards we deem necessary. We preferred models that had a separate base, allowing you to move the kettle away from the heating element, and a window that lets you view the water level. With the exception of the Bodum 5600 Curl (our Best Buy at $39.95), we disliked plastic kettles, which tended to impart an off-flavor to the water. Of the quickest kettles, we were most impressed by the Capresso Silver H2O Plus Electric Kettle ($59.95). Easy to fill, pour, and clean, its 6-cup glass carafe affords a view of bubbles rising from an orblike stainless heating element. For complete testing results, go to www.cooksillustrated.com/april.

SPEEDIER THAN THE STOVE
The sleek Capresso Silver H20 Plus Kettle brings water to a boil more quickly than the stove.

DO YOU REALLY NEED THIS? Alligator Chopper

The Alligator Chopper ($24.99) claims to deliver perfectly cubed onions and elegant batons of carrots, bell peppers, or apples with one punch of the hand-held chopper's blades against its platform base. The tool did chop half a small yellow onion (and even cut it into a fine dice, after some careful rotation and a second chomp). But with a larger red-onion half, and then a medium-sized carrot, the operation failed: We found ourselves cautiously extracting suspended vegetables from the blades and poking leftover bits through the grid with the tines of a fork.

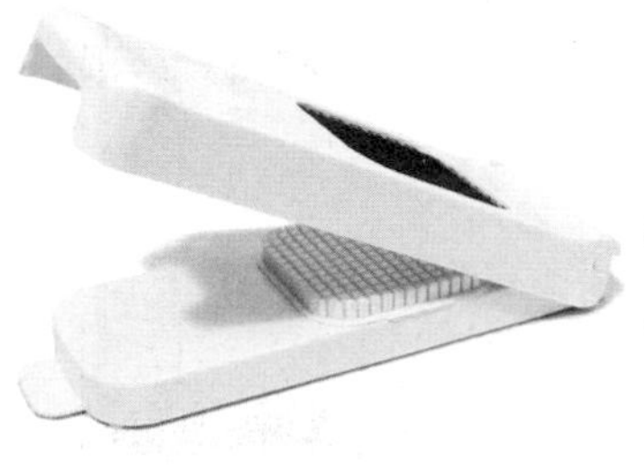

THIS CHOPPER GETS THE AX
The Alligator Chopper failed when it came to chopping anything larger than half a small onion.

NEW PRODUCT: Baker's Edge Baking Pan

This redesign of a conventional 9- by 13-inch baking pan features nothing more than three internal walls that extend across the pan. Could they really eliminate the problem of undercooked middles and burned edges when baking brownies, bar cookies, and even lasagna? When we tested this pan in our kitchen, we were pleased to discover that the answer is yes. The heavy-gauge cast aluminum pan evenly distributed heat while cooking, and because the Baker's Edge ($34.95) has six more baking surfaces than ordinary pans, it gave each serving of our brownies at least two chewy edges (a great thing if you like edge pieces). And when we made lasagna, we discovered another advantage of the interior walls—they kept the layers from sliding apart, making for easy serving. The only disadvantage when making lasagna: You must cut the noodles to fit the pan.

BAKER'S ADVANTAGE
The interior walls of this baking pan eliminate the problems of undercooked middles and burned edges in brownies and lasagna.

EQUIPMENT UPDATE: Carving Knife

Three years ago we elected the Mercer Chef Cutlery 10-Inch Wide Slicer with Granton Edge ($44.99) our favorite carving tool for its broad, round-tipped blade. Trouble is, many people—us included—have had trouble locating this knife online. A call to the company confirmed that the slicer is still available; its nomenclature has changed slightly, however, and the source's website is tricky to navigate. All three of the following websites take you to the same place: www.pcd.com, www.cookingenthusiast.com, and www.cutlery.com. Once there, enter item number WM14310 in the Catalogue Quick Order box. Alternatively, you can call to order, at 800-792-6650.

EQUIPMENT UPDATE: Wine Keepers

Since we last reviewed wine keepers in 2005, the idea has caught on, bringing many competitors into the market. At the same time, the winning system for recorking and preserving an open bottle of wine, the VacuVin Vacuum Wine Saver, now sounds a trademark click to indicate when its vacuum seal has been achieved (older models gave no clear indication). To see how this updated model compares with the new contenders, we drained 10 ounces of red wine from six identical bottles, sealed them with the VacuVin and its competitors, and refrigerated them for 10 days. At that point, we compared them all with a fresh bottle.

Tasters found little difference among the bottles. All but the V-Gauge Wine Preserver Pump & Stopper ($19.95) kept the Merlot perfectly quaffable. After that, testers limited their criticism to design flaws, most notably for the high-maintenance Epicurean Wine Saver ($79.95) and the perplexing Wine Vacuum Pump and Stopper ($17.95), which offered no written directions. For its strong seal, ease of use, and bargain price tag of $9.99, we'll stick with the new, improved VacuVin.

Sources

The following are sources for items recommended in this issue. Prices were current at press time and do not include shipping. Contact companies to confirm information or visit www.cooksillustrated.com for updates.

Page 7: CHICKENS
- D'Artagnan Whole Heritage Chicken, Blue Foot: $20.99 plus shipping, D'Artagnan (800-327-8246, www.dartagnan.com).
- Joyce Foods Poulet Rouge Fermier du Piedmont: $15–$17 plus shipping, item #218513, Joyce Foods (336-766-9900, www.joycefoods.com).

Page 13: RICER
- R.S.V.P. International Classic Kitchen Basics Potato Ricer: $11.99, item #06-1119, Cheftools (866-716-2433, www.cheftools.com).

Page 19: PROSCIUTTO
- La Quercia Prosciutto Americana: $69 for six 3-ounce packages. La Quercia (515-981-1625, www.laquercia.us).

Page 22: STAND MIXER
- Cuisinart 5.5 Quart Stainless Stand Mixer: $349, item #545981, Cooking.com (800-663-8810, www.cooking.com).

Page 25: PASTRY BAG
- Ateco Plastic Coated 18-Inch Pastry Bag: $4.45, item #708413, Cooking.com.

Page 29: SERRATED KNIVES
- Wüsthof Classic Bread Knife, 10 Inches: $79.95, item #154020, Cooking.com.
- Victorinox Forschner 10¼-Inch Bread Knife: $24.95, item #40547, Cutlery and More (800-650-9866, www.cutleryandmore.com).

Page 32: ELECTRIC KETTLE
- Capresso Silver H2O Plus Electric Kettle: $59.95, Sur la Table (800-243-0852, www.surlatable.com).

Page 32: BAKING PAN
- Baker's Edge Brownie Pan: $34.95, item #02-1290, Cheftools.

Page 32: CARVING KNIFE
- Mercer Chef Cutlery 10-Inch Wide Slicer with Granton Edge: $44.99, item #WM14310, Cooking Enthusiast (800-792-6650, www.cookingenthusiast.com).

Page 32: WINE KEEPER
- VacuVin Vacuum Wine Saver: $9.99, item #97558, Fantes (800-443-2683, www.fantes.com).

INDEX

March & April 2008

RECIPES

COOK'S LIVE Original Test Kitchen Videos **www.cooksillustrated.com**

MAIN DISHES
- **How to Make Chicken Saltimbocca**
- How do I cut chicken breasts into cutlets?

- **How to Make Crisp Roast Chicken**
- How do I carve a chicken?
- What's the difference between kosher and table salt?

- **How to Make Hearty Tuscan Bean Stew**
- How do I chop greens?

- **How to Make Oven-Roasted Salmon**
- Buying Guide: Salmon

- **How to Make Simple Italian-Style Meat Sauce**
- Can I wash mushrooms?
- Buying Guide: Tomato Paste

SIDE DISH
- **How to Make Fluffy Mashed Potatoes**

DESSERTS
- **How to Make Fluffy Yellow Layer Cake**
- Should I use a stand or hand-held mixer?
- Buying Guide: Stand Mixers

- **How to Make Foolproof Chocolate Frosting**
- How do I frost a layer cake?
- How do I melt chocolate?

- **How to Make Meringue Cookies**
- How do I use a pastry bag?
- How do I whip egg whites?

TESTING
- Behind the Scenes: Testing Serrated Knives

AMERICA'S TEST KITCHEN

Public television's most popular cooking show

Join the millions of home cooks who watch our show, *America's Test Kitchen*, on public television every week. For more information, including recipes and program times, visit www.americastestkitchen.com.

Fluffy Mashed Potatoes, 13

Roasted Vegetable Salad, 20

Hearty Tuscan Bean Stew, 15

Chicken Saltimbocca, 19

Fluffy Yellow Layer Cake, 22, with Foolproof Chocolate Frosting, 23

Crisp Roast Chicken, 7

Meringue Cookies, 25

Oven-Roasted Salmon, 11

Simple Italian-Style Meat Sauce, 9

PHOTOGRAPHY: CARL TREMBLAY, STYLING: MARIE PIRAINO

INDIAN HERBS AND SPICES

NUMBER NINETY-TWO

MAY/JUNE 2008

COOK'S ILLUSTRATED

How to Grill T-Bones

In Search of the Perfect Crust

Ultimate Stuffed Chicken Breasts

Veggie Broth Tasting

Ten Brands, Just One Winner

Reinventing Poached Salmon

New Shallow-Poach Method

Creamy Tomato Pasta Sauce

Rating Mandolines

Faster and Better Than a Knife

Ultimate Berry Fool
Mexican Pulled Pork
Spring Vegetable Risotto
Restaurant-Style Hummus
How to Cook Baby Spinach
Oatmeal Snack Cake

www.cooksillustrated.com

$5.95 U.S./$6.95 CANADA

CONTENTS

May & June 2008

COOK'S ONLINE

Go to **www.cooksillustrated.com** to access all recipes from *Cook's Illustrated* since 1993. Watch videos of all the recipes in this issue being prepared and a special report on our mandoline testing.

EDIBLE WEEDS Creeping up through sidewalks and lawns, common weeds are typically thought of as a nuisance, not a possible addition to the table. But edible varieties abound: The leaves of yellow-crowned dandelions may be enjoyed cooked or raw in salad. The astringent leaves of violets are equally good raw or cooked, and the blossoms can be candied or used for jelly. The bright acidity of wood sorrel makes it a refreshing addition to summer salads. Magenta-tinted lamb's quarter makes a vibrant contribution to salad, and it can also be used as a potherb. Stinging nettles should be handled with gloved hands and rinsed before being added to soup as a thickener. The collardlike stems of amaranth are at their best braised or in stir-fries. The grassy bite of chickweed is a good accent to salad, as are the stems of succulent purslane. The confection that takes its name from marsh mallow was developed from this wetland plant. Its pleated leaves give soups a silky texture and mild flavor. Pungent epazote is used in Mexican cooking to impart a resinous flavor to beans, soups, and sauces.

COVER (*Green Beans*): Robert Papp, BACK COVER (*Edible Weeds*): John Burgoyne

For list rental information, contact: Specialists Marketing Services, Inc., 1200 Harbor Blvd., 9th Floor, Weehawken, NJ 07087; 201-865-5800.
Editorial Office: 17 Station St., Brookline, MA 02445; 617-232-1000; fax 617-232 1572. Subscription inquiries, call 800-526-8442.
Postmaster: Send all new orders, subscription inquiries, and change-of-address notices to Cook's Illustrated, P.O. Box 7446, Red Oak, IA 51591-0446.

SUNDAYS AT THE GARAGE

Sundays in Vermont are often spent down at Tom's garage. He can be found welding a plow, fixing a three-point hitch, repainting a sander, digging test holes for a new septic system, or fixing the flat on the trailer Nate uses in the summer to transport his riding mower. Other Sundays might find us sighting in a gun or bow before deer season or trying to charge a battery that doesn't want to hold a charge. The garage is fully stocked with a drip coffee maker, nondairy creamer, a small refrigerator with a full supply of Labatt Blue (Genesee in hard times), a STIHL wall calendar featuring Nordic-looking pin-ups holding chainsaws, large bags of discount dog food, walkie-talkies for hunting, bottles of fox and skunk scent (these used to be kept cool down in the well), and more bolts, screws, washers, transmission oil, belts, and extra line for weed whackers than you could find at the average hardware store.

The other spot to find locals on a Sunday morning is at the Methodist Church. On a warm day in June, the congregation might be short a farmer or two, since hay needs to be tedded, baled, and stacked, but Old Home Day and the Christmas Eve services are packed. You can get hot coffee at both establishments—of similar quality, I might add—but the church also provides doughnuts, leftover birthday cake, or a plate of thin, store-bought oatmeal cookies. (One Sunday, a neighbor made everyone pancakes and sausage, but he was immediately censured for trying to outshine his fellow congregants, violating the first and most important rule of country living: Don't stand out.) Brightly colored juice—grape or orange—is available for the kids, who run out the back door during good weather to play tag under the large maple or sneak off to investigate the ancient two-holer hidden in the brambles. The church has a pressed tin ceiling, a 19th-century Estey pedal organ, and windows made of imperfect antique glass, the tiny bubbles distorting the view of the river valley and the Green Mountains, which emerge through the morning haze into a robin's-egg sky. The view from the garage offers only a dog kennel and a shed chock full of metal traps, but on a recent Sunday morning, a bald eagle was seen rising from the snow-covered field, wings flapping in slow motion, grabbing at the winter air as it tried to achieve elevation like a dark angel.

Christopher Kimball

Nobody is going to confuse the garage for a church. For one, Tom's garage is smaller, and nobody passes the plate in his establishment. But, over the years, I have received some pretty good advice from Tom on Sunday mornings. Make sure you know where your hunting dog is before you pull the trigger. (The last person who hit one of Tom's hunting dogs with grapeshot ended up with his shotgun barrel twisted around a large elm.) Measure twice, cut once. If you get into a bar fight, hit first and hit hard. Take the time to do it right instead of making time to do it over. Help your neighbors before they ask for help. At the church, the advice is less practical, perhaps, but "do unto others" is a message that can stand endless repetition. Both places are awash in fellowship and hot coffee. The church, however, has yet to offer anyone a cold beer.

In a garage just 50 yards down the road, Harley Smith used to have his "drinking room," a small partitioned area with a wood stove where he and his neighbor Frank Thomas would sort out the problems of the world. He once observed that "you aren't going to get any snow until the rivers are full," a rule of thumb that has proven mostly true over the years. He was also slightly sentimental, telling anyone who would listen that he shot his deer "in my Green Valley," a reference to the site of his shooting shack, hidden up in the mountains in a long, high pasture. Like his garage, it was a place of worship. Harley was the only witness to a flash flood back in the 1930s that pushed Baldwin Brook almost half a mile underground, where it remains hidden today. He also remembers the schoolhouse, right next to Tom's farmhouse, where kids used to fashion drinking cups from writing paper, twisting the sheets into cones. Nobody could afford paper cups.

Advice is cheap and Vermonters, like country preachers, speak in parables. I could write a book about all the murky advice I have received over the years about what a bear call sounds like (just like an owl, according to some locals), keeping a slow-walking horse up to speed (gently tap your feet in rhythm with its gait), distinguishing a soft maple from a hard maple (look at the branches to see if they grow at a 45-degree angle from the trunk, or check for powdery bark), and, of course, thousands of words of advice about where to locate a treestand (the short answer is, "not anywhere near mine").

In Vermont garages, one can learn much that is useful: patience, observation, hard work, and stubbornness. But my kids don't spend time in garages like I did growing up. They might stop by the saphouse to check on the timing of the next draw, cups filled with snow and spoons at the ready. But will that sweet memory teach them that life accumulates, that what they do on any one day can last forever, like syrup in a root cellar? That one has to build a life, not just live it? It may be a church, a saphouse, a garage, or a barn, but it needs a solid foundation of hard work livened with a lusty passion for wielding hammer and nail. If I have learned anything from Sundays at the garage, it is that you can't live in someone else's building—you have to find your own Green Valley. It may be simple, the roof may leak, the field mice might call it home, but it is shelter nonetheless, a place to raise your kids, share a cup of coffee, and preach to the congregation.

FOR INQUIRIES, ORDERS, OR MORE INFORMATION

www.cooksillustrated.com

At www.cooksillustrated.com, you can order books and subscriptions, sign up for our free e-newsletter, or renew your magazine subscription. Join the website and gain access to 15 years of *Cook's Illustrated* recipes, equipment tests, and ingredient tastings, as well as *Cook's Live* companion videos for every recipe in this issue.

COOKBOOKS

We sell more than 50 cookbooks by the editors of *Cook's Illustrated*. To order, visit our bookstore at www.cooksillustrated.com or call 800-611-0759 (or 515-246-6911 from outside the U.S.).

COOK'S ILLUSTRATED Magazine

Cook's Illustrated magazine (ISSN 1068-2821), number 92, is published bimonthly by Boston Common Press Limited Partnership, 17 Station St., Brookline, MA 02445. Copyright 2008 Boston Common Press Limited Partnership. Periodicals postage paid at Boston, Mass., and additional mailing offices USPS #012487. Publications Mail Agreement No. 40020778. Return undeliverable Canadian addresses to P.O. Box 875, Station A, Windsor, Ontario N9A 6P2. POSTMASTER: Send address changes to Cook's Illustrated, P.O. Box 7446, Red Oak, IA 51591-0446. For subscription and gift subscription orders, subscription inquiries, or change-of-address notices, call 800-526-8442 in the U.S. or 515-247-7571 from outside the U.S., or write us at Cook's Illustrated, P.O. Box 7446, Red Oak, IA 51591-0446.

ILLUSTRATION: RANDY GLASS

NOTES FROM READERS

COMPILED BY DAVID PAZMIÑO

Peppering Meat

I have always heard that it's better to add ground black pepper to meat after browning it to prevent the pepper from burning. Is there any truth to this?

SUSAN KAFFER
MOBILE, ALA.

To answer your question, we ground black pepper onto two steaks before cooking them and left another two steaks pepperless. Once all of the steaks were nicely browned, we removed each pair from their respective pans to rest. While they rested, we sprinkled pepper onto the steaks that had been cooked plain. After careful sampling, a few discerning tasters could detect a slightly bitter and burnt flavor in the steaks cooked with pepper, but overall, tasters found a much more significant difference in the intensity of pepper flavor. The pepper flavor was more aggressive in the steaks seasoned after cooking. If you want to preserve pepper's full flavor, season meat after cooking. If you want to tame the pepper punch, season with pepper before cooking.

Tools for Slashing Bread

Some recipes call for making slits or slashes across the top of proofed bread dough with a special tool called a *lame.* What is this tool, and is it absolutely necessary?

KARLA FAYE GEIGER
MENA, ARK.

Years of bread-baking experience have taught us that slashing free-form breads (those not cooked in loaf pans) just before baking improves their look and texture. Yeasted bread dough expands rapidly when it is placed in a hot oven, a phenomenon bakers call "oven spring." Making slashes in the dough allows gasses to escape during oven spring, giving the dough room to expand. In fact, the French have given a name to this portion of expanded dough: They refer to it as *la grigne,* or "the grin" of the bread.

French bakers swear by a tool called a lame for making precise slashes in bread dough. A lame is simply a double-edged razor attached to a plastic handle. In the test kitchen, we tried out two styles of lames, one with a straight blade and one with a curved blade. Both performed flawlessly, creating easy slashes that, once baked, developed into proper grignes.

Knowing that most home bakers don't own a lame, we gathered a handful of potential stand-ins: a serrated knife, a chef's knife, and a single-edge razor. The serrated knife sliced easily through dough, but the cuts were uneven. A sharp chef's knife was almost as good as the lame, but the heel of the knife had a tendency to snag and tear as it was dragged through the dough. The single-edge razor, however, performed just as well as the lame, producing clean slashes every time. We found it was important to use only the front tip of the razor, angling the back edge slightly up so that it wouldn't snag on the dough and create unsightly tears.

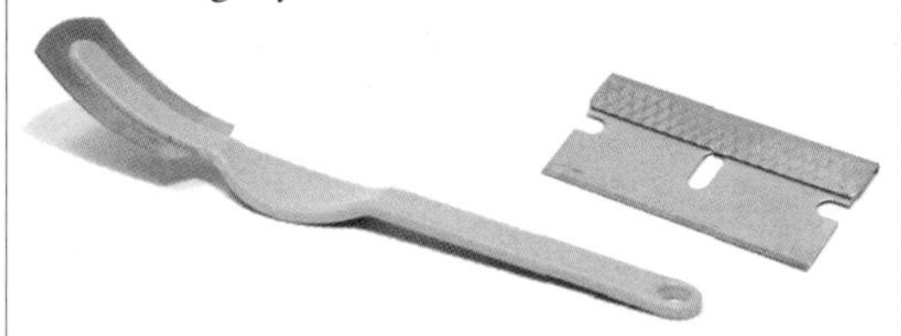

THE CUTTING EDGE
A traditional French lame is nice for slashing bread dough, but a single-edged razor works just as well.

Substituting Blackstrap Molasses

I normally keep only blackstrap molasses in my pantry, preferring it to mild molasses for its more intense flavor. Is it OK to substitute blackstrap molasses in recipes that call for mild molasses?

CHARLES JONES
PITTSBORO, N.C.

For starters, molasses is produced by boiling down sugar cane juice. Light molasses comes from the first boiling, dark from the second, and blackstrap from the third. As the molasses is boiled, the sugar caramelizes and the minerals in the sugar cane juice become more concentrated. While both light and blackstrap molasses have about the same amount of total sugar (55 to 70 percent), their mineral content differs: Light molasses contains 2 percent minerals, while blackstrap contains a whopping 10 percent.

To find out how different types of molasses affect recipes, we made batches of Boston Baked Beans (January/February 2003) and Soft and Chewy Molasses Spice Cookies (January/February 2003) with both light and blackstrap molasses. While a few tasters preferred the intense earthy and caramel flavors of the recipes made with blackstrap molasses, they were in the minority. The vast majority found it too potent. Another problem was that the beans baked with blackstrap molasses were slightly tough and mealy, a result of the higher mineral content interfering with how the beans softened.

Not giving up, we went back into the kitchen to see if we could mix blackstrap molasses with another ingredient to approximate light molasses. We replaced half of the blackstrap molasses with both light corn syrup and honey in two more batches of cookies and beans. Tasters said the batches made with honey lacked distinct molasses flavor, but declared the corn syrup–blackstrap cookies just as good as the light-molasses cookies. The corn syrup–blackstrap baked beans were tender and soft. So if you want to use blackstrap molasses in a recipe that calls for light molasses, you can temper its brashness by replacing half of it with light corn syrup.

Canola Mayonnaise

I recently noticed that Hellmann's had a new product, Canola Cholesterol Free Mayonnaise. How does it stack up to the original?

MELISSA KERRIN
PHILADELPHIA, PA.

Hellmann's Real Mayonnaise (the company is known as Best Foods west of the Rockies) was the winner of our March/April 2003 tasting. Like you, we were interested in finding out how it would fare next to its new cholesterol-free, lower-calorie cousin.

HELLMANN'S CANOLA CHOLESTEROL FREE MAYONNAISE
Is this lower-calorie mayonnaise as good as the original?

Before we started cooking, we took a close look at the ingredient label of each product. Hellmann's Real Mayonnaise contains soybean oil, water, eggs, vinegar, salt, sugar, and lemon juice and has 90 calories, 10 grams of total fat, 1.5 grams of saturated fat, and 5 milligrams of cholesterol per tablespoon. The new version differs in that water is the main ingredient, listed before the canola oil. It also contains modified food starch and a "trace amount" of whole eggs and egg yolks that allow it to be labeled mayonnaise. (According to the FDA, only products that include at least 65 percent oil by weight, an "acidifying agent"—in this case, lemon juice—and "egg yolk–containing ingredients" can bear the label "mayonnaise.") The canola mayonnaise has 45 calories, 4.5 grams of total fat, 0 grams of saturated fat, and 0 milligrams of cholesterol per tablespoon.

We compared the two mayonnaises side by side on plain white bread; in a simple macaroni salad with onion, celery, and pickles; and in our Shrimp Salad (July/August 2007). On plain bread, the canola mayo looked much whiter than the original mayo due to its lack of yolks. While

WHAT IS IT?

During a trip to Pennsylvania last year, I stopped at a flea market to look for antiques to decorate my kitchen. I stumbled across a box of old kitchen tools, and while I knew what most were, this one puzzled me. It looks like a grater—but for what?

KIMBERLY DINGWALL, EAST HADDAM, CONN.

The hundred-year-old Gem nutmeg grater efficiently grinds the spice and protects your fingertips.

Your assumption is correct. The tool is a grater. But it's not an all-purpose grater; it's designed specifically for nutmeg. In the late 1700s, nutmeg became widely available, due in part to nutmeg trees being transplanted from the Banda Islands of Indonesia to Grenada, where British merchants exported the spice. Later, different styles of nutmeg graters began appearing on the market, including yours, the Gem, which was manufactured by the Caldwell Manufacturing Company of Rochester, N.Y., in 1908. To use the Gem, place the nutmeg seed into the oval cavity and secure it with the fold-down handle, the bottom of which is covered in metal nibs that hold the nutmeg firmly in place. Holding the black wooden handle with one hand, you then rotate the nutmeg against the sharp grating teeth, producing a finely ground powder. Unlike some modern, tiny, rasp-style graters that require holding the nutmeg gingerly with your fingertips for fear of grating your knuckles, this century-old gadget offers efficient, risk-free grating.

some tasters panned the canola mayonnaise for being "sweeter" and "tangier," others liked it for its brighter flavor. When it came to the macaroni salad and Shrimp Salad, the differences were much harder to detect. The bottom line? If you're looking for a no-cholesterol, lower-calorie mayonnaise, Hellmann's Canola Cholesterol Free Mayonnaise is a fine choice.

When to Salt Sautéed Onions

I'm confused about when to salt onions. Some recipes call for salting them during sautéing and others call for salting them after sautéing. Is one way better than the other?

JOHN BARRETT
FARMINGTON HILLS, MICH.

➢ We have experienced the same dilemma in the test kitchen—each cook has a different opinion on the appropriate salting time when sautéing onions. Putting aside any preconceived notions, we set out to get to the bottom of this simple but vexing issue.

We started by sautéing 1 cup of diced onions in oil in a medium skillet over medium heat. After 6 minutes of frequent stirring, the onions were beautifully golden. After removing the onions from the skillet, we added ½ teaspoon of salt. Tasters loved the caramelized flavor but commented on the crunchiness of the onions. They also pointed out that the onions weren't seasoned throughout—only on the surface.

Next, we kept the stove on the same setting and sautéed a second cup of diced onions, this time adding ½ teaspoon of salt at the outset. After 6 minutes, the onions were not as brown as the first batch had been, so we cooked them a few more minutes until they were golden brown. When we tasted these onions, they were meltingly tender and well seasoned. The salt had drawn out their liquid, causing them to soften as they cooked. But the liquid also caused the onions to brown more slowly, tacking a few extra minutes onto the cooking time. So the controversy is over: Salt onions when they go into the sauté pan, leaving them over the heat for as long as necessary for decent browning.

Storing Vanilla Beans

Because whole vanilla beans are so expensive, I often buy them in bulk from an online source. What is the best way to store them so that they remain soft and pliable?

VALERIE GARDNER
CHUBBUCK, IDAHO

➢ We also buy vanilla beans in bulk, so we were eager to determine the best way to store them. Before we headed into the test kitchen, however, we looked into what other chefs and cookbook authors recommend. Several methods popped up: storing the beans buried in sugar or submerged in alcohol; or individually wrapping the beans in plastic wrap, placing them in a zipper-lock bag, and storing them at room temperature, in the refrigerator, or in the freezer.

We stored beans using each method, and after four weeks we split the beans in half, scraped out the seeds, and added them to our Easy Vanilla Buttercream (March/April 2005). Tasters' only negative comments concerned buttercream made with vanilla beans stored in vodka. While the alcohol didn't contribute any unwelcome flavors, the vanilla beans didn't add enough—much of their flavor seemed to have leached out into the vodka.

The real differences lay in how easy (or difficult) the beans were to handle. The vanilla beans stored in sugar, for example, dried out and shriveled, making it hard to cut the pod in half to expose the seeds. The beans stored at room temperature weren't quite as dry as those stored in sugar, but they weren't supple, either. The plumpest, softest beans were those that had been wrapped in plastic and stored in an airtight zipper-lock bag in either the refrigerator or the freezer. Both of these samples retained moisture, and little effort was required to remove the seeds.

Muddy Waters

Why do catfish and tilapia sometimes taste muddy or swampy? Is there a way to reduce or remove this unpleasant flavor?

ANN HARSTE
CHICAGO, ILL.

➢ In the test kitchen, we too have noticed a mysterious muddy flavor in some catfish and tilapia. Our research revealed that the flavor comes from a compound called *geosmin*, which is Greek for "earth smell." Geosmin is abundant in the blue-green algae found in the bottom of the man-made ponds that catfish and tilapia are raised in. When the fish swim in the geosmin-rich water, they consume the compound as they ingest the algae.

BUTTERMILK CLEANSER
An hour-long soak in buttermilk washes away the muddy flavor from freshwater fish such as catfish and tilapia.

Some cookbooks claim that soaking the fish in tap water or milk will remove the unpleasant geosmin flavors, but a quick test proved this untrue. After more research, we learned that only acidic compounds could effectively break down geosmin.

Armed with this knowledge, we decided to soak fillets in lemon water and in buttermilk before cooking them. After an hour-long soak, we battered and deep-fried half of the fillets and pan-seared the other half. The acidic baths did the trick, although tasters detected a slightly mushy texture in the fish soaked in lemon water. So if you want to enjoy clean-tasting catfish and tilapia, immerse it in buttermilk for an hour before cooking. When you're ready to cook the fish, rinse off the buttermilk, pat the fish dry, and proceed with the recipe.

SEND US YOUR QUESTIONS We will provide a complimentary one-year subscription for each letter we print. Send your inquiry, name, address, and daytime telephone number to Notes from Readers, Cook's Illustrated, P.O. Box 470589, Brookline, MA 02447, or to notesfromreaders@americastestkitchen.com.

Quick Tips

COMPILED BY YVONNE RUPERTI

Keeping Summer Salads Cold

Crystal Fouch of Clearfield, Ky., uses her enameled cast-iron Dutch oven for more than just cooking—it's also one of her favorite serving vessels for cold foods.

1. Fill an enameled cast-iron Dutch oven with ice water and let it stand until the pot is thoroughly chilled, about five minutes. Dump out the water and dry the pot.
2. Transfer chilled food, such as potato or macaroni salad, into the pot for serving. The pot will retain the cold temperature much longer than would a glass or plastic serving bowl.

Keeping Pound Cake Fresh

J.G. Quintero-Chica of Rhinebeck, N.Y., has found that the best way to keep a pound cake moist is to cut slices from the middle of the cake, not the end. The cake can then be sandwiched back together and wrapped in plastic wrap. With the cut sides insulated this way, the cake stays moist longer. This tip will also work for other items baked in a loaf pan, including quick breads.

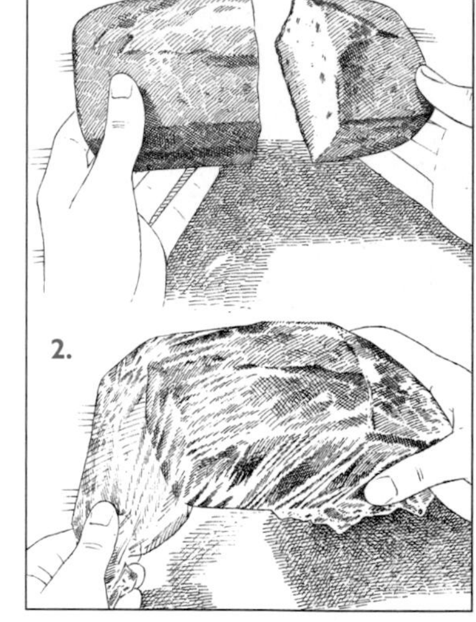

Removing Kitchen Odors

Some foods leave an unpleasant smell in the kitchen after cooking. Ann Budreski of Montpelier, Vt., offers this simple tip to freshen the air. Simmer 2 tablespoons of ground cinnamon in 2 cups of water until the offending odor is replaced with the scent of the simmering spice.

Neatly Unwrapping Vacuum-Sealed Packages

When opening poultry or meat wrapped in vacuum-sealed plastic, it's hard to prevent leakage onto your countertop. Cindy Ehlenfeldt of Charlestown, N.H., shares this simple, mess-minimizing technique.

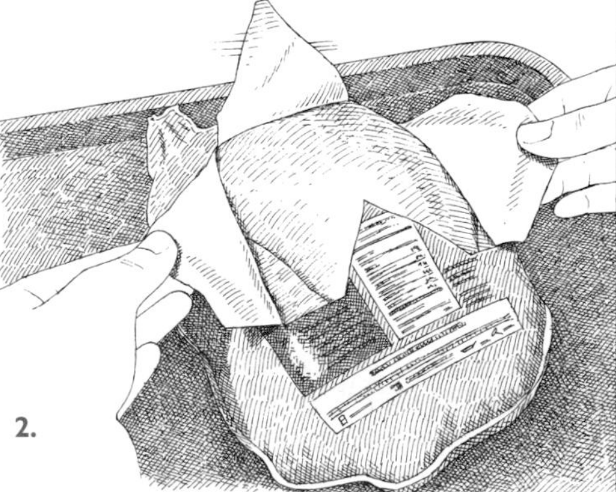

1. With a sharp knife, cut a large X in the plastic on the top of the package, being careful not to cut into the poultry or meat.
2. Gently pull the corners of the plastic away from the center of the X and remove the poultry or meat, leaving all of the juices trapped in the bottom of the package.

Peeling Garlic Cloves

Smashing a garlic clove with the side of a chef's knife is a great way to separate the skin from the clove, but what about those times when you want whole, intact cloves? Karie Menser of Chaska, Minn., came up with an efficient way to accomplish this.

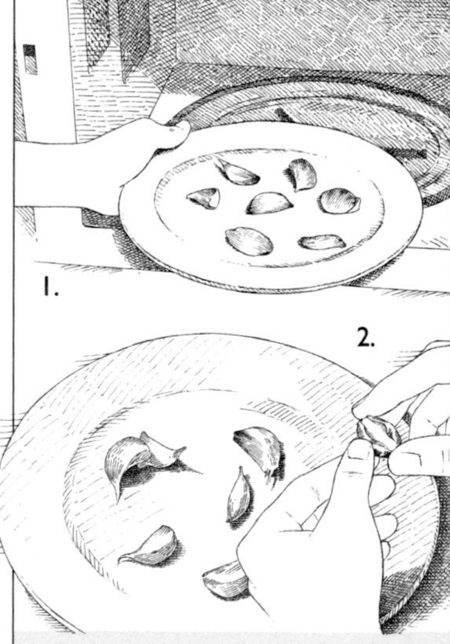

1. Place the garlic cloves on a microwave-safe plate in the microwave and cook on high power for 10 to 20 seconds.
2. Rub the skins gently to remove.

Send Us Your Tip We will provide a complimentary one-year subscription for each tip we print. Send your tip, name, and address to Quick Tips, Cook's Illustrated, P.O. Box 470589, Brookline, MA 02447, or to quicktips@americastestkitchen.com.

Easy Zesting

Tired of losing precious citrus zest in the teeth of a box grater, Stu Cohen of Arlington, Mass., uses an alternate zesting technique.

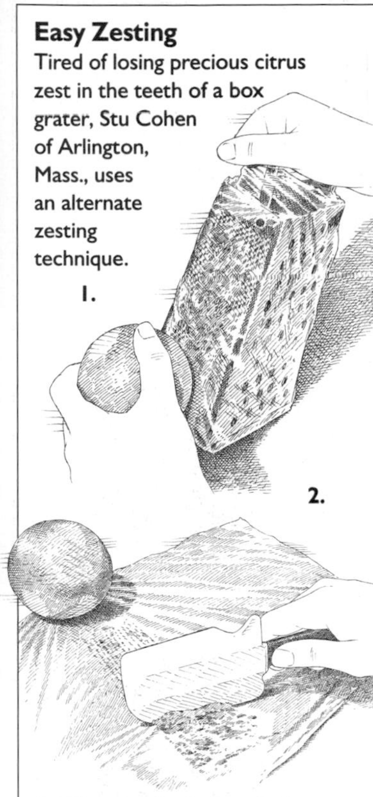

1. Wrap the fine holes of a box grater tightly with plastic wrap, then grate the citrus to remove the zest.
2. Carefully unwrap the plastic wrap and lay it flat on the work surface. Using a rubber spatula, scrape the zest from the plastic wrap.

Hassle-Free Bacon Chopping

Patti Merrell of Baytown, Texas, makes slippery bacon a cinch to mince with the following tip.

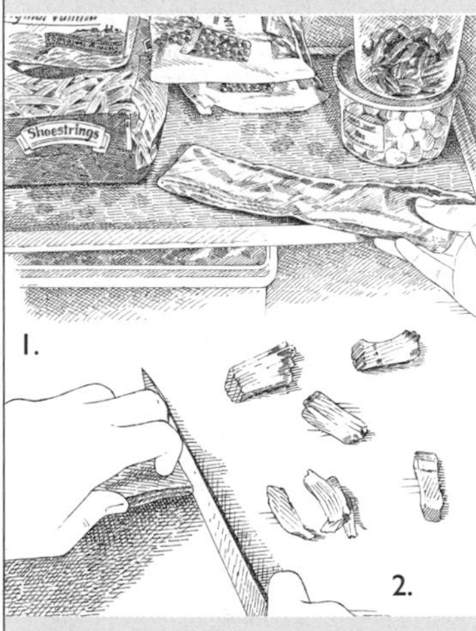

1. Wrap the bacon in plastic wrap and freeze for 15 minutes.
2. The bacon will harden just enough so that, using a chef's knife, it can be chopped as finely as needed with nary a slip.

Spotting Stray Crab Shells

A sharp eye is required to locate and pick out errant pieces of shell in fresh, frozen, or canned crabmeat. For recipes that involve warming or cooking the crab, such as crab dip or crab cakes, Christian Nahas of New York, N.Y., devised an easy method for spotting these hard-to-see shell pieces.

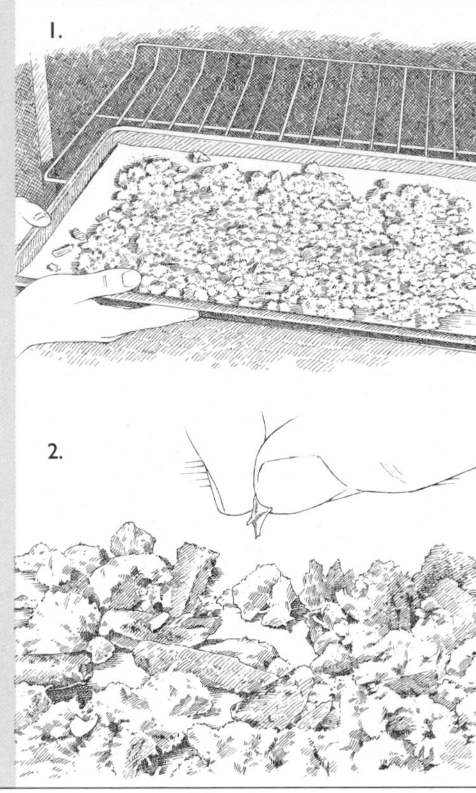

1. Spread the crabmeat evenly on a baking sheet, then place it in a 350-degree oven for about four minutes.
2. The heat will turn the transparent shell pieces opaque, making them easy to identify and discard.

Cutting Twine

Our Stuffed Chicken Breasts (page 9) call for 12 foot-long pieces of twine. Here's how to make quick work of cutting what you need.

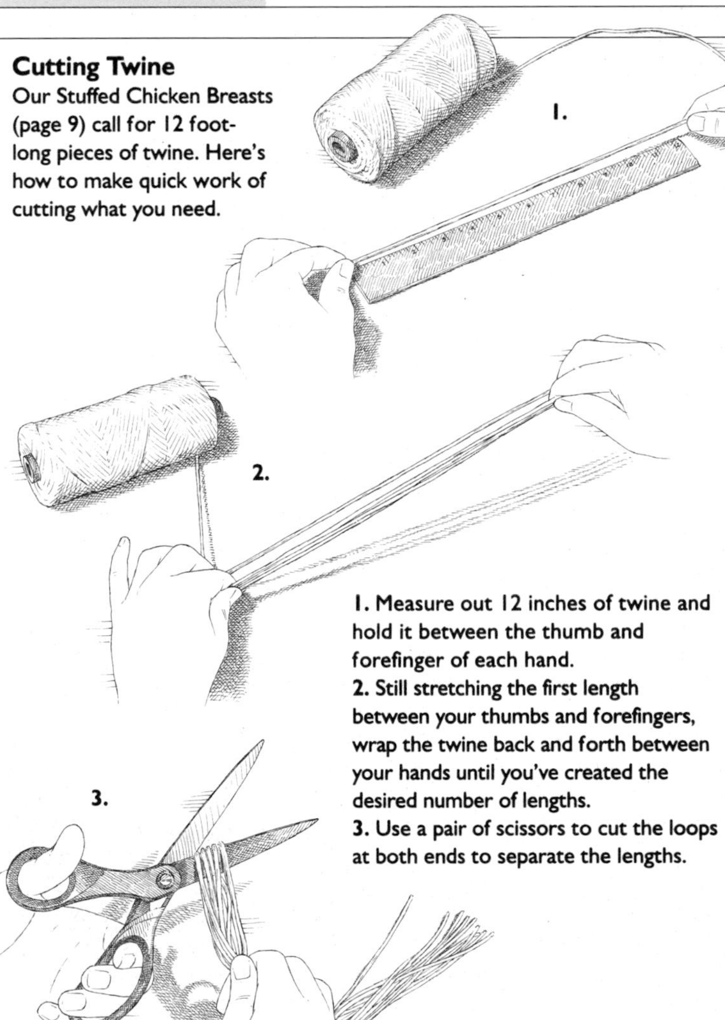

1. Measure out 12 inches of twine and hold it between the thumb and forefinger of each hand.
2. Still stretching the first length between your thumbs and forefingers, wrap the twine back and forth between your hands until you've created the desired number of lengths.
3. Use a pair of scissors to cut the loops at both ends to separate the lengths.

Cleaning Panini Grills

Because of their many grooves, panini grills, grill pans, and sandwich presses can be difficult to clean. Nancy Hemmig of Charlotte, N.C., created a customized cleaning tool with a sponge and a chef's knife.

1. Using a sharp chef's knife, cut several ½-inch-deep slits lengthwise into the sponge, spacing the slits so that they accommodate the grooves of the grill.
2. When the grill is cool and ready to be cleaned, dip the sponge into hot, soapy water and fit it into the grooves for scrubbing.

Removing Corn Silk

Susan Asanovic of Wilton, Conn., found a no-fuss way to remove the long, clingy strands of silk from ears of corn. Holding the corn under cool running water, she uses a clean, firm-bristled toothbrush to brush off the silk. The toothbrush can be cleaned in the dishwasher and used repeatedly.

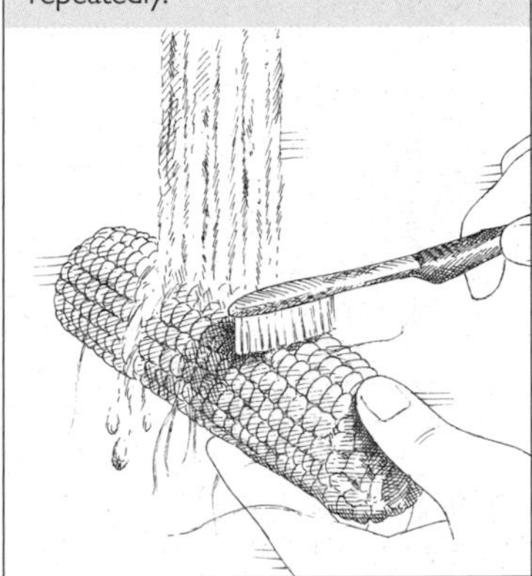

A Better Way to Grill T-Bone Steaks

At $25 per steak, charring a rich T-bone is an unacceptable—but frequent—outcome. For grilled steak perfection, we look to a Florentine prototype.

BY CHARLES KELSEY

T-bone and porterhouse steaks are the twofers of the steak world. Both cuts contain a T-shaped bone down the middle that divides a beefy, tender New York strip steak on one side from a supple, buttery piece of tenderloin on the other—two great steaks in one. The porterhouse contains a larger tenderloin, making it pricier (see "Two Types of T-Bones," below).

When it comes to figuring out the best way to cook these steaks, America's finest steakhouses and their heat-blasting broilers might come to mind for some people. But Italy is my first association. During a college semester in Florence, I experienced my first authentic *bistecca alla fiorentina*, a huge T-bone grilled over an oak fire, then sprinkled with sea salt and drizzled with olive oil. Years later, I can still recall that steak's thick, dark crust, smoky aroma, and deep grill flavor.

According to the Florentine T-Bone Steak Academy (yes, there really is such a group), the method for bistecca alla fiorentina hasn't changed in 200 years. The meat, always a thick-cut T-bone from Tuscany's native Chianina steer, is placed about eight inches above the fire and cooked for five minutes on each side. Aside from being turned once, the meat is not touched during cooking. And salt never kisses its surface until right before serving.

Finishing the steaks over indirect heat helps prevent charring.

When I've tried to re-create the thick crust of a Florentine steak on my backyard grill, I've had little success. Two factors have always worked against me: fattier American beef and the hotter fire created by charcoal briquettes. Both variables lead to fat dripping on the coals, causing flare-ups. To keep the flare-ups under control, I move the steaks off and then back on the grill until the meat has a decent sear. Ultimately, it's this back-and-forth dance that prevents the steaks from developing a good crust. American beef and charcoal briquettes were a given. But could I figure out a way to get results that were at least close to the Florentine method?

SHOPPING: Two Types of T-Bones

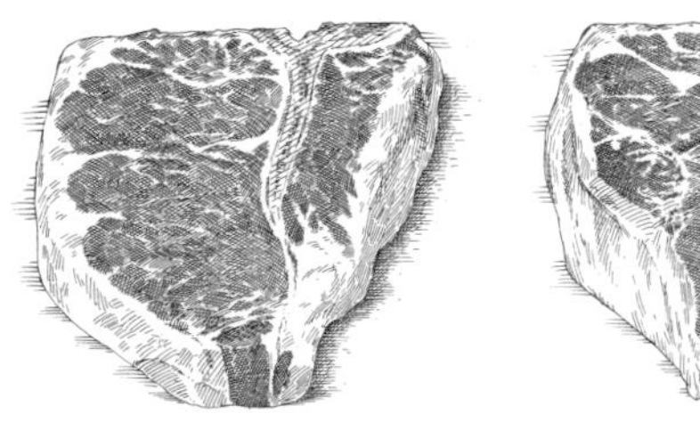

Both T-bone and porterhouse steaks contain a strip steak and a tenderloin steak connected by a T-shaped bone. Technically, a T-bone must have a tenderloin portion at least ½ inch across, and a porterhouse's tenderloin must measure at least 1¼ inches across.

Home-Grilling Renaissance

From my experience grilling at home, I already knew that cooking over a single-level fire, where the coals are spread in an even layer in the grill, wouldn't work. But what about a two-level fire, where you create hotter and cooler zones by placing more coals on one side of the grill than the other? I headed outside to the test kitchen's grilling area to try it out.

I lit a full chimney of coals, and when they were glowing I spread about 90 percent of them in a single layer over half of the grill, arranging the remaining coals on the other side. I replaced the cooking grate and let it heat up for about five minutes. The steaks gave off a good hiss when they hit the hot metal. Quickly, though, the fat melted and the too-familiar flare-ups began. These were small at first, but grew larger by the second. In another minute, my steaks would have been on fire.

I pulled the steaks to the grill's cooler half, flipping them once onto their raw sides to finish cooking. That's when I observed how the steaks reacted over a smaller fire. Dripping fat still caused flare-ups, but these flames were small and barely touched the meat. The result? A pretty good crust.

But I knew I could do better. To gain greater control, I varied the amount of charcoal, filling the chimney first one-half, then two-thirds, and finally three-quarters full. Rather than distributing the coals on both sides, I spread them evenly on only half of the grill. This way, I could get a good sear on the grill's hotter side and gently finish cooking the steaks' interiors using indirect heat on the cooler side. The steaks took about six minutes per side, and the small flare-ups helped to brown the meat.

One problem remained. Though tasters were impressed with the crust and the steaks' grilled flavor, they found the coveted tenderloin section to be somewhat tough and dry. The solution: Position the meat so that the tenderloin faces the cooler side of the grill. This allowed the delicate tenderloin to cook at a slightly slower rate and stay tender and juicy.

I was curious to see whether cooking on a gas grill would make a difference. To create hotter and cooler areas, I kept the primary burner on high and turned the others to low. Tasters preferred the smokier flavor of steaks cooked over charcoal, but the gas grill worked fine, too.

The Best Time to Season

Now that my grilling technique was nailed down, I had one last question: Would it make any difference if we salted the meat earlier in the process? I'd been following the Florentine protocol of waiting to add salt until the end, but decided to employ the test kitchen's preference for seasoning up to an hour before cooking, which enables the salt to penetrate the meat's interior. A half hour before lighting the coals, I sprinkled the meat with salt. This lengthy exposure boosted the meat's flavor from crust to bone, helping to compensate for American beef's

TECHNIQUE

GOING HOT AND COLD

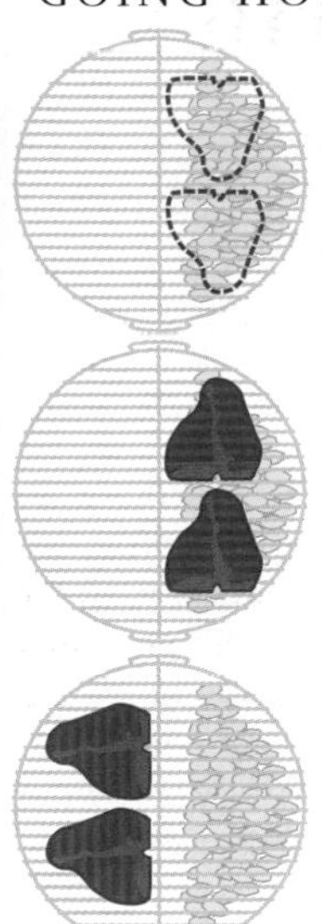

1. CREATE TWO HEAT LEVELS
Place all coals on half of grill and leave other half empty to create two heat levels. Position steaks on hotter side so smaller tenderloin portions face cooler side.

2. SEAR ON HOTTER SIDE
Flip and turn steaks so tenderloins are once again facing cooler side.

3. FINISH ON COOLER SIDE
To finish cooking meat's interior, transfer steaks to cooler side of grill, with bone sides facing fire. Cover grill to trap heat.

less complex taste. I found it necessary to remove any moisture that accumulated on the surface of the steaks with paper towels; if left in place, this moisture caused the steaks to steam a bit and the crust wasn't as thick.

For a more jazzed-up grilled steak, I brushed on a little chive butter toward the end of cooking. The Florentine T-Bone Steak Academy might not approve of such adornment, but I'm sure it would approve of my steaks' well-browned exteriors, perfectly cooked interiors, and intense beefy flavor.

CHARCOAL-GRILLED PORTERHOUSE OR T-BONE STEAKS

SERVES 4 TO 6

When arranging the lit coals in step 2, make sure that they are in an even layer. If the coals are stacked unevenly, large flare-ups may occur, causing the steaks to blacken. We highly recommend thick steaks, but if cooking thinner steaks (¾ to 1 inch thick), make the following adjustments: Reduce the kosher salt to 1 tablespoon (or 1½ teaspoons table salt) and the pepper to 1½ teaspoons. In step 2, build the fire with a full chimney (about 100 briquettes). Cook the steaks, as directed in step 3, over the hotter part of the grill for about 3 minutes per side for rare to medium-rare, or about 4 minutes per side for medium, but do not transfer them to the cooler side of the grill; they will be fully cooked at this point. For our free recipe for Chive Butter, go to www.cooksillustrated.com/june.

- 2 porterhouse or T-bone steaks, each 1 to 1½ inches thick (about 1¾ pounds each) (see note)
- 4 teaspoons kosher salt or 2 teaspoons table salt
- 2 teaspoons ground black pepper

1. Sprinkle entire surface of each steak with 2 teaspoons kosher salt (or 1 teaspoon table salt); let sit at room temperature 1 hour. Pat steaks dry with paper towels; sprinkle each with 1 teaspoon pepper.

2. About 20 minutes before grilling, light large chimney starter filled three-quarters with charcoal (4½ quarts, about 75 briquettes) and allow to burn until coals are fully ignited and partially covered with thin layer of ash. Build modified two-level fire by arranging coals over half of grill, leaving other half empty and making sure coals are in even layer. Position cooking grate over coals, cover grill, and heat grate until hot, about 5 minutes; scrape grate clean with grill brush. Grill is ready when coals are medium-hot (you can hold your hand 5 inches above grate for 3 to 4 seconds).

3. Position steaks directly over coals with tenderloin sides (smaller side of T-bone) facing cooler side of grill. Grill without moving until dark brown crust forms, about 6 minutes. (Small flare-ups will occur; if flames become constant, slide steaks to cooler side of grill and mist fire with water from spray bottle.) Flip steaks and turn so that tenderloin sides are once again facing cooler side of grill. Continue to grill until dark brown crust forms on second side, about 6 minutes.

4. Transfer steaks to cooler side of grill with bone side facing fire. Cover grill and continue cooking until instant-read thermometer inserted into center of steak registers 120 degrees for rare (about 2 minutes), 125 degrees for medium-rare (about 4 minutes), or 130 degrees for medium (about 6 minutes), flipping steaks halfway through cooking time.

5. Transfer steaks to cutting board. Let rest 10 minutes. Cut strip and tenderloin pieces off bones; cut each crosswise into ¼-inch slices. Serve immediately.

GAS-GRILLED PORTERHOUSE OR T-BONE STEAKS

If grilling thinner steaks (¾ to 1 inch thick), reduce the kosher salt to 1 tablespoon (or 1½ teaspoons table salt) and the pepper to 1½ teaspoons. Cook the steaks, as directed below, over the hotter part of the grill with the lid down for about 3 minutes per side for rare to medium-rare, or about 4 minutes per side for medium.

Follow recipe for Charcoal-Grilled Porterhouse or T-Bone Steaks through step 1. Turn all burners to high and heat with lid down until very hot, about 15 minutes. Scrape grate clean with grill brush. Leave primary burner on high and turn other burner(s) to low. Proceed with recipe from step 3, grilling steaks over hottest part of grill with lid down. For rare steaks (120 degrees), remove meat from grill after step 3. For medium-rare and medium steaks, transfer meat to cooler side of grill, turn low burner(s) off, and cook with lid down for about 2 minutes for medium-rare (125 degrees) or about 4 minutes for medium (130 degrees), flipping steaks halfway through cooking time.

TASTING: Mail-Order Steaks: Prime or Just Pricey?

Dry-aged mail-order porterhouse steaks can cost 10 times as much as steaks from the supermarket. Are they worth the premium? We grilled five and compared them with a choice-grade grocery store steak to find out. For complete tasting results, go to www.cooksillustrated.com/june. –Elizabeth Bomze

HIGHLY RECOMMENDED

BRANDT BEEF USDA Dry-Aged Prime Porterhouse Steak
Price: $46.66 per pound, plus shipping
Comments: A sky-high price tag buys "rich, buttery, smooth" texture and "fresh, complex beef flavor."

RECOMMENDED

LOBEL'S Dry-Aged American Wagyu Porterhouse Steak
Price: $130.98 per pound, plus shipping
Comments: Not the same caliber as the true steakhouse Wagyu (Japanese-bred cows known for marbled meat) but with a "distinct, nutty-cheesy flavor" and "sushilike" texture.

LOBEL'S Natural Prime Dry-Aged Porterhouse Steak
Price: $69.98 per pound, plus shipping
Comments: As popular with our tasters as its Wagyu brethren—at half the price—this "nearly perfect" steak boasted "pronounced beef flavor."

ALLEN BROTHERS Dry-Aged Prime Porterhouse
Price: $47.98 per pound, plus shipping
Comments: Tasters found this steak "well-marbled"; "beefy, tender, and juicy."

RECOMMENDED WITH RESERVATIONS

SUPERMARKET Choice Porterhouse Steak
Price: $12.99 per pound
Comments: Sampled on its own, the "mild" flavor and "tender but unremarkable" texture of this steak might have passed for higher quality, but it paled in comparison to the dry-aged mail-order beef.

NOT RECOMMENDED

PETER LUGER USDA Prime Dry-Aged Porterhouse
Price: $43.41 per pound, including shipping
Comments: This "ultrathick" steak offered "bland beef flavor" and "dry, stringy" texture.

COOK'S LIVE Original Test Kitchen Videos
www.cooksillustrated.com

HOW TO MAKE
- Charcoal-Grilled T-Bone Steaks
- Gas-Grilled T-Bone Steaks

VIDEO TIP
- What is the difference between porterhouse and T-bone steaks?

French-Style Stuffed Chicken Breasts

French chefs use a forcemeat filling to transform pedestrian chicken breasts into a four-star affair. We wanted the same filling without the fuss.

⋟ BY J. KENJI ALT ⋞

Cheesy, bready stuffing is the first thing an American cook falls back on to fill chicken breasts. This approach is fine but ho-hum. The French, however, take the concept in a different direction: a stuffing of forcemeat made from the chicken itself. The idea derives from a classic preparation known as a *ballotine.* This complex method involves skinning and boning a whole chicken, stuffing the breasts with the leg meat, and wrapping them back up in the skin. The real deal is usually made only by professional chefs in four-star restaurants. Could we come up with a version that doesn't require a culinary degree to create?

Our stuffed chicken breasts feature a meaty—not cheesy—filling.

Figuring Out the Filling

Since I wanted to make things as simple as possible, boning a whole chicken was out of the question. I decided to start with boneless, skinless breasts, which meant I'd have to come up with a stuffing that didn't rely on the traditional dark meat. I tried eliminating the meat altogether and simply using vegetables as a base. The meatless stuffing of mushrooms accented by leeks and herbs tasted great, but as soon as I cut into the chicken, the filling fell out onto the board. I needed a binder. I tried a wide assortment, including cubed white bread, ricotta cheese, and corn bread. A few of these variations tasted fine, but they took me back to producing a more pedestrian style of stuffed chicken breast.

I thought of buying one extra chicken breast to use in the filling, but most supermarkets sell them in packages of two or four. What if I bought larger breasts and trimmed a little meat off each? The trimmings, used in conjunction with the mushroom and leek stuffing I'd already developed, might make a filling that was both tasty and cohesive.

I began with a new batch of breasts that weighed 8 ounces each. I trimmed 1½ ounces off each, pureed the trimmings to a fine paste in the food processor, then folded in the sautéed mushrooms and leeks. Success! With just a small amount of meat as a binder, the filling firmed up enough to stay in place during cooking and stayed together even when I sliced the chicken into thin medallions.

Abreast of the Matter

I started off using the simple slit-and-tuck method of stuffing: cutting a pocket in the chicken, inserting the filling, and securing it with toothpicks. This technique, however, exposed the chicken's entire surface to the heat, which caused it to overcook and become dry and fibrous. The original ballotine method, in which the stuffing is spread over the pounded breast before being rolled up into a roulade, produced much better results. The chicken and stuffing were more uniformly distributed, allowing them to cook evenly and guaranteeing that each bite contained a mixture of both.

I was having difficulty pounding out the breasts to exactly the right thickness (they tended to tear apart or develop leaky holes) until I followed our technique for Chicken Kiev (March/April 2006), in which the breasts are opened up, or butterflied, before pounding. Now I could easily pound the breasts to a uniform ¼-inch thickness. But no matter how carefully I pounded the chicken, it inevitably came out unevenly shaped, making it difficult to roll into a neat roulade. There was an easy and elegant solution: Instead of trimming meat for the stuffing before pounding the chicken, I reversed the order. I first pounded the breasts, then trimmed them to form perfect, easy-to-roll rectangles, reserving the trimmings for the stuffing. Now all I had to do was spread the stuffing mixture on each breast, roll it up, and tie it with twine.

Praising Braising

Now that I had a flavorful, cohesive stuffing and a good assembly method, I shifted my attention to cooking technique. A classical ballotine is generally cooked in one of two ways: roasting or poaching. Roasting nicely browns the exterior but can produce leathery results. Poaching, on the other hand, produces meat that's very tender and moist but also bland. What if I combined the high-heat browning of a hot skillet with a gentler cooking method to finish it off? A quick braise might do the trick.

For my next test, I browned the chicken on all sides, added chicken broth and wine to the pan, covered it, and brought it to a simmer. I'd unwittingly killed two birds with one stone: I had the most flavorful, evenly cooked chicken yet and also a braising liquid that could serve as a base for a pan sauce. When the chicken was cooked through, I removed it from the pan, stirred in some mustard, and reduced the contents of the pan to create a concentrated sauce. Chopped parsley and a little butter rounded out the flavors.

Sliced into thin medallions and drizzled with the pan sauce, my stuffed chicken breasts had all the hallmarks of the French original: moist chicken wrapped around a cohesive stuffing, all enhanced with an intense sauce. Even with shortcuts, it was definitely a meal worthy of four stars.

RECIPE DIAGNOSIS: Filling Failure

The typical bread and cheese fillings in stuffed chicken breasts come with a host of problems.

PASTY AND DENSE
The bread stuffing in this breast was heavy and thick and failed to adhere to the chicken.

OVERLY OOZY
The ricotta filling in this slit-and-stuff breast oozed out while cooking, releasing curds of cheese.

STEP-BY-STEP | THE SECRETS TO SUCCESSFUL STUFFED CHICKEN BREASTS

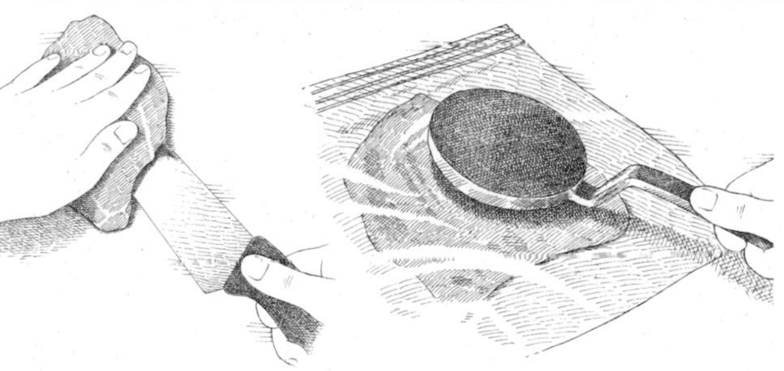

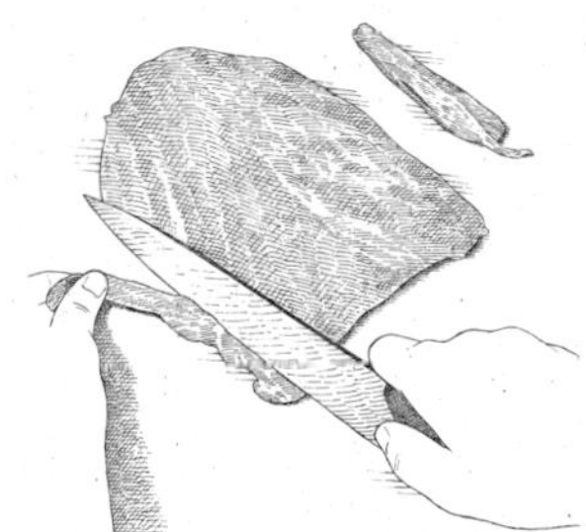

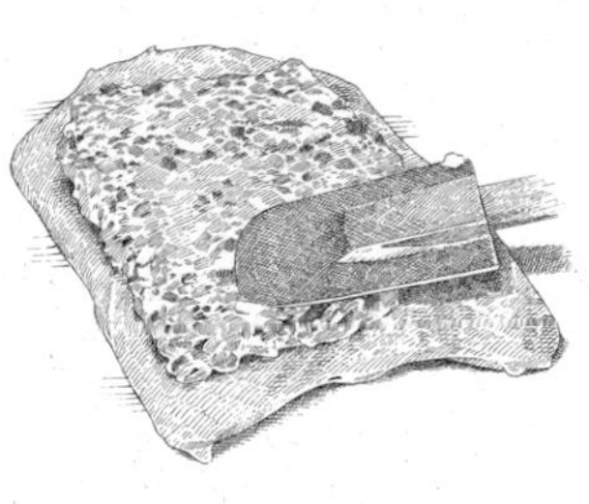

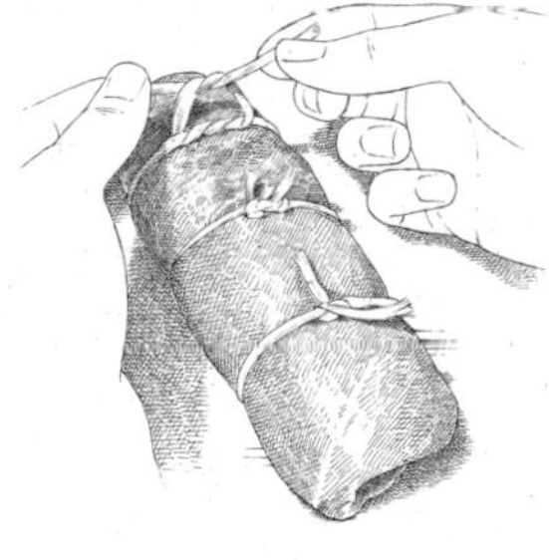

1. BUTTERFLY Slice each breast horizontally, stopping ½ inch from edges so halves remain attached.

2. POUND Open up each breast, place it in zipper-lock bag, and pound it to ¼-inch thickness.

3. TRIM Trim about ½ inch from long side of each cutlet to form 8- by 5-inch rectangle. Reserve trimmings for stuffing.

4. SPREAD Spread stuffing evenly over each cutlet, leaving ¾-inch border along short sides and ¼-inch border along long sides.

5. ROLL With short side facing you, roll up each cutlet and secure it snugly with twine (see page 5 for twine-cutting tips).

STUFFED CHICKEN BREASTS

SERVES 4 TO 6

If your chicken breasts come with the tenderloin attached, pull them off (see "Removing Chicken Tenderloins," page 31) and reserve them to make the puree in step 1. If necessary, trim these breasts to make uniform rectangles and to yield 1½ to 2 ounces total trimmings per breast. Because the stuffing contains raw chicken, it is important to check its temperature in step 5.

- 4 boneless, skinless chicken breasts (8 ounces each) (see note)
- 3 tablespoons vegetable oil
- 10 ounces white mushrooms, trimmed, wiped clean, and sliced thin
- 1 small leek, white part halved lengthwise, washed, and chopped (about 1 cup)
- 2 medium garlic cloves, minced or pressed through garlic press (about 2 teaspoons)
- ½ teaspoon chopped fresh thyme leaves
- 1 tablespoon juice from 1 lemon
- ½ cup dry white wine
- 1 tablespoon chopped fresh parsley leaves
- Table salt and ground black pepper
- 1 cup low-sodium chicken broth
- 1 teaspoon Dijon mustard
- 2 tablespoons unsalted butter

1. **FOR THE CHICKEN:** Use tip of sharp chef's knife to cut each breast horizontally, starting at thinnest end and stopping knife tip ½ inch away from edge so that halves remain attached. Open up breasts to create 4 cutlets. Place 1 cutlet at a time in heavy-duty zipper-lock bag and pound to ¼-inch thickness (cutlet should measure about 8 inches by 6 inches). Trim about ½ inch from long sides of cutlets (about 1½ to 2 ounces of meat per cutlet, or a total of ½ cup from all 4 cutlets) to form rectangles that measure about 8 by 5 inches. Process all trimmings in food processor until smooth, about 20 seconds. Transfer puree to medium bowl and set aside. (Do not wash out food processor bowl.)

2. **FOR THE STUFFING:** Heat 1 tablespoon oil in 12-inch skillet over medium-high heat until shimmering. Add mushrooms and cook, stirring occasionally, until all moisture has evaporated and mushrooms are golden brown, 8 to 11 minutes. Add 1 tablespoon oil and leek; continue to cook, stirring frequently, until softened, 2 to 4 minutes. Add garlic and thyme, and cook, stirring frequently, until fragrant, about 30 seconds. Add 1½ teaspoons lemon juice and cook until all moisture has evaporated, about 30 seconds. Transfer mixture to bowl of food processor. Return pan to heat; add wine and scrape pan bottom to loosen browned bits. Transfer wine to small bowl and set aside. Rinse and dry skillet.

3. Pulse mushroom mixture in food processor until roughly chopped, about five 1-second pulses. Transfer mushroom mixture to bowl with pureed chicken. Add 1½ teaspoons parsley, ¾ teaspoon table salt, and ½ teaspoon pepper. Using rubber spatula, fold together stuffing ingredients until well combined (you should have about 1½ cups stuffing).

4. **TO ASSEMBLE AND COOK:** With thinnest ends of cutlets pointing away from you, spread one-quarter of stuffing evenly over each cutlet with rubber spatula, leaving ¾-inch border along short sides of cutlet and ¼-inch border along long sides. Roll each breast up as tightly as possible without squeezing out filling and place seam-side down. Evenly space 3 pieces twine (each about 12 inches long) beneath each breast and tie, trimming any excess.

5. Season chicken with salt and pepper. Heat remaining tablespoon oil in skillet over medium-high heat until just smoking. Add chicken bundles and brown on 4 sides, about 2 minutes per side. Add broth and reserved wine to pan and bring to boil. Reduce heat to low, cover pan, and cook until instant-read thermometer registers 160 degrees when inserted into thickest part of chicken, 12 to 18 minutes. Transfer chicken to cutting board and tent loosely with foil.

6. **TO MAKE SAUCE AND SERVE:** While chicken rests, whisk mustard into cooking liquid. Increase heat to high and simmer, scraping pan bottom to loosen browned bits, until dark brown and reduced to ½ cup, 7 to 10 minutes. Off heat, whisk in butter and remaining 1½ teaspoons parsley and 1½ teaspoons lemon juice; season with salt and pepper. Remove twine and cut each chicken bundle on bias into 6 medallions. Spoon sauce over chicken and serve.

COOK'S LIVE Original Test Kitchen Videos

www.cooksillustrated.com

HOW TO MAKE
- Stuffed Chicken Breasts

VIDEO TIP
- How to buy and prepare leeks

EQUIPMENT UPDATE:

Meat Pounders

A good meat pounder should be able to produce thin cutlets of uniform thickness with a low number of strokes—without leaving your arm fatigued. To find a favorite, we pounded out chicken breasts with five models of various weights and shapes. Testers grew impatient with tools that weighed less than a pound: They tapped rather than pounded. Also panned were disk-shaped models whose vertical handles required a stamping motion that felt unnatural. For complete testing results, go to www.cooksillustrated.com/june.
–Elizabeth Bomze

HIGHLY RECOMMENDED

NORPRO Meat Pounder
Price: $27.99
Comments: The happy medium all around—comfortably middleweight, well-balanced, and moderately priced.

RECOMMENDED WITH RESERVATIONS

WÜSTHOF Meat Tenderizer/Pounder
Price: $179.95
Comments: Heavy and efficient, but awkwardly shaped and outrageously expensive.

NOT RECOMMENDED

OXO Good Grips i-Series Meat Pounder
Price: $16.99
Comments: Though soft and easy to grip, this vertical handle required an unnatural stamping motion.

Flavorful Poached Salmon

Poaching rarely lives up to its promise to produce silken, delicately flavored fish. We set out to eliminate chalky, tasteless poached salmon for good.

BY J. KENJI ALT

Poached salmon seems like the ideal stovetop recipe: It's fast, it requires just one pot, and there's no splattering oil to burn yourself on or strong odors to permeate the house. And, when done right, the fish has an irresistibly supple, velvety texture delicately accented by the flavors of the poaching liquid. Add a simple sauce and the dish is even more flavorful. But when done wrong, which seems to be the usual case, the fish has a dry, chalky texture and washed-out taste that not even the richest sauce can redeem.

The classic method for poaching salmon is to gently simmer an entire side of fish in a highly flavored broth called a *court-bouillon*. The salmon is cooled and served cold, often as part of a buffet. But I wasn't looking for a make-ahead method for cold salmon to serve a crowd. I wanted to produce perfectly cooked, individual portions of hot salmon and a sauce to go with them—all in under half an hour.

Lemon slices insulate the fish from direct heat, ensuring moistness.

Finessing Flavor

My first objective was to achieve great texture and flavor in the salmon itself; after that I'd focus on the sauce. First consideration: the cooking liquid. A classic court-bouillon is made by filling a pot with water, wine, herbs, vegetables, and aromatics, then boiling it all very briefly (court-bouillon is French for "short-boiled stock"). After straining the solids, you're left with an intensely flavored liquid in which to poach your fish. The broth's strong flavors are absorbed by the fish, which helps compensate for all the salmon flavor that leaches out into the liquid.

This method certainly did produce flavorful results. However, there was just one annoying little problem: To cook dinner for four, I'd just prepped a slew of ingredients (onions, carrots, celery, leeks, parsley) and bought still others (bay leaves, tomato paste, peppercorns, and white wine), only to dump them and the stock down the drain at the end. This waste isn't bothersome when you're preparing a side of fish to feed a group, but it's hardly worth it for a simple Tuesday night supper at home.

What if I used less liquid? At the very least, this would mean I'd have to buy and prep (and waste) fewer ingredients, plus using less liquid would likely mean less flavor leaching out of the salmon. I poached the salmon in just enough liquid to come half an inch up the side of the fillets. Flavor-wise, this was my most successful attempt yet. In fact, the salmon retained so much of its own natural flavor that I wondered if I could cut back even more on the quantity of vegetables and aromatics I was using in the liquid. A couple of shallots, a few herbs, and some wine proved to be all I needed. But nailing the flavor issue brought another problem into sharp relief—dry texture.

Seeking Supple Texture

Like all animal flesh, salmon has a certain temperature range at which it is ideal to eat. The proteins in salmon begin coagulating at around 120 degrees, transforming it from translucent to opaque. At around 135 degrees, the flesh is completely firm and will start to force moisture out from between its protein fibers. Any higher, and the salmon becomes dry as cardboard (like a well-done steak). I had been using an instant-read thermometer to ensure that the centers of my salmon fillets were exactly 125 degrees (medium) before removing them from the poaching liquid. But testing the temperature of various parts of the fillet showed that by the time the center was 125 degrees, most of the other thinner sections registered higher temperatures. I was concerned that the texture of these thinner areas would be dry, but found their higher fat content kept them moist (see "Benefits of Belly Fat," left).

With high cooking temperatures, the exterior of a piece of meat will cook much faster than the interior. This is great when pan-searing the skin of a salmon fillet or a beef steak, when you want a browned exterior and rare interior, but it's no good for poaching, where the goal is to have an evenly cooked piece all the way through. The most obvious solution was to lower the cooking temperature. For the next batch, I placed the salmon in the cold pan with poaching liquid and brought the liquid barely up to a simmer, then reduced the heat to its lowest possible setting and covered the pan until the salmon cooked through. Then I realized a new problem that I'd unwittingly introduced when I reduced the amount of cooking liquid: Since the salmon wasn't totally submerged in liquid, it relied on steam to deliver heat and flavor. At such a low temperature, even with a lid on, not enough steam was being created to efficiently cook the parts of the fish sticking out above the liquid. Was there a way to create more steam without increasing the temperature?

Thinking back to high school chemistry, I remembered that adding alcohol to water lowers its boiling temperature: The higher the concentration of alcohol, the more vapor will be produced as the liquid is heated. More vapor, in turn, means better heat transfer, which leads to faster cooking, even at temperatures below a simmer. I also knew that

Benefits of Belly Fat

A center-cut salmon fillet typically tapers down on one side to the fattier belly of the fish. The belly's fattiness helps keep this section of the fish moist, despite its thinner profile. The belly area is sometimes covered with a chewy white membrane, which should be trimmed away before cooking. We also like to neaten up any ragged edges that can dry out and fray during cooking.

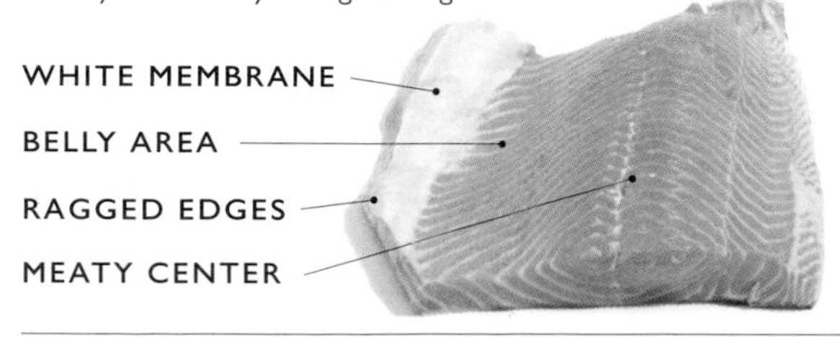

alcohol could increase the rate at which proteins denature. Therefore, if I used more alcohol in the cooking liquid, it would theoretically be able to cook the fish faster and at a lower temperature. I increased the ratio of wine to water, going from a few tablespoons of wine to ½ cup. Acid also helps fish protein denature (in addition to improving flavor), so I squeezed a little lemon juice into the liquid before adding the salmon. My hopes were high as I opened the lid to a burst of steam and salmon that appeared perfectly cooked. Everything was fine until my fork got to the bottom of the fillet. Even though the top, sides, and center were now just right, the bottom, which had been in direct contact with the pan, was still overcooked.

I knew I wasn't the first person to ever have this problem—in fact, a solution already exists: a fish poacher. This specialized pan comes with a perforated insert that elevates the fish, allowing it to cook evenly on all sides. But I wasn't about to go out and buy an expensive new pan for a technique that I'd only use a few times a year. Then I realized that I had the solution literally in my hand. Instead of squeezing lemon juice into the poaching liquid, I sliced the fruit into thin disks and lined the pan with them. By resting the salmon fillets on top of the lemon slices, I was able to insulate the fish from the pan bottom while simultaneously flavoring it. This time the salmon came out evenly cooked all the way through.

Settling the Sauce

It was time to focus on the sauce. Ticking off the list of ingredients in my super-concentrated poaching liquid, I realized I had the foundation of a *beurre blanc*, so I didn't have to make a separate sauce. This classic French sauce is made by reducing wine flavored with vinegar, shallots, and herbs and then finishing it with butter. I would need only to reduce my poaching liquid and whisk in the butter. But since a few tablespoons of butter per serving would push this dish out of the "everyday" category, I developed a vinaigrette-style variation in which I used olive oil instead of butter; tasters liked the oil version as much as the original.

This salmon-poaching method guarantees moist and delicately flavored fish and produces just the right amount of poaching liquid for a great-tasting sauce—all without boiling away any flavor or pouring ingredients down the drain.

TECHNIQUE | A FISH (ALMOST) OUT OF WATER

STANDARD POACH

The classic poaching method calls for submerging salmon completely in liquid in a deep pan, which causes flavor to leach out and leads to dry, flavorless fish.

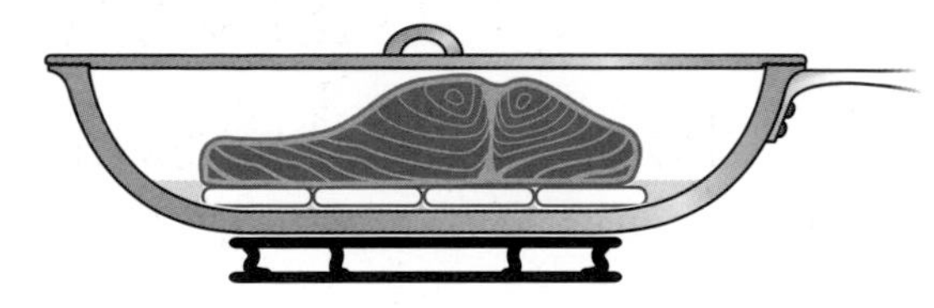

SHALLOW POACH

In our method, small amounts of liquid allow the salmon to cook at a lower temperature, preserving flavor. Lemon slices under the fillets keep their bottoms from overcooking.

POACHED SALMON WITH HERB AND CAPER VINAIGRETTE

SERVES 4

To ensure even-sized pieces of fish, we prefer to buy a whole center-cut fillet and cut it into four pieces. If a skinless whole fillet is unavailable, follow the recipe as directed with a skin-on fillet, adding 3 to 4 minutes to the cooking time in step 2. Remove the skin after cooking (see "Removing Skin from Salmon," at right). This recipe will yield salmon fillets cooked to medium. If you prefer rare salmon (translucent in the center), reduce the cooking time by 2 minutes, or until the salmon registers 110 degrees in the thickest part. For our free recipe for Poached Salmon with Bourbon and Maple, go to www.cooksillustrated.com/june.

- 2 lemons
- 2 tablespoons chopped fresh parsley leaves, stems reserved
- 2 tablespoons chopped fresh tarragon leaves, stems reserved
- 2 small shallots, minced (about 4 tablespoons)
- ½ cup dry white wine
- ½ cup water
- 1 skinless salmon fillet (1¾ to 2 pounds), about 1½ inches at thickest part, white membrane removed, fillet cut crosswise into 4 equal pieces (see note)
- 2 tablespoons capers, rinsed and roughly chopped
- 1 tablespoon honey
- 2 tablespoons extra-virgin olive oil
- Table salt and ground black pepper

1. Cut top and bottom off 1 lemon; cut into 8 to ten ¼-inch-thick slices. Cut remaining lemon into 8 wedges and set aside. Arrange lemon slices in single layer across bottom of 12-inch skillet. Scatter herb stems and 2 tablespoons minced shallots evenly over lemon slices. Add wine and water.

2. Place salmon fillets in skillet, skinned-side down, on top of lemon slices. Set pan over high heat and bring liquid to simmer. Reduce heat to low, cover, and cook until sides are opaque but center of thickest part is still translucent (or until instant-read thermometer inserted in thickest part registers 125 degrees), 11 to 16 minutes. Remove pan from heat and, using spatula, carefully transfer salmon and lemon slices to paper towel–lined plate and tent loosely with foil.

3. Return pan to high heat and simmer cooking liquid until slightly thickened and reduced to 2 tablespoons, 4 to 5 minutes. Meanwhile, combine remaining 2 tablespoons shallots, chopped herbs, capers, honey, and olive oil in medium bowl. Strain reduced cooking liquid through fine-mesh strainer into bowl with herb-caper mixture, pressing on solids to extract as much liquid as possible. Whisk to combine; season with salt and pepper to taste.

4. Season salmon lightly with salt and pepper. Using spatula, carefully lift and tilt salmon fillets to remove lemon slices. Place salmon on serving platter or individual plates and spoon vinaigrette over top. Serve, passing reserved lemon wedges separately.

COOK'S LIVE Original Test Kitchen Videos

www.cooksillustrated.com

HOW TO MAKE

- Poached Salmon with Herb and Caper Vinaigrette

VIDEO TIP

- How do I remove salmon skin?

POACHED SALMON WITH DILL AND SOUR CREAM SAUCE

SERVES 4

Follow recipe for Poached Salmon with Herb and Caper Vinaigrette through step 2, substituting 8–12 dill stems for parsley and tarragon stems and omitting capers, honey, and olive oil. Strain cooking liquid through fine-mesh strainer into medium bowl; discard solids. Return strained liquid to skillet; whisk in 1 tablespoon Dijon mustard and remaining 2 tablespoons shallot. Simmer over high heat until slightly thickened and reduced to 2 tablespoons, 4 to 5 minutes. Whisk in 2 tablespoons sour cream and juice from 1 reserved lemon wedge; simmer 1 minute. Remove from heat; whisk in 2 tablespoons unsalted butter and 2 tablespoons minced fresh dill fronds. Season with salt and pepper. Continue with recipe from step 4, spooning sauce over salmon before serving.

TECHNIQUE | REMOVING SKIN FROM SALMON

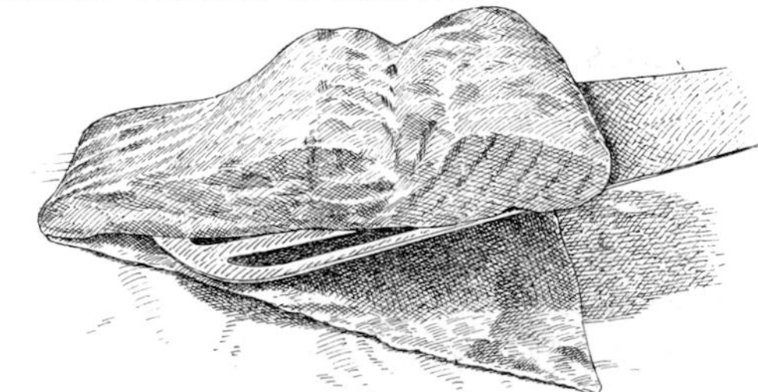

Our recipe specifies skinless salmon fillets. But if you can only find skin-on fillets, removing the skin is simple. Transfer the cooked fillet to a paper towel–lined plate and allow it to cool slightly. Gently slide a thin, wide spatula between the flesh and skin and use the fingers of your free hand to help separate the skin. It should peel off easily and in one piece.

Introducing Mexican Pulled Pork

Like the best barbecue, Mexico's version of pulled pork offers fall-apart hunks of crisp meat—but without the hassle of tending a fire.

BY CHARLES KELSEY

For pork lovers, few things can top the rich flavor and supple texture of Southern-style barbecued pulled pork. But to cook it, you have to sit outside by your smoker all day. So I was intrigued when I learned that carnitas, Mexico's version of shredded pork, is cooked indoors. Spanish for "little meats," this taquería staple is used as a filling in tacos and burritos and boasts tender chunks of pork with a lightly crisped, caramelized exterior. Unlike barbecued pulled pork, where the spice rub and tangy sauce are prominent, in carnitas, the flavor of the pork, subtly accented by earthy oregano and sour orange, takes center stage.

Most Mexican restaurants prepare carnitas by gently frying well-marbled chunks of pork in gallons of lard or oil. But home cooks often forgo all the lard in favor of a more manageable method: simmering the meat in a seasoned broth in the oven and then sautéing it in some of the rendered fat. The latter method definitely sounded more appealing—who wants to deal with deep-frying in gallons of lard at home?—but we wondered if simmering and sautéing could possibly yield the same results. I tried it anyway, gently cooking the meat in a couple quarts of water spiked with citrus and other typical carnitas flavorings, and pulling the pork out after it was softened. I then fried the meat in fat I'd skimmed from the cooking liquid.

Serve carnitas spooned into a warm corn tortilla and topped with salsa.

To my surprise, the pork turned out tender, with a browned exterior and reasonably good flavor. If I'd gotten these results without even trying, surely with a little work I could do even better. But I wouldn't consider myself successful unless I could create carnitas with the addictive taste and texture of the deep-fried versions I've enjoyed in Mexican restaurants.

South vs. South of the Border

TENDER AND SAUCY — CRISP AND CARAMELIZED

Southern-style barbecued pulled pork (at left) is cooked outdoors in a smoker to create uniformly tender meat that's served drenched in barbecue sauce. The pork in our carnitas recipe (at right) is cooked in the oven and features a soft interior and a crisp, caramelized exterior complemented by garnishes, not sauce.

Powers of Reduction

I was using a boneless Boston butt, the cut most carnitas recipes call for and the same cut American cooks use for barbecued pulled pork. Though this shoulder roast contains a good amount of fat, which can translate to deep flavor, all the liquid in the pot washed out the taste. Over the course of several tests, I went from 8 cups of liquid down to 2, the bare minimum for cooking a 3- to 4-pound roast. Braising the meat in a small amount of liquid was clearly better than completely submerging it. Still, tasters thought the pork flavor was not concentrated enough. Swapping out the water for chicken broth made little difference. And browning the meat before braising it also failed to intensify its taste. So where was the pork flavor going?

Down the drain, that's where. I'd been discarding the leftover cooking liquid after removing the meat and skimming off the fat. To capture that lost flavor, I would need to figure out how to reincorporate the liquid into the dish. Perhaps I could reduce the liquid, as the French do in their intensely flavored sauces (see "Using Reductive Powers," page 13). Back in the kitchen, I braised another batch of meat in the oven. This time, instead of pouring off the broth after I removed the pork, I left it in the pot, reducing it on the stovetop until it had the consistency of a thick, syrupy glaze.

From Braising to Broiling

With the glaze at hand, I was left wondering what my next step should be. If I added the pork back to the pot, I was afraid the glaze, which had no water left to evaporate, would burn and stick to the bottom. Because I needed to get the exterior of the pork to crisp, more cooking was a must. What about tossing the pork with the glaze and putting it into the oven? I spread the coated meat on a rimmed baking sheet and turned on the broiler. To ensure that neither glaze nor meat would burn, I placed the sheet on the same lower-middle rack I'd used for braising. Minutes later, the carnitas emerged from the broiler beautifully caramelized, the shredded parts of the meat transformed into crisp wisps with wonderfully rich flavor. The only problem: super-greasy meat.

The greasiness was my fault; I had not defatted the cooking liquid before reducing it. But when I did skim away some of the fat, I ended up with a

Don't Cut the Fat

TOO LEAN

A PERFECT 10

Leaving a ⅛-inch layer of fat on the pork is critical to imparting the best flavor and texture to the final dish. Overtrimming the meat will lead to dry, bland carnitas.

reduction that was thin and sticky and didn't flavor the meat as well. Going straight to the source, I trimmed as much fat as possible from the pork butt before cooking. This got rid of the greasiness, but it also left the carnitas too dry (see "Don't Cut the Fat," above). I was already broiling the meat. Why not let that work in my favor as a way to remove fat? Instead of spreading the carnitas directly on a baking sheet, I placed the meat on a rack set inside of it. The rack elevated the pieces of pork, allowing excess fat to drip down while the glaze stuck to the meat. The better air circulation under and around the pork also made for crispier shreds of meat and better texture overall.

All that was left was to refine the flavors in the braising liquid, which gives the pork its character. In traditional versions, other flavors take a back seat to the pork, and my recipe followed suit. Instead of garlic, I stuck with the mellow sweetness of onion. To emulate the Mexican sour oranges used in authentic carnitas, I used a mix of fresh lime and orange juices, adding the spent orange halves to the pot to impart floral notes. Bay leaves and oregano gave the meat aromatic accents. Cumin, though not a typical ingredient in carnitas, brought an earthy dimension that complemented the other flavors.

Tucked into warm corn tortillas and topped with minced onion, fresh cilantro, and a spritz of lime, the mouth-watering taste and texture of my carnitas kept tasters coming back for more. And I hadn't needed to use a speck of lard.

MEXICAN PULLED PORK (CARNITAS)

SERVES 6

We like serving carnitas spooned into tacos, but you can also use it as a filling for tamales, enchiladas, and burritos. In addition to the traditional garnishes listed below, we recommend serving the pork with our Fresh Guacamole and One-Minute Salsa recipes, available free at www.cooksillustrated.com/june.

Pork

- 1 (3½- to 4-pound) boneless pork butt, fat cap trimmed to ⅛ inch thick, cut into 2-inch chunks
- Table salt and ground black pepper
- 1 teaspoon ground cumin
- 1 small onion, peeled and halved
- 2 bay leaves
- 1 teaspoon dried oregano
- 2 tablespoons juice from 1 lime
- 2 cups water
- 1 medium orange, halved

Tortillas and Garnishes

- 18 (6-inch) corn tortillas, warmed
- Lime wedges
- Minced white or red onion
- Fresh cilantro leaves
- Thinly sliced radishes
- Sour cream

1. Adjust oven rack to lower-middle position and heat oven to 300 degrees. Combine pork, 1 teaspoon salt, ½ teaspoon pepper, cumin, onion, bay leaves, oregano, lime juice, and water in large Dutch oven (liquid should just barely cover meat). Juice orange into medium bowl and remove any seeds (you should have about ⅓ cup juice). Add juice and spent orange halves to pot. Bring mixture to simmer over medium-high heat, stirring occasionally. Cover pot and transfer to oven; cook until meat is soft and falls apart when prodded with fork, about 2 hours, flipping pieces of meat once during cooking.

2. Remove pot from oven and turn oven to broil. Using slotted spoon, transfer pork to bowl; remove orange halves, onion, and bay leaves from cooking liquid and discard (do not skim fat from liquid). Place pot over high heat (use caution, as handles will be very hot) and simmer liquid, stirring frequently, until thick and syrupy (heatsafe spatula should leave wide trail when dragged through glaze), 8 to 12 minutes. You should have about 1 cup reduced liquid.

3. Using 2 forks, pull each piece of pork in half. Fold in reduced liquid; season with salt and pepper to taste. Spread pork in even layer on wire rack set inside rimmed baking sheet or on broiler pan (meat should cover almost entire surface of rack or broiler pan). Place baking sheet on lower-middle rack and broil until top of meat is well browned (but not charred) and edges are slightly crisp, 5 to 8 minutes. Using wide metal spatula, flip pieces of meat and continue to broil until top is well browned and edges are slightly crisp, 5 to 8 minutes longer. Serve immediately with warm tortillas and garnishes.

SCIENCE:

Using Reductive Powers

We reduce liquids all the time in recipes as a way of concentrating flavor. In my Mexican Pulled Pork recipe, I reduced the braising liquid I had used to cook the pork until it took on the thick, syrupy consistency of a glaze and its flavor deepened dramatically. As familiar as the benefits of reducing liquids are to me, the glaze's intense taste made me wonder: Was all that rich flavor derived simply from evaporating the water from the braising liquid, or was there a more complex dynamic at work?

A chat with our science editor revealed the answer: The reduction's richness is in part due to the same process that makes a seared steak taste so good—the Maillard reaction. When the proteins and sugars in meat (or most any foodstuff) are subjected to a high enough temperature (around 300 to 500 degrees), they combine, leading to browning and the creation of hundreds of new flavor compounds.

In my carnitas recipe, proteins and sugars are pulled from the pork by the braising liquid, which also contains sugars from lime and orange juices. After the meat is removed, the liquid is boiled to evaporate all the water. With the water removed, the temperature of the glaze can rise higher than water's boiling point of 212 degrees, eventually kicking off the Maillard reaction. The result: a viscous, highly concentrated glaze with exceptional depth of flavor. –C.K.

AT A GLANCE | THREE STEPS TO INDOOR PULLED PORK

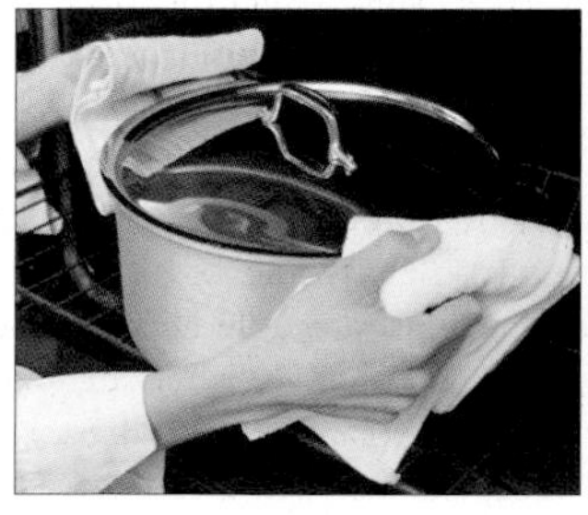

1. OVEN-BRAISE For fall-apart tender meat, oven-braise the pork at a low temperature in a covered Dutch oven for about two hours.

2. REDUCE Remove the pork and reduce the braising liquid to a glaze thick enough for a spatula to leave a trail when pulled through it.

3. BROIL Toss the pork with the glaze and broil it on the lower-middle rack in the oven to yield well-browned meat with crisp edges.

COOK'S LIVE Original Test Kitchen Videos
www.cooksillustrated.com

HOW TO MAKE
- Mexican Pulled Pork (Carnitas)
- One-Minute Salsa

Perfecting Creamy Tomato Pasta Sauce

Combining tomatoes and cream can result in a tinny-tasting mixture more akin to canned soup than pasta sauce. What's the secret to a successful marriage of the two?

BY MATTHEW CARD

I like to think there's a certain taxonomy of pasta sauces. At the top are two phyla: tomato and cream. From there, the sauces fall loosely into classes, from tomato-based marinara, puttanesca, and ragù to cream-enriched Alfredo, carbonara, and besciamella. Creamy tomato sauce, however, is its own subclass. The best examples balance the acidity of fruity tomatoes with the unctuousness of rich dairy; the worst deliver instant heartburn and make you wish the two components had never met. What's the best way to merge these seemingly incompatible ingredients in a sauce that brings out the best in each?

This hybrid sauce appears in many forms. While digging through stacks of Italian cookbooks, I found everything from simple *salsa rosate*, which took just minutes and a single pot to prepare, to long-simmered, ragùlike sauces that required the better part of a day (and a sink's worth of dishes) to pull together. I was disappointed when the recipe of one of my culinary heroes, Marcella Hazan, yielded a copper-colored slurry that tasted way too similar to canned tomato soup (all of the ingredients were simply boiled together and pureed). There were no winners among the lot, but there were plenty of thought-provoking methods and ingredients to test.

Not even heavy cream can blunt the intense tomato flavor of this pasta sauce, which is punctuated by bits of sun-dried tomatoes.

Creating the Base Notes

Traditional Italian sauces (as well as most Italian soups and stews) are built upon *soffrito*, a blend of aromatics, such as onion, carrot, celery, garlic, and parsley, stewed in lots of fat. For the richest-flavored sauce, I assumed that more was more and started with the full list of classic ingredients. As testing progressed, however, I couldn't shake the criticism that the sauce tasted too vegetal. Perhaps in this case, less was more. I cooked a batch of soffrito without celery, and tasters unanimously approved. Next I eliminated carrot, and the reaction was again positive. Left with just garlic and onion, I decided to omit long-cooked garlic in favor of a few quickly sautéed minced cloves, which packed a brighter, cleaner punch.

My goal was a smooth sauce I could make year-round, so fresh tomatoes didn't make much sense. Whole and diced canned tomatoes wouldn't do, either, even when pureed before being blended with the soffrito, because many producers douse them with calcium chloride, a firming agent that prevents the tomatoes from fully softening, regardless of whether they are ground in a processor. Crushed and pureed canned tomatoes, however, each yielded smooth sauce, with tasters preferring the brighter flavor of the crushed. The smoothest kind of canned tomatoes, tomato sauce, failed to impress anyone.

Building Bolder Flavor

A simple sauce of onion, garlic, and crushed tomatoes didn't have the legs to stand up to heavy cream, no matter how long (or short) I simmered it. In light-tasting tomato sauces, I typically eschew tomato paste, but adding a bit here made sense. A tablespoon contributed depth, and a tablespoon more proved better yet. Simply stirring it into the bubbling sauce left the paste tasting raw and tinny, so I cooked it with the softened aromatics until it darkened to brick red.

But tasters demanded still more tomato flavor. To develop deep flavor in tomato sauces and soups, the test kitchen has taken whole, drained canned tomatoes, dusted them with sugar, and then roasted them before combining them with the other ingredients. But when I tried adding tomatoes prepared with this technique, the sauce was too sweet, even when I omitted the sugar. Roasting also toughened the tomatoes' texture, which made the finished sauce decidedly pulpy.

For another of the test kitchen's pasta sauces, tomatoes are browned in a saucepan to generate a flavorful fond, which is deglazed and incorporated into the sauce. But when I tried this method with my working recipe, the fond had more undertones of caramel than tomato. There's a time and a place for the deep, caramel flavors that thorough browning can provide, but this wasn't it.

How else could I generate a bigger, brighter tomato flavor? After sifting through a list of options and testing the most promising, I landed on sun-dried tomatoes, whose sunny flavor enlivened the sauce and cut through the palate-deadening cream.

Between the tomato paste and the sun-dried tomatoes, however, the sauce's flavor had grown too sweet. A pinch of red pepper flakes helped rebalance things, and a stiff shot of wine—added prior to the

AT A GLANCE | TOMATOES THREE WAYS

CONCENTRATED
Tomato paste packs enough punch to enliven flavor-deadening heavy cream.

SUN-DRIED
With their dense, sweet-tart taste, sun-dried tomatoes round out the other flavors.

CRUSHED
Pulpy crushed tomatoes lend a bright taste and subtle texture.

crushed tomatoes and cooked down to evaporate the bitter alcohol—brought the sweetness under control and further intensified the sauce's flavor.

In my initial survey, I'd tried a recipe that included pancetta. Though the meat lent the sauce an undeniable body and depth, I had ruled it out as too assertive. If pancetta was too strong, I reasoned, perhaps milder prosciutto might work. I minced a few paper-thin slices and added it to the pan along with the onion. I'm always mindful of the effect a bit of cured pork can have on a dish (all apologies to vegetarians), and this sauce was easily the best yet. The tomatoes tasted so full and the cream so deep, I might have stirred MSG into the pot.

I liked how the sun-dried tomatoes had softened and the sauce's flavors had unified after half an hour of slow simmering, but I wondered if perhaps it tasted too homogeneous. When I make rich, meaty stews, I typically add a splash of wine to the finished dish to brighten the otherwise dark flavors. I thought it might work in this instance, too. It did—quite well. Then I decided to try adding a bit of raw crushed tomatoes at the last minute, too, a trick the test kitchen came up with for Marinara Sauce (March/April 2006). Like the wine, the raw tomatoes contributed some needed acidity, and the combination of the two cut through the dairy and brought the sauce's ingredients into sharp relief.

Finishing with Cream

From the start, I had assumed that heavy cream was the best dairy product for the job, but a few of the recipes I found used clotted cream, pureed ricotta, or mascarpone cheese instead. I quickly ruled out the clotted cream (very, very odd here), and the ricotta came across as grainy, no matter how long I processed it. To my surprise, I quite liked the flavor of the mascarpone (and turned a blind eye to its unholy calorie count), but its ultrathick texture turned the sauce gummy.

Heavy cream, then, contributed the clearest creamy flavor, but what was the best way to blend it with the tomato base? Some of the recipes I had tried reduced the cream by half to enhance its flavor and silkiness, which I felt made the sauce too sweet. Other recipes blended the tomato base with the cream and boiled it until thick, which proved dangerous; the molten sauce splattered over the stovetop—and me.

I thought the sauce tasted best and most balanced when I simply stirred the cream into the finished tomato mixture and brought it up to temperature before tossing it with the pasta. I found that half a cup was the ideal amount to make the sauce taste rich without overpowering the tomatoes.

Up to this point, I had pureed each of the finished sauces to a velvety texture, thinking that smoothness was the best way to highlight creaminess. And my sauce did taste good when smooth, but it was one-dimensional. On a whim, I left a batch unpureed, and tasters loved the bits of chewy sun-dried tomatoes, soft minced onion, and pulpy crushed tomato that punctuated the otherwise silky consistency. This was finally it: a dynamic sauce in which tomatoes and cream boosted each other's flavors and packed enough complexity to keep you coming back for more.

Italians may adhere to an orthodoxy regarding pasta shapes and the sauces with which they should be served, but I'm a bit more flexible. Maybe it's feeding a 3-year-old smitten with the curlicues of fusilli, but I loved the way the creamy sauce wrapped itself around this particular pasta's twists. Ziti and penne also worked well, as would any pasta shape that traps the sauce.

PASTA WITH CREAMY TOMATO SAUCE

SERVES 4

This sauce is best served with short pasta, such as ziti, penne, or fusilli.

- 3 tablespoons unsalted butter
- 1 ounce prosciutto, minced (about 2 tablespoons)
- 1 small onion, diced fine (about ¾ cup)
- 1 bay leaf
- Pinch red pepper flakes
- Table salt
- 3 medium garlic cloves, minced or pressed through garlic press (about 1 tablespoon)
- 2 tablespoons tomato paste
- 2 ounces oil-packed sun-dried tomatoes, drained, rinsed, patted dry, and chopped coarse (about 3 tablespoons)
- ¼ cup plus 2 tablespoons dry white wine
- 2 cups plus 2 tablespoons crushed tomatoes (from one 28-ounce can)
- 1 pound pasta (see note)
- ½ cup heavy cream
- Ground black pepper
- ¼ cup chopped fresh basil leaves
- Grated Parmesan cheese, for serving

1. Melt butter in medium saucepan over medium heat. Add prosciutto, onion, bay leaf, pepper flakes, and ¼ teaspoon salt; cook, stirring occasionally, until onion is very soft and beginning to turn light gold, 8 to 12 minutes. Increase heat to medium-high, add garlic, and cook until fragrant, about 30 seconds. Stir in tomato paste and sun-dried tomatoes and cook, stirring constantly, until slightly darkened, 1 to 2 minutes. Add ¼ cup wine and cook, stirring frequently, until liquid has evaporated, 1 to 2 minutes.

2. Add 2 cups crushed tomatoes and bring to simmer. Reduce heat to low, partially cover, and cook, stirring occasionally, until sauce is thickened (spoon should leave trail when dragged through sauce), 25 to 30 minutes.

3. Meanwhile, bring 4 quarts water to boil. Add pasta and 1 tablespoon salt and cook until al dente. Reserve ½ cup cooking water; drain pasta and transfer back to cooking pot.

4. Remove bay leaf from sauce and discard. Stir cream, remaining 2 tablespoons crushed tomatoes, and remaining 2 tablespoons wine into sauce; season to taste with salt and pepper. Add sauce to cooked pasta, adjusting consistency with up to ½ cup pasta cooking water. Stir in basil and serve immediately, passing Parmesan separately.

EQUIPMENT TESTING:

Wooden Spoons

Is there any real difference between one wooden spoon and another? In a word, yes. We used 10 models to brown beef and stir pots of thick vegetable curry. To test durability, we also tried snapping each in half. Here's what we liked: thin edges (which scrape more effectively than thick); a handle that's strong but not too bulky; and a broad bowl that covers a lot of surface area and can reach into the corners of a pot. For complete testing results, go to www.cooksillustrated.com/june. –Meredith Smith

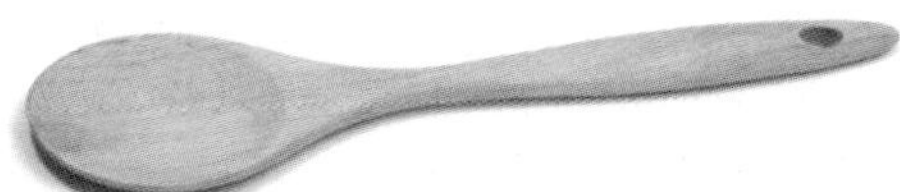

HIGHLY RECOMMENDED

MARIO BATALI 13-Inch Wooden Spoon

Price: $4.95

Comments: Strong but lightweight, with a comfortable grip and a broad, thin-edged bowl, this tool scraped and stirred its way to the top.

RECOMMENDED WITH RESERVATIONS

KITCHEN CARVERS 13-Inch Pointed Spoon You Can't Live Without

Price: $24

Comments: While useful as both a scraper and a scooper, this spoon's squared-off design made reaching all the edges of a pot awkward. We also found the notched rest in the handle (for hooking onto the pan) more of a potential hazard than a help.

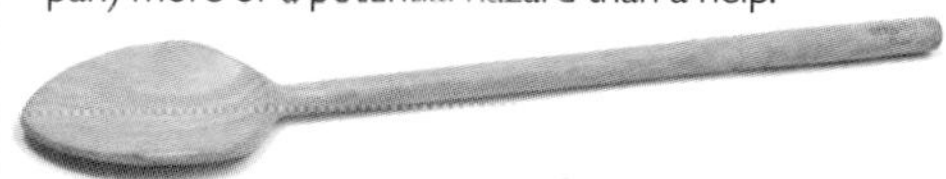

NOT RECOMMENDED

BERARD Olive Wood 13-Inch Cook's Spoon

Price: $13.95

Comments: This spoon's high-end appearance didn't translate to high-end performance. Its pointed tip meant the cook had to take more time to loosen up browned bits when creating a pan sauce. It also snapped in half under pressure.

COOK'S LIVE Original Test Kitchen Videos

www.cooksillustrated.com

HOW TO MAKE

- Pasta with Creamy Tomato Sauce

VIDEO TIPS

- How to make perfect pasta

Fish 101

When it comes to fish, the goal is straightforward: Buy good quality, keep things simple, and don't overcook. BY KEITH DRESSER

Many people find fish intimidating—both to buy and to cook. But the truth is, once you're armed with basic guidelines, fish is no more complicated to buy and cook than vegetables. The keys are learning to recognize good quality, keeping the preparation simple, and avoiding overcooking.

BUYING AND STORING BASICS

At the Store

➢ Whether it's a specialty seafood shop or a neighborhood supermarket, make sure the source is one with a high volume. High volume means high turnover, which ensures freshness. The store should smell like the sea, not fishy or sour.

➢ The fish should be stored on ice or well refrigerated. If stored on ice, the fish shouldn't be sitting in water.

➢ The flesh of fish should appear moist and shiny, not dull, and with even coloring. It should feel firm, not mushy. If possible, ask the fishmonger to press the flesh with his finger to confirm its texture.

➢ Try to have the fishmonger slice steaks or fillets to order; it's best to avoid precut.

At Home

Fish stored at 32 degrees will keep twice as long as fish stored at the typical home refrigerator temperature of 40 degrees. To create the optimum storage conditions, place fish in a zipper-lock bag on ice (or cover with ice packs) and store it at the back of the refrigerator, where it's coldest. And remember to chill the fish immediately upon getting it home.

Catch of the Day

FISH	TEXTURE	HOW TO COOK	IDEAL DONENES
Arctic Char	Medium-Firm	S, G, PS, B, P	Medium-Rare
Bluefish	Medium-Firm	S, G, PS, B, P	Medium
Catfish	Medium-Firm	S, G, PS, B	Medium
Cod	Medium, Flaky	S, B, P	Medium
Flounder	Delicate, Flaky	S	Medium
Grouper	Firm	S, G, PS, B	Medium
Haddock	Medium, Flaky	S, B, P	Medium
Halibut	Firm	G, PS, B, P	Medium
Mackerel	Medium-Firm	G, PS, B	Medium
Monkfish	Firm, Meaty	G, PS, B, P	Medium
Red Snapper	Firm, Flaky	G, PS, B, P	Medium
Salmon	Medium-Firm	G, PS, B, P	Medium-Rare
Sea Bass	Medium, Flaky	S, G, B, P	Medium
Sole	Delicate, Flaky	S	Medium
Swordfish	Very Firm, Meaty	G, PS, B	Medium
Tilapia	Medium-Firm, Dense	S, B, P	Medium
Tilefish	Firm, Flaky	G, PS, B, P	Medium
Trout	Medium-Firm	S, G, B, P	Medium
Tuna	Very Firm, Meaty	G, PS, B	Rare

KEY: S = Sauté, G = Grill, PS = Pan-Sear, B = Braise, P = Poach

PRE-COOKING PREP

Thawing Frozen Fish

Frozen fish should be fully thawed before cooking, ideally defrosted overnight in the refrigerator. Remove the fish from its packaging, lay it in a single layer on a rimmed plate (to catch any released water), and cover it with plastic wrap. Thoroughly dry fish before cooking. Alternatively, defrost fish under cold running water in its original packaging.

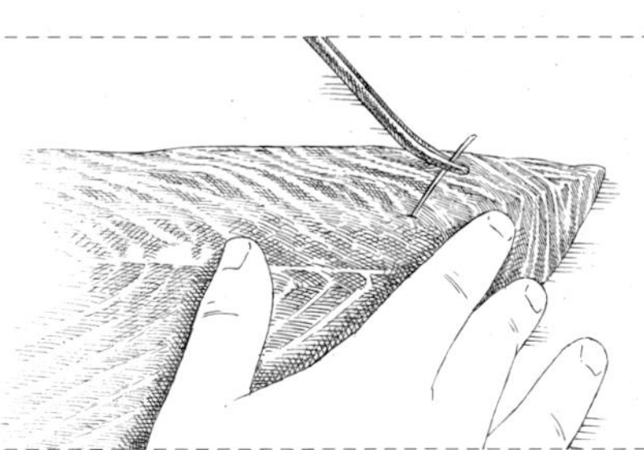

Removing Pin Bones

Pin bones are small white bones that run through the center of a fillet. Most fish is sold with the pin bones removed, but it pays to check before cooking (especially with salmon or trout). To locate pin bones, run your fingers gently over the fillet's surface, feeling for hard, tiny bumps. Use tweezers or needle-nose pliers to grasp and remove the bones.

Ensuring Even Cooking

Fish fillets often come in odd-sized pieces of uneven thickness. If your fillet has a thin, wide tailpiece, tuck it under before cooking to allow it to cook at the same rate as the thicker portion.

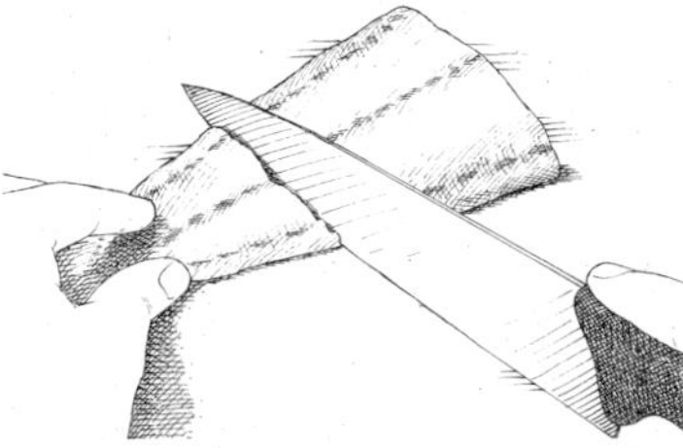

1. With sharp knife, cut halfway through flesh crosswise, 2 to 3 inches from tail end.

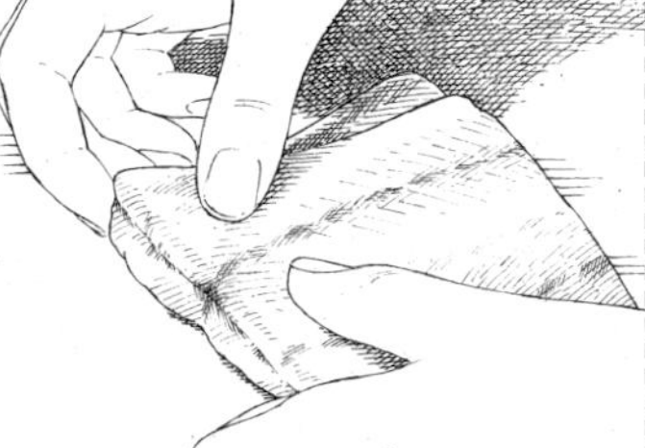

2. Fold tail end under cut seam to create fillet of relatively even thickness.

Judging Doneness

An instant-read thermometer is a useful tool to check doneness in thick fillets, but with thin fillets you have to resort to a more primitive test—nicking the fish with a paring knife and then peeking into the interior to judge color and flakiness. Whitefish, such as cod, should be cooked to medium (about 140 degrees)—that is, the flesh should be opaque but still moist and just beginning to flake; salmon is best cooked to medium-rare (about 125 degrees), with the center still translucent; and tuna is best when rare (about 110 degrees), with only the outer layer opaque and the rest of the fish translucent.

FIVE FAVORITE METHODS FOR COOKING

Successfully cooking fish fillets and steaks requires adherence to just three basic guidelines: Cook fresh fish the day you buy it (or not long after); choose a method that's appropriate for the texture and thickness of your fish; and avoid overcooking it. It really is that simple.

Sautéing

Dredging fish in flour and then sautéing it in a combination of butter and oil creates a crispy, delicate crust you can't get with other techniques. This method is best for thin fillets such as sole or flounder.

1. Pat fish dry and season both sides generously with salt. Let fish stand until it glistens with moisture, about 5 minutes.

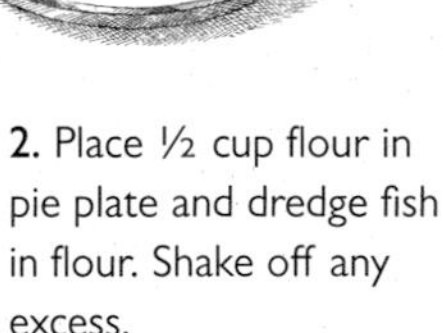

2. Place ½ cup flour in pie plate and dredge fish in flour. Shake off any excess.

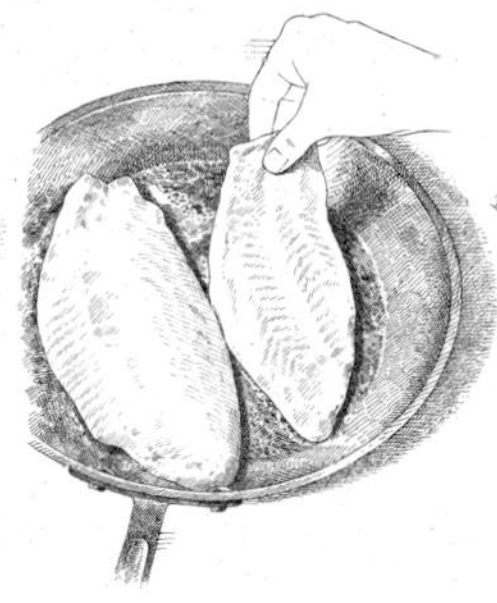

3. Heat 1 tablespoon oil in skillet over high heat; add 1 tablespoon butter and heat until foaming subsides. Reduce heat to medium-high and add fish to pan.

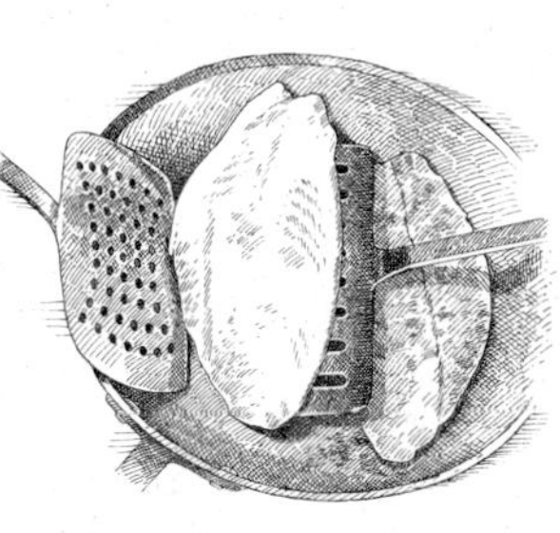

4. When bottoms are golden brown, use two spatulas to gently flip fish. Continue to cook to desired doneness.

Grilling

Grilling is a great way to accentuate flavor. Superheating the grill is the secret to preventing fish from sticking.

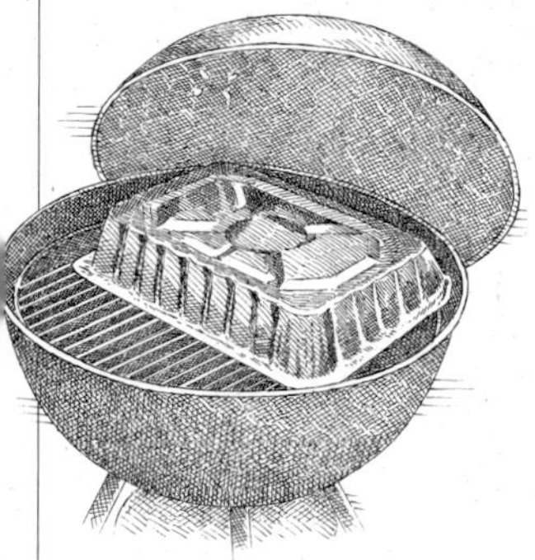

1. Place disposable aluminum pan upside down over grill. Cover for five minutes to superheat the grill and help prevent sticking.

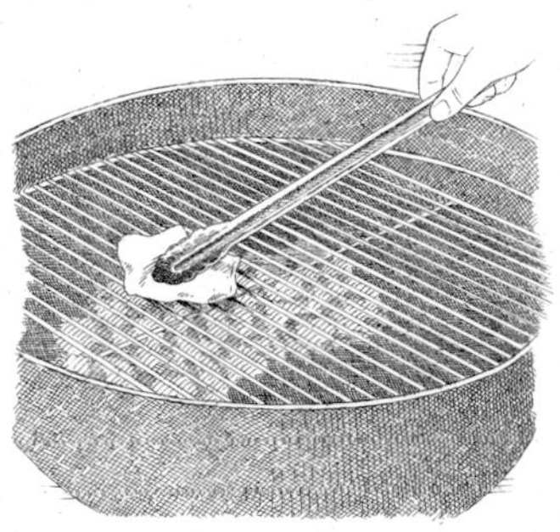

2. Scrape grate clean with grill brush, then wipe it with oil-dipped paper towels. Place fish on grill perpendicular to grates.

3. Grill fish on first side until browned, 2 to 3 minutes (if fish has skin, place skin-side up). Slide one spatula underneath fillet to lift; use another spatula to support fish while flipped. Continue to cook to desired doneness.

Pan-Searing

This method uses less fat than sautéing and calls for starting the fish in an even hotter pan. The result: a flavorful, deeply golden crust, even without the aid of flour.

1. Heat 1 tablespoon vegetable oil in nonstick skillet over high heat until just smoking. Add fish and cook for 30 seconds.

2. Reduce heat to medium-high and cook fish until it's well browned, 3 to 5 minutes. Using tongs, flip fish. Remove fish when it is still slightly translucent; residual heat will continue to cook flesh.

Braising

Braising can either add flavor to mild-flavored fish or mellow assertively flavored fish. The keys are to use low heat and a skillet with a tight-fitting lid to trap the heat so the fish partially steams and partially simmers.

1. In a skillet over medium heat, sauté 1 sliced onion and 4 cloves garlic in 2 tablespoons olive oil until softened. Stir in ½ cup white wine and 14-ounce can diced tomatoes and bring mixture to simmer.

2. Season fish with salt and pepper. Nestle fish into sauce and spoon a little sauce over it. Cover skillet, reduce heat to medium-low, and cook fish to desired doneness.

Poaching

Poaching keeps fish moist. The flavorful liquid in which the fish is cooked can be strained, reduced, and served as a sauce.

1. Bring 6 cups water, 1 cup white wine, juice of 1 lemon, 1 teaspoon table salt, ½ coarsely chopped onion, and 1 coarsely chopped carrot to simmer in large Dutch oven. A few whole peppercorns, bay leaf, and several sprigs of fresh parsley or thyme can be added. Simmer until flavors have blended, about 20 minutes.

2. Reduce heat to lowest setting and place fish into liquid. Cover pot and poach to desired doneness, 6 to 10 minutes. Remove fish using slotted spoon or spatula.

Best Hummus

Hummus requires only a handful of ingredients and five minutes to make—but that doesn't mean it's going to be good.

BY MATTHEW HERRON

Like many time-pressed cooks, I often purchase hummus at the supermarket rather than make it myself. The dip is usually unremarkable but serves its purpose as a quick snack or appetizer. A version I recently tasted at a restaurant, however, opened my eyes to how great hummus can actually be. This hummus had a light, silky-smooth texture that was far more ethereal than the dense, semigranular kinds I was accustomed to. Its flavor was memorable, too: a careful balance of pureed chickpeas, bean cooking liquid, tahini (ground sesame paste), lemon juice, garlic, and a drizzle of extra-virgin olive oil.

My efforts to re-create the restaurant hummus in the test kitchen started with an investigation of chickpeas, known as *hummus* in Arabic and *garbanzo* in Spanish. In Middle Eastern cuisine, hummus is traditionally made with dried beans, but it can also be made with canned. I made batches with each type and rounded up my colleagues for input. Although the flavor of the dried-bean hummus was superior to the canned-bean version, canned beans produced perfectly acceptable results. Given their convenience, I decided to go with canned. (But if the idea of first soaking, then cooking, dried beans doesn't bother you, see our recipe for Ultimate Hummus, page 19.) We found some surprising variation in quality among brands of canned beans, so it's important to choose carefully (see "Canned Chickpeas," page 19). Once I'd selected the brand, I patched together a working recipe that included a few tablespoons each of water (to stand in for the bean cooking liquid), extra-virgin olive oil, tahini, and fresh lemon juice, along with a clove of garlic. With this ingredient list in hand, I was ready to tackle texture.

Fresh cilantro and a hint of cumin enhance this creamy hummus.

Going against the Grain

GRAINY CREAMY

Most hummus has a coarse, dense consistency. Our hummus is characterized by its light, silky smoothness.

Puree Genius

The biggest stumbling block to a creamy, airy consistency was the chickpeas' tough outer skins, so my first thought was to remove them. I tried a ricer, then a food mill, and even rubbed the beans against a colander in my efforts to leave the fibrous skins behind—but these schemes were futile at worst and tedious at best. Perhaps I could achieve a better texture simply by pulverizing the entire bean, including the skin, in the food processor. I put all the ingredients into the workbowl of a food processor and let them whirl for several minutes. Unfortunately, no matter how long I processed, the hummus always retained a certain amount of coarse graininess. I turned to the blender, which can often produce a smoother consistency than a food processor. I had good luck with the first model, but after testing several other blenders, I found that not every one could produce an acceptably creamy dip.

It was time to regroup. I thought back to the mayonnaise-like consistency of the restaurant hummus I was so fond of. Mayonnaise gets its rich silkiness through the creation of an emulsion: a blend of two or more liquids that normally don't mix, in which one is present as tiny droplets dispersed throughout the other. In the case of hummus, my opposing ingredients were the proverbial mismatch—oil and water. Would emulsifying the two give my hummus the silky texture I was after?

I started out by making the chickpea puree as creamy as possible. I processed the beans with and without liquid and discovered that grinding them alone and then adding a small amount of water and lemon juice produced a smoother puree than processing everything at once. Adding the liquid very slowly to the ground beans further minimized grittiness. Now it was time to make an emulsion. Instead of adding the olive oil and tahini separately, as most recipes recommend, I whisked the two together and then added the mixture to the puree in a slow drizzle while processing, creating the emulsion right in the hummus. As the color of the dip changed with the dispersion of the oil, a smooth, light hummus was born.

Matters of Taste

With the technique settled, it was time to fine-tune the flavors of the dip. Tahini was up for examination first. It turns out that different brands vary significantly in fat as well as flavor, with some carrying bitter off-tastes (see "Tahini," page 19). With a good tahini, tasters liked a hefty 6 tablespoons, three times the amount usually found in homemade recipes, appreciating the nutty flavor and the silken texture it lent to the dip.

Garlic, lemon juice, spices, and olive oil are also keys to good hummus, but too much or too little of any one can throw the whole recipe off kilter. After much trial and error, I settled on 3 tablespoons of lemon juice and modest amounts of garlic and olive oil. Cumin is common in Middle Eastern cooking, and tasters liked the earthy undertone it added, along with the subtle heat from a pinch of cayenne. Garnishing the dip with a sprinkle of fresh cilantro, a drizzle of olive oil, and a smattering of whole chickpeas added visual and textural interest.

Finally, I came up with garlic, roasted red pepper,

smoked paprika, and artichoke-lemon versions that far surpassed anything similar I could buy at the supermarket. With recipes so quick and easy to make, I doubt I'll ever buy hummus again.

RESTAURANT-STYLE HUMMUS

MAKES ABOUT 2 CUPS

We recommend Joyva or Krinos tahini and Pastene chickpeas (see tasting results at right). The hummus can be refrigerated in an airtight container for 5 days. If you do not plan on serving it immediately, refrigerate the hummus and garnishes separately. When ready to serve, stir in approximately 1 tablespoon of warm water if the texture is too thick.

- 3 tablespoons juice from 1 to 2 lemons
- ¼ cup water
- 6 tablespoons tahini, stirred well (see note)
- 2 tablespoons extra-virgin olive oil, plus extra for drizzling
- 1 (14-ounce) can chickpeas, drained and rinsed (see note)
- 1 small garlic clove, minced or pressed through garlic press (about ½ teaspoon)
- ½ teaspoon table salt
- ¼ teaspoon ground cumin
- Pinch cayenne
- 1 tablespoon minced fresh cilantro or parsley leaves

1. Combine lemon juice and water in small bowl or measuring cup. Whisk together tahini and 2 tablespoons oil in second small bowl or measuring cup. Set aside 2 tablespoons chickpeas for garnish.

2. Process remaining chickpeas, garlic, salt, cumin, and cayenne in food processor until almost fully ground, about 15 seconds. Scrape down bowl with rubber spatula. With machine running, add lemon juice–water mixture in steady stream through feed tube. Scrape down bowl and continue to process for 1 minute. With machine running, add oil-tahini mixture in steady stream through feed tube; continue to process until hummus is smooth and creamy, about 15 seconds, scraping down bowl as needed.

3. Transfer hummus to serving bowl, sprinkle reserved chickpeas and cilantro over surface, cover with plastic wrap, and let stand until flavors meld, at least 30 minutes. Drizzle with olive oil and serve.

ARTICHOKE-LEMON HUMMUS

Rinse and pat dry 1 cup drained canned or jarred artichoke hearts packed in water. Chop ¼ cup artichoke hearts and set aside for garnish. Follow recipe for Restaurant-Style Hummus, increasing lemon juice to 4 tablespoons and omitting cumin. Process entire can of chickpeas (do not reserve 2 tablespoons) along with remaining ¾ cup artichokes and ¼ teaspoon grated lemon zest in step 2. Garnish hummus with reserved artichokes, 2 teaspoons chopped fresh parsley or mint, and olive oil.

HUMMUS WITH SMOKED PAPRIKA

Follow recipe for Restaurant-Style Hummus, processing entire can of chickpeas (do not reserve 2 tablespoons) in step 2 and substituting 1 teaspoon smoked paprika for cumin. Omit cilantro or parsley. Garnish hummus with 1 tablespoon thinly sliced scallion greens, 2 tablespoons toasted pine nuts, and olive oil.

ROASTED GARLIC HUMMUS

1. Remove outer papery skins from 2 heads garlic; cut top quarters off heads and discard. Wrap garlic in foil and roast in 350-degree oven until browned and very tender, about 1 hour. Meanwhile, heat 2 tablespoons olive oil and 2 thinly sliced garlic cloves in small skillet over medium-low heat. Cook, stirring occasionally, until golden brown, about 15 minutes. Using slotted spoon, transfer garlic slices to paper towel–lined plate and set aside; reserve oil. Once roasted garlic is cool, squeeze cloves from their skins (you should have about ¼ cup).

2. Follow recipe for Restaurant-Style Hummus, substituting garlic cooking oil for olive oil in step 1 and omitting cumin. Process entire can of chickpeas (do not reserve 2 tablespoons) along with roasted garlic puree in step 2. Garnish hummus with toasted garlic slices, 2 teaspoons chopped fresh parsley, and olive oil.

ROASTED RED PEPPER HUMMUS

Follow recipe for Restaurant-Style Hummus, omitting water and cumin. Process entire can of chickpeas (do not reserve 2 tablespoons) along with ¼ cup jarred roasted red peppers that have been rinsed and dried thoroughly with paper towels in step 2. Garnish hummus with 2 tablespoons toasted sliced almonds, 2 teaspoons chopped fresh parsley, and olive oil.

ULTIMATE HUMMUS

Pick through and rinse ½ cup dried chickpeas. Place beans in large bowl, cover with 1 quart water, and soak overnight. Drain. Bring beans, ⅛ teaspoon baking soda, and 1 quart water to boil in large saucepan over high heat. Reduce heat to low and simmer gently, stirring occasionally, until beans are tender, about 1 hour. Drain, reserving ¼ cup bean cooking water, and cool. Continue with recipe for Restaurant-Style Hummus, replacing tap water with cooking water.

COOK'S LIVE Original Test Kitchen Videos

www.cooksillustrated.com

HOW TO MAKE

- Restaurant-Style Hummus

VIDEO TIP

- What is the best food processor?

TASTING: Tahini

Tahini is a thick paste made from ground sesame seeds. We tasted five supermarket brands, both straight from the jar and blended into our Restaurant-Style Hummus recipe. Some brands were alarmingly bitter, but both Joyva and Krinos were pleasantly "tangy," "nutty," and "buttery." For complete tasting results, go to www.cooksillustrated.com/june. –Elizabeth Bomze

TOP TAHINIS

JOYVA Sesame Tahini
Price: $5.80 for 15 ounces
Comments: Boasting "the most tahini flavor," this brand was also "very nutty," "buttery," and almost "peanut-butterish," according to tasters.

KRINOS Tahini
Price: $5.49 for 16 ounces
Comments: Tasters appreciated the slight "lemony" tang of this "buttery," "balanced" tahini.

TASTING: Canned Chickpeas

To make hummus with great flavor and texture, you have to start at the source. We sampled six brands of canned chickpeas, both plain and pureed in our Restaurant-Style Hummus recipe, to find the best. The better brands were notable for chickpeas that were tender, creamy, and well seasoned. For complete tasting results, go to www.cooksillustrated.com/june. –E.B.

HIGHLY RECOMMENDED

PASTENE Chick Peas
Price: 79 cents for 14 ounces
Comments: "Clean," "salty—but not too salty"— flavor, and "firm yet tender" texture.

RECOMMENDED

GOYA Chick Peas
Price: 60 cents for 15.5 ounces
Comments: Highly seasoned, "creamy," and "nutty."

RECOMMENDED WITH RESERVATIONS

PROGRESSO Chick Peas
Price: $1.19 for 19 ounces
Comments: "Good" flavor, but overtly "chalky" and "pasty."

EDEN Organic Garbanzo Beans
Price: $1.69 for 15 ounces
Comments: Next-to-nothing saltwise, these were "fine" for hummus but "watery" and "bland" when eaten plain.

Rescuing Spring Vegetable Risotto

Bland flavor and mushy vegetables can ruin this Italian classic. Could we boost taste while improving the vegetables' texture?

BY KEITH DRESSER

Risotto can be a great platform for highlighting the hearty flavors of winter vegetables like butternut squash and mushrooms. But when paired with more delicate spring vegetables such as asparagus and peas, this dense, creamy rice can be overpowering. My task was straightforward: to create a memorable risotto primavera with fresh yet complex taste and vegetables that retained some crisp bite.

Risotto is medium-grain rice (traditionally Italian-grown Arborio) cooked with hot broth and stirred constantly to turn its starch into a creamy sauce. Most recipes add the broth in painstakingly small increments and stir continuously for up to 30 minutes. We've found that this is not necessary. Our method calls for adding about half the broth (3 cups) all at once at the beginning. This brings a reprieve from some of the stirring.

In Italy, some cooks bring balance to risotto primavera by lightening up the consistency of the rice, making it brothier. Could I follow suit simply by adding more liquid to our basic method? I tried this, but my tasters overwhelmingly preferred a thicker risotto. I would have to work on making the flavor and texture of the vegetables a better match for the rice.

Asparagus and leeks are a classic combination for risotto primavera, and I began there. I wasn't worried about the leeks—added to rice at the outset of cooking, they melted down and their delicate flavor was infused into the dish. My real challenge was to figure out how to keep the asparagus from turning into mush. Adding the asparagus partway through cooking was a possibility, but since cooking rice to al dente is not an exact science, the asparagus frequently over- or undercooked. Sautéing the asparagus and stirring it into the rice just before serving was the answer.

For a third vegetable, I turned to peas. Frozen peas, though not quite as sweet and tender as fresh, worked just fine and freed me from the trouble of shelling.

Still, not enough vegetable flavor was making it into the dish. It dawned on me that the tough stems of the asparagus and the leek greens, which I had been throwing away, might be sources of more flavor. Simmering them for 20 minutes in the chicken broth and water I would be using for the risotto was all it took to enrich the liquid's flavor. I then strained the broth and cooked the risotto in it.

To round out the flavors, I had been adding a splash of lemon juice at the end of cooking, but my tasters wanted even more brightness. I turned to gremolata, a garnish of minced parsley, lemon zest, and garlic that Italians traditionally use to add zip to veal shanks. Raw garlic was too strong, so I omitted it. I also added mint, which complemented the springlike flavors of the dish. I then sprinkled the mixture over the rice just before serving, for a risotto primavera full of fresh flavors and contrasting textures that was truly worthy of its name.

SPRING VEGETABLE RISOTTO

SERVES 4 AS A MAIN COURSE OR 6 AS A FIRST COURSE

To make this dish vegetarian, replace the chicken broth with vegetable broth; the test kitchen's favorite brand is Swanson Vegetarian Vegetable Broth (see "The Awful Truth about Vegetable Broth," page 26). Onions can be substituted for the leeks. If substituting onions, use 1 roughly chopped medium onion (1 cup) in the broth and 2 minced medium onions (2 cups) in the risotto. At the end of cooking, you may have up to a cup of broth left over. For our recommended brands of rice, see "Arborio Rice," page 30. For our free recipes for Spring Vegetable Risotto with Fennel and Spinach and Spring Vegetable Risotto with Carrot and Watercress, go to www.cooksillustrated.com/june.

Gremolata

- 2 tablespoons minced fresh parsley leaves, stems reserved
- 2 tablespoons minced fresh mint leaves, stems reserved
- ½ teaspoon finely grated zest from 1 lemon

Risotto

- 1 pound asparagus, tough ends snapped off and reserved, spears cut on bias into ½-inch-thick pieces
- 2 medium leeks, white and light green parts halved lengthwise, washed, and sliced thin (about 4 cups), 2 cups roughly chopped greens reserved (see note)
- 4 cups low-sodium chicken broth (see note)
- 3 cups water
- 5 tablespoons unsalted butter
- Table salt and ground black pepper
- ½ cup frozen peas
- 2 medium garlic cloves, minced or pressed through garlic press (about 2 teaspoons)
- 1½ cups Arborio rice (see note)
- 1 cup dry white wine
- 1½ ounces grated Parmesan cheese (about ¾ cup), plus extra for serving
- 2 teaspoons juice from 1 lemon

1. **FOR THE GREMOLATA:** Combine ingredients in small bowl and set aside.

2. **FOR THE RISOTTO:** Chop tough asparagus ends and leek greens into rough ½-inch pieces. Bring chopped vegetables, reserved parsley and mint stems, broth, and water to boil in large saucepan over high heat. Reduce heat to medium-low, partially cover, and simmer 20 minutes. Strain broth through fine-mesh strainer into medium bowl, pressing on solids to extract as much liquid as possible. Return strained broth to saucepan; cover and set over low heat to keep broth warm.

3. Heat 1 tablespoon butter in large Dutch oven over medium heat. When foaming subsides, add asparagus spears, pinch of salt, and pepper to taste. Cook, stirring occasionally, until asparagus is crisp-tender, 4 to 6 minutes. Add peas and continue to cook 1 minute. Transfer vegetables to plate and set aside.

4. Melt 3 tablespoons butter in now-empty Dutch oven over medium heat. When foaming subsides, add leeks, garlic, ½ teaspoon salt, and ½ teaspoon pepper. Cook, stirring occasionally, until leeks are softened, 4 to 5 minutes. Add rice and cook, stirring frequently, until grains are translucent around edges, about 3 minutes. Add wine and cook, stirring frequently, until fully absorbed, 2 to 3 minutes.

5. When wine is fully absorbed, add 3 cups hot broth to rice. Simmer, stirring every 3 to 4 minutes, until liquid is absorbed and bottom of pan is almost dry, about 12 minutes.

6. Stir in about ½ cup hot broth and cook, stirring constantly, until absorbed, about 3 minutes; repeat with additional broth 3 or 4 times until rice is al dente. Off heat, stir in remaining tablespoon butter, Parmesan, and lemon juice; gently fold in asparagus and peas. If desired, add up to ¼ cup additional hot broth to loosen texture of risotto. Serve immediately, sprinkling each serving with gremolata and passing Parmesan separately.

COOK'S LIVE Original Test Kitchen Videos

www.cooksillustrated.com

HOW TO MAKE

- Spring Vegetable Risotto

How to Cook Baby Spinach

Cooking baby spinach turns this tender green into a watery mess. Is there a way to the get water out and create a worthwhile side dish?

BY DAVID PAZMIÑO

In the test kitchen, we've always reserved delicate baby spinach for salads, turning to bigger, mature flat-leaf spinach for cooking. The reason? Tender, young baby spinach releases a lot of liquid when it hits a hot pan, which turns it into a waterlogged, mushy mess. But given how convenient baby spinach is (no stems to remove or grit to rinse out), we thought it was time to give cooking it another try.

In the past, we've solved the water problem of the baby green's grown-up cousin by wilting it first in a pan, squeezing it with tongs in a colander to remove liquid, and then returning it to the skillet. This tactic failed miserably with the more delicate baby spinach. As soon as the pressed spinach was put back in the pan, it exuded even more juices, which watered down the other ingredients in the dish.

Blanching or steaming the baby spinach first to release liquid, a technique we found successful with sturdier curly-leaf spinach, was also out. Besides the hassle of another pot to wash, why add water to something that you know will get even wetter?

How about microwaving? After all, that's the suggestion offered on the back of the spinach bag. I placed the leaves in a large glass bowl and covered it with a plate. After six minutes, the spinach was warm but still not sufficiently wilted.

I was loath to do it—but would adding just a little water (¼ cup) to the bowl help speed things up? Eureka! After three minutes, the spinach had softened and shrunk to half its size, thanks to the release of a great deal of liquid. Yet a nagging problem remained: Pressing the spinach against the colander didn't remove enough of the liquid or eliminate its tissuelike texture.

I found other recipes that called for precooking the spinach before sautéing. A few advocated chopping the wilted vegetable as a way to remove liquid. Taking up a new batch of spinach, I microwaved, pressed, and then roughly chopped it on a cutting board. Not only was the mushy texture gone, but the chopping had released even more of the water pooling around the spinach. With victory in sight, I threw the greens back in the colander for a second squeeze. This chopped and double-pressed spinach was just right: tender, sweet, and ready to be combined with complementary ingredients.

Pairings including almonds and raisins or pecans and feta introduced bold flavors and crunchy textures that enlivened this quick-cooking dish. When all was said and done, I had managed to turn a vegetable usually destined for the salad bowl into a delicious side dish with nary a stem to pick.

SAUTÉED SPINACH WITH ALMONDS AND GOLDEN RAISINS

SERVES 4

If you don't have a microwave-safe bowl large enough to accommodate the entire amount of spinach, cook it in a smaller bowl in 2 batches. Reduce the water to 2 tablespoons per batch and cook the spinach for about 1½ minutes. Our free recipes for Sautéed Spinach with Chickpeas and Sun-Dried Tomatoes and Sautéed Spinach with Leeks and Hazelnuts are available at www.cooksillustrated.com/june.

- 3 (6-ounce) bags baby spinach (about 16 cups)
- ¼ cup water
- 2 tablespoons extra-virgin olive oil, plus 2 teaspoons for drizzling
- 4 medium garlic cloves, sliced thin crosswise (about 2 tablespoons)
- ¼ teaspoon red pepper flakes
- ½ cup golden raisins
- Table salt
- 2 teaspoons sherry vinegar
- ⅓ cup slivered almonds, toasted

1. Place spinach and water in large microwave-safe bowl. Cover bowl with large microwave-safe dinner plate (plate should completely cover bowl and not rest on spinach). Microwave on high power until spinach is wilted and decreased in volume by half, 3 to 4 minutes. Using potholders, remove bowl from microwave and keep covered for 1 minute. Carefully remove plate and transfer spinach to colander set in sink. Using back of rubber spatula, gently press spinach against colander to release excess liquid. Transfer spinach to cutting board and roughly chop. Return to colander and press a second time.

2. Heat 2 tablespoons oil, garlic, pepper flakes, and raisins in 10-inch skillet over medium-high heat. Cook, stirring constantly, until garlic is light golden brown and beginning to sizzle, 3 to 6 minutes. Add spinach to skillet, using tongs to stir and coat with oil. Sprinkle with ¼ teaspoon salt and continue stirring with tongs until spinach is uniformly wilted and glossy green, about 2 minutes. Sprinkle with vinegar and almonds; stir to combine. Drizzle with remaining 2 teaspoons oil and season with salt to taste. Serve immediately.

SAUTÉED SPINACH WITH PECANS AND FETA

SERVES 4

- 3 (6-ounce) bags baby spinach (about 16 cups)
- ¼ cup water
- 2 tablespoons extra-virgin olive oil, plus 2 teaspoons for drizzling
- 3 large shallots, sliced thin crosswise (about 1 cup)
- Table salt
- 2 teaspoons red wine vinegar
- ⅓ cup chopped pecans, toasted
- 1½ ounces feta cheese, crumbled (about ¼ cup)

Follow recipe for Sautéed Spinach with Almonds and Golden Raisins through step 1. Heat 2 tablespoons oil and shallots in 10-inch skillet over medium-high heat. Cook, stirring constantly, until shallots are golden brown, 3 to 5 minutes. Add spinach to skillet, using tongs to stir and coat with oil. Sprinkle with ¼ teaspoon salt and continue stirring with tongs until spinach is uniformly wilted and glossy green, about 2 minutes. Sprinkle with vinegar and pecans; stir to combine. Drizzle with remaining 2 teaspoons oil and sprinkle with feta. Season with salt to taste and serve immediately.

Microwave Magic

PLUMPED UP — DOWNSIZED

Wilting the baby spinach in a large bowl in the microwave before sautéing makes it easy to squeeze out excess water and shrinks the spinach so that it fits easily in a skillet.

Perfecting Oatmeal Snack Cake

A caramelized broiled icing is the crowning glory on an old-fashioned oatmeal cake. But what good is a great icing if the cake itself is dense and gummy?

BY SARAH WILSON AND MATTHEW CARD

The informal title "snack cake" is applied to a broad range of simple cakes that come together with a few minutes' effort using pantry staples, making them ideal for after-school snacks, bake sales, and surprise visitors. One of the more interesting of the bunch is an oatmeal cake with a unique coconut- and pecan-studded broiled icing (broiled, that is, on top of the baked and slightly cooled cake).

The *Joy of Cooking* notes that this cake has a "loyal following," and online bulletin boards and blogs support that claim with dozens of rave reviews. Perhaps we expected too much from all the high praise, but we weren't very impressed once we'd baked a few test recipes. We assumed the cake would be moist, but instead we found it dense, gummy, and bland. The broiled icing, however, won us over: We loved its combination of chewy coconut and crunchy nuts and its butterscotch-like flavor, despite a saccharine sweetness and tendency toward greasiness. We decided that if we could make a moist (but not dense) cake and fix the icing's foibles, then we might hop on the bandwagon, too.

Batter Matters

In each of the recipes we collected, a cup or so of old-fashioned rolled oats were hydrated in water and folded into a basic batter leavened with both baking powder and baking soda. The biggest difference among recipes—outside of base ratios of ingredients—was the type of fat specified: vegetable oil, shortening, or butter. The first two provided no flavor, making butter the obvious choice. Of the recipes that called for butter, most specified a surprisingly small amount: 6 tablespoons or less. Such a scant amount of butter seemed light for a cake of this style. But with all the hydrated oats in the batter, a mere 4 tablespoons of butter was all it took to produce a cake that tasters felt was plenty moist (albeit gummy), with buttery undertones.

Our moist cake goes under the broiler to give its coconut- and pecan-studded icing a crunchy, caramelized texture.

Oats contribute starch and fiber to the cake, but little of the gluten needed for structure. For support, recipes typically include moderate amounts of all-purpose flour, usually in a 1–1 ratio with the oats. To create a lighter cake, could we use less flour than oats? Reducing the flour from 1 cup (the amount of oats we had been using) to ¾ cup helped, but the cake still wasn't light enough to suit tasters. But any less flour and the cake collapsed into crumbs when we sliced it. We'd have to look elsewhere for a solution.

Most recipes sweetened the cake with 1 cup or more of brown sugar. We hazarded a guess that the sugar's dampness contributed to the cake's density. We cut the brown sugar by half (to ½ cup) and compensated with an equal amount of granulated sugar. The cake was now sufficiently light, and its more moderate sweetness was actually better suited to the sugary icing. Still, a less dense cake did not mean a less gummy cake. It was time to address the elephant in the room: the oats.

Sorting Out the Oats

To mitigate their gumminess, we tried both toasting the oats and changing the amounts of oats and water in the batter, all to no avail. If changing the amount of oats wouldn't work, perhaps using a different type would. Chewy steel-cut oats made little sense here, but instant and quick-cooking rolled oats both did. The former bombed (precooked instant oats mostly dissolve when combined with boiling water, making the cake gluey), but the latter was a marked improvement. The cake was perceptibly less gummy, though not yet perfect.

Irrespective of type, the soaked oats were a sticky mess when we stirred them into the batter. Was that contributing to the gummy texture of the final cake? Would simply folding in dried oats suffice? No dice: The dried oats never fully hydrated, and they tasted raw and chewy in the finished cake. A chat with our science editor gave us a different idea: The hotter the water in which the oats are soaked, the more starches they release and the gluier they

SCIENCE: Goodbye to Gumminess

The unique moist yet crumbly texture of our oatmeal cake is largely due to the inclusion of oats hydrated in water. While most recipes for this cake specify old-fashioned oats soaked in boiling water, we found these cakes to be gummy and dense. We produced a cake with a much lighter texture by switching to quick-cooking oats soaked in room-temperature water. How did such a seemingly small alteration so greatly improve the cake's crumb?

It turns out that the extent to which the starch and fibers in oats absorb water is directly related to temperature: The hotter the water in which the oats are soaked, the more starches that are hydrated (and subsequently released into the mix) and the more gluey the oats become. In the case of our snack cake, all those released starches weighed down the cake's batter.

Soaking raw old-fashioned oats in tap water accomplishes little at all: Being raw, they need heat to effectively hydrate. Quick-cooking oats, however, have been steamed and then rolled into thin flakes, giving them the ability to readily absorb water at any temperature. So our success was a compromise of sorts: The quick-cooking oats absorb water and release some of their starches and fibers to moisten the cake, but not nearly as much as old-fashioned oats steeped in boiling water. –M.C.

become (see "Goodbye to Gumminess," page 23). So why not soak the oats in room-temperature, rather than boiling, water? We poured tepid tap water over a new batch of quick-cooking oats. Within a few minutes, they had absorbed the water but weren't nearly as sticky or starchy as oats "cooked" in boiling water. We baked the cake, and the results were the best yet: delightfully moist yet enticingly crumbly, and entirely free of that once-persistent gumminess.

Crunchy and Chewy

It was time to tackle the topping. The ingredients were the same in all recipes we found: sweetened, shredded coconut; pecans; light brown sugar; and butter. First we cut back on the brown sugar to make the icing less sweet. Then we examined technique. Some recipes creamed the butter and sugar until fluffy before stirring in the coconut and pecans; others simply melted the butter before stirring the ingredients together. We determined that any fluffiness achieved by creaming the butter was lost once the frosting went under the broiler, so we took the easier route and used melted butter. This produced a stiffer icing than did the creaming method, but that was easily remedied by adding a splash of milk.

After we'd charred a few cakes under the broiler, we realized that placing the cake about 9 inches from the heating element evenly browned the icing in the time it took for the texture to turn "crun-chewy." We were finally ready to give this quick, delicious, and unique cake rave reviews.

STEP-BY-STEP | FINISHING THE CAKE

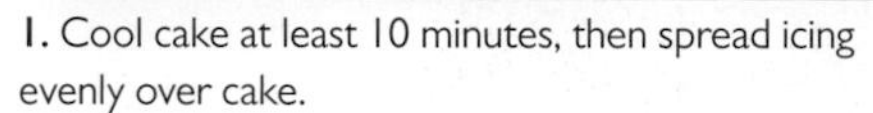

1. Cool cake at least 10 minutes, then spread icing evenly over cake.

2. Broil cake until icing is bubbling and golden brown.

OATMEAL CAKE WITH BROILED ICING

MAKES ONE 8-INCH SQUARE CAKE

Do not use old-fashioned or instant oats for this recipe. Be sure to use a metal baking dish; glass pans are not recommended when broiling. If you have a drawer-style broiler (underneath the oven), position the rack as far as possible from the broiler element and monitor the icing carefully as it cooks in step 5. A vertical sawing motion with a serrated knife works best for cutting through the crunchy icing and tender crumb.

Cake

- 1 cup (3 ounces) quick-cooking oats (see note)
- ¾ cup water, room temperature
- ¾ cup (3¾ ounces) unbleached all-purpose flour
- ½ teaspoon baking soda
- ½ teaspoon baking powder
- ½ teaspoon salt
- ¼ teaspoon ground cinnamon
- ⅛ teaspoon ground nutmeg
- 4 tablespoons (½ stick) unsalted butter, softened
- ½ cup (3½ ounces) granulated sugar
- ½ cup packed (3½ ounces) light brown sugar
- 1 large egg, room temperature
- ½ teaspoon vanilla extract

Broiled Icing

- ¼ cup packed (1¾ ounces) light brown sugar
- 3 tablespoons unsalted butter, melted and cooled
- 3 tablespoons milk
- ¾ cup sweetened, shredded coconut
- ½ cup (2½ ounces) pecans, chopped

1. **FOR THE CAKE:** Adjust oven rack to middle position and heat oven to 350 degrees. Cut two 16-inch lengths aluminum foil and fold both lengthwise to 5-inch widths. Spray 8- by 8-inch metal baking dish with nonstick cooking spray. Following illustration 1 below, fit foil pieces into baking dish, one overlapping the other, pushing them into corners and up sides of pan; allow excess to overhang pan edges. Spray foil lightly with nonstick cooking spray.

2. Combine oats and water in medium bowl and let sit until water is absorbed, about 5 minutes. In another medium bowl, whisk flour, baking soda, baking powder, salt, cinnamon, and nutmeg together.

3. In bowl of standing mixer, beat butter and sugars on medium speed until combined and mixture has consistency of damp sand, 2 to 4 minutes, scraping down bowl with rubber spatula halfway through mixing. Add egg and vanilla; beat until combined, about 30 seconds. Add flour mixture in 2 additions and mix until just incorporated, about 30 seconds. Add soaked oats and mix until combined, about 15 seconds.

4. Give batter final stir with rubber spatula to make sure thoroughly combined. Transfer batter to prepared pan and lightly tap against counter 3 or 4 times to dislodge any large air bubbles; smooth surface with spatula. Bake cake until toothpick inserted into center comes out with few crumbs attached, 30 to 35 minutes, rotating pan halfway through baking. Let cake cool slightly in pan, at least 10 minutes.

5. **FOR THE BROILED ICING:** While cake cools, adjust oven rack about 9 inches from broiler element and heat broiler. In medium bowl, whisk brown sugar, melted butter, and milk together; stir in coconut and pecans. Spread mixture evenly over warm cake. Broil until topping is bubbling and golden, 3 to 5 minutes.

6. Let cake cool in pan 1 hour. Following illustration 2, transfer cake to serving platter, then discard foil. Cut cake into squares and serve.

COOK'S LIVE Original Test Kitchen Videos
www.cooksillustrated.com
HOW TO MAKE
- Oatmeal Cake with Broiled Icing

TECHNIQUE | DOUBLE-FOIL SLING

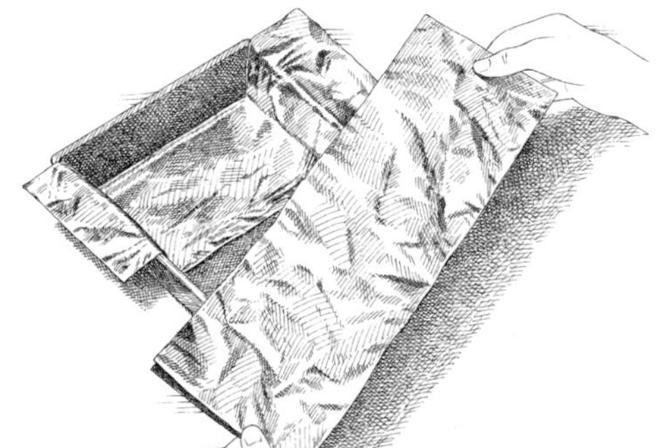

1. To transfer our exceptionally tender cake to a platter without it crumbling, we devised a novel solution. Cut two 16-inch pieces aluminum foil and fold into 5-inch widths. Press one piece foil into pan. Repeat with second piece, overlapping pieces by about 1 inch.

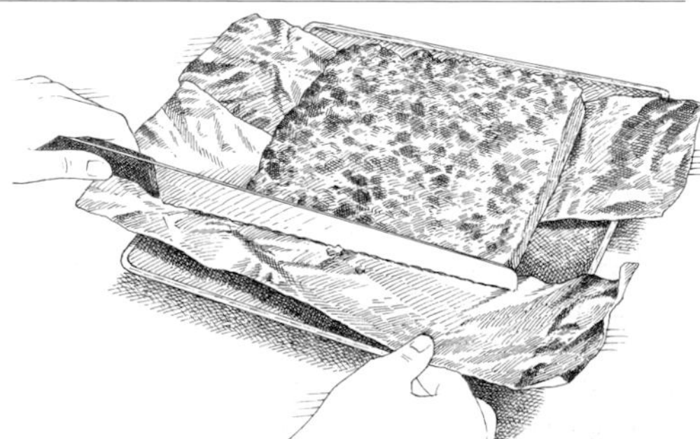

2. Once cake has cooled, pick up overhanging edges of foil and transfer cake to flat surface or platter. Gently push side of cake with knife and remove foil, one piece at a time.

Ultimate Berry Fool

Most fools are soupy and loose, with dull, overcooked fruit. The key to a fool that's both creamy and intensely fruity is all in how you thicken it.

⋟ BY DAVID PAZMIÑO ⋞

Heretical as it may sound, apple pie was not always the quintessential American dessert. Centuries ago, fruit fool held that honor. Brought to America by British colonists in the 1700s, this dessert was made by folding pureed stewed fruit (traditionally gooseberries) into a sweet custard. Gooseberry fool was important enough to show up in the recipes of Martha Washington. Two hundred years later, it was still enough of a classic to earn a place in James Beard's *American Cookery*. The origin of the dessert's name, however, remains a mystery. Some believe it comes from the French verb *fouler* (to crush or pound). Others think the etymology points to the idea that as a dessert, this concoction was a bit of sweet foolishness.

Traditional recipes call for gently heating milk, cream, sugar, and egg yolks until thickened and then folding in cooked, pureed fruit once the custard has cooled. The resulting dessert has a deep, fruity flavor and a wonderfully silken creaminess. But cooking custard is a fussy endeavor. Overheat the yolks and you produce scrambled eggs; neglect to bring the mixture up to a high enough temperature and you've made eggnog.

Sour cream and thickened fruit puree give this fool its rich body; crumbled cookies add textural interest.

Modern recipes skip the custard and use whipped cream. But most of the whipped-cream versions I tested, including one from Beard's *American Cookery*, blunted the flavor of the fruit and seemed too light and insubstantial when compared with fool made with custard. Worse, if the recipe departed from the traditional fruit choice—gooseberries—the dessert turned soupy and loose. I knew I wasn't going to be using gooseberries unless I grew them in my backyard. And I definitely didn't want to cook up custard. Could I concoct a dessert with the intense fruitiness and rich body of a traditional fool just the same?

A Sweet Finish

Though not traditional, a sprinkling of crushed sweet wheat crackers (gingersnaps and graham crackers will also work) adds subtle crunch and nutty notes that complement the berry flavors in our fool.

We're Jammin'

The reason fool made with gooseberries has a firmer texture is that this hard-to-find heritage fruit is naturally high in pectin. When exposed to heat, sugar, and acid, pectin breaks down and causes the fruit to thicken (see "Gelatin vs. Pectin," page 31). I wanted to use raspberries and strawberries, but they contain very little pectin and remain loose when cooked. Would adding a little commercially made pectin help? It did—but I needed to add so much extra sugar for the pectin to work that my puree turned into a supersweet jam.

Some fool recipes I found cooked low-pectin fruits such as raspberries and strawberries with egg yolks to thicken them up, in essence creating a fruit curd. Not surprisingly, a yolk-based fruit puree turned out to be just as temperamental as custard, requiring lots of attention to keep the fruit from turning lumpy. Furthermore, when I folded the curd into the whipped cream, the dessert no longer tasted fresh and fruity; it had an eggy flavor that superseded everything else. Cornstarch proved equally unhelpful in achieving the results I wanted. Though I used less than typically called for in a fruit pie filling, the cooked berries still lost some of their fresh, vibrant flavor, and the mixture had a slight chalkiness my tasters didn't like.

The idea of using gelatin had been percolating in the back of my mind—recipes for desserts such as mousse and Bavarian crème often use it to firm up texture. But adding it to fruit? Wouldn't that turn my puree into Jell-O? For gelatin to work, I would need to use a judicious hand. I added just 2 teaspoons, softening the gelatin in some uncooked berry puree and then combining the softened mixture with some heated puree to help melt and distribute the gelatin. After setting for a couple of hours in the refrigerator, the puree thickened to the consistency of a loose pie filling: perfect. Once I tasted the puree, I knew I had hit the jackpot—it had a far fresher and more intense fruit flavor than anything I'd managed to produce yet. And, unlike the other methods I'd tried, I didn't need to actually cook the fruit. I only needed to get the puree hot enough to melt the gelatin.

Creating a Creamier Base

All that remained was to create a richer, sturdier cream base to partner with the fruit puree. Making custard was out. But why not try to make whipped cream more custardlike? I rounded up a bunch of candidates to add density to the billowy cream: whole-milk yogurt, mascarpone cheese, crème fraîche, and sour cream. Whipped together with heavy cream, each worked surprisingly well in creating a mixture that was airy yet more substantial than plain whipped cream. Sour cream won out for adding just the right degree of richness, along with a mildly tangy undertone.

My tasters, however, were clamoring for a bit more fruit flavor, as well as contrasting fruit texture. Layering

STEP-BY-STEP | BUILDING THE ULTIMATE BERRY FOOL

1. PUREE AND STRAIN FRUIT
Puree half of the berries with sugar and then strain them to remove seeds.

2. ADD GELATIN
Thicken the berry puree with gelatin to contribute body to the final dish.

3. MACERATE BERRIES
Sprinkle the remaining berries with sugar, allow them to stand for an hour, then drain.

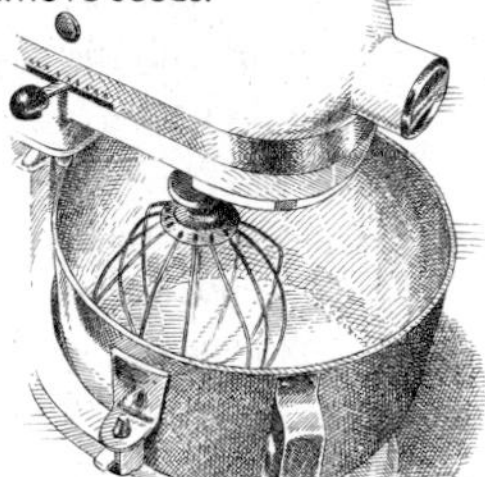

4. MAKE CREAMY BASE
Whip sour cream into the heavy cream to create a rich and creamy base.

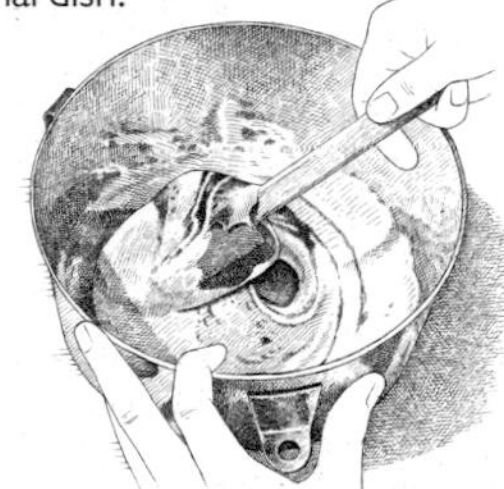

5. SWIRL PUREE INTO CREAM
Swirl the gelatin-thickened berry puree into the enriched whipped cream.

6. LAYER BERRIES
Layer the macerated berries between dollops of the creamy berry mixture to add fresh flavor.

the fruit puree and cream base with fresh berries tasted great but left pools of juice in the mixture. Letting the berries stand in a sugar mixture solved the problem by drawing out excess juice that could be strained off.

I could have left the fool well enough alone, but I had encountered several recipes that sprinkled the dessert with crumbled cookies or sweet crackers. I tried a range of these, including graham crackers and gingersnaps. Tasters' favorite was sweet wheat crackers, for the pleasant contrast their nuttiness added to the cream and fruit.

With its fruity flavor and creamy texture, I now had a modern, reliable recipe that kept only the best traits of this old-fashioned dessert.

BERRY FOOL

SERVES 6

Blueberries or blackberries can be substituted for raspberries in this recipe. You may also substitute frozen fruit for fresh, but there will be a slight compromise in texture. If using frozen fruit, reduce the amount of sugar in the puree by 1 tablespoon. The thickened fruit puree can be made up to 4 hours in advance; just make sure to whisk it well in step 4 to break up any clumps before combining it with the whipped cream. For the best results, chill your beater and bowl before whipping the cream. We like the granular texture and nutty flavor of Carr's Whole Wheat Crackers, but graham crackers or gingersnaps will also work.

- **2 quarts strawberries (about 2 pounds), washed, dried, and stemmed**
- **1 pint raspberries (about 12 ounces), washed and dried (see note)**
- **½ cup plus 4 tablespoons sugar**
- **2 teaspoons unflavored powdered gelatin**
- **1 cup heavy cream**
- **¼ cup sour cream**
- **½ teaspoon vanilla extract**
- **4 Carr's Whole Wheat Crackers, finely crushed (about ¼ cup) (see note)**
- **6 sprigs fresh mint (optional)**

1. Process 1 quart strawberries, ½ pint raspberries, and ½ cup sugar in food processor until mixture is completely smooth, about 1 minute. Strain berry puree through fine-mesh strainer into 4-cup liquid measuring cup (you should have 2½ cups puree; reserve any excess for another use). Transfer ½ cup puree to small bowl and sprinkle gelatin over top; stir until gelatin is incorporated and let stand at least 5 minutes. Heat remaining 2 cups puree in small saucepan over medium heat until it begins to bubble, 4 to 6 minutes. Remove pan from heat and stir in gelatin mixture until dissolved. Transfer gelatin-puree mixture to medium bowl, cover with plastic wrap, and refrigerate until cold, about 2 hours.

2. Meanwhile, chop remaining 1 quart strawberries into rough ¼-inch pieces. Toss strawberries, remaining ½ pint raspberries, and 2 tablespoons sugar together in medium bowl. Set aside for 1 hour.

3. Place cream, sour cream, vanilla, and remaining 2 tablespoons sugar in chilled bowl of stand mixer. Beat on low speed until bubbles form, about 30 seconds. Increase speed to medium and continue beating until beaters leave trail, about 30 seconds. Increase speed to high; continue beating until mixture has nearly doubled in volume and holds stiff peaks, about 30 seconds. Transfer ⅓ cup whipped-cream mixture to small bowl and set aside.

4. Remove thickened berry puree from refrigerator and whisk until smooth. With mixer running at medium speed, slowly add two-thirds of puree to whipped-cream mixture; mix until incorporated, about 15 seconds. Using spatula, gently fold in remaining thickened puree, leaving streaks of puree.

5. Transfer uncooked berries to fine-mesh strainer; shake gently to remove any excess juice. Divide two-thirds of berries evenly among 6 tall parfait or sundae glasses. Divide creamy berry mixture evenly among glasses, followed by remaining uncooked berries. Top each glass with reserved plain whipped-cream mixture. Sprinkle with crushed crackers and garnish with mint sprigs, if using. Serve immediately.

EQUIPMENT TESTING:
Balloon Whisks

When only a cup or so of whipped cream is needed, is it really necessary to haul out a stand mixer? Manufacturers claim the bulbous design of balloon-style whisks makes short work of whisking air into cream. We timed how long five different models took to whip a cup of heavy cream to stiff peaks, comparing the whipping times and user-friendliness of each. For complete testing results, go to www.cooksillustrated.com/june. –Elizabeth Bomze

HIGHLY RECOMMENDED
RÖSLE Balloon Whisk/Beater
Price: $26.95
Comments: This Rolls-Royce of balloon whisks whipped cream the fastest, though the price is a bit high for such a simple tool.

BEST BUY
OXO Steel 11-Inch Balloon Whisk
Price: $9.99
Comments: An all-around winner: quick whip time, comfy handle, lightweight design, and slim price tag.

RECOMMENDED WITH RESERVATIONS
CUISIPRO Duo Whisk with Wire Ball
Price: $17.99
Comments: More like a cat toy than a kitchen tool, this whisk's wire-wrapped balls failed to boost speed.

COOK'S LIVE Original Test Kitchen Videos
www.cooksillustrated.com

HOW TO MAKE
- Berry Fool

VIDEO TIPS
- What is the best way to whip cream?
- How to wash and store fresh berries

The Awful Truth about Vegetable Broth

It's no surprise that veggie broths lack meat and bones, but why do so many rely on salt and "flavor potentiators" rather than vegetables? No wonder most brands are so bad.

⇛ BY LISA McMANUS ⇚

Just 10 years ago, vegetable broth was hard to find in the supermarket. Now there are dozens of brands that come in cans and boxes, along with cubes, powders, and pastes. In the past, we've always called for canned chicken broth when we wanted to cut corners on making our own stock, even in our vegetable-based recipes. Without the advantage of meat, bones, or fat to boost their flavor, we wondered if any of these vegetable products could win us over. Are any of them more than simply second-class substitutes for those who don't use products made with meat?

We sampled 10 broths, first heated and served plain, then cooked into soup and risotto. From the first glance, it was clear that they were nothing alike. We saw broths that were opaque, others that were clear, and a few that had grit floating in the bottom of the tasting cups. Flavors ranged from bland to overpowering. Some were astonishingly salty or sweet, others oddly sour—and more than a few didn't taste anything at all like vegetables. Some were downright terrible. What could account for the extreme variety in these products that all billed themselves as vegetable broth? Clearly, if you used them interchangeably in your recipes, the results would be radically different—and possibly even disastrous.

No Rules

After noting the lack of similarity from brand to brand, we were not surprised to learn that there are no federal standards for how vegetable broth must be made. A call to Barry Swanson, a professor of food science at Washington State University, revealed that vegetable broths tend to be made from the ugly ducklings of the produce world—vegetables that, while not spoiled, are misshapen, overripe, bruised, or otherwise unsuitable for sale as whole vegetables or vegetable parts. Some broths are not even made from fresh vegetables, but use dehydrated or powdered vegetable content instead. Worse, there's no way to tell from the label whether a list of vegetable juices (carrot juice, beet juice, onion juice, etc.) came from fresh produce or were reconstituted from concentrates or powders—manufacturers are not required to reveal this. The same thing holds true for lists of what sound like whole vegetables ("organic celery," "organic carrots," etc.) but might really be vegetable extracts, concentrates, or powders.

Even more disturbing, some broths contain scant vegetable matter in any form, depending heavily on salts and sugars to stimulate the taste buds and a laundry list of enhancers known as "flavor potentiators." These include monosodium glutamate (MSG), disodium inosinate, and disodium guanylate. (Every one of these additives can also be found in commercial chicken broth.)

Taking Stock

As we shopped for our lineup, we noted that some manufacturers were calling their products vegetable "stock" rather than broth. Traditionally, stock differs from broth because it is made with bones, which release rich gelatin during a long simmer on the stove, providing body to the resulting liquid. Since vegetables have no bones, and the products claimed to be vegetarian, we assumed this had to be marketing hype. However, a call to The Hain Celestial Group, which manufactures both Imagine Organic Vegetable Stock and Imagine Organic Vegetable Broth, revealed that the company uses the term "broth" to refer to a quick-cooked liquid designed to capture fresh vegetable flavor, while "stock" refers to the more concentrated, seasoned result of a long, slow simmer. (Other manufacturers generally use the same distinction.)

Our tasters had a distinct preference for the fresher taste of broths, with the longer-cooked stocks all falling to the bottom half of the lineup. Slow-cooked stocks face another disadvantage: If the vegetables you start with are not top-notch, or if you're using scraps and peels, extended cooking can enhance and concentrate any undesirable flavors in the vegetables, such as acidity or sourness. Sure enough, our tasters noted sour, bitter, even "rotten" notes in each of the so-called stocks in our lineup. We could only wonder, then, why any manufacturer would bother to cook veggie broth long enough to turn it into stock.

Best Broth

When we looked at the labels of our broths post-tasting, we found that our preferences tended to align with those that contained vegetable content (whether derived from fresh whole vegetables, we couldn't tell) present in a high enough concentration to be listed first on the ingredient list, ahead of salt and/or water. But a higher proportion of vegetable matter, on its own, was not a guarantor of good flavor. Just as important was the presence of both a slew of heavy-hitting flavor potentiators and salt—lots of it. In fact, moderate sodium content and the lack of flavor-enhancing additives helped land nearly all of the organic brands at the bottom of the rankings. These broths shared lackluster—even off-putting—flavors that tasters likened variously to "weak V8," "musky socks," and "brackish celery water."

We've rarely had so many brands achieve such low scores in a tasting. Out of 10 brands, we can recommend just one, Swanson Vegetarian Vegetable Broth. This broth boasted the highest sodium content in the lineup—nearly double the amount of most other brands. With its mix of vegetable juices, flavor enhancers, and sweeteners such as sugar, dextrose, and high fructose corn syrup, it managed to summon up a flavor profile that more than one taster noted "actually tastes like vegetables."

And how would this one decently flavored veggie broth stack up against chicken broth? To find out, we compared batches of Creamy Potato Soup and Parmesan Risotto made with each type. For chicken broth, we chose our test kitchen favorite, Swanson's Certified Organic. Tasters were split down the middle as to which broth contributed better flavor. But taste aside, comparing the ingredient labels of the two broths disabused us once and for all of the notion that commercial vegetable broth might be the healthier alternative to commercial chicken broth. To achieve its equal footing, Swanson Vegetarian Vegetable Broth not only contains chemical flavor potentiators, it is also loaded with nearly double the sodium of our favorite chicken broth.

A Meaty (and Healthier) Alternative?

For both good taste and no chemicals in a commercial broth, we're sticking with chicken. Not only is our winning brand of vegetable broth, Swanson Vegetarian Vegetable Broth, made with artificial flavor enhancers, it's got nearly double the salt of our favorite chicken broth—Swanson's Certified Organic. All the organic vegetable broths in our lineup tanked.

FLAVORFUL AND CHEMICAL FREE

TASTING VEGETABLE BROTH

Twenty-one *Cook's Illustrated* staffers sampled 10 broths, chosen from the top-selling brands of ready-to-serve broth in the United States, according to Chicago-based market research firm Information Resources Inc. Each was tasted plain, cooked into Creamy Potato Soup and Parmesan Risotto, and tasted plain again but with salt corrected to the same level in all broths. The flavor-enhancing ingredients are listed as they appear on the product label; sodium is expressed in milligrams per 1-cup serving. Prices were paid in Boston-area supermarkets. The results of the four tastings were averaged, and the broths appear below in order of preference.

RECOMMENDED

SWANSON Vegetarian Vegetable Broth

➢ **Price:** $1.50 for 14-ounce can

➢ **Sodium:** 940 milligrams

➢ **Flavor Enhancers:** Salt, high fructose corn syrup, sugar, dextrose, autolyzed yeast extract, monosodium glutamate, disodium inosinate, disodium guanylate

Comments: "Good balance of veggie flavors—carrot and celery are distinguishable, but not overwhelming." "I'd have this as plain soup if I had a cold." The fact that it had the highest sodium level in the lineup didn't escape our tasters ("mega-salty"). With a host of chemical additives, many noted that it tasted like poultry; we had to reassure a vegetarian taster that we hadn't slipped in a chicken broth. Even when we corrected the salt levels of all of the other broths to match, this one still came out on top.

RECOMMENDED WITH RESERVATIONS

COLLEGE INN Garden Vegetable Broth

➢ **Price:** $1.09 for 14.5-ounce can

➢ **Sodium:** 590 milligrams

➢ **Flavor Enhancers:** Salt, sugar, disodium inosinate, disodium guanylate

Comments: Offering "decent, well-balanced vegetable flavor," this broth had "mostly tomato flavor," yet was still deemed "one of the best." Plain, it had a "slightly sour, tangy" taste, though cooked into risotto, it was "a good background," and in soup, "neutral."

KNORR Vegetarian Vegetable Bouillon Cubes

➢ **Price:** $1.49 for 2.1-ounce box (makes 12 cups)

➢ **Sodium:** 830 milligrams

➢ **Flavor Enhancers:** Salt, partially hydrogenated soybean and cottonseed oils, monosodium glutamate, yeast extract, sugar, disodium inosinate

Comments: "A bit salty, but good flavor," agreed tasters, noting that this broth made from pressed cubes "seems beefy, not vegetabley." Again and again, tasters were reminded of the broth that comes with packaged ramen noodles.

IMAGINE Organic Vegetable Broth

➢ **Price:** $3.59 for 32-ounce box

➢ **Sodium:** 550 milligrams

➢ **Flavor Enhancers:** Sea salt, organic spices, organic expeller-pressed canola oil and/or safflower oil and/or sunflower oil

Comments: With a "body more like soup than broth" and a flavor described as mostly "carrot—in color and flavor" (others, less flatteringly, called it "gross" and "murky"), this broth was "quite sweet," "thick," and "flat and flavorless" in soup, with only "a slight vegetable taste—but of canned vegetables." In risotto: "SO yellow" and "pretty darned bland. It's like a flavor eraser."

NOT RECOMMENDED

BETTER THAN BOUILLON Vegetable Base

➢ **Price:** $5.99 for 8-ounce jar (makes 38 cups)

➢ **Sodium:** 710 milligrams

➢ **Flavor Enhancers:** Hydrolized soy protein, salt, yeast extract, sugar, maltodextrin (from corn), partially hydrogenated soybean oil, spice extractive

Comments: Tasters agreed that broth made from this paste-style base was "a salt lick!" "metallic," and "musty," with a "smoke flavor reminiscent of a Slim Jim." The broth's origins were easily detected in every application: "Bouillon cube, I presume," wrote one taster among many who noted its "fake," "dried herb" flavors.

EMERIL'S All Natural Organic Vegetable Stock

➢ **Price:** $4.29 for 32-ounce box

➢ **Sodium:** 570 milligrams

➢ **Flavor Enhancers:** Sea salt, yeast extract, cane juice, flavor, canola oil, and flavor

Comments: "Sickeningly sweet, with a sour aftertaste." Like "weak V8" or "dirty carrot peels." It reminded tasters of "frozen onion rings that got freezer burn" and had a "weird, gelatinous texture." In soup, it was so "bland" that one taster asked: "Did you make this with water instead of broth?"

SWANSON Certified Organic Vegetarian Vegetable Broth

➢ **Price:** $4 for 32-ounce box

➢ **Sodium:** 570 milligrams

➢ **Flavor Enhancers:** Sea salt, flavoring, organic pear juice from concentrate (water, organic pear juice concentrate), organic yeast extract (organic yeast extract, salt, wheat), sugar, canola oil, flavoring

Comments: "Brackish," "thin," "bitter," and "vegetal," with a "horrible" flavor. One taster wrote, "Celery! Celery! Celery!" while another, recalling the gruel in *Oliver Twist*, called it "orphan water."

IMAGINE Organic Vegetable Cooking Stock

➢ **Price:** $3.29 for 32-ounce box

➢ **Sodium:** 580 milligrams

➢ **Flavor Enhancers:** Sea salt, natural flavors

Comments: Tasters reacted to this broth's strong flavor, described variously as "dirty tamarind water," "bitter celery leaves," "weirdly sweet and sour," and "fermented." "This is just wrong," one taster complained. "An acid punch with a carrot aftertaste," summed up another. "So this is what lighter fluid and sugar taste like."

KITCHEN BASICS Natural Vegetable Cooking Stock

➢ **Price:** $2.99 for 32-ounce box

➢ **Sodium:** 330 milligrams

➢ **Flavor Enhancers:** Natural flavor (from corn), sea salt

Comments: "Tastes like rotten vegetables." "Gross and grassy—is this houseplant broth?" Its brown color made risotto look muddy, with "watered-down caramel," "old date," "maple," "pumpkin," and "molasses" notes. In sum, it "doesn't taste anything like vegetables."

PACIFIC Natural Foods Organic Vegetable Broth

➢ **Price:** $3.99 for four 8-ounce boxes

➢ **Sodium:** 530 milligrams

➢ **Flavor Enhancer:** Sea salt

Comments: One taster deemed this broth "unnatural—terrible-tasting—not food." "I can't bring myself to taste this again, as I'm traumatized by the first taste. It tastes like dirt." "Like musky socks in a patch of mushrooms," it was redolent of "old vegetables," with an "almost rotten flavor." You get the drift.

Do You Need a Mandoline?

Long the domain of chefs churning out precision-cut produce, mandolines are increasingly targeted toward the home cook. But does this specialty slicer really give you an edge?

BY ELIZABETH BOMZE

Churning out large quantities of identically sliced fruit and vegetables is a challenge for any cook wielding only a chef's knife. Even the most skilled might wish for a faster, more precise tool. There is such a device—the mandoline. An appliance more often found in classic French or Japanese restaurants than in the home, this countertop gadget resembles a horizontal grater. It has two working surfaces: a razor-sharp blade and an adjustable platform that creates a downward cutting angle. Once the desired thickness is set, slicing requires nothing more than running a piece of food against the blade.

Despite the mandoline's speed and precision, we've always been skeptical of kitchen gadgets that perform the same function as basic tools we already own. Like most specialty kitchen tools, these slicers vary dramatically in size, price, and design. Many eat up counter space, and the most expensive can cost well over $100. And some, we discovered, even felt dangerous. Was there a mandoline that truly belonged in a home kitchen? We rounded up 13 models—from a $7 plastic tool to a souped-up $380 appliance—to find out.

The Cutting Edge

Mandolines come in two styles: Classic, French-inspired models feature a straight blade for basic slicing, as well as serrated and comb blades for fancier applications such as julienned matchsticks or waffle cuts; handheld slicers offer only a straight slicing blade, usually fit flat in a utensil drawer, and cost less (many are plastic). Either type must be sharp enough to glide through firm produce such as potatoes without bumping or jerking and slice softer foods without snagging or mangling. Most important, all good mandolines must include extensive safety features.

Nearly all models handled firm food effortlessly; a few turned out slices of potato so clean they could be reassembled into a perfect whole. Softer produce was another matter. We tried slicing ripe beefsteak tomatoes as thinly as possible, figuring a blade that could cope with something so squishy could handle anything. Tomato skins can snag on straight-bladed knives (we usually cut them with serrated knives), and we wondered if the same would hold true for mandolines. Minutes later, we had two piles: a pulverized crime scene of red juice, seeds, and skins and a towering stack of beautiful, intact tomato disks. The difference? All of the flawlessly performing mandolines had V-shaped or diagonally slanted blades, which, like the teeth on a serrated knife, cut the tough skin more readily than did a horizontal edge.

Safety First

We put a premium on the safety features of these potentially dangerous tools. Most models include hand guards to shield fingers from sharp blades and the prongs that grip the food. The safest guards were broad and ran smoothly along the slicing track. Some, shaped like derby hats, had brims whose diameters stretched at least as wide as the slicing plane. These felt far safer than guards shaped like small, plastic plates that fit in the palm of your hand.

The type of food prongs on the guards made a real difference, too. We came across three basic styles: short, blunt teeth that could only poke at hard or heavy vegetables like carrots or potatoes; sturdy skewerlike prongs of an inch or more sheathed by retractable food pushers, which worked best for both gripping produce and keeping hands out of harm's way; and the spring-loaded prongs featured on the two most expensive slicers. The spring-loaded prongs were a disaster. While the coils were supposed to create enough tension to hold the food firmly against the blade—theoretically saving the cook from pressing down while sliding the food along the slicing plane—loading this device was not easy: The food went in . . . and the food sprang back out. Finally, as much as we thought we'd like models whose food grippers locked on tracks—several guards, representing each category, could slide onto the slicing plane to prevent slipping—this feature proved irritating when the produce was too bulky to fit underneath.

Sharpest Tool in the Box

Nobody likes to have to pore over a user's manual, and more than one slicer came with cryptic instructions or sent testers through multiple steps just to change a blade. Testers awarded highest marks to models with precise, measurement-marked dials that let you set the thickness of the slice. Not only could these knobs adjust thickness, on some models they simultaneously rotated the right blade into position, eliminating contact with sharp blades.

By the time we concluded testing, it was clear that a mandoline was a welcome addition to our kitchen, but shelling out big bucks for classic French and Japanese models bought no added safety or comfort, only baffling designs and flashy storage cases. After spending between $100 and $400, we shouldn't have had to cringe in fear while slicing. For a fraction of the price, you can do better. We liked a blade-and-box combo ($39.96) from Joyce Chen Benriner, which sliced potatoes and soft tomatoes in no time and collected the contents in a handy bin. It even turned out proper julienned carrots, though testers agreed that pressing hard against the comb blade with its small guard felt dicey. For a handheld, no-frills model, a simple slicer from Kyocera ($24.95) is a real bargain—our Best Buy. Its ceramic blade is exceptionally sharp and easily adjustable, and it fits easily in a drawer.

But if we were going to own a mandoline, we figured it should do the works—slice, julienne, and waffle-cut—while keeping our hands safe. We found our winner in OXO's V-Blade Mandoline Slicer ($49.99). Testers proclaimed its V-shaped blade ideal for both firm and delicate produce. It felt safe and comfortable and came with a rimmed, long-pronged hand guard. Best of all, delicate julienne and waffle cuts were simple; with a quick blade swap and one turn of a knob, this slicer could multitask better than some of the priciest models. And just to be sure it really could earn its keep alongside a chef's knife, we put it through one final test: timing a test cook as he sliced potatoes into ⅛-inch rounds, first with a chef's knife, then with the mandoline. Not surprisingly, the mandoline's slices were far more uniform than the knife's—and they were churned out almost 30 percent faster.

Anatomy of an Ideal Mandoline

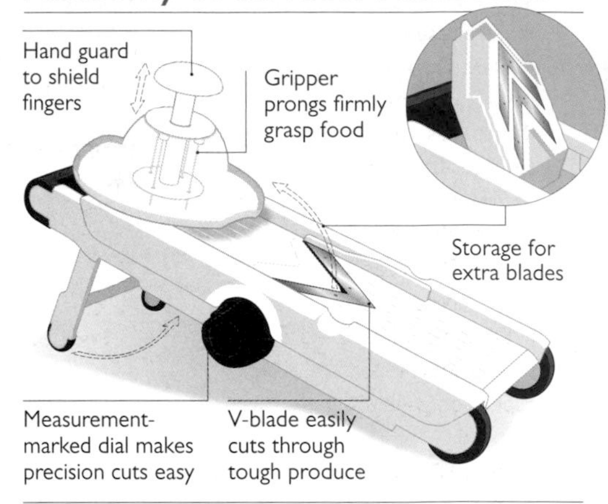

TESTING MANDOLINE SLICERS

KEY
GOOD: ★★★
FAIR: ★★
POOR: ★

We had both novice and experienced testers try out 13 mandolines, slicing russet potatoes and beefsteak tomatoes and assessing the models on safety features and user-friendliness. Where applicable, we also tested julienne and crinkle- or waffle-cutting blades. The slicers appear in order of preference. Prices were paid at Boston-area retail stores or online. Sources for the winners appear on page 32.

STRAIGHT CUTS: As our benchmark test, we used straight blades to cut russet potatoes into ⅛-inch rounds and slice beefsteak tomatoes as thinly as possible.

JULIENNE CUTS: We julienned medium carrots on models with this feature.

CRINKLE/WAFFLE CUTS: We sliced russet potatoes on the few models that offered a blade for this restaurant-style cut.

EVEN LESS RECOMMENDED: The following were eliminated in preliminary tests after failing to slice potatoes and tomatoes acceptably: Kuhn Rikon Hand-Held Mandoline Slicer with Handguard ($24.95), Progressive International Multi-Slicer ($6.99), and KitchenAid Mandoline Slicer Set ($49.99).

COOK'S LIVE
Original Test Kitchen Videos
www.cooksillustrated.com
- Behind the Scenes: Testing Mandolines

VIDEO TIP
- Buying Guide to Mandolines

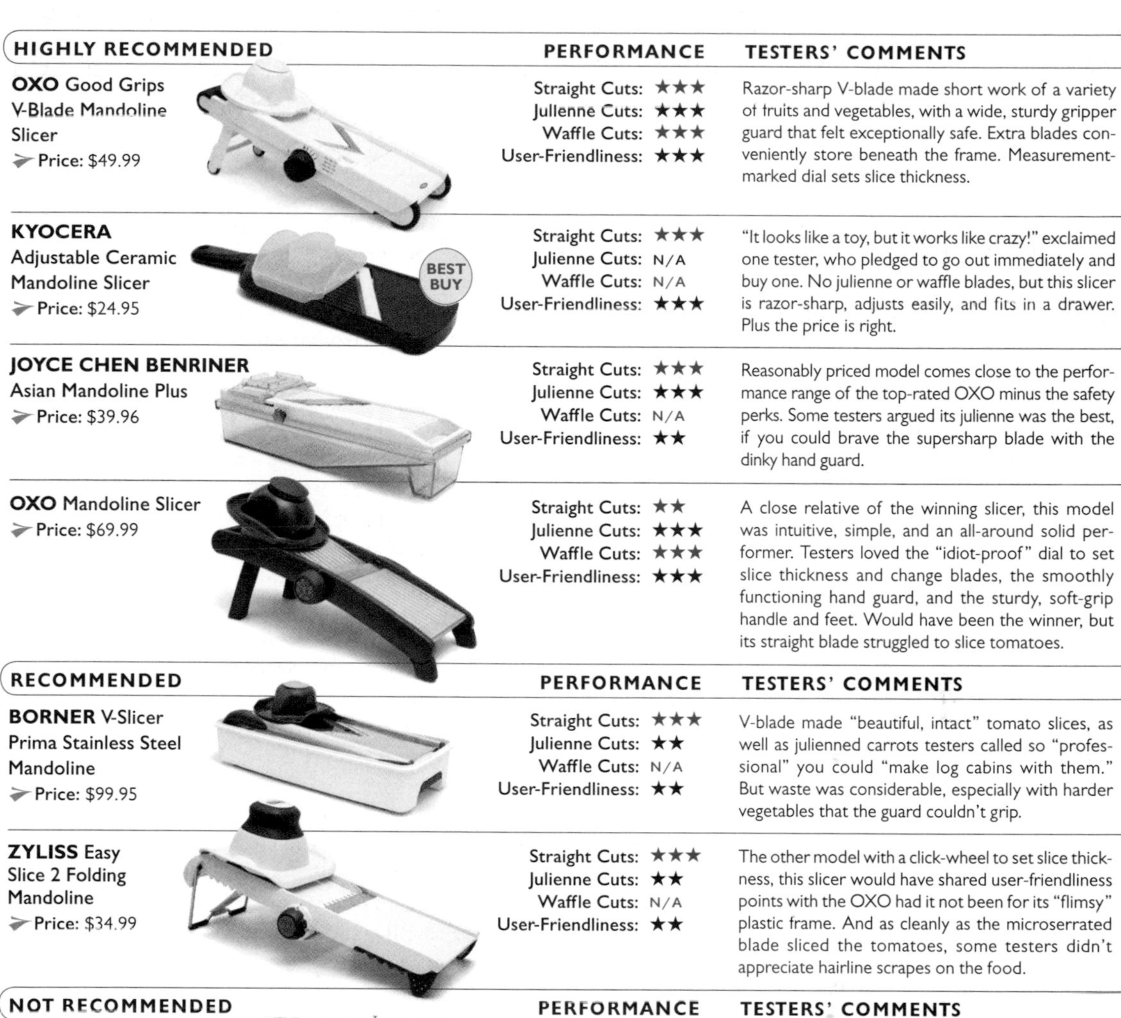

HIGHLY RECOMMENDED	PERFORMANCE	TESTERS' COMMENTS
OXO Good Grips V-Blade Mandoline Slicer Price: $49.99	Straight Cuts: ★★★ Julienne Cuts: ★★★ Waffle Cuts: ★★★ User-Friendliness: ★★★	Razor-sharp V-blade made short work of a variety of fruits and vegetables, with a wide, sturdy gripper guard that felt exceptionally safe. Extra blades conveniently store beneath the frame. Measurement-marked dial sets slice thickness.
KYOCERA Adjustable Ceramic Mandoline Slicer Price: $24.95	Straight Cuts: ★★★ Julienne Cuts: N/A Waffle Cuts: N/A User-Friendliness: ★★★	"It looks like a toy, but it works like crazy!" exclaimed one tester, who pledged to go out immediately and buy one. No julienne or waffle blades, but this slicer is razor-sharp, adjusts easily, and fits in a drawer. Plus the price is right.
JOYCE CHEN BENRINER Asian Mandoline Plus Price: $39.96	Straight Cuts: ★★★ Julienne Cuts: ★★★ Waffle Cuts: N/A User-Friendliness: ★★	Reasonably priced model comes close to the performance range of the top-rated OXO minus the safety perks. Some testers argued its julienne was the best, if you could brave the supersharp blade with the dinky hand guard.
OXO Mandoline Slicer Price: $69.99	Straight Cuts: ★★ Julienne Cuts: ★★★ Waffle Cuts: ★★★ User-Friendliness: ★★★	A close relative of the winning slicer, this model was intuitive, simple, and an all-around solid performer. Testers loved the "idiot-proof" dial to set slice thickness and change blades, the smoothly functioning hand guard, and the sturdy, soft-grip handle and feet. Would have been the winner, but its straight blade struggled to slice tomatoes.

RECOMMENDED	PERFORMANCE	TESTERS' COMMENTS
BORNER V-Slicer Prima Stainless Steel Mandoline Price: $99.95	Straight Cuts: ★★★ Julienne Cuts: ★★ Waffle Cuts: N/A User-Friendliness: ★★	V-blade made "beautiful, intact" tomato slices, as well as julienned carrots testers called so "professional" you could "make log cabins with them." But waste was considerable, especially with harder vegetables that the guard couldn't grip.
ZYLISS Easy Slice 2 Folding Mandoline Price: $34.99	Straight Cuts: ★★★ Julienne Cuts: ★★ Waffle Cuts: N/A User-Friendliness: ★★	The other model with a click-wheel to set slice thickness, this slicer would have shared user-friendliness points with the OXO had it not been for its "flimsy" plastic frame. And as cleanly as the microserrated blade sliced the tomatoes, some testers didn't appreciate hairline scrapes on the food.

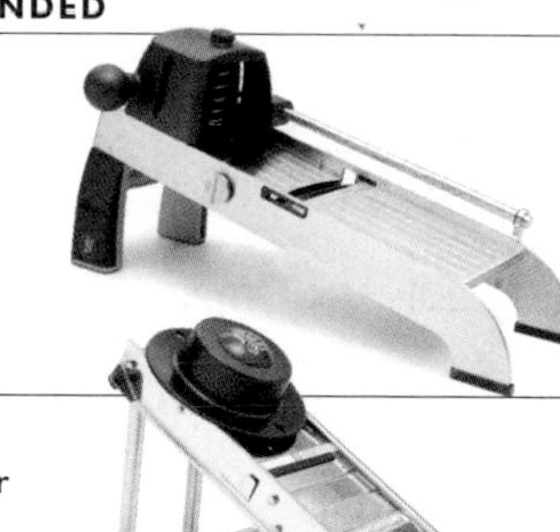

NOT RECOMMENDED	PERFORMANCE	TESTERS' COMMENTS
SHUN Mandoline Price: $379.95	Straight Cuts: ★★ Julienne Cuts: ★★ Waffle Cuts: N/A User-Friendliness: ★★	A colossal disappointment with an equally colossal price tag. Testers who were quick to compare this "beast" to a "deli machine on steroids" at first sight were shocked when the spring-loaded gripper "destroyed" tomatoes and required more than a little effort to slide across the blade. It produced "crisp, beautiful potato slices" but was an overall "pain in the neck."
BRON COUKE Stainless Steel Super Pro Mandoline Price: $179.95	Straight Cuts: ★★ Julienne Cuts: ★★ Waffle Cuts: ★★ User-Friendliness: ★	Everyone agreed that "after the setup, the results are pretty nice." Directions were "cryptic" and "confusing," and though it could make all the cuts in the book, it was "not very intuitive for novice users." Tomatoes "smeared" and "pulped" on its straight blade.
MIRCOPLANE V-Slicer Price: $39.99 	Straight Cuts: ★★ Julienne Cuts: N/A Waffle Cuts: N/A User-Friendliness: ★★	Some testers appreciated the thickness-adjusting wheel, others felt it brought fingers too close to the blade. Tomato slices were "translucent," but the heavy, juicy fruit was too weighty for the gripper. "A bit wobbly" and food "tends to get trapped" on the underside.
DE BUYER V-Pro Mandoline Price: $199.99 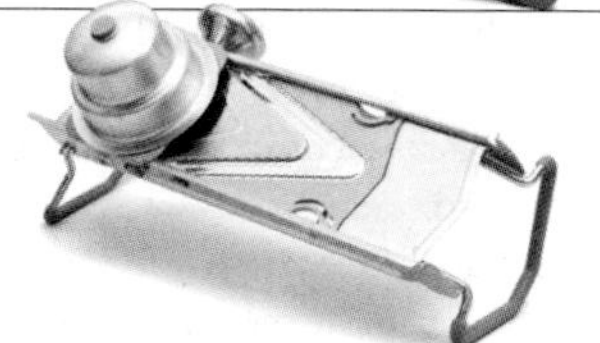	Straight Cuts: ★★ Julienne Cuts: ★★ Waffle Cuts: ★ User-Friendliness: ★	"Completely unintuitive," "uncomfortable," and "overbuilt," this brawny French model's only saving grace was its incredibly sharp V-blades. The spring-loaded guard "boinged" food across the counter.

KITCHEN NOTES

⋙ BY J. KENJI ALT ⋘

TASTING: **Arborio Rice**

The stubby, milky grains of Arborio rice, once grown exclusively in Italy, are valued for their high starch content and the subsequent creaminess they bring to risotto. But does the best Arborio rice have to come from Italy?

To find out, we cooked up batches of Parmesan risotto with two domestically grown brands of Arborio rice and four Italian imports; all brands are widely available in supermarkets. To our surprise, the winning rice hailed not from the boot, but from the Lone Star State. –Elizabeth Bomze

HIGHLY RECOMMENDED

RICESELECT Arborio Rice
Price: $7.99 for 2 lb., 4 oz.
Comments: The "creamy, smooth" grains of this Texas-grown rice won over tasters with their "good bite."

RISO BARICELLA Superfino Arborio Rice
Price: $5.99 for 2 lb.
Comments: "Great rice, awesome velvety texture," wrote one taster about this Italian import with "good flavor."

RECOMMENDED

RIENZI Premium Gourmet Arborio Rice
Price: $2.89 for 1 lb.
Comments: This Italian rice had a "springy, creamy texture."

PASTENE Superfino Italian Arborio Rice
Price: $1.99 for 16.9 oz.
Comments: This import had "good, basic flavor" but was "not as creamy as others."

NOT RECOMMENDED

LUNDBERG White Arborio Rice
Price: $4.39 for 2 lb.
Comments: Tasters complained that this California-grown rice tasted "mushy" and "chalky."

Flour Swap: King Arthur for Gold Medal

For the sake of standardization, here in the test kitchen we develop all of our baking recipes requiring all-purpose flour with Gold Medal, the best-selling brand in the United States. The number-two brand, Pillsbury, has the same protein content as Gold Medal (about 10.5 percent), and we've found that it performs on a par with Gold Medal. However, we know many of our readers keep King Arthur in the pantry. King Arthur contains roughly 11 percent more protein than Gold Medal. Protein affects gluten development: The more protein there is, the more gluten will be created during mixing and kneading. Despite the small difference, can the two brands be used interchangeably?

It depends on what you're baking. In recipes with relatively little gluten development, such as cookies, muffins, and biscuits, both flours produced virtually identical batches. But in bread recipes specifically engineered by the test kitchen to use all-purpose flour (not bread flour) to create a tender crumb, such as sandwich bread and challah, the switch mattered. The extra protein in King Arthur produced more gluten when the dough was kneaded, leading to loaves that were gummy and rubbery in comparison to loaves made from Gold Medal. After a few tests, we found an easy fix: Replacing 1 tablespoon of flour per cup with 1 tablespoon of cornstarch made King Arthur behave just like Gold Medal.

Fighting Grill Flare-Ups

While small flare-ups can impart a smoky flavor and crisp crust to grilled foods, large flare-ups can blacken your dinner, not to mention singe arm hair and eyebrows. To extinguish a flare-up, pull the food away from the offending flames (ideally to a cool spot on the grill with no coals or lit burners) and mist the spot with water from a spray bottle. If the entire grill is engulfed, food can be removed to a baking sheet while you get things under control.

Beef Primer: Buying the Best Steaks

Some of the best steaks come from two muscles found near the spine in the cow's midsection: the shell and the tenderloin. The shell is a much larger muscle, running the entire length of the cow's back, and has more fat and a more robust beef flavor than meat from the tenderloin. The rib steak is cut from the rib section of the shell. Strip steaks (also known as shell steaks) are cut from the shell muscle in the loin section. The tenderloin starts in the middle of the back, running parallel to the shell under the spine. Filet mignon steaks are cut from the tenderloin. They are extremely tender and have a mild flavor. Two of our favorite steaks, the porterhouse and the T-bone, boast the best of both worlds, containing portions of both muscles.

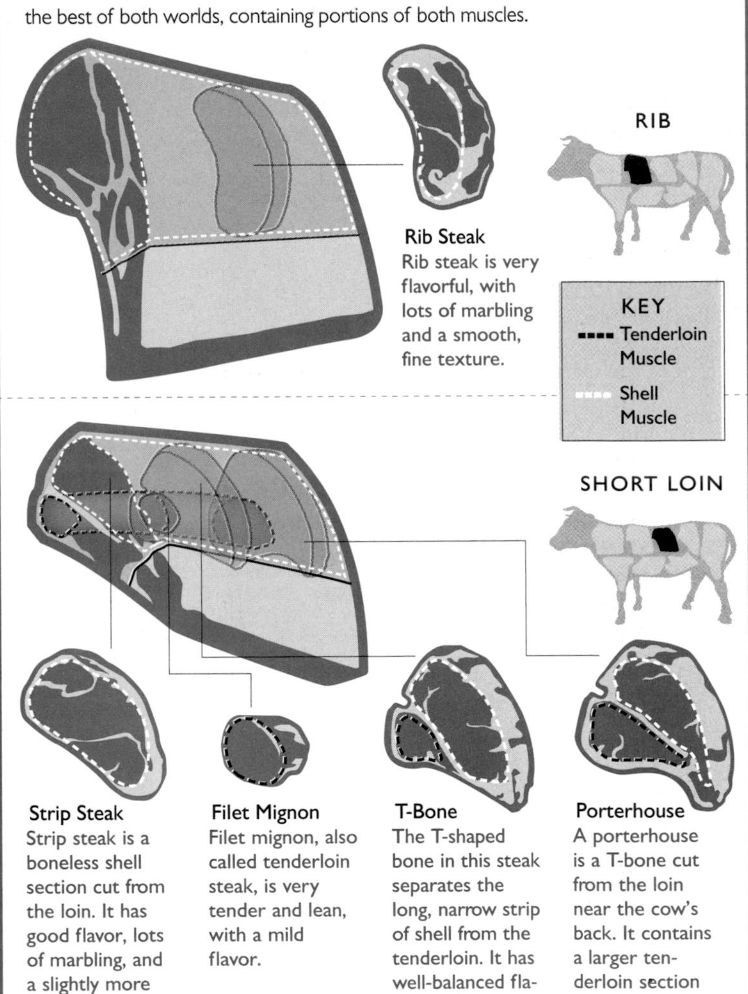

Rib Steak
Rib steak is very flavorful, with lots of marbling and a smooth, fine texture.

Strip Steak
Strip steak is a boneless shell section cut from the loin. It has good flavor, lots of marbling, and a slightly more pronounced grain than a rib steak.

Filet Mignon
Filet mignon, also called tenderloin steak, is very tender and lean, with a mild flavor.

T-Bone
The T-shaped bone in this steak separates the long, narrow strip of shell from the tenderloin. It has well-balanced flavor and texture.

Porterhouse
A porterhouse is a T-bone cut from the loin near the cow's back. It contains a larger tenderloin section than a standard T-bone.

Avoiding Bitter Orange Juice

We've noticed that fresh-squeezed orange juice has a tendency to turn bitter if it sits too long. The cause is a compound called LARL. In a whole orange, the LARL and the juice of the orange are safely separated from each other. But when the cells of the orange are ruptured, the LARL and juice mix and, with time, react to form a bitter compound called *limonin*. We tasted freshly squeezed orange juice next to juice squeezed four hours earlier, both plain and whisked into marinades. The four-hour-old orange juice was clearly more bitter than the freshly squeezed. Our advice? Squeeze your juice right before you drink it.

TECHNIQUE

REMOVING CHICKEN TENDERLOINS

The chicken tenderloin is the small piece of meat attached to the underside of each breast half. Many recipes for boneless skinless chicken (including our Stuffed Chicken Breasts, page 9) call for removing the tenderloin before cooking. Here's how to do it.

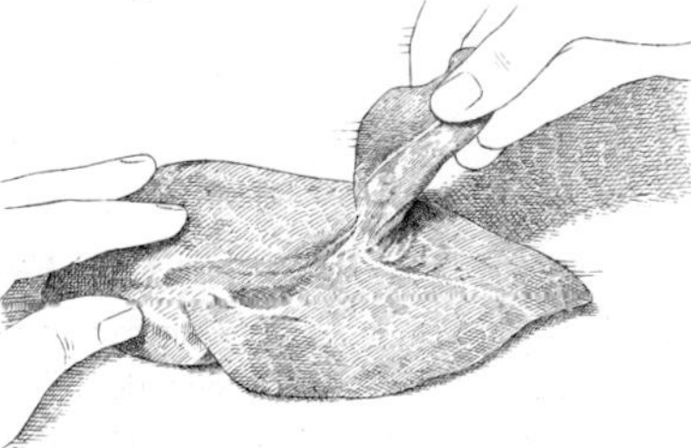

Lay the breast on the work surface smooth-side down and use one hand to locate the tenderloin. Place one hand flat against the chicken breast and hold it against the board while you gently pull the tenderloin off with your other hand.

Different Trimming Treatment for Beef and Pork

While developing our recipe for braised Mexican Pulled Pork (page 13), we found we liked the meat best when we left a thin layer of fat on the exterior of each piece. Would the same hold true for beef braised in a stew? To find out, we made batches of beef stew with meat completely trimmed, partially trimmed (leaving ⅛ inch of exterior fat and removing half of the intramuscular fat and connective tissue), and untrimmed. Tasters unanimously agreed the beef was better with all hard fat and connective tissue removed. Why the difference between pork and beef?

Beef tends to have more marbling (intramuscular ribboning of fat) than pork, so even when all the large chunks of fat are trimmed off a piece of beef, there's plenty left beneath the surface. This fat renders out and moistens the beef as it cooks, keeping it juicy and tender. The fat in pork, on the other hand, tends to be around muscles, instead of between them. So if you trim away all visible fat from pork, the remaining meat will be quite lean and, consequently, dry and fibrous once braised.

PARTIAL TRIM FOR PORK
For the optimal balance of fat and lean, leave a ⅛-inch layer of fat on pork before braising.

FULL TRIM FOR BEEF
Remove all hard fat and connective tissue (which will appear as white fibers or soft gelatinous areas) from beef before braising.

SCIENCE: Gelatin vs. Pectin

Gelatin might be a newcomer to recipes for fruit fool, but it has long been used to impart a silken texture to desserts ranging from Bavarian crème to mousse. A pure protein derived from animal bones and connective tissues, gelatin changes liquid into a semisolid state by trapping water and slowing its movement. In contrast to other thickening agents, gelatin begins to melt at body temperature, contributing to a unique sensation in the mouth. These properties worked beautifully in our Berry Fool (page 25), transforming a thin berry puree into a viscous mixture that lent silkiness to the enriched whipped cream.

Pectin is a carbohydrate that occurs naturally in fruits and vegetables and holds cell walls together like cement. When exposed to heat, sugar, and acid, pectin molecules loosen their grip on the cell walls and bond directly with each other, creating a matrix that traps water in much the same way gelatin molecules do. However, unlike gelatin, pectin requires high temperatures for its thickening action to be reversed. It also proved an unsuitable thickener for the fruit in our fool, requiring so much sugar to work that it turned the berries into jam. –David Pazmiño

RECIPE UPDATE

Manicotti with Spinach

Adding spinach to the cheese filling in our streamlined **Baked Manicotti** recipe (January/February 2007) seemed easy enough. But simply stirring chopped fresh spinach leaves into the filling resulted in bland, watery manicotti. Wilting the spinach in the microwave and squeezing it dry before adding it to the filling worked better—but, combined with the washing and chopping, microwaving added one too many steps to the process. Using chopped frozen spinach kept things simple, and tasters noticed little difference between fillings made with fresh spinach versus frozen. To boost flavor, we added salt and a pinch of nutmeg to the squeeze-dried spinach before mixing it into the cheesy filling. Go to www.cooksillustrated.com/june for our free recipe for Baked Manicotti with Spinach.

TOO WET

JUST RIGHT

Squeezing moisture from the spinach before adding it to the cheese filling in our Baked Manicotti with Spinach kept the dish from turning watery and bland.

Orange-Honey Glazed Chicken Thighs

Readers wanted to know the best way to make our **Orange-Honey Glazed Chicken Breasts** (September/October 2007) using thigh meat. The existing recipe calls for browning the bone-in breasts, simmering the orange juice–based sauce until shiny and viscous, adding the chicken to the glaze, and baking it until done. The breasts bake in the glaze skin-side down for the first half of cooking, then are turned skin-side up for the second half. When we tried our method with bone-in thighs, the meat turned out wonderfully flavorful and juicy. The skin, however, was flabby and fatty. Baking the thighs skin-side up the entire time helped render fat from the skin, making it thinner and chewier. To render even more fat, we slashed the skin before browning the thighs, which allowed the fat, once melted, to trickle down from the chicken and into the pan. Go to www.cooksillustrated.com/june for our free recipe for Orange-Honey Glazed Chicken Thighs.

Tall and Fluffy Cheddar-Chive Biscuits

Cheese seemed like it would make a tasty addition to our **Tall and Fluffy Buttermilk Biscuits** (July/August 2004). But we quickly found that high-moisture cheeses such as Monterey Jack and fontina (the Danish and Swedish varieties) turned our light biscuits dense and doughy. A judicious amount of drier types of cheese gave the biscuits rich flavor without ruining their airy texture. Tasters liked a combination of extra-sharp cheddar and Parmesan best. Finely grated Parmesan, however, made too subtle an impact. To ensure that each bite of biscuit had a good dose of its pungent, nutty notes, we shredded the Parmesan on the large holes of a box grater before adding it to the dough. Chopped fresh chives helped round out the flavors. Go to www.cooksillustrated.com/june for our free recipe for Tall and Fluffy Cheddar-Chive Biscuits.

–Charles Kelsey

If you have a question about a recipe, let us know. Send your inquiry, name, address, and daytime telephone number to Recipe Update, Cook's Illustrated, P.O. Box 470589, Brookline, MA 02447, or write to recipeupdate@americastestkitchen.com.

EQUIPMENT CORNER

BY ELIZABETH BOMZE

NEW PRODUCT: Three-Blade Peeler

Different peelers suit different requirements: Straight, traditional peelers work best for cucumbers and potatoes; serrated peelers make quick work of tender tomato and peach skins; julienne peelers turn out fine matchsticks for stir-fries and salads. A new gadget, the Prepara Trio Three Blade Peeler ($14.95), claims to do it all. Similar to a multicolor pen, this three-in-one peeler stores two blades in its grip-covered shaft while the third pops up for use. Switching blades is as simple as a click of the release button and a turn of the wheel on the base of the handle. We found each blade performed well on a range of produce and, thankfully, the blade cartridge is dishwasher-safe. A great option for those looking to save drawer space.

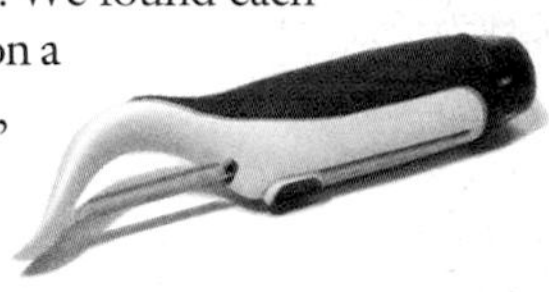

THREE TIMES A CHARM
The Prepara Trio Three Blade Peeler frees up drawer space by combining three peelers in one.

EQUIPMENT UPDATE: Grill Wizard Grill Brush

It's been five years since we crowned the Grill Wizard Grill Brush the ultimate instrument for cleaning gunked-up grill grates, and it remains our favorite. Recently it's been retooled: The 14-inch wood handle now has a lighter-weight polypropylene grip, and the two stainless steel mesh scrubbing pads have been replaced by one larger, tougher pad (with a spare included). Best of all, the price dropped from $24.95 to $10.99.

BETTER BRUSH
Recently updated, the Grill Wizard Grill Brush now comes with a more comfortable plastic handle, a tougher brush, and a more appealing price tag.

NEW PRODUCT: Cuisipro Deluxe Liquid Measuring Cup

To use a liquid measuring cup, you typically set it on a level surface, pour in the ingredient, and crouch down to see if the liquid meets the line at eye level. Then you adjust. And readjust. To streamline this process, Cuisipro introduced a cup that can be read from above. The clear plastic measure, available in 2- and 4-cup sizes ($8.95 and $11.95), is dishwasher- and microwave-safe and features a removable clip fitted with a magnetized, dual-sided red plastic marker. When you slide the outer marker to the desired measurement line, the inner tab moves with it. Then you fill to the level of the inside marker. We measured and weighed 1 cup of water to test for accuracy, then compared results with our favorite Pyrex 2-cup glass measure. The Cuisipro, read from a standing position, measured even more accurately than the Pyrex, and we like its durability and easy-to-read markings.

MEASURE FOR MEASURE
For a plastic measuring cup that can be read from a standing position, try the Cuisipro Deluxe Liquid Measuring Cup.

EQUIPMENT TESTING: Oil Misters

We love the convenience and effectiveness of nonstick sprays such as PAM. Are any of the reusable, hand-pumped aerosol misters on the market as effective? We purchased six models, filled them with olive oil, and—after reading the instructions for each—pumped away. What spritzed out ranged from a perfect mist to a splotchy dribble. Filling the Norpro mister's ($8.76) bullet-shaped vessel with the recommended ¾ cup of oil caused overflow once the cap was replaced. Others from Typhoon ($13.99), Emsa ($16.95), and R.S.V.P. Endurance ($13.49) offered clear instructions and transparent bottles to gauge fullness, but they all spat out a blotchy mess. In the end, we can only recommend models from Cuisipro ($13.95) and Misto ($9.95). Both were easy to operate and offered 10-plus seconds of drip-free spraying.

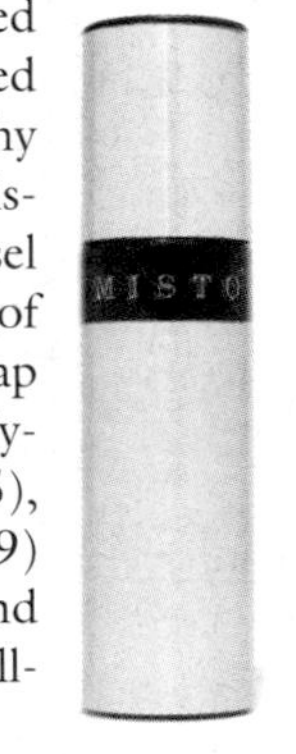

SPRAY AWAY
The Misto Gourmet Olive Oil Sprayer coated surfaces with a fine, even mist.

EQUIPMENT TESTING: Inexpensive Ice-Cream Makers

We tested seven inexpensive, pre-frozen, canister-style ice cream makers to identify which made the best dessert with the least amount of work. After 30 minutes, machines with revolving beaters—by Krups ($29.99), Hamilton Beach ($36.17), and the stand mixer attachment from KitchenAid ($69.99)—produced lighter, smoother, and creamier French-style ice cream than models with revolving canisters. If you already own a KitchenAid standing mixer, we recommend its ice-cream attachment, which produced an airy, ultracreamy ice cream. Otherwise, testers preferred the Krups Automatic Ice-Cream Maker for its smooth results and quiet action.

CREAM OF THE CROP
The Krups Automatic Ice-Cream Maker churned out smooth, creamy ice cream.

Sources

The following are sources for items recommended in this issue. Prices were current at press time and do not include shipping. Contact companies to confirm information or visit www.cooksillustrated.com for updates.

Page 7: PORTERHOUSE STEAK
- Brandt Beef USDA Dry-Aged Prime Porterhouse Steak: $46.66 per pound, plus shipping, Dean & Deluca (800-221-7714, www.deandeluca.com).

Page 9: MEAT POUNDER
- Norpro Meat Pounder: $27.99, item #06-0188, Chef Tools (866-716-2433, www.cheftools.com).

Page 15: WOODEN SPOON
- Mario Batali 13-Inch Wooden Spoon: $4.95, item #587302, Cooking.com (800-663-8810, www.cooking.com).

Page 25: WHISKS
- Rösle Balloon Whisk/Beater: $26.95, item #414616, Cooking.com.
- OXO Steel 11-Inch Balloon Whisk: $9.99, item #1050059, OXO (800-545-4411, www.oxo.com).

Page 29: MANDOLINES
- OXO V-Blade Mandoline Slicer: $49.99, item #1071480, OXO.
- Kyocera Adjustable Ceramic Mandoline Slicer: $24.95, item #CSN-202-BK, Cutlery and More (800-650-9866, www.cutleryandmore.com).

Page 32: THREE-BLADE PEELER
- Prepara Trio Three Blade Peeler: $14.95, Sur la Table (800-243-0852, www.surlatable.com).

Page 32: GRILL BRUSH
- Grill Wizard Grill Brush: $10.99, item #GRILLWIZ, BBQ Tools (800-630-8665, www.bbq-tools.com).

Page 32: LIQUID MEASURING CUP
- Cuisipro 4-Cup Deluxe Liquid Measuring Cup: $11.95, item #747101, Cutlery and More.

Page 32: OIL MISTERS
- Misto Gourmet Olive Oil Sprayer, brushed aluminum: $9.95, item #M100C3, Chef's Resource (866-765-2433, www.chefsresource.com).
- Cuisipro 8-Ounce Stainless Steel Spray Pump: $13.95, item #837530, Cutlery and More.

Page 32: ICE-CREAM MAKERS
- KitchenAid Ice-Cream Maker Attachment KICA0WH: $69.99, item #218070, Cooking.com.
- Krups Automatic Ice-Cream Maker: $29.99, item #B000LVHC7W, Amazon.com.

INDEX

May & June 2008

RECIPES

COOK'S LIVE Original Test Kitchen Videos www.cooksillustrated.com

Poached Salmon, 11

Restaurant-Style Hummus, 19

Pasta with Creamy Tomato Sauce, 15

Spring Vegetable Risotto, 20

Grilled T-Bone Steak, 7

Berry Fool, 25

Sautéed Spinach with Pecans and Feta, 21

Mexican Pulled Pork, 13

Oatmeal Cake with Broiled Icing, 23

Stuffed Chicken Breasts, 9

PHOTOGRAPHY: CARL TREMBLAY, STYLING: MARIE PIRAINO

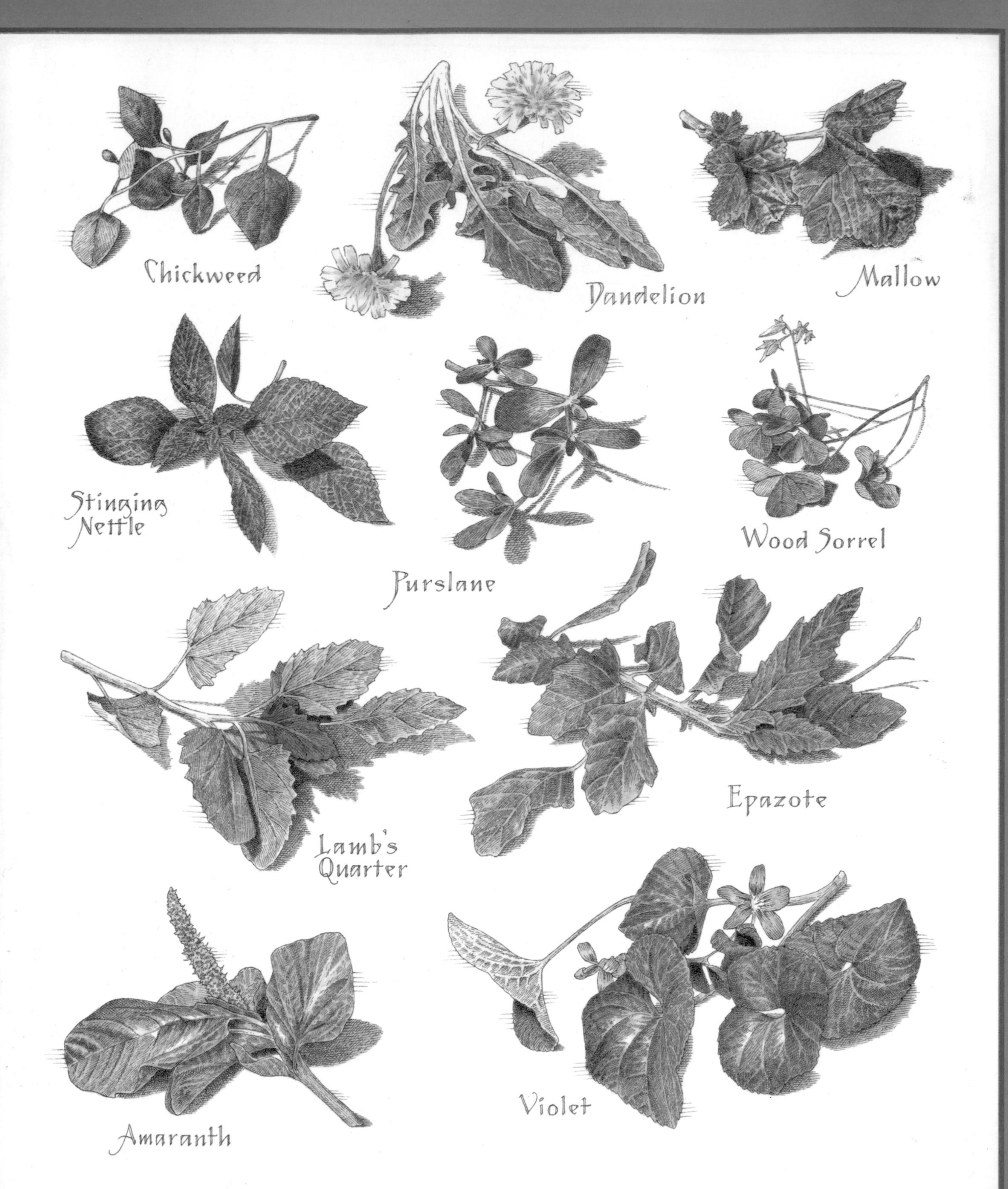

EDIBLE WEEDS

NUMBER NINETY-THREE JULY & AUGUST 2008

COOK'S ILLUSTRATED

Grilled Chicken Secrets
No More Flabby, Charred Skin

Summer Vegetable Gratin

Authentic Drive-In Burgers
Big Beef Flavor, Crisp Crust

Supermarket Olive Oil Tasting
Losers Outnumber Winners!

Best Blueberry Pie
Grated Apple for Thickener?

Keeping Produce Fresher Longer

Enchiladas Verdes

Grilled Sausages with Onions

Cherry Tomato Salads

Foolproof Peach Shortcakes

www.cooksillustrated.com

$5.95 U.S./$6.95 CANADA

CONTENTS

July & August 2008

ASIAN FRUIT The leathery crimson peel of a pomegranate conceals hundreds of jewel-like seeds that can be used in salads or pressed to make juice. Spiny durian has been banned in some hotels and airlines as too fetid to eat in public spaces, but the custardy, chestnut-flavored fruit remains prized in Indonesia and Malaysia. The meat and milk of coconut are indispensable in Asian curries, and the milk often replaces dairy in desserts. Green, unripe mangos are used for tenderizing meat while the orange flesh of the ripe fruit is used in salsas, salads, and desserts. Often candied or preserved, the grape-sized kumquat can be eaten whole, skin and all. The grapefruitlike pomelo can be as large as a melon and becomes more palatable when sprinkled with sugar. Creamy and pithy in texture, the flesh of the persimmon is best baked into desserts or dried for a snack. Named for its unique five-pointed figure when cut crosswise, the sweet-tart star fruit is ideal for chutneys and pickles. Native to China and Thailand, the milky-colored longan is similar in form and texture to lychee and is eaten raw or incorporated into desserts and soups.

COVER (*Nectarines*): Robert Papp, BACK COVER (*Asian Fruit*): John Burgoyne

For list rental information, contact: Specialists Marketing Services, Inc., 777 Terrace Ave., 4th Floor, Hasbrouck Heights, NJ 07604; 201-865-5800.
Editorial Office: 17 Station St., Brookline, MA 02445; 617-232-1000; fax 617-232-1572. Subscription inquiries, call 800-526-8442.
Postmaster: Send all new orders, subscription inquiries, and change-of-address notices to Cook's Illustrated, P.O. Box 7446, Red Oak, IA 51591-0446.

COOK'S ILLUSTRATED
www.cooksillustrated.com
HOME OF AMERICA'S TEST KITCHEN

PRINTED IN THE USA

SNAPSHOTS

The small cardboard box had been sitting for months unopened. Curiosity finally carried the day and out spilled a half-century of family snapshots: washed-out Polaroids, black and white snaps, a few sepia-toned formal portraits and then the odd exceptions to the rule, photos that still sang out boldly in oversaturated but faded shades of red and brown. I organized them into piles by time, place, and player and then realized that I had a movie of sorts, much like the storyboards used to sketch out Hollywood films. Here then is one family's story, an account that begins in Egypt in 1944.

My father stands trim, thin-lipped, well-tailored, an officer's cap mushroomed high on his head—at attention on a moonscape airfield and then astride a camel. Big staff cars with four stars on the grill—officers take turns getting chauffeured around the camp in high style. Snapshot of a Brit practicing a bayonet charge down a dune, socks pulled to the knees, and then my father again, standing upright against a bunker in an oasis. Then on to Venice where he reclines, boyishly, eyes closed, draped drunkenly in the bow of a gondola. Sailboats on the Grand Canal: The war is over.

Home again and my mother is a cross between Hepburn and Garbo, tight-waisted in a long, flowing striped skirt and closely tailored jacket. They are two future parents enjoying cocktails on the lawn, the first of many highball evenings. Big earrings, well-shined shoes, close-cropped lawns, and acres of smiles.

Then the great outdoors. My father, a crossword puzzle adventurer, is caught, like Bigfoot, doing the unthinkable: building a log cabin on a lake in Maine with a wartime buddy. The closing shot is at the end of the day, two unlikely construction workers sitting by the edge of a lake, beers in hand, gangly, sunburned, enjoying a quiet moment before the swirl of family and career. Then the camera turns to my mother, the authentic outdoorswoman, in a canoe in Canada, Bean boots hanging off the gunwale, fly rod in hand, flat fishing hat strapped to her chin, that Hepburn profile still burning bright against the expanse of rippled water and shore. Another shot, rod stretched out across the water, cigarette dangling, and heavy sunglasses under the brim. Last shot, last frame: fingers in gills, a good 16-inch trout as the day's trophy. And finally, there I am in my first scene, age 3, on my father's lap, being rowed out to a small island in a Maine lake for the first of many fishing vacations. I'll never forget my introduction to the green plastic Port-O-Potty. One more time, please: What is this thing for?

Clockwise from top left: Checking syrup at age 10. Mary Alice Kimball fishing in Canada. Ed Kimball in Egypt, 1944. My sister Kate, stirring sap.

Vermont, 1955. We build a small cabin on a piece of the old Ford farm. My mother sits in a U.S. Army Jeep, in khaki shorts, arms outstretched, looking at the sky. It is the scene on which this whole movie turns. Glamour fades and the first chords of "Moonlight in Vermont" are cued. Are we home? Has Garbo been forgotten, pushed aside for mud season, raising pigs, and the smell of creosote? I think of her wedding photo that still sits upright on our piano; the Bette Davis cheekbones, the long train, and the soft studio lighting retired for the thrill of deer season and the smell of a wood-fired Kalamazoo cookstove.

Here I am again, in a sap house, boiling syrup at age 10, holding the skimmer, looking for the hot, sweet syrup to sheet just off the edge so we know it is time to draw off. (My sister, Kate, is also captured that day, unaccountably stirring sap in the outdoor metal tank, red mountain hat on head and smiling proudly.) The steam, the smell of boiled sap, the smoke from the wood fire, and then Rob Woodcock with his sad eyes and drooping handlebar mustache, the master of the sap house. In that dark shack, the photo captures daylight filtered through a steamed window and I find a piece of the eternal mystery, the subplot of this home movie, the one with nothing more than vague suggestions as to how it will end.

More fish, more camps in Maine with rows of canoes pulled up on shore, sagging stick docks, an early morning mist over the lake and then the film fast-forwards. Kate and I in full dress, headed for some now forgotten celebration, a blindfolded child with a large stick, aiming at a hanging piñata (a family birthday tradition), many small black and white shots before the holiday tree always taken in our Vermont cabin on Christmas Eve. Kate, my father, and I arranged in a row before the icicle-draped tree, performing like drunk monkeys—we see, hear, and speak no evil. Group portraits taken with the old Country Squire station wagon as backdrop, vestigial fins still visible, memories of throwing up on road trips and passing at high speed around sharp curves late at night. I sprout up, sport a Nehru jacket at a wedding, and then the film dissolves into cousins, aunts, and uncles from which the plot never quite recovers.

I have built my own sap house and have spent countless days, like my mother and her father before her, casting for salmon on the Miramashee, Matapedia, and Restigouche rivers. But of course these things are no more than trimmings. Is it, then, my mother in her Jeep, stretching her arms heavenward as if to say how blessed she is to find her place on earth? Is it about trying to recapture that moment in time in postwar America when we could simply dream our future? Or maybe it is nothing more than the welcoming signature of wood smoke, the crack of splitting wood, the pop of a new fire in a cold Franklin stove, and the electric promise of the gray skies of November, the advent of hunting season: dark, cold mornings, sunlight seeping over the mountain, rocky fields and giant maples slowly taking shape out of mountain mists?

Like a good movie, it is not the storyboard that matters. The true story is in the details, the subtleness of delivery, the look, the acts of grace, the pulling back when we want to stand center stage. Yet to cast a fly, to draw off syrup, to sight in a gun, to hitch up a horse, to breathe the same scented mountain air my parents did a half-century before me, is unaccountably rich in satisfaction. If we can grow up to become philosophers or farmers, I choose the latter. At least I stand on firm, familiar ground.

FOR INQUIRIES, ORDERS, OR MORE INFORMATION

www.cooksillustrated.com

At www.cooksillustrated.com, you can order books and subscriptions, sign up for our free e-newsletter, or renew your magazine subscription. Join the website and gain access to 15 years of *Cook's Illustrated* recipes, equipment tests, and ingredient tastings, as well as *Cook's Live* companion videos for recipes in this issue.

COOKBOOKS

We sell more than 50 cookbooks by the editors of *Cook's Illustrated*. To order, visit our bookstore at www.cooksillustrated.com or call 800-611-0759 (or 515-246-6911 from outside the U.S.).

COOK'S ILLUSTRATED Magazine

Cook's Illustrated magazine (ISSN 1068-2821), number 93, is published bimonthly by Boston Common Press Limited Partnership, 17 Station St., Brookline, MA 02445. Copyright 2008 Boston Common Press Limited Partnership. Periodicals postage paid at Boston, Mass., and additional mailing offices USPS #012487. Publications Mail Agreement No. 40020778. Return undeliverable Canadian addresses to P.O. Box 875, Station A, Windsor, Ontario N9A 6P2. POSTMASTER: Send address changes to Cook's Illustrated, P.O. Box 7446, Red Oak, IA 51591-0446. For subscription and gift subscription orders, subscription inquiries, or change-of-address notices, call 800-526-8442 in the U.S. or 515-247-7571 from outside the U.S., or write us at Cook's Illustrated, P.O. Box 7446, Red Oak, IA 51591-0446.

NOTES FROM READERS

COMPILED BY DAVID PAZMIÑO

Whipped Butter

Can whipped butter be substituted for stick butter in recipes for baked goods?

ELEANOR PERRONE
CHICAGO, ILL.

Whipped butter is made by incorporating air into butter. Manufacturers do this to increase the butter's spreadability, especially for slathering on toast. Adding air increases the volume of the butter, not the weight. In other words, a 4-ounce stick of butter measures ½ cup in volume, and 4 ounces of whipped butter measures 1 cup. We decided to compare unsalted whipped butter and unsalted stick butter in our Glazed Butter Cookies (November/December 2003), Classic Pound Cake (January/February 2007), and Classic Vanilla Buttercream (March/April 2000).

Tasters found the cookies to be nearly identical and even slightly preferred the whipped-butter version for its "crispier" and "flakier" texture. The same held true for the pound cake. Although the butter for each cake was creamed for exactly the same time—5 minutes—some tasters deemed the cake made with whipped butter to be "lighter," "fluffier," and "more tender." The buttercream was a different story. While the stick butter produced a fluffy, off-white frosting, the whipped-butter frosting was foamy, with an intense yellow color and a "plasticlike" texture.

Can whipped butter stand in for stick?

So—unsalted whipped butter makes a fine substitute for unsalted stick butter in baked goods, but do not make the swap in uncooked applications, such as frosting. And remember to make the substitutions based on weight, not volume. A standard tub of whipped butter weighs 8 ounces, equal to two sticks of butter.

Natural Beef

I have seen "natural" beef for sale in my supermarket. How does it differ from regular beef? Does it taste better?

JILL PENATE
UNIVERSITY HEIGHTS, OHIO

To date, the term "natural" has not been approved by the USDA as a regulated term for marketing beef. But a trip to any supermarket will reveal that many beef producers now use the terms "all natural" and "naturally raised" on their packaging. Because of industry and consumer pressure, the government is in the process of holding hearings to determine what "natural" and "naturally raised" should mean. The proposed standards include: no use of synthetic or natural hormones, no antibiotics administered during the animal's life, and no feed containing mammalian or avian byproducts.

In the test kitchen, we wanted to find out if beef labeled "natural" was better than the beef that we normally buy. We decided to test the most widely available and best-selling brand of "natural" beef, Coleman Natural. In the first round of tests, we compared regular ground beef ($4.59/lb.) with Coleman Natural ground beef ($5.49/lb.) in both plain hamburgers and our Simple Italian-Style Meat Sauce (March/April 2008). There was no difference in flavor or texture; tasters liked the natural and the regular ground beef equally well.

For the second round of tests, we bought six New York strip steaks labeled "USDA Choice" ($11.99/lb.) and six Coleman Natural strip steaks ($14.99/lb.). (Coleman grades its beef, but it is not always marked for sale as "Prime," "Choice," or "Select.") Even before cooking, we noticed that the Choice steaks were more evenly marbled with fat than some of the Coleman steaks.

After cooking the steaks according to our Pan-Seared Thick-Cut Strip Steaks recipe (May/June 2007), tasters declared the USDA Choice steaks "buttery" and "tender." The Coleman steaks all tasted "beefier" than the USDA Choice steaks, but tenderness was all over the board: The steaks that had little marbling were "tough" and "chewy," while those that had more fat were "ultra-tender." Though our tests represent a limited sampling, our recommendation is to look for natural steaks labeled "Choice." If the grade isn't indicated, choose steaks that are well marbled, with flecks of fat dispersed within the meat.

Freezing Garlic

I often chop lots of garlic in my food processor and then store it in the freezer, pressed flat in a zipper-lock bag. This makes it easy to snap off a piece when I need garlic for a quick meal. Does this practice negatively affect the garlic in any way?

ELIZABETH MURPHY
KOHLER, WIS.

To find out if freezing garlic would compromise its flavor, we chopped a few dozen cloves of garlic in a food processor and froze it in a zipper-lock bag for two months. We then made two dishes with frozen and fresh garlic: Pasta with Garlic and Oil (March/April 2001) and Aioli (March/April 2005). While we fully expected the fresh garlic to have a more pungent and assertive flavor, we were surprised at just how much the garlic flavor had mellowed after two months in a deep freeze. The dishes made with frozen garlic had significantly diminished garlic flavor.

What caused the flavor decline? It turns out that the compound that gives garlic its potent taste, allicin, does not form until the cloves are chopped. But allicin is fleeting. If the chopped garlic is stored, even in the freezer, the allicin will lose strength. If you want garlic at its maximum potency, you should wait until the last minute to chop it.

Israeli Couscous

I recently noticed a product labeled Israeli couscous at my supermarket. Can you tell me about it?

CHRISTINE SPIER
NORTH SYRACUSE, N.Y.

Couscous is a starch made from durum semolina, a high-protein wheat flour that is also used to make Italian pasta. Traditional Moroccan couscous is made by rubbing coarse-ground durum semolina and water between the hands to form small, coarse granules. The couscous is then dried and cooked over a simmering stew in a steamer called a *couscoussier*. The boxed couscous found in most supermarkets is a precooked version of traditional couscous. About the size of bread crumbs, the precooked couscous needs only a few minutes of steeping in hot liquid in order to be fully cooked.

Israeli couscous, also known as pearl couscous, is larger than traditional couscous (about the size of a caper) and is not precooked. It has a unique, nutty flavor. To create well-separated grains that work well in salad, cook it as you would pasta: Boil 2 cups Israeli couscous in 2 quarts of lightly salted water for 8 to 10 minutes and then drain. For a pilaflike side dish, toast 2 cups Israeli couscous in a small amount of oil in a large skillet until light golden brown, then add 2½ cups water and ½ teaspoon table salt. Cover the skillet and simmer the couscous for 15 minutes.

ISRAELI COUSCOUS
The large, pearl-like shape of Israeli couscous makes it ideal for salads or pilaf.

Storing Defrosted Shrimp

I often buy defrosted shrimp from the fish counter of my supermarket. Are there any rules on how long they can be stored before cooking?

GERI BORGERSON
BETHANY, CONN.

➤Since almost all shrimp you buy from a fish counter have been frozen (and usually thawed by the retailer), we recommend buying individually quick-frozen shrimp rather than thawed shrimp. This puts you in control of how long the shrimp are stored once they are defrosted.

To find out how long defrosted shrimp can be stored, we defrosted 1 pound of frozen shrimp every day for a week. On the last day, we peeled and deveined the shrimp and steamed each batch separately to evaluate differences in flavor and texture. While the shrimp that had been in the refrigerator for five days were not yet rotten, they did have a mushy texture, a slight off-flavor, and a distinctly fishy and ammoniated odor. (Shrimp stored six and seven days were clearly inedible, with an odor that was even stronger.) It turns out that as raw shrimp age, enzymes begin breaking down the proteins in the flesh, creating a mealy texture. At the same time, bacteria break down an odorless compound in shrimp into trimethylamine (TMA), which has a strong ammonialike odor. The shrimp that were defrosted and cooked on the same day, on the other hand, had no unpleasant aromas and a sweet flavor that was clearly fresher than shrimp that had been stored even a day longer.

So the best approach is to buy individually quick-frozen shrimp and defrost them the same day you plan to cook them. If you want to buy defrosted shrimp at the fish counter, insist on smelling them first to assess freshness. If they're firm and have no ammonialike odor, go ahead and buy defrosted shrimp, but make sure to cook them within a day.

Rare Duck

Cookbooks always specify that chicken and turkey should be cooked to 165 degrees to kill bacteria such as salmonella. Why, then, is duck breast often served closer to rare than to well-done? Is eating duck that is less well cooked not as risky? How does the risk compare with eating a rare or medium-rare steak?

STEPHEN MASTY
STUART, FLA.

➤According to the Centers for Disease Control, all food products, especially raw meat, are susceptible to bacteria that can potentially cause illness. The U.S. Department of Agriculture (USDA) recommends cooking poultry to a minimum internal temperature of 165 degrees and cooking beef steaks to 145 degrees (or what we would consider well-done) to reduce the potential of contamination by bacterial pathogens.

We find, however, that cooking duck breast (and beef steak) past 140 degrees (or medium-rare) results in meat that is chewy, tough, and dry. Furthermore, unlike chicken and turkey, duck breast actually tastes better cooked to this lower temperature. To answer your question, the risk from eating duck cooked to 140 degrees is relatively low, or less risky than eating undercooked chicken but riskier than eating medium-rare steak. (In 2006, the latest year for which data are available, there were no confirmed cases of bacterial illness caused by consuming duck.) That said, if you have any concerns about potential bacteria, follow the USDA recommendation and cook duck to 165 degrees.

WHAT IS IT?

My brother and I found this contraption when we were cleaning out our parents' house. Do you have any idea what it is?

ARLENE PANTOJA
YORKTOWN HEIGHTS, N.Y.

This vintage ice crusher works like a charm.

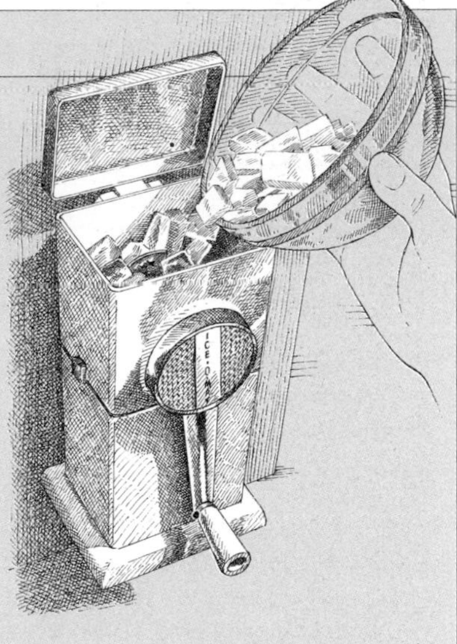

The gadget you found is a 1950s Ice-O-Matic ice crusher made by Rival. This vintage tool was designed to be attached to the wall of a kitchen or bar. We were able to locate a number of these ice crushers for sale online. To find out how this nearly 60-year-old device compares with a modern refrigerator-door ice crusher, we used the hand crank of the Ice-O-Matic to crush 10 pounds of ice. While labor intensive, the Ice-O-Matic produced chipped ice that was more uniform in size and less fine than the ice shavings from the refrigerator crusher. We also liked the handy container at the bottom of the contraption for holding the ice. While we certainly aren't ready to give up our refrigerator ice crusher, if we were setting up a retro-style bar, this item would be on the top of our list.

Locating the Middle Rack

Many of your recipes call for placing the oven rack in the middle position. My oven has six rack positions, so there is no true middle. Where is the best place to position the rack so that it works with your recipes?

KATHERYN MARTIN-DEROGATIS
WABAN, MASS.

➤In the test kitchen, we have ovens with both an even and an odd number of rack positions. If you have an odd number of racks, finding the middle position is easy. If you have an even number of racks, you can place the rack in either the upper-middle or the lower-middle position. To find out which position is preferable, we baked batches of our Lemon Sugar Cookies (January/February 2005) and Fluffy Yellow Layer Cake (March/April 2008).

With an afternoon of baking, it became clear that cookies and cakes baked on the upper-middle rack browned a little too much on top. It was better to bake both items on the lower-middle rack, which puts the food closer to the exact middle of the oven.

When to Salt Scrambled Eggs

I have come across several recipes that caution against salting beaten eggs before cooking them, for fear that early salting will make the scrambled eggs watery. Is there any truth to this?

TONY APRILE
JACKSON, N.J.

➤To put this cookbook myth to the test, we salted beaten eggs one minute before cooking and another batch right after scrambling in a hot skillet. Interestingly, tasters consistently disliked the eggs that were salted after cooking; these eggs were rubbery and firm. The eggs salted prior to cooking were tender and moist. (With these results in hand, we wondered if salting the beaten eggs an hour before cooking would make the eggs even more tender. It didn't; they were nearly identical to the eggs salted just before cooking.)

A bit of investigation revealed an explanation: Salt affects the electrical charge on the protein molecules in eggs, reducing the tendency of the proteins to bond with each other. This produces a weaker protein network, which means more tender scrambled eggs. In the absence of salt, the protein molecules interact more strongly, forming a tighter network and resulting in a firmer, more rubbery texture. We recommend salting eggs just prior to cooking.

SEND US YOUR QUESTIONS We will provide a complimentary one-year subscription for each letter we print. Send your inquiry, name, address, and daytime telephone number to Notes from Readers, Cook's Illustrated, P.O. Box 470589, Brookline, MA 02447, or to notesfromreaders@americastestkitchen.com.

Quick Tips

⋟ COMPILED BY YVONNE RUPERTI ⋞

Keeping Sponges Straight

To avoid using the same sponge for washing dishes as for cleaning grimy countertops and kitchen surfaces, Dan Cully-Rapata of San Francisco, Calif., used to assign a different color of sponge to each task. But packages of sponges always contain multiple colors, making it difficult to keep track. Now he has a better system: He snips off a corner from sponges that he intends to use for cleaning counters and stovetops, reserving uncut sponges for washing dishes.

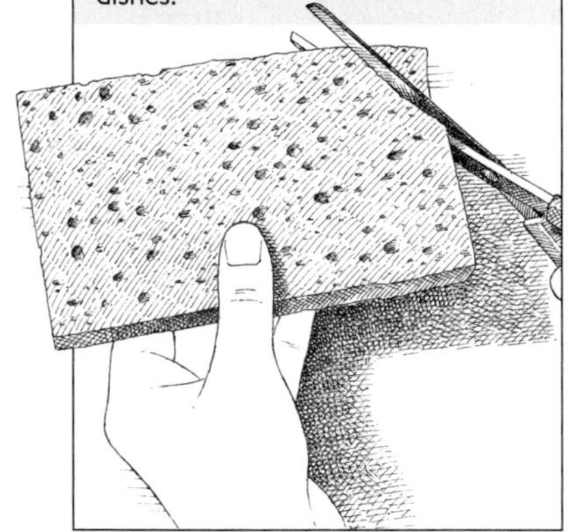

Newspaper Deodorizer

Raw garlic and onions can leave behind unpleasant odors in plastic containers, which can subsequently permeate any food stored in them. Frank Mastropaolo of Poughkeepsie, N.Y., uses newspaper to solve the problem.

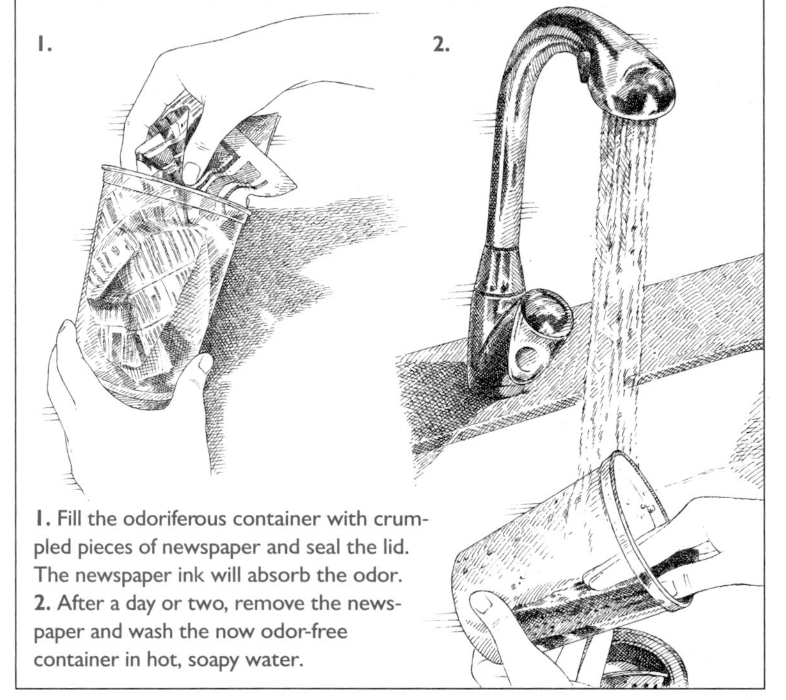

1. Fill the odoriferous container with crumpled pieces of newspaper and seal the lid. The newspaper ink will absorb the odor.
2. After a day or two, remove the newspaper and wash the now odor-free container in hot, soapy water.

Splatter-Free Tomato Crushing

When a recipe calls for crushing canned whole tomatoes by hand, things can get messy when the tomato juice squirts through your fingers and onto your clothes. Gene Hahn of Dover, Del., offers a neat solution.

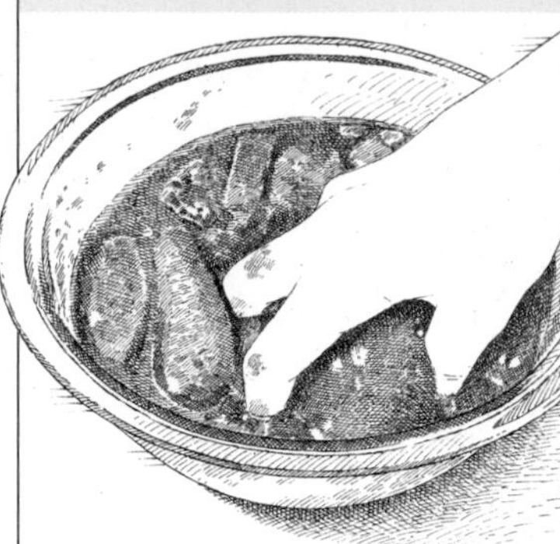

Pour the tomatoes and their juice into a medium bowl. Submerge the tomatoes under the juice and then use your hands to crush them, one at a time. The spray from the tomato does not have enough force to break through the surface of the liquid, keeping the juices contained.

Eggshell Magic

Trying to remove small bits of stray yolk or eggshell from freshly cracked eggs can test the patience of any cook. Jennifer Mulder of Saratoga Springs, N.Y., solves the problem with the egg itself.

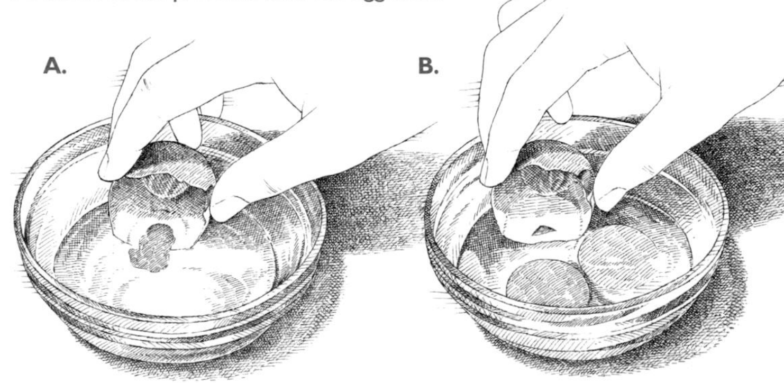

A. Dip an eggshell half into egg whites to scoop out bits of yolk. The eggshell acts as a magnet, attracting the wayward yolk.
B. An eggshell half can also be used to attract smaller pieces of eggshell that have fallen into cracked eggs.

Citrus Reamer Substitute

When Michael Wiacek of Santa Clara, Calif., needs to juice a lemon, lime, or orange, he reaches for a pair of kitchen tongs. Holding the tongs closed, he sticks the pincers into the halved fruit and uses a twisting motion to extract juice.

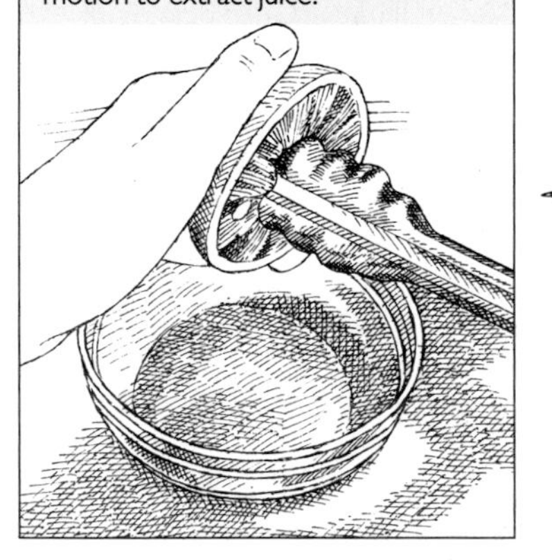

Judging Pineapple Ripeness

Because pineapples do not continue to ripen once they're picked, Jean Paul Polo of San Juan, Puerto Rico, uses this trick to choose ripe pineapples when he's at the grocery store. With one hand, gently tug at a leaf in the center of the fruit. If the leaf releases with little effort, the pineapple is ripe. If the leaf holds fast, choose a different pineapple. (Conversely, avoid pineapples with dried-out leaves and a fermented aroma—the fruit may be overripe.)

Send Us Your Tip We will provide a complimentary one-year subscription for each tip we print. Send your tip, name, and address to Quick Tips, Cook's Illustrated, P.O. Box 470589, Brookline, MA 02447, or to quicktips@americastestkitchen.com.

ILLUSTRATION: JOHN BURGOYNE

Better Way to Mince Anchovies

Tired of the scent anchovies leave on his hands after mincing, Michael Ehlenfeldt of Charlestown, N.H., developed the following approach to eliminate direct contact with the fillets.

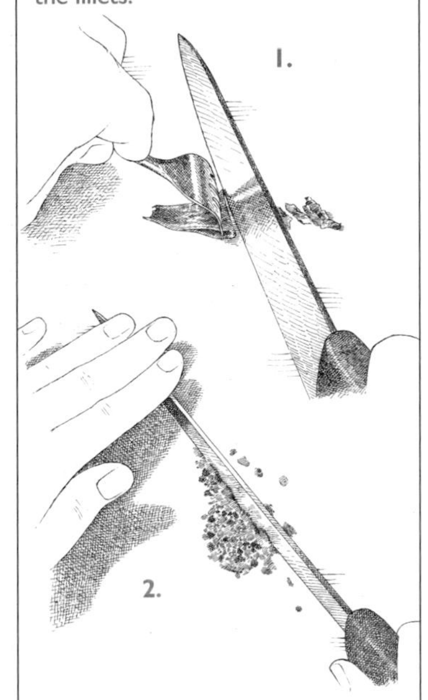

1. With a fork, remove an anchovy from its tin and place it on a work surface. Use the fork to anchor the anchovy as you cut the fillet crosswise into pieces, your hands at a safe distance away.
2. Then, use the side of the knife to gently smear the anchovy pieces against the work surface. Rock the knife back and forth to finely mince the fillets.

Giving Pastry the Brush-Off

When rolling out pastry dough, excess flour often clings to the dough, lending an unpleasant, floury taste and texture to the finished product. Extra flour can also make the pastry tough if it gets worked into the dough. Barbara Huff of Bethesda, Md., uses a pastry brush to sweep excess flour off the surface of her dough.

Lump-Free Thickening

Adding cornstarch to liquid ingredients when making pudding or pastry cream can result in lumps. Helen Konz of Pittsford, N.Y., uses the following method to smoothly blend the thickener into the liquid.

1. Instead of adding the cornstarch by itself to the liquid, mix it with the sugar from the recipe.
2. Slowly add the cornstarch-sugar mixture to the liquid. The sugar will help the cornstarch to dissolve without creating any lumps.

Makeshift Pastry Cutter

Arlene Stolley of Dallas, Texas, found herself in a bind when she was in the middle of preparing a pie dough recipe and realized it called for a pastry cutter, a tool she didn't own. With some creative thinking, she came up with the idea of using a stiff wire whisk as a substitute tool. By tilting the bowl and holding the whisk at an angle, she was able to cut the butter into the flour.

New Use for a Bath Mat

After Patrice Sheets of Enumclaw, Wash., hand-washes her pots and pans, she finds that a dish towel is never absorbent enough to soak up all of the water that trickles from the cookware. Instead of a towel, she now places a clean terrycloth bath mat beneath her dish rack to catch all of the drips. The bath mat can be laundered and used repeatedly.

A Prettier Piece of Pie

Prying out the first piece of pie usually results in a broken, messy slice. Koji Nakanishi of New York, N.Y., offers a trick to make the first piece as pretty as the rest.

1. Fold a 12- by 12-inch sheet of foil in half, then in half again to make a 6-inch square. Fold this square diagonally to form a triangle. Press one point of the triangle into the center of the pie plate and let the other two points hang over the edge.
2. After baking and cooling, slice a piece of pie following the lines of the triangle. Pull up on the overhang and use a spatula to lift out the slice.

Homemade Clip-On Thermometer

Geoff Craig of Northport, N.Y., wanted to deep-fry a batch of donuts and couldn't find the clip for his thermometer to attach it to the side of the pot. Here's how he improvised.

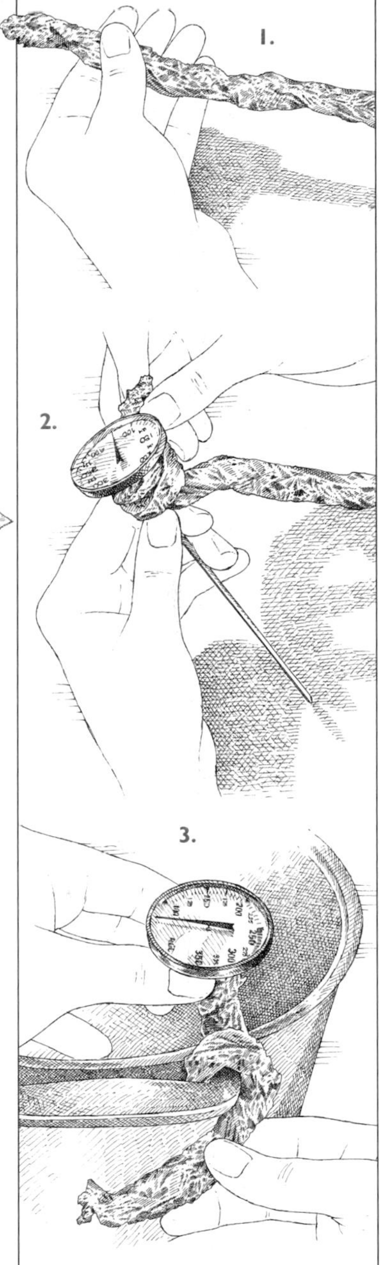

1. Crumple a 12-inch sheet of aluminum foil into a rope.
2. Wrap one end of the foil rope around the probe, directly under the face of the thermometer.
3. Add oil to the pan. Before heating it, secure the other end of the foil to the pot's handle so that the probe is stable and submerged at the desired level in the oil. (Make sure that the tip of the probe does not touch the bottom of the pot.)

Improving Enchiladas Verdes

The bright taste of their quick-cooking sauce gives enchiladas verdes an edge over the "red" kind. But not if the sauce is watery and lacks good green chile flavor.

⋟ BY CHARLES KELSEY ⋞

In Mexico, enchiladas come in myriad forms. In this country, these stuffed and baked corn tortillas are defined almost exclusively by whether they're covered in a red sauce or a green one. Red sauces boast the deep, earthy flavor of dried red chiles, while green sauces feature the brighter taste of fresh green chiles and tomatillos, the tangy little tomatolike fruit that is common in authentic Mexican cooking. For me, enchiladas topped by green sauce—enchiladas verdes—are as perfect a comfort food as any I know, especially when they include moist, tender pieces of chicken. I love the way the fresh, citrusy flavors and coarse texture of the sauce contrast with the richness of chicken wrapped in soft corn tortillas and topped with melted cheese.

For the home cook, enchiladas verdes offer a distinct advantage over red-sauce versions: To preserve its vibrant flavors, the sauce is relatively quick-cooking. (A great red sauce, on the other hand, can take the better part of a day—no small matter when, in addition to making the sauce and filling, you've got to prep the tortillas and assemble the enchiladas themselves.) But while I've had memorable enchiladas verdes with chicken in restaurants, I've never had much success re-creating them at home. The sauce is often too watery and thin, the tortillas mushy, and the filling marred by bland, dried-out chicken overpowered by cheese. Armed with a stack of recipes, I headed into the test kitchen to figure out how to get this Mexican restaurant classic right.

Thinly sliced radishes and scallions complement the bright flavors of tomatillos and green chiles in our Enchiladas Verdes.

Going Green

My first step was to nail down the sauce. I began my tests using broad, dark green poblano chiles. Poblanos have mild to moderate heat and a deep herbal flavor that is far more complex than the straightforward grassy taste of chiles such as jalapeños or serranos, making the poblano a popular choice for this kind of sauce. As for the tomatillos, I decided from the outset to use fresh instead of canned to ensure that as much of their tangy flavor as possible made it into the dish. (Luckily, the fruit is increasingly available fresh year-round in supermarkets across the country. For tips on how to buy them, see "Tomatillos" at right.) Next question: What was the best way bring out the flavors of these two key ingredients?

Traditional recipes dry-roast whole tomatillos and chiles on the stovetop until soft and charred. This method, which employs a flat cast-iron vessel known as a *comal,* imparts smokiness and concentrates flavor, all the while wicking away excess moisture that makes for a watery sauce. The blackened skins on the tomatillos have good flavor, but the chile skins taste bitter and need to be removed. These ingredients are then ground up in a mortar and pestle to form a sauce. More modern recipes skip the comal for similarly fast, intense cooking techniques such as sautéing, high-heat oven-roasting, or broiling and use a blender or food processor to create the sauce.

I quickly eliminated sautéing and oven-roasting from consideration; neither method added enough char to create the smokiness I was looking for. Broiling seemed much more promising, especially when I tossed everything with a little oil to promote the charring. The tomatillos did fine left whole on a baking sheet under the broiler, but I found that slicing the poblanos in half and placing them skin-side up under the glowing broiler helped blacken them more evenly. One taste let me know that I'd hit the jackpot: Broiling tempered the tartness of the tomatillos and brought a near-sweet richness to the poblanos.

It was now time to work on the texture of the sauce. Whirring the tomatillos and chiles in the blender made it too smooth; a few pulses in the food processor better approximated the coarse, rustic texture produced by a mortar and pestle that my tasters preferred. But I wasn't done yet. In my initial testing, tasters rejected sauces that were so thin and soupy that they turned the tortillas to mush. My sauce was now on the other end of the spectrum—overly thick and pulpy. I tried thinning it with a number of ingredients, including milk, sour cream, and chicken broth. Dairy in any form deadened the bright flavors, but just ¼ cup of chicken broth lent a subtle richness and thinned the sauce while maintaining its body. For finishing touches, I added a little raw garlic to enhance the roasted flavors and a teaspoon or so of sugar to deepen the sweetness of the tomatillos.

The Whole Enchilada

In my preliminary test, tasters preferred white meat over dark in the filling, as the mild-tasting breast complemented the flavor of the sauce rather than competing with it. But what was the best method for cooking the chicken? With an eye on keeping the recipe as streamlined as possible, I settled on the fastest, simplest approach: poaching. A brief poach in plain chicken broth wasn't enough; tasters found

SHOPPING: Tomatillos

Called *tomates verdes* (green tomatoes) in much of Mexico, small green tomatillos have a tangier, more citrusy flavor than true green tomatoes. When choosing tomatillos, look for pale-green orbs with firm flesh that fills and splits open the fruit's outer papery husk, which must be removed before cooking. Avoid tomatillos that are too yellow and soft, as these specimens are past their prime and will taste sour and muted. Canned tomatillos are a reasonable substitute for fresh, though they won't contribute the same depth of flavor. –C.K.

GREEN 'N' GOOD

TOO YELLOW 'N' MELLOW

LA PREFERIDA Tomatillos ENTEROS

FINE STAND-IN FOR FRESH

RECIPE SHORTHAND | MAKING ENCHILADAS VERDES

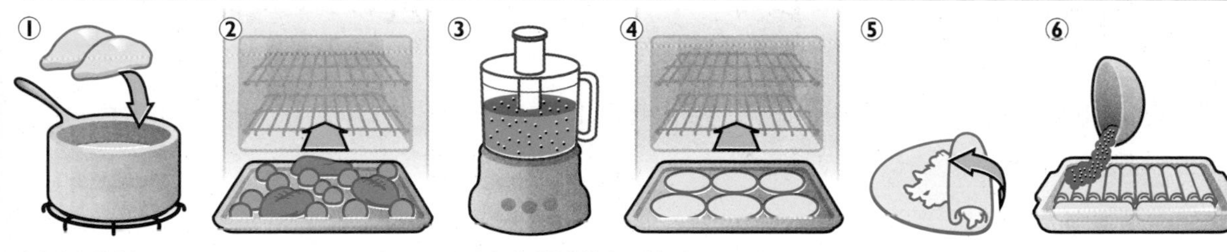

1. POACH Simmer chicken breasts in a flavored broth. **2. BROIL** Broil fresh tomatillos and chiles in the oven to intensify their flavors. **3. PUREE** Puree roasted chiles and tomatillos with poaching liquid. **4. WARM** Spray tortillas with cooking spray and briefly heat in oven to soften. **5. FILL AND ROLL** Place filling in center of each tortilla and roll up. **6. ASSEMBLE** Pour sauce over enchiladas and top with grated cheese.

the meat, which I'd shredded and chopped into bite-sized pieces, too bland. Spiking the broth with sautéed onion, garlic, and cumin before adding the chicken did the trick, infusing the meat with deeper flavor. In addition, I now had a great-tasting broth I could use to thin the sauce; I reserved ¼ cup before discarding the rest.

Many enchilada recipes lard up the filling with cheese, weighing down the dish. At first I planned to leave it out of the filling entirely, but tasters complained that the dish lacked richness, even with the traditional sprinkling of cheese on top. What if I added a moderate amount of cheese to the filling? I tried a few obvious types: pepper Jack, cheddar, and *queso fresco,* a salty, crumbly fresh cheese from Mexico resembling feta. Though queso fresco might have bested the others south of the border, it is not a melting cheese, and my tasters wanted gooeyness in their filling. Cheddar lost out to 1½ cups of shredded pepper Jack, a milder cheese that nonetheless added a spicy kick. To keep the richness of the cheese in check, I added a handful of chopped cilantro.

Traditionally, corn tortillas are dipped in hot oil to make them pliable and to keep them from breaking apart when rolled. I opted for the quicker, less messy method we've developed in the test kitchen: spraying the tortillas with vegetable oil and gently baking them for a few minutes. Once they were soft and warm, I took them out of the oven, put them on the counter, and proceeded to assemble the enchiladas: distributing filling in each, rolling them up, and placing them in a baking dish before topping them with sauce and Jack cheese. Quickly baked until heated through, then served with thinly sliced scallion, radish slices, and a dollop of sour cream, my enchiladas verdes were as good as any I'd enjoyed in my favorite Mexican restaurants.

TECHNIQUE | BROILING MAKES THE DIFFERENCE

Quickly charring the tomatillos and chiles under the broiler intensifies their taste and adds smokiness.

ENCHILADAS VERDES

SERVES 4 TO 6

You can substitute three 11-ounce cans of tomatillos, drained and rinsed, for the fresh ones in this recipe. Halve large tomatillos (more than 2 inches in diameter) and place them skin-side up for broiling in step 2 to ensure even cooking and charring. If you can't find poblanos, substitute 4 large jalapeño chiles (with seeds and ribs removed). To increase the spiciness of the sauce, reserve some of the chiles' ribs and seeds and add them to the food processor in step 3. Serve enchiladas with our recipe for Mexican Rice, available free at www.cooksillustrated.com/august.

- 4 teaspoons vegetable oil
- 1 medium onion, chopped medium (about 1 cup)
- 3 medium garlic cloves, minced or pressed through garlic press (about 1 tablespoon)
- ½ teaspoon ground cumin
- 1½ cups low-sodium chicken broth
- 1 pound boneless, skinless chicken breasts (2 to 3 breasts), trimmed of excess fat
- 1½ pounds tomatillos (16 to 20 medium), husks and stems removed, rinsed well and dried (see note)
- 3 medium poblano chiles, halved lengthwise, stemmed, and seeded (see note)
- 1–2½ teaspoons sugar
- Table salt
- Ground black pepper
- ½ cup coarsely chopped fresh cilantro leaves
- 8 ounces pepper Jack or Monterey Jack cheese, grated (2 cups)
- 12 (6-inch) corn tortillas

Garnish

- 2 medium scallions, sliced thin
- Thinly sliced radishes
- Sour cream

1. Adjust oven racks to middle and highest positions and heat broiler. Heat 2 teaspoons oil in medium saucepan over medium heat until shimmering; add onion and cook, stirring frequently, until golden, 6 to 8 minutes. Add 2 teaspoons garlic and cumin; cook, stirring frequently, until fragrant, about 30 seconds. Decrease heat to low and stir in broth. Add chicken, cover, and simmer until instant-read thermometer inserted into thickest part of chicken registers 160 degrees, 15 to 20 minutes, flipping chicken halfway through cooking. Transfer chicken to large bowl; place in refrigerator to cool, about 20 minutes. Remove ¼ cup liquid from saucepan and set aside; discard remaining liquid.

2. Meanwhile, toss tomatillos and poblanos with remaining 2 teaspoons oil; arrange on rimmed baking sheet lined with foil, with poblanos skin-side up. Broil until vegetables blacken and start to soften, 5 to 10 minutes, rotating pan halfway through cooking. Cool 10 minutes, then remove skin from poblanos (leave tomatillo skins intact). Transfer tomatillos and chiles to food processor. Decrease oven temperature to 350 degrees. Discard foil from baking sheet and set baking sheet aside for warming tortillas.

3. Add 1 teaspoon sugar, 1 teaspoon salt, remaining teaspoon garlic, and reserved cooking liquid to food processor; process until sauce is somewhat chunky, about eight 1-second pulses. Taste sauce; season with salt and pepper and adjust tartness by stirring in remaining sugar, ½ teaspoon at a time. Set sauce aside (you should have about 3 cups).

4. When chicken is cool, pull into shreds using hands or 2 forks, then chop into small bite-sized pieces. Combine chicken with cilantro and 1½ cups cheese; season with salt.

5. Smear bottom of 13- by 9-inch baking dish with ¾ cup tomatillo sauce. Place tortillas on 2 baking sheets. Spray both sides of tortillas lightly with cooking spray. Bake until tortillas are soft and pliable, 2 to 4 minutes. Increase oven temperature to 450 degrees. Place warm tortillas on countertop and spread ⅓ cup filling down center of each tortilla. Roll each tortilla tightly and place in baking dish, seam-side down. Pour remaining tomatillo sauce over top of enchiladas. Use back of spoon to spread sauce so that it coats top of each tortilla. Sprinkle with remaining ½ cup cheese and cover baking dish with foil.

6. Bake enchiladas on middle rack until heated through and cheese is melted, 15 to 20 minutes. Uncover, sprinkle with scallions, and serve immediately, passing radishes and sour cream separately.

COOK'S LIVE Original Test Kitchen Videos

www.cooksillustrated.com

HOW TO MAKE

- Enchiladas Verdes

VIDEO TIP

- How to buy and store corn tortillas

Great Grilled Bone-In Chicken Breasts

The key to avoiding the charred skin and dried-out meat that plague most grilled chicken breasts is all in how you set up the fire.

⋟ BY CHARLES KELSEY ⋞

There's a lot to admire about a perfectly grilled chicken breast. Cooked bone-in with the skin on for extra flavor and juiciness, the smoke-infused meat should be tender and succulent and the skin golden and crisp. But don't let the everyday nature of this grill favorite fool you: This dish isn't that easy to get right. Burnt, limp skin and sooty, parched meat are too often the reality.

Part of the problem is the inherent difficulty of cooking lean, delicate breast meat over the grill's dry, intense heat. The even bigger issue is that grilling, by its very nature, is an inexact cooking medium. To help inject as much precision as possible into the process, every detail counts, from how much charcoal you use, to the arrangement of the coals, to where you place the meat. But most grilled chicken recipes forgo a well-thought-out approach and focus more on marinades, sauces, and glazes—all good ways to cover up tasteless scorched meat, if you ask me. I have nothing against a grilled chicken breast embellished by a sauce, but I want the meat underneath it to be perfect.

Before even striking a match to the charcoal, I knew I would need to brine my chicken breasts for an hour or so before grilling. This would help ensure juicy, seasoned meat throughout and leave me free to focus solely on the grilling technique.

The Chicken Dance

Many recipes recommend grilling chicken over a blazing single-level fire where the coals are spread evenly over the grate. In the test kitchen, we've learned this approach doesn't work. Fat eventually starts dripping onto the coals, and before you know it, you have an inferno on your hands. The only way to keep things under control is to move the chicken on and off the grill, drying out the meat and charring more skin every step of the way. Building what we call a modified two-level fire was a more promising technique. Here, all the coals are pushed to one side of the grill to create a hot area and a cooler area. Food placed on the cooler side can cook gently through indirect heat with the cover on, with no risk of flare-ups.

A modified two-level fire produces juicy meat and golden skin.

I put the indirect-heat technique to the test, carefully arranging the breasts in a tidy row with the thicker side facing the fire to promote even cooking. Tasters praised the chicken for its "grilled" flavor and minimal char—an encouraging step in the right direction. However, the method was far from perfect. Even though I used breasts of equal size and weight, each cooked at a different rate—some took 20 minutes, others as long as 40. Because a grill's heat is always in flux, with cool and hot spots throughout its interior, I knew I'd never get all the chicken breasts to cook at exactly the same rate no matter what I did. But I wanted them to at least cook at a similar rate.

The key would be to minimize temperature fluctuation as best I could. It occurred to me that I could try a trick we sometimes use when barbecuing large cuts of meat—covering it with a piece of foil before closing the lid. The foil creates a sort of oven within an oven, trapping a layer of heat against the meat that maintains a consistent temperature. I prepped the grill by lighting a full chimney's worth of charcoal (about 100 briquettes). When the coals were glowing, I once again arranged a modified two-level fire and replaced the grill grate to heat it up. After scraping and greasing the grate, I placed the chicken breasts on the grill's cooler half skin-side down (to better render the fat), laying a large sheet of foil over them. Thirty minutes later, all six of my chicken breasts were either ready or very close to ready to come off the grill. My timing issues solved, I now had meat that was uniformly tender and juicy, with good grilled flavor. I also had a new problem: skin that was too flabby.

Easy as 1-2-3

My only choice was to start the breasts over the coals. Risking flare-ups, I tried lightly browning all sides of the chicken on the grill's hot side, keeping it there for a total of less than 10 minutes before moving it to the cooler side. This short exposure to direct heat helped crisp the skin and kept flare-ups to a minimum. But the results didn't fully satisfy my tasters. I couldn't keep the breasts over the coals any longer at the beginning of grilling or I'd be back where I started, but what about at the end of cooking? I took out a new batch of breasts, started them on the hot side, moved them to the cooler side until they were 90 percent done, then back to the hot side to finish cooking. This three-step dance was a success. Because the coals had cooled down and chicken had rendered most of its fat, the skin gently crisped and turned golden, unhindered by any violent flare-ups.

To accommodate tasters who love a glaze with their grilled chicken, I developed a few variations. But even with such embellishment, there was no question that my tender, juicy chicken, with its crisp golden skin, was the true star.

COOK'S LIVE Original Test Kitchen Videos

www.cooksillustrated.com

HOW TO MAKE

- Grilled Bone-In Chicken Breasts

VIDEO TIPS

- What is the best way to clean grill grates?
- How to mince thyme

STEP-BY-STEP | GREAT GRILLED BONE-IN CHICKEN BREASTS

1. START ON HOT SIDE
Cook chicken on all sides over hotter part of grill until lightly browned.

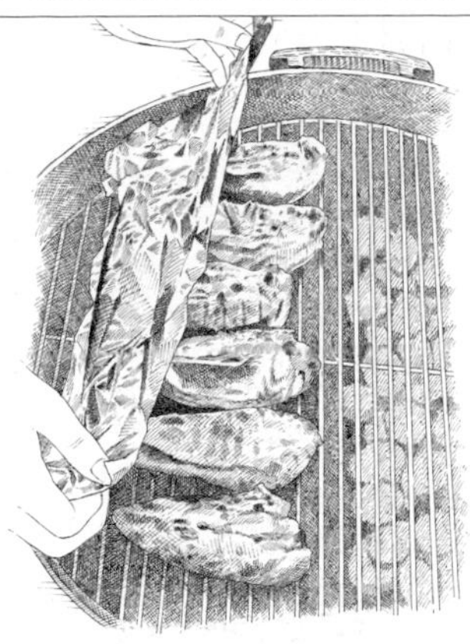

2. MOVE TO COOL SIDE
Move chicken, skin-side down, to grill's cooler half, with thicker side facing coals. Cover with foil.

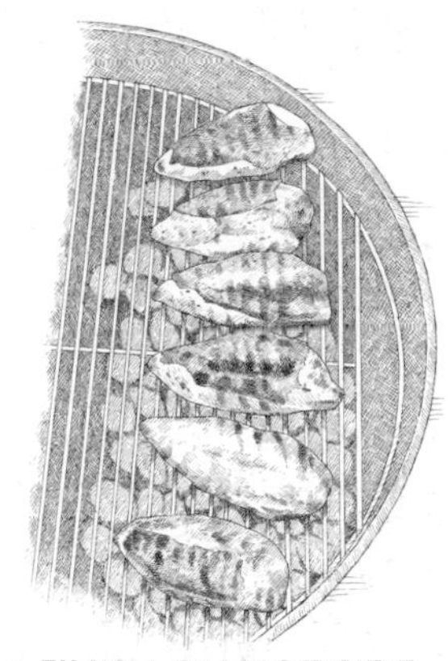

3. FINISH ON HOT SIDE
To finish, return chicken to hotter side of grill and cook on both sides until skin is brown and crisp.

CHARCOAL-GRILLED BONE-IN CHICKEN BREASTS

SERVES 6

To help ensure that each breast finishes cooking at approximately the same time, buy pieces of similar size. Barbecue sauce can replace the optional glaze in step 4. For our free recipe for Curry-Yogurt Glaze, go to www.cooksillustrated.com/august.

- ⅓ cup table salt
- 6 bone-in, skin-on chicken breast halves (about 12 ounces each), ribs removed, trimmed of excess fat and skin (see note)
- Ground black pepper
- Vegetable oil for cooking grate
- 1 recipe glaze (recipes follow; optional)

1. Dissolve salt in 2 quarts cold water in large container. Submerge chicken, cover with plastic wrap, and refrigerate 1 hour. Rinse chicken under cold water and dry thoroughly with paper towels. Season chicken with pepper.

2. Meanwhile, light large chimney starter filled with charcoal (6 quarts, or about 100 briquettes) and allow to burn until coals are fully ignited and partially covered with thin layer of ash, about 20 minutes. Build modified two-level fire by arranging all coals over one half of grill, leaving other half empty. Position cooking grate over coals, cover grill, and let grate heat up, about 5 minutes. Scrape grate clean with grill brush. Dip wad of paper towels in oil; holding wad with tongs, wipe cooking grate. Grill is ready when side with coals is medium-hot (you can hold your hand 5 inches above grate for 3 to 4 seconds).

3. Cook chicken on all sides over hotter part of grill until skin is lightly browned and meat has faint grill marks, 6 to 8 minutes. (If constant flare-ups occur, slide chicken to cooler side of grill and mist fire with water from spray bottle.) Move chicken, skin-side down, to cooler side of grill, with thicker side of breast facing coals. Cover loosely with aluminum foil, cover grill, and continue to cook until instant-read thermometer inserted into thickest part of breast registers 150 degrees, 15 to 25 minutes longer.

4. Brush bone side of chicken with glaze (if using). Move chicken, bone-side down, to hotter side of grill and cook until browned, 4 to 6 minutes. Brush skin side of chicken with glaze; turn chicken over and continue to cook until browned and instant-read thermometer inserted into thickest part of breast registers 160 degrees, 2 to 3 minutes longer. Transfer chicken to plate and let rest, tented with foil, 5 minutes. Serve, passing remaining glaze separately.

GAS-GRILLED BONE-IN CHICKEN BREASTS

Follow recipe for Charcoal-Grilled Bone-In Chicken Breasts through step 1. Turn all burners to high and heat with lid down until very hot, about 15 minutes. Follow instructions for cleaning and oiling grill in step 2. Leave primary burner on high and turn off other burner(s). Proceed with recipe from step 3, increasing browning time in step 3 to 10 to 14 minutes.

ORANGE-CHIPOTLE GLAZE

MAKES ABOUT ¾ CUP

- ⅔ cup juice plus 1 teaspoon grated zest from 2 oranges
- 1 small shallot, minced (about 1 tablespoon)
- 1–2 chipotle chiles in adobo sauce, minced (1 to 2 tablespoons)
- 2 teaspoons minced fresh thyme leaves
- 1 tablespoon light molasses
- ¾ teaspoon cornstarch
- Table salt

Combine juice, zest, shallot, chile, and thyme in small saucepan, then whisk in molasses and cornstarch. Simmer mixture over medium heat until thickened, about 5 minutes. Season with salt. Reserve half of glaze for serving and use other half for brushing on chicken in step 4.

SOY-GINGER GLAZE

MAKES ABOUT 1 CUP

Reduce the salt in the brine to ¼ cup when using this glaze.

- ⅓ cup water
- ¼ cup soy sauce
- 2 tablespoons mirin
- 1 tablespoon grated fresh ginger
- 2 medium garlic cloves, minced or pressed through garlic press (about 2 teaspoons)
- 3 tablespoons sugar
- ¾ teaspoon cornstarch
- 2 small scallions, white and green parts minced

Combine water, soy sauce, mirin, ginger, and garlic in small saucepan, then whisk in sugar and cornstarch. Simmer mixture over medium heat until thickened, about 5 minutes; stir in scallions. Reserve half of glaze for serving and use other half for brushing on chicken in step 4.

EQUIPMENT TESTING:

Barbecue Mitts

A good barbecue mitt blocks heat but doesn't impede your ability to pick up food. Choosing one, however, isn't a straightforward proposition. Mitts come in a dizzying array of fabrics, from treated cotton, leather, and rawhide to high-tech materials such as neoprene, Kevlar, Nomex, and silicone.

Testers held mitt-clad hands over a 600-degree grill to assess heat resistance in the eight styles in our lineup, then flipped zucchini slices with tongs to evaluate dexterity. A few mitts made from high-tech fabrics became burning hot and made our hands sweaty in seconds, while some treated-cotton mitts were so slick the tongs slipped from our grasp. For complete testing results, go to www.cooksillustrated.com/august.

–Elizabeth Bomze and Lindsay McSweeney

HANDS-DOWN FAVORITE
GRILL LIFE Leather Grill Gloves
Price: $12.49 per pair
Comments: These 18-inch leather gloves kept our hands and arms cool and well protected. Offered nice control when picking up food.

RUNNER-UP
CHARCOAL COMPANION
Flame Resistant BBQ Mitt
Price: $8.75 per mitt
Comments: This treated-cotton mitt kept our hands cool and performed well in dexterity testing. Flare-ups scorched but did not burn the mitt.

Reviving the Original Drive-In Burger

Sixty years ago, drive-in burgers were synonymous with freshly ground high-quality beef. Today they mean tasteless mass-produced patties. We wanted to bring back the genuine article.

BY J. KENJI ALT

Americans love hamburgers and, in spite of the myriad gourmet options featuring inch-thick patties with artisanal cheeses and dizzying arrays of toppings, fast-food burgers—as in billions served—remain the most popular choice. Our love affair with burgers began in the 1940s when a slew of drive-in hamburger restaurants sprang up in California. The best of these restaurants made their patties from freshly ground beef cooked to order. But as the biggest chains spread across the country, fresh-ground, high-quality beef gave way to preformed, deep-frozen patties made from scraps of meat you'd rather not think about.

These days, those of us outside of driving range from the few burger joints that continue to use the original methods have to be content with rubbery gray patties of questionable provenance and little beef flavor. But East Coasters got a break a couple of years ago when the Shake Shack opened in New York City. This humble stand, the brainchild of restaurateur Danny Meyer, offers burgers modeled after the drive-in original.

One taste of this burger opened my eyes to just how great the real deal could be. Like the California originals, these thin, quarter-pound burgers are made from freshly ground beef and cooked on a flat griddle. Fat rendering out of the meat collects on the griddle, frying the patty in its own grease and delivering a substantial crust. Crisp nooks and crannies riddle the patty's surface, while the interior is very loosely packed. The craggy, porous texture of this ultracrisp, ultrabrowned, ultrabeefy burger is perfect for catching the dripping juices, melted cheese, and tangy sauce that tops it.

Smitten by the experience, I returned to the test kitchen in Boston determined to develop my own recipe for drive-in burgers.

A soft bun and gooey melted American cheese are ideal complements to our burger's craggy texture.

Better Beef for a Better Burger

BONELESS SHORT RIBS SIRLOIN STEAK TIPS

Chuck is the usual choice for burgers. For the best flavor and tender juicy texture, we opted for two better cuts of beef: sirloin steak tips (right), which contribute big meaty taste, and well-marbled boneless short ribs (left), which lend the fat that keeps the burgers juicy. For best results, buy ribs with at least as much fat as the rib in the photo.

Chucking Out the Chuck

A quick test using ordinary preground chuck from the supermarket fashioned into thin patties proved disappointing. Prepackaged hamburger is ground very fine and packaged tightly, compacting it before it even comes out of the container. The result is dense, rubbery, and dry patties with little beef flavor or crisp crust, specifically lacking in the pitted surface and loose texture I wanted. To improve my burgers, I'd need freshly ground meat. But with the dearth of good butchers in the neighborhood, I was going to have to grind it myself.

I put chuck roasts through a meat grinder for my next batch of burgers. These patties were certainly less dense, but my other problems—rubberiness, dryness, and lack of beef flavor—remained. By trying over a dozen different cuts of meat and having tasters rate each sample on flavor and juiciness, I discovered that beefiness was dependent on cut, while juiciness corresponded to fat. I decided to grind my burgers from sirloin steak tips (also known as flap meat), the winner for beefiness, and to introduce an outside source of fat to increase juiciness. Butter diluted the flavor of the burger, while smoky bacon overshadowed its beefiness. On a whim, I tried mixing oil from a tin of anchovies into the beef, which added a great savory (not fishy) flavor. Unfortunately, as the meat cooked, the anchovy oil wept out, and my dryness problem persisted. What about more beef fat? Suet would be the logical choice, but it's not widely available. In the end, I found that well-marbled short ribs ground up with the sirloin tips added the perfect amount of fat without diminishing beef flavor. The combination was more complicated than buying a single cut, I admit it. But why knock something that works?

That left me with rubberiness to deal with. After looking through my food science books, I discovered the culprit: collagen. As collagen proteins get heated past 130 degrees, they start to squeeze the meat, causing it to become dense and rubbery. (At 140 degrees, the collagen will begin to unravel, turning the meat from tough to tender, but this process takes hours—far longer than the mere minutes my burger would spend on the griddle.) The more that these proteins come in contact with each other, the more shrinkage and tightening will take place. So the key to a tender burger is to keep it as loosely packed as possible.

I knew that the meat got compressed as I lifted it up and formed it into patties in my hands. What if I never picked up the meat at all? I ground up more meat, letting it fall directly from the grinding tube onto a baking sheet. Then, without lifting it, I separated it into four piles and gently pressed each one into a patty. Even as they were cooking in the pan, I could tell that these patties were going to be different. Their juices bubbled up through the meat's porous surface and dripped back down, basting the burgers as they cooked. Biting into one revealed meat so tender it virtually fell apart. Just to make sure this success really could be attributed to the loosely packed meat, I made a new batch and compared it with burgers I had molded into a tight shape. The compressed burgers were rubbery and uninspiring, whereas the loose burgers were once again an unqualified success.

A Question of Process

One more problem: Most home cooks don't own a meat grinder. Unless I could get around this roadblock, it made no difference how good the burgers were. I decided to give the food processor a shot. Almost immediately after turning the processor on, long stringy bits of fat and meat got caught up in the blade, causing the machine to jam. I patiently cleaned and re-cleaned the blade as I ground until I had what looked like a passable texture. But when I cooked the meat, the rubberiness was back. Clearly, the rough action of the food processor was mashing the meat together and reviving my old enemy, collagen.

I knew from making sausages that when meat gets too warm, it ends up being smeared instead of cleanly chopped. The same thing happened to my burger meat as it got battered in the food processor. The solution? I cut my meat into chunks and chilled them in the freezer before placing them in the food processor. This time the chunks were chopped, not pulverized, and the burgers cooked up just as perfectly tender and with as crisp a crust as those I had chopped in the meat grinder.

Topping It Off

As for the sauce, this style of burger is commonly served with a tangy and sweet Thousand Island–style dressing, and I found no reason to change that. Adding relish, sugar, and white vinegar to a mayo and ketchup base proved to be the best foil for the juicy, salty burger. Although cheddar and Swiss cheese had their proponents, most people preferred American. It filled the cracks and crevices in the patty with gooey cheese that didn't compete with the other flavors. A few thin slices of onion were preferred in lieu of "the works"—they allowed the flavor of the beef to take center stage unchallenged.

With my tender patty and toppings sandwiched by a soft toasted bun, I'd finally recaptured the flavor and texture that started a nationwide craze.

STEP-BY-STEP | KEYS TO LOOSELY PACKED PATTIES

1. FREEZE
Chill meat in freezer, separating cubes by at least ½ inch, until firm but still pliable, 15 to 25 minutes. Pulse meat in food processor.

2. SPREAD AND DIVIDE
Spread chopped meat over baking sheet and remove any large chunks or stringy connective tissue. Gently separate meat into 4 piles.

3. SHAPE
Without lifting or compressing, gently form meat into thin patties with rough edges and textured surface.

BEST OLD-FASHIONED BURGERS

MAKES 4 BURGERS

Sirloin steak tips are also labeled "flap meat" by some butchers. Flank steak can be used in its place. This recipe yields juicy medium to medium-well burgers. It's important to use very soft buns. If doubling the recipe, process the meat in three batches in step 2. Because the cooked burgers do not hold well, fry four burgers and serve them immediately before frying more. Or, cook them in two pans. Extra patties can be frozen for up to 2 weeks. Stack the patties, separated by parchment, and wrap them in three layers of plastic wrap. Thaw burgers in a single layer on a baking sheet at room temperature for 30 minutes before cooking.

- 10 ounces sirloin steak tips, cut into 1-inch chunks (see note)
- 6 ounces boneless beef short ribs, cut into 1-inch chunks
- Kosher salt and ground black pepper
- 1 tablespoon unsalted butter
- 4 soft hamburger buns (see note)
- ½ teaspoon vegetable oil
- 4 slices American cheese
- Thinly sliced onion
- 1 recipe Classic Burger Sauce (recipe follows)

1. Place beef chunks on baking sheet in single layer, leaving ½ inch of space around each chunk. Freeze meat until very firm and starting to harden around edges but still pliable, 15 to 25 minutes.

2. Place half of meat in food processor and pulse until meat is coarsely ground, 10 to 15 one-second pulses, stopping and redistributing meat around bowl as necessary to ensure beef is evenly ground. Transfer meat to baking sheet, overturning bowl and without directly touching meat. Repeat grinding with remaining meat. Spread meat over sheet and inspect carefully, discarding any long strands of gristle or large chunks of hard meat or fat.

3. Gently separate ground meat into 4 equal mounds. Without picking meat up, with your fingers gently shape each mound into loose patty ½ inch thick and 4 inches in diameter, leaving edges and surface ragged. Season top of each patty with salt and pepper. Using spatula, flip patties and season other side. Refrigerate while toasting buns.

4. Melt ½ tablespoon butter in heavy-bottomed 12-inch skillet over medium heat until foaming. Add bun tops, cut-side down, and toast until light golden brown, about 2 minutes. Repeat with remaining butter and bun bottoms. Set buns aside and wipe out skillet with paper towels.

5. Return skillet to high heat; add oil and heat until just smoking. Using spatula, transfer burgers to skillet and cook without moving for 3 minutes. Using spatula, flip burgers over and cook for 1 minute. Top each patty with slice of cheese and continue to cook until cheese is melted, about 1 minute longer.

6. Transfer patties to bun bottoms and top with onion. Spread 2 teaspoons of burger sauce on each bun top. Cover burgers and serve immediately.

CLASSIC BURGER SAUCE

MAKES ABOUT ¼ CUP

- 2 tablespoons mayonnaise
- 1 tablespoon ketchup
- ½ teaspoon sweet pickle relish
- ½ teaspoon sugar
- ½ teaspoon white vinegar
- ¼ teaspoon ground black pepper

Whisk all ingredients together in small bowl.

COOK'S LIVE Original Test Kitchen Videos
www.cooksillustrated.com
HOW TO MAKE
• Best Old-Fashioned Burgers
VIDEO TIPS
• What is the best skillet?
• How to prepare the patties

Getting the Perfect Grind

UNDERPROCESSED

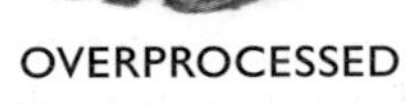

OVERPROCESSED

GROUND TO PERFECTION

Underprocessed meat will lead to gristly bits in the finished burgers and patties that don't hold together. Overprocessed meat becomes rubbery and dense as it cooks. Perfectly ground meat contains pieces that are fine enough to ensure tenderness but coarse enough that the patty will stay loose.

Rescuing Summer Vegetable Gratin

Layering summer's best vegetables into a gratin can lead to a memorable side dish—or a watery regret. This French casserole deserves better.

BY REBECCA HAYS

When summer yields a bumper crop of zucchini and tomatoes, I often consider making a simple, Provençal-style vegetable gratin. I imagine a golden brown, cheesy topping providing a rich contrast to the fresh, bright flavor of the vegetables. Then reality interrupts: As they cook, juicy vegetables exude a torrent of liquid that washes away flavors, turning my idyllic side dish into a squishy, soggy mistake.

There are plenty of vegetable gratin recipes out there, and I spent a day in the test kitchen trying a few, hoping to find the one of my dreams. But it wasn't meant to be—most were so flooded that I had to serve them with a slotted spoon. One even called for half of a loaf of sourdough bread to be layered among the vegetables, presumably to soak up some of the juices. But it didn't work. Even with 4 cups of spongy bread cubes, a deluge of liquid still ruined the dish. And with the release of juices, along went the flavor—the gratins were hopelessly bland and watery.

Our gratin releases just a little flavorful liquid as it bakes.

Testing the Waters

Before I could outline a dehydration plan, I had to determine exactly which vegetables to include. After some experimentation, I decided to stick with a fairly typical combination of tomatoes, zucchini, and summer squash. The other common choices, eggplant and bell peppers, fell short. Eggplant was simply too mushy and spongy, and red, yellow, and orange bell peppers looked pretty but took on a steamed flavor unless they were roasted before being added to the gratin. (The roasted peppers, on the other hand, tasted great and are worth the extra effort, so I used them in a recipe variation.)

My first move was to bake the casserole uncovered. The practice of covering the gratin with foil during baking (recommended by most recipes to speed cooking) was keeping too much moisture in. This was a step in the right direction, but my gratin was still waterlogged. To rid the zucchini and squash of some of their liquid, precooking methods such as grilling, broiling, or sautéing came to mind. While these methods were workable, I didn't want to spend all day at the grill, oven, or stove just to make a mere side dish. Salting, a technique frequently used to draw moisture from vegetables, made more sense. This method worked like a charm on the zucchini and summer squash, drying them out and thoroughly seasoning them as well. The tomatoes, however, were still exuding more liquid than I wanted. Should I go one step further and remove their watery jelly and seeds before salting them?

To my surprise, when I tried this, the gratin lacked deep tomato flavor. I wanted to make sure my results weren't a fluke, so I prepared two gratins—one with salted seedless tomatoes and one with salted tomatoes with the seeds and jelly intact—and tasted them side by side. The gratin made with tomatoes that had jelly and seeds was significantly richer and fuller in flavor than the one without them. After some research, I learned why: These two components contain far more flavorful glutamate compounds than the tomato flesh (see "Keeping the Taste in Tomatoes," page 13). If I wanted a gratin with intense tomato flavor, it was actually in my best interest to leave the jelly and seeds in, even if it meant a little extra liquid in the dish.

In my testing, I found the spots where the edges of the tomatoes peeked through the layers of zucchini were particularly good, having taken on the appealing qualities of oven-roasted tomatoes. To capitalize on this effect, I remodeled the architecture of the casserole, moving the tomatoes to a single top layer where they could really roast and caramelize. This worked well, especially when I drizzled the tomatoes with an aromatic garlic-thyme oil. The fragrant oil

STEP-BY-STEP | ASSEMBLING THE GRATIN

1. Toss salted zucchini and squash in half of garlic-thyme oil, then arrange in greased baking dish.

2. Spread caramelized onions in even layer on top of zucchini and squash.

3. Slightly overlap salted tomatoes in single layer on top of onions, then top with remaining garlic-thyme oil.

4. When vegetables are tender, sprinkle gratin with bread-crumb mixture, then bake until golden brown.

SCIENCE EXPERIMENT:

Keeping the Taste in Tomatoes

Removing the seeds from tomatoes is a common practice intended to improve the texture of a finished dish. But how does that affect flavor?

EXPERIMENT

We prepared two gratins, one made with intact tomatoes and another where the tomato seeds and jelly had been removed.

FULL OF FLAVOR

RESULTS

The gratin with the intact tomatoes had a decidedly richer, deeper flavor than its stripped-down counterpart.

STRIPPED AWAY

EXPLANATION

According to a study published in the *Journal of Agricultural and Food Chemistry*, that's because the seeds and jelly actually contain three times the amount of flavor-enhancing glutamic acid as the flesh. (This is the compound that supplies the savory quality known as umami in many foods.) So the next time a recipe calls for removing the seeds from tomatoes, you may want to ignore the instructions. You'll be saving time—and flavor. –R.H.

was so good that I decided to toss the zucchini and squash in it as well.

To add complexity, I inserted a layer of caramelized onions between the zucchini/squash and tomato layers and sprinkled the gratin with Parmesan bread crumbs. When my gratin came out of the oven leaking very little juice, I knew my rescue mission was a success.

SUMMER VEGETABLE GRATIN

SERVES 6 TO 8 AS A SIDE DISH OR 4 AS A LIGHT ENTRÉE

The success of this recipe depends on good-quality produce. Buy zucchini and summer squash of roughly the same diameter. While we like the visual contrast zucchini and summer squash bring to the dish, you can also use just one or the other. A similarly sized broiler-safe gratin dish can be substituted for the 13- by 9-inch baking dish. Serve the gratin alongside grilled fish or meat and accompanied by bread to soak up any flavorful juices.

COOK'S LIVE Original Test Kitchen Videos

www.cooksillustrated.com

HOW TO MAKE

- Summer Vegetable Gratin
- Roasted Bell Peppers

VIDEO TIP

- Why do I need to salt some vegetables?

- 6 tablespoons extra-virgin olive oil
- 1 pound zucchini, ends trimmed and sliced crosswise into ¼-inch-thick slices (see note)
- 1 pound yellow summer squash, ends trimmed and sliced crosswise into ¼-inch-thick slices (see note)
- 2 teaspoons table salt
- 1½ pounds ripe tomatoes (3 to 4 large), sliced ¼ inch thick
- 2 medium onions, halved lengthwise and sliced thin pole to pole (about 3 cups)
- ¾ teaspoon ground black pepper
- 2 medium garlic cloves, minced or pressed through garlic press (about 2 teaspoons)
- 1 tablespoon minced fresh thyme leaves
- 1 large slice white sandwich bread, torn into quarters
- 2 ounces grated Parmesan cheese (about 1 cup)
- 2 medium shallots, minced (about ¼ cup)
- ¼ cup chopped fresh basil leaves

1. Adjust oven rack to upper-middle position and heat oven to 400 degrees. Brush 13- by 9-inch baking dish with 1 tablespoon oil; set aside.

2. Toss zucchini and summer squash slices with 1 teaspoon salt in large bowl; transfer to colander set over bowl. Let stand until zucchini and squash release at least 3 tablespoons of liquid, about 45 minutes. Arrange slices on triple layer paper towels; cover with another triple layer paper towels. Firmly press each slice to remove as much liquid as possible.

3. Place tomato slices in single layer on double layer paper towels and sprinkle evenly with ½ teaspoon salt; let stand 30 minutes. Place second double layer paper towels on top of tomatoes and press firmly to dry tomatoes.

4. Meanwhile, heat 1 tablespoon oil in 12-inch nonstick skillet over medium heat until shimmering. Add onions, remaining ½ teaspoon salt, and ¼ teaspoon pepper; cook, stirring occasionally, until onions are softened and dark golden brown, 20 to 25 minutes. Set onions aside.

5. Combine garlic, 3 tablespoons oil, remaining ½ teaspoon pepper, and thyme in small bowl. In large bowl, toss zucchini and summer squash in half of oil mixture, then arrange in greased baking dish. Arrange caramelized onions in even layer over squash. Slightly overlap tomato slices in single layer on top of onions. Spoon remaining garlic-oil mixture evenly over tomatoes. Bake until vegetables are tender and tomatoes are starting to brown on edges, 40 to 45 minutes.

6. Meanwhile, process bread in food processor until finely ground, about 10 seconds. (You should have about 1 cup crumbs.) Combine bread crumbs, remaining tablespoon oil, Parmesan, and shallots in medium bowl. Remove baking dish from oven and increase heat to 450 degrees. Sprinkle bread-crumb mixture evenly on top of tomatoes. Bake gratin until bubbling and cheese is lightly browned, 5 to 10 minutes. Sprinkle with basil and let sit at room temperature 10 minutes before serving.

EQUIPMENT TESTING:

Broiler-Safe Gratin Dishes

As an all-purpose baking dish, Pyrex holds its own—it was the first dish we turned to for baking our gratin. But it has one main drawback: Pyrex is not broiler-safe, a necessary feature for melting cheese on many casseroles. As alternatives to Pyrex, we tested three broiler-safe baking dishes of similar size (around 3 quarts) made of clay or porcelain. All produced well-browned, evenly cooked food and each sported large, easy-grip handles for trouble-free maneuvering. –Elizabeth Bomze

HIGHLY RECOMMENDED

EMILE HENRY 3-Quart Gratin Dish
Price: $54.95
Comments: This heavy-duty clay casserole dish is a great, broiler-safe alternative to glassware Pyrex.

RECOMMENDED

REVOL ECLIPSE 3½-Quart Graphite Baker
Price: $79.95
Comments: Large offset handles make this pricey charcoal-colored casserole dish easy to transfer into and out of the oven; its porcelain finish is a cinch to clean.

ALL-CLAD Porcelain 3¼-Quart Baker with Stainless Steel Trivet
Price: $99.95
Comments: This shallow porcelain pan browns food nicely and cleans up easily, but without its trivet, the handles are skimpy.

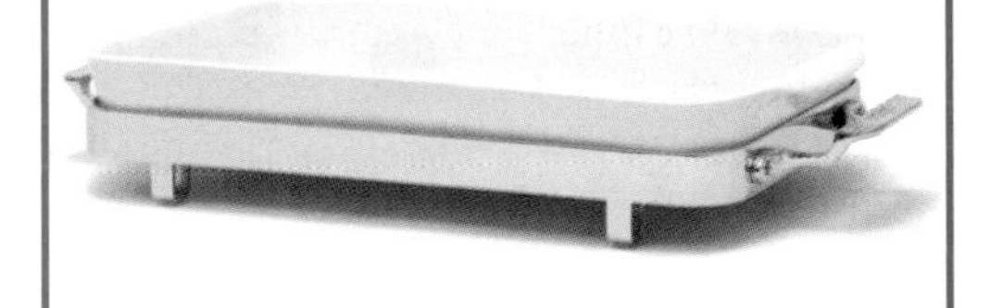

SUMMER VEGETABLE GRATIN WITH ROASTED PEPPERS AND SMOKED MOZZARELLA

For our free recipe for Roasted Bell Peppers, go to www.cooksillustrated.com/august.

Follow recipe for Summer Vegetable Gratin, substituting 4 ounces shredded smoked mozzarella (1 cup) for Parmesan and 3 roasted red peppers, skinned and cut into 1-inch pieces, for summer squash (do not salt roasted peppers).

Better Grilled Sausages with Onions

This classic pairing sounds tailor-made for the grill. But the reality is usually onions that are both crunchy and charred and sausages that either dry out or—even worse—catch fire.

BY DAVID PAZMIÑO

On the surface, few things sound easier than grilling up a few sausages—all you need is meat and a fire. But as any cook who's grilled his fair share can tell you, nicely browned links with juicy interiors are an elusive goal. Fatty sausages drip grease on the coals, causing flare-ups that can quickly turn exteriors into carbon while the insides remain barely cooked. Leaner sausages made from chicken or turkey may escape charring, but the intense heat of the grill can all too easily dry them out and turn their texture mealy. Things don't get any better when you throw onions into the mix—they usually wind up raw and sooty instead of tender and golden. I wanted a foolproof method that would work with any sausage I put on the grill and would let me offer sweet caramelized onions as part of the bargain.

Our grill method yields not only juicy, browned sausages but also tender onions and peppers infused with meaty flavor.

The best grilled sausages and onions I've ever eaten have come from the street vendors just outside Fenway Park. The Red Sox ballpark is just a short walk from the test kitchen, and I've had lots of opportunities to watch these grill masters at work. The secret to their technique is precooking the meat with the onions on a griddle that sits on the grill grate. They thinly slice the onions, spread them over the griddle, top them with sausages, and put the griddle over the fire. Once the onions are nearly done and full of flavor from the meat's dripping fat, the partially cooked sausages are put directly over the flames. Because most of the meat's fat has been rendered, flare-ups are minimal. The sausage can crisp and finish cooking all the way through without risk of blackening.

The closest thing I had to a griddle was my skillet, and I really didn't want to put it on top of a searing-hot grill. Perhaps a campfire technique from my Boy Scout days might serve the same purpose. On camping trips, we would toss onions, potatoes, and ground meat into aluminum foil packages we called hobo packs and throw them into the fire. In 20 to 30 minutes, the food would be cooked and the flavors blended. What if I adopted the same method but removed the sausage from the foil for the last few minutes to brown over the coals?

I sliced a few onions pole to pole, placed them on a sheet of foil, and topped them with sausages. I then placed the folded-up pack on a single-level fire with the coals evenly distributed over the grill bottom. After 15 minutes, the sausages were nearly cooked through, so I removed them from the foil and placed them directly over the coals. Six minutes later, I had nicely browned links infused with onion flavor. The onions themselves, however, left a lot to be desired. Some were tender, others still crunchy. Maybe spreading them out over a bigger surface would help.

For my next test, I placed the sausages and onions in a disposable roasting pan that I covered with foil. This improved matters, but not enough. I tried building a bigger fire, but that didn't work either, causing some onions to burn while others remained stubbornly crunchy. What if I tried a different tack and gave the onions a jump-start before putting them on the grill? I tried sautéing them first, seasoned with a little thyme and some salt and pepper, but it took nearly 20 minutes for them to soften. Although I'd never microwaved onions before, I figured it was worth a shot. As it turned out, the microwave achieved the same results as the

STEP-BY-STEP | A BETTER METHOD FOR GRILLING SAUSAGES AND ONIONS

1. MICROWAVE ONIONS
Microwave onions to jump-start cooking and ensure uniformly tender texture.

2. TOP ONIONS WITH SAUSAGES
Placing sausages on top of hot onions in aluminum pan allows their rendered fat to flavor onions.

3. PLACE FOIL-COVERED PAN ON HOT GRILL
Cooking onions in foil-covered pan makes them tender, not crunchy.

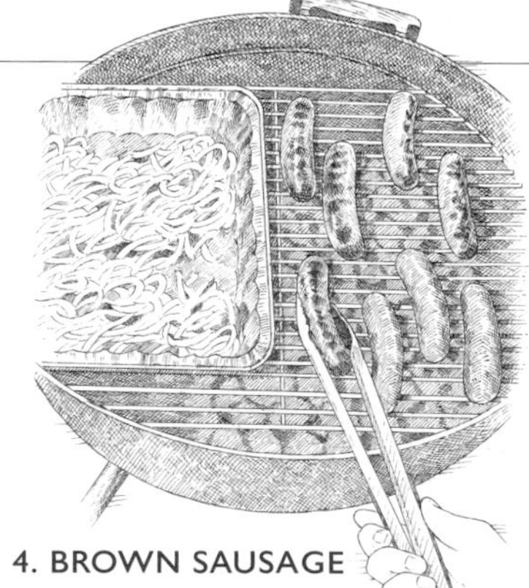

4. BROWN SAUSAGE OVER COALS
With most of their fat rendered, sausages can finish cooking over coals with little risk of flare-ups.

TASTING: Coarse-Grain Mustard

Mustard aficionados argue that the coarse-grained condiment improves any ham sandwich or grilled sausage—unless you pick the wrong jar. The fate of our lunch at stake, we sampled 11 brands.

Tasters appreciated spiciness, tanginess, and the pleasant pop of seeds. They disliked mustards with superfluous ingredients such as xanthan gum, artificial flavors, and garlic and onion powders. But the more noteworthy factor turned out to be salt. Mustards with a meager quantity (such as Westbrae) ranked low, while the winners contained roughly twice as much of this flavor amplifier. Tying for first place, both the familiar "nasal-clearing" Grey Poupon Country Dijon and the newer, "poppier" Grey Poupon Harvest Coarse Ground make good pantry staples. For complete tasting results, go to www.cooksillustrated.com/august. –Elizabeth Bomze

HIGHLY RECOMMENDED

GREY POUPON
Harvest Coarse Ground Mustard
Price: $3.79 for 8 oz.
Comments: This mustard boasts "a real burst of mustard flavor" with "big, round, crunchy seeds," "good heat," and just enough vinegar.

GREY POUPON
Country Dijon Mustard
Price: $3.79 for 8 oz.
Comments: Tasters noted this "classic," "moderately coarse" mustard with "wasabi-like heat" was particularly suited to grilled sausage.

skillet, but in just 4 minutes. I then layered the raw sausages over the hot onions in the disposable pan and placed the pan on the grill. This time around, all the onions were perfectly soft and tender. To deepen their flavor, I allowed them to caramelize in the pan on the grill for an extra 5 to 10 minutes after taking the sausages off.

With only a little more work than it takes to throw links on the fire, I now had juicy, browned, grilled sausages and sweet caramelized onions as good as any I've eaten in the shadow of Fenway Park.

CHARCOAL-GRILLED SAUSAGES WITH ONIONS

SERVES 4

This recipe will work with any raw, uncooked sausage. Serve sausages as is or in toasted buns.

- 2 large onions, halved and cut pole to pole into ¼-inch-thick slices
- 1 teaspoon fresh thyme leaves
- ½ teaspoon table salt
- ¼ teaspoon ground black pepper
- 13- by 9-inch disposable aluminum roasting pan
- 2 pounds sweet or hot Italian sausages (8 to 12 links) (see note)

1. Light large chimney starter filled with charcoal (6 quarts, or about 100 briquettes) and allow to burn until coals are fully ignited and partially covered with thin layer of ash, about 20 minutes. Build single-level fire by arranging coals evenly across bottom of grill. Position cooking grate over coals, cover grill, and heat until grate is hot, about 5 minutes; scrape grate clean with grill brush.

2. Meanwhile, combine onions, thyme, salt, and pepper in medium microwave-safe bowl. Cover with plastic wrap and microwave on high power until onions begin to soften and tips turn slightly translucent, 4 to 6 minutes, stirring once halfway through cooking (be careful of steam). Transfer onions to disposable roasting pan. Place sausages in single layer over onions and wrap roasting pan tightly with foil.

3. Place roasting pan in center of grill, cover grill, and cook 15 minutes. Move pan to one side of grill and carefully remove foil cover. Using tongs, place sausages on grate directly over coals. Grill sausages, uncovered, turning every 1 to 2 minutes, until golden brown on all sides, 5 to 7 minutes. Transfer sausages to platter and loosely tent with foil. Cover grill and continue cooking onions, stirring occasionally, until liquid evaporates and onions begin to brown, 5 to 10 minutes longer. Serve sausages, passing onions separately.

GAS-GRILLED SAUSAGES WITH ONIONS

Follow recipe for Charcoal-Grilled Sausages with Onions, turning all burners to medium-high and heating grill with lid down until very hot, about 15 minutes. Scrape grate clean with grill brush. Proceed from step 2, grilling sausages with lid down.

GRILLED SAUSAGES WITH PEPPERS AND ONIONS

Follow recipe for Charcoal-Grilled Sausages with Onions through step 1. In step 2, omit thyme and add 3 seeded and quartered medium red bell peppers to roasting pan along with sausages. In step 3, transfer pepper pieces directly over coals with sausages and cook, turning once, until charred patches form, 5 to 7 minutes. Remove peppers with sausages and continue to cook onions as directed.

GRILLED BRATWURST WITH SAUERKRAUT AND APPLES

Follow recipe for Charcoal-Grilled Sausages with Onions through step 1. In step 2, omit onions and thyme and combine 3 peeled and coarsely shredded medium Granny Smith apples, 2 cups drained sauerkraut, and ½ teaspoon minced fresh sage leaves in roasting pan (do not microwave before adding to pan). Replace sausages with 2 pounds bratwurst. Put bratwurst on top of sauerkraut mixture and cook as directed in step 3.

SHOPPING: Fresh Sausage

For grilling, links are better than long coils, which cook unevenly on the grill. We also avoid precooked sausages (these often come in shrink-wrapped packages), as grilling tends to dry them out and turn their texture mealy. Here are some of the most common types of links you'll find at the supermarket.

SWEET OR HOT ITALIAN SAUSAGE
Sweet versions of this pork sausage are flavored with fennel seeds, while the hot kind is spiked with chiles. Both types have a meaty flavor that makes them great for grilling, but they're also very fatty and should be carefully monitored when grilled directly over the coals (even after precooking) to avoid flare-ups.

FRESH BRATWURST
Authentic versions of these pale, mild German sausages made from pork and veal have a smooth, almost emulsified texture, with all the fat blended thoroughly with the meat, helping to reduce flare-ups.

FRESH CHICKEN SAUSAGE
Because chicken sausages tend to be lean, we prefer varieties that contain cheese. The extra fat helps keep the sausage from drying out on the grill and doesn't add to the risk of flare-ups.

FRESH POLISH SAUSAGE
The thicker casings of these mild pork sausages mean they may need a little more time over the coals to ensure fully cooked interiors. The smoked, dried version, called kielbasa, usually comes precooked and should be avoided when grilling.

GRILLED SAUSAGE WITH FENNEL

Follow recipe for Charcoal-Grilled Sausages with Onions through step 1. In step 2, substitute 2 thinly sliced, cored fennel bulbs for 1 onion and 2 tablespoons minced fennel fronds for thyme, microwaving as directed. Continue with recipe as directed.

COOK'S LIVE Original Test Kitchen Videos
www.cooksillustrated.com
HOW TO MAKE
- Grilled Sausages with Peppers and Onions

VIDEO TIPS
- Starting a fire in a charcoal grill
- How to slice fennel
- Tong primer

How to Keep Produce Fresher Longer

Proper storage is the key to longer-lasting fruits and vegetables. BY KEITH DRESSER

Most people tend to treat all fruits and vegetables the same, fitting them wherever there's room in the fridge. The reality is, different types of produce have different storage requirements. Some need to be placed in the coldest part of the refrigerator, some need humidity, and some don't need to be chilled at all. Storing your produce under the appropriate conditions is the key to prolonging its shelf life.

REFRIGERATOR MICROCLIMATES

We often think of our refrigerator as having a single temperature: around 34 degrees Fahrenheit, the average temperature recommended for a home refrigerator. In fact, every refrigerator has its own microclimates, with warmer, cooler, and more humid zones. When we hooked up a special device to one of our refrigerators in the test kitchen to monitor temperatures in various locations, we found that temperature ranged from as low as 33 degrees to as high as 43. You can make this temperature variation work to your advantage by learning which fruits and veggies do best where.

COLD ZONE: BACK, TOP TO MIDDLE
The top and middle shelves at the back of the fridge are normally the coldest, with temperatures that can dip below 34 degrees. Fruits and vegetables that are not prone to chill-injury should be stored here.

MODERATE ZONE: FRONT, MIDDLE TO BOTTOM
The areas at the front of our refrigerator, from the middle to the bottom shelves, were the most moderate, with temperatures above 37 degrees. Put fruits and vegetables that need refrigeration but are sensitive to chill-injury here.

HUMID ZONE: CRISPER DRAWER
Crispers provide a humid environment that helps keep produce with a high water content from shriveling and rotting. However, if the humidity is too high, water can build up on fruits and vegetables and hasten spoilage. You can regulate humidity by adjusting the vents; the more cold air that is let in, the less humid the environment.

STORAGE BASICS

Ethylene: Enemy of Freshness

As produce ripens, it emits small amounts of the ripening hormone ethylene. If ethylene is allowed to build up (in the closed environment of a plastic bag, for example, or a crisper), the gas will activate enzymes that break down and soften the cell walls of produce, speeding moisture loss and spoilage. Most storage techniques are designed to slow the production of ethylene or mitigate its impact.

When to Wash

With the exception of berries (see "Better Berry Treatment," page 17), it's best to wash produce just before you use it. Moisture promotes the growth of mold, which in turn causes spoilage. If you do wash ahead of time, make sure to dry the produce thoroughly before storing.

It's a Wrap

In general, it's a good idea to store produce in the packaging in which it was sold. Sometimes ready-made packaging has a function beyond simple convenience and can actually help to preserve the contents. For example, though they appear solid, the bags in which spinach and other greens are now sold are made of a polymer that allows ripening gases to pass through freely (see "Ethylene: Enemy of Freshness," left), staving off spoilage. Other types of packaging often feature small perforations or other openings (such as the bags in which celery is sold); here, too, the intent is to allow gases to escape while also protecting the produce from the drying effects of air.

WHERE TO STORE PRODUCE

Keep in the Front of the Fridge

These items are sensitive to chill-injury and should be placed in the front of the fridge, where the temperatures tend to be higher.

- Berries
- Citrus
- Corn on the cob
- Melons
- Peas

Best in the Crisper

These items do best in the humid environment of the crisper.

Artichokes	Chiles	Mushrooms
Asparagus	Cucumbers	Peppers
Beets	Eggplant	Radishes
Broccoli	Fresh herbs	Scallions
Cabbage	Green beans	Summer squash
Carrots	Leafy greens	Turnips
Cauliflower	Leeks	Zucchini
Celery	Lettuce	

Chill Anywhere

These items are not prone to chill-injury and can be stored anywhere in the fridge (including its coldest zones), provided the temperature doesn't freeze them.

- Apples
- Cherries
- Grapes

On the Counter

Some produce is sensitive to chill-injury and is subject to dehydration, internal browning, and/or internal and external pitting if stored in the refrigerator.

Apricots	Papayas
Avocados*	Peaches
Bananas	Pears
Kiwis*	Pineapple
Mangos	Plums
Nectarines	Tomatoes

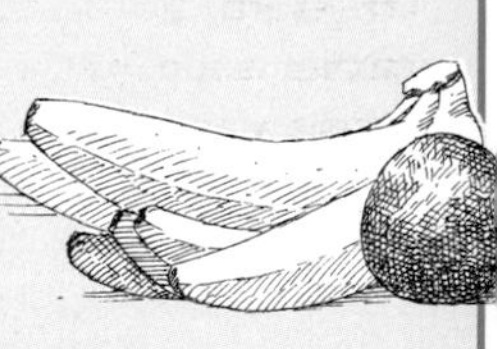

*Once they've reached their peak ripeness, these fruits can be stored in the refrigerator to prevent overripening, but some discoloration may occur.

In the Pantry

The following produce should be kept at cool room temperature and away from light to prevent sprouting (in the case of potatoes) and to prolong shelf life.

Garlic	Shallots
Onions	Sweet potatoes
Potatoes	Winter squash

STORAGE TECHNIQUES

Herb Keeper

Because stores sell fresh herbs in larger bundles than called for in most recipes, we are always interested in finding new ways to maximize the shelf life of leftovers. In the test kitchen, our preferred method for storing herbs has been to wrap them in a damp paper towel, then place them in a plastic bag in the refrigerator. However, that changed when we found the Herb Keeper ($12.99), an acrylic canister that holds long-stemmed herbs upright in water. It has a rubber lid and a removable bottom piece that can be unscrewed to refill with fresh water every three to four days. The jar fits inside refrigerator door shelves, making it easy to store. Compared with our standard storage method, we found that the Herb Keeper added three to four days to an herb's life.

Water Your Spears

Asparagus stored in the fridge can quickly dry out and become tough. To keep spears tender and flavorful, trim the ends and store them upright in cool water. Limp broccoli and celery benefit from the same treatment.

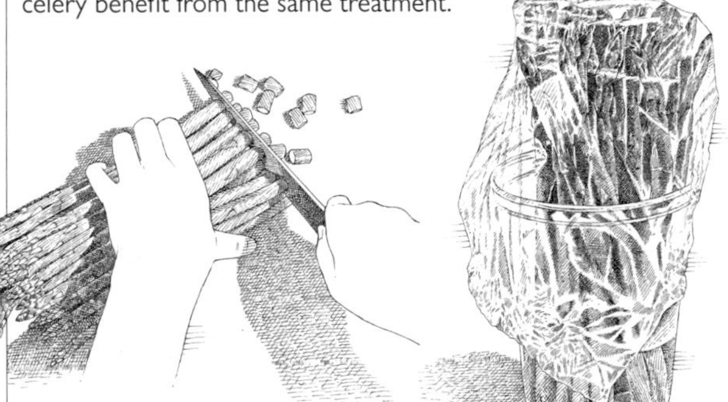

Keeping Lettuce Crisp

When lettuce and other leafy greens come in bags, store them in their original packaging (see "It's a Wrap," page 16). Store lettuce without packaging as follows.

1. **SHORT-TERM STORAGE** Wash and dry lettuce, then line the empty salad spinner with paper towels. Layer in the lettuce, covering each layer with additional paper towels.

2. **LONGER-TERM STORAGE** Loosely roll the washed and dried lettuce in a kitchen towel or paper towels and then place inside a large zipper-lock bag; leave the bag open to allow gases to escape. Lettuce will keep for up to one week.

Better Berry Treatment

While damp berries turn mushy faster than dry berries, we've discovered that cleaning with a mild vinegar solution and carefully drying destroys bacteria and mold spores, extending a berry's life.

1. Wash the berries in a bowl with 3 cups water and 1 cup white vinegar. Drain in a colander and rinse under running water.

2. Place the berries in a salad spinner lined with three layers of paper towels. Spin for 15 seconds or until the berries are completely dry. Store in a loosely covered paper towel–lined container.

Keeping Corn Sweet

The general rule with corn is to eat it the same day you buy it, as its sugars start converting to starches as soon as it is harvested, causing the corn to lose sweetness. Never refrigerate corn without wrapping it—and letting it sit on the counter is worse still.

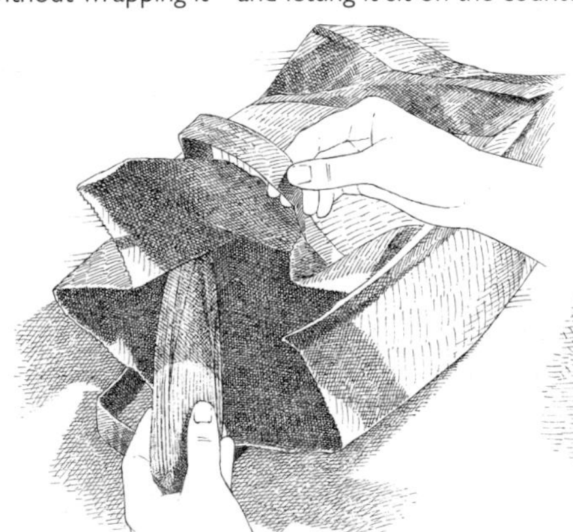

1. Wrap the unshucked corn in a wet paper bag to slow down the conversion from sugar to starch.

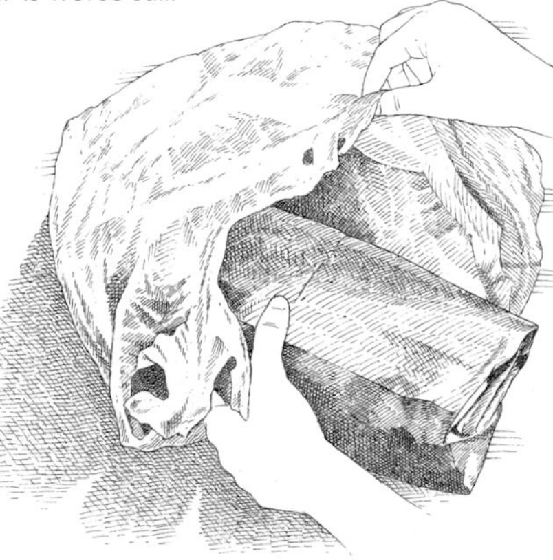

2. Place the wet paper bag in a plastic bag (any shopping bag will do) and refrigerate.

PRODUCE FOUNTAIN OF YOUTH?

Two products now in the produce aisles of some supermarkets claim to slow the aging process of greens as well as fruits and other vegetables. One is Evert-Fresh Green Bags, green plastic bags used to store produce; the other is ExtraLife, green plastic disks that are tossed into the crisper drawer. Both products use a mineral called zeolite that is said to absorb ethylene, the ripening gas emitted by most fruits and vegetables (see "Ethylene: Enemy of Freshness," page 16).

To test the effectiveness of these products, we refrigerated red leaf lettuce, green beans, cucumbers, and cantaloupes according to the products' instructions. A third set of produce was stored without any life-extending product.

The ExtraLife disks ($3.98 for one, which is to last for three months) were a complete waste of money, doing nothing to extend the life of the fruit or the vegetables. The Evert-Fresh bags ($3.98 for 10) seemed to have no effect on the melon or the cucumber, but did buy the lettuce and the beans a couple of extra days.

Perfecting Caponata

This sweet and sour eggplant relish from Sicily provides a great complement to meat or fish—but not if the vegetables are mushy and the flavors out of balance.

BY FRANCISCO J. ROBERT

Every Sicilian village has its own spin on caponata—a dish revered in Italy for hundreds of years, but far less well known in other parts of the world. If you've never encountered caponata, imagine a soft mélange of stewed vegetables—typically eggplant, celery, onion, red pepper, and tomato—augmented by the bolder flavors and textures of such Mediterranean stalwarts as capers, anchovies, olives, raisins, and pine nuts. The mixture is enriched by the viscous, deeply flavorful cooking liquid from the vegetables, enhanced by sugar and a splash of wine vinegar. This relish is typically used as a topping for bruschetta or as an accompaniment to grilled meat or fish—but I find it so addicting I can simply eat spoonfuls from a bowl. It is always served warm or at room temperature, never cold.

Although its ingredients may vary, caponata's preparation is usually the same: The vegetables are first sautéed, then simmered in liquid with the other components to meld the flavors. While the method sounded simple enough, a first trial of recipes revealed that it wasn't foolproof. I found that the problems almost always stemmed from caponata's star ingredient: eggplant.

Pine nuts add crunch to this caponata full of well-balanced flavors and tender vegetables.

The Taming of the Eggplant

Eggplant is essentially a sponge, consisting of a maze of tiny air pockets ready to absorb anything, especially the medium it's cooked in. It's also packed with water. I knew from experience that both properties make eggplant troublesome to cook. When it is sautéed, for example, the air pockets will suck up any oil in the pan, forcing the cook to keep adding oil to prevent sticking or burning. Meanwhile, the moisture inside turns to steam. This one-two punch transforms the eggplant into oil-soaked mush before it has a chance to caramelize.

In the test kitchen, we get around these problems by salting the eggplant, then pressing it between paper towels. Salt on the surface of the eggplant draws out the moisture from within, while pressing forces out even more moisture and also collapses the eggplant's cell walls, helping to eliminate air pockets.

But when I tried this treatment—cutting the eggplant into cubes, sprinkling them with salt, allowing them to drain in a colander for the recommended two hours before pressing on them—the eggplant didn't dry out quite as much as I'd hoped. After sautéing, it was still too greasy for my liking. I could let the eggplant macerate for a few more hours before pressing, but that seemed like an excessive amount of prep time for what was ultimately just a relish.

Was there a faster, more effective way to dehydrate the eggplant? A colleague teasingly suggested that I put it in the microwave—everyone's favorite way to speed things up. But when I thought about it, I realized the microwave was potentially a brilliant solution. After all, this appliance works by causing the water molecules in food to oscillate rapidly and generate steam. Food left in the microwave long enough will eventually transition from merely heating up to actually dehydrating. Better yet, for my purposes, dehydration would occur in a matter of minutes (see "A Cure for What Ails Eggplant," page 19).

It was definitely worth a try. And since dehydration would occur anyway, was there any point in salting the eggplant? I decided there was, as salt not only draws out moisture but also seasons the eggplant throughout. I placed the cubed, salted eggplant in a single layer on a plate and nuked it for 10 minutes. Lots of water leached out, all right—but it also pooled on the plate, poaching the eggplant into a soupy mess.

A box of coffee filters sitting on the counter nearby caught my eye. I placed a few under the next batch of eggplant I put in the microwave. They absorbed moisture so well that the eggplant shriveled to one-third its size, eliminating any need for pressing and making me wonder if I'd gone overboard. But all was well when I proceeded with the rest of the recipe. I was able to sauté the dried eggplant in the smallest amount of oil yet (1 tablespoon versus the nearly ½ cup I had been using). I then removed it from the pan while I sautéed some onion and other vegetables, returning it when I was ready to stew them all together. Once I added liquid to the pan, the eggplant plumped back up, nicely absorbing the flavors of the other ingredients instead of just oil.

Optimizing the Auxiliary Ingredients

In the best versions of caponata I've sampled, tomatoes are almost as integral to the dish as eggplant,

Caponata's Supporting Players

V8 JUICE
Though not traditional, a little V8 juice enhances caponata's tomato flavor.

ANCHOVY
A few minced fillets add dimension without imparting an overtly fishy taste.

RED WINE VINEGAR
Red wine vinegar brings the right degree of acidity.

BROWN SUGAR
Brown sugar adds more complexity than white sugar.

OLIVES
Black olives lend fruitiness and bump up the robust flavors of the relish.

providing a rich, fruity sweetness that nothing else can replicate. As it was summer, there was no question that I was going to use fresh tomatoes in my own rendition. The question was, when should I add them? If I added them too early, they lost their fresh taste; if I added them just before taking the pan off the heat, they gave the dish the texture of fresh salsa rather than blending into a harmonious medley. I struck the perfect balance by gently simmering the tomatoes with the browned eggplant and other ingredients at the very end of cooking. About five minutes over medium-low heat incorporated the tomatoes' sweet juiciness while preserving their bright freshness.

Now I wondered if I could achieve the deep tomato flavor that makes a great caponata so memorable. Adding canned tomatoes as well as fresh seemed like a good idea, but while tasters praised their concentrated flavor, they didn't care for their pulpy texture. Tomato paste also proved problematic, contributing intensity but camouflaging the delicate flavor of the fresh tomatoes. Running out of options, I gave V8 juice a try. A small amount was just enough to provide another layer of tomato flavor, while still allowing the fresh tomatoes to shine.

With the major problems solved, I needed to focus on the sweet and sour finish that is essential to traditional caponata (and helps distinguish it from the stewed eggplant specialty from France, ratatouille). I tried each of the sweeteners suggested in the recipes I found in my research. Honey, molasses, and maple syrup all overpowered the other flavors in the dish; brown sugar was the winner, lending more complexity than white. As for the sour note, traditional caponata calls for the use of wine vinegar. White wine vinegar proved too sharp and one-dimensional, while balsamic was overly concentrated and rich. Red wine vinegar, however, provided just the right bracing degree of tartness.

Tasters agreed that the customary inclusion of raisins and olives was a must. After trying a dozen different olive varieties, I made the happy discovery that almost any olive would work. A few anchovy fillets deepened the overall flavor of the dish, and a toss of toasted pine nuts provided an aromatic crunch. At last I had a simple, well-balanced recipe for an authentic caponata that tasted great as an appetizer, a relish, or just straight from the bowl.

STEP-BY-STEP | HOW TO MAKE CAPONATA

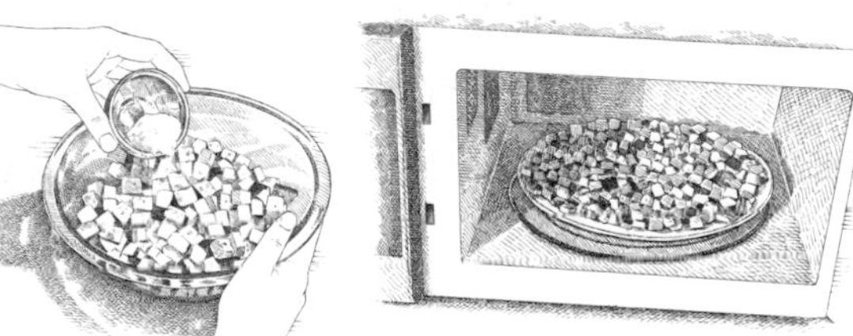

1. SALT eggplant and toss it in bowl to distribute salt evenly.

2. MICROWAVE eggplant on coffee filters until almost all of moisture has evaporated.

3. SAUTÉ eggplant first, then set it aside and sauté other vegetables.

4. SIMMER all ingredients until cooking liquid thickens and coats vegetables.

A Cure for What Ails Eggplant

To rid the eggplant of excess moisture and collapse the air pockets that make it soak up oil like a sponge, we came up with a novel solution: salting it and then heating it in the microwave. The salt pulls out liquid from inside the eggplant at the same time the microwave causes it to steam. In addition, the microwave helps to compress the eggplant, making it less spongy. To keep the eggplant from poaching in the liquid it released, we set it on a layer of coffee filters. By absorbing all of that liquid, the filters also helped to maintain a superhigh salt concentration on the exterior of the eggplant, which caused even more unwanted moisture to be drawn out. –F.J.R.

RAW DEAL
Without pretreatment, the raw eggplant looks good but cooks up oily and mushy.

MICROWAVE MAGIC
Salted, microwaved eggplant isn't as pretty, but the shrunken cubes soak up far less oil.

SICILIAN EGGPLANT RELISH (CAPONATA)

MAKES 3 CUPS

Serve caponata spooned over slices of toasted baguette or alongside grilled meat or fish. Adjust the vinegar as necessary, depending on the acidity of your tomatoes and what you are serving with the caponata. If coffee filters are not available, food-safe, undyed paper towels can be substituted when microwaving the eggplant. To allow the steam released by the eggplant to escape, remove the plate from the microwave immediately. Although the test kitchen prefers the complex flavor of V8 vegetable juice, tomato juice can be substituted. Caponata is best made in advance and can be refrigerated for up to 1 week in an airtight container.

- 1 large eggplant (about 1½ pounds), cut into ½-inch cubes (about 7 cups)
- ¾ teaspoon kosher salt
- ¾ cup V8 vegetable juice (see note)
- ¼ cup red wine vinegar, plus extra for seasoning (see note)
- 2 tablespoons light brown sugar
- ¼ cup minced fresh parsley leaves
- 1½ teaspoons minced anchovy fillets (2 to 3 fillets)
- 8 ounces ripe tomatoes (2 medium), cored, seeded, and cut into ½-inch dice (about 1 cup)
- ¼ cup raisins
- 2 tablespoons minced black olives
- 2 tablespoons extra-virgin olive oil
- 1 celery rib, cut into ¼-inch dice (about ½ cup)
- 1 small red bell pepper, seeded and cut into ¼-inch dice (about ½ cup)
- 1 small onion, diced fine (about ½ cup)
- ¼ cup pine nuts, toasted

1. Toss eggplant and salt together in medium bowl. Line entire surface of large microwave-safe plate with double layer of coffee filters and lightly spray with nonstick cooking spray. Spread eggplant in even layer over coffee filters. Microwave on high power until eggplant is dry and shriveled to one-third of its size, 8 to 15 minutes (eggplant should not brown). (If microwave has no turntable, rotate plate after 5 minutes.) Remove eggplant from microwave and immediately transfer to paper towel–lined plate.

2. Meanwhile, whisk vegetable juice, vinegar, brown sugar, parsley, and anchovies together in medium bowl. Stir in tomatoes, raisins, and olives.

3. Heat 1 tablespoon oil in 12-inch nonstick skillet over medium-high heat until shimmering. Add eggplant and cook, stirring occasionally, until edges are browned, 4 to 8 minutes, adding 1 teaspoon oil if pan appears dry. Transfer to bowl and set aside.

4. Add remaining 2 teaspoons oil to now-empty skillet and heat until shimmering. Add celery and red pepper; cook, stirring occasionally, until softened and edges are spotty brown, 2 to 4 minutes. Add onion and continue to cook until vegetables are browned, about 4 minutes longer.

5. Reduce heat to medium-low; stir in eggplant and vegetable juice mixture. Bring to simmer and cook until vegetable juice is thickened and coats vegetables, 4 to 7 minutes. Transfer to serving bowl and cool to room temperature. Taste and season with up to 1 teaspoon additional vinegar. Sprinkle with pine nuts before serving.

COOK'S LIVE Original Test Kitchen Videos
www.cooksillustrated.com
HOW TO MAKE
- Sicilian Eggplant Relish

VIDEO TIPS
- How to core and seed tomatoes
- How to toast pine nuts

Really Good Cherry Tomato Salad

How do you transform juicy cherry tomatoes into a great salad? For starters, get rid of some juice.

⋟ BY DAVID PAZMIÑO ⋞

Cherry tomatoes are often considered a support player in salad. But when summertime cherry tomatoes are especially sweet and juicy, they are more than worthy of taking center stage. I knew from experience, however, that I couldn't merely slice them in half, toss them with vinaigrette, and call it a salad. Like bigger, meatier beefsteak and plum varieties, cherry tomatoes exude lots of liquid when cut, quickly turning a salad into soup.

In the test kitchen, we often slice larger tomatoes, sprinkle them with salt, and allow them to drain to remove liquid and concentrate flavors. Following suit, I tossed 2 pints of halved cherry tomatoes with ¼ teaspoon salt (plus a pinch of sugar to accentuate sweetness) and let them drain in a colander. After 30 minutes, only a paltry 2 tablespoons of liquid had leached out. What if I exposed even more of the tomatoes' surface area to salt? I tried again with a fresh batch of tomatoes, cutting each one along the equator and then in half again. Progress: The salted, quartered tomatoes netted ¼ cup of liquid. But even this wasn't enough to prevent the salad from turning soggy when I tossed the tomatoes with oil and vinegar.

Some tomato salad recipes call for removing the watery seed pockets of the tomatoes, thus eliminating a major source of liquid. I wasn't about to cut open 40 or so cherry tomatoes and painstakingly push out the jelly and seeds with my thumb; I needed a more efficient method. That's when I thought of a salad spinner. The centrifugal force of the whirling bowl spins water off lettuce and herbs. Why wouldn't it have the same effect on tomatoes? It did—spinning salted and drained tomatoes resulted in the release of ½ cup of liquid.

My tomatoes were no longer liquidy, but when I tossed them with dressing, I noticed they tasted a little dull. This was not too surprising, as the jelly is the most flavorful part of the tomato (see "Keeping the Taste in Tomatoes," page 13), and I had stripped it away. If I added the jelly to the oil and vinegar I was already using to dress the tomatoes, I'd be putting the liquid I'd taken such pains to remove right back in. But how about reducing the jelly to concentrate its flavor? I strained the seeds from the jelly and then boiled it in a small saucepan with a chopped shallot and balsamic vinegar. After cooling the mixture and combining it with olive oil, I tossed it with the cherry tomatoes. This time I nailed it, with every bite of the salad delivering sweet tomato flavor.

COOK'S LIVE Original Test Kitchen Videos
www.cooksillustrated.com
HOW TO MAKE
• Greek Cherry Tomato Salad

GREEK CHERRY TOMATO SALAD

SERVES 4 TO 6

If in-season cherry tomatoes are unavailable, substitute vine-ripened cherry tomatoes or grape tomatoes from the supermarket. Cut grape tomatoes in half along the equator (rather than quartering them). If you don't have a salad spinner, after the salted tomatoes have stood for 30 minutes, wrap the bowl tightly with plastic wrap and gently shake to remove seeds and excess liquid. Strain the liquid and proceed with the recipe as directed. The amount of liquid given off by the tomatoes will depend on their ripeness. If you have less than ½ cup of juice after spinning, proceed with the recipe using the entire amount of juice and reduce it to 3 tablespoons as directed (the cooking time will be shorter). For our free recipes for Cherry Tomato and Watermelon Salad and Cherry Tomato Salad with Mango and Lime Curry Vinaigrette, go to www.cooksillustrated.com/august.

- 2 pints ripe cherry tomatoes, quartered (about 4 cups) (see note)
- Table salt
- ½ teaspoon sugar
- 2 medium garlic cloves, minced or pressed through garlic press (about 2 teaspoons)
- ½ teaspoon dried oregano
- 1 medium shallot, minced (about 3 tablespoons)
- 1 tablespoon red wine vinegar
- 2 tablespoons extra-virgin olive oil
- Ground black pepper
- 1 small cucumber, peeled, seeded, and cut into ½-inch dice
- ½ cup chopped pitted kalamata olives
- 4 ounces feta cheese, crumbled (about 1 cup)
- 3 tablespoons chopped fresh parsley leaves

1. Toss tomatoes, ¼ teaspoon salt, and sugar in medium bowl; let stand for 30 minutes. Transfer tomatoes to salad spinner and spin until seeds and excess liquid have been removed, 45 to 60 seconds, stirring to redistribute tomatoes several times during spinning. Return tomatoes to bowl and set aside. Strain tomato liquid through fine-mesh strainer into liquid measuring cup, pressing on solids to extract as much liquid as possible.

2. Bring ½ cup tomato liquid (discard any extra), garlic, oregano, shallot, and vinegar to simmer in small saucepan over medium heat. Simmer until reduced to 3 tablespoons, 6 to 8 minutes. Transfer mixture to small bowl and cool to room temperature, about 5 minutes. Whisk in oil and pepper to taste until combined. Taste and season with up to ⅛ teaspoon table salt.

3. Add cucumber, olives, feta, dressing, and parsley to bowl with tomatoes; toss gently and serve.

CHERRY TOMATO SALAD WITH BASIL AND FRESH MOZZARELLA

Follow recipe for Greek Cherry Tomato Salad, substituting balsamic vinegar for red wine vinegar and omitting garlic and oregano in step 2. Substitute 1½ cups lightly packed fresh basil leaves, roughly torn, and 8 ounces fresh mozzarella, cut into ½-inch cubes and patted dry with paper towels, for cucumber, olives, feta, and parsley in step 3.

CHERRY TOMATO SALAD WITH TARRAGON AND BLUE CHEESE

Follow recipe for Greek Cherry Tomato Salad, substituting cider vinegar for red wine vinegar, omitting garlic and oregano, and adding 2 teaspoons Dijon mustard and 4 teaspoons honey to tomato liquid in step 2. Substitute ½ cup roughly chopped toasted pecans, 2 ounces crumbled blue cheese, and 1½ tablespoons chopped fresh tarragon leaves for cucumber, olives, feta, and parsley in step 3.

TECHNIQUE | AVOIDING WATERLOGGED CHERRY TOMATO SALAD

1. SPIN
Spinning the quartered tomatoes in a salad spinner removes excess liquid that can make salad watery.

2. REDUCE
Simmering the strained tomato liquid creates a concentrated tomato base for the vinaigrette.

Improving Pasta with Olives, Garlic, and Herbs

Made in Italy with the very best local olives and extra-virgin olive oil, this simple dish can be superb. But how good can it get with ingredients from the supermarket?

⋟ BY DAVID PAZMIÑO ⋞

Pasta dressed with nothing more than olives and garlic warmed in olive oil is an Italian classic. In Italy, with locally pressed extra-virgin olive oil and the very best olives at your disposal, what else would you need? However, if your starting points are supermarket olives and mass-produced olive oil—as they are for most of us in this country—the results are a little one-dimensional. Could I retool the dish with a few more pantry staples to boost its flavors?

My first task was to settle on the type of olive. After tasting a dozen green and black varieties, my tasters chose the bold yet well-rounded flavors of widely available kalamata olives. Next up: how best to incorporate them into the dish? I could puree the kalamatas into a paste with the garlic and olive oil, or I could coarsely chop them with a knife and mix them with minced garlic and oil. My tasters most liked how chunks of fleshy olive meat distributed bursts of flavor throughout the dish, so the latter method won out. Following tradition, I warmed the chopped olives and garlic in a couple of tablespoons of extra-virgin olive oil to mellow their flavors before adding them to the pasta.

Now it was time to look for other pantry staples to bring additional dimension to the dish. My first thought was to toss in a few anchovies. Many cooks shy away from these salty little fish, fearing their pungency will overpower everything else. But I found that by limiting myself to a tablespoon of minced fillets, I deepened the other flavors without contributing any overt fishiness at all.

I wondered if a small amount of tomato would add welcome acidity and sweetness. Fresh tomatoes were out—their flavor wouldn't be concentrated enough. I also didn't want to open a can of crushed or diced tomatoes. But I did reach for a tube of tomato paste. One tablespoon was enough to help bring balance to the other flavors. And for a more concentrated form of sweetness that could go head-to-head with the olives, I turned to a few chopped sun-dried tomatoes. Adding a little hot water from the boiling pasta to the skillet helped turn all these disparate ingredients into a cohesive sauce.

Tossing in grated Parmesan cheese was a given. But a few rustic Italian pasta dishes skip the Parmesan in favor of toasted bread crumbs. Why not use both? With fresh parsley and basil stirred in to add bright herbal flavor, I now had a dish that tasted so good I hardly noticed the fact that my ingredients came from the grocery store, not the olive estate down the road.

PASTA WITH OLIVES, GARLIC, AND HERBS

SERVES 4 TO 6

For a milder olive flavor, use manzanilla olives in place of kalamata. Be sure to rinse the pitted olives before chopping them to remove excess salt. In addition to mezze rigatoni or farfalle, any short, tubular, or molded pasta will work well.

- 5 tablespoons extra-virgin olive oil
- 6 medium garlic cloves, minced or pressed through garlic press (about 2 tablespoons)
- 1 tablespoon minced anchovy fillets (4 to 6 fillets)
- 1 tablespoon tomato paste
- ¼–½ teaspoon hot red pepper flakes
- ¼ cup drained oil-packed sun-dried tomatoes, rinsed, patted dry, and cut into thin strips
- 1 cup pitted kalamata olives, rinsed and coarsely chopped (see note)
- 2 large slices white sandwich bread (about 3 ounces), torn into quarters
- 1¾ teaspoons table salt
- 1 pound mezze rigatoni or farfalle (see note)
- 2 ounces finely grated Parmesan cheese (about 1 cup)
- 3 tablespoons chopped fresh parsley leaves
- 1½ cups lightly packed fresh basil leaves, roughly torn
- Ground black pepper
- 1 lemon, cut into wedges

1. Combine 3 tablespoons olive oil, 1 tablespoon garlic, anchovies, tomato paste, red pepper flakes, sun-dried tomatoes, and olives in medium bowl. Set aside.

2. Pulse bread in food processor until coarsely ground, about 16 one-second pulses. Heat remaining 2 tablespoons oil in 12-inch skillet over medium heat until shimmering. Add bread crumbs and cook, stirring frequently, until beginning to brown, 4 to 6 minutes. Stir in remaining tablespoon garlic and ¼ teaspoon salt. Continue to cook, stirring constantly, until garlic is fragrant and bread crumbs are dark golden brown, 1 to 2 minutes longer. Transfer to plate to cool. Wipe out skillet with paper towels.

3. Meanwhile, bring 4 quarts water to boil in Dutch oven over high heat. Add rigatoni and remaining 1½ teaspoons salt. While pasta is cooking, return now-empty skillet to medium heat and add olive mixture. Cook until olive mixture is aromatic and oil has turned rusty red, 4 to 6 minutes. Remove ¾ cup pasta cooking water from pot and add to skillet. Bring to simmer and cook for 2 minutes. Remove pan from heat while pasta finishes cooking.

4. When pasta is just shy of al dente, drain pasta, reserving ½ cup of pasta cooking water, and transfer back to Dutch oven. Add olive mixture to pasta and toss over medium heat until pasta absorbs most of liquid, about 2 minutes. Stir in ½ cup Parmesan. Adjust consistency of sauce with reserved pasta water. (Sauce should cling to pasta but not be too loose or runny.) Remove pot from heat and stir in parsley and basil; adjust seasoning with pepper. Serve, passing lemon wedges, remaining Parmesan, and bread crumbs separately.

Bread crumbs and sun-dried tomatoes add complexity to our pasta.

Foolproof Peach Shortcakes

Ripe farmstand peaches lead to shortcakes drenched in sweet juice. But what if you're stuck with hard, mealy supermarket peaches?

BY J. KENJI ALT

Berry shortcake is the ultimate carefree dessert, requiring little more than tossing berries with sugar, sandwiching them inside a split biscuit, and topping it with whipped cream. With such a simple procedure, you would think the recipe would be easy to adapt to any number of fresh fruits. But that's not the case. Take peaches. If you begin with ripe farmstand fruit dripping in juice, the results can be spectacular. But try making shortcake with the hard, mealy peaches that are the typical supermarket offering and you end up with flavorless filling and a dry, crumbly biscuit. My goal was to develop a foolproof recipe for peach shortcake that would work with any peach, regardless of quality.

We designed our shortcake biscuits to be porous enough to absorb the peach juice but firm enough to stand up under the weight of the fruit.

Getting the Juices Going

Scanning cookbooks for peach shortcake recipes, I found that most were tacked-on modifications of berry shortcakes that simply called for replacing the berries with peaches. Comparing shortcakes made with ordinary supermarket strawberries and less-than-perfect supermarket peaches side by side, the difference was clear. The strawberry biscuits were soaked in sweet juice, while the peach biscuits remained bone dry. Figuring that berries must simply have more liquid than peaches, I consulted our science editor. Surprisingly, peaches (even unripe ones) actually contain ever so slightly more juice than berries—88 percent versus 87 percent.

There's more to the story: Both fruits had been macerated in sugar, a technique designed to not only extract juice from the fruit but improve on nature by sweetening it. When sugar comes in contact with fruit, it will dissolve in the small amount of moisture present on the fruit's surface, creating a super-concentrated sugar solution. Inside the cells of the fruit is a much weaker solution—the juice. Whenever an imbalance like this occurs, liquid inside the cells will flow outside to bring the two sugar solutions into equilibrium in a process called osmosis.

Two major factors can influence the efficiency of osmosis: the structure of the cell walls and the fruit's surface area. The cell walls of a berry are weaker and more permeable than those of a peach, and a berry's nubby exterior is covered in nooks and crannies that add up to more surface area than there is on a smooth peach chunk. Consequently, even though it contains less juice, a berry will release more liquid than a peach chunk in the presence of sugar.

To help level the playing field, my first step was to increase the surface area of the peaches so that more of it would come in contact with the sugar. Chopping the peaches up very finely would be one way, but I knew my tasters would miss the bigger pieces. Alternatively, I could slice the peaches as thinly as possible. When I tried this, the thin slices produced far more liquid than the thicker ones had, but not enough to guarantee shortcakes saturated in juice. Was there any other method besides maceration that I could use to pull moisture out of the fruit?

My next thought was to cook the peaches, which would cause the cell walls to rupture and release juice. Unfortunately, even a little cooking made the slices turn to mush and lose their fresh flavor. This gave me an idea: Instead of cooking all of the peaches a little, I'd cook a few of the peaches a lot. For my next batch of shortcakes, I removed a quarter of the sliced peaches and cooked them in a bowl in the microwave with some sugar until completely tender. I mashed them with a potato masher, then used the resulting peachy jam with the remaining peaches, which I had macerated as usual. When I assembled the shortcakes, I found their juiciness was greatly improved.

As a final measure to guarantee enough juice in my shortcakes even with the mealiest peaches, I tried to think of an outside source for liquid. Orange juice worked pretty well; it added a sweet, fruity background without being overly assertive. In the end, however, I found that peach schnapps worked best. By microwaving it along with the peaches destined for mashing, most of the raw alcohol flavor disappeared, so that my tasters hardly detected it.

A Peach of a Biscuit

Now that I'd found a way to guarantee the presence of lots of juice in my shortcake, it was time to focus on the biscuits. Drop biscuits held the most promise. All the work can be done directly in a bowl, and the craggy results are perfect for catching liquid. Starting with our existing recipe (November/December 2007), I removed a little of the salt and increased the amount of sugar, converting the biscuits from side dish to dessert. But when topped with peaches, the biscuits were a little too airy for my purposes. To increase their density so that they would hold up better under the weight of the fruit, I added an egg to the batter. I also played with the mixing method, stirring the dough vigorously with a wooden spoon for 30 seconds to encourage gluten formation. The dough was noticeably tackier (a sign of gluten) when I dropped it onto the baking sheet, and I held high hopes for the biscuits as they baked.

My hopes were rewarded. The biscuits were tender and porous enough to absorb all the juices yet firm enough to stand up to the fruit. I always

AT A GLANCE | BUMPING UP JUICE AND FLAVOR

Macerating fruit in sugar is the traditional method for releasing its juices. But for peaches, this step alone was not enough. Here's how we supplemented maceration.

PEACH SCHNAPPS
A splash of peach schnapps brings even more liquid into the mix—without diluting fresh peach flavor.

MICROWAVING
Microwaving some of the peaches to soften their cell walls makes the cells more susceptible to rupturing (and releasing juice).

MASHING
Mashing the microwaved peaches completely breaks down their cell walls, increasing the amount of juice they release.

thought berry shortcakes were the pinnacle of summer desserts, but since my recipe works with even less-than-perfect peaches, I may have discovered a new year-round contender.

PEACH SHORTCAKES
SERVES 6

This recipe works well with any peaches, regardless of quality. If your peaches are firm, you should be able to peel them with a sharp vegetable peeler. If they are too soft to withstand the pressure of a peeler, you'll need to blanch them in a pot of simmering water for 15 seconds and then shock them in a bowl of ice water before peeling. If buttermilk is not available, substitute ½ cup of low-fat yogurt mixed with 3 tablespoons of milk. Orange juice or orange liqueur can be used in place of the peach schnapps. The biscuits may be made up to 24 hours in advance.

Fruit

- 2 pounds ripe but firm peaches (4 to 5 medium), peeled, pitted, and cut into ¼-inch-thick wedges (see note)
- 6 tablespoons sugar
- 2 tablespoons peach schnapps (see note)

Biscuits

- 2 cups (10 ounces) unbleached all-purpose flour
- 2 teaspoons baking powder
- 2 tablespoons sugar
- ¾ teaspoon table salt
- ⅔ cup cold buttermilk (see note)
- 1 large egg
- 8 tablespoons unsalted butter, melted and cooled slightly

Whipped Cream

- ½ cup heavy cream
- 1 tablespoon sugar
- ½ teaspoon vanilla extract

1. **FOR THE FRUIT:** Gently toss three-quarters of peaches with 4 tablespoons sugar in large bowl. Let stand 30 minutes. Toss remaining peaches with remaining 2 tablespoons sugar and schnapps in medium microwave-safe bowl. Microwave on high power until peaches are bubbling, about 1 to 1½ minutes, stirring twice during cooking. Using potato masher, crush peaches into coarse pulp. Let stand 30 minutes.

2. **FOR THE BISCUITS:** Adjust oven rack to middle position and heat oven to 475 degrees. While peaches macerate, whisk flour, baking powder, 1 tablespoon sugar, and salt in large bowl. Whisk together buttermilk and egg in medium bowl; add melted butter and stir until butter forms small clumps.

3. Add buttermilk mixture to dry ingredients and stir with wooden spoon until dough comes together and no dry flour remains. Continue stirring vigorously for 30 seconds. Using greased ⅓ cup dry measure, scoop up mound of dough and drop onto parchment-lined rimmed baking sheet (if dough sticks to cup, use small spoon to pull it free). Repeat with remaining dough, spacing biscuits about 1½ inches apart, to create 6 biscuits. Sprinkle remaining tablespoon sugar evenly over top of biscuits. Bake until tops are golden brown and crisp, about 15 minutes. Transfer to wire rack and let cool 15 minutes before assembling.

4. **FOR THE WHIPPED CREAM:** Using hand mixer or stand mixer fitted with whisk attachment, beat cream, sugar, and vanilla on low speed until bubbles form, about 30 seconds. Increase speed to medium; continue beating until beaters leave trail, about 30 seconds longer. Increase speed to high; continue beating until nearly doubled in volume and whipped cream forms soft peaks, 30 to 45 seconds longer.

5. **TO ASSEMBLE:** Split each biscuit in half and place bottoms on individual serving plates. Spoon portion of crushed peach mixture over each bottom, followed by peach slices and any exuded juices. Top peaches with 2 tablespoons whipped cream, cap with biscuit top, and dollop each shortcake with some of remaining whipped cream. Serve immediately.

COOK'S LIVE Original Test Kitchen Videos
www.cooksillustrated.com
HOW TO MAKE
• Peach Shortcakes
VIDEO TIP
• How to peel, pit, and slice peaches

EQUIPMENT TESTING:

Dry Measuring Cups

Dry measuring cups vary tremendously in material, shape, weight, and price. We rounded up 11 sets to compare their differences. To test accuracy, we filled each cup to the brim with water and checked whether it fell within 5 percent of the target weight. (We have found that eyeballing fluid in a cup yields a more precise measurement than filling it with a dry ingredient like flour, where the amount can vary widely, depending on who is doing the measuring.) As we measured, we discovered we preferred stainless steel over plastic for its heft and durability. We also liked long handles that extend straight out; angled or raised handles obstructed our ability to draw a straight edge across the rim to level off the ingredient. For complete testing results, go to www.cooksillustrated.com/august.

–Elizabeth Bomze and Lindsay McSweeney

HIGHLY RECOMMENDED
AMCO Stainless Steel 4-Piece Measuring Cup Set
Price: $9.95
Comments: This stainless steel set offers accuracy, good weight balance, and long, level, well-marked handles.

RECOMMENDED
OXO GOOD GRIPS 7-Piece Soft Handled Measuring Cup Set
Price: $7.95
Comments: Of the plastic sets, this was our favorite. Accuracy was good—off by less than 1 percent—plus, the set includes ⅔ and ¾ cups (and an egg separator)—a nice bonus.

NOT RECOMMENDED
CALPHALON Set of 4 Stainless Steel Measuring Cups
Price: $19.99
Comments: We liked the shovel-like shape and long, comfortable silicone handles on these cups, but their accuracy was off by almost 10 percent.

Best Blueberry Pie

Sweet, delicate blueberries are easily overshadowed by a dull thickener. Our goal was a sliceable pie with bright, fresh flavor.

⋟ BY YVONNE RUPERTI ⋞

There's nothing like blueberry pie to shake the confidence of even the most experienced baker. Unlike apple pie, which requires little (if any) starch to thicken the fruit, the filling in blueberry pie needs special attention because the berries are so juicy. The very first slice reveals success or failure. Triumph brings a firm, glistening filling full of fresh, bright flavor and still-plump berries. Defeat can range from a wedge that collapses into a soupy puddle topped by a sodden crust to filling so dense that cutting into it is like slicing through gummi bears.

In the Thick of It

I started my search for a juicy yet sliceable pie by filling our Foolproof Pie Dough (November/December 2007) with a fairly standard mixture of 6 cups fresh blueberries, ¾ cup sugar, and our usual thickener for berry pies, tapioca. (I knew to avoid cornstarch or flour—in the test kitchen we've found they mute fresh fruit flavor.) The 6 tablespoons recommended on the back of the tapioca box produced a stiff, congealed mass, so I slowly cut back the amount. At 4 tablespoons, the filling was still too congealed for my tasters' liking, but this amount proved to be the tipping point; any less and the pie needed to be served with a spoon.

The problem, of course, was the juiciness of the berries. Could I reduce some of their liquid by cooking them before they were baked in the pie shell? I put all 6 cups in a pan. As the berries simmered, I mashed them with a potato masher to release their juices. Excess liquid did indeed boil away—but so did a lot of fresh berry flavor.

After some experimentation, I found that cooking just half of the berries was enough to adequately reduce the liquid. I then folded the remaining raw berries into the mixture, creating a satisfying combination of intensely flavored cooked fruit and bright-tasting fresh fruit that allowed me to cut the tapioca down to 3 tablespoons. Encouraged by this success, I wondered if I could decrease the tapioca even further.

This pie has it all—a juicy yet firm filling full of fresh blueberry flavor.

Pectin Power

As I watched the blueberries for my pie bubble away in the pot, I thought about blueberry jam. Well-made jam boasts a soft, even consistency that is neither gelatinous nor slippery. The secret to this great texture is pectin, a carbohydrate found in fruit. Blueberries are low in natural pectin, so commercial pectin in the form of a liquid or powder is usually added when making blueberry jam. The only downside to commercial pectin is that it needs the presence of a certain proportion of sugar and acid in order to work. I added an ounce of pectin, which required me to bump up the sugar to 2½ cups. This increase in sugar overpowered the berries, making the filling sickeningly sweet. A test with "no sugar needed" pectin set up properly, but this additive contains lots of natural acid, which compensates for the lack of extra sugar—and its sourness made my tasters wince. I was ready to give up when a colleague offered a suggestion: Since apples contain a lot of natural pectin, could an apple be added to the blueberries to help set the filling?

I folded one peeled and grated Granny Smith apple into a new batch of fresh and cooked berries I had mixed with 2 tablespoons of tapioca. I baked the pie, then waited impatiently while it cooled. When I finally tried a slice, I knew I'd hit on a great solution. Combined with a modest 2 tablespoons of tapioca, the apple provided enough thickening power to set the pie beautifully, plus it enhanced the flavor of the berries without anyone guessing my secret ingredient. (For more information, see "The Apple of My Pie," page 25.) Just as important, it left no evidence of its own texture. To make sure the tapioca was equally unobtrusive—thickening the filling without leaving any telltale pearls—I pulverized it in a spice grinder before adding it to the filling.

The Crust of the Matter

Tweaking the crust was the last step. I found that baking the pie on a heated baking sheet on the bottom rack of the oven produced a crisp, golden bottom crust that didn't get soggy. As for the top crust, berry pies are often made with a decorative lattice topping that allows the steam from the berries to gently escape. But after making more than 50 lattice tops, I was determined to find a faster, easier approach. I decided to try making a crust I had seen in my research that had vents in the form of simple round cutouts. After rolling out the dough, I used a small biscuit cutter to cut out circles, then transferred the dough onto the pie. This method saved time and made an attractive, unusual-looking top crust that properly vented the steam from the berry filling as it baked. At long last, my blueberry blues had turned to blueberry bliss.

RECIPE DIAGNOSIS: **Looks Can Be Deceiving**

PRETTY BUT PASTY
Too much tapioca (or the wrong thickener, such as flour or cornstarch) results in a filling that holds its shape but tastes gluey and dull.

FRESH BUT SOUPY
With no thickener at all, there is plenty of fresh berry flavor, but the filling is loose and runny.

TECHNIQUE | NO-FUSS TOP CRUST

We used a 1¼-inch biscuit cutter to cut holes in the dough, but a spice-jar lid will also do the trick.

BLUEBERRY PIE

MAKES ONE 9-INCH PIE

This recipe was developed using fresh blueberries, but unthawed frozen blueberries (our favorite brands are Wyman's and Cascadian Farm) will work as well. In step 4, cook half the frozen berries over medium-high heat, without mashing, until reduced to 1¼ cups, 12 to 15 minutes. Grind the tapioca to a powder in a spice grinder or mini food processor. If using pearl tapioca, reduce the amount to 5 teaspoons. Vodka is essential to the texture of the crust and imparts no flavor; do not substitute.

Foolproof Pie Dough

- 2½ cups (12½ ounces) unbleached all-purpose flour, plus more for work surface
- 1 teaspoon table salt
- 2 tablespoons sugar
- 12 tablespoons (1½ sticks) cold unsalted butter, cut into ¼-inch slices
- ½ cup cold vegetable shortening, cut into 4 pieces
- ¼ cup cold vodka (see note)
- ¼ cup cold water

Blueberry Filling

- 6 cups (about 30 ounces) fresh blueberries (see note)
- 1 Granny Smith apple, peeled and grated on large holes of box grater
- 2 teaspoons grated zest and 2 teaspoons juice from 1 lemon
- ¾ cup (5¼ ounces) sugar
- 2 tablespoons instant tapioca, ground (see note)
- Pinch table salt
- 2 tablespoons unsalted butter, cut into ¼-inch pieces

- 1 large egg, lightly beaten with 1 teaspoon water

1. **FOR THE PIE DOUGH:** Process 1½ cups flour, salt, and sugar in food processor until combined, about two 1-second pulses. Add butter and shortening and process until homogenous dough just starts to collect in uneven clumps, about 15 seconds; dough will resemble cottage cheese curds and there should be no uncoated flour. Scrape bowl with rubber spatula and redistribute dough evenly around processor blade. Add remaining cup flour and pulse until mixture is evenly distributed around bowl and mass of dough has been broken up, 4 to 6 quick pulses. Empty mixture into medium bowl.

2. Sprinkle vodka and water over mixture. With rubber spatula, use folding motion to mix, pressing down on dough until dough is slightly tacky and sticks together. Divide dough into 2 even balls and flatten each into 4-inch disk. Wrap each in plastic wrap and refrigerate at least 45 minutes or up to 2 days.

3. Remove 1 disk of dough from refrigerator and roll out on generously floured (up to ¼ cup) work surface to 12-inch circle, about ⅛ inch thick. Roll dough loosely around rolling pin and unroll into pie plate, leaving at least 1-inch overhang on each side. Working around circumference, ease dough into plate by gently lifting edge of dough with one hand while pressing into plate bottom with other hand. Leave dough that overhangs plate in place; refrigerate while preparing filling until dough is firm, about 30 minutes.

4. **FOR THE FILLING:** Adjust oven rack to lowest position, place rimmed baking sheet on oven rack, and heat oven to 400 degrees. Place 3 cups berries in medium saucepan and set over medium heat. Using potato masher, mash berries several times to release juices. Continue to cook, stirring frequently and mashing occasionally, until about half of berries have broken down and mixture is thickened and reduced to 1½ cups, about 8 minutes. Let cool slightly.

5. Place grated apple in clean kitchen towel and wring dry. Transfer apple to large bowl. Add cooked berries, remaining 3 cups uncooked berries, lemon zest, juice, sugar, tapioca, and salt; toss to combine. Transfer mixture to dough-lined pie plate and scatter butter pieces over filling.

6. Roll out second disk of dough on generously floured (up to ¼ cup) work surface to 11-inch circle, about ⅛ inch thick. Using 1¼-inch round biscuit cutter, cut round from center of dough. Cut another 6 rounds from dough, 1½ inches from edge of center hole and equally spaced around center hole. Roll dough loosely around rolling pin and unroll over pie, leaving at least ½-inch overhang on each side.

7. Using kitchen shears, trim bottom layer of overhanging dough, leaving ½-inch overhang. Fold dough under itself so that edge of fold is flush with outer rim of pie plate. Flute edges using thumb and forefinger or press with tines of fork to seal. Brush top and edges of pie with egg mixture. If dough is very soft, chill in freezer for 10 minutes.

8. Place pie on heated baking sheet and bake 30 minutes. Reduce oven temperature to 350 degrees and continue to bake until juices bubble and crust is deep golden brown, 30 to 40 minutes longer. Transfer pie to wire rack; cool to room temperature, at least 4 hours. Cut into wedges and serve.

SCIENCE EXPERIMENT:

The Apple of My Pie

When making our blueberry pie filling, we found that if we used more than 2 tablespoons of tapioca, the texture of the filling took on a gummy consistency we didn't like. But 2 tablespoons or less resulted in a filling that was too loose. Could we solve this problem with pectin, a gentle thickener that occurs naturally in fruit?

EXPERIMENT

As a control, we thickened one pie with 2 tablespoons tapioca. We then compared it with a second pie thickened with 2 tablespoons tapioca and a grated apple, which is high in pectin and has a mild flavor. (We hoped that grating the apple would make it less noticeable in the baked pie.)

RESULTS

As expected, the pie thickened with tapioca alone was loose and soupy. But the pie thickened with tapioca plus an apple had a naturally gelled texture that was just right. The apple bits seemed to melt into the berry filling during baking, boosting fruity flavor but leaving no textural sign of their presence.

EXPLANATION

Pectin is a natural substance, found in fruits and vegetables, that creates structure in a plant by helping to bind its cell walls together. This same substance is used to thicken jams and jellies into a set, but soft, mass. Pectin content varies from fruit to fruit and also within a plant (more pectin is found in the skin of a fruit than in its flesh, for example). Apples are a great source of pectin because they contain high levels of high-methoxy pectin, the best natural pectin for making gels. By mashing some of the blueberries and grating the apple, we helped to release the pectin from the fruits' cell walls so that it could thicken the pie filling. –Y.R.

ON THE LOOSE

Pie filling thickened without enough tapioca won't firm up. But too much tapioca leads to gumminess.

ALL FIRMED UP

A little tapioca plus a grated apple created a juicy but sliceable filling.

The Problem with Supermarket Olive Oils

You get what you pay for with most supermarket extra-virgin olive oils: bland, bottom-of-the-barrel, and boring. Is there a brand worth buying?

⋟ BY LISA McMANUS ⋞

When you set out to buy superior extra-virgin olive oil at the supermarket, good luck. Rows of bottles fill the shelves, with even the most ordinary of grocery stores offering more than a dozen choices. It's a booming business: The United States imported 261,000 metric tons of extra-virgin olive oil last year, up from 163,000 metric tons a decade ago. But given the cost—an average of $18.99 per liter for the oils in our lineup—should you just grab the cheapest or try for something better from a gourmet shop or online seller?

To find out if there were any extra-virgin olive oils truly worth bringing home from the supermarket, we chose 10 of the top-selling brands and conducted a blind tasting—first plain, and then warmed and tossed with pasta. (Because high heat destroys the distinctive, fruity taste of extra-virgin olive oil, we reserve it for mixing into pasta dishes and vinaigrettes or drizzling on grilled steak and vegetables; for cooking, we turn to cheaper, lower-grade olive oil.)

Here's the not-so-great news: Our highest average scores barely reached 5 out of a possible 10 points. While a few supermarket oils passed muster, most ranged from plain Jane to distinctly unpleasant, even tasting a bit old, though all were purchased only a few days before we tasted them.

Top of the Line

Extra-virgin is the highest grade of olive oil. At its best, it's simply fresh olive juice, extracted from any of hundreds of olive varieties that were picked at the grower's desired level of ripeness and pressed as soon as possible. (In general, an earlier harvest yields greener, more peppery oil; oil from a later harvest is more golden and mild.) To be designated "extra-virgin," the oil should meet certain standards set by the International Olive Council (IOC) in Madrid. It must be pressed—or, more commonly today, spun out using a centrifuge—without using heat or chemicals, which can extract more oil from the olives, but at the cost of flavor and quality. It must have less than 0.8 percent oleic acid, a measure of quality based on the level of free fatty acids, a product of deterioration. Finally, it can have absolutely no chemical or flavor defects, as determined by both laboratory tests and tasting experts. If an oil doesn't make it as extra-virgin, it can be classified, in descending order, as virgin, pure, or lampante olive oil, the last of which is fit only for industrial use.

While these stringent olive oil standards sound good, it's important to note: They don't apply in the U.S. This country has never adopted the IOC standards, instead holding to unrelated grades of "fancy," "choice," "standard," and "substandard."

Mix and Match

By now it's common knowledge that while the majority of mass-market olive oil manufacturers have Italian-sounding names, most do not sell Italian oils—Italy alone can't supply enough olives to meet demand. Italian companies buy olive oil from all over the Mediterranean, including relatively cheap sources such as Turkey and Tunisia, then ship it in-country for bottling and sell it as a "product of Italy." (All the brands we tasted, however, do specify the countries of origin on the label, a recent development.) At each company, experts blend these various oils to match the brand's characteristic flavor profile.

After our tasting, we had to wonder if the majority of olive oil destined for the American market isn't intentionally blended to be bland. (A number of experts we spoke to said yes, many European producers assume Americans want their olive oil to be as neutral as vegetable oil.) Worse, we wondered whether some of the oils that arrive here labeled "extra-virgin" are even extra-virgin at all.

Standard Oil

Having read reports of the fraudulent adulteration of mass-market olive oils with cheaper oils such as soybean or hazelnut, we sent our samples to an independent laboratory for analysis. All were confirmed to be made only from olives. But in the absence of any regulatory standards in the U.S., that's all we were able to confirm. Companies importing olive oil are free to label their products "extra-virgin"—even if the same oils wouldn't qualify for that appellation in Europe, as many impassioned olive oil advocates believe is the case. Nancy Loseke, editor of *Fresh Press*, a newsletter devoted to olive oil, put it bluntly: "Americans mostly shop the world's olive oil dregs, the low-rung stuff."

Organizations such as the North American Olive Oil Association (NAOOA), which represents the interest of olive-oil importers (including six out of the 10 we tasted), claim to provide oversight the government does not. According to president Bob Bauer, the NAOOA independently buys and tests the oils of member companies at a European laboratory with IOC certification, and he asserts that NAOOA members meet international standards. But in our own tasting, these assurances meant little. None of the top three oils in our lineup were members. Furthermore, the NAOOA currently performs a chemical analysis but does not test for flavor defects that are an equally important "sensory" part of the IOC standards.

And what about those flavor defects our tasters identified so readily? These included soapy, metallic, or chemical notes; dirty, rotten, or medicinal aspects; even "kitty litter" smells. According to Alexandra Devarenne, a California-based olive oil consultant trained in sensory evaluation of olive oil according to IOC standards, many of these flaws are due to delays between harvesting and pressing olives. In countries where abundant varieties of olives can't be harvested quickly enough before they become overripe, fall off the trees, and begin to rot, such flavor defects are common. Poor sanitary conditions on the processing machinery may also contribute to off-flavors.

In addition, the oil can sometimes be a victim of poor storage. Olive oil has a shelf life of 12 to 18 months, but supermarkets frequently do not rotate their supply of olive oil accordingly. And while high-end oils usually indicate the harvest year, most mass-market brands do not, and lack sell-by dates on their labels; less than half our lineup had them. Oils that are beginning to break down have a "greasy" rather than rich texture—a flaw our tasters noted several times.

Pressing Choice

Despite all we didn't like about most of the olive oils in our tasting, we did find two acceptable products. Perhaps not surprisingly, origin did make a difference—both are made from all-Italian olives (though a third, much cheaper, all-Italian oil did not

TASTING SUPERMARKET EXTRA-VIRGIN OLIVE OIL

Twenty-one *Cook's Illustrated* staffers sampled 10 extra-virgin olive oils, selected from the top-selling supermarket brands in the United States, according to Chicago-based market research firm Information Resources, Inc. The supermarket oils were tasted plain as well as heated and tossed with pasta. We then tasted them plain a second time with our favorite high-end extra-virgin olive oil, Columela, available in better supermarkets. Prices were paid in Boston-area supermarkets, with per-liter price calculated for comparison. Information about the national origin of the oils was provided by the manufacturers. The results of the tastings were averaged, and the oils appear below in order of preference. A source for the winning oil is on page 32.

HIGHLY RECOMMENDED

COLUMELA Extra Virgin Olive Oil
Price: $17.95 for 17 oz ($35.90 per liter)
Origin: Spain
Comments: Our favorite premium extra-virgin olive oil from a previous tasting, Columela is composed of a blend of intense Picual, mild Hojiblanca, Ocal, and Arbequina olives. This oil took top honors for its fruity flavor and excellent balance. Tasters praised it as having "big olive aroma, big olive taste" with a "buttery" flavor that is "sweet" and "full," with a "peppery finish." One taster summed it up this way: "It's very green and fresh—like a squeezed olive." Another simply wrote: "Fantastic."

RECOMMENDED

LUCINI ITALIA Premium Select Extra Virgin Olive Oil
Price: $19.99 for 500 ml ($39.98 per liter)
Origin: Italy
Comments: Tasters noted this oil's flavor was "much deeper than the other samples," describing it as "fruity, with a slight peppery finish," "buttery undertones," and a "clean, green taste" that was "aromatic, with a good balance." "It has the flavor that some good EVOOs have," said one admiring taster.

COLAVITA Extra Virgin Olive Oil
Price: $17.99 for 750 ml ($23.98 per liter)
Origin: Italy
Comments: Virtually tied for second place, this oil was deemed "round and buttery," with a "light body" and flavor that was "briny and fruity," "very fine and smooth," and "almost herbal," with "great balance." "Good olive flavor. I could smell it and taste it," approved one taster. In a word, "pleasant."

RECOMMENDED WITH RESERVATIONS

BERTOLLI Extra Virgin Olive Oil
Price: $12.49 for 750 ml ($16.65 per liter)
Origin: Italy, Greece, Spain, and Tunisia
Comments: A clear step down from the top oils, tasters noted "overall mild" flavor and "very little aroma," with only a "hint of green olive" and a "hint of spiciness at the end." In pasta, it was initially "not complex," but gradually "bloomed in your mouth." Overall, it was "worthy of a second bite."

FILIPPO BERIO Extra Virgin Olive Oil
Price: $10.99 for 750 ml ($14.65 per liter)
Origin: Italy, Spain, Greece, and Tunisia
Comments: While some tasters found this oil "sweet" and "buttery" with "medium body" and "slight spice at the end," others complained that it had "zero olive flavor" and was "so floral it's almost like eating perfume"; still others noted a "bitter" aftertaste. In pasta, it was "extremely mild" to the point of being "boring."

RECOMMENDED WITH RESERVATIONS *(CONTINUED)*

GOYA Extra Virgin Olive Oil
Price: $13.99 for 1 liter
Origin: Spain
Comments: The best comments tasters could muster were "mild" and "neutral." Some liked it on pasta (though one called it "Snoozeville"), but complaints were myriad: "metallic," "soapy," "briny," "hints of dirt." Carped one taster, "I can't imagine what is in here, but they have a nerve calling it EVOO."

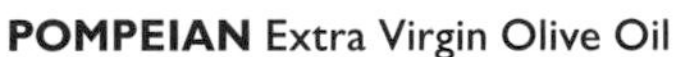

POMPEIAN Extra Virgin Olive Oil
Price: $9.99 for 473 ml ($21.12 per liter)
Origin: Spain
Comments: While some tasters called this oil "mild" and "smooth," others found it "thin, greasy" and "not very interesting." "I bet the cooking water had more olive flavor," speculated one taster; "could be canola—it is so bland," mused another. A few noted an objectionable aftertaste that was "soapy, chemical" or "menthol—think Vicks VapoRub."

BOTTICELLI Extra Virgin Olive Oil
Price: $10.99 for 1 liter
Origin: Italy
Comments: While a few tasters liked this "potent" oil, others said they detected "mushroom," "rotten walnuts," "a Band-Aid wrapped in a cherry blossom," and a quality that was "downright medicinal—Triaminic, anyone?" Several deemed it "overpowering" and "musky," with a "rank, off-flavor." "Tastes not like olives but like the armpits of olive laborers," shuddered one.

NOT RECOMMENDED

CARAPELLI Extra Virgin Olive Oil
Price: $10.99 for 750 ml ($14.65 per liter)
Origin: Italy, Greece, Spain, Tunisia, Turkey, Cyprus, Morocco, and Syria
Comments: "Nothing remarkable here—just greasy, no flavor," summarized one taster. "Where did the olive go?" said another. This oil was judged to have a "kind of rancid" aftertaste that was reminiscent of not only "soil," "tree resin," and "ammonia and grass," but even "kitty litter smells" and "a set of sweaty hockey pads."

DAVINCI Extra Virgin Olive Oil
Price: $17.99 for 1 liter
Origin: Italy, Greece, Spain, Tunisia, and Turkey
Comments: Although this oil won top place in a previous tasting, because olive oil is an agricultural product, it can differ from year to year. This time, tasters found it "washed out and muted," if "nice, in a totally bland and unremarkable way." Tasted plain, objections ranged from "insipid, with no real complexity" to "tastes like EVOO mixed with vegetable oil."

STAR Extra Virgin Olive Oil
Price: $11.99 for 750 ml ($15.99 per liter)
Origin: Spain, Italy, Greece, and Tunisia
Comments: "Boring" and "not very complex," this oil came across as "plastic-y and industrial; some hint of olives, but it fades quickly." Tasters identified off-flavors that were "unpleasant, dirty," "like rubber and metal, with a sour aftertaste," or at least "a bit funky," with a "strange taste" that was "spicy, but in a motor oil kind of way." One simply wrote, "Blech."

fare well). Price stood out, too: Our top picks were the two most expensive oils. In fact, our favorite cost almost $40 per liter, nearly twice the average price of the rest of the lineup, and as much as many high-end olive oils from gourmet stores. This front-runner was Lucini Italia Premium Select Extra Virgin Olive Oil, made (according to the manufacturer) from olives grown on Italian estates, hand-picked, and pressed within 24 hours. It was closely followed by Colavita Extra Virgin Olive Oil, also described as being made exclusively from olives harvested and pressed in Italy.

But in the end, while these two oils stood out among the supermarket sampling, they were easily bested in a second blind tasting that included our favorite premium extra-virgin olive oil by Columela, which is made with a blend of Picual, Hojiblanca, Arbequina, and Ocal olives grown in Spain; tasters found it offered exceptionally fruity and well-balanced flavor. At about $36 per liter, Columela is actually cheaper than Lucini, our top supermarket brand. This raises the question: Is the supermarket the best place to buy your extra-virgin olive oil? Unfortunately, we'd have to say no.

Seeking a Better Spatula

Newfangled silicone spatulas are rife with issues—either too flimsy or too rigid, weirdly shaped, or uncomfortable to hold. Do any deliver a better tool?

BY LISA McMANUS

Hardly anyone spends more than two minutes a year thinking about problems with their spatulas. With a tool that costs only a couple of bucks, why bother? But the fact is, every spatula has its issues. Old-fashioned rubber spatulas melt in high heat. Newfangled kinds made from silicone are heat-resistant and come in all sorts of new shapes and designs, but many seem more gimmicky than useful. Some are so stiff they can't fold egg whites. Others are so flexible they bend when confronted with thick cookie dough. And still others have handles that are such instruments of torture they must have been designed by Torquemada. Why can't manufacturers come to the rescue and design a better spatula?

In my quest to find one spatula that could do it all, I singled out 10 silicone contenders with features promising greater convenience, versatility, or comfort. All were dishwasher-safe and priced between $7 and $19. My testers and I put each one through a series of nine tests that included everything from delicate mixing to high-heat cooking and heavy-duty stirring—we even tried to stain, melt, and destroy them. After all, what good is a great spatula if it isn't going to last?

Heads Up

The business end of a spatula, the head, is its single most critical feature. In many ways the ideal material for the head is silicone, which is heat-resistant, inert (it doesn't release chemicals into the air or your food), and endlessly customizable. Manufacturers have added curves and swoops to serve any number of purposes, some of which only became clear as we worked with the spatulas. One model boasted a small rectangular "rest" that kept the head from touching the counter when it was laid down and also sported a useful notch for swiping the rim of a jar or bowl. Tips could be pointed to get into pan corners or squared off to scrape the bottom of a saucepan clean—and sometimes both features could be found on the same spatula. Not all shapes worked.

As we assessed the range of design variations in our lineup, we discovered certain preferred characteristics. First was the character of the silicone. Our favorite spatulas had heads that were not only soft and flexible enough to sweep all traces of batter out of a mixing bowl but stiff enough to remove sticky brown bits, or fond, from a skillet. We also decided that the top edge of the head had to be flat, fairly rigid, and squared off (in other words, not unlike the design of the traditional rubber spatula). Spatulas with pointed, floppy, or particularly curvy tips just made us work harder to scrape up food. The edge of the tip and sides also had to be thin enough to maneuver into hard-to-reach corners, rounded bowls, or the edges of a skillet.

We learned that the face of the spatula head should be as flat as possible, so it would scrape clean in one stroke against the rim of a pot or bowl. Flat "cheeks" also came in handy for swirling and blending pan sauces or slipping under the delicate edge of an omelet. A number of models have a central ridge where the handle is attached, which left batter stuck on either side, requiring multiple swipes.

Getting a Grip

With spatulas, handles are nearly as important as heads. They can help or hurt when you're stirring for an extended time or pushing against stiff dough. And after folding dozens and dozens of whipped egg whites into batter for angel food cake and stirring pot after pot of steaming-hot risotto, we concluded that we liked a long handle on our spatulas to keep our hands a safe distance from the food. But length alone wasn't enough—handles also had to be rigid enough to provide leverage: A few of our models had handles that literally flopped like a wet noodle just when you needed them to have a backbone. Try blending Parmesan into a finished risotto with a spatula that can barely push through the rice.

Comfort was equally important. One spatula cut into our fingers with its hard plastic edge, making it a little painful to push through cookie dough. Another sported such an extreme curve that it forced our wrists to twist unnaturally as we stirred our way around a pan sauce. Others felt comfortable and easy as we shifted hand positions for different tasks, turning the spatula horizontal to a pan to fold over an omelet or vertical to scrape down a mixing bowl, or providing a firm grip as we pushed through stiff cookie dough to mix in nuts and chocolate chips.

And while flat, Popsicle-stick-style handles are the classic choice in a rubber spatula, we broke with tradition by preferring rounded handles, whether smooth like a dowel or with indentations for the thumb. We also liked our spatula handle to be as heat-resistant as the head—one handle actually melted as it rested on the edge of a hot skillet. A few handles with metal inserts heated up, as did a metal logo placed on the grip of another.

Tough Enough

What good is a spatula that has a great shape and comfy handle if it can't hold up for years of hard cooking in your kitchen? Or one that stains and smells like the last thing you cooked? We concocted a witches' brew of curry and tomato sauce—the worst offenders—and tossed in all the spatulas for an hour-long simmer. Then we ran them through a home-style dishwasher twice. The dark-colored spatulas came clean, while lighter models stained. Depending on the formulation of the silicone in each brand, some spatulas absorbed odors, while others didn't. (As I write, the scent of turmeric is wafting up from a few of these spatulas—not too appealing if the next thing I want to use them for is making cookies.)

Putting the claims of heat resistance to the test, we also tried to melt the spatulas in a cast-iron skillet by firmly pressing their tips against the bottom of a hot pan for two minutes (using a thermocouple to monitor temperature). None of the spatulas lost their shape or showed signs of disintegrating, but a few turned brown or lost color at the point of contact. None gave off fumes or odors.

The Final Turn

After all the flipping, folding, scraping, and stirring was done, we declared a pair of winners. The Rubbermaid Professional 13½-Inch Heat Resistant Scraper ($18.99) is a workhorse with an extra-long handle and a generously sized head that resembles a bigger, better version of the brand's traditional rubber spatula.

The Tovolo Silicone Spatula ($8.99) boasts a snazzy blue head and a brushed stainless steel handle that never got hot and proved remarkably comfortable to hold. Both designs feature heads large enough to move volumes of food, with tips rigid enough to lift fond from a skillet. Their handles were easy to manipulate at any angle and didn't dip your fingers in the food. Neither showed signs of melting or discoloring, even when we left them in a hot pan at higher-than-recommended temperatures. The Tovolo's good looks and nice price make it hard to resist, but, in the end, the larger overall size and sturdiness of the Rubbermaid won our highest accolades.

COOK'S LIVE Original Test Kitchen Videos
www.cooksillustrated.com
• Behind the Scenes: Spatula Testing

KEY

GOOD: ★★★

FAIR: ★★

POOR: ★

TESTING SILICONE SPATULAS

We evaluated 10 silicone spatulas, all dishwasher-safe, running each through nine tests, including lifting omelets, scraping the bowl of a food processor, hand-mixing nuts and other ingredients into stiff cookie dough, folding whipped egg whites into cake batter, making a pan sauce, and stirring risotto. We also simmered the spatulas in a pot of tomato-curry sauce for an hour to see if they would stain and absorb odors, and ran them through the dishwasher twice to see if they would come through clean and odor-free. And we tested their heat-safe claims, trying to melt them in a cast-iron skillet as hot as we could get it—up to 674 degrees Fahrenheit. Finally, we asked a variety of test cooks to weigh in on the spatulas' comfort and performance. The spatulas appear below in order of preference. Sources for the winning spatulas are on page 32.

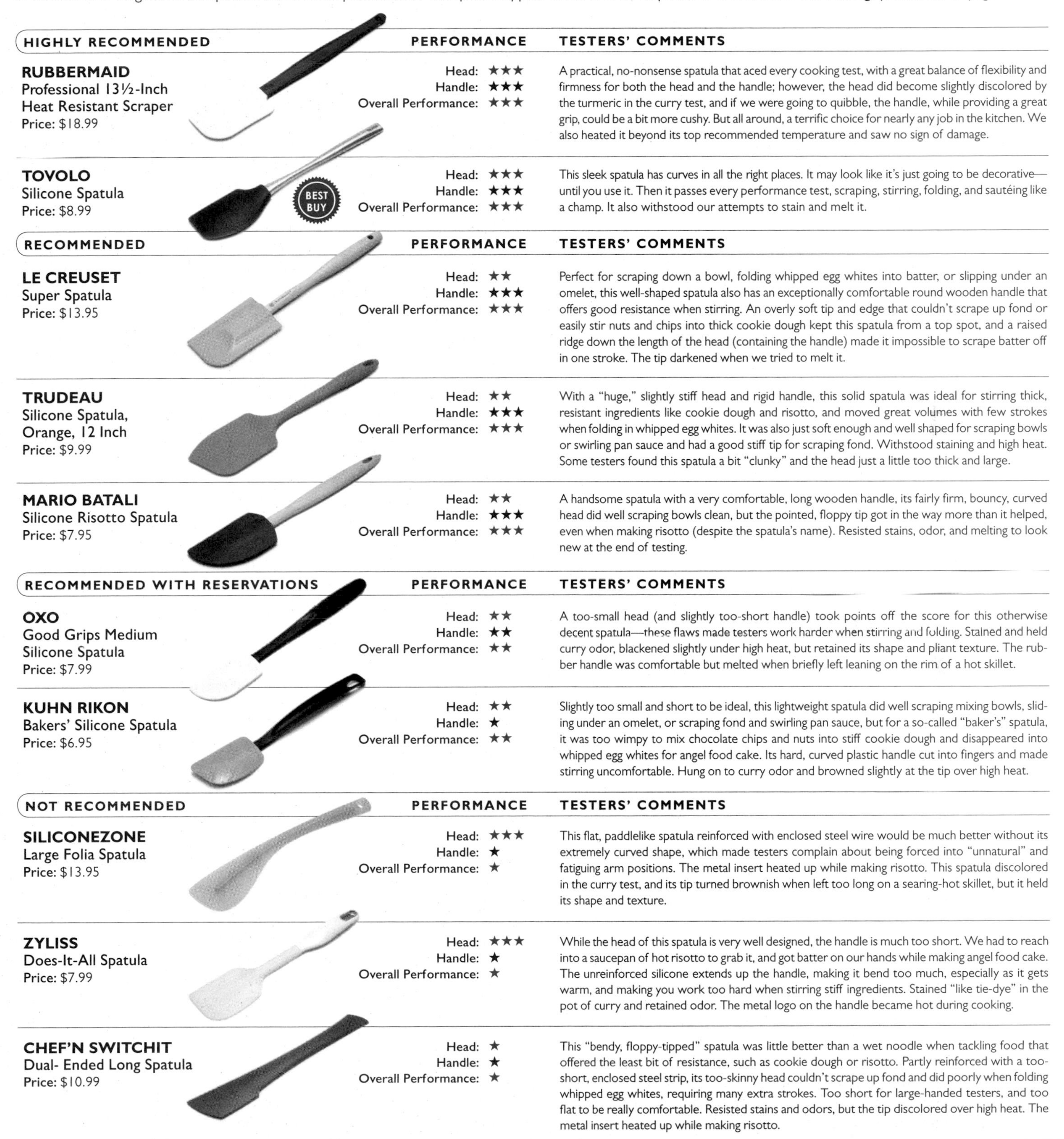

HIGHLY RECOMMENDED	PERFORMANCE	TESTERS' COMMENTS
RUBBERMAID Professional 13½-Inch Heat Resistant Scraper Price: $18.99	Head: ★★★ Handle: ★★★ Overall Performance: ★★★	A practical, no-nonsense spatula that aced every cooking test, with a great balance of flexibility and firmness for both the head and the handle; however, the head did become slightly discolored by the turmeric in the curry test, and if we were going to quibble, the handle, while providing a great grip, could be a bit more cushy. But all around, a terrific choice for nearly any job in the kitchen. We also heated it beyond its top recommended temperature and saw no sign of damage.
TOVOLO Silicone Spatula Price: $8.99	Head: ★★★ Handle: ★★★ Overall Performance: ★★★	This sleek spatula has curves in all the right places. It may look like it's just going to be decorative—until you use it. Then it passes every performance test, scraping, stirring, folding, and sautéing like a champ. It also withstood our attempts to stain and melt it.

RECOMMENDED	PERFORMANCE	TESTERS' COMMENTS
LE CREUSET Super Spatula Price: $13.95	Head: ★★ Handle: ★★★ Overall Performance: ★★★	Perfect for scraping down a bowl, folding whipped egg whites into batter, or slipping under an omelet, this well-shaped spatula also has an exceptionally comfortable round wooden handle that offers good resistance when stirring. An overly soft tip and edge that couldn't scrape up fond or easily stir nuts and chips into thick cookie dough kept this spatula from a top spot, and a raised ridge down the length of the head (containing the handle) made it impossible to scrape batter off in one stroke. The tip darkened when we tried to melt it.
TRUDEAU Silicone Spatula, Orange, 12 Inch Price: $9.99	Head: ★★ Handle: ★★★ Overall Performance: ★★★	With a "huge," slightly stiff head and rigid handle, this solid spatula was ideal for stirring thick, resistant ingredients like cookie dough and risotto, and moved great volumes with few strokes when folding in whipped egg whites. It was also just soft enough and well shaped for scraping bowls or swirling pan sauce and had a good stiff tip for scraping fond. Withstood staining and high heat. Some testers found this spatula a bit "clunky" and the head just a little too thick and large.
MARIO BATALI Silicone Risotto Spatula Price: $7.95	Head: ★★ Handle: ★★★ Overall Performance: ★★★	A handsome spatula with a very comfortable, long wooden handle, its fairly firm, bouncy, curved head did well scraping bowls clean, but the pointed, floppy tip got in the way more than it helped, even when making risotto (despite the spatula's name). Resisted stains, odor, and melting to look new at the end of testing.

RECOMMENDED WITH RESERVATIONS	PERFORMANCE	TESTERS' COMMENTS
OXO Good Grips Medium Silicone Spatula Price: $7.99	Head: ★★ Handle: ★★ Overall Performance: ★★	A too-small head (and slightly too-short handle) took points off the score for this otherwise decent spatula—these flaws made testers work harder when stirring and folding. Stained and held curry odor, blackened slightly under high heat, but retained its shape and pliant texture. The rubber handle was comfortable but melted when briefly left leaning on the rim of a hot skillet.
KUHN RIKON Bakers' Silicone Spatula Price: $6.95	Head: ★★ Handle: ★ Overall Performance: ★★	Slightly too small and short to be ideal, this lightweight spatula did well scraping mixing bowls, sliding under an omelet, or scraping fond and swirling pan sauce, but for a so-called "baker's" spatula, it was too wimpy to mix chocolate chips and nuts into stiff cookie dough and disappeared into whipped egg whites for angel food cake. Its hard, curved plastic handle cut into fingers and made stirring uncomfortable. Hung on to curry odor and browned slightly at the tip over high heat.

NOT RECOMMENDED	PERFORMANCE	TESTERS' COMMENTS
SILICONEZONE Large Folia Spatula Price: $13.95	Head: ★★★ Handle: ★ Overall Performance: ★	This flat, paddlelike spatula reinforced with enclosed steel wire would be much better without its extremely curved shape, which made testers complain about being forced into "unnatural" and fatiguing arm positions. The metal insert heated up while making risotto. This spatula discolored in the curry test, and its tip turned brownish when left too long on a searing-hot skillet, but it held its shape and texture.
ZYLISS Does-It-All Spatula Price: $7.99	Head: ★★★ Handle: ★ Overall Performance: ★	While the head of this spatula is very well designed, the handle is much too short. We had to reach into a saucepan of hot risotto to grab it, and got batter on our hands while making angel food cake. The unreinforced silicone extends up the handle, making it bend too much, especially as it gets warm, and making you work too hard when stirring stiff ingredients. Stained "like tie-dye" in the pot of curry and retained odor. The metal logo on the handle became hot during cooking.
CHEF'N SWITCHIT Dual- Ended Long Spatula Price: $10.99	Head: ★ Handle: ★ Overall Performance: ★	This "bendy, floppy-tipped" spatula was little better than a wet noodle when tackling food that offered the least bit of resistance, such as cookie dough or risotto. Partly reinforced with a too-short, enclosed steel strip, its too-skinny head couldn't scrape up fond and did poorly when folding whipped egg whites, requiring many extra strokes. Too short for large-handed testers, and too flat to be really comfortable. Resisted stains and odors, but the tip discolored over high heat. The metal insert heated up while making risotto.

KITCHEN NOTES

⋟ BY J. KENJI ALT ⋞

Dutch Oven Conversion

Our recipe for Almost No-Knead Bread (January/February 2008), calls for preheating a Dutch oven to 500 degrees. After we published our recipe, it was called to our attention that the manufacturers of both our favorite Dutch oven (the 7¼-Quart Round French Oven by Le Creuset) and our Best Buy Dutch oven (the 6.5-Quart Cast Iron Dutch Oven by Tramontina) recommend against heating the pots to this temperature, due to the phenolic knobs used on the lids.

Fortunately, there are two simple solutions. The knobs on both lids are secured with a single screw that is easily removed. Once the knob is removed, you can replace it with an inexpensive all-metal drawer handle purchased from a hardware store. Alternatively, Le Creuset has introduced a stainless steel replacement knob for its Dutch ovens that is completely heatproof (and also happens to fit perfectly on the also-recommended Lodge Color Enamel Dutch Oven and Chefmate Dutch Oven), available for about $10. To fit this knob on the Tramontina Dutch Oven, you'll need a single ⅜-inch-diameter, ¾-inch-long machine screw—the ½-inch screw that comes with the knob is not long enough to fit through the thicker lid of the Tramontina.

A $10 stainless steel replacement knob from Le Creuset allows your Dutch oven to be heated to 500 degrees.

SCIENCE: When to Salt Fresh-Ground Meat

During testing, we thought that we could improve the flavor of our Best Old-Fashioned Burgers (page 11) by salting the meat before grinding it, but the burgers ended up very dense. What was going on? From research we've done on brining and salting larger cuts of meat, we know that when exposed to a strong concentration of salt, meat proteins will dissolve. This breakdown is desirable in steaks or chops—the action of dissolving the protein allows the meat to hold on to more moisture, making it juicier when cooked. In our burgers, however, the dissolved meat proteins act as a sort of glue, binding the ground bits together very tightly to create a rubbery, almost sausagelike texture. So while you may be tempted to add salt to the meat before grinding, we recommend waiting until you've formed the patties. Salting just the exterior will maintain the tender, open structure we're after with this recipe.

TIGHTLY WOUND
The meat for this patty was salted before it was ground, leading to a dense, rubbery texture.

LOOSENED UP
Salt just on its exterior helped this patty maintain the loose structure we wanted.

SHOPPING: Olive Quartet

Jarred olives come in three basic types at the supermarket: brine-cured green, brine-cured black, and salt-cured black (often erroneously labeled "oil-cured"). Curing is the process that removes the bitter compound oleuropein from olives to make them suitable for consumption. Brine-cured olives are soaked in a salt solution; salt-cured olives are packed in salt until nearly all their liquid has been extracted, then covered in oil to be re-plumped. Both processes traditionally take weeks or even months. To quickly leach the oleuropein out of canned California olives, producers use lye, which "ripens" olives artificially in a matter of days, then further process the olives to turn their green flesh black.

We tasted several varieties of olives in both our Pasta with Olives, Garlic, and Herbs (page 21) and our Sicilian Eggplant Relish (page 19) and found that brine-cured black or green olives can be used in either recipe, based on personal preference. Often labeled "Spanish" olives, green olives are picked before fully ripened and add a bright, acidic dimension to food. Picked when mature, black olives lend a more robust taste. Only a few olive aficionados favored the concentrated, bitter taste of salt-cured olives—we don't recommend cooking with them unless a recipe specifically calls for them. And canned olives? Their bland flavor and firm yet oddly slippery texture helped land them at the bottom of our taste test.

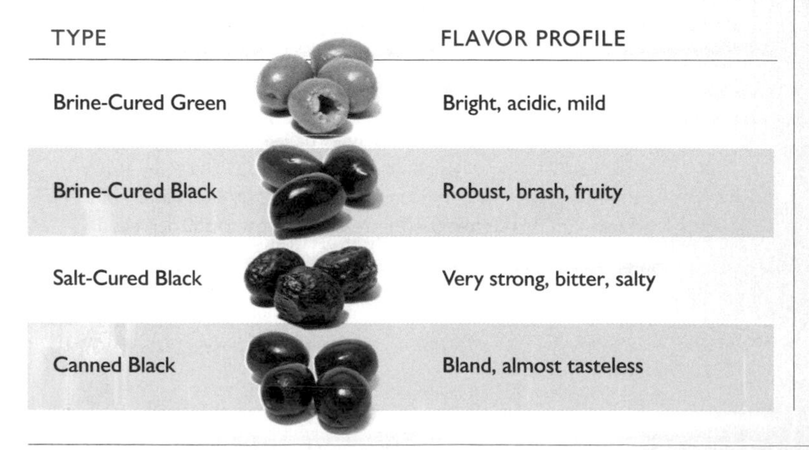

TYPE	FLAVOR PROFILE
Brine-Cured Green	Bright, acidic, mild
Brine-Cured Black	Robust, brash, fruity
Salt-Cured Black	Very strong, bitter, salty
Canned Black	Bland, almost tasteless

SCIENCE The Chill Factor in Mealy Peaches

Can refrigerating peaches make them mealy? According to the *Journal of Experimental Botany*, the answer is yes. A study in the August 13, 2004, edition found that storage at temperatures at or below 40 degrees Fahrenheit can destroy the activity of certain enzymes in the peach that normally break down pectin in its cell walls during the ripening process. If these enzymes are deactivated before the fruit is ripe, the pectin will remain intact and the peach will have a mealy texture.

To test this finding ourselves, we divided a single case of peaches into two batches, allowing one to ripen immediately without refrigeration and storing the other for a week in the fridge, before allowing it to finish ripening for a couple of days at room temperature. Both sets of peaches were placed in containers sealed with plastic wrap in order to prevent moisture from evaporating. True to the study, our tasters found that despite being soft and ripe to the touch, the peaches that spent time in the fridge were significantly mealier than those kept at room temperature. Moral of the story: Don't refrigerate your peaches unless you're sure they're ripe. You may prolong their shelf life, but the loss of quality isn't worth it.

SCIENCE Lengthening the Life of Tomatoes

We've heard that storing a tomato with its stem end facing down can prolong shelf life. To test this theory, we placed one batch of tomatoes stem-end up and another stem-end down and stored them at room temperature. A week later, nearly all the stem-down tomatoes remained in perfect condition, while the stem-up tomatoes had shriveled and started to mold. Why the difference? We surmised that the scar left on the tomato skin where the stem once grew provides both an escape for

STEM UP

STEM DOWN

Storing a tomato stem-end down (room temperature is best) prevents air from entering and moisture from exiting its scar, prolonging shelf life.

moisture and an entry point for mold and bacteria. Placing a tomato stem-end down blocks air from entering and moisture from exiting the scar. To confirm this theory, we ran another test, this time comparing tomatoes stored stem-end down with another batch stored stem-end up, but with a piece of tape sealing off their scars. The taped, stem-end-up tomatoes survived just as well as the stem-end-down batch.

SCIENCE Goodbye to Sticky Milk Film

When scalding milk, a difficult-to-remove film of browned whey proteins can develop on the bottom of the pan. We learned from food-science guru Harold McGee's book *On Food and Cooking* that a thin film of water can discourage these proteins from adhering. We also know that the longer proteins are heated, the more browning occurs. Could preheating the pot further minimize sticking by speeding up the rate at which the milk heats? We heated milk three ways: in a cold empty pot, in a cold pot with a little water, and in a preheated pot with a little water. The third pot finished nearly film-free. So whenever a recipe calls for scalding milk, we suggest adding a thin film of water to the pan (just enough to cover the bottom) and preheating it until the water is boiling before adding your milk.

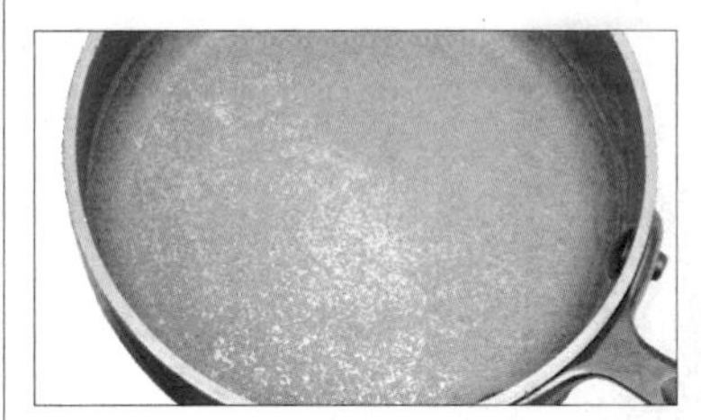

COLD START
Scalding milk in a dry non-preheated pot results in a large deposit of browned proteins in the bottom.

IN HOT WATER
Preheating a thin film of water before adding the milk inhibits proteins from sticking and browning, resulting in an easier-to-clean pot.

TASTING: UglyRipe Tomatoes

Most supermarket tomatoes are bred for their uniform spherical appearance and are picked well before ripening (even so-called vine-ripened kinds) in order to be able to withstand the rigors of cross-continental shipping. The results are notoriously juiceless and flavorless. But the Santa Sweets tomato company of Plant City, Florida, claims that its UglyRipe brand of tomatoes was bred with only flavor in mind. In addition, this tomato is supposedly allowed to stay on the living vine to a much later stage, resulting in a riper, juicier product. (In fact, the fruit is so ripe when packed that it comes individually foam-wrapped for protection.)

To put these claims to the test, we performed blind taste tests of UglyRipe tomatoes against tomatoes labeled "vine-ripened" (which are picked when just 10 percent of the fruit has turned from green to red), sampling them raw and cooked into sauce. The UglyRipes were unanimously favored in both tests for their sweet tomato flavor. We also noticed that as they cooked, the UglyRipes released nearly twice as much juice as vine-ripe tomatoes—an indication that the company's claim of a later harvest is true. We'll still go for locally grown farmers' market tomatoes in the summer, but the UglyRipes, even at $3.99 per pound (versus $3.49 per pound for the vine-ripe fruit), are worth every extra cent in winter.

WATER RETENTION
Tomatoes picked when not fully ripe won't release enough liquid to deliver good tomato flavor, even when cooked.

TOTAL RELEASE
Because UglyRipe Tomatoes are allowed to ripen further on the vine, they release more flavor and sugar-rich juice when cooked.

RECIPE UPDATE

Grilled Greek-Style Lamb Pita Sandwiches

Fans of our pan-fried Greek-Style Lamb Pita Sandwiches (July/August 2007) wanted a way to make them on the grill. Our existing recipe calls for pan-frying 12 small patties (3 per sandwich) of a garlicky ground lamb mixture until well browned and cooked through. Small patties were difficult to manage on the grill, so the first thing we did was to fuse them together to make four large rectangular shapes (which would each fit neatly in the wrapped pita sandwich). The next adjustment was to cut down on the amount of panade (a paste made of fresh bread crumbs combined with a liquid ingredient) that we added to the ground lamb. The purpose of the panade is to keep the small patties moist during their high-heat sear, but they actually caused too much moisture retention in the big patties, giving them a mushy, wet texture. With less panade, the patties grilled up with a nice crust on the outside and tender but firm meat on the inside. Go to www.cooksillustrated.com/august for our free recipe for Grilled Greek-Style Lamb Pita Sandwiches.

GREAT FOR THE PAN

BETTER FOR THE GRILL

While smaller gyro patties (left) work well for pan-frying, we found them difficult to deal with on a grill. Our solution? Combine three patties into one large shape (right) for easier grilling.

Grilled Potatoes with Oregano and Lemon

Changing the flavors of our Grilled Potatoes with Garlic and Rosemary (July/August 2007) to oregano and lemon (keeping with the Greek theme above) was not quite as simple as merely swapping the ingredients. Our existing recipe flavors the spuds with a cooked garlic-herb oil made with a lot of garlic (9 cloves) and just a little fresh rosemary (1 teaspoon). Because of the more subtle floral character of oregano, which is easily overpowered by stronger flavors, we found it necessary to cut down the garlic in the oil to 3 cloves and to increase the herb to 2 tablespoons. We also added some lemon zest. To reinforce these flavors in the final dish, we tossed the cooked potatoes with an extra dose of uncooked minced oregano and zest. A squeeze of fresh lemon juice brightened all the flavors. Go to www.cooksillustrated.com/august for our free recipe for Grilled Potatoes with Oregano and Lemon.

Classic Pound Cake in a Tube Pan

Readers wanted to know how to bake our Classic Pound Cake (January/February 2007) in a tube pan instead of the traditional loaf pan. A logical request, considering that a tube pan (sometimes called an angel-food cake pan) works perfectly for dense baked goods like pound cake. The pan's center tube helps conduct heat to the middle of the cake, allowing for even cooking and a stable structure. The first step was to double the pound cake batter to fill the tube pan's larger capacity. Due to the center tube's heat conductivity, the cake took less time to bake (by about 10 minutes). However, it baked up very dense; clearly, a tube pan full of batter couldn't get enough lift from the 325-degree oven. Increasing the heat to 350 degrees made the cake lighter but created an exterior verging on burnt. Starting the cake in a 350-degree oven for 15 minutes, then reducing the temperature to 325 degrees led to the perfect amount of rise and a nicely golden brown exterior. Go to www.cooksillustrated.com/august for our free recipe for Classic Pound Cake in a Tube Pan.

–Charles Kelsey

EQUIPMENT CORNER

BY ELIZABETH BOMZE

EQUIPMENT TESTING **Ice Cream Scoops**

Even badly designed ice cream scoops do the job—but they make you work much harder than necessary, with their uncomfortable handles, thick edges that can't penetrate hard-packed surfaces, bowls that won't release the ice cream, or scoop sizes that won't fit in an ordinary cone. To find the perfect dipper, we scooped up six models, both traditional and innovative. We quickly eliminated the dwarf-sized Tovolo Standz Ice Cream Scoop ($4.99), concluding that nobody needs a scoop that stands upright. Another nontraditional model, the Van Vacter Ice Cream Knife ($18.95), also didn't make the cut, marring even the hardest ice cream with its big, blunt teeth. The beak-nosed OXO i-Series Scoop ($14.99) rolled gawky, pointed scoops, as did the elongated scoop from KitchenAid ($9.99). The three remaining models, including a sleeker update of our previous favorite from Zeroll ($16.95), all scooped capably and easily, but the perfect orbs made by the thin-rimmed stainless steel Rösle Ice Cream Scoop ($20.00) impressed us most. For complete testing results, go to www.cooksillustrated.com/august.

HERE'S THE SCOOP
The exceptionally thin edge on the Rösle Ice Cream Scoop rolled up flawless ice cream spheres.

NEW PRODUCT **Pie Gate**

Leftover pie doesn't last long, but when there is some to spare, a Pie Gate ($6.95) from Progressive International promises to keep the filling intact. This plastic tool, which looks like two wings attached on a central hinge, adjusts to fit any angle—and most pie plates. Its flexible silicone edge does the job of neatly and tightly sealing in leaky fillings. The device can also double as a dam for cut rounds of creamy, oozy cheeses such as Brie or Camembert.

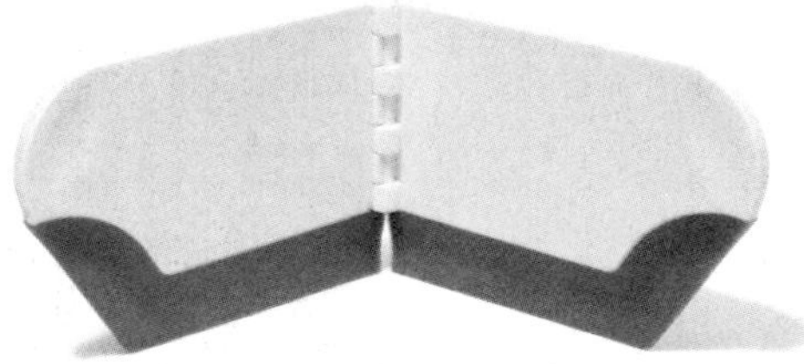

SURPRISINGLY USEFUL
Runny pie fillings and oozy cheeses stay intact with the Progressive International Pie Gate.

NEW PRODUCT **Cake Pan Liners**

Lining cake pans with parchment paper ensures easy release of baked goods, but cutting parchment to fit can be tedious and wasteful. We like Regency Parchment Rounds ($1.99), which are a bargain compared with a roll of supermarket parchment. One package contains 24 liners for 8- to 9-inch round cake pans and tube pans, 12 for each shape.

EQUIPMENT TESTING
Electric Citrus Juicers

Though we find a handheld citrus squeezer fine if we only need a little juice, we prefer plugging into a more powerful tool when we want a lot. A heavy stainless steel model from Breville ($169.95) extracted every last drop of juice smoothly and efficiently. Pressing on the handle squeezes the fruit while starting a motorized reamer. If juicing is a top priority, this "Rolls-Royce of juicers" is a nice investment. Meanwhile, juice flowed almost as freely from smaller (and much cheaper) electric juicers from Black & Decker ($19.21), Delonghi ($29.99), and Cuisinart ($29.95). The Black & Decker won us over with its mess-free squeezing, easy pouring, and bargain price. If you happen to own a KitchenAid food processor, the KitchenAid Citrus Press attachment ($39.99) performed well.

KING OF THE JUICERS
Fresh-juice aficionados will appreciate the ultimate citrus press from Breville.

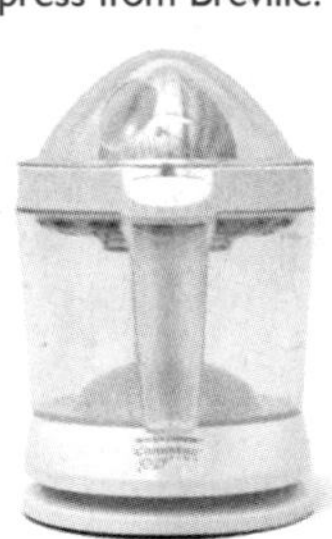

BEST BUY
For easy, mess-free squeezing at a bargain price, look to the Black & Decker CitrusMate Plus.

EQUIPMENT UPDATE
Snow River Cutting Board

Shortly after we applauded the durability and convenience of the Snow River Utility Cutting Board ($16.99) in a recent test, we were disappointed to learn that the company discontinued the board. It is now producing another dishwasher-safe board, the Snow River Grande Epicure Pro ($19.95), which, like its predecessor, boasts a composite core sandwiched between sheets of real maple. But instead of being 7/16 inch thick, the new board has a thickness of just 3/16 inch.

We subjected the Grande Epicure Pro to the same battery of tests as the other boards. We sliced onions, whacked chicken thighs through the bone with a cleaver, cut on it 750 times with a new knife, minced deep-staining chipotle chiles, ran it through the dishwasher, and dropped it on the floor. Fresh out of the box, the board was noticeably curved, and it had warped dramatically by the end of testing. Cutting on it felt hard and unpleasant under the knife. And as for the maple surface, our cuts left raggedy fissures and deep scars. We can't recommend the Grande Epicure Pro as a replacement for the Utility Board. For a cheaper, dishwasher-safe alternative to our winning board, we'll stick with the plastic Architec Gripper Nonslip Cutting Board ($14.95).

NOT SO GRANDE
The Snow River Grande Epicure Pro came out of our testing chewed up and misshapen.

Sources

The following are sources for items recommended in this issue. Prices were current at press time and do not include shipping. Contact companies to confirm information or visit www.cooksillustrated.com for updates.

Page 9: BARBECUE GLOVES
- Grill Life Leather Grill Gloves: $12.49 per pair, item #8167470, Ace Hardware Outlet (800-985-6017, www.acehardwareoutlet.com).

Page 13: GRATIN DISH
- Emile Henry 3-Quart Gratin Dish: $54.95, item #578951, Cooking.com (800-663-8810, www.cooking.com).

Page 23: DRY MEASURING CUPS
- Amco Stainless Steel 4-Piece Measuring Cup Set: $9.95, item #708231, Cooking.com.

Page 27: EXTRA-VIRGIN OLIVE OIL
- Columela Extra Virgin Olive Oil: $17.95 for 17 oz., item #569178, Sur La Table (800-243-0852, www.surlatable.com).

Page 29: SPATULAS
- Rubbermaid Professional 13½-Inch Heat Resistant Scraper, $18.99, item #B0000CFO2Y, www.amazon.com.
- Tovolo Silicone Spatula, $8.99, item #B000ILRG5I, www.amazon.com.

Page 32: ICE CREAM SCOOP
- Rösle Ice Cream Scoop: $20.00, item #12741, Cutlery and More (800-650-9866, www.cutleryandmore.com).

Page 32: PIE GATE
- Progressive International Pie Gate: $6.95, item #BE0045, Kitchen Krafts (800-776-0575, www.kitchenkrafts.com).

Page 32: CAKE PAN LINERS
- Regency Parchment Rounds and Tube Pan Liners: $1.99 for 24, item #080988202023, The Kitchen Store.com (800-458-2616, www.thekitchenstore.com).

Page 32: CITRUS JUICERS
- Breville Citrus Press: $169.95, item #392748, Cooking.com.
- Black & Decker CitrusMate Plus Citrus Juicer: $19.21, item #B00004SC51, www.amazon.com.
- KitchenAid Citrus Press 12-Cup Food Processor Attachment: $39.99, item #KFP7CP, KitchenAid (800-541-6390, www.kitchenaid.com).

Page 32: CUTTING BOARD
- Architec Gripper Nonslip Cutting Board: $14.95, item #186325, Cooking.com.

INDEX

July & August 2008

RECIPES

COOK'S LIVE Original Test Kitchen Videos www.cooksillustrated.com

Grilled Bone-In Chicken Breasts, 9

Best Old-Fashioned Burgers, 11

Enchiladas Verdes, 7

Pasta with Olives, Garlic, and Herbs, 21

Blueberry Pie, 25

Sausages with Peppers and Onions, 15

Sicilian Eggplant Relish, 19

Greek Cherry Tomato Salad, 20

Summer Vegetable Gratin, 13

Peach Shortcake, 23

PHOTOGRAPHY: CARL TREMBLAY, STYLING: MARIE PIRAINO

Star Fruit
Longans
Mango
Kumquats
Persimmon
Pomegranate
Lychees
Pomelo
Durian
Coconut

ASIAN FRUIT

NUMBER NINETY-FOUR

SEPTEMBER & OCTOBER 2008

COOK'S ILLUSTRATED

Herbed Roast Chicken

Rating Premium Bacon
Supermarket vs. Mail Order

Creamy Tomato Soup
Without the Cream!

Best Steak Tacos

Drip Coffee Makers
Should You Spend $50 or $250?

No-Roll Pizza
Thick, Extra Chewy Crust

Skillet Apple Pie
Half the Work, Twice the Flavor

Grilled Rack of Lamb
Pork Lo Mein
Glazes for Grilled Chicken
Crisp Oven-Fried Fish
Sticky Toffee Pudding Cakes

www.cooksillustrated.com
$5.95 U.S./$6.95 CANADA

CONTENTS

September & October 2008

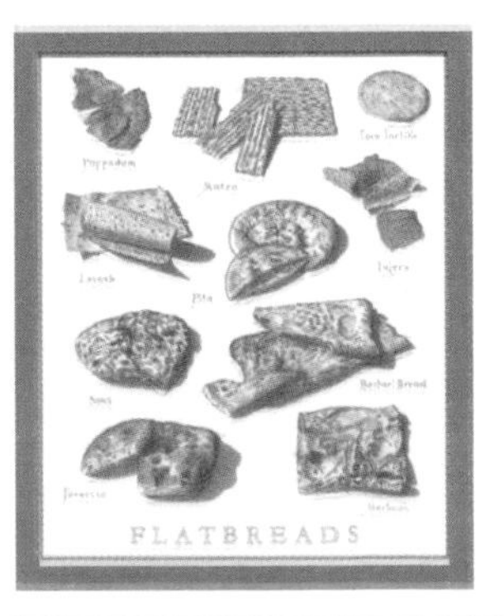

FLATBREADS As ancestors to today's modern loaves, flatbreads have many expressions. Touted as the world's oldest bread, pocketed Middle Eastern pita can be stuffed, rolled, or served as an edible plate. Leavened rounds of naan are baked in a tandoor oven to produce a blistered exterior. Pappadam is an Indian staple, the crisps typically served with chutneys. Corn tortillas are integral to Mexican and Central American diets. Injera is a spongy, crêpelike bread from the Ethiopian highlands that serves as both a plate and, when torn into pieces, an eating utensil. Similarly in the Levant region of the Middle East, large, paper-thin sheets of markook are used to scoop up the main dish. Armenian lavash, a central component of the wrap sandwich, can also be dried to resemble a large matzo, the crackerlike, unleavened bread eaten during the Jewish holiday of Passover. Long, soft loaves of Barbari bread, originated by the Barbars of Persia, are typically split and filled with cheese or yogurt. Italian focaccia is a dimpled, pizzalike flatbread that varies regionally but is often seasoned with herbs and olive oil.

COVER (*Grapes*): Robert Papp, BACK COVER (*Flatbreads*): John Burgoyne

America's TEST KITCHEN

America's Test Kitchen is a very real 2,500-square-foot kitchen located just outside of Boston. It is the home of *Cook's Illustrated* and *Cook's Country* magazines and is the workday destination for more than three dozen test cooks, editors, food scientists, tasters, and cookware specialists. Our mission is to test recipes over and over again until we understand how and why they work and until we arrive at the best version. We also test kitchen equipment and supermarket ingredients in search of brands that offer the best value and performance. You can watch us work (in our actual test kitchen) by tuning in to *America's Test Kitchen* (www.americastestkitchen.com) on public television. Subscribe to *Cook's Illustrated* magazine at www.cooksillustrated.com or *Cook's Country* magazine at www.cookscountry.com.

COOK'S ILLUSTRATED

For list rental information, contact: Specialists Marketing Services, Inc., 777 Terrace Ave, 4th Floor, Hasbrouck Heights, NJ 07604; 201-865-5800.

Editorial Office: 17 Station St., Brookline, MA 02445; 617-232-1000; fax 617-232-1572. Subscription inquiries, call 800-526-8442.

Postmaster: Send all new orders, subscription inquiries, and change-of-address notices to Cook's Illustrated, P.O. Box 7446, Red Oak, IA 51591-0446.

PRINTED IN THE USA

THE SPECIALIST

In 1929, Charles Sale authored a small book of humor entitled *The Specialist*, about a country handyman, Lem Putt, who one day decided to become "the champion privy builder of Sangamon County." He took all aspects of his craft seriously, first and foremost the question of location. He suggests building a privy near a woodpile since "a timid woman . . . is too bashful to go direct out so she'll go to the woodpile, pick up the wood, and go back to the house to watch her chance." This means that the wood box will get filled by noon. He suggests beams over joists since nobody likes a "diggin' party." ("Aunt Emmy ain't gettin' a mite lighter. Some day she might be out there when them joists give way and there she'd be—catched.") He prefers lean-to roof designs over a pitched roof (less room for wasp nests), a hook and eye over a spool and thread to fasten the door ("either the spool or thread will give way and there you are . . ."), crescent moon designs over a window for ventilation, and a nail to hang the catalog as well as a box for the corn cobs ("Pa's of the old school and would prefer the box"). When asked how long the average mail-order catalog ought to last he opines, ". . . by placin' the catalog in there, say in January—when you get your new one—you should be into the harness section by June." He also railed against Mr. Sears Roebuck, who put too many stiff colored pages in the catalog. It was "hard to figger."

In 1687, when Sir Isaac Newton published his Principia Mathematica, he established, in just three sentences, the laws of motion that allowed the human race to, at last, penetrate everything from the movement of a pea on a plate to figuring out how to send men to the moon less than three centuries later. It was a time when a keen observer of natural phenomena could, without the benefit of a laboratory, penetrate the great mysteries of life.

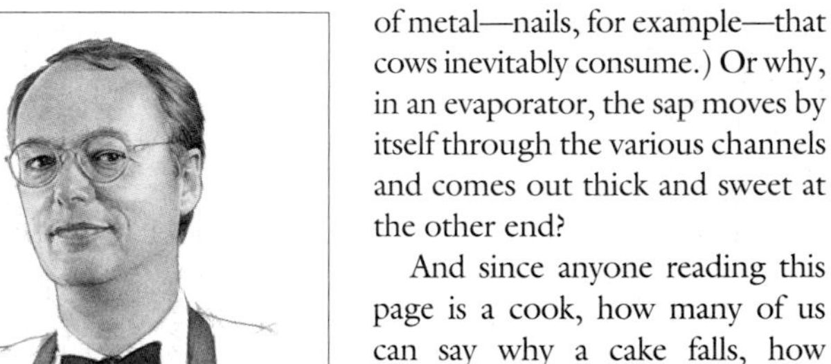

Christopher Kimball

In the country, the common man can still observe and then answer the question, "How does it work?" One can lift up the hood, tear off old drywall, dig out the septic, or poke holes in rotten joists to get at the answers. Maybe the submersible pump had gone bad (or the electric connections had crimped and broken) and that's why the neighbors ran out of water. Or the distributor cap was cracked and the truck wouldn't start. Or the hot water recirculator had sprung a leak. Or maybe it was simpler—the battery connections were fouled and the posts needed a brushing along with the connectors and now the old Farmall fires right up.

Our town has more than one Lem Putt. Old man Woodcock, when hired to take a daily ride up Red Mountain to feed trout in a flatlander's pond, figured he could cut down his visits by shooting a woodchuck and stringing it up over the water. (Trout love maggots.) Russell Bain invented a homemade rotisseric for the annual Ox Roast using mattress springs to keep the steamship rounds firmly attached to the spit. When Dotty and Jim first built their house out of sprayed concrete, many of the windows were purchased at automobile junkyards—some of them still show their inspection stickers.

Slowly, the world reveals itself. Did you know that carpenters have a "Blue Book" that tells them the exact angles to cut wood for roofs and stairways? Or why a V-8 is referred to as a "V"? (The cylinders are set at an angle to each other, reducing an engine's size and weight.) Or why vets make cows swallow a large lozenge-shaped magnet? (To attract the bits of metal—nails, for example—that cows inevitably consume.) Or why, in an evaporator, the sap moves by itself through the various channels and comes out thick and sweet at the other end?

And since anyone reading this page is a cook, how many of us can say why a cake falls, how much alcohol is burned off during cooking, whether a sirloin steak is related to a sirloin tip, or how brining works? Given a lifetime of experience, we become specialists—unlike those who just go out to eat. They might know where the kitchen is, but not what to do once they get there.

If satisfaction is to be found on earth, and some people might argue the point, it most likely comes from knowledge and a job well done, whether on the farm or in the kitchen. Allow me to end with the words of Mr. Putt, the man who specialized in privies.

"Sometimes when I get to feelin' blue and thinkin' I hitched my wagon to the wrong star. . . I just pack the little woman and the kids in the back of my car and start out, aimin' to fetch up at Elmer's place along about dusk. When we gets to the top of the hill overlookin' his place, we stops. There sits that privy on that knoll near the woodpile, painted red and white, mornin' glories growin' over her and Mr. Sun bathin' her in a burst of yeller color as he drops back of them hills. I heaves a sigh of satisfaction, my eyes fill up and I sez to myself, 'Folks are right when they say that next to my eight holer that's the finest piece of construction work I ever done. I know I done right in Specializin'; I'm sittin' on top of the world.' "

ILLUSTRATION: RANDY GLASS

FOR INQUIRIES, ORDERS, OR MORE INFORMATION

www.cooksillustrated.com

At www.cooksillustrated.com, you can order books and subscriptions, sign up for our free e-newsletter, or renew your magazine subscription. Join the website and gain access to 15 years of *Cook's Illustrated* recipes, equipment tests, and ingredient tastings, as well as Cook's Live companion videos for every recipe in this issue.

COOKBOOKS

We sell more than 50 cookbooks by the editors of *Cook's Illustrated*. To order, visit our bookstore at www.cooksillustrated.com or call 800-611-0759 (or 515-246-6911 from outside the U.S.).

COOK'S ILLUSTRATED Magazine

Cook's Illustrated magazine (ISSN 1068-2821), number 94, is published bimonthly by Boston Common Press Limited Partnership, 17 Station St., Brookline, MA 02445. Copyright 2008 Boston Common Press Limited Partnership. Periodicals postage paid at Boston, Mass., and additional mailing offices USPS #012487. Publications Mail Agreement No. 40020778. Return undeliverable Canadian addresses to P.O. Box 875, Station A, Windsor, Ontario N9A 6P2. POSTMASTER: Send address changes to Cook's Illustrated, P.O. Box 7446, Red Oak, IA 51591-0446. For subscription and gift subscription orders, subscription inquiries, or change-of-address notices, call 800-526-8442 in the U.S. or 515-247-7571 from outside the U.S., or write us at Cook's Illustrated, P.O. Box 7446, Red Oak, IA 51591-0446.

NOTES FROM READERS

COMPILED BY DAVID PAZMIÑO

Enameled Cast-Iron Safety

I was excited to make your Almost No-Knead Bread (January/February 2008) but noticed that the recipe calls for placing the empty pot in the oven and then heating the oven to 500 degrees. The manufacturer of my pot does not recommend heating it past 375 degrees. What should I do?

JAMES A. RUDDY
WESTLAKE VILLAGE, CALIF.

The main reason that manufacturers of enameled cast-iron pots give this recommendation concerns the phenolic (plasticlike) knob on the lid. This material tends to give off fumes and crack when heated past 375 degrees. In the July/August 2008 Kitchen Notes, we offered recommendations for replacing the knob with one that can withstand higher temperatures.

We were surprised to learn that in certain instances, the pot itself might crack. The enamel coating on cast-iron pots is made of vitrified glass. Although this material is built to withstand years of cooking, it can crack if the pot is dropped, the enamel has been improperly applied, or thermal shock occurs. Thermal shock may occur if a cold, empty pot is placed in a hot oven; if an empty pot is heated and then filled with cold food; or if a hot pot is placed on a cold surface.

According to Le Creuset and Lodge (two of the leading manufacturers of enameled cast iron), the risk for thermal shock with our Almost No-Knead Bread recipe is low. The recipe calls for placing a cold pot in a cold oven, heating the oven to 500 degrees, and then placing room-temperature dough into the pot. Both manufacturers agree that there would be a much greater risk of thermal shock if cold food, liquid, or oil were placed in the hot pot. To prevent thermal shock when the pot is removed from the oven, place it on a wire rack or trivet or on the cooking grate of the stove.

When to Freeze Casseroles

I often prepare casseroles for my family and in-laws to keep in their freezers. Should I cool casseroles completely before freezing them?

KAREN SCHOENIKE
OCONOMOWOC, WIS.

We, too, wondered how freezing cooled versus still-warm casseroles would affect quality, as well as how the casseroles would affect the temperature of the freezer. We recommend maintaining a freezer temperature of about 0 degrees Fahrenheit. At temperatures higher than 7 to 10 degrees, the foods in the freezer will begin to defrost, affecting their quality and safety.

We baked two batches of Classic Macaroni and Cheese (May/June 2004). We cooled the first batch for 15 minutes, wrapped it in aluminum foil, and placed it in a freezer registering -2 degrees. The ambient temperature in the freezer immediately jumped to 23 degrees and after one hour registered 16 degrees. This increase in temperature had the potential to partially defrost foods close to the casserole, causing freezer burn. It took a full four hours for the freezer to return to our recommended 0 degrees. We cooled the second casserole on the counter for two hours, wrapped it in foil, and then placed it in the freezer. The temperature in the freezer rose just 2 degrees; after 30 minutes, it had fallen to 0 degrees.

FREEZE FRAMES
The top casserole was cooled just 15 minutes before freezing and developed an icy layer that impacted taste and texture. The bottom casserole was cooled to room temperature before freezing and tasted far better when reheated.

After three days, we unwrapped each casserole. The casserole that had gone into the freezer warm sported a thick, fuzzy layer of frozen condensed steam. Once reheated, it had a soggy texture and an off-flavor. The casserole that had been completely cooled had no condensation and tasted fine. Our recommendation: Cool any casserole to room temperature (about two hours) before freezing.

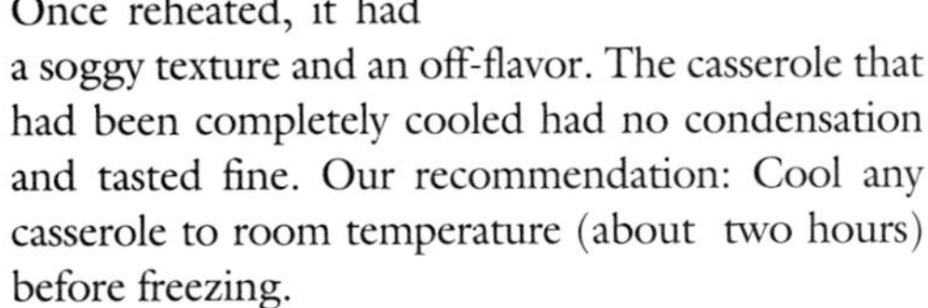

Next-Day Flavor

The headnote to your Best French Onion Soup recipe (January/February 2008) explains that the flavor of the soup improves when it is made in advance. This got me wondering: Why do soups and stews taste better the next day?

HENRY ARMIJO
WASHINGTON, D.C.

To get to the bottom of this issue, we had a conversation with our science editor. He explained that even after cooking ceases, many chemical reactions continue to take place in foods. In the case of a soup or stew containing milk or cream, the lactose breaks down into sweeter-tasting glucose. Similarly, the carbohydrates in onions develop into sugars such as fructose and glucose. Proteins in meat turn into individual amino acids that act as flavor enhancers. Finally, starches in potatoes and flour break down into flavorful compounds.

To verify this, we made batches of Best French Onion Soup (January/February 2008), Simple Beef Chili (March/April 2003), Ultimate Cream of Tomato Soup (November/December 1999), and Black Bean Soup (January/February 2005) and refrigerated them. Two days later, fresh batches of each recipe were served hot alongside the reheated soups and stews. Tasters unanimously preferred the onion, tomato, and black bean soups that had been held for two days, calling them "sweeter," "more robust-tasting," and "well rounded." When it came to the chili, most tasters made the same comments, but some preferred the fresh sample—as it sat, the chile flavors became sweeter and less sharp. If you like vibrant chile flavor, it's best to serve chili the same day you make it.

Salt Content of Brined Foods

I love what brining does to pork chops and chicken breasts. How much salt does the meat soak up during a 30-minute brine?

KIALA REICH
WOBURN, MASS.

We have been brining meat for years and were also interested in finding out how much sodium penetrates during the process. To answer your question, we brined natural pork chops and boneless, skinless chicken breasts in standard quick-brine solutions of ½ cup table salt dissolved in 2 quarts of cold water. After 30 minutes, we removed the pork and chicken, patted them dry, and cooked them in different skillets. We also cooked an "enhanced" pork chop (injected with a saltwater solution) and a kosher chicken breast that had been salted during processing.

We sent the samples to a food lab to measure sodium content. The brined pork chops had a sodium content of 245 milligrams per 100 grams of meat (just under ⅛ teaspoon per serving); the enhanced pork had a bit more, with 268 milligrams. The kosher chicken breast weighed in at 252 milligrams of sodium. The brined chicken came in with the most sodium of all, at 353 milligrams (just over ⅛ teaspoon per serving). The USDA recommends limiting your daily sodium intake to 2,300 milligrams, about 1 teaspoon.

Why did the chicken absorb more salt during brining than the pork? The loose white muscle fibers in chicken absorb salt water more quickly than the tighter muscle fibers in pork.

Iodized Salt

I was surprised to read that your recipes call for table salt. Doesn't it contain lots of additives, including iodine?

JOHN MORROW
OAKDALE, MINN.

➢We do call for table salt in our recipes, but not for iodized table salt. Many producers add iodine to salt because at one time many people in this country were deficient in this natural element found mostly in seafood. To hide the mineral aftertaste of iodine in salt, many producers add dextrose, a form of sugar. It's worth noting that nowadays most people get sufficient iodine from baked goods and dairy products (iodine is in dairy cow feed and is used to wash their udders before milking).

To confirm the test kitchen's preference, we made two batches of buttered popcorn and seasoned one with plain salt and the other with iodized salt. Some tasters couldn't detect a difference, but a few noticed a slight chemical aftertaste in the batch seasoned with iodized salt. While using iodized salt certainly won't ruin a recipe, we prefer to stick with the clean taste of plain salt.

CLEAN TASTE CHEMICAL TASTE
The test kitchen prefers plain salt to iodized salt.

Cooling Baked Goods

Recipes often call for cooling baked goods on a wire rack. Is a wire rack really necessary, or is it OK to cool foods on a flat surface?

JENNA DURST
LARGO, FLA.

➢The chief concern when cooling baked goods is preventing sogginess. When an item is cooled on a wire rack, air can circulate beneath it, allowing steam to escape, rather than condensing and causing the food to turn mushy. To prove this theory, we baked up two batches of our Thin and Crispy Oatmeal Cookies (January/February 2008) and Deep-Dish Apple Pie (September/October 2005). We cooled one batch of each recipe on a wire rack and compared it to batches cooled directly on a heatproof counter. The cookies cooled on a rack were crisp and evenly textured from the edge to the center. The counter-cooled cookies were less crisp overall and chewy in the center. The pie test was equally convincing: The bottom crust of the pie cooled on the wire rack maintained its crispness despite the moist apple filling. The pie cooled on the counter, on the other hand, developed a gummy and wet bottom crust.

WHAT IS IT?

My brother found this tool at a flea market. We can't figure out what it's used for. Can you help?

DIANE THOMSON
MILFORD, MASS.

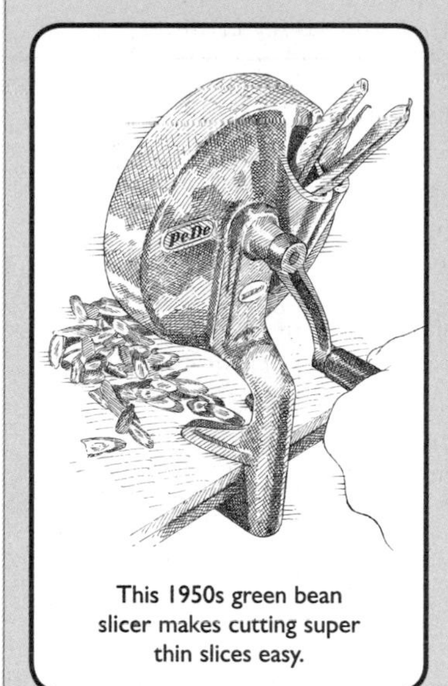

This 1950s green bean slicer makes cutting super thin slices easy.

The photo you sent stumped us, too. We spent weeks paging through antique catalogs and searching online markets before finally identifying this gadget. It's a double-feed green-bean slicer. Made by the Peter Dienes company (Pe De for short), this implement was manufactured in Holland during the 1950s. To use the slicer, the bottom must be affixed to a countertop or heavy-duty cutting board. Each of the two chutes accommodates two green beans; with a few turns of the handle, a blade cuts them on the bias into 1-inch long, 1/16-inch-thick slices. This paper-thin cut makes mature, tough green beans taste less fibrous.

How does the Pe De slicer compare to a knife? It took us just five minutes to cut 1 pound of green beans into uniform, ultrathin cuts using the slicer and more than 15 minutes to cut far less precise slices with a knife. If you're faced with mountains of green beans, then the Pe De slicer is a useful tool.

Rice Bran Oil

I recently noticed a new cooking oil in my supermarket made from rice bran. The importer, California Rice Oil Company, claims that it has a neutral flavor and a really high smoke point. Have you tried it?

DIANA JESSIE
FAIRBANKS, ALASKA

➢Produced in Thailand, the rice bran oil imported by California Rice Oil Company is available in specialty markets and natural foods stores. Oils with a high smoke point (such as canola and peanut) are recommended for high-heat cooking techniques such as stir-frying and pan-frying. The higher the smoke point, the less likely the oil is to burn.

To compare rice bran oil to canola oil, we placed 2 tablespoons of canola in a cold skillet and set it over high heat. After 3 minutes and 30 seconds, the oil began to smoke, and the pan registered 456 degrees on an infrared thermometer. (Peanut oil also has a smoke point of about 450 degrees.) When we repeated the test with rice bran oil, it took almost 4 minutes for the oil to smoke, and the pan registered 497 degrees.

Rice bran oil from California Rice Oil Company has a higher smoke point and lighter flavor than canola oil.

Rice bran oil won the smoke point test; how would it fare in a taste test? We compared canola and rice bran oil in three applications: a basic vinaigrette, a beef stir-fry, and a pan-fried breaded chicken cutlet. In all three tests, the rice bran oil passed with flying colors. Tasters thought the rice bran oil vinaigrette was "lighter" in flavor than the canola vinaigrette. When the oils were heated, the differences were even more striking. The beef and chicken cooked in canola oil tasted "heavier" and "more oily" compared with those cooked in rice bran oil. The bottom line: Even at 12 cents per ounce for rice bran oil (versus 6 cents per ounce for canola oil), we think it's worth the expense, especially when stir-frying or pan-frying.

Wooden Spoon Clarification

In our testing of wooden spoons in the May/June 2008 issue, we didn't fully explain the reservation in our recommendation of Kitchen Carvers' The Pointed Spoon You Can't Live Without. While the notched rest in the handle allows the spoon to sit on the rim of the pan and provides an innovative solution for keeping the utensil handy, we felt that using it on a gas stove at high heat might turn this helpful feature hazardous.

SEND US YOUR QUESTIONS We will provide a complimentary one-year subscription for each letter we print. Send your inquiry, name, address, and daytime telephone number to Notes from Readers, Cook's Illustrated, P.O. Box 470589, Brookline, MA 02447, or to notesfromreaders@americastestkitchen.com.

Quick Tips

COMPILED BY YVONNE RUPERTI

Storing Kitchen Tongs

Spring-loaded tongs without a locking mechanism can easily get tangled up in a utensil drawer. For sleek storage and easy retrieval, Deanna Mishlu of Syracuse, Ind., slips a heavy-duty rubber band around the pincer tips of the tongs to keep them tightly closed.

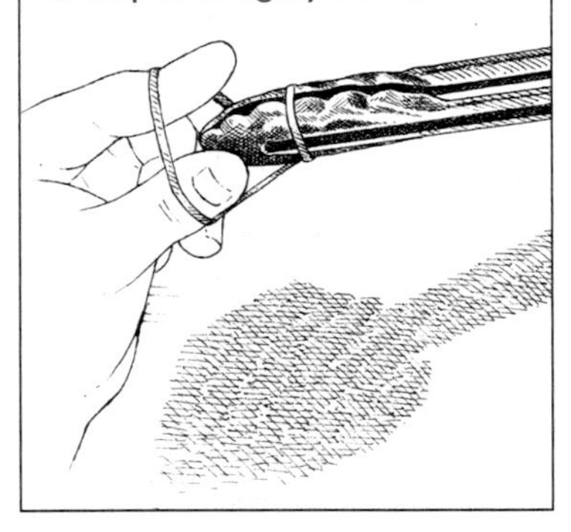

Clump-Free Caper Chopping

Adriana Lopez of New York, N.Y., finds tiny, slippery capers difficult to chop when they roll around on the cutting board. She uses the following technique to stabilize them.

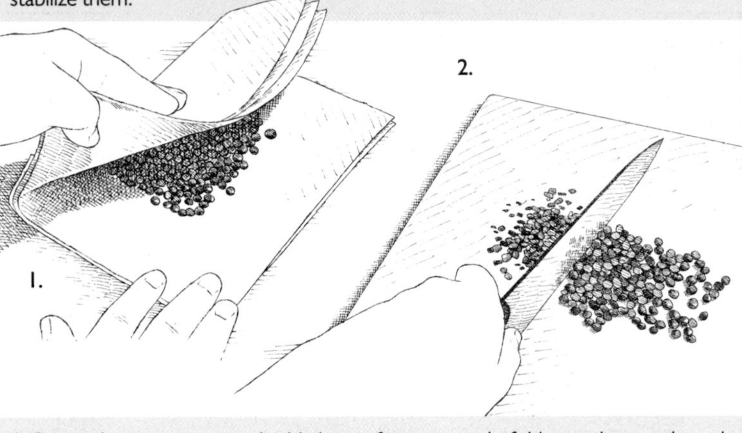

1. Spoon the capers onto a double layer of paper towels, fold over the towels, and push down firmly on them to flatten.
2. Transfer the dry, flat capers to a cutting board for chopping.

Storing Bacon Grease

Handling hot bacon drippings is a messy proposition. LaDorna C. Fox of Olean, N.Y., offers a great tip for neatly storing the drippings for later use.

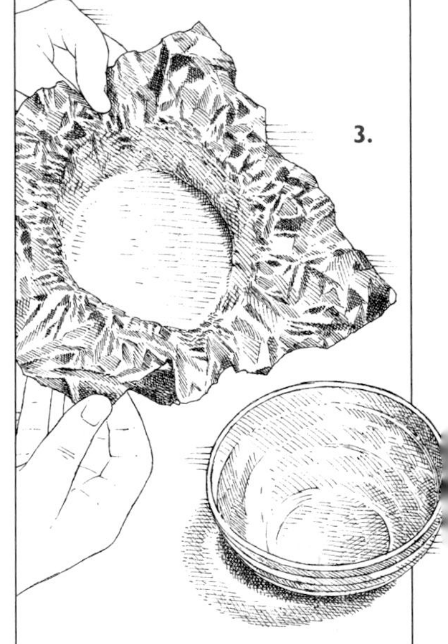

1. Line a small heatproof bowl with two small sheets of heavy-duty aluminum foil.
2. Carefully pour the hot bacon fat into the foil-lined bowl.
3. After the fat cools and solidifies, lift out the foil and fold it over the fat. The fat can then be refrigerated or frozen.

Safer Grater Storage

A rasp-style grater can nick fingers when it is left unprotected in a drawer. Lee Hiteshew of Newtown, Conn., fearlessly stores his grater by slipping it into an empty paper-towel tube before sliding it into the drawer.

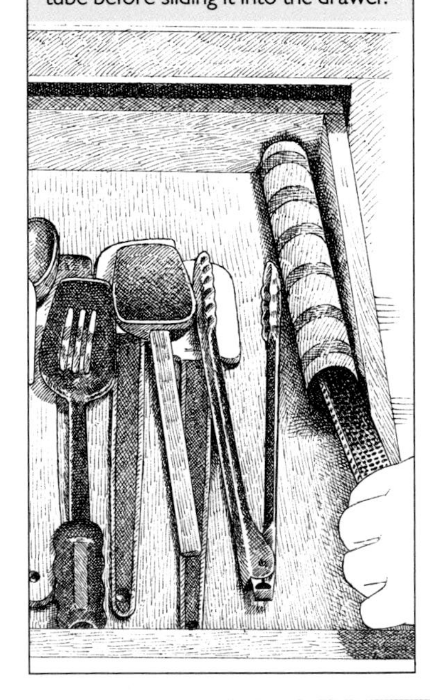

Cleaning an Immersion Blender

Scrubbing the blade of an immersion blender with a thick sponge can be a frustrating, dangerous task. Leevi Ernits of Stanfordville, N.Y., found a better approach. Fill a bowl with hot soapy water and place it in the sink. Place the dirty blender blade in the water. Turn the blender on to whirl away the stuck-on food, then rinse it clean with hot water.

Defatting Ground Meat

Mark Fourman of Cambridge, Mass., has a mess-free method for removing excess fat from fried ground beef, poultry, or pork. He transfers the cooked meat to a colander set inside a bowl. After the grease drains away, he returns the meat to the pan and continues with his recipe.

Send Us Your Tip We will provide a complimentary one-year subscription for each tip we print. Send your tip, name, and address to Quick Tips, Cook's Illustrated, P.O. Box 470589, Brookline, MA 02447, or to quicktips@americastestkitchen.com.

Sorting Dried Beans

It is important to pick over dried beans to remove any stones or debris before cooking. Douglas Durning of Saratoga Springs, N.Y., offers an easy way to accomplish the task.

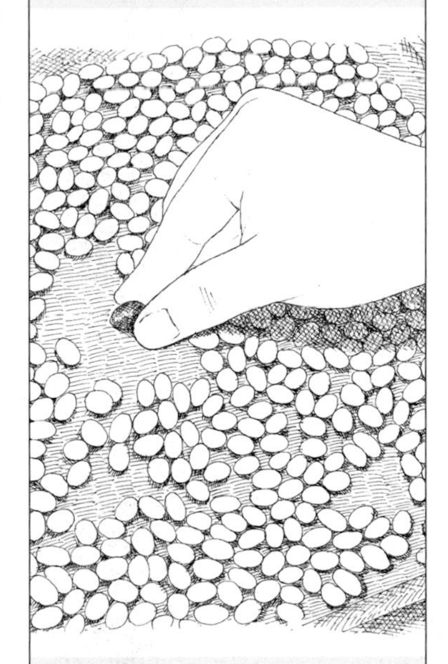

Arrange the beans in a single layer on a rimmed baking sheet. Sort through the beans, pushing the "checked" beans to one side of the sheet and discarding debris as you go. Rinse the beans before cooking them.

No-Slip Mixing

When using a hand-held mixer to make cookies or cake, Livie Zuccaro of Westlake, Ohio, likes to keep one hand free for adding ingredients to the mixing bowl. She keeps the bowl from sliding around by placing it on a rubber shelf liner or silicone baking sheet liner. The mixing bowl sticks to the liner and keeps it stable.

Easy-to-Clean Recipe Cards

Paper recipe cards often get stained in the kitchen and become difficult to read. Jenny Hansell of Sharon, Conn., keeps her recipes pristine by printing them on heavy-weight photo paper. The paper is sturdy enough to prop up during cooking and can easily be wiped clean with a damp towel.

Resuscitating Stale Cookies

To restore the warm and chewy "just out of the oven" texture to stale, hardened cookies, Heather Paxson of Cambridge, Mass., places them on a microwave-safe plate and heats them in the microwave on high power for 10 seconds to make them soft and chewy again. Be careful if the cookies are hot, but eat them before they cool completely and lose their softness.

Just Enough Wine for Cooking

When a recipe requires only a small amount of wine, Michael Pignotti of Tinley Park, Ill., doesn't always want to uncork a whole bottle. He solves the problem by keeping four-packs of miniature bottles of red and white wine on hand.

New Use for Cookie Cutters

Finding herself without a roasting rack, Susan Chi of Lawrence, Kan., improvised by placing several open-style metal cookie cutters in the bottom of a roasting pan. She then placed the item to be roasted on the cutters, successfully suspending it above the bottom of the pan.

Cheesier Sandwiches

Large, round slices of cheese such as provolone can be too big to fit onto a piece of sandwich bread. For a neater fit, Juliet Pusateri of Ellicott City, Md., uses this clever trick, which is especially useful for making grilled cheese, when you don't want any of the cheese to leak out.

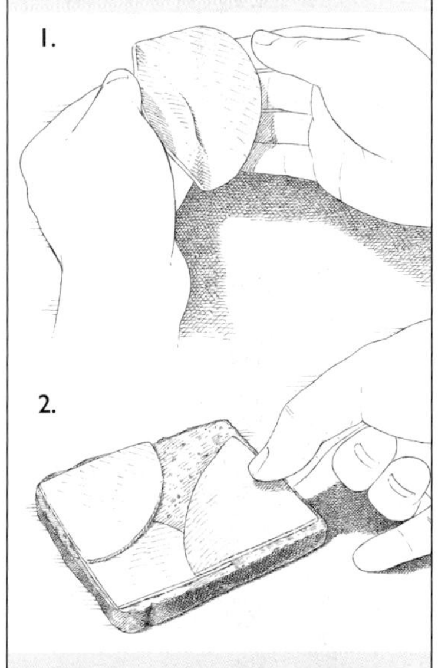

1. Fold the cheese slice into quarters, breaking it into four pieces.
2. Arrange the cheese on the bread with the squared edges facing out and the rounded edges facing in.

Improving Herbed Roast Chicken

Most herbed roast chicken has so little herb flavor it's hardly worthy of the name. We set out to roast a chicken with herbs in every bite.

⋟ BY CHARLES KELSEY ⋞

Adding herb flavor to roast chicken sounds easy enough—even downright simple. The reality is that this is one of the hardest culinary tasks to get right. For starters, the delicate flavor of herbs does not easily penetrate deep into the bird. Then there's the heat of the oven, which tends to wilt fresh herbs, dulling their flavor. The most common approach—spreading herb butter under the skin of the breast—only succeeds in flavoring the chicken weakly at best. My goal was ambitious: getting the entire bird—not just the breast—seasoned with herbs throughout.

Our skillet-roasted bird has both crisp skin and potent herb flavor.

Seeking a Flavor Infusion

To succeed where even the best chefs have failed, I would need to think outside the box. What if I could get herb flavor into the bird before it went into the oven? We typically brine whole chickens in a saltwater solution an hour or so before roasting to season the meat and keep it juicy. If I added herbs to the brine, would their flavor migrate into the meat along with the salt? Sadly, no matter how many bunches of herbs I used or how long I soaked the chicken, little of their flavor seemed to penetrate. A quick conversation with our science editor explained why: The flavor compounds in herbs are oil soluble and thus, in a water-based solution, have no conduit for traveling into the meat. Would I have better luck marinating the chicken in oil mixed with herbs—a technique we've used successfully to flavor chicken kebabs? I soaked the bird for an hour, two hours, even a full day—all with little success. While a marinade may inject flavor directly into skinless chunks of chicken, the skin, bones, and moisture of a whole bird were too much of a barrier.

I was back at square one: spreading herb butter under the skin. But instead of spreading it just under the skin of the breast, what if I applied it under the skin of the whole bird? I devised a basic rosemary-parsley paste (I'd perfect the exact combination later) and went about separating the skin from the bird to make room for spreading it. As soon as I tried lifting up under the thin, tight skin of the legs and thighs, I knew why recipes rarely call for this: No matter how delicate my efforts, I wound up tearing much of it. Pushing on, I roasted the tattered chicken in a V-rack placed inside a roasting pan. As the chicken cooked, herbs slipped out from the tears in the skin with the rendering fat. Worse, the skin pulled apart at these openings, exposing much of the breast meat and causing it to cook up dry and leathery. Hello failure.

Clearly, if I were going the herbs-under-the-skin route, I'd have to stick with just the breast meat. But what if I supplemented this by slathering the whole chicken with more of the paste midway through cooking? (Any earlier and the herbs would scorch.) In addition, I decided to try a technique I'd come across in my research: slashing shallow cuts in the dark meat. The cuts would not only help the skin to render better, they would create pockets to trap herbs. These methods yielded mixed success. While the cuts did provide traction for some of the herbs and the whole top of the bird cooked up with a beautiful herb-infused crust, the paste still didn't effectively cling to the parts of the legs and thighs on the underside of the chicken. (Argh, gravity!)

I needed to find a way to get the herb paste to stay on the whole chicken without it sloughing off. Mixing in ingredients with sticking power—such as mustard, mayo, and egg whites—merely introduced odd textures and interfering flavors. Why not make it easier for the herbs to stay put in the first place? Back in the kitchen, I butterflied a chicken, removing the backbone and pressing down on the breastbone so the whole bird would lie flat. I then slashed the dark meat as usual, brined the bird, and applied herb paste under the skin of the breast. Instead of the usual V-rack, I roasted the chicken directly on the roasting pan so it would lie flat.

Midway through cooking, I slathered on the herb butter. Though the butter in the paste melted and ran off, the herbs stayed put. When tasters tucked into the chicken, they were pleasantly surprised by the generous herb-to-meat ratio in each bite, even in the dark meat.

STEP-BY-STEP | PREPPING CHICKEN FOR AN HERBAL INFUSION

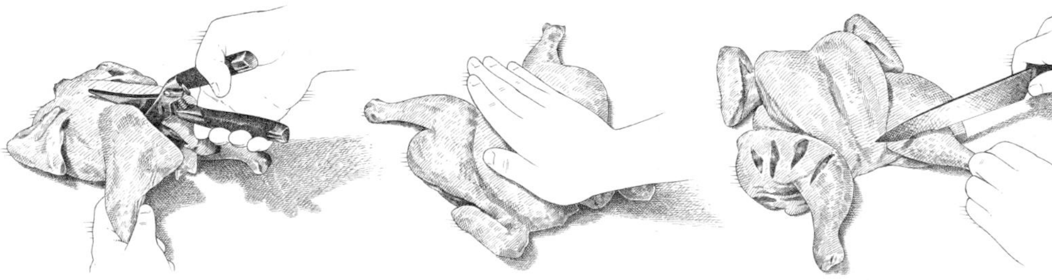

1. BUTTERFLY Herbs rolled right off whole chicken. To help herbs stay put, flatten bird, first removing backbone.

2. PRESS Use heel of your hand to press firmly on breastbone so chicken will lie flat, helping herbs stay on top.

3. SCORE Make shallow cuts on legs and thighs to create pockets that can trap herbs.

AT A GLANCE | HERBS THREE WAYS

To ensure herbs in every bite, we made a paste of tarragon, thyme, scallions, and butter and deployed it three ways.

1. UNDER SKIN Before roasting, spread herb butter evenly under loosened skin of breast meat.

2. OVER SKIN Midway through cooking, coat skin of entire bird with herb butter.

3. ON THE SIDE Serve chicken with pan sauce enriched with herb butter.

Herbaceous Triple Threat

Up to this point, the skin of my chicken was not the golden, crisp-thin sheath I wanted. Blasting the oven to 500 degrees for the first half of cooking and then finishing the chicken at a lower temperature didn't improve things. Neither did beginning at a low temperature and then kicking up the heat to high. Broiling the bird near the end of cooking rendered the skin better, but at the expense of the herbs, which scorched under the broiler's intense heat. Could it be that the moisture in both the herbs and butter (butter is nearly 20 percent water) were slowing down the melting of fat in the skin? Why not speed things up by starting the bird on the stovetop? I could keep the chicken in the skillet when I transferred it to the oven. This approach worked perfectly: Boosted by the browning, the rendering process was well underway as the chicken entered the oven. And by the time I slathered on the herb paste halfway through cooking, the skin had fully rendered.

With the cooking technique settled, I turned my attention to the best herb combinations. Dried herbs were not an option as their potency weakened dramatically during roasting and their texture turned gritty. For a balance of flavors and textures, I tried pairings of soft, delicately flavored herbs like parsley, cilantro, basil, tarragon, or chives with tougher, potent herbs like rosemary, oregano, thyme, or sage.

After numerous tests I found at least one herb that tasters could agree on: chives. They contributed a fresh, grassy flavor that everybody loved. But to get the level of flavor I wanted took three to four bunches. Would the tops from a single bunch of scallions work just as well? This, combined with tarragon and thyme, two other herbs my tasters favored, worked incredibly well, and a little minced garlic mixed into the paste boosted all of its flavors.

Just to make sure that every bite of chicken was bursting with herb flavor, I made a quick pan sauce using the drippings in the skillet, finishing it off with a couple tablespoons of extra herb butter and a few drops of lemon juice. Now, with triple layers of herb flavor in my recipe—roasted into the meat, spread over the skin, and drizzled onto each serving—it was nearly impossible to have a bite of plain ol' chicken.

Secret Ingredient: Scallions

Though unusual for an herb paste, we liked the robust, grassy flavor that scallion tops brought to our herb butter, preferring them to more delicate chives.

HERBED ROAST CHICKEN

SERVES 3 TO 4

If you like, substitute an equal amount of basil for tarragon and replace the thyme with rosemary, oregano, or sage. Do not use dried herbs, which lose potency during cooking and turn the dish gritty. For best flavor, buy a high-quality chicken such as Bell & Evans. The chicken should not exceed 5 pounds or it won't fit in the skillet. The chicken may slightly overhang the skillet at first, but once browned it will fit.

Chicken

- 1 whole chicken (about 5 pounds), trimmed of excess fat, giblets discarded (see note)
- ½ cup plus ¼ teaspoon table salt
- ¼ cup lightly packed fresh tarragon leaves (see note)
- 1 tablespoon fresh thyme leaves (see note)
- 6 medium scallions, green parts sliced thin (about ⅔ cup), whites reserved for another use
- 1 medium garlic clove, minced or pressed through garlic press (about 1 teaspoon)
- Ground black pepper
- 6 tablespoons unsalted butter, softened
- 1 tablespoon vegetable oil

Sauce

- 1-1½ cups low-sodium chicken broth
- 2 teaspoons unbleached all-purpose flour
- 1 teaspoon juice from 1 lemon

1. **FOR THE CHICKEN:** Following illustrations on page 6, butterfly chicken and flatten breastbone. Tuck wings behind back. Using sharp knife, lightly score skin of thighs and legs, making 2 shallow cuts on each part about ⅛ inch into meat and about ¾ inch apart. Dissolve ½ cup salt in 2 quarts cold water in large container. Submerge chicken in brine, cover with plastic wrap, and refrigerate 1 hour.

2. Meanwhile, adjust oven rack to middle position and heat oven to 450 degrees. Place tarragon, thyme, scallions, garlic, remaining ¼ teaspoon salt, and ¼ teaspoon pepper on cutting board; mince to fine paste. Transfer herb paste to medium bowl and add butter. Using fork or stiff rubber spatula, mix until combined. Transfer 2 tablespoons herb butter to small bowl and refrigerate; set aside remainder at room temperature.

3. Remove chicken from brine and rinse under cold running water; pat dry with paper towels. Following illustrations on page 31 and using fingers, carefully separate skin from each side of breast to form pocket. Place 1 tablespoon softened herb butter in each pocket. Using spoon or fingers, spread butter over breast meat. Season skin with pepper.

4. Heat oil in ovensafe 12-inch skillet over medium-high heat until just smoking. Place chicken skin-side down in skillet and reduce heat to medium. Cook until lightly browned, 8 to 10 minutes. Transfer skillet to oven and roast chicken 25 minutes. Using tongs, flip chicken so skin-side is facing up. Using spoon or spatula, evenly coat chicken skin with remaining softened herb butter and return to oven. Roast chicken until skin is golden brown and instant-read thermometer inserted in thickest part of breast registers 160 degrees and 175 degrees in thickest part of thigh, 15 to 20 minutes. Transfer chicken to carving board and let rest, uncovered, 20 minutes.

5. **FOR THE SAUCE:** While chicken rests, pour pan juices into fat separator; allow liquid to settle 5 minutes. Pour juices into 2-cup measuring cup and add enough chicken broth to measure 1½ cups. Add 2 teaspoons fat from fat separator to skillet and place over medium heat. When fat is shimmering, add flour and cook, stirring constantly, until golden, about 60 seconds. Add broth and bring to simmer, scraping pan bottom to loosen browned bits. Simmer rapidly until reduced to 1 cup, 5 to 7 minutes. Stir in any accumulated chicken juices from carving board; return to simmer and cook 30 seconds. Remove pan from heat, whisk in cold herb butter and lemon juice; season with salt and pepper. Carve chicken and serve, passing sauce separately.

COOK'S LIVE Original Test Kitchen Videos

www.cooksillustrated.com

HOW TO MAKE

- Herbed Roast Chicken

VIDEO TIPS

- How to butterfly a chicken
- The basics of brining poultry
- What's the best way to carve a butterflied chicken?

Perfecting Grilled Rack of Lamb

At nearly $20 a pound, rack of lamb had better be good. What's the key to achieving the rich crust and pink interior that make the most of this prime piece of meat?

⋟ BY KEITH DRESSER ⋞

Rack of lamb is like prime rib: You don't cook an expensive cut like this very often, and when you do, you want it to be spectacular. The meat should be pink and juicy, surrounded by a well-browned crust that provides a contrast in texture to the lush, ultratender interior. While it's possible to achieve these results in the oven, lamb and the grill have unbeatable chemistry. The intense heat of the coals produces a great crust and melts away the meat's abundance of fat, distributing flavor throughout. Plus grilling imparts a smokiness that's the perfect complement to lamb's rich, gamey flavor. The only hitch: I'd have to figure out how to keep all the rendering fat from creating the meat-scorching flare-ups and sooty flavors that are the surest way to ruin this pricey cut.

Reckoning with the Fat of the Lamb

Before I looked into the best way to grill the racks, I needed to figure out which type to buy. The racks sold by supermarkets are typically domestic or imported from Australia or New Zealand. My tasters in the test kitchen preferred the milder domestic lamb to the imported meat, which is bred for gamier flavors. Domestic lamb also has the advantage of coming in bigger sizes. (On average, the domestic racks I found weighed about 1½ pounds—a half pound more than the imported racks. For more information on the differences between the domestic and imported lamb, see "Lamb Flavor," below.) While I knew that the larger racks would be a challenge to cook evenly, I also figured a heftier size would translate to a longer stay on the grill, thus better grilled flavor.

For foolproof results with this expensive cut, we reversed the usual order of things and saved searing over direct heat for last.

The key to lamb's unique flavor and tenderness is its high proportion of fat, most of which covers one side of the rack like a cap. I knew from experience that leaving on the fat would lead to aggressive flare-ups virtually as soon as I put the lamb over the coals. But removing all of the cap wasn't the solution either. When I did this, the racks ended up dry with very little of the distinctive lamb flavor that makes this meat superb. As a compromise, I left a thin layer of fat over the loin and removed most of the fat between the bones.

Even when it was trimmed of fat, I knew I couldn't treat lamb like any old piece of chicken or pork cooked directly over the coals the entire time. Lamb still has enough interior fat that it would only be a matter of minutes before the flare-ups started. When grilling fattier meat, we often build a two-level fire by pushing all the coals to one side of the grill to create hot and cool areas. We then brown the meat over the hot coals, sliding it to the cooler side of the grill to finish. When I tried this method, the racks cooked to medium-rare at the center and had decent grilled flavor. However, many tasters found the outer layers of the meat to be overdone and tough. Plus, starting the racks on the hot side of the grill still led to flare-ups if I wasn't paying close attention.

Reverse Logic

It then dawned on me that my order of cooking should be reversed. What I needed was to start the lamb over indirect heat to allow the fat to render first. Once that fat was sufficiently rendered, I could move the racks to direct heat to brown the exterior. Testing this hypothesis, I had much better results. The only drawback was that because of the lamb's size, I had to crowd the racks on one side of the grill, leaving them catty-cornered to the fire, which caused them to cook unevenly. This method also left small pockets of unrendered fat that made the meat taste greasy instead of rich.

To solve this problem, I turned to a solution we devised for other large cuts: Instead of a traditional two-level fire with all the coals on one side, I heaped two smaller mounds on either side of the grill and placed an aluminum pan between them to act as a divider. (The pan would also serve as a drip tray to catch rendering fat.) I then positioned the lamb racks over the cooler center of the grill. Situated this way, all parts of the meat were exposed to the same amount of heat, allowing the racks to cook more

SCIENCE: Lamb Flavor

Domestic lamb is distinguished by its larger size and milder flavor, while lamb imported from Australia and New Zealand features a far gamier taste. The reason for this difference in taste boils down to diet—and the chemistry of lamb fat. Imported lamb is pasture-fed on mixed grasses, while lamb raised in the U.S. begin on a diet of grass but finish with grain. The switch to grain has a direct impact on the composition of the animal's fat, reducing the concentration of the medium-length branched fatty-acid chains that give any lamb its characteristic "lamb-y" flavor—and ultimately leading to sweeter-tasting meat.

DOMESTIC
American-raised lamb boasts bigger racks and a sweet, mild flavor.

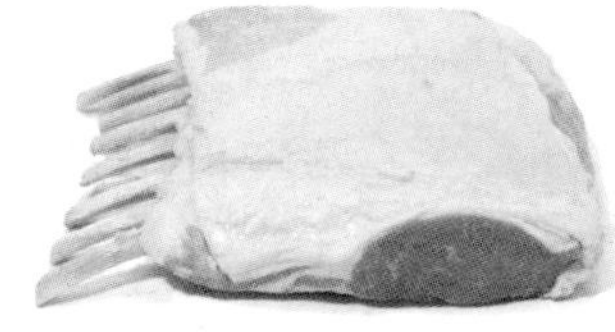

DOWN UNDER
Racks from Australia (as well as New Zealand) come smaller with a stronger, gamier flavor.

COOK'S LIVE Original Test Kitchen Videos
www.cooksillustrated.com
HOW TO MAKE
• Grilled Rack of Lamb
VIDEO TIP
• How do you trim a rack of lamb?

evenly. And because the heat was more diffuse, the fat also rendered more thoroughly. When the racks were lightly browned and the fat sufficiently rendered, I could then slide them over to the hot sides for just a short while to brown the exterior without fear of flare-ups. (Concerned that this setup might be hard to replicate on a gas grill, I did some quick tests. I found that because of the larger surface area of the gas grill, I could abandon the split-fire method and simply leave one burner on high and turn the others off.)

My biggest challenge met, I set out to flavor the lamb. Because lamb tastes so good on its own, I wanted to enhance the meat's flavor without overwhelming it. Many recipes call for marinating the lamb before grilling, but the several I tried only succeeded in making the lamb mushy. A dry rub, applied to the racks before they went on the grill, did add some flavor, but with my particular cooking method, much of the spice rub trickled away with the rendering fat, ending up in the drip pan. I tried applying the spice rub partway through cooking, but I just ended up with burnt fingers and the dusty taste of raw spices. The best option turned out to be a wet rub consisting of garlic and a couple of robust herbs (rosemary and thyme) mixed with a little oil (just enough to adhere the flavorings to the lamb without causing flare-ups). Brushed on the racks as they browned over the direct heat, the wet rub added just the right note to the perfectly cooked meat.

TECHNIQUE | TRIMMING FAT FROM THE RACK

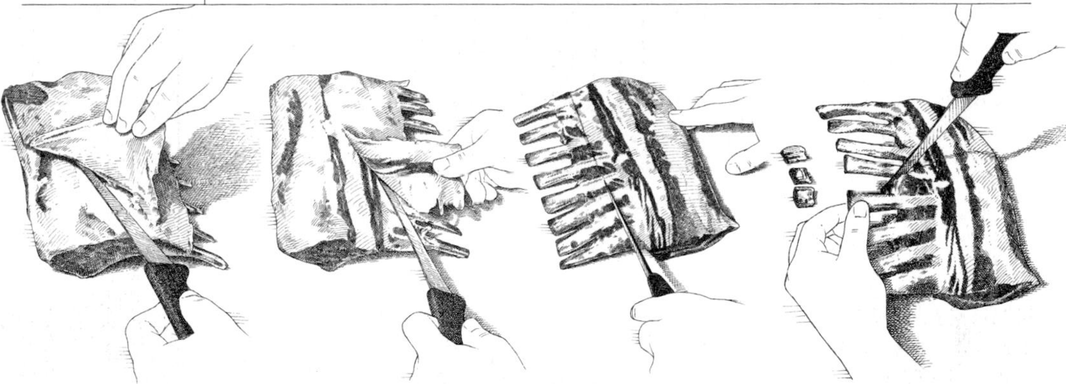

1. Peel back the thick outer layer of fat from the rack. Cut any tissue connecting the fat cap to the rack.

2. Trim the remaining thin layer of fat that covers the loin, leaving the thin strip of fat between the loin and the bone.

3. Make a straight cut along the top side of the bones, an inch up from the small eye of meat.

4. Remove any fat above this line and scrape any remaining meat or fat from the exposed bones.

GRILLED RACK OF LAMB

SERVES 4

We prefer the milder taste and bigger size of domestic lamb, but you may substitute imported lamb from New Zealand and Australia. Since imported racks are generally smaller, follow the shorter cooking times given in the recipe. While most lamb is sold frenched (meaning part of each rib bone is exposed), chances are there will still be some extra fat between the bones. Remove the majority of this fat (see illustrations, above), leaving an inch at the top of the small eye of meat. Also, make sure that the chine bone (along the bottom of the rack) has been removed to ensure that it will be easy to cut between the ribs after cooking. Ask the butcher to do it; it's very hard to cut off at home.

- Disposable 12- by 8-inch aluminum pan
- 4 teaspoons olive oil
- 4 teaspoons chopped fresh rosemary leaves
- 2 teaspoons chopped fresh thyme leaves
- 2 medium garlic cloves, minced or pressed through garlic press (about 2 teaspoons)
- 2 racks of lamb (1½ to 1¾ pounds each), rib bones frenched, meat trimmed of all excess fat (see note, illustrations above)
- Table salt and ground black pepper

1. Light large chimney starter filled with charcoal (6 quarts, or about 100 briquettes) and allow to burn until coals are fully ignited and partially covered with thin layer of ash, about 20 minutes. Place aluminum pan in center of grill. Empty coals into grill, creating equal-sized piles on each side of pan. Position cooking grate over coals, cover grill, and heat until grate is hot, about 5 minutes; scrape grate clean with grill brush. Grill is ready when coals are medium-hot.

2. Combine 3 teaspoons oil, rosemary, thyme, and garlic in small bowl; set aside. Rub lamb with remaining teaspoon oil and season generously with salt and pepper. Place racks bone-side up on cooler center of grill over aluminum pan with meaty side of racks very close to, but not quite over, hot coals. Cover and grill until meat is lightly browned, faint grill marks appear, and fat has begun to render, 8 to 10 minutes.

3. Flip racks over, bone-side down, and move to hotter parts of grill. Grill, without moving, until well-browned, 3 to 4 minutes. Brush racks with herb-garlic mixture. Flip racks so bone-side is up and continue to grill over hotter parts of grill until well browned, 3 to 4 minutes. Stand racks up and lean them against each other; continue to grill over one hotter side of grill until bottom is well-browned and instant-read thermometer inserted from side of rack into center, but away from any bone, registers 120 degrees for medium-rare or 125 degrees for medium, 3 to 8 minutes longer.

4. Remove lamb from grill and allow to rest, tented with foil, 15 minutes (racks will continue to cook while resting). Cut between ribs to separate chops and serve immediately.

RECIPE SHORTHAND | GRILLING RACKS OF LAMB

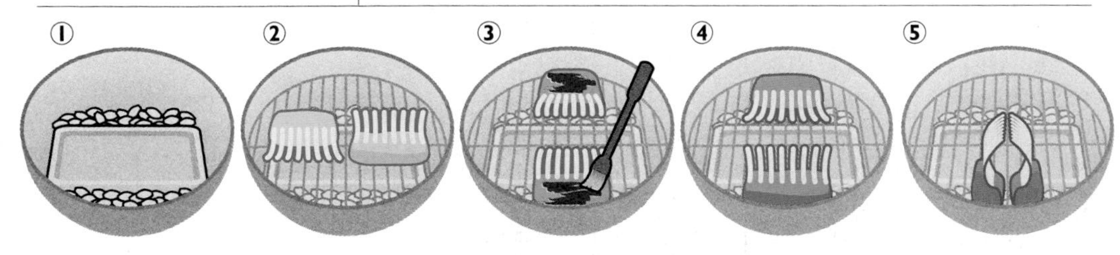

1. BUILD SPLIT FIRE Place aluminum pan between two mounds of coals to create cooler center area flanked by 2 hotter areas. **2. START OVER INDIRECT HEAT** Place racks bone-side up on cooler center of grill and grill until lightly browned. (On gas grill, place racks on cool side of grill.) **3. TRANSFER TO DIRECT HEAT** Grill racks, bone-side down, over hotter sides of grill for 3 to 4 minutes, and then brush with herb paste. **4. FLIP MEAT** Flip each rack so bone-side is up and brown meat. **5. BROWN RACK BOTTOMS** Stand racks together and brown their bottoms.

GRILLED RACK OF LAMB ON A GAS GRILL

Follow recipe for Grilled Rack of Lamb, omitting disposable pan, turning all burners to high, and heating grill with lid down until very hot, about 15 minutes. Scrape grill grate clean with grill brush. Proceed with recipe from step 2, leaving primary burner of grill on high, turning off other burner(s), and cooking with lid down.

GRILLED RACK OF LAMB WITH SWEET MUSTARD GLAZE

Follow recipe for Grilled Rack of Lamb, omitting rosemary and adding 3 tablespoons Dijon mustard, 2 tablespoons honey, and ½ teaspoon grated lemon zest to oil, thyme, and garlic in step 2. Brush racks with mustard glaze as directed in step 3, reserving 2 tablespoons. Brush racks with reserved glaze once removed from grill in step 4.

Bringing Steak Tacos Indoors

Who says that a great steak taco has to begin on the grill? We wanted a way to cook juicy, flavorful steak indoors so we could enjoy beefy tacos all year long.

BY KEITH DRESSER

Beef tacos made indoors are typically the pedestrian ground-beef kind, stuffed into a crisp corn tortilla and loaded with cheese and shredded lettuce. More upscale steak tacos, modeled after authentic Mexican *carne asada,* are generally reserved for the grill. Here a thin cut of beef, typically skirt or flank steak, is marinated, then grilled, cut into pieces, and served in a soft corn tortilla with simple garnishes. Done properly, the meat has rich, grilled flavor and the tacos themselves are simple to throw together.

Given the choice, I'd almost always prefer the beefier (and let's face it—better) flavors of a steak taco over a ground beef one, but what about those times when cooking outdoors isn't possible? I wanted to develop a method for bringing steak tacos indoors that would yield meat as tender, juicy, and rich-tasting as the grilled kind. I also wanted the technique to have the same success rate as grilling, without some of the common problems of cooking indoors: weak burners, poor ventilation, or a tendency to turn down the heat too soon so that by the time a crust develops, the center of the steak is overcooked.

Staking Out the Steak

My first task was to choose the right cut of meat. I decided from the outset to shy away from steaks like rib eye and top loin—though both are exceptionally beefy and tender, paying $15 to $20 for meat that you are just going to wrap up in a tortilla seemed a waste. Traditional Mexican recipes typically call for skirt or flank steak for taco meat, both of which come from the belly of the cow. I also wanted to try two other inexpensive cuts: blade steak, which comes from the shoulder, and steak tips (also called flap meat), from the sirloin of the animal. I pan-seared each type to determine which would work best. Tasters liked the well-marbled steak tips and skirt steak, but I found that availability of these cuts was spotty. The flavor of the blade steak was great, but it contained too much internal gristle. Flank steak proved to be the best choice all around. It had a nice beefy flavor and, when sliced thinly against the grain, was very tender.

The beefy flavor of flank steak proved best for these soft tacos.

Unadorned, the flank steak was good, but I wondered if I could render the meat even juicier. Referring back to our recipe for Grilled Flank Steak (May/June 2005), I found that sprinkling the meat with a liberal dose of salt and allowing it to sit for an hour markedly boosted juiciness, similar to brining. I was able to reduce that time to just 30 minutes by poking holes into the steak with a fork, which allowed the salt to sink more quickly into the meat's interior.

Given that the grill was the inspiration for this recipe, I wanted to try to mimic the browned exterior and crisp, brittle edges of grilled meat as much as possible. I figured that the intense heat of the oven's broiler would most closely resemble that of a grill and decided to start there. But after several tests, I knew the oven would never work with a thin cut like flank steak. While the broiler was able to brown the exterior of the meat, this didn't occur until the ¾-inch steak was way overcooked.

Pan-searing proved to be a much more promising method that allowed me to achieve some decent browning. But I wanted more. I tried increasing the surface area by laying the steak flat on the cutting board and slicing it in half, parallel to the board—a technique known as butterflying—but this was a tedious process that didn't yield significantly better results. Next I experimented with cutting the steak lengthwise with the grain into four long strips about 2½ inches wide and 1 inch thick. The results were great. Because the strips were relatively thick, I could brown them on four sides instead of two, which gave me even more exposed edges that became crisp and super-flavorful. I had two more tricks up my sleeve to promote caramelization and boost flavor even further: I sprinkled the steak pieces with a little sugar before browning and increased the oil I was cooking them in from 2 teaspoons to 2 tablespoons. Thanks to the salting and to the fact that the meat was in the skillet only briefly, the steak never dried out.

Marinades and Other Matters

With a successful cooking method squared away, I now looked at adding some other flavor dimensions to the steak. Reviewing my recipe, my first thought was to incorporate a dry spice rub when I salted the meat, which would not only add flavor, but might also help with the surface texture of the meat. But after a couple of tests I found that the spice rub just tasted dusty and raw. A wet rub or paste, provided it was removed before cooking so it wouldn't impede browning, seemed a better option. After looking into traditional marinades, I settled on a combination of cilantro, scallions, garlic, and jalapeño. Processed into a pestolike paste with some oil, this marinade added fresh flavors to the steak. And when coupled with the salt, the oil-based marinade was pulled into the steak, flavoring it throughout. I reserved some of the marinade to toss with the steak

SHOPPING: Corn Tortillas for Tacos

The rule of thumb when buying tortillas is to buy a brand made with nothing more than ground corn treated with lime (an alkali that removes the germ and hull) and water. Look for brands sold in the refrigerator case of the supermarket, as these have few, if any, preservatives and tend to be more moist and flavorful.

COOK'S LIVE Original Test Kitchen Videos

www.cooksillustrated.com

HOW TO MAKE

- Steak Tacos
- Sweet and Spicy Pickled Onions

VIDEO TIP

- How to warm tortillas

STEP-BY-STEP | KEYS TO TENDER, FLAVORFUL BEEF

1. **CUT** Slice flank steak into strips that can be browned on all sides.

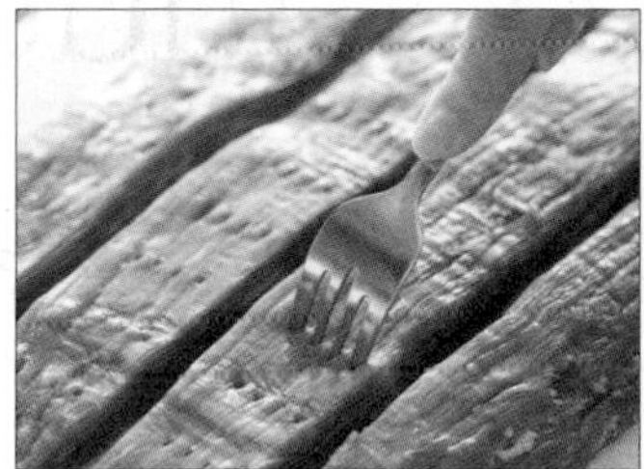

2. **POKE** Pierce steak pieces with fork to allow herb paste to penetrate.

3. **SALT** Season meat and coat with herb paste; let stand at least 30 minutes.

4. **SEAR** Cook steak in generous 2 tablespoons oil to promote browning.

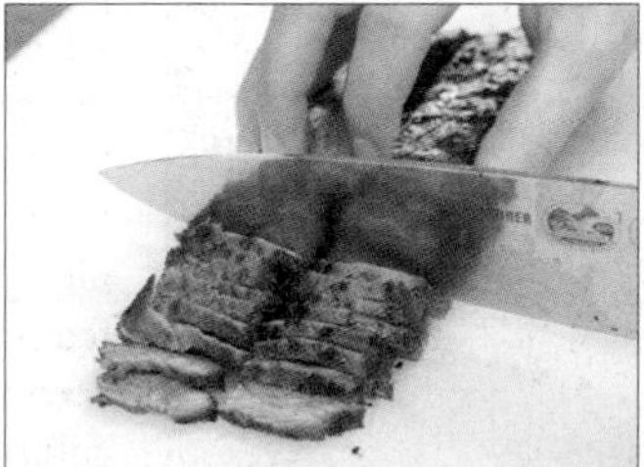

5. **SLICE** Cut steak thinly across grain to ensure tenderness.

6. **TOSS** Mix steak with more herb paste and lime juice to brighten flavors.

after it was sliced. This brightened the flavor and presentation considerably.

For garnishes, I chose raw onion, cilantro leaves, and lime wedges—all of which echoed the flavors in my marinade. Tasters also liked thinly sliced radishes and cucumber for the contrast in texture they provided to the steak. Lastly, I experimented with making some quick pickled vegetables, which I loosely based on *curtido* (a relish commonly served in Latin America). Tasters loved onions I "pickled" in a mixture of sugar and red wine vinegar enlivened by a couple of jalapeños. I now had a great-tasting alternative to the ubiquitous ground beef taco—one that could even be made in the middle of winter and in no time at all.

TECHNIQUE | HOW TO WARM TORTILLAS

Our preferred method for warming tortillas is to place each one over the medium flame of a gas burner until slightly charred, about 30 seconds per side. We also like toasting them in a dry skillet over medium-high heat until softened and speckled with brown spots, 20 to 30 seconds per side. You can also use the oven: Divide the tortillas into 2 stacks and wrap each stack in foil. Heat the tortillas on the middle rack of a 350-degree oven for 5 minutes.

Keep the warmed tortillas wrapped in foil or a kitchen towel until ready to use or they will dry out. (If your tortillas are very dry, pat each with a little water before warming.)

STEAK TACOS

SERVES 4 TO 6

For a less spicy dish, remove some or all of the ribs and seeds from the jalapeños before chopping them for the marinade. In addition to the toppings suggested below, try serving the tacos with Sweet and Spicy Pickled Onions (recipe follows), thinly sliced radishes or cucumber, or salsa.

Herb Paste

- ½ cup packed fresh cilantro leaves
- 3 medium garlic cloves, roughly chopped
- 3 medium scallions, roughly chopped (about ⅓ cup)
- 1 medium jalapeño chile, stemmed and roughly chopped (see note)
- ½ teaspoon ground cumin
- ¼ cup vegetable oil
- 1 tablespoon juice from 1 lime

Steak

- 1 flank steak (1½ to 1¾ pounds), trimmed of excess fat and cut lengthwise (with grain) into 4 equal pieces (see photo above)
- 1 tablespoon kosher salt or 1½ teaspoons table salt
- ½ teaspoon sugar
- ½ teaspoon ground black pepper
- 2 tablespoons vegetable oil

Tacos

- 12 (6-inch) corn tortillas, warmed (see photo below)
- Fresh cilantro leaves
- Minced white onion
- Lime wedges

1. **FOR THE HERB PASTE:** Pulse cilantro, garlic, scallions, jalapeño, and cumin in food processor until finely chopped, ten to twelve 1-second pulses, scraping down sides as necessary. Add oil and process until mixture is smooth and resembles pesto, about 15 seconds, scraping down sides of workbowl as necessary. Transfer 2 tablespoons herb paste to medium bowl; whisk in lime juice and set aside.

2. **FOR THE STEAK:** Using dinner fork, poke each piece of steak 10 to 12 times on each side. Place in large baking dish; rub all sides of steak pieces evenly with salt and then coat with remaining herb paste. Cover with plastic wrap and refrigerate at least 30 minutes or up to 1 hour.

3. Scrape herb paste off steak and sprinkle all sides of pieces evenly with sugar and pepper. Heat oil in 12-inch heavy-bottomed nonstick skillet over medium-high heat until smoking. Place steak in skillet and cook until well browned, about 3 minutes. Flip steak and sear until second side is well browned, 2 to 3 minutes. Using tongs, stand each piece on a cut side and cook, turning as necessary, until all cut sides are well browned and internal temperature registers 125 to 130 degrees on an instant-read thermometer, 2 to 7 minutes. Transfer steak to cutting board and let rest 5 minutes.

4. **FOR THE TACOS:** Using sharp chef's knife or carving knife, slice steak pieces across grain into ⅛-inch-thick pieces. Transfer sliced steak to bowl with herb paste–lime juice mixture and toss to coat. Season with salt. Spoon small amount of sliced steak into center of each warm tortilla and serve immediately, passing toppings separately.

SWEET AND SPICY PICKLED ONIONS

MAKES ABOUT 2 CUPS

The pickled onions can be refrigerated in an airtight container for up to 1 week.

- 1 medium red onion, halved and sliced thin (about 1½ cups)
- 1 cup red wine vinegar
- ⅓ cup sugar
- 2 jalapeños, stemmed, seeded, and cut into thin rings
- ¼ teaspoon table salt

Place onions in medium heat-resistant bowl. Bring vinegar, sugar, jalapeños, and salt to simmer in small saucepan over medium-high heat, stirring occasionally, until sugar dissolves. Pour vinegar mixture over onions, cover loosely, and let cool to room temperature, about 30 minutes. Once cool, drain and discard liquid.

Super Crisp Oven-Fried Fish

Oven-fried fish is typically fraught with soggy coatings and dry, overcooked flesh. We set out to bake flaky fillets in an ultracrisp crust.

⋺ BY J. KENJI ALT ⋲

When it comes to cooking fish in a flavorful coating, batter-fried is the gold standard. Done right, the fish is flaky and moist, encased in a crisp, delicate crust. But it's also a messy operation that splatters hot oil all over the stove and spreads fishy odors throughout the house. Most home cooks forgo the grease and smells of stovetop frying for the far greater convenience of "oven-fried" fish. Here, the fillets are simply dipped in liquid, covered in bread crumbs, and baked in the oven.

The trouble is, most recipes for this dish are disappointing. The fish is often dry and overcooked, while the bread crumb coating ranges from thin and sandy to soggy and crumbly. Is it possible, I wondered, to bake moist and flavorful fillets in a crunchy crust that would not merely play second fiddle to batter-fried fish, but stand out as a worthy dish in its own right?

Fresh toasted bread crumbs help put the "crisp" in our coating.

A Crumb-y Situation

My first task was to select the fish. I immediately ruled out dense varieties such as swordfish from consideration as their meaty textures wouldn't provide the contrast I wanted between crust and interior. Thin fillets such as sole and flounder were also out; they would overcook well before the coating had a chance to brown and harden. The flaky flesh of cod or haddock (the traditional choices for fried fish) was the best bet.

As for the coating, I knew better than to even think of cutting corners with bread crumbs from a can or box. These stale-tasting products are the key culprits behind gritty, insubstantial coatings. But fresh crumbs made from sandwich bread also present problems: Even the thickest fish fillet will cook through too rapidly, leaving fresh crumbs undercooked and soft. And once out of the oven, any crumbs that manage to get crunchy quickly turn soggy from escaping steam and fail to adhere to the moist fish.

Why not start with something that was already dry and crisp? I went to our pantry and pulled out a few things that looked promising: saltine crackers, potato chips, and Melba toast. I pulsed each in the food processor and applied them to three different batches of fish, using the standard breading method: I dusted the fillets in flour, dipped them in a basic egg wash, then pressed on the crumbs. The results were mixed. The saltines delivered a crust that was too soft. While the chips created crusts with definite crunch, their distinctive flavor wasn't appreciated by most of my tasters. The neutral flavor of the Melba toast worked better, but it produced a crust so crunchy it bordered on tough.

The best option, it seemed, was to stick with fresh bread crumbs. We've had success toasting fresh crumbs before using them in breading for meat or chicken, and I followed suit. I pulsed white bread in a food processor along with some melted butter. I spread the buttery crumbs on a baking sheet and baked them in a 350-degree oven until deep golden brown. Then I pressed the crumbs firmly on a batch of fillets. When I pulled the fillets out of the oven 20 minutes later, I could see that the breading on the top and sides of the fish was crisp, but the bottom crust remained soggy. I tried again with a new batch of larger, more coarsely processed crumbs. While this helped, it wasn't enough. Placing the fish on a wire rack set inside the baking sheet to allow air to circulate underneath was another step in the right direction, but I still needed something more.

Moisture leaking out of the fish as it cooked was the source of the sogginess. What if I tried to remove some of this moisture before cooking? I'd already been patting the fish dry with paper towels before

STEP-BY-STEP | KEYS TO A CRISP CRUST

Soft, moist fish needs an extra-thick coating of bread crumbs to add flavor and crunch. Here's how we lay it on thick:

1. PULSE Processing fresh crumbs very coarsely maximizes crunch.

2. TOAST Prebaking buttered crumbs ensures that they are brown and crisp when fish is done.

3. DIP Thickening batter with flour and mayonnaise prevents toasted crumbs from turning soggy and glues them firmly to fish.

4. COAT Pressing down gently on crumbs helps to pack thick layer on fish.

5. ELEVATE Baking fish on wire rack set inside baking sheet allows air to circulate underneath.

breading it, but a bit of salt might help pull out excess moisture. I salted the fillets and left them to sit on a rack. Twenty minutes later, I blotted away the drops of water that had begun beading on the fish's surface. But my hopes were dashed when I took this batch of fish out of the oven: Not only were the bottom crusts still soggy, the fish was too salty.

Maybe the solution would be found not in the fish or the crumbs, but in the egg wash. What if I were to thicken it up, turning it into a kind of buffer zone between the moist fish and the dry bread crumbs? Casting back to deep-fried fish for inspiration, I added a few tablespoons of flour to the egg wash, thickening it to a viscous batterlike texture. I also remembered that in the past we've added mustard to egg wash to give it more flavor. Mustard was too strong for the fish, but mayonnaise worked beautifully, adding richness and a welcome note of acidity. I covered the fillets in a generous layer of this revamped wash before pressing on the bread crumbs. When this fish came out of the oven, I held my breath as I turned a few over to check their bottom crusts. Success! The crust was crisp and dry all the way around and firmly bonded to the fish.

Fishing for Flavor

Having achieved a crunchy crust, I could focus on finessing flavor. Up to this point, I had seasoned the fish with nothing more than a little salt and pepper. I mixed a range of herbs and aromatics into the bread crumbs, including two common additions to breading: garlic and thyme. In the end, my tasters preferred the subtler flavors of shallots and parsley.

Now, what could I do to liven up the egg wash? Many deep-fried fish recipes call for paprika and cayenne pepper in their batter, and I found the same seasonings worked equally well in the egg wash. Still, the dish needed something more. I experimented with both Worcestershire and hot pepper sauce, but neither did the trick. Horseradish adds kick to cocktail sauce; would introducing it to the coating have a positive effect? I whisked a couple of teaspoons into the egg wash. Most of my tasters couldn't identify its flavor in the cooked fillets—just a new, fresh bite to the fish. As a final touch, I whipped up a tartar sauce with mayonnaise, capers, and sweet relish.

With or without sauce, these moist, tender fillets in their crisp, flavorful crust could definitely hold their own as a lighter and far easier alternative to fried fish any day.

CRUNCHY OVEN-FRIED FISH

SERVES 4

To prevent overcooking, buy fish fillets at least 1 inch thick. The bread crumbs can be made up to 3 days in advance, cooled, and stored at room temperature in an airtight container. Serve with Sweet and Tangy Tartar Sauce or lemon wedges.

- 4 large slices white sandwich bread, torn into 1-inch pieces
- 2 tablespoons unsalted butter, melted
- Table salt and ground black pepper
- 2 tablespoons minced fresh parsley leaves
- 1 small shallot, minced (about 2 tablespoons)
- ¼ cup plus 5 tablespoons unbleached all-purpose flour
- 2 large eggs
- 2 teaspoons prepared horseradish (optional)
- 3 tablespoons mayonnaise
- ½ teaspoon paprika
- ¼ teaspoon cayenne pepper (optional)
- 1¼ pounds cod, haddock, or other thick white fish fillet (1 to 1½ inches thick), cut into 4 pieces (see note)
- Lemon wedges

1. Adjust oven rack to middle position and heat oven to 350 degrees. Pulse bread, melted butter, ¼ teaspoon salt, and ¼ teaspoon pepper in food processor until bread is coarsely ground, eight 1-second pulses (you should have about 3½ cups crumbs). Transfer to rimmed baking sheet and bake until deep golden brown and dry, about 15 minutes, stirring twice during baking time. Cool crumbs to room temperature, about 10 minutes. Transfer crumbs to pie plate; toss with parsley and shallot. Increase oven temperature to 425 degrees.

2. Place ¼ cup flour in second pie plate. In third pie plate, whisk eggs, horseradish (if using), mayonnaise, paprika, cayenne pepper (if using), and ¼ teaspoon black pepper until combined; whisk in remaining 5 tablespoons flour until smooth.

3. Spray wire rack with nonstick cooking spray and place in rimmed baking sheet. Dry fish thoroughly with paper towels and season with salt and pepper. Dredge 1 fillet in flour; shake off excess. Using hands, coat with egg mixture. Coat all sides of fillet with bread crumb mixture, pressing gently so that thick layer of crumbs adheres to fish. Transfer breaded fish to wire rack. Repeat with remaining 3 fillets.

4. Bake fish until instant-read thermometer inserted into centers of fillets registers 140 degrees, 18 to 25 minutes. Using thin spatula, transfer fillets to individual plates and serve immediately with lemon wedges.

SWEET AND TANGY TARTAR SAUCE

MAKES ABOUT 1 CUP

This sauce can be refrigerated in an airtight container for up to 1 week.

- ¾ cup mayonnaise
- ½ small shallot, minced (about 1 tablespoon)
- 2 tablespoons drained capers, minced
- 2 tablespoons sweet pickle relish
- 1½ teaspoons white vinegar
- ½ teaspoon Worcestershire sauce
- ½ teaspoon ground black pepper

Mix all ingredients together in small bowl. Cover with plastic wrap and let stand to blend flavors, about 15 minutes. Stir again before serving.

TASTING: Tartar Sauce

The French created tartar sauce as a simple gherkin-filled mayonnaise. These days, the condiment regularly comes loaded with myriad additions: from horseradish and onions to capers, cabbage, and celery. We compared eight brands with our own homemade version to find a worthy sauce.

None compared to homemade. Most tasted gloppy and saccharine, though we found two acceptable stand-ins. Though not widely available, Legal Sea Foods Tartar Sauce stood apart for its creamy, balanced base chock full of cucumber, onion, cabbage, celery—even red bell pepper—and McCormick Original Tartar Sauce was almost as good. For complete testing results, go to www.cooksillustrated.com/october. –Elizabeth Bomze

GREAT BUT HARD TO FIND

LEGAL SEA FOODS Tartar Sauce

Price: $2.75 for 8 oz.

Comments: Lots of vegetable chunks and a "sweet/tart balance" made this condiment from New England's most famous seafood destination taste less like bottled.

PLENTY OF PICKLES

McCORMICK Original Tartar Sauce

Price: $2.49 for 8 oz.

Comments: Tasters praised this "rich, eggy" sauce with "good acidity" and an abundance of sweet pickle bits.

HEAVY ON THE HEAT

BOOKBINDER'S Tartar Sauce

Price: $2.79 for 8.25 oz.

Comments: This sauce from one of Philadelphia's oldest seafood establishments ran too heavy on the horseradish.

NOT PREMIUM AT ALL

HEINZ Premium Tartar Sauce

Price: $2.99 for 12.5 oz.

Comments: Tasters condemned this "artificially thick," "greasy" sauce with "Miracle Whip" sweetness.

OFFENSIVELY SWEET

HELLMANN'S Tartar Sauce

Price: $2 for 10 oz.

Comments: "Custard-like" and overly sweet, this bore no resemblance to the tartar sauce we wanted.

COOK'S LIVE Original Test Kitchen Videos

www.cooksillustrated.com

HOW TO MAKE

- Crunchy Oven-Fried Fish

VIDEO TIPS

- What's the best way to store fish?
- Buying frozen fish

Rescuing Stir-Fried Noodles with Pork

Pork lo mein is full of ingredients we love—fresh egg noodles, smoky barbecued pork, and pungent Chinese vegetables. So why can't takeout joints deliver a winning version?

⋟ BY FRANCISCO J. ROBERT ⋞

Pork lo mein is like fried rice: Order it from your typical takeout joint, and the dish invariably disappoints with greasy flavors and sodden vegetables. A few years back, we revamped fried rice with our own lighter, fresher renditions. That got me wondering: Could I do the same with pork lo mein? I wanted a dish representative of the best any good Chinese home cook could turn out: chewy noodles tossed in a salty-sweet sauce and accented with bits of smoky *char siu* (barbecued pork) and still-crisp cabbage.

Chewy noodles, still-crisp vegetables, and chunks of caramelized pork give our lo mein real bite.

Pinning Down the Pork

My first task was to find a suitable replacement for the char siu. This Cantonese specialty takes the better part of a day to prepare, and while enterprising cooks might attempt it themselves (we featured a streamlined approach in a past issue), it's more the provenance of restaurants and professional kitchens. A trip to Boston's Chinatown for some char siu wouldn't be out of the question on some occasions, but I wanted a dish I could whip up any time with ingredients from home. I would already be stir-frying the vegetables. As part of my makeover, why not stir-fry the pork as well?

But what cut would work best? I considered pork tenderloin, which we've used with great success in stir-fries. The only problem is that tenderloin, while tender, can be a little bland—worlds apart from the richly flavored, well-marbled pork shoulder traditional to char siu. Pork shoulder itself was out—it requires hours of cooking to become fall-apart tender. Pork belly is popular in Chinese cooking, but this fat-streaked meat from the underside of the pig is also the cut of choice for most bacon made in this country, and I could only find it smoked or cured. The most sensible option was country-style pork ribs. Though fatty, these meaty ribs from the upper side of the rib cage have the same rich flavor of pork shoulder; plus, they're naturally tender.

Following the protocol for char siu, I knew I wanted to marinate the pork before cooking. To avoid a dish that was overly greasy, I first trimmed the ribs of surface fat and cut them into thin strips that would allow the marinade to penetrate more efficiently. I then soaked the meat in a classic Chinese mixture of hoisin sauce, oyster sauce, soy sauce, toasted sesame oil, and five-spice powder, an aromatic blend of cinnamon, star anise, and other spices (see "Five-Spice Powder," on page 15). After 20 minutes, I removed the pork from the liquid and seared it quickly over high heat in a cast-iron skillet. (Because more of its surface is in contact with the burner, a large skillet provides more sizzle and sear than a wok, whose conical bottom was not designed for a Western stovetop.) One bite and I knew I had hit on a very good thing on my first try. The meat cooked up tender and juicy on the inside with a crisp, browned exterior. I took the flavor one step further by adding a few drops of liquid smoke for a little of that smoky flavor I love so much in char siu.

Noodling Around

Pork issues settled, I was ready to tackle the noodles. Lo mein literally translates to "tossed noodles," referring to the way the strands, made from wheat and egg and resembling thick spaghetti, are tossed in sauce. Traditionally the dish calls for fresh noodles, as these absorb the flavors of the sauce better than dried kinds. We tried a variety of fresh Chinese egg noodles, but only the ones labeled "lo mein" from the Asian grocery near the test kitchen boasted the good, wheaty taste and firm texture we were after. These came in a loose tangle packaged in a simple plastic bag. Disappointingly, the more readily available fresh "Chinese-style" egg noodles from the supermarket, sold in vacuum-packed containers in the produce aisle, had a pasty texture and an inferior taste that sent me seeking a better alternative. Back in the test kitchen, I scanned the shelves of our pantry. My eyes landed on a box of dried linguine. Despite its flat shape, these long Italian strands are similar in width to Chinese noodles. Cooked to al dente, they worked beautifully, sharing the same firm chewiness of the fresh Chinese noodles. (For more on noodle options, see "Noodles for Lo Mein," on page 30.)

In restaurants, for expediency's sake, the noodles are typically cooked well ahead of serving, rinsed in cold water, and then slathered in oil to keep them from clumping together as they wait to be added to the stir-fry. This not only makes the noodles excessively oily, but also prevents the sauce from clinging to them. Home cooking offered an advantage in this area—I could simply boil the noodles (fresh lo mein takes just four to five minutes) before tossing them with the sauce, avoiding the need for extra oil.

All that was left was to figure out the vegetables and the sauce. I opted for traditional choices—cabbage, scallions, and shiitake mushrooms—stir-frying them in a little vegetable oil with garlic and fresh ginger after cooking the meat. As for the sauce, my tasters decided the same mixture I had been using for the meat marinade would serve just fine as a base, with a little chicken broth and a teaspoon of cornstarch added for body. The final step: tossing the stir-fried meat and vegetables with the drained noodles in the pot I'd just used for boiling them, with a little Asian garlic-chili sauce for some added kick.

Traditionally, noodles are the star of lo mein,

COOK'S LIVE Original Test Kitchen Videos

www.cooksillustrated.com

HOW TO MAKE

- Pork Stir-Fry with Noodles (Lo Mein)

VIDEO TIPS

- Asian noodles 101
- How do you peel ginger?
- Tips for stir-fry success

A Hot Contest: Skillet vs. Wok

We have always preferred a skillet to a wok in our stir-fry recipes. Its flat-bottom design allows more of its surface area to come in direct contact with the flat burner of a Western stove, delivering more heat over more of its parts than a wok—and enabling it to remain hot even after food is added.

To quantify their differences, we heated oil in a wok and a heavy 12-inch skillet over high heat on gas burners. Once the oil was smoking (at around 415 degrees), we added stir-fry ingredients to each pan. The wok's temperature plummeted dramatically, to 220 degrees at its center, rising only another 50 degrees over the course of cooking. The skillet's temperature dipped to 345 degrees, then recovered quickly, continuing to rise to almost 500 degrees. This higher heat translated to better browning and more flavor.

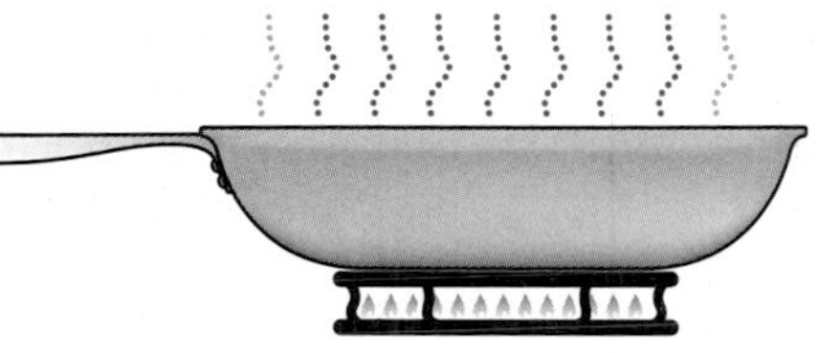

FLAT-BOTTOM BENEFITS

The flat bottom of a 12-inch skillet is better suited to a flat burner, maintaining heat (and even continuing to rise) after food is added.

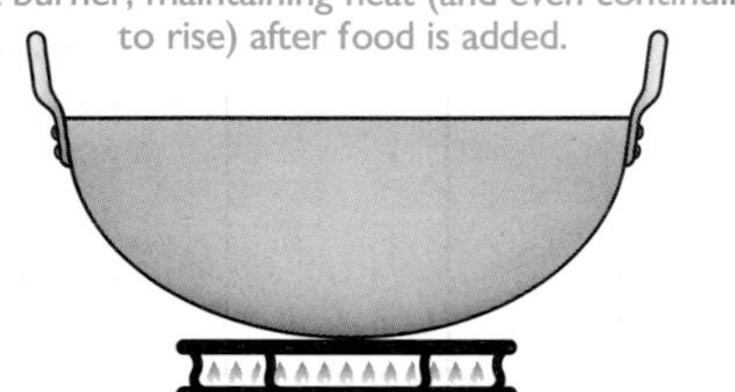

CONICAL COMPROMISE

The conical bottom of a traditional wok was designed for a pit-style stove. On a flat Western burner, it heats inefficiently, dropping its temperature when food is added.

while the meat and vegetables serve as little more than garnishes. To meet the demands of my American tasters, I quadrupled the amount of pork from 4 ounces to a pound and increased the vegetable amounts by several cups. The net effect was a richer yet fresher-tasting dish.

At last I had the kind of pork lo mein that Chinese takeout rarely delivers: chewy noodles coated in a flavorful sauce and full of tender, browned pork and pungent-tasting vegetables.

PORK STIR-FRY WITH NOODLES (LO MEIN)

SERVES 4

Use a cast-iron skillet for this recipe if you have one—it will help create the best sear on the pork. When shopping for Chinese rice wine, look for one that is amber in color; if not available, sherry wine may be used as a substitute. If no hoisin sauce is available, substitute 1 tablespoon of sugar. If boneless pork ribs are unavailable, substitute 1½ pounds of bone-in country-style ribs, followed by the next-best option, pork tenderloin. Liquid smoke provides a flavor reminiscent of the Chinese barbecued pork traditional to this dish. It is important that the noodles are cooked at the last minute to avoid clumping. See page 30 for information on buying noodles.

- 3 tablespoons soy sauce
- 2 tablespoons oyster sauce
- 2 tablespoons hoisin sauce (see note)
- 1 tablespoon toasted sesame oil
- ¼ teaspoon five-spice powder
- 1 pound boneless country-style pork ribs, trimmed of surface fat and excess gristle and sliced crosswise into ⅛-inch pieces (see note)
- ¼ teaspoon liquid smoke (optional)
- ½ cup low-sodium chicken broth
- 1 teaspoon cornstarch
- 2 medium garlic cloves, minced or pressed through garlic press (about 2 teaspoons)
- 2 teaspoons grated fresh ginger
- 4½ teaspoons vegetable oil
- 4 tablespoons Chinese rice cooking wine (Shao-Xing) or dry sherry (see note)
- ½ pound shiitake mushrooms, stems trimmed, caps cut in halves or thirds (about 3 cups)
- 2 bunches scallions, whites thinly sliced and greens cut into 1-inch pieces (about 2 cups)
- 1 small head Napa cabbage, halved, cored, and sliced crosswise into ½-inch strips (about 4 cups)
- 12 ounces fresh Chinese noodles or 8 ounces dried linguine (see note)
- 1 tablespoon Asian garlic-chili sauce

1. Bring 4 quarts water to boil in Dutch oven over high heat.

2. Whisk soy sauce, oyster sauce, hoisin sauce, sesame oil, and five-spice powder together in medium bowl. Place 3 tablespoons soy sauce mixture in large zipper-lock bag; add pork and liquid smoke, if using. Press out as much air as possible and seal bag, making sure that all pieces are coated with marinade. Refrigerate at least 15 minutes or up to 1 hour. Whisk broth and cornstarch into remaining soy sauce mixture in medium bowl. In separate small bowl, mix garlic and ginger with ½ teaspoon vegetable oil; set aside.

3. Heat 1 teaspoon vegetable oil in 12-inch cast-iron or nonstick skillet over high heat until just smoking. Add half of pork in single layer, breaking up clumps with wooden spoon. Cook, without stirring, 1 minute. Continue to cook, stirring occasionally, until browned, 2 to 3 minutes. Add 2 tablespoons wine to skillet; cook, stirring constantly, until liquid is reduced and pork is well coated, 30 to 60 seconds. Transfer pork to medium bowl and repeat with remaining pork, 1 teaspoon oil, and remaining 2 tablespoons wine. Wipe skillet clean with paper towels.

4. Return skillet to high heat, add 1 teaspoon vegetable oil, and heat until just smoking. Add mushrooms and cook, stirring occasionally, until light golden brown, 4 to 6 minutes. Add scallions and continue to cook, stirring occasionally, until scallions are wilted, 2 to 3 minutes longer; transfer vegetables to bowl with pork.

5. Add remaining teaspoon vegetable oil and cabbage to now-empty skillet; cook, stirring occasionally, until spotty brown, 3 to 5 minutes. Clear center of skillet; add garlic-ginger mixture and cook, mashing mixture with spoon, until fragrant, about 30 seconds. Stir garlic mixture into cabbage; return pork-vegetable mixture and chicken broth–soy mixture to skillet; simmer until thickened and ingredients are well incorporated, 1 to 2 minutes. Remove skillet from heat.

6. While cabbage is cooking, stir noodles into boiling water. Cook, stirring occasionally, until noodles are tender, 3 to 4 minutes for fresh Chinese noodles or 10 minutes for dried linguine. Drain noodles and transfer back to Dutch oven; add cooked stir-fry mixture and garlic-chili sauce, tossing noodles constantly, until sauce coats noodles. Serve immediately.

TASTING: Five-Spice Powder

Though recipes for five-spice powder can vary, its trademark warmth and pungency traditionally derive from cinnamon, cloves, fennel seed, star anise, and Szechuan peppercorns (white pepper and ginger are common substitutes). Grinding whole spices produces the freshest and most aromatic results, but we wondered if we could save time and money with a commercial blend. All five brands we tested turned out to be acceptable, but the best offered a "mellow" yet "sweet" and "fragrant" backdrop not too far from our homemade blend. For complete tasting results, go to www.cooksillustrated.com/october. –Elizabeth Bomze

BALANCED BLEND

DEAN & DELUCA Five Spice Blend

Price: $6.50 for 1.4 oz.

Comments: White pepper and a goodly amount of star anise contributed to the "nice depth" and "balanced heat and sweetness" that landed this mail-order brand in first place.

MORE SWEET THAN SPICE

PENZEYS Chinese Five Spice Powder

Price: $5.19 for 2.1 oz.

Comments: The strong presence of China cassia cinnamon gave this blend more sweetness than spice, which some tasters liked and others deemed "overwhelming."

MILDLY MEDICINAL

McCORMICK Gourmet Collection Chinese Five Spice

Price: $4.76 for 1.75 oz.

Comments: A heavy hand with fennel and star anise made this familiar supermarket brand taste "mildly medicinal."

Mushrooms 101

A comprehensive guide to buying, storing, and preparing mushrooms. BY CHARLES KELSEY

Long gone are the days when the only mushrooms in the produce aisle were white button, portobello, or cremini. Some stores display up to a dozen different kinds; many once available only seasonally are now farmed almost year-round. Cultivated or wild, common or rare, mushrooms are easy to prepare and add an intense flavor boost to everything from soups, stews, and sauces to meats, stuffings, and egg dishes.

BUYING

We recommend buying loose rather than prepackaged mushrooms so you can inspect their condition and quality. Look for mushrooms with whole, intact caps; avoid those with discoloration or dry, shriveled patches. The mushrooms should feel faintly damp, but not moist or slimy. Their texture should be springy and light, never spongy. Aroma is another important indicator of quality and intensity—the stronger the sweet, earthy scent, the more potent and flavorful the mushrooms. Sour or fishy-smelling mushrooms should always be avoided. Pick mushrooms with large caps and minimal stems since the latter are often discarded.

STORING

Due to their high moisture content, mushrooms are very perishable. They can go from plump to shriveled and slimy in no time. Over the years we've tested numerous storage methods to find the best approach.

DON'T wrap mushrooms in a paper bag—as directed by many sources—as it turns the fungi spongy and wrinkly.

DON'T cover mushrooms with a damp paper towel (another common technique), as it only speeds up their deterioration.

DO store loose mushrooms in a partially open zipper-lock bag, which maximizes air circulation without drying out the mushrooms. Leaving the bag slightly open allows for the release of the ethylene gas emitted from the mushrooms.

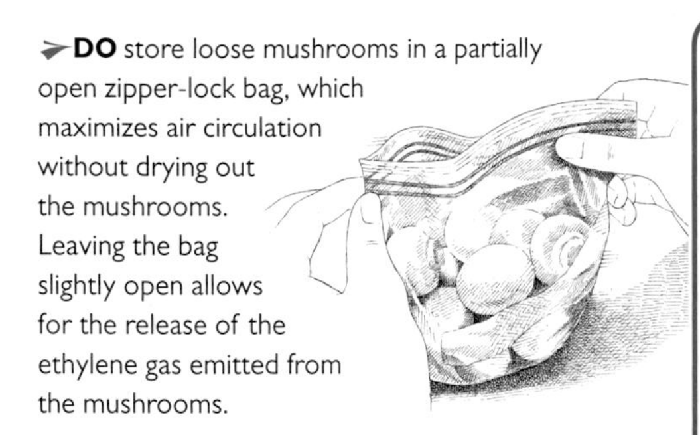

DO store packaged mushrooms in their original containers. These containers are designed to "breathe," maximizing the life of the mushrooms by balancing the retention of moisture and release of ethylene gas. If you open a sealed package of mushrooms but don't use all the contents, simply re-wrap the remaining mushrooms in the box with plastic wrap.

CLEANING

Many sources advise against washing mushrooms to avoid their soaking up any additional moisture and suggest brushing them instead. But after we learned that mushrooms are over 80 percent water, we began to question their ability to absorb more liquid. To find out, we rinsed mushrooms in cold water, weighing them before and after their wash. We found that six ounces of mushrooms gained only about a quarter ounce of water, and most of this was beaded on the surface. Cut mushrooms are another story. The exposed flesh will absorb water like a sponge, so rinse mushrooms before slicing them. And be careful not to wash mushrooms until you are ready to cook them or they will turn slimy.

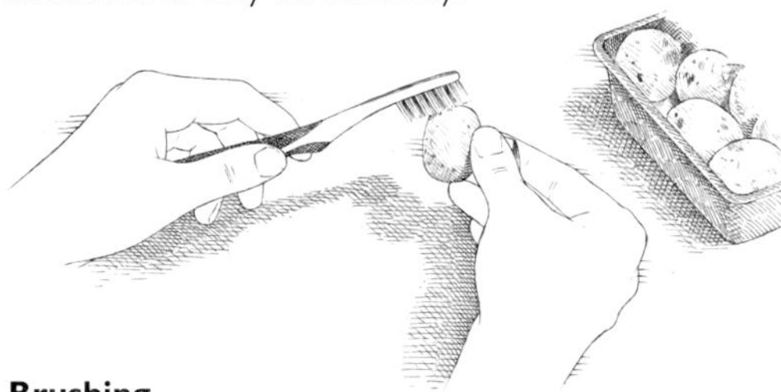

Brushing

Brushing off mushrooms with a dry toothbrush makes sense when you plan to serve them raw, as rinsing can cause discoloration.

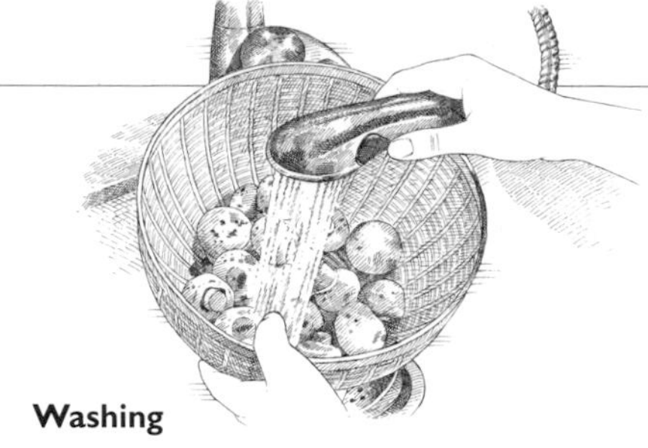

Washing

1. Place mushrooms in a salad spinner basket and spray with water until dirt is removed.

2. Put the basket into the salad spinner and spin the mushrooms dry. Use a paper towel to blot up any remaining moisture.

How to Use Dried Mushrooms

To boost mushroom flavor in soups, stews, stuffings, and risottos, we often turn to dried porcini, also known as cèpes.

Buying

Look for packages with large, thick, tan or brown (not black) pieces. Avoid packages with lots of dust and crumbled bits and keep an eye out for small pinholes, telltale signs that worms got into the mushrooms.

Rehydrating

Place the dried porcini in a small strainer and rinse. Transfer them to a microwave-safe bowl, add water to cover, and seal the bowl with plastic wrap. Cut steam vents in the plastic wrap and microwave on high power for 30 seconds. Remove the bowl from the microwave and let stand, covered, until the mushrooms soften, about 5 minutes.

Getting Rid of Grit

1. Use a fork to lift the rehydrated mushrooms from the soaking liquid without stirring up the sand. If the mushrooms still feel gritty, rinse them briefly under cool running water.

2. To remove grit from the soaking liquid, pour it through a strainer lined with a coffee filter or a paper towel set over a measuring cup. Save this flavorful liquid for other uses.

MUSHROOM VARIETIES

PORTOBELLO

Ranging in diameter from 4 to 6 inches, portobellos are the giants of the Agaricus clan. Their dense flesh is steaklike, with a robust flavor.

Buying: Choose portobellos with fully intact caps and dry gills; avoid those with wet, damaged gills.

Prepping: To avoid a muddy-looking sauce, gently scrape out the portobello's black gills with a spoon before cooking.

Best ways to cook: Grill, Sauté, Roast

SHIITAKE

This variety is tan to dark brown. The caps have a chewy texture and nutty flavor, but the stems are tough, woody, and inedible and should be trimmed and discarded.

Buying: Look for smaller shiitakes that have domed, thick caps, with edges that curl under the cap (a sign of freshness). They should be dry—but not desiccated or wrinkly—with a nutty, earthy aroma.

Best way to cook: Sauté

WHITE BUTTON

The mild flavor of this most common cultivated variety becomes rich and meaty when cooked.

Best ways to cook: Grill, Sauté, Roast

CREMINI

Basically miniature portobellos harvested before reaching maturity, cremini are browner and firmer than white buttons and have a more intense flavor.

Best ways to cook: Grill, Sauté, Roast

OYSTER

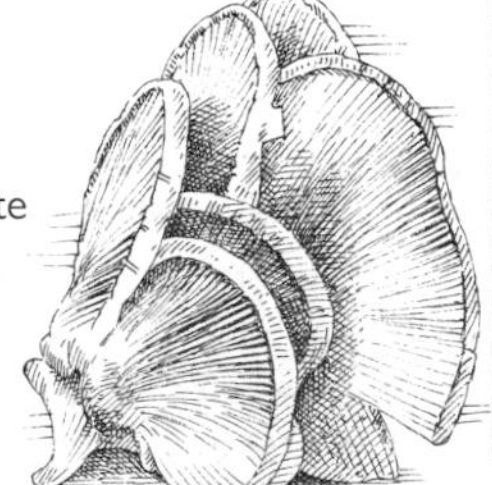

These large, fan-shaped mushrooms are commonly beige, cream, or gray. Delicate and best cooked only briefly, they have a springy texture and subtle briny flavor.

Best way to cook: Sauté

BLACK TRUMPET/HORN OF PLENTY

Related to chanterelles, black trumpets are hollow and drier. They have a chewy texture and an almost smoky flavor.

Buying: Avoid dried-out, leathery mushrooms and those that are solid black (a sign of old age).

Cleaning: These particularly dirty mushrooms need to be rinsed in several changes of water. Halve them first to loosen any grit hiding inside their hollow center.

Best way to cook: Sauté

MOREL

Ranging from blond to black, morels are hollow and porous with a mild, nutty flavor that's less potent than other wild mushrooms.

Buying: When buying wild morels, pick mushrooms with minimal grit and be sure to check inside the hollow center for insects.

Cleaning: While the cultivated kind is very clean, wild morels need to be thoroughly washed. After trimming off and discarding the bottoms of the stems, halve the mushrooms and rinse them in several changes of water.

Best way to cook: Sauté

MAITAKE/ HEN-OF-THE-WOODS

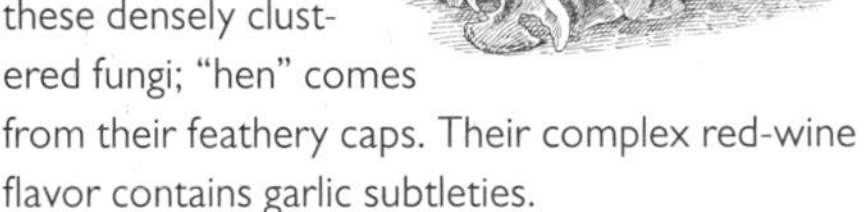

Maitake is the Japanese name for these densely clustered fungi; "hen" comes from their feathery caps. Their complex red-wine flavor contains garlic subtleties.

Best way to cook: Sauté

CHANTERELLE

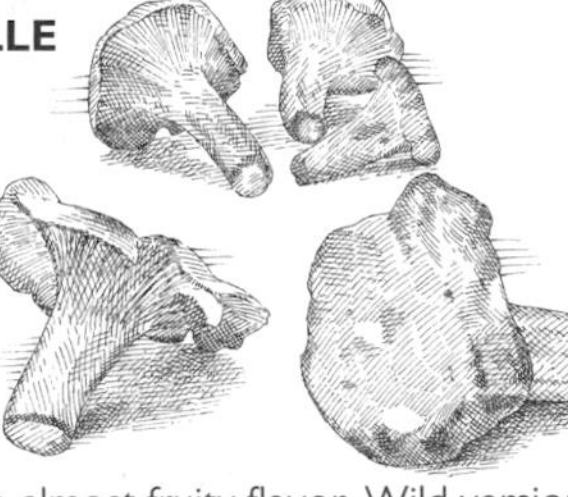

Pale yellow to deep orange, chanterelles are trumpet-shaped and dense. They have an assertively nutty, almost fruity flavor. Wild versions are intensely flavored.

Best way to cook: Sauté

Simple Mushroom Recipes

High-heat cooking methods are a must for mushrooms, causing them to shed excess liquid quickly so they can start to brown, thus deepening their flavors.

GRILLED MUSHROOMS

SERVES 4

Portobello, button, and cremini mushrooms are our favorites for grilling.

For portobellos: Brush 4 mushrooms—cleaned, stems removed—with 2 tablespoons olive oil and season with salt and pepper to taste. Grill over medium-hot fire, turning once, until browned and tender, 8 to 12 minutes.

For button/cremini mushrooms: Toss 1 pound mushrooms—cleaned, stems trimmed—with 2 tablespoons olive oil and salt and pepper to taste. Skewer mushrooms (see illustration below) and grill over medium-hot fire, turning several times, until browned and tender, 8 to 12 minutes.

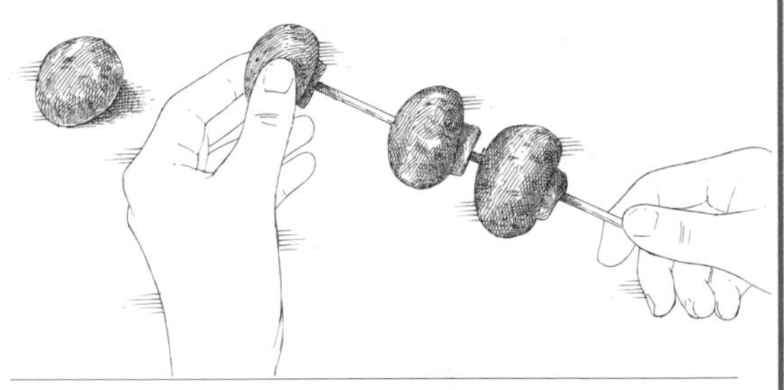

SAUTÉED MUSHROOMS

SERVES 4

All mushroom varieties respond well to sautéing.

1. Heat 1 tablespoon oil in 12-inch skillet over medium-high heat. Add 1½ pounds mushrooms—cleaned, stems trimmed, quartered (if large) or halved (if small)—and cook, stirring occasionally, until mushrooms release liquid, about 5 minutes.
2. Increase heat to high and cook, stirring occasionally, until liquid has evaporated, about 8 minutes.
3. Add 1 tablespoon unsalted butter, reduce heat to medium, and continue to cook, stirring once every minute, until mushrooms are dark brown, about 8 minutes.
4. Add 1 medium shallot, minced, and 1 tablespoon minced fresh thyme and cook until softened, about 3 minutes.
5. Add ¼ cup dry Marsala and cook until liquid has evaporated, about 2 minutes. Season with salt and pepper.

ROASTED MUSHROOMS

SERVES 4

Roasting helps wick away moisture from dense, meaty mushrooms such as button, cremini, and portobello.

1. Adjust oven rack to lowest position and heat oven to 450 degrees. Toss 1 pound mushrooms—cleaned, stems trimmed, quartered or halved—with 2 tablespoons olive oil and salt and pepper to taste.
2. Arrange in single layer on rimmed baking sheet; roast until released juices have nearly evaporated and mushroom surfaces touching baking sheet are browned, 12 to 15 minutes.
3. Turn mushrooms with spatula. Continue to roast until liquid has evaporated and mushrooms are brown, 5 to 10 minutes longer.

Creamless Creamy Tomato Soup

Plain tomato soup can be thin and sharp. Adding cream—the usual stodgy solution—merely dulls it. We wanted to tame the tartness without losing flavor.

BY J. KENJI ALT

Tomato soup should have it all: good looks, velvety smoothness, and a bright, tomatoey taste balanced by the fruit's natural sweetness. But poor versions are the norm, either featuring an acidic, watery broth or an overdose of cream. Though it's meant to tame tartness and lend body, I've always found that adding any amount of cream goes hand-in-hand with muting flavor. I wanted soup with rich tomato flavor and a satisfying texture. Could I get there without the cream?

The first step in the process was to pass over fresh tomatoes for canned, which are almost always far better than your average supermarket tomato, boasting more consistently rich and concentrated flavor. Plus they're already peeled—a big timesaver for soup. I opted for whole tomatoes rather than diced or crushed; the latter two types often contain calcium chloride, an additive that prevents them from breaking down completely, compromising texture. I then developed a simple working recipe, sautéing onions and garlic in butter, stirring in the tomatoes and a can of chicken broth, and then giving the whole thing a quick spin in the blender. The results were decent, but dull.

If cream subdues tomato flavor, could the milk solids in the butter be tamping it down as well? I substituted extra-virgin olive oil for the butter and found that the soup brightened as a result. A few more small changes—a bay leaf and a pinch of red pepper flakes sautéed with the onions—upped the flavor significantly. To compensate for the flavor the oil lost as it cooked, I drizzled a little more over the soup before it went into the blender. Most tasters also welcomed a couple tablespoons of brandy.

Taming Tartness

Now that I had my flavor profile nailed down, I was on to bigger problems: tartness and thin texture. Sugar is often used as a means to combat tartness. We preferred brown sugar to one-dimensional white sugar and corn syrup, but sugar could only take us so far—add enough to tone down tartness and the soup becomes unpalatably sweet.

I needed a thickener that would also help temper the acid. Flavor-dulling dairy ingredients were definitely out, but what about a starch? Cooking flour along with the onions to form a roux made for a thicker soup, but the texture turned slimy instead of creamy, and it did nothing for flavor. Cornstarch produced similar results. I scoured our cookbook library before I found inspiration in another tomato-based soup: gazpacho. This Spanish classic is made from tomatoes, olive oil, and garlic, along with an unusual element for thickening: bread. But gazpacho is served cold. Would bread work as a thickener for hot soup?

I tore several slices of sandwich bread into pieces and stirred them into the pot with the tomatoes and chicken broth as they simmered. When I processed the mixture in the blender, I ended up with bread chunks that swam in a sea of broth and resisted being sucked down into the blender's spinning blades. To cut back on the liquid in the blender, I decided to try leaving out the broth until the very end. With my next batch of soup, I pureed the tomatoes with the aromatics and bread before returning the mixture to the pan and whisking in the broth. One taste and I knew I'd hit on just the right solution. My tomato soup had the same velvety texture as the creamy kind, but with bright, fresh flavor. None of my tasters even guessed that my soup contained a secret ingredient. Only after the pot was empty did I divulge it.

Bread—not cream—is the secret to our soup's creamy texture.

CREAMLESS CREAMY TOMATO SOUP

SERVES 6 TO 8

If half of the soup fills your blender by more than two-thirds, process the soup in three batches. You can also use an immersion blender to process the soup directly in the pot. For an even smoother soup, pass the pureed mixture through a fine-mesh strainer before stirring in the chicken broth in step 2. Serve this soup with Grilled Cheese Sandwiches for a Crowd or topped with Butter Croutons (for our free recipes, go to www.cooksillustrated.com/october).

- ¼ cup extra-virgin olive oil, plus more for drizzling
- 1 medium onion, chopped medium (about 1 cup)
- 3 medium garlic cloves, minced or pressed through garlic press (about 1 tablespoon)
- Pinch hot red pepper flakes (optional)
- 1 bay leaf
- 2 (28-ounce) cans whole tomatoes packed in juice
- 1 tablespoon brown sugar
- 3 large slices good-quality white sandwich bread, crusts removed, torn into 1-inch pieces
- 2 cups low-sodium chicken broth
- 2 tablespoons brandy (optional)
- Table salt and ground black pepper
- ¼ cup chopped fresh chives

1. Heat 2 tablespoons oil in Dutch oven over medium-high heat until shimmering. Add onion, garlic, red pepper flakes (if using), and bay leaf. Cook, stirring frequently, until onion is translucent, 3 to 5 minutes. Stir in tomatoes and their juice. Using potato masher, mash until no pieces bigger than 2 inches remain. Stir in sugar and bread; bring soup to boil. Reduce heat to medium and cook, stirring occasionally, until bread is completely saturated and starts to break down, about 5 minutes. Remove and discard bay leaf.

2. Transfer half of soup to blender. Add 1 tablespoon oil and process until soup is smooth and creamy, 2 to 3 minutes. Transfer to large bowl and repeat with remaining soup and oil. Rinse out Dutch oven and return soup to pot. Stir in chicken broth and brandy (if using). Return soup to boil and season to taste with salt and pepper. Serve soup in individual bowls. Sprinkle each portion with pepper and chives and drizzle with olive oil.

Quick Glazes for Grilled Chicken

Most glazes are too sweet and require too much work. Our goal was bold flavor in a no-hassle glaze.

BY DAVID PAZMIÑO

Most glazes are distractingly sweet and one-dimensional, relying on sugary ingredients for sticking power. A super sweet glaze made mostly of honey, maple syrup, or brown sugar is fine for a rich, salty ham, but when it comes to mild chicken, something more savory makes sense. I wanted to develop a variety of glazes that would complement grilled chicken. Because I would already be out at the grill, I wanted glazes that wouldn't require much stovetop cooking.

My first stop was the test kitchen pantry, where I scanned the shelves for ingredients thick enough to serve as a base. Fruit preserves stood out, as they are commonly used in glazes; I would just need to keep their sweetness in check. I also decided to try ketchup, peanut butter, and hoisin sauce. None are overly sweet, and all have a thick, sticky consistency that I hoped would cling nicely to the chicken during grilling.

I began by adding hefty amounts of tangy Dijon and whole-grain mustards to apricot preserves, then pulsing the mixture in a food processor to puree it. This glaze was only mildly sweet and complemented the grilled chicken beautifully. Next, I created a glaze based on the flavors of a traditional barbecue sauce, spiking ketchup with soy sauce, cider vinegar, and mustard for salty and sour notes. Peanut butter and hoisin sauce were my final challenges. Once thinned with coconut milk and rice vinegar, respectively, they were transformed into Indonesian- and Asian-inspired glazes.

Because these glazes weren't gloppy and thick like sugar-based glazes, a thin coating was all that clung to the chicken. No matter: Adding bold ingredients such as garlic, ginger, herbs, and spices made a little go a long way, and passing extra glaze at the table to use as a dipping sauce boosted the flavor of every bite.

Out at the grill, I found it best to wait to apply the glaze until the chicken was nearly cooked; because of the high sugar content, brushing it on any earlier caused burning. (That meant waiting until breasts reached an internal temperature of 155 degrees and legs or thighs reached 170 degrees; see "How to Glaze Grilled Chicken," at left below.) These four glazes can be used on bone-in or boneless chicken parts.

How to Glaze Grilled Chicken

1. Grill chicken until instant-read thermometer inserted into thickest part registers 155 degrees for breasts and 170 degrees for legs or thighs.

2. Brush one side of chicken pieces with half of glaze reserved for grilling, then turn chicken glaze-side down and cook 2 minutes.

3. Brush second side of chicken with remaining glaze reserved for grilling, then turn chicken and cook until browned and instant-read thermometer registers 160 degrees for breasts and 175 degrees for legs or thighs, 1 to 3 minutes longer. Let chicken rest 5 minutes. Serve, passing remaining glaze at table.

APRICOT-MUSTARD GLAZE

MAKES ABOUT 1½ CUPS, ENOUGH TO GLAZE 4½ POUNDS CHICKEN

- ¾ cup apricot preserves
- ¼ cup whole-grain mustard
- 3 tablespoons Dijon mustard
- 4 tablespoons unsalted butter, melted and cooled
- 2 medium shallots, chopped coarse
- ½ teaspoon table salt
- 3 tablespoons water

Process all ingredients in food processor until thoroughly combined, 20 to 30 seconds, scraping down sides of workbowl as needed. Reserve half of glaze for serving and use other half to brush on chicken while grilling (see "How to Glaze Grilled Chicken," left).

HOISIN-SESAME GLAZE

MAKES ABOUT 1½ CUPS, ENOUGH TO GLAZE 4½ POUNDS CHICKEN

- ⅔ cup hoisin sauce
- ¼ cup rice vinegar
- 2 tablespoons dry sherry
- 1 tablespoon vegetable oil
- 2 teaspoons toasted sesame oil
- 1 (1-inch) piece fresh ginger, peeled and sliced thin
- 2 medium garlic cloves, chopped coarse
- 6 scallions, chopped coarse
- ½ teaspoon ground white pepper (optional)

Process all ingredients in food processor until thoroughly combined, 20 to 30 seconds, scraping down sides of workbowl as needed. Reserve half of glaze for serving and use other half to brush on chicken while grilling (see "How to Glaze Grilled Chicken," left).

INDONESIAN PEANUT GLAZE

MAKES ABOUT 1½ CUPS, ENOUGH TO GLAZE 4½ POUNDS CHICKEN

- ½ cup creamy peanut butter
- ⅓ cup coconut milk
- ⅓ cup lightly packed fresh cilantro leaves
- ¼ cup honey
- 1 teaspoon grated zest and 5 tablespoons juice from 2–3 limes
- 2 tablespoons water
- 1 tablespoon fish sauce
- ½ teaspoon hot red pepper flakes
- 1 (1-inch) piece fresh ginger, peeled and sliced thin
- 2 garlic cloves, chopped coarse
- ½ teaspoon curry powder (optional)

Process all ingredients in food processor until thoroughly combined, 20 to 30 seconds, scraping down sides of workbowl as needed. Reserve half of glaze for serving and use other half to brush on chicken while grilling (see "How to Glaze Grilled Chicken," left).

BARBECUE GLAZE

MAKES ABOUT 1½ CUPS, ENOUGH TO GLAZE 4½ POUNDS CHICKEN

- 1 cup ketchup
- ¼ cup packed light brown sugar
- 2 tablespoons soy sauce
- 2 tablespoons cider vinegar
- 2 tablespoons Dijon mustard
- 2 medium garlic cloves, chopped coarse
- 1½ teaspoons chili powder
- ½ teaspoon liquid smoke

Process all ingredients in food processor until thoroughly combined, 20 to 30 seconds, scraping down sides of workbowl as needed. Reserve half of glaze for serving and use other half to brush on chicken while grilling (see "How to Glaze Grilled Chicken," left).

Introducing Pizza Bianca

Italians have a way to create a superbly crisp, chewy crust that sidesteps the single biggest hassle of making pizza: rolling out the dough. What's their secret?

BY DAVID PAZMIÑO

During a trip to Rome a few years ago, I couldn't help but notice the lines of people waiting outside local bakeries for a regional specialty: pizza bianca. Intrigued, I waited my turn. When a server handed me a piece taken from a long, rectangular plank, it looked like no pizza I'd ever seen. With no cheese or sauce—just a gloss of olive oil and flakes of salt—it looked more like focaccia than pizza. But one bite into its crisp exterior and chewy, bubbly middle and I immediately forgot all about nomenclature—even toppings. I headed right back to the end of the line for more.

When I got home I collected a few pizza bianca recipes and even spent a day working with an American practitioner of the craft, cookbook author Daniel Leader, owner of Bread Alone, a bakery in Boiceville, New York. I discovered it's made from the same basic ingredients as our familiar pizza crusts: flour, water, yeast, and salt (plus a little sugar). And the general method is no more difficult: Mix the ingredients, knead them until dough forms (we use a stand mixer fitted with a dough hook), allow the dough to rise for a couple of hours, and you're good to go. So what's the difference?

Classic pizza bianca, above, makes a great snack, but adding mozzarella and tomatoes (not shown) turns the same chewy crust into dinner.

As it turns out, there's a big one: Italians use significantly more water, creating a dough so wet it's impossible to roll out. While most pizza doughs don't exceed 60 percent hydration—meaning there are 6 ounces of water for every 10 ounces of flour—pizza bianca dough ranges from 70 to over 100 percent. In Italy, pizza makers use a long-handled wooden peel, or paddle, to deposit and stretch the gloppy dough across the far end of the oven.

There was no way I was going to try stretching dough out in my own oven, no matter how good the resulting crust. But if I could simply press this very wet dough into a baking sheet—and add a few toppings to turn a snack into dinner—I might never go back to making any other kind of pizza again.

Working with Wet Dough

I was ready to get to work. I combined flour, water, yeast, and salt in a mixing bowl, opting for a hydration level around 90 percent. More water might make the dough gooey and difficult to handle; any less and I wouldn't get the super chewy, bubbly interior I was hoping for (see "Pizza Water Works," page 21). Though I knew wet batter would require a lengthy kneading time, I wasn't prepared for the 30 minutes it took for dough to form, even with the mixer on high. At high speed (a must for wet dough), I had to baby-sit the mixer to keep it from wobbling off the countertop. Unless I could cut down the kneading process to 5 to 10 minutes, as for other types of bread or pizza, this dough would be more hassle than it was worth.

I took a step back and thought about the mechanics of bread-making. The goal in making any dough is to create gluten, the strong elastic network of cross-linked proteins that give bread its crumb structure. Kneading aids gluten formation by bringing the protein molecules in flour into alignment so they can bind. I remembered from our No-Knead Bread recipe (January/February 2008) that a far different approach—a long rest—has the same exact effect. In that recipe, we let the dough sit for 8 hours, which produced so much gluten, it only took a few seconds of kneading to create a loaf with a very open, chewy texture. I didn't want to wait around for a day just to make pizza, but what if I allowed the flour and water to sit for a modest interval—say, less than an hour? After experimenting, I found that 20 minutes of resting was enough to reduce the kneading time to less than 10 minutes—a perfectly acceptable length of time to stand over my mixer.

Next step in the proceedings: transferring my dough to an oiled bowl and leaving it to rise. Two hours later, the dough had tripled in volume. Though sticky, the wet dough proved remarkably easy to shape. As I pressed it out over an 18- by 13-inch baking sheet, it showed little of the "spring back" that can make firmer dough annoying to work with. And with no rolling out, I was avoiding the single biggest challenge of pizza-making: getting the dough from the counter onto the baking stone without tearing it and having to start over.

Now ready to bake, I tried our typical protocol for pizza recipes: Let the dough rest 5 to 10 minutes, then place it on a heated pizza stone positioned on a lower rack of a 500-degree oven. (I found that setting the baking sheet on a hot stone was a must for a crisp exterior.) But when I tried to remove the baked pizza from the pan, it stuck resolutely, leaving behind swaths of crust—a clear sign that not enough moisture had cooked off. The solution: I reduced the oven temperature to 450 degrees and baked the dough on the middle rack, which allowed me to leave it in the oven longer. The pizza I pulled from the oven was as golden and crisp on the outside, and as chewy and flavorful on the inside, as any pizza bianca I had sampled in Italy.

COOK'S LIVE Original Test Kitchen Videos
www.cooksillustrated.com
HOW TO MAKE
- Pizza Bianca

VIDEO TIPS
- What's the difference between instant and active dry yeast?
- How water amounts affect pizza crust texture

A Question of Toppings

Up to now, I had been loyal to authentic versions, adorning pizzas with nothing more than salt, a handful of rosemary (added halfway through cooking to avoid burning), and a thin coat of olive oil brushed on at the end. As good as this was, I wanted a pizza I could serve as a meal. I settled on tomato sauce and mozzarella for a variation I knew would please even the pickiest eaters in my household, and sausage for another. Adding these toppings halfway through baking was the key—spreading them over the raw dough at the beginning led to a gummy crust. Using a light hand was also essential, as too much of any one ingredient overpowers the flavor of the crust and detracts from its texture.

With the technique for dealing with wet dough perfected, and toppings successfully added, I had discovered how to adapt a classic Italian recipe for my kitchen at home. This easy, all-purpose pizza crust is one I'll return to again and again.

AT A GLANCE | SECRETS TO NO-ROLL PIZZA

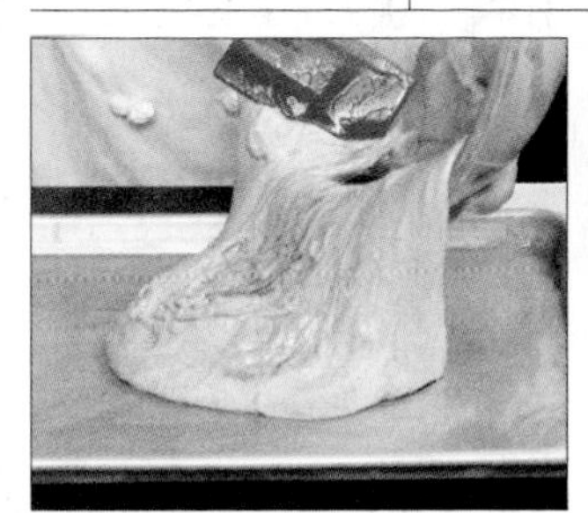

1. The dough for pizza bianca is far too wet to roll out. Instead, pour it onto a well-oiled baking sheet.

2. Shaping is easy: Press the dough from its middle toward the edges of the pan.

3. To cook the moisture off, bake the crust on a pizza stone on the middle rack of a 450-degree oven.

PIZZA BIANCA

SERVES 6 TO 8

Serve the pizza by itself as a snack or with soup or salad for a light meal. Once the dough has been placed in the oiled bowl, it can be transferred to the refrigerator and kept for up to 24 hours. Bring the dough to room temperature, 2 to 2½ hours, before proceeding with step 4. When kneading the dough on high speed, the mixer tends to wobble and move on the counter. Place a towel or shelf liner under the mixer and watch it at all times during mixing. Handle the dough with slightly oiled hands. Resist flouring your fingers or the dough might stick. This recipe was developed using an 18- by 13-inch baking sheet. Smaller baking sheets can be used, but because the pizza will be thicker, baking times will be longer. If not using a pizza stone, increase the oven temperature to 500 degrees and set the rack to the lowest position; the cooking time might increase by 3 to 5 minutes and the exterior won't be as crisp. For our free recipe for Pizza Bianca with Caramelized Onions and Gruyère, go to www.cooksillustrated.com/october.

- 3 cups (15 ounces) unbleached all-purpose flour
- 1⅔ cups (13½ ounces) water, room temperature
- 1¼ teaspoons table salt
- 1½ teaspoons instant yeast
- 1¼ teaspoons sugar
- 5 tablespoons extra-virgin olive oil
- 1 teaspoon kosher salt
- 2 tablespoons whole fresh rosemary leaves

1. Place towel or shelf liner beneath stand mixer to prevent wobbling. Mix flour, water, and table salt in bowl of stand mixer fitted with dough hook on low speed until no patches of dry flour remain, 3 to 4 minutes, occasionally scraping sides and bottom of bowl. Turn off mixer and let dough rest 20 minutes.

2. Sprinkle yeast and sugar over dough. Knead on low speed until fully combined, 1 to 2 minutes, occasionally scraping sides and bottom of bowl. Increase mixer speed to high and knead until dough is glossy, smooth, and pulls away from sides of bowl, 6 to 10 minutes. (Dough will only pull away from sides while mixer is on. When mixer is off, dough will fall back to sides.)

3. Using fingers, coat large bowl with 1 tablespoon oil, rubbing excess oil from fingers onto blade of rubber spatula. Using oiled spatula, transfer dough to bowl and pour 1 tablespoon oil over top. Flip dough over once so it is well coated with oil; cover tightly with plastic wrap. Let dough rise at room temperature until nearly tripled in volume and large bubbles have formed, 2 to 2½ hours.

4. One hour before baking pizza, adjust oven rack to middle position, place pizza stone on rack, and heat oven to 450 degrees.

5. Coat rimmed baking sheet with 2 tablespoons oil. Using rubber spatula, turn dough out onto baking sheet along with any oil in bowl. Using fingertips, press dough out toward edges of pan, taking care not to tear it. (Dough will not fit snugly into corners. If dough resists stretching, let it relax for 5 to 10 minutes before trying to stretch again.) Let dough rest in pan until slightly bubbly, 5 to 10 minutes. Using dinner fork, poke surface of dough 30 to 40 times and sprinkle with kosher salt.

6. Bake until golden brown, 20 to 30 minutes, sprinkling rosemary over top and rotating baking sheet halfway through baking. Using metal spatula, transfer pizza to cutting board. Brush dough lightly with remaining tablespoon oil. Slice and serve immediately.

SCIENCE: Pizza Water Works

To achieve its chewy, bubbly texture, our recipe for Pizza Bianca calls for 9 parts water to 10 parts flour—an almost 30 percent higher level of hydration than in most other pizza dough. Water aids the development of gluten, the network of crosslinked proteins that gives bread its internal structure and chew. Up to a point, the more water in the dough, the stronger and more elastic the gluten strands and the chewier the bread. These strands, in turn, help to support the air bubbles formed as the dough bakes, preventing them from bursting and creating an open, airy crust.

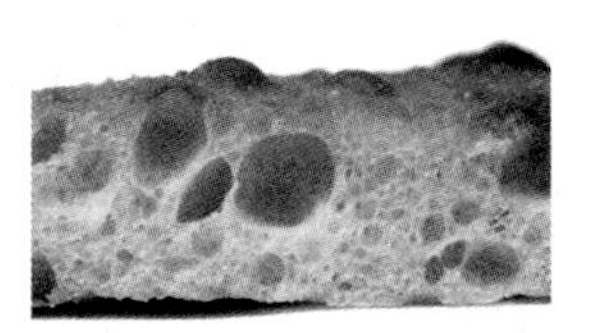

90% HYDRATION
More water, bubblier crust.

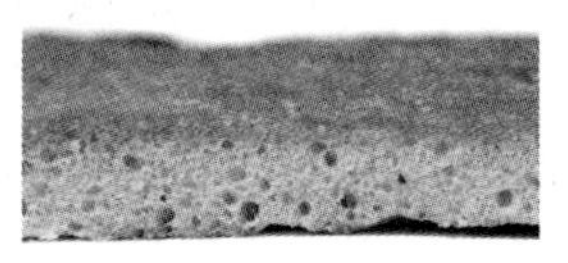

60% HYDRATION
Less water, denser crust.

PIZZA BIANCA WITH TOMATOES AND MOZZARELLA

Place 28-ounce can of crushed tomatoes in fine-mesh strainer set over medium bowl. Let sit 30 minutes, stirring 3 times to allow juices to drain. Combine ¾ cup tomato solids, 1 tablespoon olive oil, and ⅛ teaspoon table salt. (Save remaining solids and juice for another use.) Follow recipe for Pizza Bianca, omitting kosher salt and rosemary. In step 6, bake pizza until spotty brown, 15 to 17 minutes. Remove pizza from oven, spread tomato mixture evenly over surface, and sprinkle with 6 ounces (1½ cups) shredded mozzarella (do not brush pizza with oil). Return pizza to oven and continue to bake until cheese begins to brown in spots, 5 to 10 minutes longer.

PIZZA BIANCA WITH TOMATOES, SAUSAGE, AND FONTINA

Remove ¾ pound sweet Italian sausage from casings. Cook sausage in large nonstick skillet over medium heat, breaking into small pieces with wooden spoon, until no longer pink, about 8 minutes. Transfer to paper towel–lined plate. Follow recipe for Pizza Bianca with Tomatoes and Mozzarella, substituting 8 ounces (2 cups) shredded fontina cheese for mozzarella and sprinkling sausage over pizza with cheese.

Introducing Sticky Toffee Pudding

Studded with dates and coated in a sweet toffee sauce, this moist, rich cake is a British favorite. How would it translate to the American kitchen?

⋟ BY THE COOK'S ILLUSTRATED TEST KITCHEN ⋞

Similar to plum pudding, sticky toffee pudding is a sophisticated, richly flavored, grown-up dessert; one that has roots reaching deep into the Anglo culinary past. What the Brits call a "pudding" is not pudding by American standards. Rather, it's a rich, spongy cake full of dates and lots of butter. This cake, baked in individual ramekins or a single baking dish, is smothered in an unapologetically sweet toffee sauce created from butter, cream, and sugar.

This is a wickedly good dessert—one that is truly worth its calories and the little bit of fuss it takes to make. But in bringing this dessert into the American home kitchen, we wanted to make a few adjustments. Our primary goals were to make the texture of the cake foolproof and showcase the deep fruity flavor of the dates while keeping the sweetness in check. And we'd have to find a substitute for treacle, the molasseslike sweetener traditional to this dessert that's nearly impossible to find in American supermarkets.

Holes poked in the cake allow toffee sauce to seep into its center.

Proof in the Pudding

After reviewing a slew of recipes, we realized there was nothing terribly complicated about this dish; no separated eggs, sifted flour, or finicky mixing techniques. Most recipes followed either a standard creaming method (sugar and butter whipped until light and fluffy, eggs beaten in, and finally, the dry ingredients incorporated) or a basic quick-bread method (dry and wet ingredients mixed separately and then combined). Working with a basic ingredient list of 1¼ cups flour, two eggs, ¾ cup water, 1½ cups chopped dates, 1 cup granulated sugar (we'd find a substitute for treacle later), and a stick of butter, we compared the two mixing methods head to head. The cakes made with the creaming method had a light, delicate texture that turned to mush when soaked in toffee sauce. Happily, the easier quick-bread technique produced a denser, springier, coarser crumb—just what we wanted. It was important, however, to mix the batter gently. Overmixing encouraged gluten development and resulted in tough cakes.

With a full stick of butter, the cakes were spectacularly rich and somewhat greasy. We reduced the amount tablespoon by tablespoon, finally settling on four tablespoons of butter and 1¼ cups of flour—half as much butter as many recipes call for. With this adjustment, the cakes were still appropriately rich but didn't leave a slick coating on the tongue.

The next step was to find a suitable replacement for the treacle, a byproduct of refined sugar similar to molasses. A straight-up molasses substitution overwhelmed the fruity flavor of the dates. Reducing the molasses to just a couple tablespoons and combining it with granulated sugar yielded acceptable results, but using brown sugar (made commercially by mixing white sugar with molasses) was easier. Dark brown sugar provided a robust richness, while light brown sugar was subtler. Since tasters were evenly split between light and dark, we decided to leave the matter up to personal preference. A modest amount of brown sugar (¾ cup) yielded a sweet but not cloying cake.

To bake the cakes, some recipes call for simply placing the ramekins in the oven, while others specify the gentler, more even cooking method of baking the batter-filled ramekins in a bain-marie, or water bath. Baked without steam, the puddings ended up with an unappealing, dry consistency. We got the moist, springy crumb we wanted when we placed the batter-filled ramekins in a roasting pan, added boiling water, covered the pan with aluminum foil, and baked them. During baking, the water filled the pan with steam, cooking the cakes and maintaining moisture. The key to effective steaming, we found, is to make sure that the aluminum foil forms an airtight seal around the pan.

The Dating Game

Next issue: date flavor. The chopped dates for this cake are traditionally soaked in baking soda–laced water, intended to soften their papery skins (see "A Remedy for Tough Dates," page 23), and though the dates were certainly tender prepared this way, their concentrated fruity flavor didn't permeate the cake. Replacing the water in the cake batter with an equal amount of soaking liquid from the dates improved matters, but we needed to take a more drastic step.

What if we were to completely pulverize the dates before incorporating them, so that the batter would be studded with minuscule bits of dates? For our next batch, we placed half the dates in the food processor with the brown sugar and processed them until the dates were chopped into very fine pieces. Bingo. Every bite of cake was now full of fruity date

TECHNIQUE

STEAMING THE PUDDINGS

Our sticky toffee pudding recipe results in a dessert that's neither a pudding (as most American cooks understand the term) nor a conventional cake. Here, pudding refers to a moist, spongy cake that achieves its unique texture from being steamed in a water bath in the oven.

Place the batter-filled ramekins in a roasting pan, add freshly boiled water to the pan, and cover the pan tightly with aluminum foil to create a super moist environment that steams the puddings.

SCIENCE:

A Remedy for Tough Dates

Most recipes for sticky toffee pudding call for softening the tough, papery skins of dried dates by soaking them in baking soda–laced water.

EXPERIMENT

To verify the validity of this practice, we compared dates that had been soaked in baking soda–water to dates soaked in plain water.

RESULTS

The dates soaked in baking soda–water were indeed soft and tender, while the skins of the plain water dates were leathery.

EXPLANATION

The skins of dried dates contain pectin, an acidic compound that acts as a glue, holding the cells of the date skin together. Soaking the dates in alkaline baking soda water sparks an acid-alkaline chemical reaction. When an acid and an alkaline come in contact, they react to form sodium salts (not to be confused with table salt). The sodium salts are soluble in water and thus get washed away from between the cells of the date skins, weakening and softening them. –J. Kenji Alt

flavor, and the cakes still had plenty of larger chunks of sticky dates.

A Sticky Subject

With perfectly moist, spongy cakes and full date flavor, we moved on to our next task: dealing with the "sticky," or the toffee sauce. Every single British recipe we found called for a simple blend of butter, brown sugar or treacle, and heavy cream. We found these sauces to be tooth-achingly sweet, even when we increased the cream and reduced the sugar. The solution? A squeeze of lemon juice and a capful of rum. Together, they cut through the sugar and add brightness.

As we poured the sauce over the puddings, one last problem revealed itself: The cakes refused to absorb enough sauce, and we wanted them to be thoroughly soaked. Poking the cakes with a toothpick before anointing them with sauce solved the problem. Our next and final batch of puddings truly lived up to its "sticky" moniker.

INDIVIDUAL STICKY TOFFEE PUDDING CAKES

SERVES 8

To make the cakes ahead of time, cover and refrigerate the unbaked batter for up to 24 hours; bake as directed in step 4. The sauce can be made up to 2 days ahead of time; reheat on medium-high heat in the microwave, stirring often, until hot, about 3 minutes. When baking, it is important to form a tight seal with the foil to trap the steam inside the roasting pan.

Pudding Cakes

- 4 tablespoons (½ stick) unsalted butter, melted, plus extra for ramekins
- 1¼ cups (6¼ ounces) unbleached all-purpose flour, plus extra for ramekins
- 8 ounces whole pitted dates (about 1½ cups lightly packed), cut crosswise into ¼-inch slices
- ¾ cup warm water
- ½ teaspoon baking soda
- ½ teaspoon baking powder
- ½ teaspoon table salt
- ¾ cup packed (5¼ ounces) light or dark brown sugar
- 2 large eggs
- 1½ teaspoons vanilla extract

Toffee Sauce

- 4 tablespoons (½ stick) unsalted butter
- 1 cup packed (7 ounces) light or dark brown sugar
- ¼ teaspoon table salt
- 1 cup heavy cream
- 1 tablespoon rum
- ½ teaspoon juice from 1 lemon

1. **FOR THE PUDDING CAKES:** Adjust oven rack to middle position and heat oven to 350 degrees. Grease and flour eight 4-ounce ramekins. Set prepared ramekins in large roasting pan lined with clean dish towel. Bring kettle or large saucepan of water to boil over high heat.

2. Combine half of dates with water and baking soda in liquid measuring cup (dates should be submerged beneath water) and soak 5 minutes. Meanwhile, whisk flour, baking powder, and salt together in medium bowl.

3. Process remaining dates and brown sugar in food processor until no large date chunks remain and mixture has texture of damp coarse sand, about 45 seconds, scraping down bowl as needed. Drain soaked dates and add soaking liquid to processor workbowl. Add eggs, vanilla, and melted butter and process until smooth, about 15 seconds. Transfer mixture to bowl with dry ingredients and sprinkle softened dates on top.

4. With rubber spatula or wooden spoon, gently fold wet mixture into dry mixture until just combined and date pieces are evenly dispersed. Distribute batter evenly among prepared ramekins (should be two-thirds filled). Add boiling water to roasting pan until water comes ¼ inch up sides, making sure not to splash water into ramekins. Cover pan tightly with aluminum foil, crimping edges to seal. Bake 40 minutes until puffed and surfaces are spongy, firm, and moist to touch. Immediately transfer ramekins from water bath to wire rack; cool 10 minutes.

5. **FOR THE TOFFEE SAUCE:** While cakes cool, melt butter in medium saucepan over medium-high heat. Whisk in brown sugar and salt until smooth. Continue to cook, stirring occasionally, until sugar is dissolved and slightly darkened, 3 to 4 minutes. Add ⅓ cup cream and stir until smooth, about 30 seconds. Slowly pour in remaining ⅔ cup cream and rum, whisking constantly until smooth. Reduce heat to low and simmer until frothy, about 3 minutes. Remove from heat and stir in lemon juice.

6. **TO SERVE:** Using toothpick, poke 25 holes in each cake and spoon 1 tablespoon toffee sauce over each cake. Let rest 5 minutes until sauce is absorbed. Invert each ramekin onto plate or shallow bowl and remove ramekin. Divide remaining toffee sauce evenly among cakes and serve immediately.

EQUIPMENT TESTING:

Digital Scales

Handy as they are, measuring cups will never measure up to the accuracy of a digital scale. We've found different cooks can be off by as much as 10 percent measuring dry ingredients using a "dip and sweep" method—a variance that, in baking, can mean the difference between a dense cake and a fluffy crumb. We tested nine different scales and, happily, found them all acceptably accurate (within 2 grams). We then assessed them for user-friendliness, ranking models most highly for roomy platforms, at least 7-pound capacity, and a large, clear readout display. For complete testing results, go to www.cooksillustrated.com/october. –Elizabeth Bomze

TOP OF THE SCALE

OXO Food Scale

Price: $49.99

Comments: Besides its spacious platform, backlit display, and clear buttons, the OXO Food Scale's screen can be pulled out from the large, removable (i.e., washable) platform when weighing bulky items.

BEST BUY

SOEHNLE 65055 Digital Scale

Price: $29.75

Comments: Our previous favorite, this scale still impresses with its sexy design and recently slashed price, though its non-compact structure makes storage a challenge.

LARGE STICKY TOFFEE PUDDING CAKE

SERVES 8

Follow recipe for Individual Sticky Toffee Pudding Cakes, substituting 8-inch square baking dish, buttered and floured, for ramekins. Bake until outer 2 inches develop small holes and center is puffed and firm to touch, about 40 minutes. Cool as directed. Using toothpick, poke about 100 holes in cake and glaze with ½ cup toffee sauce. Let rest 5 minutes until sauce is absorbed. Cut cake into squares and pour remaining toffee sauce over each square before serving.

COOK'S LIVE Original Test Kitchen Video

www.cooksillustrated.com

HOW TO MAKE

- Individual Sticky Toffee Pudding Cakes

Rethinking Apple Pie

A simple, old-fashioned dessert called apple pandowdy promises apple pie appeal with none of the fuss. Is it time for an apple pie makeover?

⋟ BY YVONNE RUPERTI ⋞

As great as apple pie is, let's face it: It's not a dish most of us make that often. Making a perfect filling, let alone a top and bottom crust, requires a few too many steps for everyday occasions. So when I came across a recipe for a humbler cousin to apple pie called apple pandowdy, I was immediately intrigued. A colonial New England original, pandowdy is essentially an apple pie filling baked with a top crust. During or after baking, the cook breaks the pastry and pushes it into the filling, a technique known as "dowdying" (and a reference, perhaps, to the dessert's resulting "dowdy" appearance). Rustic looks aside, I loved the idea of this no-frills approach. With no fussy crimping, no filling that must be finessed to make it sliceable, and no bottom crust that could get soggy, this kind of pie sounded manageable enough to make all the time.

A skillet proved key to producing tender, flavorful apples and a beautifully browned crust.

Testing the Basics

I wondered if I could make apple pandowdy by simply putting an apple pie filling in a baking dish and topping it with dough. I decided to try this with the test kitchen's favorite apple pie filling, which incorporates sweet and tart apples, sugar, and lemon juice. As for the topping, a traditional pandowdy may be topped with a cakelike batter, biscuit dough, or pie pastry. Because I was drawn to the idea of a simple apple pie, I decided to stick with a pie pastry topping.

When the dessert came out of the oven, I gave dowdying a try, using the back of a spoon to push the crust into the filling. The results were disappointing. The crust quickly became soggy and bloated—not what I wanted at all. In colonial times, dowdying was likely practiced in order to soften a tough dough with the juice from the apples. My tender modern dough was much more delicate than its sturdy ancestors, and dowdying just didn't make sense. I made the radical decision to skip the dowdying and pursue a dessert modeled on a one-crust pie.

Even after abandoning the dowdying step, there were adjustments to be made. First and foremost, the apple filling was dry and lacked flavor. I wanted a juicy, rich filling that really tasted of apples. Unlike a pie, which needs to be thick and sliceable (a challenge because apples never cook up the same way twice; see "Mushy Apples," page 25), my pandowdy could afford to be somewhat saucy—and then I could concentrate on building superior flavor without having to worry about sliceability.

Perhaps I could produce a juicier filling by drawing out some of the liquid in the apples? I tried macerating the apples in sugar to coax out moisture (a technique we use in various other fruit desserts), but this was unsuccessful: Apples aren't as juicy as berries or stone fruits. I would have to add some extra liquid to the apples. An additional ½ cup of apple juice made the filling moist but diluted its taste. Simmering a cup of apple juice until it was reduced by half intensified the flavor, but using apple cider was easier—it provided resonant apple flavor straight from the jug. My apple filling was now pleasantly juicy and bursting with the taste of apples. I thickened the cider with two teaspoons of cornstarch, yielding a juicy filling with just the right amount of body.

To enhance the flavor of the apples, I experimented with different sweeteners and spices. Pandowdies were originally sweetened with molasses, maple syrup, or brown sugar. Compared with these old-fashioned choices, the granulated sugar that I had been using tasted plain and boring. But not all the traditional sweeteners were equally appealing. Molasses lent the filling a dark color and somewhat overpowering flavor. Both dark and light brown sugars also turned out to be too imposing. One-third of a cup of maple syrup, however, struck the perfect balance, complementing the natural sweetness of the apples without being cloying. As a bonus, the extra moisture from the maple syrup made my juicy filling even juicier. After trying—and dismissing—a few different spices, tests proved that a classic pinch of cinnamon was a nice optional addition.

History Lesson

At this point I had a succulent, juicy apple filling and could focus on improving the crust. I wanted it to be extra-crisp to stand up to the moist, saucy fruit. After some trial and error, I found that the best approach was to use a standard pie crust that had been brushed with egg white and sprinkled with sugar, then bake the pandowdy in a 500-degree oven on the upper-middle rack. The egg white and sugar combination created a wonderful, crackly finish. But there was a problem: Although the crust was browned and crisp with a beautiful golden color, the apples were

COOK'S LIVE Original Test Kitchen Videos

www.cooksillustrated.com

HOW TO MAKE

- Skillet Apple Pie

VIDEO TIPS

- What's the best way to core an apple?
- Best apples for baking

SCIENCE: Mushy Apples

While developing my Skillet Apple Pie recipe, I noticed that the apple filling occasionally turned mushy. After a chat with our science editor, I learned that apples that aren't going to be sold within a few weeks of harvest are placed in refrigerated "controlled atmosphere" (CA) storage with regulated levels of oxygen and carbon dioxide. Because apples continue to ripen after harvest, these conditions are designed to halt the ripening process. The problem is that once the apples are removed from CA storage and put on display at the grocery store, they begin an accelerated ripening process. The apple's structure will then quickly break down upon cooking. The longer the apples are kept in CA storage (and they may be stored as long as 10 months), the faster they ripen once removed, and the more likely they are to turn mushy during baking.

Because it is impossible to know how long or under what conditions supermarket apples have been stored, your best bet is to use fresh, local apples whenever possible. If you purchase fresh apples, refrigerate and use them as soon as you can. –Y.R.

sadly undercooked. Lowering the oven temperature eventually cooked the apples through, but left the crust pale.

As I struggled to solve this dilemma, I wondered if colonial American cooks had faced similar problems with this otherwise straightforward dish. I turned to my historical sources again and rediscovered a chief point about early pandowdies: They were cooked in a heavy skillet or pot that was placed directly over the heat source. An idea began to form in my mind. Could I mimic this old-fashioned technique by starting my pandowdy in a skillet on the stovetop? I could give the apples a head start by sautéing them first, then add the crust and quickly brown it in a hot oven. Envisioning a skillet filled with sizzling, cider-sauced apples topped by an impeccably crisp crust, I headed into the kitchen to test this promising whim.

Eureka. My new method worked beautifully, yielding apples that were richly flavored and perfectly cooked. In fact, caramelizing the apples before baking them made the filling taste even better than a traditional apple pie filling. The total cooking time was only about 20 minutes (much less than a traditional pie, which can take an hour or more). In this time, the apples baked evenly, the sauce was nicely thickened and sticky around the edges, and the crust developed a lovely deep brown hue.

As a final touch, I cut the dough into six squares before the pandowdy went into the oven. Prepared this way, each square of pastry baked up with multiple crisp, flaky edges. The cider-enriched filling bubbled up and caramelized nicely around the edges of the tender pastry. With results so good and so simple to come by, I might never go back to conventional apple pie again.

SKILLET APPLE PIE

SERVES 6 TO 8

If your skillet is not heatproof, precook the apples and stir in the cider mixture as instructed, then transfer the apples to a 13- by 9-inch baking dish. Roll out the dough to a 13- by 9-inch rectangle and bake it as instructed. If you do not have apple cider, reduced apple juice may be used as a substitute—simmer 1 cup apple juice in a small saucepan over medium heat until reduced to ½ cup (about 10 minutes). Serve the pie warm or at room temperature with vanilla ice cream or whipped cream. Use a combination of sweet, crisp apples such as Golden Delicious and firm, tart apples such as Cortland or Empire.

Crust

- 1 cup (5 ounces) unbleached all-purpose flour, plus more for dusting work surface
- 1 tablespoon sugar
- ½ teaspoon table salt
- 2 tablespoons vegetable shortening, chilled
- 6 tablespoons (¾ stick) cold unsalted butter, cut into ¼-inch pieces
- 3–4 tablespoons ice water

Filling

- ½ cup apple cider (see note)
- ⅓ cup maple syrup
- 2 tablespoons juice from 1 lemon
- 2 teaspoons cornstarch
- ⅛ teaspoon ground cinnamon (optional)
- 2 tablespoons unsalted butter
- 2½ pounds sweet and tart apples (about 5 medium), peeled, cored, halved, and cut into ½-inch-thick wedges (see note)

- 1 egg white, lightly beaten
- 2 teaspoons sugar

1. **FOR THE CRUST:** Pulse flour, sugar, and salt in food processor until combined. Add shortening and process until mixture has texture of coarse sand, about ten 1-second pulses. Scatter butter pieces over flour mixture and process until mixture is pale yellow and resembles coarse crumbs, with butter bits no larger than small peas, about ten 1-second pulses. Transfer mixture to medium bowl.

2. Sprinkle 3 tablespoons ice water over mixture. With blade of rubber spatula, use folding motion to mix. Press down on dough with broad side of spatula until dough sticks together, adding up to 1 tablespoon more ice water if dough does not come together. Turn dough out onto sheet of plastic wrap and flatten into 4-inch disk. Wrap dough and refrigerate 30 minutes, or up to 2 days, before rolling out. (If dough is refrigerated longer than 1 hour, let stand at room temperature until malleable.)

3. **FOR THE FILLING:** Adjust oven rack to upper-middle position (between 7 and 9 inches from heating element) and heat oven to 500 degrees. Whisk cider, syrup, lemon juice, cornstarch, and cinnamon (if using) together in medium bowl until smooth. Heat butter in 12-inch heatproof skillet over medium-high heat. When foaming subsides, add apples and cook, stirring 2 or 3 times until apples begin to caramelize, about 5 minutes. (Do not fully cook apples.) Remove pan from heat, add cider mixture, and gently stir until apples are well coated. Set aside to cool slightly.

4. **TO ASSEMBLE AND BAKE:** Roll out dough on lightly floured work surface, or between 2 large sheets of plastic wrap, to 11-inch circle. Roll dough loosely around rolling pin and unroll over apple filling. Brush dough with egg white and sprinkle with sugar. With sharp knife, gently cut dough into 6 pieces by making 1 vertical cut followed by 2 evenly spaced horizontal cuts (perpendicular to first cut). Bake until apples are tender and crust is a deep golden brown, about 20 minutes. Let cool 15 minutes; serve.

STEP-BY-STEP | KEYS TO A FLAKY, FLAVORFUL SKILLET APPLE PIE

1. CARAMELIZE APPLES Precook apples in butter to deepen their flavor.

2. ADD CIDER Coat apples with ½ cup apple cider to create juicy, flavorful filling.

3. CUT DOUGH Score before baking to allow juices to bubble up and caramelize around edges.

4. BAKE IN HOT OVEN Precooked apples need less time in oven than traditional apple pie.

Bringing Home Better Bacon

Artisanal bacon takes time, hand labor, and real wood smoke. But at double or even triple the cost of supermarket bacon, is it worth it?

BY LISA McMANUS

While there's probably no such thing as terrible bacon, we know from previous tastings that there is definitely better bacon, with mass-market supermarket strips, for example, varying a lot from producer to producer. In recent years we've been hearing about small, artisanal producers crafting premium bacon using old-fashioned curing methods and hand labor. Before you factor in shipping (most of these products are only available through mail order), premium pork can cost double or even triple the price of ordinary bacon. Could such a dramatic difference in price really be worth it?

We bought six artisanal bacons by mail order in a single style—applewood smoked—so we could sample different brands' treatment of this traditional approach that adds a mildly sweet, fruity note to familiar bacon. We then pitted these premium strips against applewood-smoked bacon from the supermarket (we found just two brands, both a cut above true mass-market bacons like Hormel or Oscar Mayer). We cooked them all to a uniform doneness and tasted them blind.

Ham-Made

American-style bacon is made from pork bellies that have been cut into slabs, cured, smoked, and sliced. But the similarity between most supermarket bacon and artisanal bacon generally ends there. Mass-produced bacon is made in a matter of hours and by machine. Artisanal bacon is made over days or even weeks, and much of the work is done by hand.

Mass-produced bacon often starts with frozen pork bellies that are thawed and tumbled in a metal drum to soften the meat, then placed on hangers and pumped full of a liquid cure solution. This solution includes curing salts such as sodium erythorbate and sodium nitrite, along with phosphates that bind the water to the cells in the meat, plumping it up (and also causing it to shrink in the pan when cooked). The meat is not actually smoked—liquid smoke and other flavorings such as sweeteners, herbs, and spices are added to the cure. After curing for a few hours, the bellies are often sprayed with more liquid smoke and heated in a thermal processing unit (often referred to as "the smokehouse") to destroy bacteria and infuse smoke flavor throughout the meat. Finally, the slab is quickly chilled, machine-pressed into a uniform shape, sliced, and packaged for sale.

By contrast, artisanal bacon takes much more time, as well as hand labor and real wood smoke. It begins with fresh pork bellies, which artisanal producers say make bacon with superior texture and flavor compared to starting with frozen bellies. While the pork is sometimes soaked in a "wet" cure, it is traditionally dry-cured, which means the meat is hand-rubbed with a dry mixture of herbs, sugars, salt, and curing salts. Artisanal producers leave the bacon to cure for anywhere from a day to a month, then slow-smoke it over wood fires, generally from one to three days, depending on the maker. The extended curing time intensifies the pork flavor and shrinks the meat so that the bacon doesn't shrivel much as it cooks. While most producers in our lineup burn real applewood sawdust or wood chips to create smoke, one burns dried apple pomace, the residue left after squeezing apples for cider.

The ingredients of the cure, the method of smoking, and the timing of each step determine each bacon's unique flavor. The age, gender, and breed of the pig and what it is fed are other factors that determine the final flavor of the bacon. For instance, most bacon producers won't use a sow that has given birth (too tough) or a male that isn't castrated (testosterone can give the meat an off-flavor) and call for a slaughter weight that is not too heavy to keep the bacon fat in proportion to the meat. In contrast to mass-produced bacon, where the pork bellies must be similar in size for machine processing, artisanal bacon has a much more irregular shape.

On the Scales

In spite of the fact that all of the bacons in our lineup were applewood-smoked or apple-flavored, they were remarkably different. Great bacon is all about a balance of sweet, smoky, salty, and meaty—and striking that flavor balance turned out to be the biggest factor for success with our tasters. In fact, tasters downgraded most of the premium mail-order brands for being too much of any one thing—too smoky, too fatty, or too sweet.

Only two of the six achieved enough of a balance to bring genuine raves. Tasters extolled Vande Rose Farms for having it all: a "nice balance of sweetness to salt, great deep complex ham flavor, very meaty." They also singled out Nodine's Smokehouse for its "hulking slices of delectable pork belly, sure to satisfy sweet and smoky fans." In addition to sharing that desirable balance of sweet, smoky, and salty flavors, both bacons provided the largest, thickest-cut slices of the lineup (33 grams and 37 grams, respectively, compared to other slices that were as slight as 4 grams), which gave our tasters the meaty, substantial bacon texture they preferred.

The two bacons at the bottom of the heap, Niman Ranch and Nueske's, got slammed for opposite reasons. Tasters assailed the Niman Ranch strips for a lack of flavor and the Nueske's bacon for its "overwhelming smoke flavor" that was like licking an "ashtray."

But in the biggest surprise of the tasting, the next highest-rated bacons were not premium mail-order bacons at all, but our two supermarket brands. Both were a step up from the usual mass-produced bacon, straddling the gap between artisanal and more mainstream supermarket styles. Applegate Farms' Uncured Sunday Bacon is smoked over real hardwood from apple trees. While it is described as "uncured" because the company does not use sodium nitrite (the chemically produced curing salt that creates the deep red color and characteristic flavor of bacon), it is cured just as thoroughly with naturally occurring sodium nitrate from celery juice. Farmland (called Carando in the Northeast) uses its own pigs, which allows it to start the process with fresh, versus frozen, pork bellies that absorb the cure more evenly. Farmland also uses real smoke from applewood chips, not liquid smoke. While these bacons didn't receive quite the raves of the two top-ranked premium bacons, tasters praised them both for good meaty flavor and mild smokiness.

Factoring in the Premium Price

So where does that leave us? As delicious as the best premium pork can be, there's no getting around the fact that mail-order bacon is far more expensive than even higher-end supermarket bacon. Applegate Farms costs about $11 per pound, while Farmland costs just $6. Even after we shopped around for the best price, one 12-ounce package of Vande Rose Farms bacon set us back $13.95 plus $22 in shipping (second-day delivery), adding up to nearly $36 for not even a full pound of bacon. (If you order a few pounds of bacon at the same time, you might get the total cost down to just over $20 per pound—still well over supermarket bacon prices.) Unfortunately for most of us, such a high price tag for what's basically breakfast food is a pretty steep barrier to bringing these bacons home.

TASTING PREMIUM APPLEWOOD BACONS

Twenty *Cook's Illustrated* staffers sampled eight bacons, six mail-order artisanal brands and two higher-end brands from the supermarket, all smoked with applewood or cured with apple cider. We cooked them to a uniform doneness on a rimmed baking sheet, using our recipe for Oven-Fried Bacon (go to www.cooksillustrated.com/october for our free recipe), and rated them on saltiness, sweetness, smokiness, and meatiness, as well as overall appeal. Sodium and fat content were provided by the manufacturers. Because pork bellies are an agricultural product, some variation from package to package in flavor and in fat-to-meat ratio could be expected. To ensure that any variation was within an acceptable range, we tasted multiple batches of our two top-rated bacons months apart. A source for the winning brand appears on page 32. Based on our experience, shipping for this brand and the other mail-order bacons will cost $20 or more.

HIGHLY RECOMMENDED

FAT/SODIUM | **TESTERS' COMMENTS**

VANDE ROSE FARMS Artisan Dry Cured Bacon, Applewood Smoked
Price: $13.95 for 12 ounces, plus shipping
Description: Dry-cured with brown sugar, salt, and pepper; hand-rubbed; applewood-smoked

Size of slice: 33 g
Sodium per slice: 260 mg
Fat per slice: 13 g

Tasters raved that this bacon—which scored a distinct few notches higher than the rest of the lineup—had it all: "Nice balance of sweetness to salt, great deep complex ham flavor, very meaty," with a "faint fruity taste, sweet and salty." "A nice, thick cut, very hearty and substantial." "Classic bacon, but with lots more genuine smoke flavor and in every way better." "Now you're talking! This has lots of sex appeal—good balance of everything." In sum: "A winner."

RECOMMENDED

FAT/SODIUM | **TESTERS' COMMENTS**

NODINE'S SMOKEHOUSE Apple Smoke Flavored Bacon
Price: $8 for 16 ounces, plus shipping
Description: Wet-cured with brown sugar, salt, and spices; smoked over dried apple pomace and hickory or maple hardwood

Size of slice: 37 g
Sodium per slice: 330 mg
Fat per slice: 18 g

"Wow, this is some huge piece of amazing bacon. Slices very wide and thick, and even the fat tastes great." "That's good eatin'—hulking slices of delectable pork belly, sure to satisfy sweet and smoky fans." "Nice meatiness" and "great depth here." "Apple flavor is subtle and it isn't too smoky." While it had "good pork flavor," several tasters felt it "needs more salt."

APPLEGATE FARMS Uncured Sunday Bacon
Price: $5.39 for 8 ounces
Description: Wet-cured with water, sea salt, celery juice, evaporated cane juice, and lactic acid starter culture; smoked over applewood

Size of slice: 7 g
Sodium per slice: 145 mg
Fat per slice: 2.5 g

SUPERMARKET BEST BUY

One taster praised this nitrite-free supermarket brand for a "subtle smokiness, sweetness of pork, but not sugary. Woodsy but not overly smoky. This is log-cabin bacon." Another noted, "You get the sense this is right off the pig; natural-tasting." "Interesting flavor, almost like a cured sausage or ham." Two identified it as supermarket bacon, "with its heavy salt and mild smoke," though one taster added, "As a salt-lover, I like it."

RECOMMENDED WITH RESERVATIONS

FAT/SODIUM | **TESTERS' COMMENTS**

FARMLAND/CARANDO Apple Cider Cured Bacon, Applewood Smoked
Price: $5.99 for 16 ounces
Description: Wet-cured with water, sugar, salt, sodium phosphate, natural apple flavoring, sodium erythorbate, and sodium nitrite; smoked over applewood

Size of slice: 7.5 g
Sodium per slice: 125 mg
Fat per slice: 3 g

SUPERMARKET BEST BUY

Some found this "sugary" supermarket bacon far too sweet: "a deal breaker for me in bacon," "like cotton candy!" Others enjoyed its "applelike flavor" and "subtle apple cider undertones," describing it as "caramelized," with cinnamon and maple syrup notes, "like it's been hanging with French toast already," as well as being "light on smoke and salt, and quite meaty. Delicious!"

OSCAR'S SMOKE HOUSE Applewood Smoked Bacon
Price: $9.95 for 16 ounces, plus shipping
Description: Wet-cured with brown sugar and honey; applewood-smoked

Size of slice: 4 g
Sodium per slice: 96 mg
Fat per slice: 2 g

A few tasters noted an "almost Asian" flavor to this bacon, describing it as like "teriyaki bacon, sweet and tangy" or "soy sauce." Several noted a "chewy" (a few said "tough") texture and "relatively meaty" consistency, with "good pork flavor but not really bacon-y," according to one taster. Others found it "too sweet," "out of balance," and "one-dimensional" and deemed it "nothing special."

NORTH COUNTRY SMOKEHOUSE Applewood Smoked Bacon
Price: $18.50 for 2 pounds, plus shipping
Description: Wet-cured in maple syrup and spices; smoked and cooked for eight hours

Size of slice: 12 g
Sodium per slice: 350 mg
Fat per slice: 3 g

Smoke flavor dominated, according to our tasters, and those who liked smokiness liked this bacon. "Pretty smoky, and very meaty and chewy. Thick, hearty, and fairly hamlike," said one taster. "Delicious." But the majority disagreed: "Wow, a lot of smoke, like barbecued bacon. Too much for me."

NOT RECOMMENDED

FAT/SODIUM | **TESTERS' COMMENTS**

NIMAN RANCH Applewood Smoked Dry-Cured Bacon
Price: $7.98 for 12 ounces, plus shipping
Description: Dry cured, smoked over applewood chips

Size of slice: 15 g
Sodium per slice: 140 mg
Fat per slice: 7 g

"A fairly average piece of bacon," "thin," "not sweet or deeply flavorful," "needs more sweetness." One taster noted it "tastes like smoke, but not much else; very fatty." Another agreed: "I felt like I was eating straight fat with no flavor. Disgusting." A few noted a distinctly "gamy," "funky" taste.

NUESKE'S Applewood Smoked Bacon
Price: $19.95 for 2 pounds, plus shipping
Description: Wet-cured with salt, sugar, sodium phosphate, sodium erythorbate, and sodium nitrite for 24 hours; hung to dry for 24 hours, then applewood-smoked for 24 hours

Size of slice: 9 g
Sodium per slice: 180 mg
Fat per slice: 3.5 g

Despite the company's claims of using particularly lean hogs, our tasters found this bacon "very fatty" with "hardly any meat," and many complained of its "overwhelming smoke flavor," which was akin to licking a "wood-burning stove" or "ashtray."

Searching for the Perfect Drip Coffee Maker

Most models turn costly beans into mediocre coffee: too weak, too flat, or too bitter. What's so hard about making a decent drip coffee maker?

≥ BY LISA McMANUS ≤

In this age of Starbucks, Americans have gotten much more sophisticated about the complexities of coffee flavor. Now when we make our coffee at home, that old Mr. Coffee on the counter—never all that great to begin with—increasingly doesn't measure up. As we surveyed the latest models on store shelves, we wondered if manufacturers might have caught up with our coffee obsession and finally developed an automatic drip coffee maker that can produce a terrific brew.

From previous tests, we knew that a thermal carafe would be essential; the usual hot plate under a glass carafe starts turning fresh coffee acrid in a matter of minutes. We found eight brands with thermal carafes and at least a 10-cup capacity at prices from $47 to nearly $300. Most were programmable, meaning you can fill them with coffee and water and set the time you want the pot to turn itself on. Two came with an attached burr-style coffee grinder. With hope—and more than 30 pounds of freshly roasted, house-blend coffee beans from Stumptown Coffee Roasters in Portland, Oregon—we set to work.

Better Brew

Brewing a full pot in each machine, we asked tasters to judge the coffees' aroma, body, complexity of flavor, level of bitterness, and overall appeal. Our hopes for the new generation of coffee makers were quickly crushed. Most of those eight stainless steel machines made the same kind of mediocre coffee we've come to expect: bitter, weak, or one-dimensional.

What was the problem? Aside from using fresh, high-quality coffee beans and good-tasting cold water, the two most important factors in making good coffee are the water temperature as it passes through the grounds and the length of time the grounds are exposed to the water. These factors determine which of the more than 1,000 volatile flavor and aroma compounds identified in roasted coffee beans make it into your cup and which get left behind (only a limited number of them—approximately 30—produce the best-tasting coffee). Studies have shown that the most flavorful, aromatic compounds are released by water between 195 and 205 degrees Fahrenheit, at a brew time of six minutes, for drip coffee makers. The ideal cup of coffee contains 18 to 22 percent suspended solids extracted from the ground coffee. Too fast a brew time and the extraction of solids will be less than 18 percent, and your coffee will be weak; too slow a brew time leads to overextraction (more than 22 percent suspended solids) and a bitter brew. If the coffee maker is too slow and the water is not sufficiently hot, you can even wind up with coffee that is both weak and bitter.

We made more coffee, this time measuring the water temperature throughout the brew cycle. And here we made a key discovery: Most of these machines were too cool, spending most of the brewing cycle struggling to bring the water into the right temperature range. Many didn't reach the correct temperature until the last minute or two of brewing—and then kept climbing, scorching the grounds as the last few cups dripped into the carafe.

Next, we timed three pots in each coffee maker with a stopwatch and averaged the results. Once again, our lousy coffee could be explained: Most of the machines never reached that ideal time frame for water to pass through the coffee grounds, though two came much closer than the rest. The slowest machine took 18 minutes to make one pot of very bitter coffee. The fastest took just four minutes, and tasters found its coffee weak, thin, and flat.

Tasters' Choice

How can manufacturers keep getting away with these crimes against good coffee? They know consumers can't taste the coffee before they buy the machine; most choose a coffee maker based on looks and price. New models are dressed up to be enticing, with graceful carafes, backlit digital displays, and multiple features. Why can't the flavor match up? "To sell their coffee makers competitively, these machines have to be made cheaply," said Mané Alves, chair of the technical standards committee for the Specialty Coffee Association of America. "And the most expensive part of the coffee maker is the heating element."

In the end, only one coffee maker stood out in our tests as exceptional. The Technivorm Moccamaster (model KBT741), made in the Netherlands, consistently brewed smooth, full-flavored coffee that our tasters ranked highest. Tellingly, it was the only model to get close to the ideal six-minute brewing time, averaging 7½ minutes to completely finish dripping, though the water was fully dispensed within six minutes. Unlike any of the other coffee makers, its internal heating element brought the brewing water to the correct temperature range within seconds and kept it there through the brewing cycle.

It turns out that in contrast to most coffee maker heating elements, which are made of aluminum, the Technivorm's heating element is made of far more expensive copper. In coffee makers, the heating element usually runs alongside a tube containing water. As the cool water drips down from the tank, it passes through the heated channel, then boils up to the top of the machine, and finally drips down onto the grounds. A copper heating element has higher thermal conductivity than aluminum, meaning it is more responsive and can reach a higher temperature more quickly. The Technivorm is also more powerful, operating at a higher electrical wattage than most coffee makers—with 1,400 watts compared to the average 900 watts of the rest of the lineup—making its brew time correspondingly more efficient.

The $240 Question

Its sophisticated internal workings aside, the rest of the Technivorm is simple, with a cone to hold the coffee and a nine-hole sprayer to disperse water evenly. A switch lets you stop the flow of water to pour a cup. There's just one problem with the Technivorm—its price. Could we really justify spending $240 when we know that great coffee can be had through far cheaper methods? To make sure, we compared coffee made in the Technivorm to coffee from a French press, the method favored by many coffee connoisseurs. (We used the Bodum Chambord, which sells for $39.95.) To our surprise, while our tasters enjoyed the French press coffee's rich aroma and flavor, the Technivorm coffee won the day with even better flavor—and with no need to go through the French press's multiple steps of separately heating the water to 200 degrees, then pouring, stirring, waiting four minutes (according to manufacturer instructions), and pressing.

The Technivorm's price tag is high, but its consistently full-flavored, smooth brew—made with all the convenience of that old Mr. Coffee—will pay for itself when you start skipping a few trips to Starbucks.

TESTING AUTOMATIC DRIP COFFEE MAKERS

We tested eight automatic drip coffee makers with thermal carafes and a capacity of at least 10 cups. In our ratings, we placed greatest emphasis on the taste of the coffee. Prices were paid through online retail sources or Boston-area retailers. The coffee makers appear below in order of preference. A source for the winner appears on page 32.

KEY
GOOD: ★★★
FAIR: ★★
POOR: ★

BREWING: Highest scores went to machines that brewed a pot close to the ideal six minutes' brewing time; kept brewing water temperature between 195 and 205 degrees; produced brewed coffee at the ideal serving temperature between 155 and 175 degrees; made a half-pot at the same strength as a full pot; and had a carafe that kept coffee at the proper serving temperature for an hour.

FLAVOR: We ranked freshly brewed coffee on aroma, body, complexity, bitterness, and overall appeal.

USER-FRIENDLINESS: We preferred clear, intuitive controls; water tanks that were easy to fill and check; carafes that opened, closed, and poured easily; and filters that kept used grounds contained and easy to remove.

HIGHLY RECOMMENDED

HIGHLY RECOMMENDED		PERFORMANCE	TESTERS' COMMENTS
TECHNIVORM Moccamaster Coffeemaker, Model KBT741 **Price:** $239.95		Brewing: ★★★ Flavor: ★★★ User-friendliness: ★★★	Fast, very simple to operate. Tasters described coffee as "a dynamic and clean cup, flavorful and expressive," "very good; robust but smooth." Achieved perfect temperatures for brewing and serving and was the closest of all the coffee makers to reaching the ideal brewing time. Pieces disassemble easily for cleaning. Though not programmable, this machine was so fast and easy to use, we didn't mind.

RECOMMENDED WITH RESERVATIONS

RECOMMENDED WITH RESERVATIONS		PERFORMANCE	TESTERS' COMMENTS
KRUPS 10-Cup Programmable Thermal Coffee Machine, Model FMF5 **Price:** $95.93		Brewing: ★ Flavor: ★★ User-friendliness: ★★★  BEST BUY	Compact and attractive, this programmable machine is simple to use, but it lost points for too-slow and slightly too-hot brewing. Thin water line down front of machine magnifies as water is added, making it easy to read levels. Optional beeper indicates when brewing is complete. Tasters deemed its coffee "slightly too bitter." Half-pot was weaker than the full pot.
CUISINART Grind & Brew Thermal 12-Cup Automatic Coffeemaker, Model DGB-900BC **Price:** $199		Brewing: ★ Flavor: ★★ User-friendliness: ★★	"As loud as a jet taking off," the attached burr grinder will wake anyone who isn't already up in the morning. Controls and carafe were well designed, but brewing water spent most of the cycle well below optimal temperature, reaching it only for the last three minutes. While a few tasters called the coffee "mellow," others deemed it "watery," "bitter," and "thin."
BLACK & DECKER 10-Cup Thermal Stainless Steel Coffeemaker, Model TCM830 **Price:** $59.99		Brewing: ★ Flavor: ★★ User-friendliness: ★★	Innovative lift-out water reservoir you can take to the sink and fill, but controls could use improvement: A temporary sticker explained that one button turned the machine on and off and set programs with different numbers of pushes. Tasters found the coffee "strong," but "nothing exceptional"; some remarked on its bitterness. Brewing water remained too cool for most of the cycle, then spiked up too high near the end. Half-pot was slightly weaker.

NOT RECOMMENDED

NOT RECOMMENDED		PERFORMANCE	TESTERS' COMMENTS
HAMILTON BEACH Stay or Go Deluxe 10-Cup Thermal Coffeemaker, Model 45238 **Price:** $89.99		Brewing: ★ Flavor: ★ User-friendliness: ★★★	This programmable machine is easy to use and fill, with simple controls, and we liked the two commuter cups you can brew into directly. But it's by far the slowest coffee maker in the lineup, taking 18 minutes to produce a pot. Brewing water was too cool and took 16 minutes of the brew cycle to reach the proper temperature. Tasters found the coffee "strong" but too "bitter."
MR. COFFEE 10-Cup Thermal Programmable Coffee Maker, Model FTTX95 **Price:** $47.24		Brewing: ★ Flavor: ★ User-friendliness: ★★	Attractive machine, but water filter is fussy to put in correct direction, with tiny, raised print the only indication. Condensation dripped neatly into tank when lid was opened. Tasters found the coffee the most bitter of the lineup, calling it "harsh," "like cowboy coffee," and rated it near the bottom for complexity of flavor. Brewing temperature fluctuated between too high and too low.
BUNN-O-MATIC Home Brewer, Model BTX **Price:** $131.32		Brewing: ★ Flavor: ★ User-friendliness: ★	This super-fast machine brews a full pot in just four minutes, but the coffee is "weak," "thin," and "flat." You can't see into the water reservoir or check water level; you must leave unit on at all times to keep water preheated and ready to brew (at the cost of fresh flavor), or wait 15 minutes for preheating before brewing. No "on" button; closing reservoir lid starts brewing. Turbulent water spray strews grounds over and around filter. Water never reached 195 degrees.
CAPRESSO CoffeeTEAM Therm, Model 455 **Price:** $299		Brewing: ★ Flavor: ★ User-friendliness: ★	Deluxe machine is enjoyable to watch as the filter fills, then swings over to begin brewing, but for the price, the coffee should taste better, and it takes up too much counter space. Coffee was brewed at too high a temperature, making it "too hot to drink," "weak and watery," and "too bitter"; it received the lowest overall tasting scores. Delicate, tiny parts for top of brew basket were fussy, easily lost, and had to be in exactly the right place for proper function.

Inexpensive Alternative?

Coffee connoisseurs willing to overlook the precise calibration and multiple steps required by the French press rave about the complex flavors of its brew. And few drip coffee makers can beat its price (our favorite, the 8-cup Bodum Chambord, at right, costs just $39.95). Nevertheless, our winning drip coffee maker, the Technivorm, beat it in a head-to-head tasting.

CHEAPER BREW

 KITCHEN NOTES 

BY J. KENJI ALT

How Long Does Wine Last?

We've all had the unpleasant experience of wine that tastes sour the day after being opened. There is a way of extending its shelf life: Use a Vacu Vin Vacuum Wine Saver, which prevents wine from oxidizing and keeps it palatable for weeks. If you don't own one of these gadgets, how long can you expect the wine to stay fit for cooking? Taking a bottle of red and a bottle of white, we cooked up pan sauces every day for a week, corking the bottle and storing it in the refrigerator after each daily batch. The white wine remained usable until the end of the week; the red fared less well, developing off-flavors after just four days. The culprit is a class of chemical compounds called phenols, which reacts to oxygen and turns the wine astringent and vinegary. Red wine has five times the level of phenols as white wine; if you need to keep red wine longer than 2 to 3 days, we suggest you buy half bottles or boxed wine (which contains an inner bag that deflates as it is used, preventing exposure to oxygen).

SHOPPING: Noodles for Lo Mein

Developing the recipe for our Pork Stir-Fry with Noodles (page 15), we discovered that not any old noodle will do.

BEST BET
The slightly dry and curly fresh egg noodles labeled "lo mein" from an Asian market boasted firm texture and the best flavor.

BEST ALTERNATIVE
Dried linguine, though not authentic, offered a firm chewiness similar to lo mein.

NO THANKS
Vacuum-packed fresh noodles from the grocery store labeled "Chinese-style" were gummy and pasty.

Turning Cheap Vodka into Premium Spirits

When cooking with vodka (such as in our Penne alla Vodka recipe, November/December 2006), we've always recommended buying a premium bottle. Vodka is made by fermenting and then distilling starch (usually potatoes). It is then passed through a charcoal filtration system to remove impurities before being diluted with water. Generally, the better the vodka, the more highly filtered it is and the more neutral its flavor. If the key to good vodka's clean flavor is charcoal filtration, we wondered: Could we improve cheap vodka by passing it through a home water filtration system? To find out, we held a blind tasting of three bottles of vodka: Grey Goose, Ruble (the cheapest vodka we could find), and "doctored" Ruble passed four times through a Brita water filter. We still preferred Grey Goose straight up, but in mixed drinks and Penne alla Vodka, Grey Goose and filtered Ruble both had supporters. So while straight-vodka connoisseurs may prefer to spring for a premium bottle, home-filtered cheap vodka is fine for cooking and cocktails.

BRITA WATER FILTER JUG + CHEAP VODKA = PREMIUM VODKA

SCIENCE: Staling Bread

Many recipes that call for stale bread give you two options: using naturally staled, day-old bread, or bread that is "quick staled" by drying in a low oven. Does it matter which technique you use? We staled three types of bread (a French baguette, an egg-enriched challah, and supermarket sliced white bread) in two ways: unwrapped on the counter for three days and in a 225-degree oven for about 35 minutes. We then used the breads to make stuffing, berry puddings, and bread crumbs. Tasters arrived at the same surprising conclusion for all three recipes: The oven-dried versions were the best. The recipes made with oven-dried bread had a fresher taste and a superior structure; the naturally staled bread turned gummy once combined with the other ingredients.

As bread stales naturally, its starch molecules recrystallize in a process called retrogradation, causing the bread to become hard and crumbly, but not necessarily dry. The naturally staled bread was still too moist to produce optimal results. Staling bread quickly in the oven, on the other hand, mostly hardens bread through the removal of moisture, not through retrogradation (which works best at cooler temperatures), ultimately leading to a drier—and better—structure. And though the counter-staled bread produced acceptable results, we'll stick with the faster, more foolproof "oven staling" from now on.

Sizing Up Herbs

Herbs come in all shapes, sizes, and weights. If a recipe calls for ½ cup chopped basil, how many ounces should you buy? Here's a chart to help you gauge.

TYPE OF HERB	WHOLE LEAVES PER ½ OUNCE	FINELY MINCED LEAVES PER ½ OUNCE
Woody: Thyme, Rosemary	½ cup	2–2½ tablespoons
Leafy: Parsley, Cilantro, Dill, Tarragon, Mint, Basil	¾ cup	3 tablespoons
Other: Chives	No whole leaves	4 tablespoons
Delicate (fluffy): Oregano, Marjoram, Sage	¾ cup	5 tablespoons

The Best Bay Leaf: Fresh or Dried?

Fresh bay leaves have become available in many supermarkets. In the test kitchen, we use fresh herbs more often than dried—bay leaves being an exception. To decide whether we should switch, we made two batches of a béchamel sauce, simmering dried bay leaves in one and fresh in the other. Surprisingly, they finished in a dead heat. Here's why: The aromatic molecules in most herbs are more volatile than water. When an herb is dried, most of the flavor evaporates along with the water. Herbs that grow in hot, arid environments—like bay leaves—are different: Their aromatic molecules are less volatile, retaining flavor even after water evaporates. Similarly, in long-cooked applications, we've found that rosemary, thyme, oregano, sage, and other herbs native to hot, arid environments do as well as their fresh counterparts. (And bay leaves are used only in long-cooked recipes.) Since they are cheaper and keep for months in the freezer, we'll continue using dried bay leaves (about 10 cents per leaf), instead of springing for fresh, which cost twice as much.

TECHNIQUE:

Butter Up Your Bird

Many chicken and turkey recipes, including our Herbed Roast Chicken (page 7), call for loosening the skin and applying butter directly on the meat before roasting. We find that the easiest way to do this is with your fingers and a spoon.

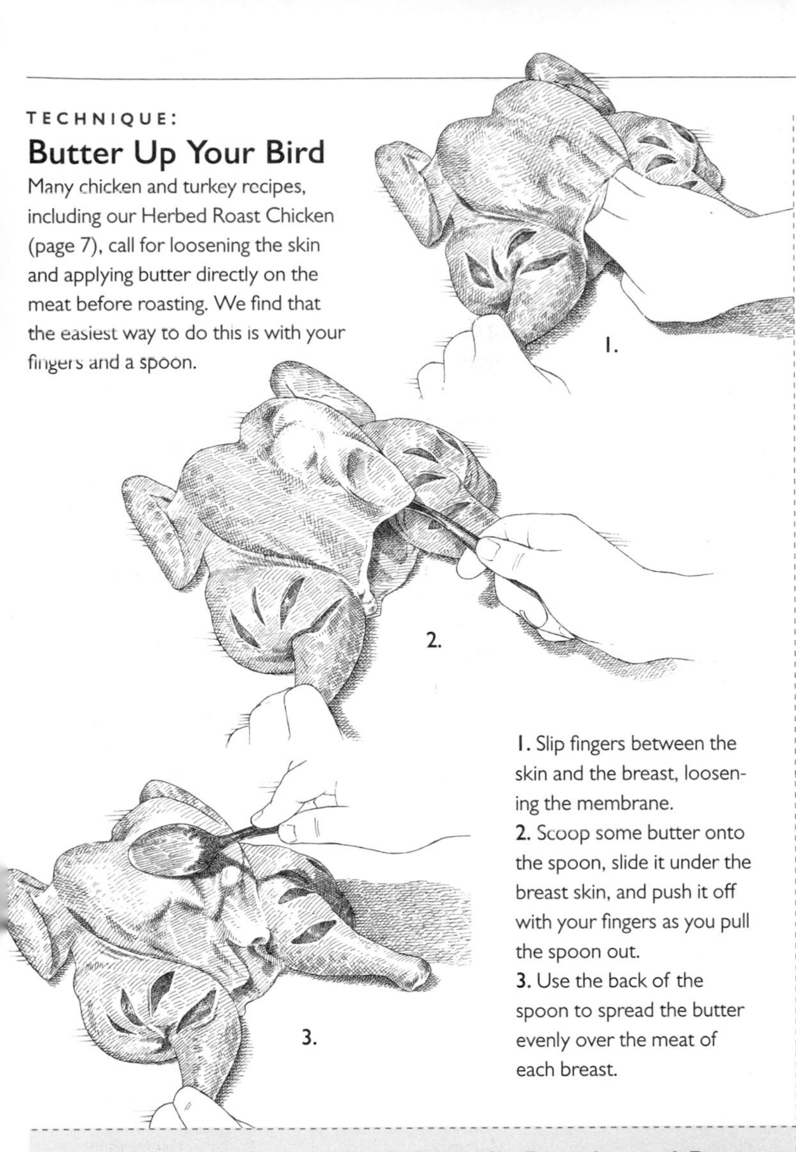

1. Slip fingers between the skin and the breast, loosening the membrane.
2. Scoop some butter onto the spoon, slide it under the breast skin, and push it off with your fingers as you pull the spoon out.
3. Use the back of the spoon to spread the butter evenly over the meat of each breast.

COOKING CLASS 101:

Boil, Blanch, Poach, and Braise

Boiling, blanching, poaching, and braising all involve cooking in a pot of hot water, but that's where their similarities end.

➢ **BOILING:** Water is as hot as possible (212 degrees at sea level), with many large bubbles constantly breaking the surface. This method is reserved mainly for cooking pasta or starchy foods such as potatoes. Since prolonged boiling can compromise color and flavor, we don't recommend it for most vegetables.

➢ **BLANCHING:** Blanching involves quickly plunging food into boiling water, then transferring it into ice water (called "shocking"). We like to blanch green vegetables—such as green beans, broccoli rabe, and snap peas—to help set their color and remove any bitterness. Blanching also helps loosen the skins of nuts or soft fruits such as tomatoes and peaches.

➢ **POACHING:** This technique uses water between 160 and 180 degrees (depending on the delicacy of the item being cooked), at which point small bubbles just begin to break the surface. This gentle cooking method is good for delicate foods such as fruit, fish, or eggs. The poaching liquid is often seasoned with aromatics or alcohol to induce an exchange of flavors between the food and the liquid.

➢ **BRAISING:** This method calls for slowly simmering food in a small amount of liquid in a tightly covered pot. (The temperature of the simmering liquid is 180 to 190 degrees.) Braising is most often used for tough cuts of meat that need to cook gently until tender. Braised items are usually browned in hot oil before aromatics and flavorful liquids such as wine or stock are added.

TASTE TEST:

Cucumbers

Supermarkets carry two kinds of slicing cucumbers: seedless English and standard American. To assess which we prefer, we tasted them grated in a yogurt sauce, salted in a salad, and plain. We found that the American cucumbers had the crispest texture and the most concentrated cucumber flavor, while the English were much milder and more watery.

It turns out that cucumbers contain a "softening" enzyme that breaks down cell walls when the vegetable is cut open. Due to genetic differences between the English and American varieties as well as differences in how they are grown (English cucumbers are almost exclusively raised in greenhouses, while most American kinds grow outdoors), English cucumbers have weaker cell walls that are more easily broken down by the enzyme. Weak cells lead to less-than-crisp texture and flavor that leaks out. And salting cucumbers (which we regularly do for salads) makes the problem worse.

What about the seedless advantage? We'd gladly suffer the minor inconvenience of seeding our own cukes than having to wade through watery salads.

WEAK AND SOGGY
English cucumbers have a weak cellular structure that turns them mushy when cut and salted.

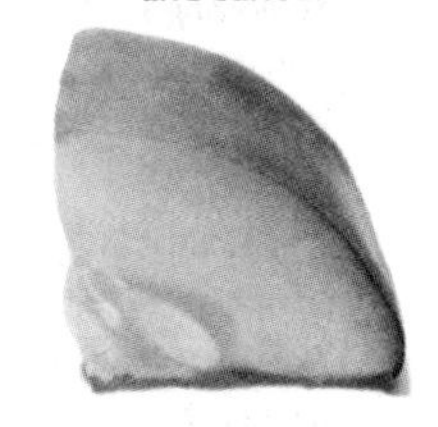

STRONG AND CRISP
Regular American cukes retain their crunch with the same treatment.

SHOPPING:

Frozen Fish

How do the individually frozen fish from the freezer section compare to fresh fish sold at the fish counter? We gathered every type and brand of frozen fish we could find, defrosted them, and compared them to fresh fish. We found that doing a "quick thaw" by leaving the vacuum-sealed bags under cool running tap water for 30 minutes produced results identical to an overnight thaw in the refrigerator. We figured the fresh fish would win by a landslide, but testing turned up a few surprises.

TYPE OF FISH	SHOULD I BUY IT FROZEN?
Delicate/Thin: Flounder, Sole	**RECOMMENDED:** Thin fillets freeze quickly, minimizing moisture loss. When thawed, most tasters couldn't tell the difference, with some tasters even preferring frozen fillets over fresh.
Firm: Halibut, Snapper, Tilapia, Salmon	**RECOMMENDED WITH RESERVATIONS:** When cooked beyond medium-rare, most tasters couldn't tell the difference, but lower degrees of doneness revealed a dry, stringy texture.
Medium-Firm/Flaky: Cod, Haddock, Sea Bass	**NOT RECOMMENDED:** Flaky fish tended to fall apart while defrosting, breaking into small pieces before it even made it to the pan.
Very Firm/ Dense: Tuna, Swordfish	**NOT RECOMMENDED:** Defrosted fish was discolored and cooked unevenly (spotty browning). Lots of moisture escaped during cooking, making the fish dry.

WHAT'S IN THE BAG?
Avoid fish in opaque packaging that doesn't allow you to inspect what's inside.

CLEAR VIEW
This packaging allows you to see the individual fillets before you pay for them.

EQUIPMENT CORNER

BY ELIZABETH BOMZE

EQUIPMENT UPDATE
Mini Adjust-A-Cup

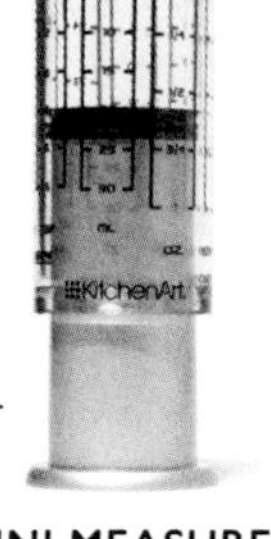

MINI MEASURE
Our favorite measuring tool for sticky, gooey ingredients now has a shorter sibling for smaller amounts.

For measuring sticky ingredients such as honey or peanut butter, we have always liked the KitchenArt Adjust-A-Cup. Available in one- and two-cup capacities, this plunger-fitted tube forces the food out of the cup with a slow, steady push of the sliding base. Now, a new Mini Adjust-A-Cup ($2.99) is ideal for measuring just a few teaspoons, tablespoons, milliliters, or ounces. It works with the ease of its larger counterpart and, at just under three inches tall, stores handily in a drawer.

NEW PRODUCT
Battery-Powered Blender

We thought a portable blender could be useful for car camping or backyard bartending, so we charged the battery, crushed some ice, and blended up milk shakes and margaritas in the Coleman Rechargeable Portable Blender ($59.99), which runs on rechargeable batteries or plugs into a car lighter.

The very loud motor was powerful enough, but the poorly designed, hand-wash-only jar didn't taper sufficiently. Margaritas fared better than thick milk shakes (these required multiple scrape-downs), but the crevices still trapped food away from the blade, which struggled to crush ice and chop large chunks of frozen strawberries. Still, our tasters deemed the results good enough for a camping trip (though maybe not a backyard barbecue), and the long-lasting battery charge was impressive. In sum, this is no replacement for your home blender, but works well enough for making simple frozen drinks or smoothies outdoors.

NOT A BETTER BLENDER
Though convenient for outdoor excursions, the Coleman Rechargeable Portable Blender doesn't stand up to a countertop model.

EQUIPMENT TESTING
Tube Pans

Tube pans are not just for looks—they also help cakes bake faster and more evenly. When we baked simple yellow and angel food cakes in five tube pans, however, we discovered a range of problems.

First, there was leaking. Pans with removable bottoms made from lightweight materials (under 1 pound) by Wilton ($16.99) and Williams-Sonoma ($22) let batter seep under the bottom, gluing it to the rest of the pan, while the heavier model from Chicago Metallic (1.65 pounds; $19.95) stayed grounded. No leaking, no sticking.

Poor browning was another common flaw. Pale, tinny finishes on the Wilton and Williams-Sonoma pans, as well as on heavy-duty one-piece models from Fante's ($37.99) and Bridge Kitchenware ($43.60), left cakes pallid and sticky. We worried that the dark nonstick coating on the Chicago Metallic pan might prevent the batter from rising, but both cakes baked in it emerged tall and evenly burnished. This model also has handy feet on the rim to elevate the upturned pan for cooling. It's our new favorite tube pan.

ANGELIC PAN
Removing cakes is easy with this nonstick pan from Chicago Metallic—you just pull up the tube attached to the removable bottom.

EQUIPMENT TESTING
Thermal Carafes

We love the thermal carafe feature of our new favorite coffee maker, the Technivorm, but for high-volume entertaining—or for those who own a nonthermal machine—we wanted a separate heat-keeping carafe. We tested six models. All kept liquids between a drinkable 120 and 160 degrees for three hours (we probably wouldn't want to drink coffee any older than that). Of these, our favorite—the 51-ounce Thermos Nissan Stainless Steel Carafe ($46)—won praise for being dishwasher-safe and for its sleek, compact design, single-handed pouring, and superior durability that survived a fall to the floor in our final "tip-over test."

HOT POT
This Thermos carafe is dishwasher-safe and offers excellent temperature retention, convenient one-handed pouring, and a stable, leak-free design.

NEW PRODUCT
Tabletop Food Tents

We love to entertain outside in summer, but fighting off insects can force the party indoors. One solution is to pop open a food tent. We tested a variety of these mesh shelters, including dome-shaped models from Patio Companion (a 17-inch tent for $4.95, and a 48- by 24-inch model meant to cover a table for $9.95) and a cylindrical trio from Improvements ($14.99 for a set of 12½-, 14½-, and 16½-inch covers). All were large enough for most standard serving platters, and all were collapsible for storage and transportation. Of these two brands, we preferred the set from Improvements for its range of sizes and finer, sturdier mesh.

BUG OFF
Tabletop food tents, like this cylindrical model from Improvements, protect outdoor meals from flies.

Sources

The following are sources for items recommended in this issue. Prices were current at press time and do not include shipping. Contact companies to confirm information or visit www.cooksillustrated.com for updates.

Page 15: FIVE-SPICE POWDER
- Dean & DeLuca Five Spice Blend: $6.50 for 1.4 oz., item #511078, Dean & DeLuca (800-221-7714, www.deandeluca.com).

Page 23: DIGITAL SCALES
- OXO Food Scale: $49.99, item #1130800, OXO (800-545-4411, www.oxo.com).
- Soehnle 65055 Digital Scale: $29.75, Chef's Corner (877-372-4535, www.chefscorner.com).

Page 27: BACON
- Vande Rose Farms Applewood Smoked Bacon: $13.95 for 12 oz., Grateful Palate (888-472-5283, www.gratefulpalate.com).

Page 29: COFFEE MAKER
- Technivorm Moccamaster Coffeemaker: $239.95, item #KBT741, Roastmasters (888-950-0888, www.roastmasters.com).

Page 32: MINI ADJUST-A-CUP
- KitchenArt Mini Adjust-A-Cup: $2.99, item #22100, KitchenArt (800-239-8090, www.kitchenart.com).

Page 32: PORTABLE BLENDER
- Coleman Rechargeable Portable Blender: $59.99, item #850-865, Coleman (800-835-3278, www.coleman.com).

Page 32: TUBE PAN
- Chicago Metallic Professional Nonstick Angel Food Cake Pan with Feet: $19.95, item #394876, Cooking.com (800-663-8810, www.cooking.com).

Page 32: THERMAL CARAFE
- Thermos Nissan Stainless Steel Carafe: $46, item #00002369, Bald Mountain Coffee (866-393-9155, www.baldmountaincoffee.com).

Page 32: FOOD TENTS
- Collapsible Food Covers: $14.99 for three, item #297029, Improvements (800-634-9484, www.improvementscatalog.com).

INDEX

September & October 2008

RECIPES

COOK'S LIVE Original Test Kitchen Videos **www.cooksillustrated.com**

Herbed Roast Chicken, 7

Steak Tacos, 11

Quick Glazes for Grilled Chicken, 19

Pork Stir-Fry with Noodles, 15

Grilled Rack of Lamb, 9

Pizza Bianca, 21

Crunchy Oven-Fried Fish, 13

Creamless Creamy Tomato Soup, 18

Individual Sticky Toffee Pudding Cakes, 23

Skillet Apple Pie, 25

PHOTOGRAPHY: CARL TREMBLAY, STYLING: MARIE PIRAINO

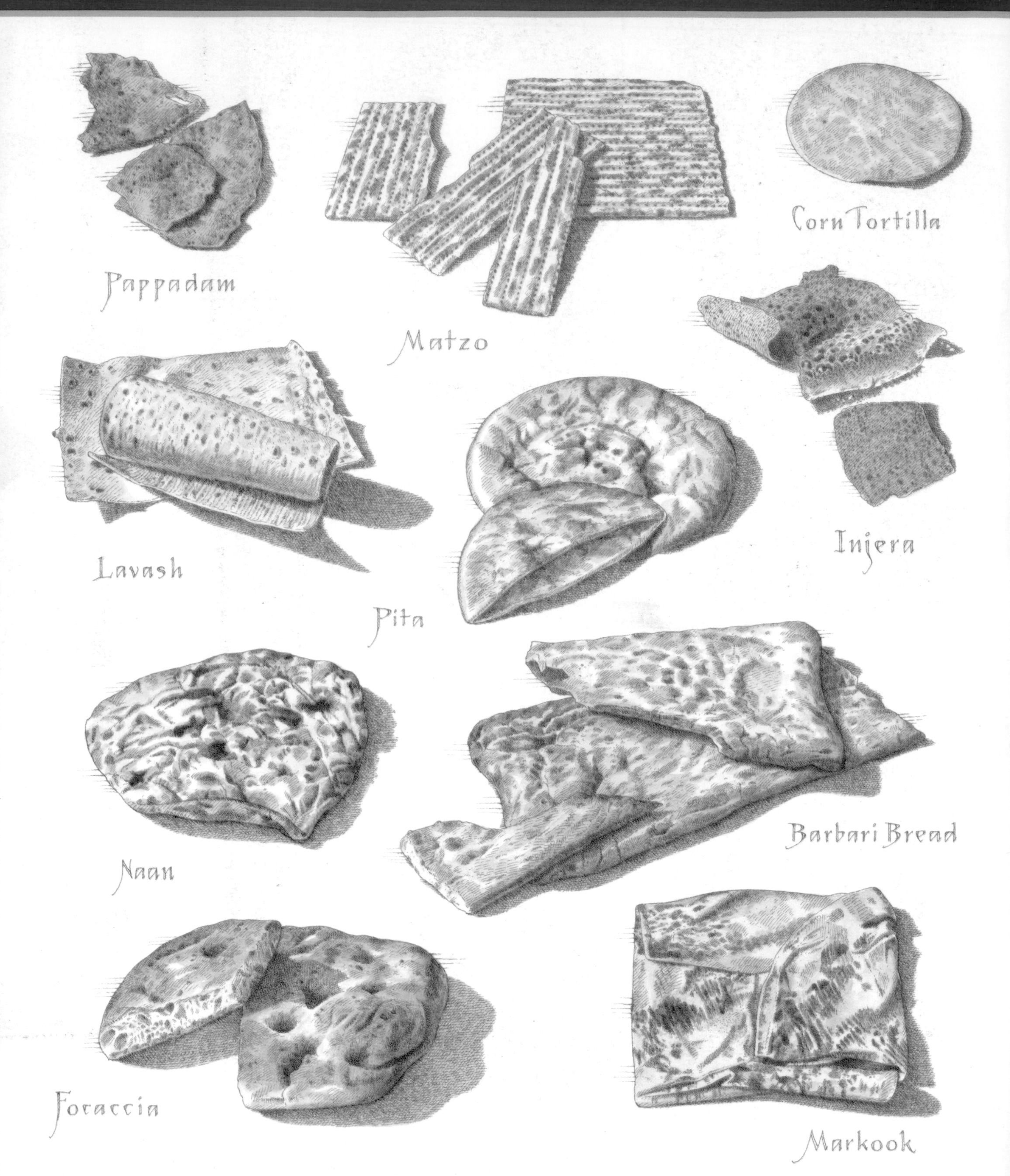
Pappadam
Matzo
Corn Tortilla
Injera
Lavash
Pita
Naan
Barbari Bread
Focaccia
Markook

FLATBREADS

NUMBER NINETY-FIVE

NOVEMBER & DECEMBER 2008

COOK'S ILLUSTRATED

Quick Roast Chicken
30-Minute Skillet Technique

Easy Green Beans

No-Fuss Roast Turkey
Juicy Meat without the Brine

Rating Slicing Knives

Best Black Pepper
Brand Really Does Matter!

Better Pumpkin Pie
Secret Ingredients Improve Flavor

Chef's Knife Primer
Essential Tips for Every Cook

Authentic Hungarian Beef Stew
Foolproof Rustic Dinner Rolls
Ultimate Stuffed Mushrooms
French Butter Cookies
Garlic Shrimp Pasta
Roasted Sweet Potatoes

www.cooksillustrated.com
$5.95 U.S./$6.95 CANADA

CONTENTS

November & December 2008

ITALIAN COOKIES Licorice-y anise is the darling of Italian cookie flavorings, though lemon and vanilla are also commonly featured in cookies like Anginetti. Anisette cookies are iced with a confectioners' sugar glaze and sometimes topped with confetti sprinkles. Biscotti are baked twice to create a crunchy dipping cookie for soaking up coffee or wine. Mildly sweetened sesame cookies make an equally good accompaniment to coffee. Meringuelike pignoli cookies take their name from the pine nuts that are dispersed throughout this airy confection. Crimped and folded, lemon flips resemble mini turnovers with their citrusy filling and pie pastry shell. Waffle irons press wafer-thin pizzelle into lacy patterns. Florentine crisps are cooked in a skillet to develop their candylike texture before being coated in chocolate. Cakey tricolor rainbow cookies are layered with marzipan and glazed with chocolate. Pink and green leaf-shaped butter cookies sandwich a thin layer of chocolate. Made with a similar butter dough, esse cookies are named for their serpentine shape and can be flavored with a variety of extracts and sprinkled with sugar. Italian fig cookies are everything that Fig Newtons aspire to be—and more.

COVER (*Clementines*): Robert Papp, BACK COVER (*Italian Cookies*): John Burgoyne

COOK'S ILLUSTRATED

Founder and Editor Christopher Kimball
Editorial Director Jack Bishop
Executive Editor Amanda Agee
Test Kitchen Director Erin McMurrer
Managing Editor Rebecca Hays
Senior Editors Keith Dresser, Lisa McManus
Features Editor Lisa Glazer
Copy Editor Amy Graves
Associate Editors J. Kenji Alt, Charles Kelsey, David Pazmiño
Production Editor, Special Issues Elizabeth Bomze
Test Cooks Francisco J. Robert, Yvonne Ruperti
Assistant Test Kitchen Director Matthew Herron
Assistant Editors Meredith Butcher, Peggy Chung
Executive Assistant Meredith Smith
Editorial Assistant Jacqueline Valerio
Senior Kitchen Assistant Nadia Domeq
Kitchen Assistants Maria Elena Delgado, Ena Gudiel, Edward Tundidor
Producer Melissa Baldino
Contributing Editors Matthew Card, Dawn Yanagihara
Consulting Editors Scott Brueggeman, Guy Crosby
Proofreader Jean Rogers

Online Managing Editor David Tytell
Online Editor Kate Mason
Online Media Producer Peter Tannenbaum
Online Assistant Editor Leaya Lee

Design Director Amy Klee
Art Director, Magazines Julie Bozzo
Senior Designer Christine Vo
Designer Jay Layman
Staff Photographer Daniel J. van Ackere

Vice President Marketing David Mack
Circulation Director Doug Wicinski
Circulation & Fulfillment Manager Carrie Horan
Circulation Assistant Elizabeth Dayton
Partnership Marketing Manager Pamela Putprush
Direct Mail Director Adam Perry
Direct Mail Analyst Jenny Leong
Marketing Database Analyst Ariel Gilbert-Knight
Product Operations Director Steven Browall
Product Promotions Director Randi Lawrence
E-Commerce Marketing Director Hugh Buchan
Associate Marketing Manager Laurel Zeidman
Marketing Copywriter David Goldberg
Customer Service Manager Leann Fowler
Customer Service Representative Jillian Nannicelli

Sponsorship Sales Director Marcy McCreary
Retail Sales & Marketing Manager Emily Logan
Corporate Marketing Associate Bailey Vatalaro

Production Director Guy Rochford
Traffic & Projects Manager Alice Cummiskey
Senior Production Manager Jessica L. Quirk
Production & Imaging Specialist Lauren Pettapiece
Imaging & Color Specialist Andrew Mannone

Vice President New Technology Craig Morrow
Systems Administrator S. Paddi McHugh
Web Production Coordinator Evan Davis
Support Technician Brandon Lynch

Chief Financial Officer Sharyn Chabot
Human Resources Director Adele Shapiro
Controller Mandy Shito
Senior Accountant Aaron Goranson
Staff Accountant Connie Forbes
Accounts Payable Specialist Steven Kasha
Office Manager Tasha Bere
Receptionist Henrietta Murray
Publicity Deborah Broide

For list rental information, contact: Specialists Marketing Services, Inc., 777 Terrace Ave., 4th Floor, Hasbrouck Heights, NJ 07604; 201-865-5800.

Editorial Office: 17 Station St., Brookline, MA 02445; 617-232-1000; fax 617-232-1572. Subscription inquiries, visit www.americastestkitchen.com/customerservice or call 800-526-8442.

Postmaster: Send all new orders, subscription inquiries, and change-of-address notices to Cook's Illustrated, P.O. Box 7446, Red Oak, IA 51591-0446.

PRINTED IN THE USA

LISTEN TO THE RIVER

Back in 1970, two friends and I bought a station wagon in Baltimore for the price of two Friendly's fried clam platters and headed out West for spring break. I eventually ended up in Taos, where I stumbled across Wavy Gravy's famous hippie commune, the Hog Farm. It was an experiment in dropping out, but it reminded me of a poorly run summer camp: The kitchen was filthy, the diet was mostly goat's milk and undercooked brown rice, everyone's hair was smoky and snarled, and I almost froze to death the first night since nobody knew how to bank a fire. I spent a long weekend scrubbing the kitchen and cooking, an early sign of my eventual career path. Today, they probably all trade oil futures.

Fast forward 40 years, and I am so far on the grid that I am not sure I would know how to get off. Sure, we produce a lot of our own food—and, yes, we can heat our farmhouse with our wood furnace, and we can't get cell phone service except when I stand exactly 15 feet down the driveway, perched on the south side. Yet I have a fair number of frequent flyer miles, my passport is well stamped, and I can tell you the best place for lunch in Saigon.

Unlike our parents' generation, whose core values were drawn from two world wars and the Great Depression, my generation has little to show for its life philosophy other than the peace sign and a brightly painted VW bus. "Give Peace a Chance" and "All You Need Is Love" turned out to be nothing more than pleasant mantras. Religions understand that an approach to life has to be simple and actionable. The Golden Rule ("Do unto others . . .") is perfect in that regard or, as I once summarized the essence of Christianity in a Sunday sermon, "Don't be a jerk." Harsh, perhaps, but easy to follow.

My story is the story of a generation. I left for college, became a lifelong Deadhead, spent more than one evening skinny dipping in cold Vermont beaver ponds after listening to Cat Stevens and eating carrot cake, and studied Foxfire books to learn about a future dressing out hogs, building my homestead cabin, and running a pick-your-own operation. I stood on a stage next to Allen Ginsberg on May Day 1970 in New Haven, chanting "Nam Myoho Renge Kyo" while being teargassed by police, marched on the administration building at Columbia, drove a 1961 VW Beetle with a sunroof and a large sheepdog for company, and spent more time than I care to admit eating burnt oatmeal at rainy rock concerts from upstate New York (Watkins Glen) to the state of Washington. My bible was *Living the Good Life* by the Nearings, who lived, serendipitously enough, not far from our present farm. Their philosophy of hard physical labor in the morning followed by a long, lovingly prepared lunch and then an afternoon of intellectual and musical pursuits is still my life goal.

Christopher Kimball

Our movement skidded ingloriously in the mud of Woodstock, which defined the '60s only by its music—a dissonant, howling version of our national anthem played by a soon-to-be-dead rock star who overdosed on drugs. Hmm. Not an ideal last chapter.

So here we are, a generation later, in need of a new, improved philosophy. The irony is beyond ironic. War. Earth endangered. Mass consumerism. And Bob Dylan is still giving sold-out concerts.

My Vermont neighbors never dropped out, nor did they succumb to the siren song of platitudes. They simply got up early every day in an effort to be useful. They still bake birthday cakes flavored with locally picked butternuts, can tomatoes and green beans, and know how to switch out blades on a mower. They regularly send their sons and daughters off to serve their country. In hard times they might complain a bit—don't mention the price of gas—but they make do and still find time to hunt and fish. And when a neighbor needs a lift or a casserole, they are quick to provide.

They might think nothing of sitting starkers outside their roadside sauna on Sunday afternoons, watching chickens and traffic, unlike the made-for-media nakedness of Woodstock. They know that the old sayings are perfectly true: Make hay while the sun shines; a penny saved is a penny earned. They have an independent streak with words: "I'm so broke that I can't even pay attention," "I wouldn't run uphill after it," and, one of my all-time favorites, "I'm so hungry I could eat the north end of a southbound skunk." Shopping is not a sport (unless it's Cabela's); it is merely a necessity. And where they live is no small thing—the full moon rises over our upper horse pasture, bathing the farmhouse with a pure, spectral glow. The moonlight whispers that there is redemption in the little things, in trying hard and in self-reliance.

Ken Kesey, the voice of the Beat Generation, lost his son in a car accident and found himself not long after at a Grateful Dead concert. When they played "Brokedown Palace" he cried, realizing that art is not about politics but about the personal. We sing along: "Going home, going home, by the riverside I will rest my bones," and then we end with, "Listen to the river sing sweet songs to rock my soul."

Life is a mystery. It isn't what we think or even what we hope. It is always just one step beyond our understanding; once in a while, it comes back around to offer us a second chance. Across America, we now realize, there were people better than us who had always lived within the sound of the river.

Last summer, after the brook had dried up, a midnight thunderstorm drove through the valley, dropping an inch of rain. The next day, I sat on the porch and heard something familiar. Having been gone for so long, the river sounded particularly sweet.

FOR INQUIRIES, ORDERS, OR MORE INFORMATION

www.cooksillustrated.com

At www.cooksillustrated.com, you can order books and subscriptions, sign up for our free e-newsletter, or renew your magazine subscription. Join the website and gain access to 15 years of *Cook's Illustrated* recipes, equipment tests, and ingredient tastings as well as Cook's Live companion videos for every recipe in this issue.

COOKBOOKS

You will find more than 50 cookbooks from the editors of *Cook's Illustrated* in our bookstore at www.cooksillustrated.com.

COOK'S ILLUSTRATED Magazine

Cook's Illustrated magazine (ISSN 1068-2821), number 95, is published bimonthly by Boston Common Press Limited Partnership, 17 Station St., Brookline, MA 02445. Periodicals postage paid at Boston, Mass., and additional mailing offices USPS #012487. Publications Mail Agreement No. 40020778. Return undeliverable Canadian addresses to P.O. Box 875, Station A, Windsor, Ontario N9A 6P2. POSTMASTER: Send address changes to Cook's Illustrated, P.O. Box 7446, Red Oak, IA 51591-0446. For subscription and gift subscription orders, subscription inquiries, or change-of-address notices, visit us at www.americastestkitchen.com/customerservice or write to us at Cook's Illustrated, P.O. Box 7446, Red Oak, IA 51591-0446.

NOTES FROM READERS

COMPILED BY DAVID PAZMIÑO

Dealcoholized Wine

I know that not all of the alcohol in wine evaporates during cooking. I recently saw bottles of alcohol-free wine that claimed they had as much flavor as the real thing. Have you ever tried this as a substitute for regular wine?

TRAVIS BUCKMAN
WALNUT CREEK, CALIF.

Before heading into the kitchen, we sampled both red and white versions of two national brands of dealcoholized wine, Ariel and Fre. Neither brand had the complexity of real wine, but the Fre red and white beverages were a step up from mere grape juice. To find out what factors might contribute to the differences between the brands, we looked into how each producer removes alcohol from wine. Ariel uses a cold filtration process, repeatedly passing the wine along meshlike membranes to remove the alcohol. The resulting alcohol-free syrup is then diluted with water. Fre wines, on the other hand, are produced with a technique known as the "spinning-cone" method, in which the wine cascades down spinning, cone-shaped cylinders in a thin stream. Nitrogen gas is sprayed over this thin layer of wine to prevent any of the flavor compounds from becoming volatile and escaping. When the wine is subsequently heated to remove the alcohol, the nitrogen shield protects the flavors of the wine. In the end, the alcohol is reduced from 10 to 12 percent to 0.3 to 0.5 percent. Since some liquid evaporates in the process, a small amount of unfermented grape juice is added to the wine. Though sweet, wines that are dealcoholized with the spinning-cone method retain distinct wine aromas and flavors.

Fre dealcoholized wine is an acceptable substitute for the real thing.

To see how the dealcoholized Fre would stand up to the real deal in cooking, we made our Sautéed Chicken Cutlets with Shallots and White Wine Sauce (January/February 2005) and our Daube Provençal (November/December 2005). While all tasters could easily detect the sweet and less acidic notes of the dealcoholized wine in both dishes, most thought it was still quite acceptable. When we added some lemon juice or wine vinegar to cut the sweetness, both dishes got near-universal compliments. If you want to avoid wine with alcohol, the only national brand we found that uses the spinning-cone method is Fre, which is made by Sutter Home.

Cannellini Bean Substitute

I often make recipes that call for dried cannellini beans, but these beans are hard to find in my supermarket. Are dried great Northern or navy beans a good substitute?

ALISON HALÁSZ
MEMPHIS, TENN.

All three beans come from a common ancestor: the pole bean. But are they interchangeable? To find out, we soaked several different brands of each type separately for 12 hours and then cooked them in fresh water. The flavor was nearly identical in all three, but the texture was not. Cannellini beans (measuring an average of 0.9 inch long after cooking) had the thickest skins, which kept the inside texture creamy. The great Northern beans (0.69 inch long when cooked) had more tender skins and slightly less creamy flesh. Navy beans (0.52 inch long) were tender and soft, but their thin skins slipped off easily and contributed an almost chewy texture.

Next, we tested each bean in our Tuscan White Bean Soup (January/February 2001). While tasters generally preferred the creamy texture and larger size of the cannellini beans, most found that the great Northern beans tasted nearly as good. Because the navy beans' skins came off so readily, however, these beans yielded too high a ratio of skins to flesh. While navy beans are great in soups specifically designed for them or in dishes like baked beans (where the acidic molasses aids in keeping bean skins intact during the long cooking), we would avoid using them as a substitute for cannellini beans. If you can't find cannellini beans, great Northern beans are the best stand-in.

Whole Grain White Bread

I have followed your ingredient recommendations for years, especially when it comes to staples like bread. I have been happy with your favorite, Pepperidge Farm White Sandwich Bread. When visiting my supermarket, I was surprised to find that Pepperidge Farm has a new product, Whole Grain White Sandwich Bread. How does this differ from white bread and is it as good?

ROXANNE BILOSKIRKA
NEWTON, MASS.

We too had noticed Pepperidge Farm Whole Grain White Sandwich Bread (made from white whole wheat flour) and decided to pit it head to head against their regular white bread. Since we often use white bread to make bread crumbs, we first decided to make crumbs out of each for our Crisp Breaded Chicken Cutlets (September/October 2001). The results: The whole grain white bread was nearly indistinguishable from the regular white bread. In the second round of tests, we used each loaf for a simple bread stuffing. Again, the whole grain white bread was deemed identical to the white bread. Then came the moment of truth—eating it plain. The differences here were more apparent: The whole grain white bread was called "sweeter" and had a "coarser texture."

According to Chuck Walker, a grain specialist and professor at Kansas State University, white whole wheat is not sweeter than its darker whole wheat cousins; it simply contains less bitter compounds, called phenolics, in the outer bran layer. When people eat bread made from white whole wheat flour, it tastes surprisingly sweet. Unlike white flour where the outer bran layers are removed, white whole wheat flour contains the whole grain. This means it has more fiber compared to white flour (3 grams of fiber per 2 slices compared to less than 1 gram for regular white bread). If you are looking to add a bit more fiber to your diet, using Whole Grain White Sandwich Bread from Pepperidge Farm would certainly be the way to go, especially when cooking.

Adding Eggs One at a Time

I find that some recipes call for adding eggs one at a time to creamed butter and sugar. I use an electric stand mixer to make batters and doughs for cakes and cookies. Would it really matter if I simply added the eggs all at once to save on mixing time?

JIM MILESKI
NORTH QUINCY, MASS.

Looking into our archives, we noticed that almost all of our cake and cookie recipes that call for more than one egg either add them one at a time or premix the eggs and then add them in a steady stream. Your letter made us wonder why this extra effort is involved and whether it is necessary. First, we made a batch of our Chocolate Chip Oatmeal Cookies (January/February 1997). When the two eggs in the recipe were added one at a time, it took about 30 seconds to incorporate each into the creamed butter and sugar, compared with slightly over two minutes when both were added at once. While the difference in time might not seem significant, the difference in the finished cookies was. Eggs added one at a time led to cookies that were thick and chewy; eggs added all at once produced cookies that spread, became unevenly shaped, and were not as chewy. We encountered similar differences with our Chocolate Sour Cream Bundt Cake (January/February 2004) and Classic Pound Cake (January/February 2007). In both recipes, when the eggs were added together, it took longer to incorporate them and the cakes turned out denser and slightly rubbery.

WHAT IS IT?

I found this gadget while rummaging around in my grandmother's attic last summer. It has a long handle, a sharp blade, and two sides with blunt and spiky metal parts. The only label on it says K.D.&S. Chicago. Do you have any idea how my grandmother might have used this tool in her kitchen?

JENNIFER MEISENKOTHEN
MARYSVILLE, OHIO

➤The item you uncovered in your grandmother's attic is a "combination kitchen tool" from the early 1900s. This somewhat menacing-looking gadget (a 6-inch-long blade attached to a 4½-inch handle) actually played an important role in the pre-electric kitchen. By pressing a metal button near the blade face that activates a locking mechanism, the blade can turn 90 degrees so that either the blunt or the jagged edges may be employed. The blunt edge was used to tenderize tough cuts of meat. The sharper and more triangular edges served to chip ice from large ice blocks used to cool early refrigerators. When locked in its flatter position, the tool could also be used like a cleaver to chop meat or vegetables. If all these applications weren't enough, its neck includes a working bottle opener, making this gadget the Swiss Army knife of the kitchen.

We tried out the tool, finding it did a passable job chopping onions and carrots and hacking through chicken breasts. Flipped into the upright position, it also did a decent job of tenderizing meat. But the only area where it really excelled? Breaking ice cubes into small pieces. While we're not ready to give up our automatic ice crusher, it's good to know there's still a gadget around that can get the job done with simple manpower.

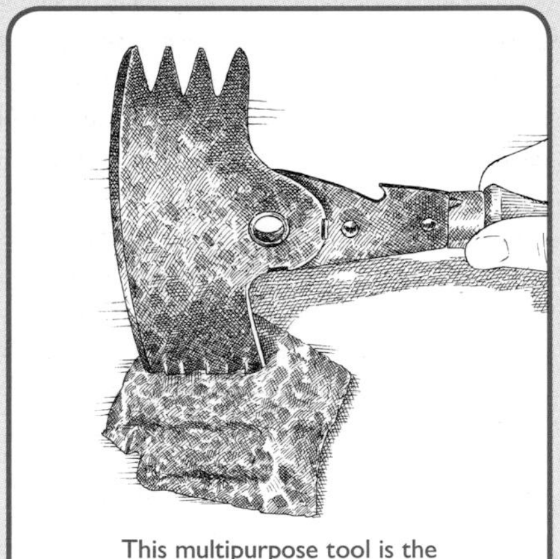

This multipurpose tool is the Swiss Army knife of the kitchen.

The fact is, like oil and vinegar, eggs and butter don't mix naturally. It's a matter of chemistry: Butter is at least 80 percent fat, while eggs contain large amounts of water. So any time you add more than a single egg to creamed butter, it's best to do it slowly to give the mixture time to thicken and emulsify.

Disposable Baking Pans

During the holidays, I typically need lots of bakeware for transporting casseroles, cakes, and pastries to parties and potlucks. I would like to use disposable aluminum pans but am afraid they might not work well for baked goods. What do you think?

BECKY GEORGE-KURBER
GREENFIELD, MASS.

➤To see how disposable aluminum baking pans would perform, we made a batch of our New York–Style Crumb Cake (May/June 2007) in a disposable aluminum 8-inch square pan and our Sticky Buns with Pecans (September/October 2004) in a disposable aluminum 13- by 9-inch pan. When compared to batches made in traditional metal pans, there was a clear difference. The cake and buns made in the disposable pans had not browned and were unevenly cooked, and the caramel on the sticky buns was a lighter shade.

Another drawback of the disposable pans was that they were hard to transfer out of the oven, since they tended to be wobbly. Borrowing an idea for browning and crisping the bottoms of pies, we next put the filled disposable pans directly on a preheated baking sheet. This solved both problems. The baked goods now browned evenly, and the baking sheet made it easy to transfer the pans out of the oven.

Dry versus Liquid Measuring Cups

Before I read your magazine, I always measured flour, milk, and most other ingredients in the same glass Pyrex measuring cup. You always say to use a dry measuring cup for dry ingredients and a liquid measuring cup for liquid ingredients. Is this absolutely necessary?

JEAN HESSEY
SARASOTA, FLA.

➤To demonstrate how each type of measuring cup fared, we asked 18 people, both cooks and non-cooks, to measure 1 cup of all-purpose flour in both dry and liquid measuring cups. We then weighed the flour to assess accuracy (a properly measured cup of all-purpose flour weighs 5 ounces). With the dry measuring cup, the measurements were off by as much as 13 percent. This variance can be attributed to how each person dipped the cup into the flour; a more forceful dip packs more flour into the same volume. Measuring flour in a liquid measuring cup, where it's impossible to level off any excess, drove that variance all the way up to 26 percent.

The same people then measured 1 cup of water (which should weigh 8.345 ounces) in both dry and liquid measuring cups. The dry cup varied by 23 percent, while the liquid cup varied by only 10 percent. In this case, it was much easier to gauge the volume of water in the liquid measuring cup, as its transparency allowed measurers to see when the meniscus—the bottom of the curved surface line of the liquid—had touched the 1-cup line. There was a greater variance when measuring water in a dry cup because it was so easy to overfill, as the surface tension of water allows it to sit slightly higher in this type of vessel.

When measuring a dry ingredient, it is best to scoop it up with a dry measuring cup and then sweep off the excess with a flat utensil, a method we call "dip and sweep." To fill a liquid measuring cup, we recommend placing it on the counter, bending down so that the cup's markings are at eye level, and then pouring in liquid until the meniscus reaches the desired marking. And whenever you want to be nearly 100 percent accurate, use a scale.

SAVE FOR DRY ONLY FOR LIQUIDS

For the greatest accuracy, use the appropriate measuring cup.

Erratum

➤"Searching for the Perfect Drip Coffee Maker" on page 28 of the September/October 2008 issue contained incorrect information. A testing error led us to report an incorrect average time to brew a 10-cup pot of coffee in the Hamilton Beach Stay or Go Deluxe 10-Cup Thermal Coffeemaker. Due to a confusing button design, we tested the machine with the wrong setting, using the 1-4 cup mode for a full pot, which slowed the brewing time to an average of 18 minutes. When we retested the coffee maker using the correct settings, the average brewing time for a full pot of coffee dropped to 12 minutes, 23 seconds. However, this brewing time is still unsatisfactory. To earn a recommendation, the machine must brew 10 cups in six minutes or less. We also found that the faster brewing time did not markedly improve the flavor of the coffee. We stand by our original assessment of this product, and do not recommend it.

SEND US YOUR QUESTIONS We will provide a complimentary one-year subscription for each letter we print. Send your inquiry, name, address, and daytime telephone number to Notes from Readers, Cook's Illustrated, P.O. Box 470589, Brookline, MA 02447, or to notesfromreaders@americastestkitchen.com.

Quick Tips

COMPILED BY YVONNE RUPERTI

Twine Dispenser

Kitchen twine can be unwieldy to unravel, and the roll often gets dirty in the process. Melissa Murphy of Kingston, N.H., keeps her twine clean by assembling a homemade dispenser. Stand a roll of twine upright on a saucer, then cover it with an overturned clay flowerpot.

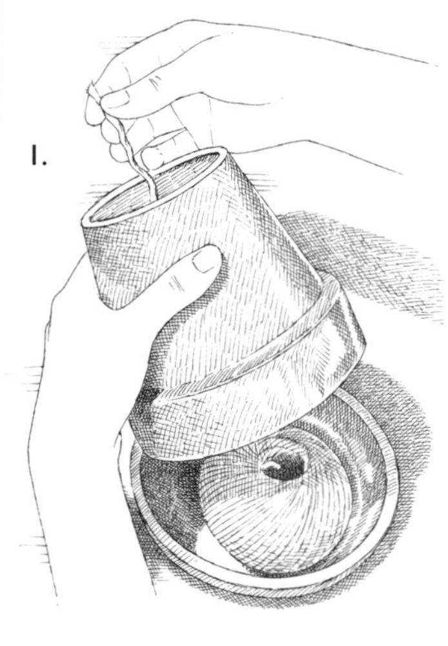

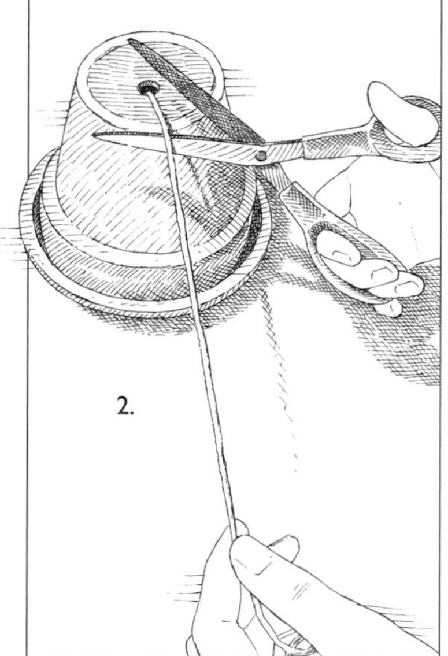

1. Feed the twine through the hole in the bottom of the pot, pulling out as much as you need for each use.
2. Snip at the desired length.

Recycling Rubber Gloves

No-skid rubber mats are useful for stabilizing cutting boards and preventing them from slipping around on the counter. Instead of buying a no-skid mat, Megan Carroll of New York, N.Y., recycles unlined rubber kitchen gloves.

1. Use scissors to cut off the hand portion of a glove at the wrist; discard the hand. Slit the wrist section to open into a flat piece, then cut the piece in half lengthwise.
2. Place the rubber pieces on the work surface and then place the cutting board on top.

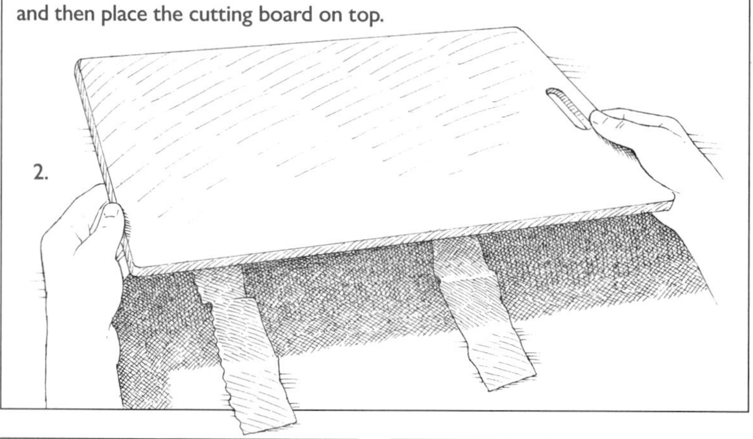

Preventing Microwave Splatters

Food often splatters when it is being heated in the microwave. Jane Weis of Elk Rapids, Mich., found that a basket-style coffee filter is ideal for covering food and keeping the walls of the microwave clean.

Reviving Stale Marshmallows

Marshmallows have a tendency to become hard and stale over time. Patricia Craig of Hopewell Jct., N.Y., offers this simple tip to restore their freshness. Place the stale marshmallows and 1 slice of white sandwich bread in an airtight container. After 24 hours, the marshmallows will be soft and ready for snacking or floating on hot chocolate. Discard the bread.

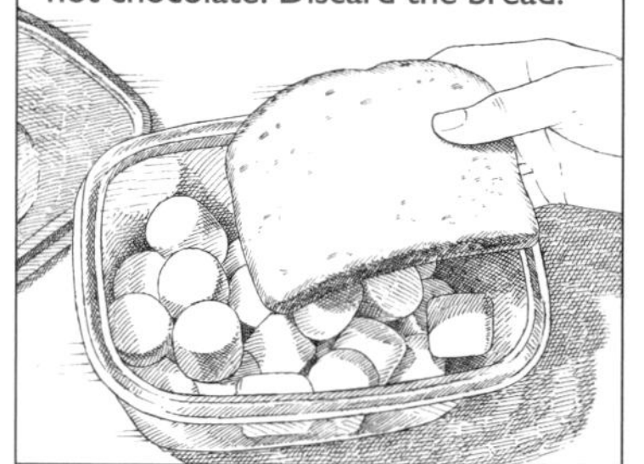

Funnel in a Flash

To create a funnel to fill small kitchen tools such as a pepper mill without spilling, Jeff Katz of New York, N.Y., offers this crafty tip.

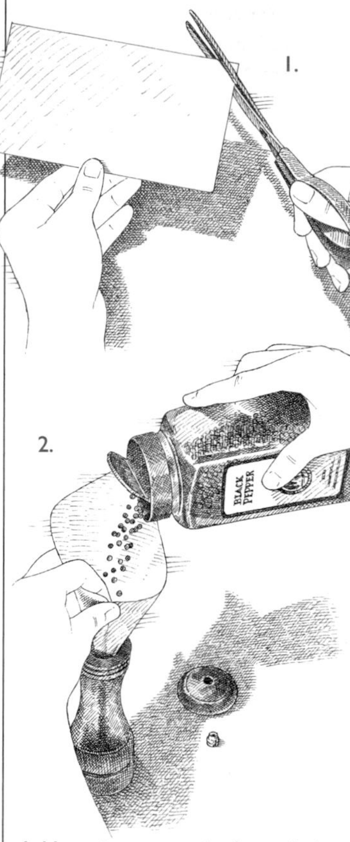

1. Use scissors to snip the sealed corner from an envelope to create a funnel of the desired width.
2. Crack open the envelope, insert the funnel into the container, and pour in ingredients.

Turkey Leftovers

Microwaving or reheating leftover turkey in the oven often dries it out. Elaine Parker of Edmonton, Alberta, Canada, found an ingenious way to keep the meat moist. Place slices of leftover turkey in a steamer basket set in a pot of simmering water, then cover the pot with a lid and check it every few minutes. The turkey heats up quickly and stays juicy.

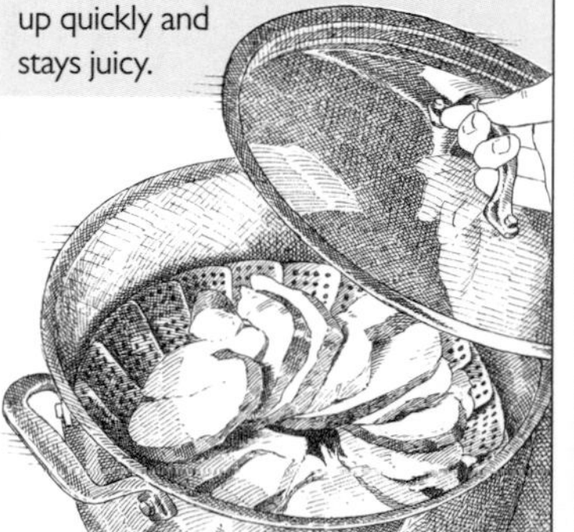

Send Us Your Tip We will provide a complimentary one-year subscription for each tip we print. Send your tip, name, and address to Quick Tips, Cook's Illustrated, P.O. Box 470589, Brookline, MA 02447, or to quicktips@americastestkitchen.com.

ILLUSTRATION: JOHN BURGOYNE

Precise Cookie Cutting

When cookie cutters are used to create intricate shapes from a thin sheet of dough, transferring the shapes to a baking sheet with a spatula can distort or ruin their appearance. Liz Baak of Landisville, Pa., uses this clever method instead.

1.

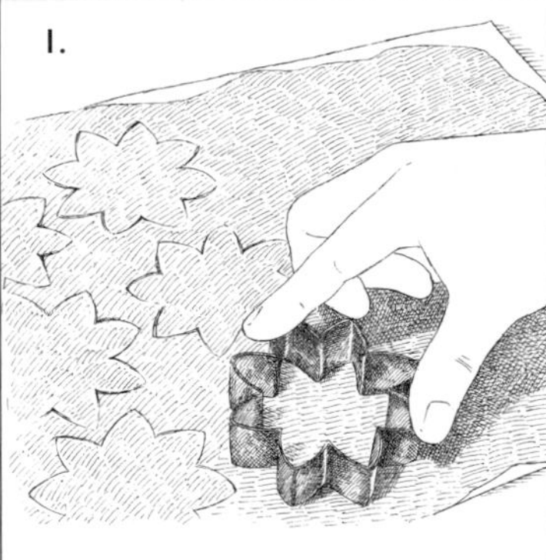

2.

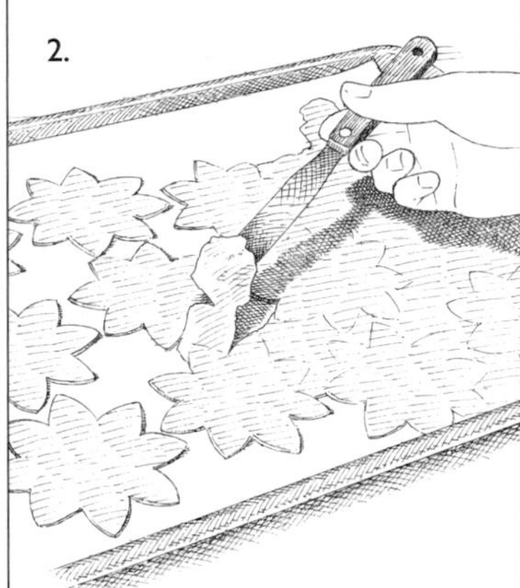

1. Roll the cookie dough out on a piece of parchment paper or on a nonstick baking liner, then use a cookie cutter to cut shapes. Transfer the filled parchment or baking liner to a baking sheet.
2. Use a small spatula to carefully remove the excess scraps of dough from around the shapes, leaving behind perfectly formed cookies.

Toasted Nuts, at the Ready

Eileen McMurrer of West Hartford, Conn., often uses toasted nuts in recipes such as pesto or cookies, but becomes impatient when it comes to toasting small amounts for each dish. Looking for ways to streamline her approach, she found a method to ensure that she always has toasted nuts at the ready.

1. Toast several cups of nuts on a baking sheet in a 350-degree oven for 3 to 5 minutes.
2. When the nuts are cool, transfer them to a zipper-lock bag, then freeze them. Do not use pretoasted frozen nuts for recipes in which a crisp texture is desired, such as salads.

1.

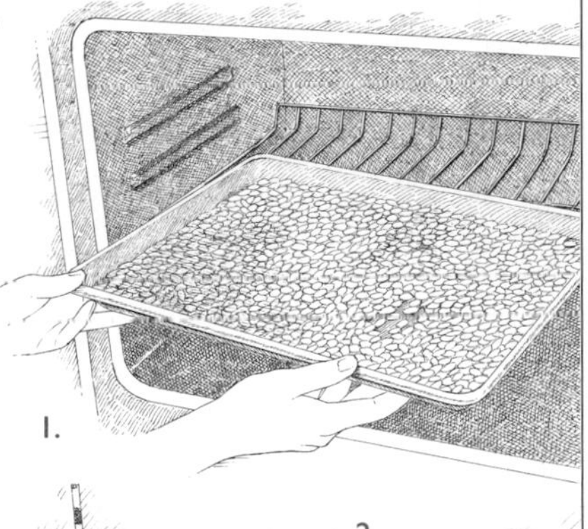

2.

Sausage Casing Solution

When eating hard sausage or salami, Janet Gilbert of Eugene, Ore., finds it a nuisance to peel off the sticky white casing from each individual slice. If the casing won't peel off the whole sausage easily before slicing, she uses a vegetable peeler to quickly remove the casing in advance.

Keep a Lid on It

Transporting a casserole to a potluck can be a messy task. To secure the glass lid of a casserole dish and prevent spills, Patricia Potts of Hidden Valley Lake, Calif., uses this technique.

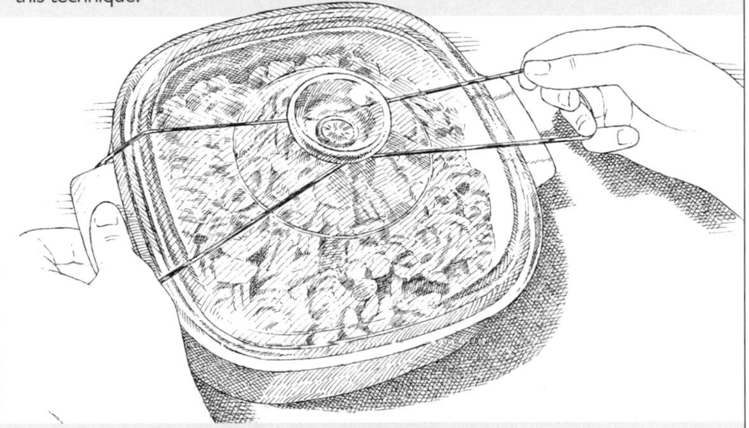

Secure a rubber band on the handle of the lid and stretch it to attach it to one of the side handles of the dish. Then secure a second rubber band on the handle of the lid and stretch it to attach it to the other side handle of the dish.

Crisp Stuffing Tops

Norma Wrenn of Abilene, Texas, has a family that prizes the crisp topping of baked stuffing. To please everyone at the table, she bakes individual portions of stuffing in muffin tins so that there is plenty of crispness to go around: The sides and top of each "muffin" become browned and crunchy. (A bonus: the baking time for the stuffing is also reduced.)

Perfect Parchment Lining

When preparing parchment to line the bottom of a tube pan, the center tube can make it tricky to cut out that perfect "circle within a circle." Patricia Jassir of Tampa, Fla., suggests this foolproof technique.

1.

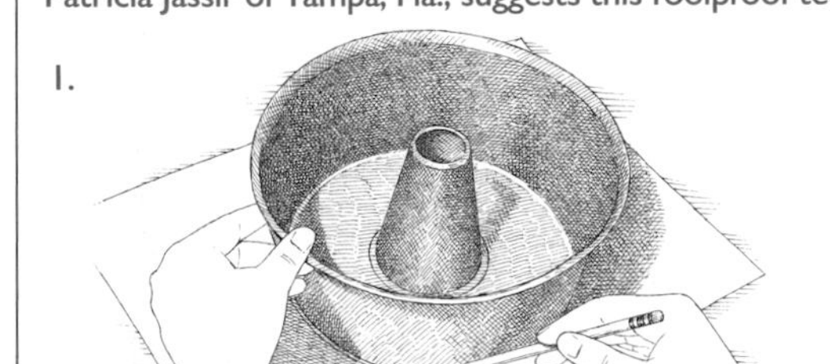

2.

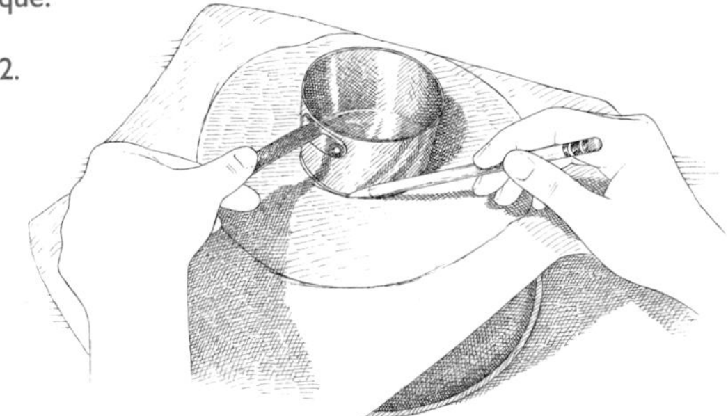

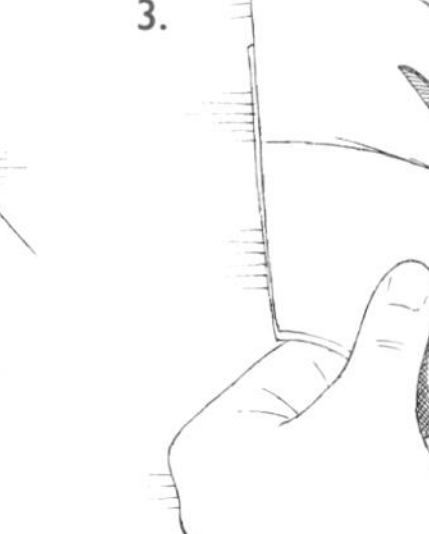

3.

1. Place the pan right-side up and trace the outside perimeter.
2. Turn the pan upside down, place the parchment on top of the pan, and then place a measuring cup that fits the opening of the center hole right in the middle of traced circle, where the hole is. Use it as a guide to trace the center hole.
3. Fold the parchment into quarters and cut out the hole. Finally, cut out the circle.

Stovetop Roast Chicken

One skillet and a trick from Chinese cookery were all we needed to produce the speediest crisp and juicy roast chicken that never saw the inside of an oven.

BY J. KENJI ALT

Roasting chicken in the oven is the usual route to crisp skin and moist meat, but sometimes you want your oven for something else. Plus the fond created from the drippings is typically greasy (or burned) and firmly bonded to the bottom of the roasting pan—so if one of your goals is making a pan sauce, it's more trouble than it's worth. Cooking chicken pieces in a skillet easily yields a pan sauce, but the skin on the chicken is often flabby and the meat unevenly cooked. Was there a way to combine the best aspects of each method? My goals were high: crisp, golden skin; evenly cooked, juicy meat; and a flavorful sauce—all produced in a single large skillet that would never go into the oven.

These crisp-skinned chicken pieces are served with a quick pan sauce.

Steaming Up the Process

To suit everyone's taste, I wanted my recipe to work with any combination of white and dark meat, so I did my initial testing on a standard set of mixed chicken parts: four breast halves, two drumsticks, and two thighs. First I cooked the chicken pieces in the simplest way I could think of. I fit the eight pieces snugly into a 12-inch skillet, where I browned the skin for 5 minutes over medium-high heat (any higher and the skin tended to burn in patches). I flipped the pieces over, browned the second side, then turned the heat down to low (trying to cook the chicken through at a higher temperature ended up burning it). Then I waited. And waited. And waited. Forty-nine minutes later, the eight chicken pieces had reached their optimal temperature (160 degrees for breast meat and 170 degrees for legs and thighs), but the bottom layer of chicken that had been in contact with the pan was dry and leathery.

Next I tried starting the chicken pieces skin-side up, then flipping and finishing them skin-side down with a cover on the skillet. The idea was that the skin would act as an insulating buffer, protecting the meat from overcooking and becoming leathery. The long, slow rendering process produced some of the crispest skin I'd ever had, and the cover speeded things up a bit, but it still took over 40 minutes. Plus the meat wasn't as juicy as I'd hoped.

What if I introduced a little liquid into the mix? Water transfers heat much more efficiently than dry air (as an example, putting your hand in 200-degree water can cause burns, while you can safely reach into a 200-degree oven). So if I created a moist, steamy environment for the chicken, I should be able to cook it much more quickly. For my next test, I browned the chicken on both sides, added some broth to the pan, put on the lid, and let the chicken cook undisturbed over low heat.

This technique worked—almost. Cooking the chicken at a very gentle simmer (instead of a blazing 450-degree oven, as in oven roasting) meant that the meat came out tender and juicy every time, as long as I didn't overcook it. Unfortunately, the limp, steamed skin wasn't in the same league as the perfectly cooked, moist meat underneath.

Achieving Crisp Skin

Traditionally, chicken parts are seared before being cooked through. What if I tried reversing that convention? I started the chicken off in the simmering broth, waited until it cooked through, poured off the liquid, and then returned the pieces skin-side down to the hot pan to brown the skin. I was sure I had solved the problem by the smell of browning skin and the decisive sizzle of the meat. But upon removing the pieces from the pan, I discovered that the skin had shrunk to almost half its size, leaving the chicken looking like someone trying to fit into a jacket four sizes too small. Clearly I had to sear the chicken and its skin before steaming (to learn why, see "Keeping Skin from Shrinking," page 7), but how could I keep the skin crisp until the very end? I was toying with the idea of removing the skin after searing and serving it separately (a technique I've used in restaurants in the past) when an idea struck me.

Growing up, my favorite meal was my mom's Chinese potstickers. First she seared the dumplings, which set the size and shape of the bottoms and produced a golden brown crust (the same process that happens with chicken skin). Then she added water to the pan, covered it with a lid, and gently cooked them through. Finally, she re-seared the dumplings after steaming, creating a bottom crust that was even crisper than after the initial sear.

Since I had the same goal in mind for my chicken, why not use the same method? After searing and steaming the pieces, I poured off all the liquid from the pan (reserving it for my pan sauce) and returned the chicken skin-side down. The second searing produced just the deep, russet-hued crisp skin I had hoped for. I softened a little chopped shallot in the hot skillet, added some flour and the reserved liquid, then whisked in lemon juice, parsley, chives, and butter off heat to create a flavorful pan sauce.

With a simple 30-minute technique, I had managed to produce juicy meat with skin that's thinner and crisper than that of any oven-roasted chicken (not to mention a great pan sauce!).

COOK'S LIVE Original Test Kitchen Videos
www.cooksillustrated.com

HOW TO MAKE
- Stovetop Roast Chicken with Lemon-Herb Sauce

VIDEO TIP
- How to cut up a chicken

TECHNIQUE | KEYS TO CRISP SKIN AND JUICY MEAT

1. SEAR the raw chicken pieces to jump-start the cooking process and crisp the skin.

2. STEAM the chicken in broth to cook it quickly and evenly and to render fat from the skin.

3. RE-CRISP the chicken pieces in the cleaned skillet to create super thin, ultracrisp skin.

STOVETOP ROAST CHICKEN WITH LEMON-HERB SAUCE

SERVES 4

A whole 4-pound chicken, cut into 8 pieces, can be used instead of the chicken parts. Use a splatter screen when browning the chicken. For our free recipe for Stovetop Roast Chicken with Sake Glaze, go to www.cooksillustrated.com/december.

Chicken

- 3½ pounds bone-in, skin-on chicken parts (breasts, thighs, and drumsticks, or a mix, with breasts cut in half), trimmed of excess fat (see note)
- Table salt and ground black pepper
- 1 tablespoon vegetable oil
- 1–1¼ cups low-sodium chicken broth

Lemon-Herb Sauce

- 1 teaspoon vegetable oil
- 1 medium shallot, minced (about 3 tablespoons)
- 1 teaspoon unbleached all-purpose flour
- 1 tablespoon juice from 1 lemon
- 1½ tablespoons minced fresh parsley leaves
- 1½ tablespoons minced fresh chives
- 1 tablespoon cold unsalted butter
- Table salt and ground black pepper

1. **FOR THE CHICKEN:** Pat chicken dry and season with salt and pepper. Heat 2 teaspoons oil in 12-inch nonstick skillet over medium-high heat until shimmering. Add chicken pieces skin-side down and cook without moving until golden brown, 5 to 8 minutes.

2. Using tongs, flip chicken pieces skin-side up. Reduce heat to medium-low, add ¾ cup broth to skillet, cover, and cook until instant-read thermometer inserted into thickest part of chicken registers 155 degrees for breasts and 170 degrees for legs and thighs, 10 to 16 minutes (smaller pieces may cook faster than larger pieces). Transfer chicken to plate, skin-side up.

3. Pour off liquid from skillet into 2-cup measuring cup and reserve. Using tongs, wipe skillet with paper towels. Add remaining teaspoon oil to skillet and heat over medium-high heat until oil is shimmering. Return chicken pieces skin-side down and cook undisturbed until skin is deep golden brown and crisp and it reaches 160 degrees for breasts and 175 degrees for legs and thighs, 4 to 7 minutes. Transfer to serving platter and tent loosely with foil. Using spoon, skim fat from reserved cooking liquid and add enough broth to measure ¾ cup.

4. **FOR THE SAUCE:** Heat oil in now-empty skillet over low heat. Add shallot and cook, stirring frequently, until softened, about 1 minute. Add flour and cook, stirring constantly, 30 seconds. Increase heat to medium-high, add reserved cooking liquid, and bring to simmer, scraping skillet bottom with wooden spoon to loosen browned bits. Simmer rapidly until reduced to ½ cup, 2 to 3 minutes. Stir in any accumulated juices from resting chicken; return to simmer and cook 30 seconds. Off heat, whisk in lemon juice, parsley, chives, and butter; season with salt and pepper. Pour sauce around chicken and serve immediately.

STOVETOP ROAST CHICKEN WITH SPICY THAI SAUCE

- 3 tablespoons juice from 2 limes
- ¼ cup light brown sugar
- 2 garlic cloves, minced or pressed through garlic press (about 2 teaspoons)
- 1 tablespoon fish sauce
- 1 teaspoon Thai red curry paste
- 2 tablespoons chopped fresh cilantro leaves

Follow recipe for Stovetop Roast Chicken with Lemon-Herb Sauce through step 3. Add 2 tablespoons lime juice, sugar, garlic, fish sauce, and curry paste to now-empty skillet. Cook over medium-high heat, scraping skillet bottom with wooden spoon to loosen browned bits, until spoon leaves wide trail when dragged through sauce, about 2 minutes. Add reserved cooking liquid; return to simmer and cook until reduced to ½ cup, 2 to 3 minutes. Stir in any accumulated juices from resting chicken; return to simmer and cook 30 seconds. Off heat, stir in cilantro and remaining tablespoon lime juice. Pour sauce around chicken and serve immediately.

STOVETOP ROAST CHICKEN WITH GRAPEFRUIT-TARRAGON SAUCE

- 1 teaspoon vegetable oil
- 1 medium shallot, minced (about 3 tablespoons)
- 1 grapefruit, rind and pith removed and segments cut into ½-inch pieces, juice reserved (about ½ cup)
- 1 tablespoon honey
- 1 tablespoon chopped fresh tarragon leaves
- 1 tablespoon cold unsalted butter
- Table salt and ground black pepper

Follow recipe for Stovetop Roast Chicken with Lemon-Herb Sauce through step 3. Heat oil in now-empty skillet over low heat. Add shallot and cook, stirring frequently, until softened, about 1 minute. Increase heat to medium-high, add reserved cooking liquid and reserved grapefruit juice; bring to simmer, scraping skillet bottom with wooden spoon to loosen browned bits. Simmer rapidly until reduced to ¼ cup, 4 to 6 minutes. Add grapefruit segments, honey, and any accumulated juices from resting chicken and return to simmer. Off heat, stir in tarragon and butter; season with salt and pepper. Pour sauce around chicken and serve immediately.

SCIENCE:

Keeping Skin from Shrinking

PROBLEM: While creating our recipe for Stovetop Roast Chicken, we tried a variety of approaches to achieve both moist meat and perfectly crisp skin. One method, steaming the raw chicken in broth and then searing it in a hot pan, skin-side down, crisped the skin but shrunk it to half its size.

EXPLANATION: Chicken skin is composed of protein, fat, and water. When steamed (which occurs at a relatively low temperature of about 212 degrees), the fat slowly renders out, water evaporates, and the proteins tighten, causing the skin to shrink dramatically.

SOLUTION: We seared the chicken first, then steamed it. Searing at a very high temperature (close to 500 degrees) causes the proteins inside the skin to rapidly crosslink, setting the skin into a firm shape before it has time to shrink. Even subsequent steaming will not lead to major shrinkage. –J.K.A.

STEAMED, THEN SEARED

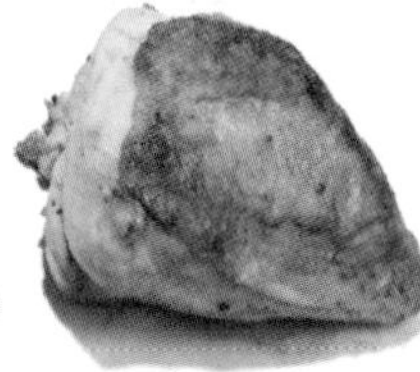

SEARED, THEN STEAMED

Real Hungarian Beef Stew

Stews overloaded with vegetables and sour cream give goulash a bad name. We wanted to set the record straight.

BY DAVID PAZMIÑO

Though you'd never guess it from the gussied-up versions served in this country, traditional Hungarian goulash is the simplest of stews, calling for little more than beef, onions, and paprika. Sour cream has no place in the pot, nor do mushrooms, green peppers, or most herbs. Least welcome of all are the ketchup and Worcestershire sauce that were standard ingredients in my mother's renditions. Instead, the best goulash features the simple heartiness of beef melded with the sweetness of long-cooked onions. But the real revelation is the paprika. Instead of being a mere accent, its fruity, almost chocolaty flavors infuse the meat and help transform the braising liquid into a rich, thick sauce.

Ignoring the countless recipes with ingredient lists as long as my arm, I set out to bring a humble but delicious stew back to its roots.

Great goulash is all about the meat—and the paprika.

Sorting Out the Essentials

The Hungarian herdsmen who developed this campfire stew used tough cuts of meat such as shin (a cross-section from the front leg that includes both bone and meat), cooking it for hours over a low fire until tender. While many modern recipes still call for shin, it is not widely available in this country. I settled on chuck-eye roast, a flavorful center cut from the upper shoulder that is a test kitchen favorite for stew. I bought a whole roast and cut it myself to ensure uniform pieces that would cook evenly. In keeping with the authentic recipes I found, I cut large pieces—$1\frac{1}{2}$ inches—a size that kept the meat from turning stringy or falling apart during cooking.

As for the paprika, my tasters affirmed that the traditional sweet kind was best, preferring its floral, fruity qualities to the spiciness of hot paprika. Fresh, high-quality paprika is a must (see "Sweet Paprika," on page 9), but to achieve the desired level of intensity, some recipes call for as much as half a cup per 3 pounds of meat. I found that once I reached 3 tablespoons, the spice began contributing a gritty, dusty texture I didn't like.

To eliminate grittiness, I tried steeping the paprika in broth and then straining it through a coffee filter. This captured plenty of paprika flavor without a trace of its texture, but straining took nearly 30 minutes—a deal breaker. Processing the paprika and broth in a blender proved futile, as the spice was already too fine to be broken down further. After consulting with chefs at a few Hungarian restaurants, I was turned on to a new idea: paprika cream, a condiment my sources told me was as common in Hungarian cooking as the dried spice. No stores I could find stocked it, so I ordered it online. "Paprika cream" turned out to be a deep red paste, packaged in a metal tube, that contained ground paprika camouflaged in a puree of red bell peppers. When I added it to my stew, it created vibrant paprika flavor without any offensive grittiness.

This convenience product was great, but I didn't want to have to hunt it down every time I made goulash. Why not create my own paprika cream? I went to the test kitchen pantry for a jar of roasted red peppers (their tender texture would be better for my purposes than fresh). I drained the peppers and pureed them in a food processor along with the paprika. To better approximate the lively yet concentrated flavors of the cream from the tube, I also added a couple of tablespoons of tomato paste and a little vinegar. Bingo! I was able to add up to $\frac{1}{3}$ cup paprika without the stew seeming as if I'd dumped a handful of sand into the pot.

Stewing Things Up

To ensure the most tender meat possible, I had been salting the beef and allowing it to stand for a few minutes before cooking—a method we often use in the test kitchen. As the salt penetrates, it helps break down the proteins, tenderizing the meat fibers. Up to now I had also been following the standard stew protocol: Sear the meat in batches, cook aromatics (in this case, just onions), return the beef to the pot along with broth and other ingredients, and cook until the meat is tender. But once I introduced paprika paste into the mix, I found the flavor of the seared meat competed with the paprika's brightness. Referring back to the hundreds of goulash recipes I had gathered in my research, I found an interesting trend: Many did not sear the meat. Instead, the

Smooth Spice Solution

The large quantity of paprika in authentic Hungarian goulash can turn it gritty. Here are two solutions.

COMMERCIAL CONVENIENCE
Hard-to-find Hungarian paprika cream is a smooth blend of paprika and red bell peppers.

HOMEMADE SOLUTION
We created our own quick version by pureeing dried paprika with roasted red peppers and a little tomato paste and vinegar.

SCIENCE: Skipping the Sear, but Not the Flavor

Most stews begin by browning meat on the stovetop to boost flavor. They also call for lots of added liquid. Our recipe skips the sear and goes into a moderate 325-degree oven. Though this relatively low temperature can't compare with the sizzling heat of a 500-degree skillet, over time, the dry top layer of meat will reach 300 degrees—the temperature at which the meat begins to brown, forming thousands of new flavor compounds. But only the top of the meat will brown; due to the surrounding liquid, the submerged part of the meat can't rise above the boiling point of water, or 212 degrees Fahrenheit. –D.P.

RISING ABOVE IT ALL
Even at a relatively low oven temperature, our method still triggers browning—but only on the "dry" part of the meat above the liquid.

onions went into the pot first to soften, followed by the paprika and meat, and then the whole thing was left to cook. That's it. No liquids were ever added.

Intrigued, but dubious that this method would work, I cooked the onions briefly in oil, added the paprika paste and meat, and placed the covered pot in the oven. (We have found that the gentle, steady heat of a low oven provides better results for stew than the stove.) Sure enough, the onions and meat provided enough liquid to stew the meat. As I cooked batch after batch using this no-sear method, I noticed something peculiar: The meat above the liquid actually browned during cooking. In effect, I was developing similar (though not quite as intense) flavors as if I had seared the beef. Toward the end of cooking, after the meat browned, I added a little broth to thin out the stewing liquid and make it more saucelike.

COOK'S LIVE Original Test Kitchen Videos
www.cooksillustrated.com
HOW TO MAKE
- Hungarian Beef Stew

VIDEO TIPS
- Why do I need to cut my own stew meat?
- Paprika 101

In keeping with authentic goulash, the only vegetables in the pot were onions. But in deference to my American tasters, who wanted at least a few vegetables in their stew, I incorporated carrots into the mix, finding that I also appreciated the sweetness and textural contrast they provided. For those tasters who wanted the extra richness of sour cream, I found ¼ cup did the trick. Even with these slight adulterations, my Hungarian goulash was the real deal: a simple dish of tender braised beef packed with paprika flavor.

HUNGARIAN BEEF STEW
SERVES 6

Do not substitute hot, half-sharp, or smoked Spanish paprika for the sweet paprika in the stew (see our recommended brands at right), as they will compromise the flavor of the dish. Since paprika is vital to this recipe, it is best to use a fresh container. We prefer chuck-eye roast, but any boneless roast from the chuck will work. Cook the stew in a Dutch oven with a tight-fitting lid. (Alternatively, to ensure a tight seal, place a sheet of foil over the pot before adding the lid.) The stew can be cooled, covered tightly, and refrigerated for up to 2 days; wait to add the optional sour cream until after reheating. Before reheating, skim the hardened fat from the surface and add enough water to the stew to thin it slightly. Serve the stew over boiled potatoes or egg noodles.

- 1 boneless beef chuck-eye roast (about 3½ pounds), trimmed of excess fat and cut into 1½-inch cubes (see note)
- Table salt
- ⅓ cup sweet paprika (see note)
- 1 (12-ounce) jar roasted red peppers, drained and rinsed (about 1 cup)
- 2 tablespoons tomato paste
- 3 teaspoons white vinegar
- 2 tablespoons vegetable oil
- 4 large onions, diced small (about 6 cups)
- 4 large carrots, peeled and cut into 1-inch-thick rounds (about 2 cups)
- 1 bay leaf
- 1 cup beef broth, warmed
- ¼ cup sour cream (optional; see note)
- Ground black pepper

1. Adjust oven rack to lower-middle position and heat oven to 325 degrees. Sprinkle meat evenly with 1 teaspoon salt and let stand 15 minutes. Process paprika, roasted peppers, tomato paste, and 2 teaspoons vinegar in food processor until smooth, 1 to 2 minutes, scraping down sides as needed.

2. Combine oil, onions, and 1 teaspoon salt in large Dutch oven; cover and set over medium heat. Cook, stirring occasionally, until onions soften but have not yet begun to brown, 8 to 10 minutes. (If onions begin to brown, reduce heat to medium-low and stir in 1 tablespoon water.)

TASTING: Sweet Paprika

Some cooks think of paprika as merely a coloring agent. But the best versions of this sweet Hungarian spice (made from a different variety of red pepper than hot or smoked paprika) pack a punch that goes beyond pigment. We sampled six brands, two from the supermarket and four ordered online. Our findings? It pays to mail-order your paprika—the supermarket brands had little flavor and even less aroma. For complete testing results, go to www.cooksillustrated.com/december.

–Elizabeth Bomze

FIRST-RATE FRUITINESS
THE SPICE HOUSE
Hungarian Sweet Paprika
Price: $3.28 for 2.5 oz.
Comments: This specialty brand outshone the competition with the complexity of its "earthy," "fruity" flavors and "toasty" aroma, making the slight inconvenience of mail-ordering it well worthwhile.

BOLD STATEMENT
PENZEYS Hungary Sweet Paprika
Price: $4.75 for 2.4 oz.
Comments: Tasters described noticeably more "heat" (despite being a sweet variety) and a slightly more "vegetal bite" in this second-place paprika.

SUPERMARKET STANDBY
McCORMICK Paprika
Price: $3.99 for 2.12 oz.
Comments: Some tasters found this supermarket staple (which finished fourth out of six brands) perfectly respectable, but most considered it "one-dimensional," even "flavorless."

3. Stir in paprika mixture; cook, stirring occasionally, until onions stick to bottom of pan, about 2 minutes. Add beef, carrots, and bay leaf; stir until beef is well coated. Using rubber spatula, scrape down sides of pot. Cover pot and transfer to oven. Cook until meat is almost tender and surface of liquid is ½ inch below top of meat, 2 to 2½ hours, stirring every 30 minutes. Remove pot from oven and add enough beef broth so that surface of liquid is ¼ inch from top of meat (beef should not be fully submerged). Return covered pot to oven and continue to cook until fork slips easily in and out of beef, about 30 minutes longer.

4. Skim fat off surface; stir in remaining teaspoon vinegar and sour cream, if using. Remove bay leaf, adjust seasonings with salt and pepper, and serve.

The Problem with Roast Turkey

Roasting a whole turkey is a race to keep the white meat from drying out while the dark meat cooks through. So who says you have to roast it whole?

BY J. KENJI ALT

For most of us, juicy, perfectly cooked roast turkey shrouded in crisp, burnished skin is like a desert mirage: a beautiful idea, yes, but one that always seems just out of reach. Here's the crux of the problem: getting the dark meat up to temperature and the skin crisp without overcooking the white meat. Breast meat needs to reach about 160 degrees and not much more or its muscle proteins will tighten up, squeezing out juices. At the same time, dark meat must be cooked to 170 degrees. Another problem is that dark meat cooks especially slowly, particularly the thighs, which due to the anatomy of a turkey are shielded from direct oven heat.

Enter two safeguards we've long advocated in the test kitchen: salting the turkey or brining it in saltwater. Both measures change the structure of the bird's muscles, allowing it to retain more moisture, especially at the exterior of the breast, the area most prone to overcooking. But neither measure is foolproof, and each takes the better part of a day. I wanted to cut out at least one kitchen task this Thanksgiving and skip that extra step. My goal was no less than the perfect turkey recipe, an approach that would get my fowl from supermarket to table in just a few hours, with meat as moist as prime rib and crisp, crackling skin. And since this would be the ideal recipe, I wanted to end up with great and easy gravy, too.

Roasting turkey parts helps avoid the need for a brine.

Taking Turkey's Temperature

To find out exactly how much of the turkey was hitting the 160-degree mark, I roasted a turkey using our standard method (start in a 400-degree oven breast-down and finish breast-up at 325 degrees). I took the temperature of the breast meat at ¼-inch intervals all the way from the coolest point (which registered 160 degrees) to the very exterior. This test showed that more than 50 percent of the turkey breast was reaching temperatures above 180 degrees, with some parts reaching nearly 200 degrees. No wonder brining is usually necessary to ensure meat that isn't completely dried out!

This problem was nearly identical to a dilemma I had encountered last year when developing a recipe for thick-cut steaks (May/June 2007), when I found that high-heat cooking caused the outer layers to overcook. The solution? Lower the heat. I baked the steaks in a gentle 275-degree oven before finishing them in a hot pan, resulting in perfectly and evenly cooked meat. Maybe, I reasoned, a slow-roasted turkey might also be the key to juicy meat.

I roasted my next turkey at 275 degrees, again taking its temperature at ¼-inch intervals once the center had reached 160 degrees. This time, the majority of the meat stayed reasonably close to the 160-degree mark, with only the outermost layers reaching between 170 and 180 degrees—a marked improvement that was verified by correspondingly juicier breast meat (see "Don't Leave Your Turkey High and Dry" on page 11). But three problems had emerged. The most obvious was the pale and flabby skin, which failed to brown at the lower temperature. Second was the extremely long cooking time (over five hours), which not only tied up the oven but left the meat in the 40- to 140-degree "danger zone" (the range at which bacteria flourish) for too long. Finally, with the lower temperature, while the breast meat stayed closer to 160 degrees, so, unfortunately, did the legs and thighs. By the time the breast was done cooking, the thighs were still a disquieting pale pink.

Separation Anxiety

I knew from past chicken recipes that spreading the legs out from the breast helps them to cook faster. Could separating them completely help even more? Even the most sentimental cook would surely give up their Norman Rockwell dream of a whole golden brown bird emerging from the oven in exchange for the juiciest turkey with the simplest preparation.

Rather than go through the hassle of breaking down a whole turkey, I bought a turkey breast along with two leg quarters (thighs and drumsticks). I roasted them elevated on a rack over a baking sheet to promote air circulation. This time, after just under three hours in the oven, the breast had reached 160 degrees. And without the insulating effect of the turkey's backbone and breast meat, the thighs and drumsticks serendipitously reached 175 degrees just as the breast finished cooking! Cutting into the breast revealed tender, juicy meat.

The only remaining problem was the skin. Most turkey recipes achieve crisp skin by starting the bird in a hot oven to brown it, then lowering the heat to finish cooking. But a higher starting temperature meant a higher oven temperature the whole way through, which led to dried-out meat. Increasing the heat near the end seemed more promising, but ultimately proved untenable; leaving the turkey in the oven as it heated up slowly also caused it to overcook. But what if I allowed the turkey to cool before popping it back in the oven to crisp the skin? I roasted more parts, this time removing them from the oven before raising the temperature as high as it would go—500 degrees. I allowed the turkey to rest for a full half hour until the temperature of the meat had dropped to around 130 degrees. After the turkey was in the oven for 15 minutes, I hesitantly poked my instant-read thermometer into the skin, which made an encouraging crack. The

SHOPPING: Turkey Parts

Most supermarkets carry whole bone-in turkey breasts as well as leg quarters and individually packaged thighs and drumsticks. Try to avoid breasts that have been injected with a saline solution (often called "self-basters"), as we find it masks the natural flavor of the turkey. Also, ignore any pop-up timer that may come with the breast; the meat will be long overcooked by the time the popper pops.

SCIENCE:
Don't Leave Your Turkey High and Dry

EXPERIMENT: We roasted two non-brined turkeys, one using our standard high-heat approach (start in a 400-degree oven and finish at 325 degrees), the other roasted at 275 degrees the entire time. Once the center of each breast hit 160 degrees (the ideal temperature for moist, tender white meat), we recorded its temperature at ¼-inch intervals to the very exterior.

RESULTS: The outermost layers of the high-heat breast topped a moisture-obliterating 210 degrees. The exterior of the slow-roasted breast reached a much more moderate 176 degrees—proving that if you can roast at low heat, the meat will still be moist, even without a brine. –J.K.A.

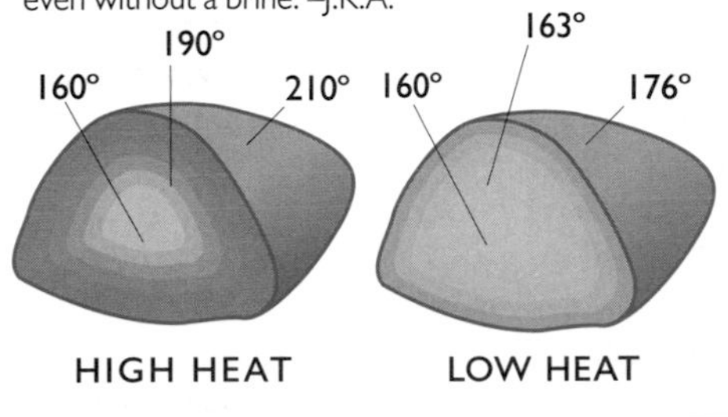

thermometer revealed what one taste soon confirmed—the turkey was perfectly cooked from center to edge and surrounded by flawlessly rendered, crisp skin.

The Gravy Train

My remaining task was to find a simple way to create rich gravy. For a foundation, I placed a mixture of carrots, celery, onions, and flavorings under the turkey with some chicken broth. After a couple hours in the oven, the savory roasted vegetables were further seasoned by turkey drippings. Once the meat was cooked (but before crisping the skin), I strained the liquid and added more canned broth. The turkey's resting period gave me plenty of time to cook up a dark golden roux from flour and butter that I whisked into the broth. Barely 20 minutes later, the roux and broth had thickened into an intense gravy.

I'll still brine a turkey whenever I get the urge to provide a picture-perfect Thanksgiving centerpiece. But I have a feeling most times I won't even start worrying about the bird until the afternoon of the big day, knowing that I can easily produce juicy turkey with crisp skin—and a rich gravy—all in time for dinner.

SLOW-ROASTED TURKEY WITH GRAVY
SERVES 10 TO 12

Instead of drumsticks and thighs, you may use 2 whole leg quarters, 1½ to 2 pounds each. The recipe will also work with turkey breast alone; in step 2, reduce the butter to 1½ tablespoons, the salt to 1½ teaspoons, and the pepper to 1 teaspoon. If you are roasting kosher or self-basting turkey parts, season the turkey with only 1½ teaspoons salt.

Turkey

- 3 medium onions, chopped medium
- 3 medium celery ribs, chopped medium
- 2 medium carrots, peeled and chopped medium
- 5 sprigs fresh thyme
- 5 medium garlic cloves, peeled and halved
- 1 cup low-sodium chicken broth
- 1 whole bone-in, skin-on turkey breast (5 to 7 pounds), trimmed of excess fat and patted dry with paper towels (see note)
- 4 pounds turkey drumsticks and thighs, trimmed of excess fat and patted dry with paper towels (see note)
- 3 tablespoons unsalted butter, melted
- 1 tablespoon table salt
- 2 teaspoons ground black pepper

Gravy

- 2 cups low-sodium chicken broth
- 3 tablespoons unsalted butter
- 3 tablespoons unbleached all-purpose flour
- 2 bay leaves
- Table salt and ground black pepper

1. **FOR THE TURKEY:** Adjust oven rack to lower-middle position and heat oven to 275 degrees. Arrange onions, celery, carrots, thyme, and garlic in even layer on rimmed baking sheet. Pour broth into baking sheet. Place wire rack on top of vegetables (rack will rest on vegetables, not on bottom of baking sheet).

2. Brush turkey pieces on all sides with melted butter. Sprinkle salt and pepper evenly over turkey. Place breast skin side down and drumsticks and thighs skin-side up on rack on vegetable-filled baking sheet, leaving at least ¼ inch between pieces.

3. Roast turkey pieces 1 hour. Using wads of paper towels, turn turkey breast skin-side up. Continue roasting until instant-read thermometer registers 160 degrees when inserted in thickest part of breast and 170 to 175 degrees in thickest part of thighs, 1 to 2 hours longer. Remove baking sheet from oven and transfer rack with turkey to second baking sheet. Allow pieces to rest at least 30 minutes or up to 1½ hours.

4. **FOR THE GRAVY:** Strain vegetables and liquid from baking sheet through colander set in large bowl. Press solids with back of spatula to extract as much liquid as possible. Discard vegetables. Transfer liquid in bowl to 4-cup liquid measuring cup. Add chicken broth to measuring cup (you should have about 3 cups liquid).

5. In medium saucepan, heat butter over medium-high heat; when foaming subsides, add flour and cook, stirring constantly, until flour is dark golden brown and fragrant, about 5 minutes. Whisk in broth mixture and bay leaves and gradually bring to boil. Reduce heat to medium-low and simmer, stirring occasionally, until gravy is thick and reduced to 2 cups, 15 to 20 minutes. Discard bay leaves. Remove gravy from heat and adjust seasonings with salt and pepper. Keep gravy warm.

6. **TO SERVE:** Heat oven to 500 degrees. Place baking sheet with turkey in oven. Roast until skin is golden brown and crisp, about 15 minutes. Remove baking sheet from oven, transfer turkey to cutting board, and let rest 20 minutes. Carve and serve, passing warm gravy separately.

COOK'S LIVE Original Test Kitchen Video
www.cooksillustrated.com
HOW TO MAKE
• Slow-Roasted Turkey with Gravy

STEP-BY-STEP | SLOW-ROASTED TURKEY WITH GRAVY

1. ADD AROMATICS
Aromatics and broth catch drippings and help flavor gravy.

2. ARRANGE MEAT
Arrange turkey on rack set over vegetables to allow air circulation. Roast at 275 degrees.

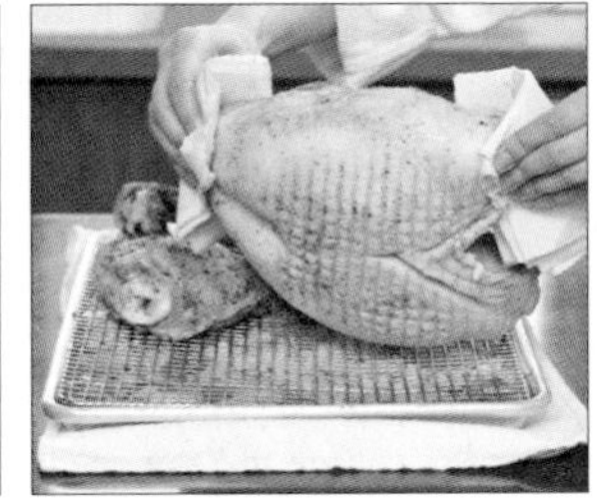

3. FLIP BREAST
Flip breast partway through cooking to ensure uniform doneness.

4. REST, THEN CRISP
Let turkey rest to allow juices to redistribute before final crisping in 500-degree oven.

5. MAKE GRAVY
Strain vegetables and broth, then use this flavorful liquid as a base for gravy.

Simplifying Sautéed Green Beans

Parboiling, shocking, drying, sautéing—do you really need a four-step process to produce tender, evenly cooked beans?

BY KEITH DRESSER

Perfect sautéed green beans cooked in just one pan.

The standard technique in most recipes for sautéed green beans goes something like this: parboil, shock in ice water, dry with towels, and finally, sauté. While the method has advantages—it allows you to do most of the prep work in advance—sometimes I want things a little more streamlined. Could I achieve tender, lightly browned, fresh-tasting beans, without all the fuss and in just one pan?

First, I tried simply sautéing the raw beans in a skillet in oil—big mistake. The dry heat took so long to penetrate the beans that their exteriors blackened before the interiors cooked through. Water was clearly going to be necessary. My next thought was to do a variation on parboiling. I threw beans and a small amount of water into a cold pan, covered it, and brought it to a simmer. Once the beans were almost cooked, I removed the lid and waited for the water to evaporate. I then added a little oil and sautéed the beans until browned. While promising, the method wasn't foolproof. If the water took too long to evaporate, the beans turned flaccid before they could brown. And even when I achieved lightly browned and properly cooked beans, the caramelized flavor seemed superficial.

Why not reverse the process and sauté the beans first? Following this line of thinking, I briefly sautéed the beans until they were spotty brown but not yet cooked through, then added ¼ cup water to the pan. As soon as the water hit the skillet, it turned to steam, and I quickly covered the pan. Once the beans were almost cooked (an efficient process in this steamy environment), I removed the lid and let the excess moisture evaporate. This produced just the right crisp-tender texture I was looking for and, at least initially, the caramelized flavor was deeper. But once I added water to the skillet, it seemed to wash off some of that intensified flavor, making my veggies taste more like ordinary steamed beans.

The solution: I simply steamed the beans for a minute or so less so they remained slightly undercooked, then blasted the heat once the lid was removed. This quickly evaporated what little water was left in the pan and allowed me to promote additional browning before the beans fully cooked through. I also found that adding a little softened butter to the skillet once the water had evaporated (softened butter was quicker to melt and faster to brown than cold) added some welcome richness and further aided browning.

As far as additional flavors, I decided to limit extras to herbs, spices, and a few pantry items. Mixed into the butter (or in some cases, oil), combinations such as garlic and herbs, smoked paprika and almonds, and ginger and sesame added complexity without tampering with the dish's one-pan simplicity.

SAUTÉED GREEN BEANS WITH GARLIC AND HERBS

SERVES 4

This recipe yields crisp-tender beans. If you prefer a slightly more tender texture (or you are using large, tough beans), increase the water by a tablespoon and increase the covered cooking time by 1 minute. To serve 6, increase all of the ingredients by half and increase the covered cooking time by 1 to 2 minutes. Do not attempt to cook more than 1½ pounds of green beans with this method. For our free recipe for Sautéed Green Beans with Tarragon and Lime, go to www.cooksillustrated.com/december.

- 1 tablespoon unsalted butter, softened
- 3 medium garlic cloves, minced or pressed through garlic press (about 1 tablespoon)
- 1 teaspoon chopped fresh thyme leaves
- 1 teaspoon olive oil
- 1 pound green beans, stem ends snapped off, beans cut into 2-inch pieces
- Table salt and ground black pepper
- ¼ cup water
- 2 teaspoons juice from 1 lemon
- 1 tablespoon chopped fresh parsley leaves

Combine butter, garlic, and thyme in small bowl; set aside. Heat oil in 12-inch nonstick skillet over medium heat until just smoking. Add beans, ¼ teaspoon salt, and ⅛ teaspoon pepper; cook, stirring occasionally, until spotty brown, 4 to 6 minutes. Add water, cover, and cook until beans are bright green and still crisp, about 2 minutes. Remove cover, increase heat to high, and cook until water evaporates, 30 to 60 seconds. Add butter mixture and continue to cook, stirring frequently, until beans are crisp-tender, lightly browned, and beginning to wrinkle, 1 to 3 minutes longer. Transfer beans to serving bowl, toss with lemon juice and parsley; adjust seasoning with salt and pepper. Serve immediately.

SAUTÉED GREEN BEANS WITH SMOKED PAPRIKA AND ALMONDS

Follow recipe for Sautéed Green Beans with Garlic and Herbs, omitting chopped thyme and parsley. Stir ¼ teaspoon smoked paprika into softened butter with garlic. Sprinkle cooked beans with ¼ cup toasted slivered almonds before serving.

SPICY SAUTÉED GREEN BEANS WITH GINGER AND SESAME

Combine 1 teaspoon toasted sesame oil, 1 teaspoon grated fresh ginger, and 1 tablespoon chili-garlic paste in small bowl. Follow recipe for Sautéed Green Beans with Garlic and Herbs, substituting vegetable oil for olive oil and increasing amount to 2 teaspoons. Cook as directed, replacing butter mixture with sesame oil mixture and omitting lemon juice and parsley. Sprinkle cooked beans with 2 teaspoons toasted sesame seeds before serving.

SAUTÉED GREEN BEANS WITH ROASTED RED PEPPERS AND BASIL

Combine 2 teaspoons olive oil, 1 medium shallot, minced, and ⅛ teaspoon red pepper flakes in small bowl. Follow recipe for Sautéed Green Beans with Garlic and Herbs, replacing butter mixture with oil-shallot mixture. Add ⅓ cup roasted red peppers, cut into ½-inch pieces, to pan with oil-shallot mixture. Substitute 1 teaspoon red wine vinegar for lemon juice and 2 tablespoons chopped fresh basil leaves for parsley.

COOK'S LIVE Original Test Kitchen Video
www.cooksillustrated.com
HOW TO MAKE
- Sautéed Green Beans with Garlic and Herbs

PHOTOGRAPHY: CARL TREMBLAY

Better Roasted Sweet Potatoes

Too often, roasted sweet potatoes turn out starchy and wan. To hit their sweet spot, was it time to throw out a cardinal rule of roasting?

⋟ BY DAVID PAZMIÑO ⋞

Sweet potatoes destined for the casserole dish during the holidays often languish under marshmallow toppings, smothered in sweeteners. I've always found this a poor way to treat food that needs little fuss to taste great on its own. Instead, I prefer to call on a method I use for regular potatoes: slice, toss with oil, then roast at a high temperature. When all goes well, the potatoes emerge from the oven with a nicely caramelized exterior, smooth creamy interior, and an earthy sweetness that needs little enhancement.

Trouble is, sweet potatoes don't always behave like their white and yellow-fleshed brethren. Handled the same way, they can come out of the oven tasting starchy and wan. Returning them to the oven for crisping doesn't usually solve the problem—and can even worsen it by burning their edges. Could I figure out a way to tweak this very simple procedure so that it would produce perfect roasted sweet potatoes every time?

A thin spatula is ideal for transferring the sticky potatoes.

The most common shape for roasted potatoes is the wedge, which is easy to cut and allows many pieces to fit on a rimmed baking sheet. But I found wedges unsuitable: The thinner tips finished cooking long before the sides had softened. Cutting the potatoes into 1-inch chunks can help ensure more even dimensions with regular spuds, but the knobby shapes and tapered ends of the sweet potatoes made creating uniform cubes impossible. In the end, I took shape out of the equation and simply cut the sweet potatoes into rounds. While the diameter varied, each round was the same height on the pan; ¾ inch thick turned out to be just right.

On to the cooking method. Roasted at 425 degrees (the temperature often recommended for regular spuds), the sweet potatoes browned nicely, but their interiors were starchy and fibrous and lacked sweetness. As I experimented with the oven temperature to get better results, I noticed a curious trend: the lower the temperature, the less browning that occurred but the sweeter the potatoes became. After a little digging, I found an explanation: The starch in sweet potatoes is converted into sugars between 135 and 175 degrees. Once the internal temperature of the potato exceeds 175 degrees, no further conversion occurs. Thus the lower the oven temperature, the longer the potatoes would stay within this range and the sweeter the spuds.

But dropping the temperature would also mean more time in the oven, and I didn't want a simple side dish to take all day. That's when I remembered a technique I'd come across that totally turned the standard approach to roasting on its head by starting the sweet potatoes in a cold, versus preheated, oven—a different way to keep their internal temperature lower longer. It was worth a try.

I put a batch of potato rounds on a baking sheet, placed them in a cold oven, then cranked the heat to 425, inserting a remote digital thermometer in one of the rounds to track its temperature. After 20 minutes, the thermometer registered 175. I cooked the potatoes for 25 minutes more until the bottom edges browned, then flipped them to let the other side brown. These potatoes tasted vastly better than the ones roasted in a preheated oven, but could I get them sweeter still?

I prepped a new batch, but to further delay heating, I covered them in foil before placing them in a cold oven. This time, the potatoes took 30 minutes to reach 175. I then removed the foil and continued to roast them as before. The 10-minute difference was small but significant. These potatoes were perfect—super-sweet and tender, with a slightly crisp, caramelized exterior. The only problem was they stuck to the pan, easily remedied in my next batch by covering the bottom of the pan with foil and coating it with cooking spray.

At last, I had roasted sweet potatoes that were simple to make and consistently sweet.

ROASTED SWEET POTATOES

SERVES 4 TO 6

Note that this recipe calls for starting the potatoes in a cold oven. Choose potatoes that are as even in width as possible; trimming the small ends prevents them from burning. If you prefer not to peel the potatoes, just scrub them well before cutting. For our free recipes for Roasted Sweet Potatoes with Maple-Thyme Glaze and Roasted Sweet Potatoes with Spiced Brown Sugar Glaze, go to www.cooksillustrated.com/december.

- 3 pounds sweet potatoes (about 6 medium), ends trimmed, peeled, rinsed, and cut into ¾-inch-thick rounds (see note)
- 2 tablespoons vegetable oil
- 1 teaspoon table salt
- Ground black pepper

1. Toss potatoes in large bowl with oil, salt, and pepper to taste until evenly coated. Line 18- by 13-inch heavy-duty rimmed baking sheet with aluminum foil and coat with nonstick cooking spray. Arrange potatoes in single layer on baking sheet and cover tightly with aluminum foil. Adjust oven rack to middle position and place potatoes in cold oven. Turn oven to 425 degrees and cook potatoes 30 minutes.

2. Remove baking sheet from oven and carefully remove top layer of foil. Return potatoes to oven and cook until bottom edges of potatoes are golden brown, 15 to 25 minutes.

3. Remove baking sheet from oven and, using thin metal spatula, flip slices over. Continue to roast until bottom edges of potatoes are golden brown, 18 to 22 minutes longer. Remove from oven; let potatoes cool 5 to 10 minutes; transfer to platter and serve.

COOK'S LIVE Original Test Kitchen Videos
www.cooksillustrated.com
HOW TO MAKE
• Roasted Sweet Potatoes
VIDEO TIP
• Sweet potato primer

Perfecting Rustic Dinner Rolls

Turning flour, water, and yeast into crusty, airy rolls is one of the hardest bits of kitchen wizardry around. We wanted to make the process foolproof.

BY CHARLES KELSEY

I have always had a weakness for European-style dinner rolls. These lean, rustic rolls boast an airy crumb and yeasty, savory flavor worlds away from their richer American cousins. But the best part is their crust—so crisp it practically shatters when you bite into it, yet chewy enough to offer satisfying resistance.

This magnificent crust is what keeps these rolls the provenance of professionals, who typically rely on a steam-injected oven to expose the developing crust to moisture. I didn't have a steam-injected oven, but I did have a library of cookbooks and a kitchen full of experienced test cooks to consult. With these reinforcements and a little ingenuity, I was sure I could create a reliable recipe for rustic dinner rolls that looked—and tasted—like they came from an artisanal bakery.

Our rolls feature a chewy, bubbly crumb that's worlds apart from the soft, dense interior of typical American-style rolls.

Roll Calls

After testing various recipes, I found the best rolls had two things in common: no butter or oil, and the use of bread flour instead of all-purpose. This made sense, as fat inhibits gluten formation while the higher protein content of bread flour encourages it. (Gluten is the network of proteins that gives bread its chew.) For a working recipe, I settled on 3 cups bread flour, 10 ounces water, 1¼ teaspoons instant yeast, and salt. Following bread-making protocol, I mixed and kneaded the dough in a stand mixer, then transferred it to a bowl to rise. A couple hours later, I shaped the dough into balls, let them rise briefly, and baked them in a 425-degree oven.

My first batch emerged looking the part, with appealingly burnished exteriors. When I broke open a roll, however, I discovered a dense, bland crumb beneath a thin, leathery crust. The flavor was easy enough to improve; replacing 3 tablespoons of bread flour with whole wheat flour contributed subtle earthiness, while 2 teaspoons honey (tasters preferred it over molasses or sugar) added some sweetness yet left the rolls' savory profile intact. On to the next task: creating an airy crumb.

Liquid Assets

First I tried increasing the yeast, hoping that more rise would open up the crumb. But I was able to add only a scant ¼ teaspoon before the rolls took on a sour, fermented flavor. This modest addition provided some lift, but not enough.

That's when two fellow test cooks suggested making the dough wetter. Their logic was simple: During baking, the water within the dough turns to steam, creating hollow pockets as moisture rushes to escape. In addition, extra water creates looser dough, which allows the steam bubbles to expand more easily. The higher the hydration level, the theory goes, the airier the crumb.

Determining the hydration of my dough to be nearly 60 percent (the water's weight divided by the flour's weight), I assembled several batches of dough with varying amounts of water. Sure enough, increasing the hydration opened the crumb considerably. Working my way up, I found about 72 percent hydration to be optimal before the dough started getting too wet to shape into rolls. (By contrast, our Best American Dinner Roll dough, September/October 2006, with its tight, tender crumb, has around 53 percent hydration.)

From past experience, I knew that giving the dough a couple turns (gently folding it over on itself when partially risen) would encourage the yeast to produce more carbon dioxide, creating even more bubbles in the dough and thus an airier crumb. (For more information, see "One Good Turn," page 30.) This technique was indeed effective, yielding the airiest and chewiest texture yet.

A Half-Baked Plan

Using more water improved the finished rolls, but it also made the dough extremely sticky, oozy, and hard to shape. In fact, the very process of forming rolls sometimes caused the delicate dough to deflate, making its texture too dense. Wondering if I could forgo

Secrets of Rustic Dinner Rolls

WHOLE WHEAT FLOUR
A little whole wheat flour contributes nice earthiness.

BIT O' HONEY
Honey adds subtle sweetness while leaving the savory profile of the rolls intact.

VERY WET DOUGH
Lots of water in the dough means more steam bubbles during baking and, in turn, an airier crumb.

PHOTOGRAPHY: CARL TREMBLAY

A Burst of (Oven) Spring

Cranking up the heat when the rolls go into the oven maximizes what professional bakers call "oven spring," the rapid rise in volume that all yeasted dough experiences when it first hits a hot oven. The higher this initial lift, the higher the finished bread.

HIGHER HEAT= HIGHER RISE

LOWER HEAT= LESS LIFT

shaping altogether, I tried using a bench scraper to divide the dough into rough (but even) pieces. Bingo! With less handling, these rolls retained far more of the open texture I had taken such pains to achieve. Still, a problem remained: how to keep the soft dough from spreading and baking into a squat shape.

I flirted with the idea of baking the pieces in a muffin tin—but who wants a dinner roll shaped like a breakfast item? Moving on, I tried crowding the dough in a cake pan. I coated these pieces lightly with flour to keep them from fusing together during baking and to make them easier to pull apart afterward. This batch looked good, but the spots where the rolls had rested against each other stayed soft. The solution: I removed the rolls from the oven halfway through baking, pulled them apart, and returned them to the oven spaced out on a baking sheet. With this two-stage baking method, they finished uniformly golden and crisp.

My rolls were now airy, with excellent flavor and an appealing shape. But I still wasn't satisfied with their crust. I wanted the shattering crispness I'd admired on rustic dinner rolls from good bakeries. We had achieved just such a crust on our Almost No-Knead Bread (January/February 2008) by using a Dutch oven to trap steam. But this seemed impractical for my two-stage baking method (who wants to reach into a hot pot to pluck out rolls?), plus, fitting all the pieces would require multiple Dutch ovens.

Playing around with oven temperature, I tried an old baking technique (popularized by Fannie Farmer in the late 19th century) of starting the rolls at a high temperature, then reducing the heat to finish them. Instead of 20 minutes at 425 degrees, I baked the rolls at 500 degrees for 10 minutes, separated them on a baking sheet, and lowered the heat to 400 degrees. This initial blast of heat made all the difference between a so-so crust and one with real crackling crispness. It had another advantage—boosting the oven spring (the rise that yeasted dough experiences when it first hits the heat of the oven), so the crumb was even airier than before. Misting the rolls with water before baking (a nod to steam-injected ovens) made the crust even crisper. Finally, I had rustic dinner rolls from my home oven. Light, chewy, and shatteringly crisp, with a perfectly airy crumb, they could give any artisanal bakery rolls a run for the money.

COOK'S LIVE Original Test Kitchen Videos
www.cooksillustrated.com
HOW TO MAKE
• Rustic Dinner Rolls
VIDEO TIPS
• Why free-form rustic dinner rolls are better
• How can I tell when my dough is properly proofed?

RUSTIC DINNER ROLLS

MAKES 16 ROLLS

Because this dough is sticky, keep your hands well floured when handling it. Use a spray bottle to mist the rolls with water. The rolls will keep for up to 2 days at room temperature stored in a zipper-lock bag. To re-crisp the crust, place the rolls in a 450-degree oven 6 to 8 minutes. The rolls will keep frozen for several months wrapped in foil and placed in a large zipper-lock bag. Thaw the rolls at room temperature and re-crisp using the instructions above.

- **1½ cups plus 1 tablespoon water (12½ ounces), room temperature**
- **1½ teaspoons instant or rapid-rise yeast**
- **2 teaspoons honey**
- **3 cups plus 1 tablespoon bread flour (16½ ounces), plus extra for forming rolls**
- **3 tablespoons whole wheat flour (about 1 ounce)**
- **1½ teaspoons table salt**

1. Whisk water, yeast, and honey in bowl of stand mixer until well combined, making sure no honey sticks to bottom of bowl. Add flours and mix on low speed with dough hook until cohesive dough is formed, about 3 minutes. Cover bowl with plastic wrap and let sit at room temperature 30 minutes.

2. Remove plastic wrap and evenly sprinkle salt over dough. Knead on low speed (speed 2 on KitchenAid) 5 minutes. (If dough creeps up attachment, stop mixer and scrape down using well-floured hands or greased spatula.) Increase speed to medium and continue to knead until dough is smooth and slightly tacky, about 1 minute. If dough is very sticky, add 1 to 2 tablespoons flour and continue mixing 1 minute. Lightly spray 2-quart bowl with nonstick cooking spray; transfer dough to bowl and cover with plastic wrap. Let dough rise in warm, draft-free place until doubled in size, about 1 hour.

3. Fold dough over itself; rotate bowl quarter turn and fold again. Rotate bowl again and fold once more. Cover with plastic wrap and let rise 30 minutes. Repeat folding, replace plastic wrap, and let dough rise until doubled in volume, about 30 minutes. Spray two 9-inch round cake pans with nonstick cooking spray and set aside.

4. Transfer dough to floured work surface, sprinkle top with more flour. Using bench scraper, cut dough in half and gently stretch each half into 16-inch cylinders. Divide each cylinder into quarters, then each quarter into 2 pieces (you should have 16 pieces total), and dust top of each piece with more flour. With floured hands, gently pick up each piece and roll in palms to coat with flour, shaking off excess, and place in prepared cake pan. Arrange 8 dough pieces in each cake pan, placing one piece in middle and others around it, with long side of each piece running from center of pan to edge and making sure cut-side faces up. Loosely cover cake pans with plastic wrap and let rolls rise until doubled in size, about 30 minutes (dough is ready when it springs back slowly when pressed lightly with finger). Thirty minutes before baking, adjust rack to middle position and heat oven to 500 degrees.

5. Remove plastic wrap from cake pans, spray rolls lightly with water, and place in oven. Bake 10 minutes until tops of rolls are brown; remove from oven. Reduce oven temperature to 400 degrees; using kitchen towels or oven mitts, invert rolls from both cake pans onto rimmed baking sheet. When rolls are cool enough to handle, turn right-side up, pull apart, and space evenly on baking sheet. Continue to bake until rolls develop deep golden brown crust and sound hollow when tapped on bottom, 10 to 15 minutes; rotating baking sheet halfway through baking time. Transfer rolls to wire rack and cool to room temperature, about 1 hour.

TECHNIQUE

BROWNED ALL AROUND

For uniformly crisp, golden rolls, we devised a two-step baking process.

1. Partially baking the rolls in a cake pan helps set their shape but leaves soft spots where they touch.

2. Separating the rolls and returning them to the oven on a baking sheet ensures finished rolls that are golden and crisp all around.

Making the Most of Your Chef's Knife

With a little know-how, your chef's knife can be a workhorse that handles 90 percent of your kitchen cutting jobs—from chopping onions to mincing herbs and butchering chicken.

BY CHARLES KELSEY

ANATOMY OF A CHEF'S KNIFE

Handle
The knife handle helps balance the blade's weight. A good handle should virtually disappear in your grip, making the knife the oft-cited "extension of your hand." When choosing a knife, try gripping it before making your choice. The handle should be comfortable and resist slipping, even when your hand is wet or greasy.

Blade Curve
A good chef's knife blade should have a long, gently sloping curve suited to the rocking motion of mincing and chopping.

Blade Length
An 8-inch blade provides plenty of power without being unwieldy.

Blade Material
We prefer knives made with high-carbon stainless steel that, once sharpened, stay that way. Some purists prefer carbon steel knives, which may take a sharper edge but don't retain it for as long. Expensive ceramic blades are ultrasharp but equally fragile.

Forged vs. Stamped Blades
Forged blades—made by pouring molten steel into molds—are weightier than stamped blades, which are punched out of steel. Both perform equally well. The blade above is stamped.

Winning Chef's Knives

The inexpensive, lightweight Victorinox Fibrox 8-Inch Chef's Knife ($24.95; above, left) is a test kitchen favorite. Though far more expensive, we also like the Glestain Indented-Blade 8.2-Inch Gyutou Chef's Knife ($157.50) for its razor-sharp blade and double row of granton-style oval hollows on one side to minimize resistance between blade and food. For the complete results of our testing of chef's knives, go to www.cooksillustrated.com/december.

BLADE MAINTENANCE

A Knife's Life Cycle

A sharp blade tapers down to a thin edge (below, left). However, even a few minutes of cutting can make that edge roll over (below, center) and cause the blade to feel slightly dull. A quick steeling will remove the folded edge and restore sharpness. After the sharp angles become rounded and very dull (below, right), the knife needs a new edge, achievable only through true sharpening, not steeling.

VERY SHARP

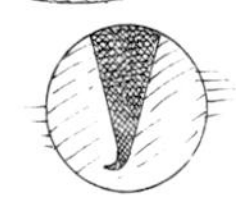

SLIGHTLY DULL

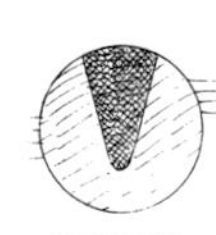

VERY DULL

Is It Sharp?

Even the best knives dull quickly with regular use. To determine if your knife needs sharpening, put it to the paper test.

Hold a folded, but not creased, sheet of newspaper by one end. Lay the blade against the top edge at an angle and slice outward. If the knife fails to slice clearly, try steeling it. If it still fails, it needs sharpening.

Make It Sharp

To reshape the edge of a dull knife, you have three choices: You can send it out, you can use a whetstone (tricky for anyone but a professional), or—the most convenient option—you can use an electric or manual sharpener. In the test kitchen, our favorite electric model is the Chef'sChoice 130 ($159) and our preferred manual tool is the AccuSharp Knife and Tool Sharpener ($11.71), a simple plastic hand-held device with a single tungsten carbide V-shaped blade.

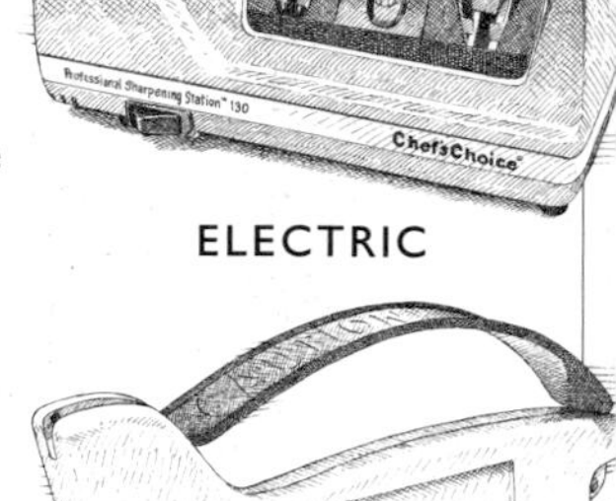

ELECTRIC

MANUAL

Dull and Dangerous

A dull knife is a dangerous knife. Here's why: The duller the blade, the more force it takes to do the job—and the easier it is for the blade to slip and miss the mark (slippery ingredients like onions are the worst offenders), quickly sending the knife toward your hand. With a sharp knife, the blade does the work—and the razorlike edge is far less likely to slip. To protect your knife from dulling, avoid hard cutting surfaces such as glass or acrylic (stick with bamboo and plastic cutting boards) and keep it out of the dishwasher, where getting knocked around might damage its edge.

When to Use a Sharpening Steel

A so-called sharpening steel, the metal rod sold with most knife sets, doesn't sharpen at all: It's a tuneup device. As you cut with a sharp knife, the edge of the blade can actually get knocked out of alignment. The knife may seem dull, but its edge is simply misaligned. Running the knife blade over the steel repositions that edge. But it can't reshape a blade that's rounded and worn down—that's when you need a sharpener to cut away metal and restore the standard 20-degree angle of each side of the edge.

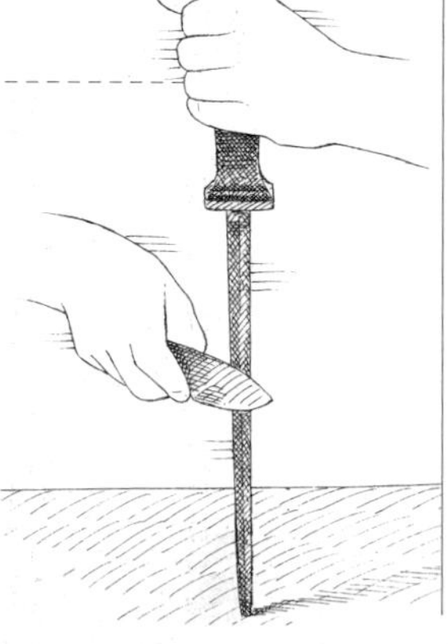

MAKING THE CUT

Different cuts make use of different parts of the blade. Here's how to utilize all parts of the blade safely and efficiently.

Whole Blade

To make fast work of mincing fresh herbs, garlic, and the like, place one hand on the handle and rest the fingers of the other hand lightly on the knife tip. This lighter two-handed grip facilitates the up-and-down rocking motion needed for quick mincing. To make sure the food is evenly minced, pivot the knife as you chop.

Get a Grip

Most people tend to hold a chef's knife by keeping their fingers entirely on the handle (top). For added control, choke up on the knife, with the thumb and index finger actually gripping the heel of the blade (bottom).

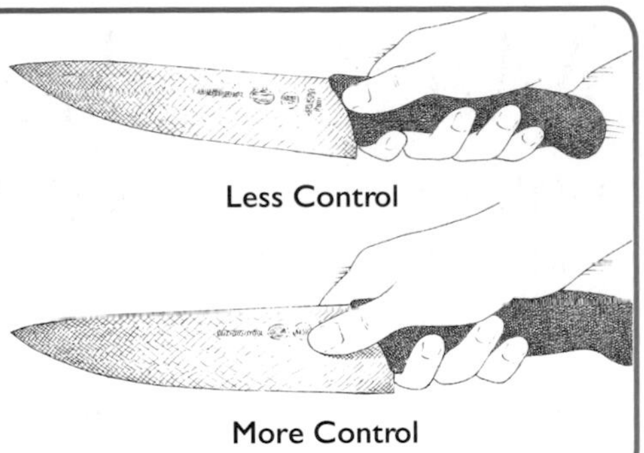

Tip

We rarely use a cutting motion that brings the blade toward the body. However, when using the tip, drawing the knife inward is unavoidable.

1. To use this technique safely, place the knife into the food with the tip facing slightly down. Pivot the blade so the tip slices through the ingredient and rests on the board.
2. Drag the knife toward you, making sure to keep the tip against the board as you pull.

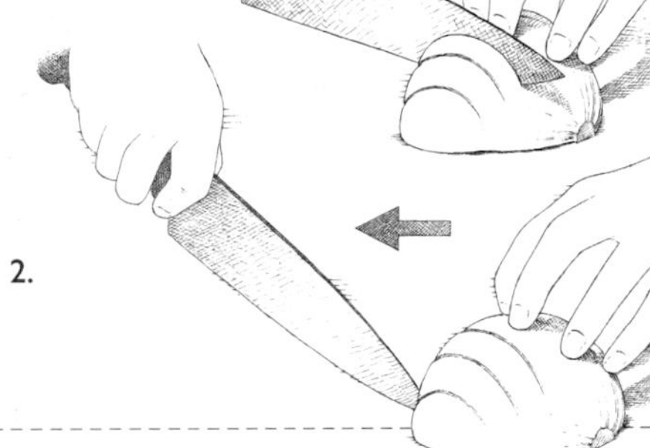

Middle

While using the blade's curve to guide the knife through a series of smooth cutting strokes, push the blade forward and down. If the food is small enough (e.g., celery or scallions), the tip of the blade should touch the cutting board at all times (top). However, for large ingredients such as eggplant or sweet potatoes, the tip of the blade should come off the board while making smooth cutting strokes through the ingredient (bottom).

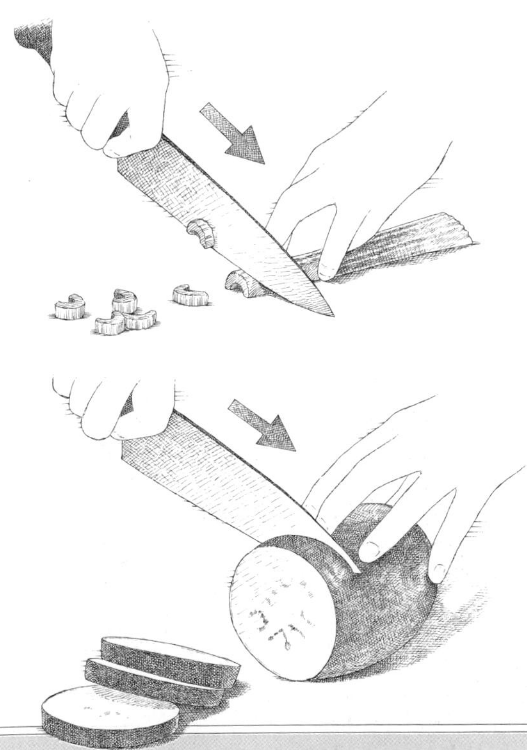

Heel

The heel is the sturdiest part of the blade, offering a flat cutting edge for hacking up chicken bones, divvying up a large piece of hard Parmesan, or splitting winter squash. To apply a lot of force using the heel, hold the handle and place the flat palm of your other hand over the top of the blade (use a towel to cushion your hand) and cut straight down on the item. Use utmost caution and make sure your knife, hands, and cutting surface are completely dry (to avoid slippage).

COOK'S LIVE
Original Test Kitchen Videos
www.cooksillustrated.com
VIDEO TIPS
- How to dice a potato
- How to mince an onion
- How to mince or chop a carrot
- Basic chef's knife skills

Safety Basics

Stabilized for Safety

Knife work and wobbly ingredients don't mix—the combination is unsafe and leads to uneven cuts. Halve round foods like onions to create a flat, stable side and place each half cut-side down before slicing or dicing. For narrow ingredients such as carrots, remove a thin sliver from one side to create a stable edge (below).

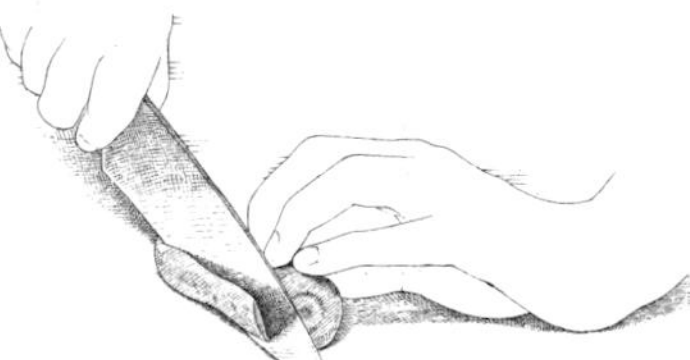

1. Create a stable edge.

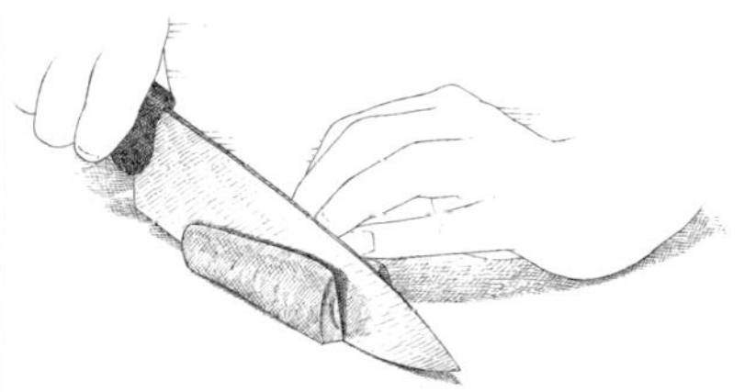

2. Flip carrot onto stable edge and cut.

Positioned for Protection

Prevent slippage, control cut size, and protect your fingers by curling the ingredient-holding hand.

Tuck your fingertips away from the knife in a "bear claw" to hold the food in place, while the knuckles rest against the side of the blade, providing guidance while minimizing danger. During the upward motion of slicing, reposition your guiding hand for the next cut.

ILLUSTRATION: JOHN BURGOYNE

Ultimate Stuffed Portobellos

We set out to transform this humdrum party food into a first-rate side dish worth making after the holidays are over.

⇛ BY FRANCISCO J. ROBERT ⇚

The key to filling that stays together is to remove moisture from the mushrooms before stuffing them.

Come holiday time, stuffed mushrooms compete with mini quiches as the most ubiquitous hors d'oeuvre on the party platter. Stuffed mushrooms aren't bad—but I've never eaten any worth raving about. For one thing, they're often marred by a soggy, gluey, or just plain messy filling. Furthermore, although white button mushrooms have an ideal shape for finger food, they're no prize in terms of flavor and are easily overshadowed—even by an imperfect filling. I wanted the ultimate stuffed mushroom: meaty, earthy, and intense, with a filling that contributed complementary flavors and textures. In short, stuffed mushrooms good enough to break out after New Year's Eve as a dressed-up side dish.

Returning to Earth(iness)

First, I needed more mushroom flavor. Many exotic mushrooms fit that requirement, but they're the wrong shape for stuffing. Two cultivated kinds stood out for consideration: creminis (also called "baby bellas") and portobellos. Both boast rich flavor and are widely available. I went with portobellos for two reasons. As mushrooms mature, their flavor intensifies, giving portobellos the edge on that front. And while small mushrooms are great for passing on trays to grazing guests, a sit-down meal with knife and fork calls for one large mushroom per portion. Armed with a parcel of portobellos and a bucket of basic bread crumb stuffing, I headed to the test kitchen to get started.

Many recipes call for simply stuffing the raw caps and placing them in the oven. But like all fungi, portobellos are 80 to 90 percent water, and it stood to reason that to avoid a soggy filling, some water should come out before any stuffing went in. In the test kitchen, we often salt watery vegetables such as eggplant and zucchini to extract moisture. So I tossed the caps with salt and placed them in a colander to drain. Two hours later, the mushrooms had merely turned slimy but remained as waterlogged as ever. A little research revealed that a protective water-repellent coating on the mushroom's surface was to blame (see "Mushrooms and Moisture," page 19).

I'd have to resort to the usual approach of eliminating moisture from mushrooms—precooking. But with mushrooms this big, sautéing was clearly not an option unless I wanted to spend an hour at the stove. Instead, I placed a batch of portobello caps in a 400-degree oven and waited for the moisture to exit. And waited. Forty minutes later, the mushrooms were dry, with deep flavor, albeit a little leathery from the long exposure to heat.

I was on the right track, though. A colleague suggested scoring the mushrooms with shallow cuts (on the smooth, non-gill side) before precooking to expedite the release of moisture. Brilliant. The mushrooms lost enough water after just 20 minutes, leaving them intensely flavored and sufficiently dry (but not leathery) in half the time. I wondered if I could achieve even more intense flavor by caramelizing the exterior—easy to do with the direct heat of the stovetop, a bit harder in the oven's ambient heat. I tried preheating the baking sheet before placing the mushrooms on top, mimicking the effects of a hot skillet. The results were exemplary: beautiful, caramelized exteriors and deep, earthy flavor.

Binders, Keepers

When it comes right down to it, you can stuff a mushroom with anything so long as it fits in the cap. But after testing dozens of combinations, I developed some basic rules. First, chopped stems make a good stuffing base. Portobello caps hold plenty of filling, so it made sense to use the parts already on hand rather than rely solely on new ingredients. Next, some sort of binder is essential. The most common are bread crumbs and béchamel, but I

RECIPE SHORTHAND | STUFFED PORTOBELLO MUSHROOMS

1. SCORE mushrooms on non-gill side. **2. ROAST** gill-side up on preheated baking sheet, then flip and roast gill-side down. **3. TOAST** bread crumbs in skillet. **4. SAUTÉ** stuffing ingredients in batches. **5. FILL** mushrooms with stuffing and sprinkle with bread crumbs. **6. BROIL** until golden brown.

PHOTOGRAPHY: CARL TREMBLAY ILLUSTRATION: JAY LAYMAN

found that each had its share of problems. The bread crumb fillings were typically soggy and did nothing for flavor, while the béchamel versions turned out gluey and were a pain to make. Could I simply use cheese as a binder? After sautéing the chopped stems, I added ½ cup of cheddar with a splash of cream and crossed my fingers. Success: The cheese kept the stuffing intact, and the cream added welcome lushness. Tasters then sampled a few different kinds, preferring goat cheese for its tangy flavor, with blue cheese coming in a close second.

With a solid structure for the filling, it was all a matter of tweaking. The best fillings combined bright and earthy flavors with soft and creamy textures and a contrasting crunch. In the end, tasters liked the tangy mineral taste of fresh spinach, the crunchiness of toasted chopped walnuts, the savory flavors of onion and garlic, and the fragrant addition of thyme. To get the right volume, I added a couple of extra chopped portobellos. As a final flourish, I toasted some fresh bread crumbs in a skillet with butter and oil and sprinkled them over each stuffed mushroom. With every ingredient precooked, all these mushrooms needed was a few minutes under the broiler to come out sizzling, with enough sophistication to serve long after the holidays are over.

STUFFED PORTOBELLO MUSHROOMS WITH SPINACH AND GOAT CHEESE

SERVES 8 AS A SIDE DISH OR 4 AS A MAIN COURSE

The filling can be made up to 2 days ahead and refrigerated. Rewarm the filling before stuffing the mushrooms. We do not recommend roasting the mushrooms in advance, as they become leathery once rewarmed. When shopping, choose dense mushrooms with a cupped shape. Blue cheese can be substituted for the goat cheese. This recipe can be easily halved. For our free recipe for Stuffed Portobello Mushrooms with Cheddar and Prosciutto, go to www.cooksillustrated.com/december.

- 10 portobello mushrooms (each 4 to 5 inches), stems removed and reserved, caps wiped clean
- 4 tablespoons olive oil
- Table salt
- 2 (6-ounce) bags baby spinach (about 10 cups)
- 2 tablespoons water
- 2 large slices white sandwich bread, torn into quarters
- 2 tablespoons unsalted butter
- 2 medium onions, diced small (about 2 cups)
- 4 medium garlic cloves, minced or pressed through garlic press (about 4 teaspoons)
- ½ cup dry sherry
- 2 tablespoons chopped fresh thyme leaves
- 4 ounces goat cheese, crumbled (about 1 cup) (see note)
- ¼ cup heavy cream
- 1 cup walnuts, toasted and roughly chopped
- 2 teaspoons juice from 1 lemon
- Ground black pepper

1. Adjust oven rack to upper-middle position, place rimmed baking sheet on rack, and heat oven to 400 degrees. Using sharp knife, cut ¼-inch slits, spaced ½ inch apart, in crosshatch pattern on surface (non-gill side) of 8 mushrooms. Dice remaining 2 mushroom caps and reserved stems into ½-inch pieces; set aside (you should have about 3 cups).

2. Brush both sides of caps with 2 tablespoons oil and sprinkle evenly with 1 teaspoon salt. Carefully place caps, gill-side up, on preheated baking sheet. Roast until mushrooms have released some of their juices and begin to brown around edges, 8 to 12 minutes. Flip caps over and continue to roast until liquid has completely evaporated and caps are golden brown, 8 to 12 minutes longer. Remove mushrooms from oven and heat broiler.

3. Meanwhile, place spinach and water in large microwave-safe bowl. Cover bowl with large dinner plate (plate should completely cover bowl and not rest on spinach). Microwave on high power until spinach is wilted and decreased in volume by half, 3 to 4 minutes. Using potholders, remove bowl from microwave and keep covered 1 minute. Carefully remove plate and transfer spinach to colander set in sink. Using back of rubber spatula, gently press spinach against colander to release excess liquid. Transfer spinach to cutting board and roughly chop. Return spinach to colander and press again. Set aside.

4. Pulse bread in food processor until coarsely ground, about 16 one-second pulses (you should have about 1½ cups). Heat 1 tablespoon oil and 1 tablespoon butter in 12-inch skillet over medium heat until butter is melted. Add bread crumbs and ¼ teaspoon salt; cook, stirring frequently, until light golden brown, 5 to 8 minutes. Transfer crumbs to small bowl and wipe out skillet with paper towels.

5. Return now-empty skillet to medium-high heat, add remaining tablespoon oil, and heat until smoking. Add chopped mushrooms and cook without stirring for 2 minutes. Continue cooking, stirring occasionally, until lightly browned, 4 to 6 minutes longer. Transfer to medium bowl.

6. Add remaining tablespoon butter and onions to skillet; cook, stirring occasionally, until onions are light brown, 5 to 6 minutes. Add garlic and cook until fragrant, about 30 seconds. Stir in sherry and cook until almost no liquid remains, 1 to 2 minutes. Reduce heat to low and stir in reserved cooked mushrooms, spinach, thyme, goat cheese, cream, and walnuts. Continue cooking until cheese is melted and vegetables are well coated, 1 to 2 minutes. Remove pan from heat, stir in lemon juice, and season with salt and pepper to taste.

7. Flip caps, gill-side up, and distribute filling evenly among mushroom caps; top each with 2 tablespoons bread crumb mixture. Broil mushrooms until crumbs are golden brown, 1 to 3 minutes. Serve immediately.

SCIENCE:

Mushrooms and Moisture

To extract moisture from the whole mushroom caps in our stuffed portobello recipe, we tried salting and draining them before cooking—a trick we often use with watery veggies such as eggplant and zucchini. But the method succeeded only in making the caps slimy. It turns out that the exterior of any mushroom is covered with a layer of hydrophobic (water-repellent) proteins that prevents water from going in—and keeps moisture from going out. Instead, we removed liquid by cutting slits in the caps, which allowed water to drip out and evaporate as we precooked the mushrooms in a 400-degree oven. –F.J.R.

WATERTIGHT Whole caps have a protective coating that keeps moisture in—even when salted.

FREE-FLOWING We slit the caps to allow water to be released as the mushrooms cooked.

EQUIPMENT TESTING:

Flipping Fish . . . and Beyond

Fish spatulas—elongated versions of a standard pancake flipper—are designed expressly for shimmying underneath delicate fillets. But we've found no better tool for extracting sticky vegetables from a baking sheet—or transferring a loaded-up portobello to a plate. The best fish spatulas we tested were strong yet pliable, and not too long. Tapered edges made easy work of digging beneath caramelized potatoes, while a gentle upward curve at the tip cradled slippery foods with panache. For complete testing results, go to www.cooksillustrated.com/december.

–Elizabeth Bomze

CURVE APPEAL
WÜSTHOF Gourmet 7.5-Inch Slotted Turner/Fish Spatula
Price: $34.95
Comments: A curved shape and tapered edge made the Wüsthof our winner.

DISTURBING THE PIECE
OXO Good Grips Fish Turner
Price: $11.99
Comments: The OXO's "absurdly large" nearly 10-inch blade was too long for adequate control, landing it in last place.

COOK'S LIVE Original Test Kitchen Videos
www.cooksillustrated.com
HOW TO MAKE
• Stuffed Portobellos
VIDEO TIP
• All about portobello mushrooms

Taming Garlic Shrimp Pasta

Delicate shrimp, volatile garlic, and a whole mess of oil—what could possibly go wrong?

BY FRANCISCO J. ROBERT

In theory, garlic shrimp pasta has all the makings of an ideal weeknight meal. Toss a few quick-cooking ingredients—shrimp, garlic, oil, wine—with boiled dried pasta, and only the salad's left holding up dinner.

As with most theories, of course, reality has a way of rearing its ugly head. Delicate shrimp cooks fast, which translates to overcooked in a matter of seconds. Meanwhile, volatile garlic is all over the map: Like a high-maintenance friend, it can become overbearing or bitter (or simply disappear), depending on how it's treated. Add to that the challenge of getting a brothy sauce to coat the pasta, and this simple recipe turns into a precarious balancing act. But I still wanted it all: al dente pasta and moist shrimp bound by a supple sauce infused with a deep garlic flavor.

Before facing the garlic problem, I tackled the shrimp. Because most shrimp are frozen once caught—and the flavor and texture degrade quickly once thawed—the test kitchen prefers buying IQF (individually quick frozen) shrimp and thawing it ourselves (which takes only minutes in a colander under cold running water). We've also found that freezing prepeeled, deveined shrimp sabotages flavor, so it's worth saving those tasks for home, too. I ruled out medium-sized shrimp because they cook too fast, as well as expensive extra-large and jumbo, landing on midpriced-but-meaty large shrimp (21 to 25 per pound).

In most shrimp pasta recipes, the shrimp are cooked separately, then tossed with the sauce and pasta at the end. But how to cook them? Searing quickly over high heat was too risky, yielding an overcooked texture. Poaching in a court-bouillon (water enhanced with wine and aromatics) kept the shrimp moist but didn't contribute much flavor. I tentatively settled on sautéing them gently in garlic and oil while building the sauce.

Starting with a basic working recipe, I sautéed the shrimp with three cloves of minced garlic in a modest amount of olive oil. Removing the shrimp, I added a pinch of red pepper flakes and a cup of white wine, reduced the sauce, then tossed it with the shrimp and boiled linguine. The results were just OK: weak garlic, moist but lackluster shrimp, and a thinnish sauce that dripped off the pasta.

Upping the garlic by increments until I reached six cloves gave me indisputably garlicky pasta. But now I had a new problem: All that garlic cooked unevenly. Sautéed too little, and the pasta suffered that raw flavor that (literally) takes your breath away; too long, and random burnt granules impart a bitter taste. Turning the heat to the lowest setting and simmering the garlic longer yielded a sweet, nutty taste, but we missed the brasher notes.

Borrowing tricks from our recipe for Spanish-Style Garlic Shrimp (January/February 2008), I split the difference. First, I slowly simmered the oil with smashed garlic cloves (more effective in this task than minced) over low heat, discarded the toasted cloves, and built the sauce using the infused oil. Just before adding the wine, I quickly sautéed a smaller amount of minced garlic (just long enough to bloom the flavor). With sweet low notes from the infused oil and brasher high notes from the minced, I finally had the balanced, deeply layered garlic flavor I wanted. When tasters noted that the shrimp itself was still short on flavor, I marinated it for 20 minutes with additional minced garlic.

Next, I tinkered with the sauce. To deglaze the pan, I tried replacing the wine with sherry, Marsala, and Madeira, but tasters preferred the cleaner taste of vermouth or white wine. Bottled clam broth added after the vermouth contributed seaworthy complexity, bolstering the shrimp flavor. To get the sauce to cling to the pasta, I stirred a little flour into the oil as a thickener just before adding the liquid and added some cold butter to finish.

Presumably at the finish line, I served up my deep-flavored, luxurious-textured pasta. But tasters remarked that the shrimp stayed hidden in a tangle of linguine, and there simply weren't enough bites. Swapping out traditional linguine for a chunky tubular pasta (we liked mezze rigatoni) made it easy to find the shrimp, and cutting each shrimp into thirds before cooking ensured that nearly every bite boasted a tasty morsel.

COOK'S LIVE Original Test Kitchen Video
www.cooksillustrated.com
HOW TO MAKE
• Garlicky Shrimp Pasta

GARLICKY SHRIMP PASTA

SERVES 4

Marinate the shrimp while you prepare the remaining ingredients.

- **5 medium garlic cloves, minced or pressed through garlic press (about 5 teaspoons), plus 4 medium cloves, smashed**
- **1 pound large (21–25) shrimp, peeled, deveined, each shrimp cut into 3 pieces**
- **3 tablespoons olive oil**
- **Table salt**
- **1 pound short tubular pasta such as fusilli, campanelle, or mezze rigatoni**
- **¼–½ teaspoon red pepper flakes**
- **2 teaspoons unbleached all-purpose flour**
- **½ cup dry vermouth or white wine**
- **¾ cup clam juice**
- **½ cup chopped fresh parsley leaves**
- **3 tablespoons unsalted butter**
- **1 teaspoon lemon juice plus 1 lemon, cut into wedges**
- **Ground black pepper**

1. Toss 2 teaspoons minced garlic, shrimp, 1 tablespoon oil, and ¼ teaspoon salt in medium bowl. Let shrimp marinate at room temperature 20 minutes.

2. Heat 4 smashed garlic cloves and remaining 2 tablespoons oil in 12-inch skillet over medium-low heat, stirring occasionally, until garlic is light golden brown, 4 to 7 minutes. Remove skillet from heat and use slotted spoon to remove garlic from skillet; discard garlic. Set skillet aside.

3. Bring 4 quarts water to boil in large Dutch oven over high heat. Add 1 tablespoon salt and pasta. Cook until just al dente, then drain pasta, reserving ¼ cup cooking water, and transfer pasta back to Dutch oven.

4. While pasta cooks, return skillet with oil to medium heat; add shrimp with marinade to skillet in single layer. Cook shrimp, undisturbed, until oil starts to bubble gently, 1 to 2 minutes. Stir shrimp and continue to cook until almost cooked through, about 1 minute longer. Using slotted spoon, transfer shrimp to medium bowl. Add remaining 3 teaspoons minced garlic and pepper flakes to skillet and cook until fragrant, about 1 minute. Add flour and cook, stirring constantly, for 1 minute; stir in vermouth and cook for 1 minute. Add clam juice and parsley; cook until mixture starts to thicken, 1 to 2 minutes. Off heat, whisk in butter and lemon juice. Add shrimp and sauce to pasta, adding reserved cooking water if sauce is too thick. Season with black pepper. Serve, passing lemon wedges separately.

All Clammed Up

We sampled three brands of bottled clam juice and found the fresh, bright taste of Bar Harbor boosted our pasta's seafood flavor best, keeping the shrimp from getting stranded in a sea of garlic. For complete tasting results, go to www.cooksillustrated.com/december.

TOP CLAM JUICE

Introducing Sablé Cookies

These French butter cookies offer sophistication and style from simple pantry ingredients. That is, if you can capture their elusive sandy texture.

BY YVONNE RUPERTI

During the holidays, butter cookies are the go-to choice for many American bakers. Shaped with cookie cutters, these simple cookies serve mainly as a backing for sugary frostings and fanciful decorations. Standard butter cookie dough includes just four main ingredients: all-purpose flour, butter, granulated sugar, and eggs. But don't let the brief ingredient list fool you—not all butter cookies are alike.

Take, for example, French butter cookies, or sablés. The best have a lightness and inviting granular texture that is decidedly different from sturdy American butter cookies. (*Sablé* is French for "sandy," as befits their crisp crumble.) They are often made as icebox cookies, in which the dough is shaped into a log, chilled, sliced into rounds, and baked, so there's no need to fuss with cookie cutters. And because they are delicate and refined, sablés require only a sprinkle of sugar to be ready for the holiday table.

Searching for Sandiness

After reviewing dozens of recipes, I was perplexed by what appeared to be only slight differences in ingredient proportions between American and French butter cookie recipes. To create the hallmark sandy texture of sablés, I would have to do some detective work. I began by assembling a basic recipe using the typical method of creaming butter and sugar in a stand mixer, then adding egg and flour. I rolled the dough into a log, chilled it, then sliced and baked.

French butter cookies lend themselves to myriad festive shapes.

With just one taste, I knew my cookies were missing the delicate crumbliness that defines sablés. I studied my ingredients list—1½ cups flour, ⅓ cup sugar, 12 tablespoons butter, and one egg—and then consulted our science editor, who suggested that I reduce the moisture in the dough. When cookie dough is prepared with a small amount of liquid, only a portion of the sugar will dissolve, leaving behind intact granules that deliver a sandy consistency. (When the cookies are baked, some of the sugar will liquefy, but when they cool, the sugar will recrystallize, restoring sandiness.) The bottom line: I needed to decrease the liquid in my dough so there would be less moisture to dissolve the sugar particles.

So, the two candidates for cutbacks were the butter and the egg. Butter is 20 percent water; with 12 tablespoons in my recipe, I decided to start there. But as cookie dough needs enough butterfat to coat the flour and provide tenderness, I found I could eliminate only 2 tablespoons before the cookies became tough. Luckily, minute adjustments to baking recipes can often have a big impact, and even this small reduction proved helpful—the cookies were now somewhat sandy. Still, I wanted even more crumbliness.

With just one ingredient left to fiddle with—the egg—my options were few. Eliminating the egg altogether yielded somewhat tough, pallid cookies. What if I just got rid of the egg white, which is nearly 90 percent water? A yolk-only dough was a giant step in the right direction: These cookies were just about where I wanted them to be. But I wanted to push this recipe further, eliminating even more moisture to produce supremely sandy, crystalline sablés. After mulling things over, I went out on a limb. Because flour is about 14 percent water, I wondered if toasting would drive off some moisture. I gave it a try, browning the flour in a skillet before adding it to the creamed butter and sugar. But my hopes were dashed when I sampled the resulting cookies: I didn't detect enough of a difference to make it worth the bother.

STEP-BY-STEP | SHAPING PERFECT COOKIES

1. Roll each log of dough in parchment or wax paper.

2. Twist one end of parchment paper.

3. Stand log on twisted end. Squeeze dough into cylinder while twisting upper end. Chill.

4. To slice, rotate chilled dough ¼ turn after each cut.

Boiling It Down

I dug deeper into the stacks of the test kitchen library. A few sablé recipes called for something I'd never heard of in years of baking: adding a hard-cooked yolk to the dough. These recipes claimed that the hard-cooked yolk would deliver a sandy cookie. Skeptical but intrigued, I hard-cooked and cooled an egg and then added the mashed yolk

SCIENCE: Invoking the Yolk

When we came across sablé recipes that called for a hard-cooked egg yolk, we were tempted to ignore this unlikely ingredient. What could it possibly do—aside from fleck our cookies with unwelcome bits of yolk? But when we actually gave the cooked yolk a try, we were surprised by the results.

EXPERIMENT

We prepared one batch of sablé cookies with a raw yolk and compared it with another batch made with a hard-cooked yolk that had been pressed through a fine-mesh strainer.

RESULTS

The cookies prepared with the hard-cooked egg yolk were markedly sandier than those prepared with the raw yolk. Even better, we could detect no bits of cooked yolk, just rich flavor.

EXPLANATION

An egg yolk consists of about 50 percent water by weight. When boiled, the proteins in the yolk form a solid matrix that locks in that water, making it unavailable. The sandiness in sablé cookies comes from undissolved sugar crystals. By reducing the amount of water available to dissolve the sugar, the cooked yolk promotes a crystalline texture in the finished cookies. By contrast, the liquid in the raw egg yolk dissolved the sugar, making the texture of the cookies smoother. –Y.R.

to the butter and sugar during creaming. Voilà! This unusual step eliminated even more moisture from the cookies and really improved their texture (for more information, see "Invoking the Yolk," above). Because yolks are about 50 percent water, the subtraction of moisture from just one yolk was small but significant.

With the texture of the cookies perfected, I focused on tweaking flavor. To amplify buttery taste, I added 1/4 teaspoon of salt and 1 teaspoon of vanilla (due to its alcohol base, vanilla extract quickly evaporates during baking, so its moisture didn't affect the texture). After rolling portions of the dough in parchment paper (plastic wrap was too flimsy) to form cylinders, I refrigerated them for an hour. The chilled logs were easy to cut into slices. Brushing the cookies with a beaten egg white and sprinkling them with coarse turbinado sugar added a delicate crunch and an attractive sparkle. For the oven, a standard butter cookie temperature of 350 degrees was best. With my French butter cookie recipe complete, I used the sablé dough to form some simple but striking European-style variations.

COOK'S LIVE Original Test Kitchen Videos

www.cooksillustrated.com

HOW TO MAKE

- French Butter Cookies (Sablés)

VIDEO TIPS

- How to hard-cook an egg
- How to make Checkerboard Cookies
- What are turbinado and Demerara sugars and how do you use them?

FRENCH BUTTER COOKIES (SABLÉS)

MAKES ABOUT 40 COOKIES

Turbinado sugar is commonly sold as Sugar in the Raw. Demerara sugar, sanding sugar, or another coarse sugar can be substituted. Make sure the cookie dough is well chilled and firm so that it can be uniformly sliced. After the dough has been wrapped in parchment, it can be double-wrapped in plastic and frozen for up to 2 weeks. For our free recipe for Checkerboard Cookies, go to www.cooksillustrated.com/december.

- 1 large egg
- 10 tablespoons (1 1/4 sticks) unsalted butter, softened
- 1/3 cup plus 1 tablespoon (2 3/4 ounces) granulated sugar
- 1/4 teaspoon table salt
- 1 teaspoon vanilla extract
- 1 1/2 cups (7 1/2 ounces) unbleached all-purpose flour
- 1 large egg white, lightly beaten with 1 teaspoon water
- 4 teaspoons turbinado sugar (see note)

1. Place egg in small saucepan, cover with 1 inch water, and bring to boil over high heat. Remove pan from heat, cover, and let sit 10 minutes. Meanwhile, fill small bowl with ice water. Using slotted spoon, transfer egg to ice water and let stand 5 minutes. Crack egg and peel shell. Separate yolk from white; discard white. Press yolk through fine-mesh strainer into small bowl.

2. In bowl of stand mixer fitted with paddle attachment, beat butter, granulated sugar, salt, and cooked egg yolk on medium speed until light and fluffy, about 4 minutes, scraping down sides of bowl and beater with rubber spatula as needed. Turn mixer to low, add vanilla, and mix until incorporated. Stop mixer; add flour and mix on low speed until just combined, about 30 seconds. Using rubber spatula, press dough into cohesive mass.

3. Divide dough in half; roll each piece into log about 6 inches long and 1 3/4 inches in diameter. Wrap each log in 12-inch square of parchment paper and twist ends to seal and firmly compact dough into tight cylinder (see illustrations 1 through 3 on page 21). Chill until firm, about 1 hour.

4. Adjust oven racks to upper-middle and lower-middle positions and heat oven to 350 degrees. Line 2 rimmed baking sheets with parchment paper. Using chef's knife, slice dough into 1/4-inch-thick rounds, rotating dough so that it won't become misshapen from weight of knife (illustration 4). Place cookies 1 inch apart on baking sheets. Using pastry brush, gently brush cookies with egg white mixture and sprinkle evenly with turbinado sugar.

5. Bake until centers of cookies are pale golden brown with edges slightly darker than centers, about 15 minutes, rotating baking sheets front to back and top to bottom halfway through baking. Cool cookies on baking sheet 5 minutes; using thin metal spatula, transfer cookies to wire rack and cool to room temperature. Store cooled cookies between sheets of parchment paper in airtight container for up to 1 week.

TASTING: Premium Butter

Do boutique butters deserve their rave reviews? To find out, we tasted seven premium unsalted butters, cultured and sweet cream (plus our favorite supermarket stick from Land O' Lakes), plain and in butter cookies. While you hear a lot about the higher fat content in premium butters, they actually contain only about a gram more per tablespoon than regular butter, and the difference is not discernible to most palates. Our tasters' preferences came down to culture. Culturing, or fermenting cream before churning it into butter, is standard practice in Europe and builds tangy, complex flavors that our tasters almost unanimously preferred tasted plain. Baked into cookies, however, these nuances were harder to detect, even in our winner, Lurpak ($4.99 for 8 oz.). For complete tasting results, go to www.cooksillustrated.com/december. –Elizabeth Bomze

CREAM OF THE CROP

LURPAK Unsalted Butter

Price: $4.99 for 8 oz.
Comments: This Danish cultured butter tasted "creamy" and "nutty" on its own and baked up into cookies with a "near-perfect," "tight crumb."

A GOOD TANG

VERMONT BUTTER & CHEESE COMPANY Unsalted Butter

Price: $4.50 for 8 oz.
Comments: A favorite for those who liked a subtle "cheesy tang," this small-batch log earned second place for being "rich" and "creamy."

LAND O' THE BLAND

LAND O' LAKES Unsalted Butter

Price: $4.69 for 1 pound
Comments: Most tasters had no trouble picking out this "bland" supermarket staple, which finished fifth out of the eight brands tested, when tasted plain. But it baked up well in cookies.

CHOCOLATE SABLÉS

Follow recipe for French Butter Cookies, reducing flour to 1 1/3 cups (6 2/3 ounces) and adding 1/4 cup (1 ounce) Dutch-processed cocoa with flour in step 2.

TECHNIQUE | FORMING SANDWICH COOKIES

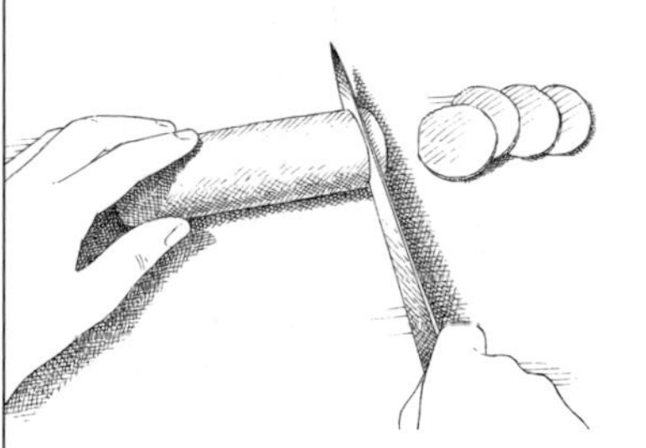

1. Slice 1 dough log into 1/8-inch-thick rounds.

2. Bake 10 to 13 minutes. Repeat with second log.

3. When cookies are cool, spread melted chocolate on bottom of 1 cookie.

4. Place second cookie on top, slightly off-center, so some chocolate shows.

TECHNIQUE | FORMING PRETZEL COOKIES

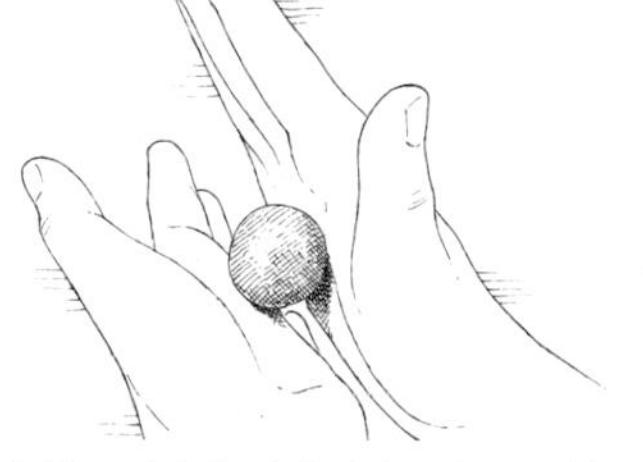

1. Slice slightly chilled dough into 1/4-inch-thick rounds and roll into balls.

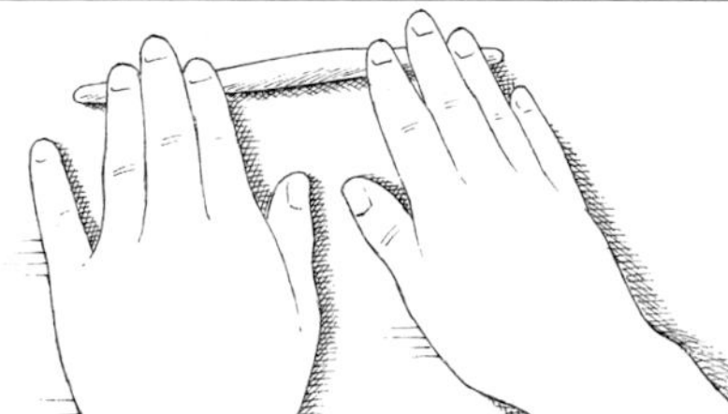

2. Roll each ball into 6-inch rope, tapering ends.

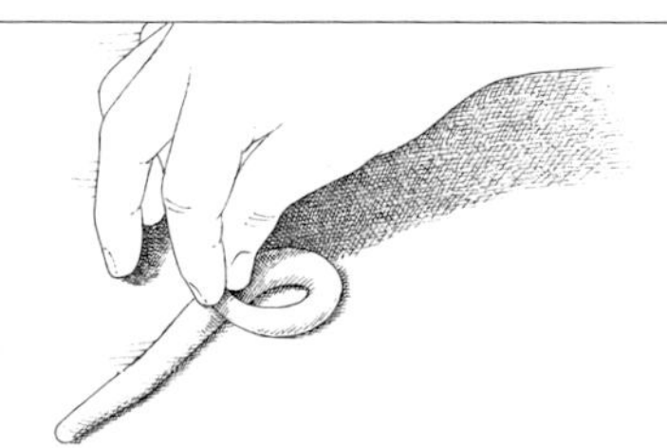

3. Pick up 1 end of rope and cross it over to form half of pretzel shape.

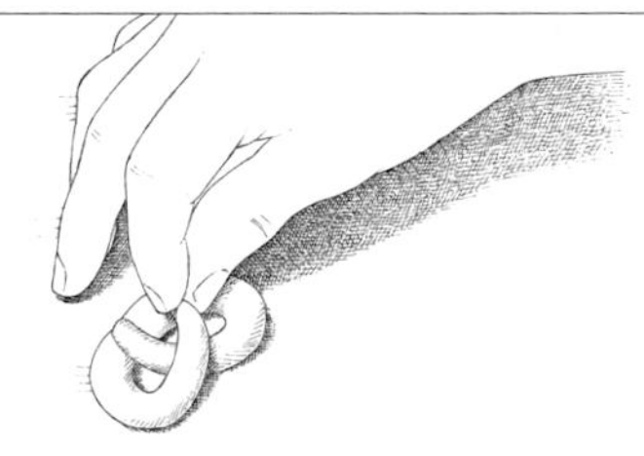

4. Bring second end over to complete pretzel shape.

TECHNIQUE | FORMING SPIRAL COOKIES

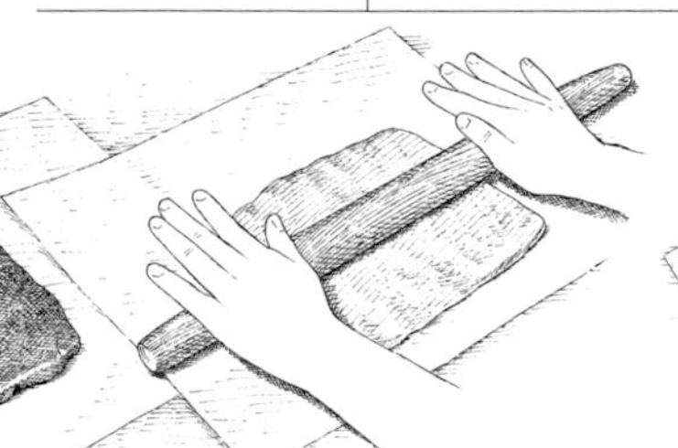

1. Halve each batch of dough. Roll out each portion on parchment paper into 6- by 8-inch rectangle, 1/4 inch thick. Briefly chill dough until firm enough to handle.

2. Using bench scraper, place 1 plain cookie dough rectangle on top of 1 chocolate dough rectangle. Repeat to make 2 double rectangles.

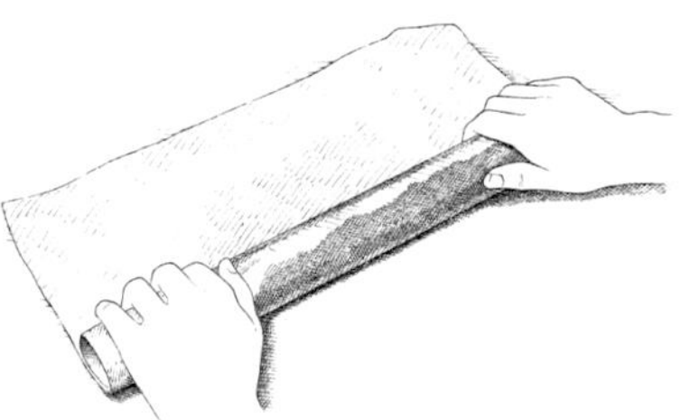

3. Roll out each double rectangle on parchment into 6- by 9-inch rectangle (if too firm, let rest until malleable). Starting at long end, roll each into tight log.

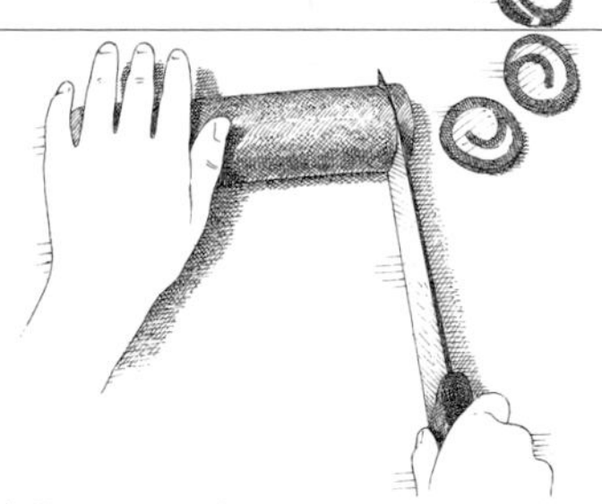

4. Twist ends of parchment to seal and chill logs 1 hour. Slice logs into 1/4-inch rounds.

LEMON SABLÉS

Follow recipe for French Butter Cookies, adding 4 teaspoons grated lemon zest with vanilla in step 2. Omit egg white mixture and turbinado sugar. Once cookies have cooled, dust with confectioners' sugar.

TOASTED COCONUT SABLÉS

Follow recipe for French Butter Cookies, adding 1/3 cup finely chopped toasted sweetened coconut to dough with flour in step 2. Omit turbinado sugar. After brushing cookies with egg white mixture, sprinkle with 1/3 cup finely chopped untoasted sweetened coconut.

ALMOND SABLÉS

Follow recipe for French Butter Cookies, substituting 1 1/2 teaspoons almond extract for vanilla extract and adding 1/3 cup finely ground sliced almonds to dough with flour. Omit turbinado sugar. After brushing cookies with egg white mixture, gently press 3 almond slices in petal shape in center of each cookie.

BLACK AND WHITE SPIRAL COOKIES

MAKES ABOUT 80 COOKIES

Follow recipes for French Butter Cookies and Chocolate Sables through step 2, omitting egg white mixture and turbinado sugar in both recipes. Following "Forming Spiral Cookies" illustrations above, form doughs into spiral logs. Proceed with French Butter Cookie recipe from step 4, slicing logs into 1/4-inch-thick rounds and baking as directed.

CHOCOLATE SANDWICH COOKIES

MAKES ABOUT 40 COOKIES

Follow recipe for French Butter Cookies through step 3, omitting egg white mixture and turbinado sugar. In step 4, slice 1 dough log into 1/8-inch-thick rounds. Bake cookies as directed in step 5, reducing baking time to 10 to 13 minutes. Repeat with second dough log. When all cookies are completely cool, melt 3 1/2 ounces dark or milk chocolate and cool slightly. Following "Forming Sandwich Cookies" illustrations above, assemble cookies.

VANILLA PRETZEL COOKIES

MAKES ABOUT 40 COOKIES

Follow recipe for French Butter Cookies through step 3, increasing vanilla extract to 1 tablespoon and reducing chilling time to 30 minutes (dough will not be fully hardened). Slice dough into 1/4-inch-thick rounds and roll into balls. Roll each ball into 6-inch rope, tapering ends. Following "Forming Pretzel Cookies" illustrations above, form ropes into pretzel shapes. Proceed with recipe, brushing with egg white mixture, sprinkling with turbinado sugar, and baking as directed.

Revisiting Pumpkin Pie

The best thing about pumpkin pie is that you only have to eat it once a year. If any Thanksgiving tradition deserves a fresh approach, it's this one.

⋙ BY FRANCISCO J. ROBERT ⋘

Serving pumpkin pie at Thanksgiving is an exercise in futility. After a rich, filling repast, the last part of the ritual appears, problematic as ever: grainy, canned-pumpkin custard encased in a soggy crust. If pumpkin pie is so important that it wouldn't be Thanksgiving without it, why not make it a first-class finish to the meal? Our recipe from 15 years ago was good, but not everything it could have been (lately we've found it overspiced and dense). Could we turn this classic holiday dessert into more than an obligatory endnote for already-sated guests?

This pumpkin pie combines creaminess with punched-up flavor.

Pumping Up Pumpkin Flavor

All too often, pumpkin pie does a poor job of showcasing the flavor of its star ingredient. But I knew better than to think the answer was to use fresh pumpkin. In numerous tests, we've found that very few tasters can distinguish between fresh and canned pumpkin once it's baked in a pie—and cooking a fresh pumpkin is a whole lot of work. The real problem is that pumpkin, fresh or canned, contains a lot of moisture, which ultimately dilutes the pie's flavor. This point was driven home when I wrapped the contents of a can of pumpkin puree in cheesecloth and left it overnight in a colander to drain. By the next morning, the pumpkin had released copious amounts of liquid. Out of curiosity, I tasted a spoonful of the liquid and was surprised to find it had an intense flavor.

To maximize flavor, it made sense to concentrate the pumpkin's liquid rather than just remove it. I took a cue from our 1993 recipe, in which we found cooking the pumpkin on the stovetop to be beneficial. I emptied a can of puree into a saucepan along with some sugar and spices, then cranked up the heat. I whisked in some dairy and eggs and poured the filling into a prebaked shell of Foolproof Pie Dough (November/December 2007). Cooking the pumpkin not only improved its flavor, but the hot filling also allowed the custard to firm up quickly in the oven, preventing it from soaking into the crust and turning it soggy. But I wasn't done: Tasters still complained about an overabundance of spices.

Now that I had great flavor, did I even need the spices? My tasters unanimously agreed that a small amount complemented the pumpkin, singling out nutmeg, cinnamon, and ginger as their favorites and rejecting pungent clove (which also gave the pie a dirty brown appearance). Substituting a couple of teaspoons of freshly grated ginger for the dry equivalent was a hit, imparting a bright, almost fruity flavor to the pie. Cooking the ginger and spices along with the pumpkin puree intensified their taste—the direct heat bloomed their flavors. I also experimented with a number of different sweeteners, including honey, maple syrup, and brown sugar. On their own, maple syrup and honey were overpowering; brown sugar resulted in a grainier texture and a too-distinct flavor. In the end, tasters favored a combination of white sugar and a small amount of maple syrup, which added a layer of complexity. But not enough complexity—tasters still craved a more flavorful pie.

On a whim, I borrowed a few roasted sweet potatoes that a colleague was testing for a side dish and mashed them into my pumpkin mixture without telling anyone. Tasters immediately recognized a new and deeper flavor in the pie. I had hit on a secret ingredient! But I didn't really want to take the time to roast the sweet potatoes for this effect. Would it work just as well to microwave them? I tried this, and my tasters liked this pie just as much. Could I streamline the method even further and use canned sweet potatoes? I drained the sugar syrup from a can of sweet potatoes (commonly labeled yams) and cooked them with the canned pumpkin. Once again, my tasters loved the pie and never guessed the true source of the flavor.

Key Flavoring Ingredients

SWEET POTATOES
Sweet potatoes intensify pumpkin flavor.

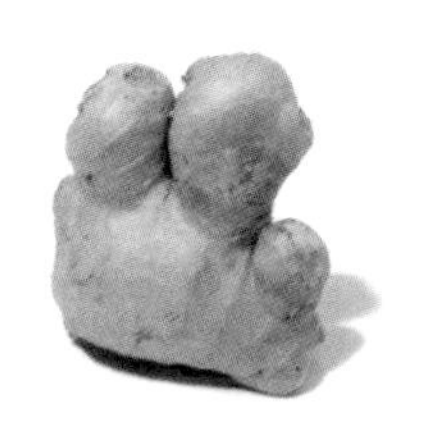

FRESH GINGER
Grated ginger packs more punch than dried ginger.

MAPLE SYRUP
Maple syrup boosts pumpkin's natural sweetness.

The Search for a Silky Texture

With richly flavored filling at hand, it was time to tackle the texture. My goal was to eliminate the graininess that plagues most custard for a creamy, sliceable, not-too-dense pie. To achieve this, I first played with the type of dairy and quantity of eggs. Whole milk yielded a looser pie than one made with cream, but tasters found the latter too rich. Using equal amounts of whole milk and cream provided balance. But this filling was barely sliceable, and using extra whole eggs to firm it up just made the pie taste too eggy. Since the white contains most of the water in an egg, I replaced a few of the whole eggs with yolks to firm up the custard, settling on a ratio

COOK'S LIVE Original Test Kitchen Videos
www.cooksillustrated.com
HOW TO MAKE
- Pumpkin Pie

VIDEO TIPS
- Adding a decorative edge to a pie shell
- How to blind bake a pie shell

RECIPE TESTING:

Keeping Custard from Curdling

OVERCOOKED
A pie cooked at 425 degrees the whole time curdles and becomes watery and grainy.

SILKY SMOOTH
Starting the pie at 400 degrees and finishing it at 300 degrees allows it to bake without curdling.

of 3 whole eggs to 2 yolks. I then whisked the milk, cream, and eggs with some vanilla into the cooked pumpkin–sweet potato mixture and passed the filling through a fine-mesh strainer to remove any stringy bits, ensuring a smooth texture.

Most pumpkin pie recipes call for a high oven temperature to expedite cooking time. But baking any custard at high heat has its dangers. Once the temperature of custard rises above 175 degrees it curdles, turning the filling coarse and grainy. This is exactly what happened when I baked the pie at 425 degrees, the temperature recommended by most recipes. Lowering the temperature to 350 degrees wasn't the solution: I now had a pie that curdled and overcooked at the outer edges but was still underdone in the center. I tried the opposite extreme—baking the pie at 300 degrees, a temperature that would give me a wide margin of safety. The problem was that for the pie to cook through, I needed to leave it in the oven for nearly two hours. What if I combined both approaches: a high initial oven temperature for 15 minutes to give the already-warm filling a blast of heat, followed by a gentle 300 degrees for the remainder of the baking time? Not only did this reduce the total baking time to less than an hour, the dual temperatures produced a creamy pie fully and evenly cooked from edge to center.

Months of testing and hundreds of pies later, I had finally created a pumpkin pie destined to be a new classic: velvety smooth, packed with pumpkin flavor, and redolent of just enough fragrant spices. This year I'll see if anyone can turn down a slice—even after the heavy meal.

TECHNIQUE

COOKING THE FILLING

Simmering the filling for pumpkin pie is an unusual step, but its benefits are threefold. First, cooking the pumpkin and sweet potatoes drives off moisture and concentrates their taste. Second, cooking the spices along with the pumpkin allows their flavors to bloom. Third, heating the filling allows it to firm up quickly in the oven, rather than soaking into the pastry and causing the crust to become soggy.

PUMPKIN PIE

MAKES ONE 9-INCH PIE

If candied yams are unavailable, regular canned yams can be substituted. The best way to judge doneness is with an instant-read thermometer. The center 2 inches of the pie should look firm but jiggle slightly. The pie finishes cooking with residual heat; to ensure that the filling sets, cool it at room temperature and not in the refrigerator. To ensure accurate cooking times and a crisp crust, the filling should be added to the prebaked crust when both the crust and filling are warm. Serve at room temperature with whipped cream. Vodka is essential to the texture of the crust and imparts no flavor; do not substitute.

Crust

- 1¼ cups (6¼ ounces) unbleached all-purpose flour
- ½ teaspoon table salt
- 1 tablespoon sugar
- 6 tablespoons (¾ stick) cold unsalted butter, cut into ¼-inch slices
- ¼ cup cold vegetable shortening, cut into 2 pieces
- 2 tablespoons cold vodka (see note)
- 2 tablespoons cold water

Filling

- 1 cup heavy cream
- 1 cup whole milk
- 3 large eggs plus 2 large yolks
- 1 teaspoon vanilla extract
- 1 (15-ounce) can pumpkin puree
- 1 cup drained candied yams from 15-ounce can (see note)
- ¾ cup sugar
- ¼ cup maple syrup
- 2 teaspoons grated fresh ginger
- ½ teaspoon ground cinnamon
- ¼ teaspoon ground nutmeg
- 1 teaspoon table salt

1. **FOR THE CRUST:** Process ¾ cup flour, salt, and sugar in food processor until combined, about two 1-second pulses. Add butter and shortening and process until homogenous dough just starts to collect in uneven clumps, about 10 seconds; dough will resemble cottage cheese curds with some very small pieces of butter remaining, but there should be no uncoated flour. Scrape bowl with rubber spatula and redistribute dough evenly around processor blade. Add remaining ½ cup flour and pulse until mixture is evenly distributed around bowl and mass of dough has been broken up, 4 to 6 quick pulses. Empty mixture into medium bowl.

2. Sprinkle vodka and water over mixture. With rubber spatula, use folding motion to mix, pressing down on dough until dough is slightly tacky and sticks together. Flatten dough into 4-inch disk. Wrap in plastic and refrigerate at least 45 minutes or up to 2 days.

3. Adjust oven rack to lowest position, place rimmed baking sheet on rack, and heat oven to 400 degrees. Remove dough from refrigerator and roll out on generously floured (up to ¼ cup) work surface to 12-inch circle about ⅛ inch thick. Roll dough loosely around rolling pin and unroll into pie plate, leaving at least 1-inch overhang on each side. Working around circumference, ease dough into plate by gently lifting edge of dough with one hand while pressing into plate bottom with other hand. Refrigerate 15 minutes.

4. Trim overhang to ½ inch beyond lip of pie plate. Fold overhang under itself; folded edge should be flush with edge of pie plate. Using thumb and forefinger, flute edge of dough. Refrigerate dough-lined plate until firm, about 15 minutes.

5. Remove pie pan from refrigerator, line crust with foil, and fill with pie weights or pennies. Bake on rimmed baking sheet 15 minutes. Remove foil and weights, rotate plate, and bake 5 to 10 additional minutes until crust is golden brown and crisp. Remove pie plate and baking sheet from oven.

6. **FOR THE FILLING:** While pie shell is baking, whisk cream, milk, eggs, yolks, and vanilla together in medium bowl. Combine pumpkin puree, yams, sugar, maple syrup, ginger, cinnamon, nutmeg, and salt in large heavy-bottomed saucepan; bring to sputtering simmer over medium heat, 5 to 7 minutes. Continue to simmer pumpkin mixture, stirring constantly and mashing yams against sides of pot, until thick and shiny, 10 to 15 minutes.

7. Remove pan from heat and whisk in cream mixture until fully incorporated. Strain mixture through fine-mesh strainer set over medium bowl, using back of ladle or spatula to press solids through strainer. Rewhisk mixture and transfer to warm prebaked pie shell. Return pie plate with baking sheet to oven and bake pie for 10 minutes. Reduce heat to 300 degrees and continue baking until edges of pie are set (instant-read thermometer inserted in center registers 175 degrees), 20 to 35 minutes longer. Transfer pie to wire rack and cool to room temperature, 2 to 3 hours. Cut into wedges and serve.

TASTING: **Premade Pie Dough**

TIME-SAVER
Pillsbury Pie Crusts is the best of the convenience products sold in supermarkets.

The Best Black Peppercorns

You only use a grind or two on your food, so does it really matter what brand of peppercorn you buy?

BY LISA McMANUS

We take black pepper for granted. But this pantry staple was once so deeply coveted that the kingdoms of Europe launched voyages (including the one that led Columbus to America) to find better trade routes to India with an eye toward controlling the crop. In the Middle Ages, rent could be paid in peppercorns instead of cash. When the Visigoths held Rome ransom, they demanded gold, silver—and 3,000 pounds of peppercorns. Beyond its heat and sharp bite, black pepper also enhances our ability to taste food, stimulating our salivary glands so we experience flavors more fully.

This effect only comes from freshly ground pepper. Once the hard, black shell of the peppercorn is cracked open, its aroma immediately starts to fade, and most of its flavor and scent disappear within a half hour. Not surprisingly, we have never found a preground pepper worth buying. In fact, replacing your pepper shaker with a good pepper mill is one of the simplest ways to enhance your cooking. But can choosing a better variety of peppercorn improve it even more?

Sharp Differences

Until recently, spice brands sold in supermarkets never specified the origin or variety of their peppercorns, as they simply bought the cheapest they could get. But specialty spice retailers offering multiple varieties bearing exotic names such as Sarawak, Lampong, Malabar, and Tellicherry have raised consumer awareness; now, two of the largest supermarket brands, McCormick and Spice Islands, have added "gourmet" Tellicherry peppercorns to their lines. Though Tellicherry is generally considered to be the world's finest pepper, all true peppercorns—black, green, and white—actually come from the same plant, *Piper nigrum*. Native to India, this flowering vine is now grown in many other tropical areas close to the equator, including Vietnam, Indonesia, Malaysia, Ecuador, Brazil, and Madagascar. It sprouts clusters of berries that are dried and treated to become peppercorns. Like grapes, coffee beans, and cacao beans, the flavor of peppercorns depends on exactly where it is cultivated, when the berries are picked, and how they are processed. But all peppercorns are defined by the heat-bearing compound piperine, which perks up our taste buds. Their complex flavor and aroma also come from volatile oils called terpenes, which contribute notes of turpentine, clove, and citrus; pyrazines provide earthy, roasty, green vegetable aromas.

While most peppercorns are picked as soon as the immature little green berries appear on the vine, Tellicherry berries (named after a port town in the state of Kerala on India's Malabar Coast) are left to ripen the longest. This allows the pepper's flavor to fully develop, becoming deeper and more complex, even a little fruity—not just sharp, hot, and bright like peppercorns made from younger berries. But given that we generally use just a few grinds of pepper on our food, would we actually be able to detect such differences?

To find out, we sampled Tellicherry peppercorns from McCormick and Spice Islands against six of the other most popular supermarket brands. Priced from about $1.35 to $2.22 per ounce, most of these brands did not specify variety. As we tasted each black pepper freshly ground with optional white rice, it was immediately clear that there were significant differences among brands. Some were searingly hot, others mild; some one-dimensional, others complex. Only two peppers impressed our tasters enough to be recommended without reservation: McCormick Tellicherry and the organic, Indonesian-grown Lampong peppercorns from a lesser-known brand, Morton & Bassett. The most widely available peppercorns in the country, ordinary McCormick Whole Black Peppercorns, were not recommended at all, finishing dead last.

Special Delivery

If the fancier supermarket peppercorns were good, would peppercorns from specialty merchants taste even better? We decided to order some online to find out. After all, peppercorns are extremely light, so shipping is cheap. A few ounces last many months, and online prices are only a few dollars higher than supermarket prices. We focused on Tellicherry peppercorns for their stellar reputation, choosing six mail-order brands to pit against our two supermarket winners. Once again, we tasted the freshly ground pepper plain or with white rice.

Though tasters detected a range of flavor nuances from brand to brand, the final rankings among these peppercorns were close. We gave top marks to highly aromatic peppercorns with complex flavor and preferred moderate rather than strong heat, which tended to overpower any other taste. Peppercorns also lost points for having an alluring aroma with no flavor to back it up. Our favorite peppercorn was the fresh, earthy, and only moderately hot Tellicherry sold by the Manhattan emporium Kalustyan's, available online ($6.99 plus shipping for 2.5 ounces). Coming in as a close second, however, was one of the supermarket winners, Morton & Bassett Whole Black Peppercorns ($5.39 for 2 ounces). As with Kalustyan's Tellicherry, tasters praised this pepper for being spicy but not too hot, as well as fresh, fragrant, and floral. Sampled against this steep competition, our other supermarket brand, McCormick Gourmet Collection Tellicherry Black Peppercorns ($4.99 for 1.87 ounces), was deemed "unremarkable."

Don't Make This Mistake

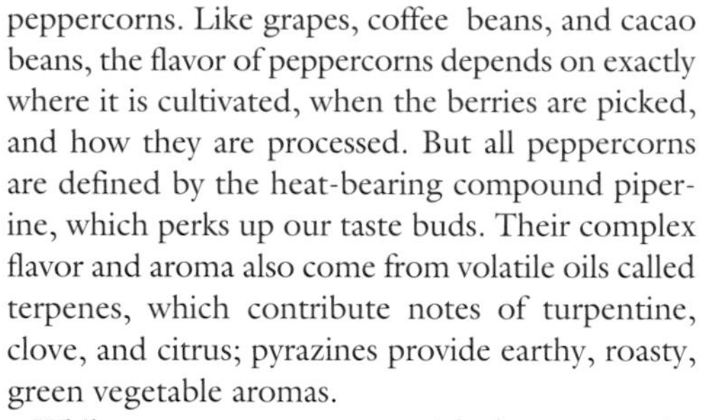

Preground pepper quickly loses all flavor and aroma and is not worth buying.

Single-Estate Pepper

IN A CLASS OF ITS OWN

While shopping for peppercorns, we kept running across purveyors praising Parameswaran's Special Wynad Estate Peppercorns ($30 for 200 grams/7 ounces). Unlike most black pepper, which comes from multiple plantations, this organic, hand-picked black pepper is grown on one estate on the Wynad Plateau in Kerala, India, using best practices of black pepper cultivation. It is made from two particular varieties of black pepper, Karimunda and Panniyur, and grown without chemical pesticides or fertilizers. The peppercorn berries are allowed to ripen to maximum size and flavor, then picked by hand and sun-dried. Even more important, they are vacuum-packed on the estate to preserve freshness and flavor, avoiding the typical ills of transport. Tasters praised this pepper's "rich," "beautiful floral fragrance," with a "ripe, floral, lavenderlike warmth" and flavor that is "earthy and smooth," with "moderate heat that builds gradually, not ferociously." This special estate pepper is worth a special order. –L.M.

So what would account for differences in the flavor and heat levels of the Tellicherry peppercorns, when they all come from the same region? The most important factor probably has to do with differences in cultivars, or varieties, of the plant itself, which grows on plantations in the state of Kerala, an area about the size of the Netherlands. Though none of the spice companies we spoke to would share details of the processing methods used by their suppliers, these approaches can also influence taste—peppercorns can be picked by hand or by machine, dried in the sunlight or a kiln, even boiled. Storage also has an impact on flavor. Peppercorns that are subjected to too much heat or moisture grow musty-smelling mold and bacteria, all the while losing flavor. In fact, some peppercorns, including our winner from Kalustyan's, get a special cleaning in the United States before they go on sale, restoring freshness after months at sea.

The Leveling Effect of Cooking?

Now that we had our winners, an important question remained: Would a better pepper's complexity actually be evident if we just added the usual pinch or two in cooking? We chose polar opposites—top-ranked Kalustyan's and bottom-ranked McCormick Whole Black Peppercorns from our supermarket tasting—and sampled them stirred into scrambled eggs and tomato soup. Interestingly, with pepper as a mere accent, the distinctions between these two very differently rated brands became quite difficult to detect: Votes were split as to which brand tasted better.

But what if peppercorns are one of the main attractions, as in steak au poivre, which is thickly crusted with crushed peppercorns and pan-seared? We compared steaks made with Kalustyan's Tellicherry, Morton & Bassett's Lampong, and the McCormick Tellicherry. This time, the nuances of the peppercorns came through, with tasters echoing their original assessments. Kalustyan's impressed tasters most for its "fruity, pungent, really complex berrylike flavors," while Morton & Bassett came in right behind it with a "very bold, full flavor." The McCormick Tellicherry ranked a few steps down from those top two—just as it had in the plain tasting.

The verdict? In applications that call for a small dose, just about any pepper will be fine as long as it is freshly ground. But if you're cooking a peppery specialty, or you like to grind fresh pepper over your food before eating, choosing a superior peppercorn can make a difference. Given that it costs only a few dollars more than supermarket pepper, we'll be filling the test kitchen's pepper mills with Kalustyan's Tellicherry Peppercorns. If you can't be bothered to mail-order peppercorns, look for Morton & Bassett Organic Whole Black Peppercorns in the supermarket.

COOK'S LIVE Original Test Kitchen Video
www.cooksillustrated.com
VIDEO TIP
- Buying Guide to Pepper Mills

TASTING BLACK PEPPER

Nineteen *Cook's Illustrated* staff members tasted eight samples of freshly ground whole black peppercorns plain or with white rice. The samples included six mail-order Tellicherry peppercorns and two supermarket brands. The supermarket peppercorns were singled out as favorites in an earlier tasting of the eight top-selling brands, identified by research compiled by the Chicago-based market research firm Information Resources, Inc. We were joined by chefs Ana Sortun of Oleana (author of *Spice: Flavors of the Eastern Mediterranean*) and Tony Maws of Craigie Street Bistrot; both restaurants are in Cambridge, Mass. We rated the peppercorns on aroma, heat, complexity, and overall taste. They appear below in order of preference. Sources for top brands appear on page 32.

RECOMMENDED — **TESTERS' COMMENTS**

KALUSTYAN'S
Indian Tellicherry Black Peppercorns
Price: $6.99 for 2.5-ounce jar ($2.80 per ounce)

With high marks for "enticing" aroma and complex flavor, and with only "moderate" heat, tasters praised these peppercorns for a "beautiful scent," "like licorice, sweet and spicy; rich, a little smoky," "winey," "floral," with a "hint of sweetness," and a "fruity" taste with "mild heat that gradually builds." Tasters enjoyed notes of pine or eucalyptus and an aroma "reminiscent of a fire on a cold day" or "like newly varnished wood" that was "smoky, earthy, sweet—a very nice pepper."

MORTON & BASSETT
Organic Whole Black Peppercorns
Price: $5.39 for 2-ounce jar ($2.70 per ounce)

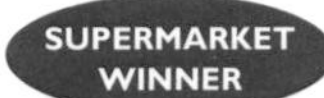

"Spicy but not hot," this organic Lampong pepper from Indonesia (sold by a San Francisco–based spice company) won our initial supermarket-brand tasting, and was the only non-Tellicherry pepper to make it to our final lineup. It won praise for being "very fragrant and floral and piney, very spicy," with notes of "cinnamon" and "citrus," "sharp and fresh" with "some good berry notes." "The heat came at the end—a slow burn." In sum: "A classic pepper—what I expect pepper to taste like."

ZINGERMAN'S
Tellicherry Peppercorns
Price: $8 for 2.53-ounce jar ($3.16 per ounce)

"This smells like green peppercorns, ripe, pungent, sharp and hot," noted one taster of this pepper from a Michigan-based gourmet catalog and retailer, while others described its "creeping heat and lovely floral undertones," including "herb, lavender, and rosemary," and called it "bright," "lively," and "grassy, with balanced heat and spice, nice and aromatic."

RECOMMENDED WITH RESERVATIONS — **TESTERS' COMMENTS**

VANNS SPICES
Tellicherry Peppercorns
Price: $3.77 for 2.25-ounce jar ($1.68 per ounce)

With a "bright, fresh scent" and a "mellow bite," this pepper from a Baltimore spice purveyor was described as "floral" and "fruity" with hints of "currants," "mulling spice," "nutmeg," and "orange," while others less flatteringly mentioned "slightly pungent barnyard flavors," "gravelly undertones," and "no depth of flavor."

McCORMICK Gourmet
Collection Tellicherry Black Peppercorns
Price: $4.99 for 1.87-ounce jar ($2.67 per ounce)

While several tasters noted this supermarket pepper's "very nice" "floral" aroma, with notes of "coffee grounds, clove, turpentine, pine" and "menthol," they also noted that, compared to other samples, it was "bland" and "flat" and offered "not as complicated or layered flavors." Overall: "Taste is unremarkable."

PENZEYS India
Tellicherry Peppercorns
Price: $3.49 for 2.2-ounce jar ($1.59 per ounce)

Tasters enjoyed this gourmet spice purveyor's offering for its "piney, rosemary scent" with "citrus" and "lavender" notes, but many complained of "a lot of burning heat" that was "not very pleasant." "I taste mostly heat, not flavor," said one unhappy taster. "It finishes very hot but without much depth."

THE SPICE HOUSE
Tellicherry Black Peppercorns
Price: $2.98 for 2.5-ounce jar ($1.19 per ounce)

With a "super strong aroma" that was "very appealing—piney, citrus, fresh Christmas tree," these peppercorns from the Chicago spice purveyor founded by a branch of the Penzey family also came across with a peppery intensity that "is really assertive—a smack-you-in-the-face kind of heat." "It reminds me of Fireballs, sharp and somehow sweet." But reactions were mixed: Several found it "slightly bitter" and "stale."

DEAN & DELUCA
Tellicherry Peppercorns
Price: $5.75 for 2-ounce tin ($2.88 per ounce)

Tasters noted this pepper's "mild aroma and flavor"—described as "soft," "faint," and even "dull"—and "barely detectable heat." What little flavor and aroma tasters did perceive they mostly liked: "almost like cloves or allspice," "a cinnamony aroma" that was "a little chocolatey on the finish." Overall: "Not great; smells better than it tastes."

NOTE: We eliminated the following brands in a preliminary tasting of eight top-selling supermarket brands: Vigo Whole Black Peppercorns (also sold as Alessi), Badia Whole Black Pepper, Spice Islands Tellicherry Black Peppercorns, Tone's Whole Black Peppercorns (also sold as Durkee), Drogheria & Alimentari All Natural Black Peppercorns, and plain McCormick Whole Black Peppercorns.

Why You Need a Slicing Knife

Slicing a roast, ham, or turkey doesn't require expert knife skills. But producing thin, even slices of meat can be next to impossible if you don't have the right knife.

⋟ BY PEGGY CHUNG ⋞

At big holiday meals, I'm often called upon to carve a large roast. I usually feel I'm up to the task—until I'm handed someone's trusty 8-inch chef's knife. Like lots of people, my family assumes that a sharp, good-quality knife is all that the job requires (especially in the hands of a culinary school graduate like me). But after too many debacles carving roast beef into lopsided, haphazard slices with the wrong knife, I know better.

When a knife breaks through the surface of meat, it cuts through muscle fibers and connective tissue bundled together like multiple strands of twisted, plastic-covered telephone wire. Depending on how the knife is designed, the fiber and tissue can split apart cleanly or unevenly. To produce thin, uniform slices, heft and sharpness are important—but so are the length and shape of the blade. So while the wide, triangular blade of a chef's knife is excellent for everyday kitchen tasks such as chopping vegetables or hacking raw chicken into pieces, it is really too thick and blunt to slice meat precisely and too short to get through a big roast in a single stroke. Even worse, the pointed tip wedges into the meat, forcing you to saw back and forth to finish the task. The result: thick, ridged, uneven slices.

But if you set out to buy a knife specifically for slicing, catalogs and cutlery stores present a confounding array of choices. Blades can be narrow, wide, or extra-wide; rigid or flexible; measuring 8 inches to 14 inches. Tips are pointed or round. The cutting edges are straight, serrated, wavy, or hollowed, a feature sometimes called a granton or kullenschliff edge. Prices range from $19 to $199. No wonder so many cooks just stick with their chef's knife.

Origins of the Granton Edge

"Granton-edge" knives have oval scallops carved into both sides of the blade. While it's touted for its nonstick quality, we like the design because it allows for a thinner cutting edge without sacrificing the heft carried by the top of the blade. It also helps to preserve some beneficial rigidity in the blade.

William Grant, founder of the Granton Knives Company in Sheffield, England, patented this innovative edge in 1928. The company still hand-makes granton-edge knives with scallops carved all the way down to the cutting edge (imitators have scallops that stop just above it). Because the knives have a limited distribution in the United States, we chose not to include them in our lineup. But we did test an original 12-inch Granton-Edge knife ($40) against our winning Forschner Fibrox Granton Edge slicer ($44.95). The British knife was razor sharp but its 1-inch-wide blade was no match for the 1½-inch width of the Forschner's blade when it came to easily slicing a thick roast. –P.C.

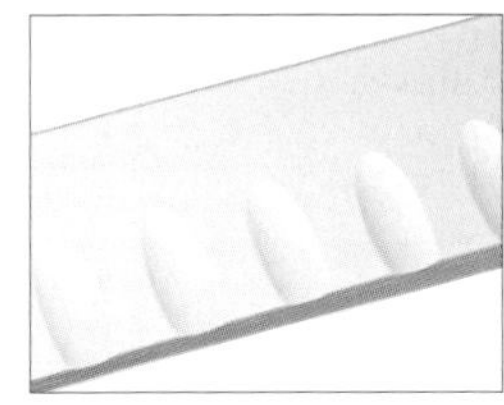

ON EDGE
The original granton-edge knife has recesses cut all the way to the cutting edge.

Making the Cut

We decided to take on the challenge of finding the best slicer. Past evaluations of knives gave us some criteria to look for: an extra-long blade that could slice through large cuts of meat in one easy glide, enough sturdiness to ensure a straight cutting path, and a round tip that wouldn't get caught coming down. We also knew to single out knives with a hollow or granton edge. These knives have small oval scallops carved out on both sides of the blade. By chiseling out recesses close to the cutting edge, a thinner edge can be achieved without sacrificing the heft or rigidity carried by the top of the blade—all the better for producing the thinnest slices with the least amount of effort. (For more on this design, see "Origins of the Granton Edge," left.) We also knew to eliminate carving knives, sometimes advertised as slicing knives, because their pointed tip and narrow blade make them too agile to maintain a straight cutting path. (Their specialty is detail work such as cutting meat off the bone or maneuvering into turkey joints—tasks a chef's knife can easily handle.) In the end, we chose nine models for testing.

To see how each knife dealt with different textures, thicknesses, and issues related to different types of meat, we cooked more than 180 pounds of roast beef, ham, turkey, flank steak, brisket, and smoked salmon and began cutting. Slicing a large roast and a ham put the length of the blade to the test. The ideal knife requires minimal motion to create a straight slice. In the past, the test kitchen has recommended 10-inch slicing knives, but we found that a few extra inches greatly helped testers create a slice in a single stroke, especially with these large cuts. Our conclusion: About 12 inches is ideal.

Flexibility was another key factor. Knives with an overly stiff blade were too clunky to make thin slices. Very flexible knives permitted too much movement and wobbled on a big cut of meat; however, their flexibility helped when slicing smoked salmon and flank steak, which are cut on the bias, as opposed to perpendicular to the cutting board. For an all-purpose knife, the best choice is somewhere in between.

Weight was also important. Heavier knives—those weighing more than 6 ounces—tended to be more stable, maintaining a straight path and requiring less effort pushing through thick cuts. Lightweight knives felt flimsy and almost toylike, even against smaller cuts like turkey breast. But weight alone did not make for a better knife—how well the weight was balanced made all the difference. Blade-heavy knives with light handles felt as cumbersome as meat cleavers, while knives that carried weight in both the blade and the handle translated their heft into force and power, making slicing effortless.

Top-Notch Tapering

As we continued slicing our way through meat and fish, we made another discovery: All of the top knives tapered significantly, with the thickness of the blade narrowing from the handle to the tip. Measuring, we noted that our top three knives tapered by 24 percent to 35 percent, whereas poorer performers tapered only by 5 percent to 17 percent. The thinness near the tip helped testers control the knife, while the thicker base of the knife preserved the weight needed to cut cleanly. Research confirmed that tapering is a traditional characteristic of the very best knives, a key factor in precision, control, and responsiveness.

In the end, three knives were jockeying for the top spot. All offered granton edges, generous length, and good balance and helped even our most unskilled testers produce consistently thin, professional-looking slices. Our winner is the Forschner Fibrox 12" Granton Edge Slicing Knife, which received testers' highest marks for comfort. It's also moderately priced at $44.95.

COOK'S LIVE Original Test Kitchen Video
www.cooksillustrated.com
BEHIND THE SCENES
• Testing slicing knives

TESTING SLICING KNIVES

Seven testers with knife skills ranging from beginner to advanced used nine knives to slice cooked meats and cold smoked salmon. Prices were paid in Boston-area retail stores or online. Knives are listed in order of preference. A source for the winning knife appears on page 32.

KEY
GOOD: ★★★
FAIR: ★★
POOR: ★

LENGTH & WIDTH: Length was measured from tip to heel. Longer, wider blades were preferred.

WEIGHT: Heftier knives with good balance between blade and handle were easier to control.

TAPERING: Measured from base to tip of blade. Dramatic tapering was most responsive.

COMFORT: Balanced knives with easy-to-grip handles were considered well constructed.

RIGIDITY: Tested by flexing blade against counter, rigidity was measured on scale of 0 to 10, with 10 as most rigid. Fairly rigid knives—those that rated between 7 and 8—performed best.

SLICING: Average of testers' scores, determined through slicing meats and cold smoked salmon.

SHARPNESS: Sharper blades cut meat with less effort and permitted thin slicing.

HIGHLY RECOMMENDED

	PERFORMANCE	TESTERS' COMMENTS
FORSCHNER Fibrox 12-Inch Granton Edge Slicing Knife Model 47645 **Price:** $44.95 **Length:** 11 15/16 inches **Width:** 1½ inches **Weight:** 6.4 oz. **Rigidity:** 7.5 **Tapering:** 35%	Slicing: ★★★ Sharpness: ★★★ Comfort: ★★★	This "basic, but well-made" knife was our favorite for a number of reasons: Moderately heavy, it had enough heft and rigidity to make straight cuts, while a slight flexibility gave a feeling of control. The thin, tapered, razor-sharp blade was long and wide enough to draw through a large roast in one stroke.

RECOMMENDED

	PERFORMANCE	TESTERS' COMMENTS
WÜSTHOF Gourmet 12-Inch Roast Beef Slicer Hollow Edge Model 4515 **Price:** $99.95 **Length:** 12¾ inches **Width:** 1½ inches **Weight:** 7.2 oz. **Rigidity:** 7 **Tapering:** 29%	Slicing: ★★★ Sharpness: ★★★ Comfort: ★★	This "good-looking, well-crafted" knife was the longest of the lineup. Testers applauded the extra length as well as the heavy yet balanced feel of the blade and handle. Though most were impressed by the "solid, hefty" construction of the knife, testers with smaller hands found it a bit awkward.
MESSERMEISTER 12-Inch Park Plaza Extra Wide Kullenschliff Slicer Model 8096-12 **Price:** $49.99 **Length:** 12 inches **Width:** 1½ inches **Weight:** 8.8 oz. **Rigidity:** 8 **Tapering:** 24%	Slicing: ★★★ Sharpness: ★★★ Comfort: ★★	This "very heavy" knife won accolades for the way it used heft to its advantage, and testers found the weight well balanced. A sharp and rigid yet slightly flexible blade helped to make "effortless, uniform slices." However, its large, "blocky" handle felt uncomfortable.

RECOMMENDED WITH RESERVATIONS

	PERFORMANCE	TESTERS' COMMENTS
KERSHAW SHUN Classic 12-Inch Hollow Edge Slicing Knife Model DM0745 **Price:** $199.95 **Length:** 12⅜ inches **Width:** 1¾ inches **Weight:** 9.6 oz. **Rigidity:** 9 **Tapering:** 8%	Slicing: ★★ Sharpness: ★★★ Comfort: ★★	By far the heaviest, widest, and most expensive knife we tested, testers called it a "samurai sword for meat." Though the stiff, razor-sharp blade made very straight and uniform cuts, testers had trouble making thin slices. Testers called it "clunky" and "too much knife."
MERCER Chef Cutlery Wide Slicer with Granton Edge, 10-Inch Model WM14310 **Price:** $44.99 **Length:** 10 inches **Width:** 1⅜ inches **Weight:** 6.4 oz. **Rigidity:** 8 **Tapering:** 12%	Slicing: ★★ Sharpness: ★★ Comfort: ★★	This knife, our previous winner, literally fell short against the longer knives, though its moderately heavy, gradually tapered, and fairly rigid yet flexible blade led it to perform well on smaller roasts. The short length gave us "short, choppy strokes" on larger roasts.

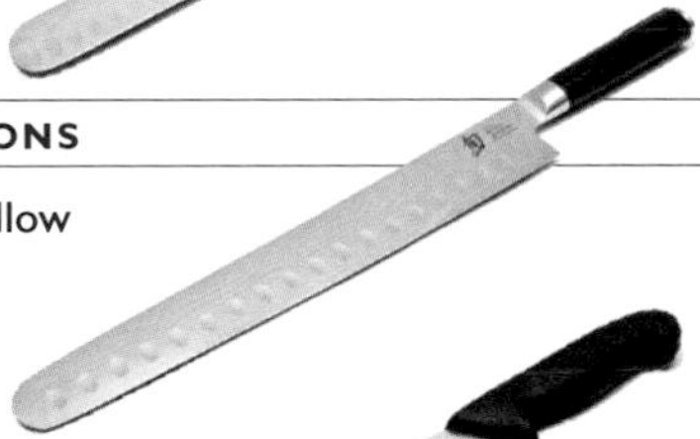

NOT RECOMMENDED

	PERFORMANCE	TESTERS' COMMENTS
MERCER Millennia 11-Inch Granton Edge Slicer Model M23011 **Price:** $20.97 **Length:** 11 inches **Width:** 1¼ inches **Weight:** 5.6 oz. **Rigidity:** 6 **Tapering:** 9%	Slicing: ★ Sharpness: ★ Comfort: ★★	While testers thought the 11-inch blade was long enough for many tasks, this knife felt flimsy, light, and not sharp enough on large roasts. Testers commented that the lack of heft required them to use "extra pressure." The light, "cheap" plastic handle made the knife feel unbalanced.
MUNDIAL Slicer Knife, Granton Edge 12-Inch Model 5627-12GE **Price:** $20.50 **Length:** 11¼ inches **Width:** 1 inch **Weight:** 5.6 oz. **Rigidity:** 3 **Tapering:** 17%	Slicing: ★ Sharpness: ★★ Comfort: ★	A sharp blade with a fair amount of precision, it lacked heft; the handle "felt cheap," and the weight was unbalanced. Testers had to saw to get through thicker cuts of meat to achieve uniform slices.
BERGHOFF 12-Inch Granton Edge Slicing Knife Model 2213582 **Price:** $19 **Length:** 12 inches **Width:** 1 inch **Weight:** 5.6 oz. **Rigidity:** 4.5 **Tapering:** 5%	Slicing: ★ Sharpness: ★ Comfort: ★	"Flimsy as a toy sword," this knife's flexible, thin, lightweight blade had good precision only when we sliced salmon. On most meat, testers had to "force the knife through" and employ a great deal of sawing.
LAMSONSHARP PRO Kullenschliff Slicer, White Handle, 12-Inch Model 31004 **Price:** $40.50 **Length:** 12 inches **Width:** 1⅜ inches **Weight:** 5.6 oz. **Rigidity:** 4.5 **Tapering:** 5%	Slicing: ★ Sharpness: ★ Comfort: ★	This knife offered a fair amount of precision due to its thin blade and flexibility, but was too lightweight to get through a roast without effort. Testers complained that the handle was slippery and that the knife looked and felt cheaply constructed.

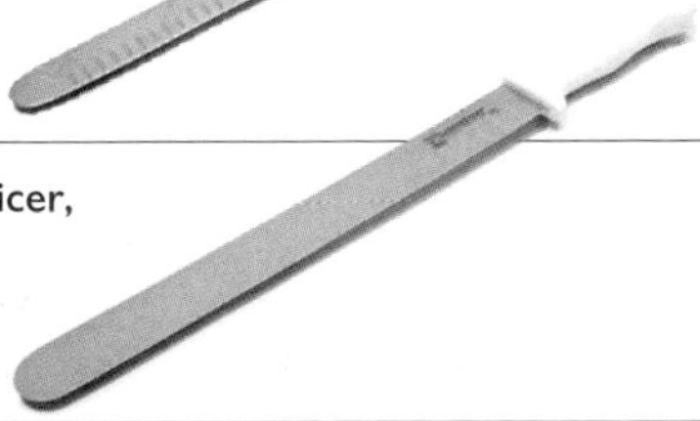

KITCHEN NOTES

BY J. KENJI ALT

SHOPPING:

Experiencing the Prime of Paprika

When preparing dishes like our Hungarian Beef Stew (page 9), which calls for ⅓ cup (about 1.35 ounces) of paprika, it may be tempting to buy the spice in bulk to save money (most jars in the supermarket range between 1.5 and 3 ounces). Don't do it. We cooked Hungarian Beef Stew and our Chicken Paprikash (March/April 2002) recipe with fresh paprika and paprika from jars that had been lurking in the spice racks of staff members for six months or longer. The difference was striking. The dishes prepared with fresh paprika had bright, fresh flavor, while the old paprikas imparted a stale, dusty taste to the food and a lingering bitter aftertaste. Stored in a cool, dark place (heat and sunlight dull its color and flavor), paprika will retain its freshness for only about six months. We recommend buying only as much paprika as you think you'll use in that time.

BIG WASTE
A big jar of paprika can sit in the spice rack for years, slowly losing flavor.

A Shell Game

We've always heard that fresh eggs are for frying and old eggs are for boiling, as the older an egg is, the easier it is to peel. But who keeps different boxes of eggs of different ages in their refrigerator? We wanted to find a way to make peeling even a fresh egg more foolproof. To this end, we hard-cooked 120 eggs and tested every egg-peeling myth, old wives' tale, and urban legend we could find. Ultimately, while we found that basics like peeling under running water and starting from the fat end (where the air pocket makes it easier to remove this first bit of shell) helped, only one trick nearly guaranteed perfectly peeled eggs: shocking the egg in ice water as soon as it is done cooking. Here's why: As an egg cooks, the layer of protein in the white known as albumin that's closest to the outer shell will slowly bond with it. An egg left at room temperature or even under cold running water will cool relatively slowly, giving the hot albumin plenty of time to form a strong bond with the shell. Shocking the egg in ice water quickly halts this bonding process. In addition, the sudden cooling causes the cooked egg white to shrink and pull away from the shell, making it much easier to remove.

So, for best results, shock your hard-cooked eggs in ice water; roll them on the counter to crack their entire surface; and peel under cool running water, starting from the fat end.

TEST KITCHEN TIP:

Heating Up a Better Brew

If you're dissatisfied with the quality of brew from your drip coffee maker, two factors may be contributing: The brew time may be too long (studies have shown that six minutes is optimal in a drip coffee maker) or the machine may not be heating water to the ideal temperature range necessary to produce a really good cup. You can't adjust the brew time, but here's something that may help with the water temperature: Try adding warm, versus cold, water to the coffee maker.

Our testing of automatic drip coffee makers (September/October 2008) turned up three models that failed to brew perfect cups because they were unable to heat water to the ideal 195 to 205 degrees before dripping it over the grounds: the Black & Decker 10-Cup Thermal Stainless Steel Coffeemaker, the Cuisinart Grind & Brew Thermal 12-Cup Automatic Coffeemaker, and the Hamilton Beach Stay or Go Deluxe 10-Cup Thermal Coffeemaker. When we brewed coffee in these three machines starting with water that had been preheated on the stove to 100 degrees, we found the flavor of the coffee improved significantly—even with a too-long brew time. For best results, make sure you start with cold tap water, as hot tap water contains fewer dissolved minerals than cold and can impart a flat taste to your brew. (Note: Our advice contradicts manufacturers' instructions to add regular cold water to coffee makers.)

SCIENCE:

Storing Sweet Potatoes

We normally store sweet potatoes away from light at a cool room temperature, but we wondered if storing them in the refrigerator would have any detrimental effects.

EXPERIMENT

We bought a case of sweet potatoes and divided it into two batches. We stored each batch for four weeks, one at room temperature (in a cabinet, between 55 and 65 degrees) and one in the refrigerator (between 34 and 38 degrees). After four weeks, we removed the sweet potatoes from the refrigerator and allowed them to come to room temperature before cutting both batches of potatoes into pieces and roasting them in a 400-degree oven for 45 minutes. We then tasted them to see if we could spot any differences.

RESULTS

Both batches of potatoes looked the same coming out of storage, but cooking them told a different story. While the room-temperature potatoes were creamy and soft all the way through, the refrigerated potatoes remained hard at the center. To see if another cooking method would produce different results, we repeated the test, this time boiling sliced potatoes for 40 minutes. The outcome was the same: The refrigerated potatoes had tough centers.

EXPLANATION

It turns out that sweet potatoes contain an enzyme called demethylase that normally lies dormant. But if the potato is subjected to temperatures below 55 degrees for a prolonged period, this enzyme kicks into gear, weakening the pectin that holds the potato's cells together so that it binds with calcium ions that are also present. This calcium strengthens the cells' walls so that they can't be broken down—even by prolonged cooking.

SHOPPING:

Home on the Range

We recently noticed a new item in the supermarket meat aisle—vacuum-sealed packages of ground bison (the same animal as buffalo). Bison has a lower fat content than beef, and the National Bison Association touts it as being more flavorful and tender as well. To find out if bison lives up to its billing, we sampled the meat in four different applications: spicy chili, long-cooked Bolognese sauce, grilled hamburgers, and Italian meatballs. Despite its low fat content, the bison remained remarkably tender cooked in burgers and meatballs. But this tenderness turned to mush when the bison simmered for hours in chili and Bolognese sauce. As for flavor, tasters found bison to be slightly sweeter and gamier than beef in the burgers; these differences were less pronounced when the meat was paired with the competing flavors in the other recipes. The bottom line: We prefer the meatier texture of beef over bison.

MUSHY GROUND
Ground bison is slightly sweeter than beef and very tender, but this softer texture turns to mush with prolonged cooking.

One Good Turn

Some bread recipes call for punching the dough down after its initial rise, while others call for merely "turning" it (gently folding the sides over into the center). To see what worked best for our Rustic Dinner Rolls (page 15), we tried both methods, along with an untouched batch of dough as a control. The untouched dough produced bland rolls that lacked chewiness, while the simple turn yielded the highest rise and the most open texture. Why? As the dough gets jostled around, the yeast cells are introduced to new food sources that allow them to continue multiplying, improving flavor and creating gas to help it rise. While turning does this in a very gentle way that helps the dough retain its air pockets, punching actually deflates the dough—great for dense, fine-crumbed bread like a sandwich loaf, but not for airy, open-crumbed rustic rolls.

EQUIPMENT: Do You Need a Nonstick Roasting Pan?

We've long been satisfied with the traditional stainless steel roasting pans made by our top-rated brands, All Clad and Calphalon. But since both companies also manufacture nonstick versions, we thought we would give them a try. For us, a great roasting pan should brown food evenly in the oven and produce a substantial fond when searing food over a burner. (Fond is the flavorful browned bits that form when drippings from a roast or bird fall to the bottom of the pan, creating a flavorful base for gravy or sauces.) We roasted chicken and potatoes as well as a whole prime rib (searing it first over two burners) in each type of pan.

Both types of pan performed identically in most applications—including browning the food evenly and preventing it from sticking. Where differences arise was in making gravy, specifically when it came to fond. Oftentimes, the fond is cooked over a burner while the roast rests, before being deglazed and made into gravy. The problem is, the dark color of the nonstick pan makes it very difficult to gauge not only how much fond you have but how dark the fond has become, leading us to accidentally burn one batch as we prepared to deglaze it. The final word? We'll stick to the traditional choice.

HIDDEN PROBLEM
The dark coating in a nonstick roasting pan makes it hard to judge how dark your fond is.

STICK WITH IT
If you allow food to brown properly, sticking is never an issue with a traditional roasting pan, plus fond shows up clearly against the shiny background.

COOKING CLASS 101: Searing vs. Sautéing

Searing and sautéing both involve cooking food in a shallow pan on the stovetop, but their similarities end there. Searing is a surface treatment used to produce a flavorful brown crust on thick cuts of protein. Sautéing is used to cook smaller pieces of food or thinner cuts of meat all the way through.

METHOD	OBJECTIVE	KEYS TO SUCCESS
Searing	• Produce a flavorful, well-browned crust on thick steaks, chops, fish, or poultry before the interior of the food is finished with a gentler method. It does not "lock in" juices, as is commonly believed. • Create fond (brown bits stuck to the pan) for use in a sauce or braising liquid.	• Use a conventional, rather than nonstick, skillet; it helps fond to develop. • Use high heat and preheat the pan properly; the oil should just start to smoke. • Do not move the food until a browned crust develops.
Sautéing	• Quickly cook thin cuts of meat and fish all the way through, as well as small pieces of food such as chopped vegetables. • Soften onions, garlic, or other aromatics to build a flavorful base for a sauce, stew, or braise.	• Use a slope-sided skillet to facilitate flipping and stirring. • Use moderate heat to ensure even cooking; higher heat can cause the ingredients on the bottom of the pan to overbrown or burn before the ingredients on top have a chance to cook through. • For smaller ingredients, stir and shake the pan to make sure exposure to heat is even.

TEST KITCHEN TIP: Don't Toast Your Peppercorns

We often recommend toasting whole spices before grinding them to intensify their taste, but what about black pepper? Is it worth the trouble to toast whole peppercorns before you put them in your pepper mill? We took two batches of Kalustyan's (our winning brand of peppercorns), toasted one in a dry skillet and left the other alone; and tasted each plain, ground over scrambled eggs, and crushed and pan-seared in steak au poivre. The untoasted pepper won every test. While tasters noted that the flavor of the toasted pepper was smokier, it lacked the pungency of the untoasted pepper. This is because pepper's piquancy comes from a volatile molecule called piperine. When pepper is heated, piperine is one of the first chemicals to vaporize and disappear. Without piperine, pepper has no bite, and without bite, pepper has no purpose. (For more information on our recommended brands of black peppercorns, see "Tasting Black Pepper" on page 27.)

INGREDIENTS: A Sweet Exchange

It's happened to all of us: A recipe calls for a sweetener such as confectioners', brown, or superfine sugar, but the only thing on hand is plain old white. However, given that all three of these sweeteners are nothing more than commercially processed white sugar, we wondered—could we "process" the white stuff ourselves to serve as a stand-in?

Once we came up with the formulas, we tested our homemade sugar substitutes in various applications to see how they would hold up against their commercial counterparts. We compared the superfine sugars in butter cookies; the confectioners' sugars in glazes; and the light and dark brown sugars in brown-sugar cookies and sticky toffee puddings. The upshot? Though it's certainly more convenient to buy a particular sugar when you need it, each of our substitutes worked just fine.

SUPERFINE SUGAR

What It Is: Finely ground granulated white sugar

Common Uses: Its small granules dissolve almost instantly, making superfine sugar ideal for sweetening drinks as well as for baked applications such as sugar cookies in which a grit-free texture is desired.

Granulated Sugar Substitute: Process 1 cup plus 2 teaspoons white sugar in a food processor for 30 seconds. Yield: 1 cup superfine sugar

CONFECTIONERS' SUGAR

What It Is: Very finely ground granulated white sugar, with 3 percent cornstarch added to prevent caking

Common Uses: This sugar is mainly used for dusting finished desserts; also for making glazes and sweetening some meringues.

Granulated Sugar Substitute: Pulverize 1 cup white sugar with 1 teaspoon cornstarch in a spice grinder or blender (a food processor cannot crush the sugar fine enough) for at least 1 minute until fully powdered (if your spice grinder is not large enough or the sugar sticks to the side of the blender, you may need to process the sugar in two batches). Strain through a fine-mesh strainer to remove any large particles that remain. Yield: 1 cup confectioners' sugar

BROWN SUGAR

What It Is: Unlike unrefined, naturally brown sugars (such as Demerara or turbinado), most commercial brown sugar is made by adding molasses to white sugar (about 3.5 percent for light brown, 6.5 percent for dark).

Common Uses: Its ability to retain water means that brown sugar helps to keep baked goods such as cookies moist. We also use it to add complex flavor to countless other desserts and many savory sauces and glazes.

Granulated Sugar Substitute: Pulse 1 cup white sugar with 1 teaspoon dark molasses (2 teaspoons for dark brown) in a food processor until fully combined. (The resulting sugars will not look as dark as store-bought brown sugars, but should perform similarly in recipes.) Yield: 1 cup light or dark brown sugar

EQUIPMENT CORNER

BY MEREDITH BUTCHER AND PEGGY CHUNG

EQUIPMENT UPDATE:
KitchenAid Spiral Dough Hook

The only quibble we've had with the KitchenAid Professional 6-Quart Stand Mixer since it became our "mixer for all reasons" in 2005 was a less-than-perfect dough hook. Tacky pizza dough rode up the C-shaped metal claw, sticking instead of being churned into the mix. This flaw allowed the Cuisinart 5.5-Quart Stand Mixer to take top honors as the test kitchen favorite. But KitchenAid has risen to the challenge. Its latest Professional 600 model comes with a new and improved Spiral Dough Hook that's also available as an attachment ($19.99) for older machines. Rather than grasping the dough, this pigtail-shaped attachment rolls the dough over in the bottom of the bowl, kneading it better and faster than the old C-hook.

With this improvement, the KitchenAid is back on the counter alongside the Cuisinart stand mixer as a highly recommended model.

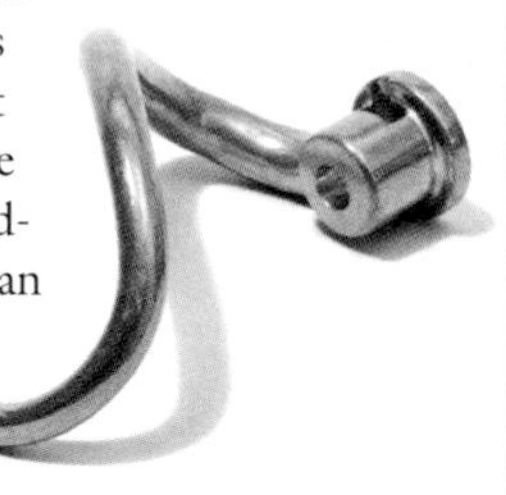

MEETING A KNEAD
The new KitchenAid Spiral Dough Hook makes kneading sticky dough easy.

NEW PRODUCT:
Victorinox Knife Sharpener

In the style of our favorite manual knife sharpener, the AccuSharp Knife and Tool Sharpener ($10.48), Victorinox has created its own plastic hand-held sharpener ($16.93). Both use a single tungsten-carbide V-shaped blade, and both work the same way, with the knife blade face-up on the counter and the sharpener running over the blade. We used each model to sharpen two moderately dull knives (for really dull knives, an electric sharpener is best)—a forged knife with a bolster and a stamped, bolsterless knife. Both newly honed knives cut paper—our simple test of a knife's sharpness—and ripe tomato equally well. As for the sharpening itself, testers liked the Victorinox's comfortable grip and its sturdy, rigid hand guard, which felt secure as the sharpener straddled the knife blade. Overall, both tools are safe and comfortable to use, and either is an excellent choice. But since the AccuSharp is a few bucks cheaper, we're sticking with it as our favorite.

DO YOU REALLY NEED THIS?
Battery-Operated Flour Sifter

Sifting flour can be monotonous and messy if you're using a traditional squeeze-handled model. Those who want to sift through the process a little faster (and don't mind a low buzz in their ears) might like Norpro's Battery-Operated Flour Sifter ($15.99). Its "on" button is handily located next to your thumb, and its plastic grip activates a motor that makes quick, tidy work of sifting up to 4 cups of flour, cocoa powder, or confectioners' sugar. To clean, a swipe of a pastry brush or soft, dry cloth will dust away any lingering powder. Is it a little supercharged for such a simple task? Almost certainly (for sifting, we generally opt for nothing more high tech than a spoon and a fine-mesh sieve). On the other hand, the sooner the flour is sifted, the sooner the cake's out of the oven.

SWIFTER SIFTER
Gadget lovers will appreciate the ease of Norpro's Battery-Operated Flour Sifter.

NEW PRODUCT: **Gripper Mat**

We love the ingenious rubber feet covering the underside of our favorite plastic cutting board, the Architec Gripper Nonslip Cutting Board. Now, with the introduction of the Architec Gripper Smart Mat ($9.99), we can use this grippy surface under any cutting board, mixing bowl, or appliance. This 20-by-15-inch silicone mat (which can be cut to fit) tightly grabs a surface with its multitude of skid-proof disks—and does so more securely and durably than our usual trick of using a piece of shelf liner.

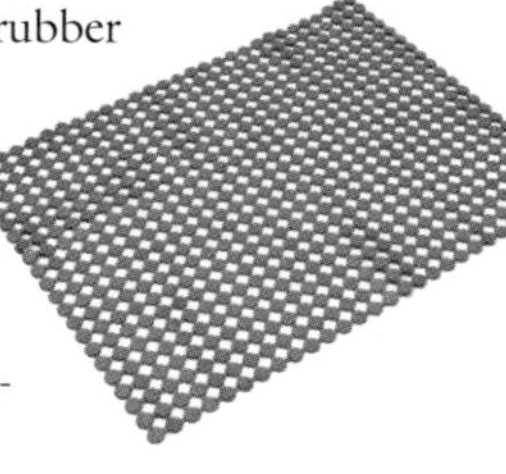

GETTING A GRIP
The Architec Gripper Smart Mat keeps things grounded.

NEW PRODUCT:
Handheld Espresso Makers

We tested two hand-powered portable espresso makers: the Aerobie AeroPress Coffee and Espresso Maker ($29.95) and the Handpresso Wild Portable Espresso Maker ($149.99) to see if they could do the job of an espresso machine. While neither produced the deep, rich brew you might find at a gourmet coffee outlet, both made flavorful espresso quickly and easily. The bicycle pump–like Handpresso, which requires a coffee pod (ground coffee beans in their own filter), pressed out brew with a hearty aroma; however, tasters commented on its muddiness and bitter finish. The lightweight plastic AeroPress did better. Using freshly ground beans, it produced smooth espresso that, according to tasters, combined the slightly heavier body of French press coffee and the cleanness of drip coffee. With good reason—the AeroPress mimics the technology of both. To make a cup, you insert a disk-shaped paper filter, add coffee to the chamber with hot water, mix, and press. At $149.99, the Handpresso is just not worth the expense, but for a single-cup brewer at a reasonable price, the AeroPress does the job.

EXPRESS PRESS
The AeroPress Coffee and Espresso Maker quickly produces a smooth cup of espresso.

Sources

The following are mail-order sources for items recommended in this issue. Prices were current at press time and do not include shipping. Contact companies to confirm or visit www.cooksillustrated.com for updates.

PAGE 9: PAPRIKA
- The Spice House Hungarian Sweet Paprika: **$3.28 for 2.5 oz.**, The Spice House (312-274-0378, www.thespicehouse.com).

PAGE 19: METAL SPATULA
- Wüsthof Gourmet 7.5-Inch Slotted Turner/Fish Spatula: **$34.95, item #4433,** Cutlery and More (800-650-9866, www.cutleryandmore.com).

PAGE 27: BLACK PEPPERCORNS
- Kalustyan's Indian Tellicherry Black Peppercorns: **$6.99 for 2.5 oz., item #332B640,** Kalustyan's (800-352-3451, www.kalustyans.com).
- Parameswaran's Special Wynad Estate Peppercorns: **$30 for 200 g.,** Zingerman's (888-636-8162, www.zingermans.com).

PAGE 29: SLICING KNIFE
- Forschner Fibrox 12-Inch Granton Edge Slicing Knife: **$44.95, model #40645,** Cutlery and More.

PAGE 32: DOUGH HOOK
- KitchenAid Burnished Spiral Dough Hook: **$19.99, item #KNS256BDH,** KitchenAid (800-334-6889, www.kitchenaid.com).

PAGE 32: KNIFE SHARPENER
- AccuSharp Knife and Tool Sharpener: **$10.48, item #633677,** Cooking.com (800-663-8810, www.cooking.com).

PAGE 32: BATTERY-OPERATED SIFTER
- Norpro Battery-Operated Flour Sifter: **$15.99,** Target (800-591-3869, www.target.com).

PAGE 32: GRIPPER MAT
- Architec Gripper Smart Mat: **$9.99, item #B000MD7YTA,** Amazon.com.

PAGE 32: PORTABLE ESPRESSO MAKER
- Aerobie AeroPress Coffee and Espresso Maker: **$29.95,** Sur la Table (800-243-0852, www.surlatable.com).

INDEX

November & December 2008

RECIPES

COOK'S LIVE Original Test Kitchen Videos **www.cooksillustrated.com**

MAIN DISHES
- **How to Make Garlicky Shrimp Pasta**
- **How to Make Hungarian Beef Stew**
- Why do I need to cut my own stew meat?
- Paprika 101
- **How to Make Slow-Roasted Turkey with Gravy**
- **How to Make Stovetop Roast Chicken**
- How to cut up a chicken
- **How to Make Stuffed Portobello Mushrooms**
- All about portobello mushrooms

SIDE DISHES
- **How to Make Roasted Sweet Potatoes**
- Sweet potato primer
- **How to Make Rustic Dinner Rolls**
- Why free-form rustic dinner rolls are better
- How can I tell when my dough is properly proofed?
- **How to Make Sautéed Green Beans**

DESSERTS
- **How to Make French Butter Cookies (Sablés)**
- How to hard-cook an egg
- What are turbinado and Demerara sugars and how do you use them?
- How to make Checkerboard Cookies
- **How to Make Pumpkin Pie**
- Adding a decorative edge to a pie shell
- How to blind bake a pie shell

TASTING AND TESTING
- Behind the Scenes: Testing Slicing Knives
- Buying Guide to Pepper Mills

Making the Most of Your Chef's Knife
- How to dice a potato
- How to mince an onion
- How to mince or chop a carrot
- Basic chef's knife skills

Stuffed Portobello Mushrooms, 19

Slow-Roasted Turkey with Gravy, 11

Sautéed Green Beans, 12

Rustic Dinner Rolls, 15

Stovetop Roast Chicken, 7

Hungarian Beef Stew, 9

French Butter Cookies, 22

Pumpkin Pie, 25

Roasted Sweet Potatoes, 13

Garlicky Shrimp Pasta, 20

PHOTOGRAPHY: CARL TREMBLAY, STYLING: MARIE PIRAINO

ITALIAN COOKIES